ASCENT
CENTER FOR TECHNICAL KNOWLEDGE

AF818832

Autodesk® Revit® 2018 MEP Fundamentals

Student Guide
Metric - 1st Edition

AUTODESK.
Authorized Publisher

CONTINUING EDUCATION AIA

ASCENT - Center for Technical Knowledge®
Autodesk® Revit® 2018 MEP
Fundamentals

Metric - 1st Edition

Prepared and produced by:

ASCENT Center for Technical Knowledge
630 Peter Jefferson Parkway, Suite 175
Charlottesville, VA 22911

866-527-2368
www.ASCENTed.com

Lead Contributor: Martha Hollowell

ASCENT - Center for Technical Knowledge is a division of Rand Worldwide, Inc., providing custom developed knowledge products and services for leading engineering software applications. ASCENT is focused on specializing in the creation of education programs that incorporate the best of classroom learning and technology-based training offerings.

We welcome any comments you may have regarding this student guide, or any of our products. To contact us please email: feedback@ASCENTed.com.

AS-RME1801-FND1MT-SG // IS-RME1801-FND1MT-SG

Contents

Preface

To take full advantage of Building Information Modeling, the *Autodesk® Revit® 2018 MEP: Fundamentals* student guide has been designed to teach the concepts and principles of creating 3D parametric models of MEP system from engineering design through construction documentation.

The student guide is intended to introduce students to the software's user interface and the basic HVAC, electrical, and piping/plumbing components that make the Autodesk Revit software a powerful and flexible engineering modeling tool. The student guide will also familiarize students with the tools required to create, document, and print the parametric model. The examples and practices are designed to take the students through the basics of a full MEP project from linking in an architectural model to construction documents.

Topics Covered:

- Working with the Autodesk Revit software's basic viewing, drawing, and editing commands.
- Inserting and connecting MEP components and using the System Browser.
- Working with linked architectural files.
- Creating spaces and zones so that you can analyze heating and cooling loads.
- Creating HVAC networks with air terminals, mechanical equipment, ducts, and pipes.
- Creating plumbing networks with plumbing fixtures and pipes.
- Creating electrical circuits with electrical equipment, devices, and lighting fixtures and adding cable trays and conduits.
- Creating HVAC and plumbing systems with automatic duct and piping layouts.
- Testing duct, piping and electrical systems.
- Creating and annotating construction documents.
- Adding tags and creating schedules.
- Detailing in the Autodesk Revit software.

Note on Software Setup

This student guide assumes a standard installation of the software using the default preferences during installation. Lectures and practices use the standard software templates and default options for the Content Libraries.

Students and Educators can Access Free Autodesk Software and Resources

Autodesk challenges you to get started with free educational licenses for professional software and creativity apps used by millions of architects, engineers, designers, and hobbyists today. Bring Autodesk software into your classroom, studio, or workshop to learn, teach, and explore real-world design challenges the way professionals do.

Get started today - register at the Autodesk Education Community and download one of the many Autodesk software applications available.

Visit www.autodesk.com/joinedu/

Note: Free products are subject to the terms and conditions of the end-user license and services agreement that accompanies the software. The software is for personal use for education purposes and is not intended for classroom or lab use.

Lead Contributor: Martha Hollowell

Martha incorporates her passion for architecture and education into all her projects, including the student guides she creates on Autodesk Revit for Architecture, MEP, and Structure. She started working with AutoCAD in the early 1990's, adding AutoCAD Architecture and Autodesk Revit as they came along.

After receiving a B.Sc. in Architecture from the University of Virginia, she worked in the architectural department of the Colonial Williamsburg Foundation and later in private practice, consulting with firms setting up AutoCAD in their offices.

Martha has over 20 years' experience as a trainer and instructional designer. She is skilled in leading individuals and small groups to understand and build on their potential. Martha is trained in Instructional Design and has achieved the Autodesk Certified Instructor (ACI) and Autodesk Certified Professional designations for Revit Architecture.

Martha Hollowell has been the Lead Contributor for *Autodesk Revit MEP Fundamentals* since its initial release in 2011.

In this Guide

The following images highlight some of the features that can be found in this Student Guide.

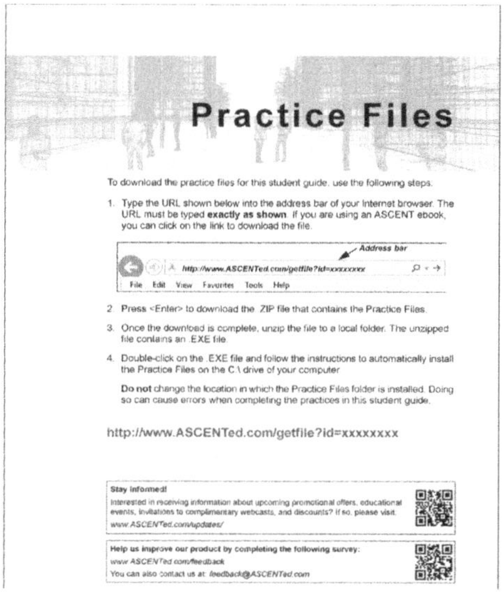

Practice Files

To download the practice files for this student guide, use the following steps.

1. Type the URL shown below into the address bar of your Internet browser. The URL must be typed **exactly as shown**. If you are using an ASCENT ebook, you can click on the link to download the file.

2. Press <Enter> to download the .ZIP file that contains the Practice Files.
3. Once the download is complete, unzip the file to a local folder. The unzipped file contains an .EXE file.
4. Double-click on the .EXE file and follow the instructions to automatically install the Practice Files on the C:\ drive of your computer.

   Do not change the location in which the Practice Files folder is installed. Doing so can cause errors when completing the practices in this student guide.

http://www.ASCENTed.com/getfile?id=xxxxxxxx

Stay Informed!
Interested in receiving information about upcoming promotional offers, educational events, invitations to complimentary webcasts, and discounts? If so, please visit: *www.ASCENTed.com/updates/*

Help us improve our product by completing the following survey:
www.ASCENTed.com/feedback
You can also contact us at: *feedback@ASCENTed.com*

FTP link for practice files

Practice Files

The Practice Files page tells you how to download and install the practice files that are provided with this student guide.

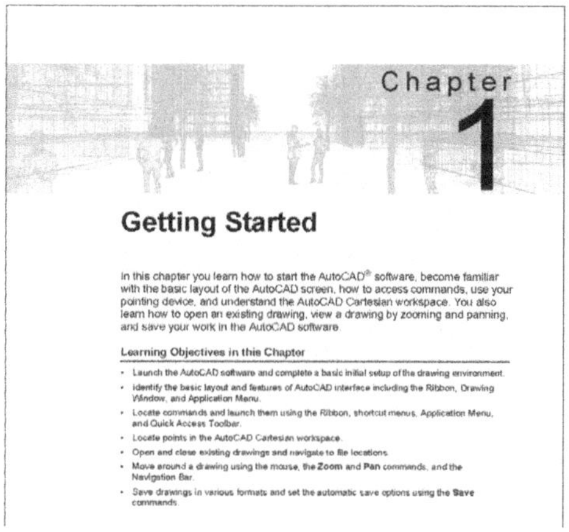

Chapter 1

Getting Started

In this chapter you learn how to start the AutoCAD® software, become familiar with the basic layout of the AutoCAD screen, how to access commands, use your pointing device, and understand the AutoCAD Cartesian workspace. You also learn how to open an existing drawing, view a drawing by zooming and panning, and save your work in the AutoCAD software.

Learning Objectives in this Chapter

- Launch the AutoCAD software and complete a basic initial setup of the drawing environment.
- Identify the basic layout and features of AutoCAD interface including the Ribbon, Drawing Window, and Application Menu.
- Locate commands and launch them using the Ribbon, shortcut menus, Application Menu, and Quick Access Toolbar.
- Locate points in the AutoCAD Cartesian workspace.
- Open and close existing drawings and navigate to file locations.
- Move around a drawing using the mouse, the **Zoom** and **Pan** commands, and the Navigation Bar.
- Save drawings in various formats and set the automatic save options using the **Save** commands.

Learning Objectives for the chapter

Chapters

Each chapter begins with a brief introduction and a list of the chapter's Learning Objectives.

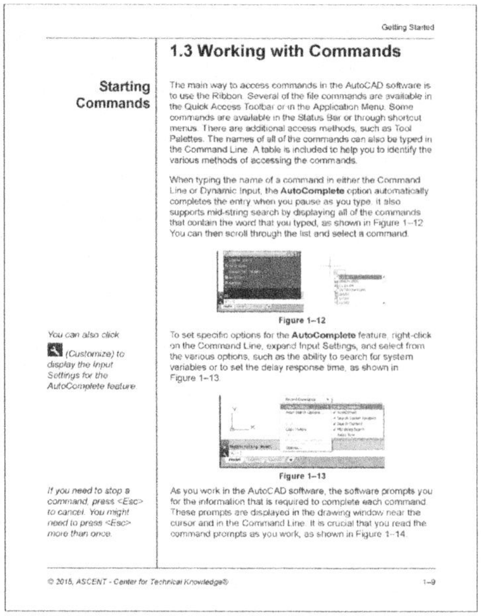
Getting Started

1.3 Working with Commands

Starting Commands

The main way to access commands in the AutoCAD software is to use the Ribbon. Several of the file commands are available in the Quick Access Toolbar or in the Application Menu. Some commands are available in the Status Bar or through shortcut menus. There are additional access methods, such as Tool Palettes. The names of all of the commands can also be typed in the Command Line. A table is included to help you to identify the various methods of accessing the commands.

When typing the name of a command in either the Command Line or Dynamic Input, the **AutoComplete** option automatically completes the entry when you pause as you type. It also supports mid-string search by displaying all of the commands that contain the word that you typed, as shown in Figure 1–12. You can then scroll through the list and select a command.

Figure 1–12

You can also click (Customize) to display the Input Settings for the AutoComplete feature.

To set specific options for the **AutoComplete** feature, right-click on the Command Line, expand Input Settings, and select from the various options, such as the ability to search for system variables or to set the delay response time, as shown in Figure 1–13.

Figure 1–13

If you need to stop a command, press <Esc> to cancel. You might need to press <Esc> more than once.

As you work in the AutoCAD software, the software prompts you for the information that is required to complete each command. These prompts are displayed in the drawing window near the cursor and in the Command Line. It is crucial that you read the command prompts as you work, as shown in Figure 1–14.

© 2015, ASCENT - Center for Technical Knowledge® 1–9

Instructional Content

Each chapter is split into a series of sections of instructional content on specific topics. These lectures include the descriptions, step-by-step procedures, figures, hints, and information you need to achieve the chapter's Learning Objectives.

Side notes

Side notes are hints or additional information for the current topic.

Practice Objectives

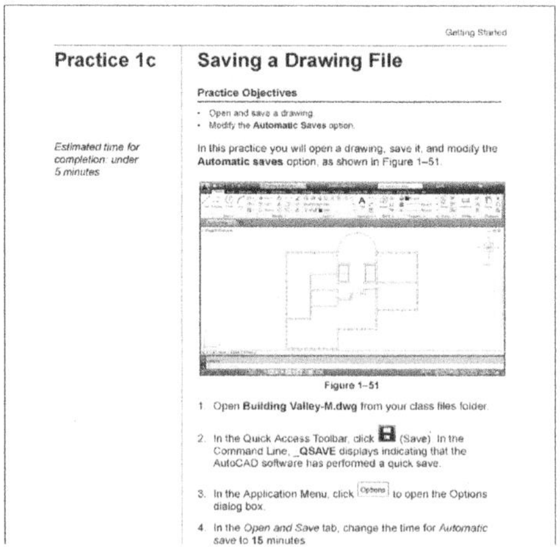
Getting Started

Practice 1c Saving a Drawing File

Practice Objectives

- Open and save a drawing.
- Modify the **Automatic Saves** option.

Estimated time for completion: under 5 minutes

In this practice you will open a drawing, save it, and modify the **Automatic saves** option, as shown in Figure 1–51.

Figure 1–51

1. Open **Building Valley-M.dwg** from your class files folder.
2. In the Quick Access Toolbar, click (Save). In the Command Line, **_QSAVE** displays indicating that the AutoCAD software has performed a quick save.
3. In the Application Menu, click Options to open the Options dialog box.
4. In the *Open and Save* tab, change the time for *Automatic save* to **15** minutes.

Practices

Practices enable you to use the software to perform a hands-on review of a topic.

Some practices require you to use prepared practice files, which can be downloaded from the link found on the Practice Files page.

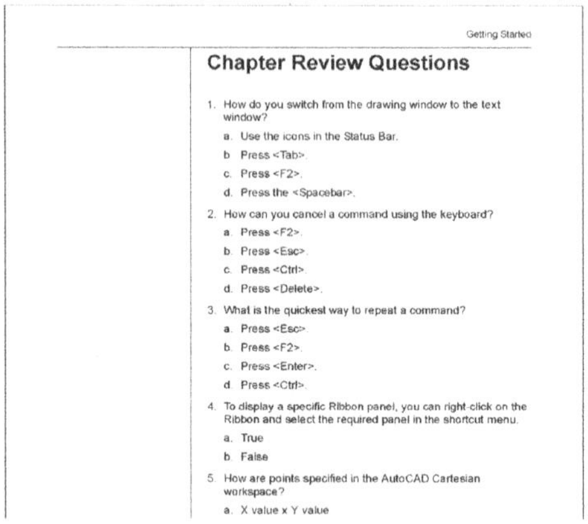
Getting Started

Chapter Review Questions

1. How do you switch from the drawing window to the text window?
   a. Use the icons in the Status Bar.
   b. Press <Tab>.
   c. Press <F2>.
   d. Press the <Spacebar>.
2. How can you cancel a command using the keyboard?
   a. Press <F2>.
   b. Press <Esc>.
   c. Press <Ctrl>.
   d. Press <Delete>.
3. What is the quickest way to repeat a command?
   a. Press <Esc>.
   b. Press <F2>.
   c. Press <Enter>.
   d. Press <Ctrl>.
4. To display a specific Ribbon panel, you can right-click on the Ribbon and select the required panel in the shortcut menu.
   a. True
   b. False
5. How are points specified in the AutoCAD Cartesian workspace?
   a. X value x Y value

Chapter Review Questions

Chapter review questions, located at the end of each chapter, enable you to review the key concepts and learning objectives of the chapter.

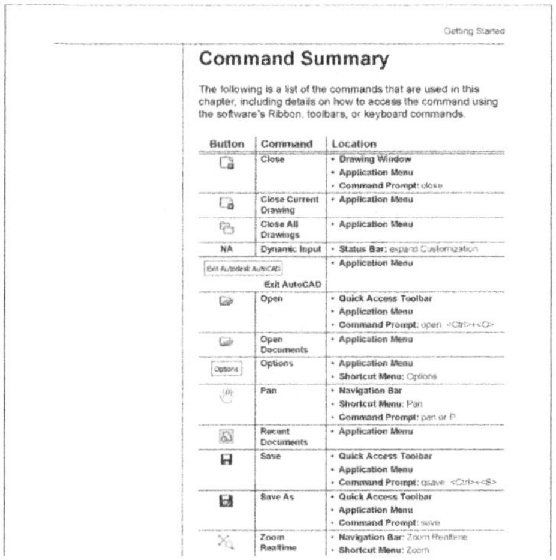
Getting Started

Command Summary

The following is a list of the commands that are used in this chapter, including details on how to access the command using the software's Ribbon, toolbars, or keyboard commands.

Button	Command	Location
	Close	• Drawing Window • Application Menu • Command Prompt: close
	Close Current Drawing	• Application Menu
	Close All Drawings	• Application Menu
NA	Dynamic Input	• Status Bar: expand Customization
Exit Autodesk AutoCAD	Exit AutoCAD	• Application Menu
	Open	• Quick Access Toolbar • Application Menu • Command Prompt: open, <Ctrl>+<O>
	Open Documents	• Application Menu
Options	Options	• Application Menu • Shortcut Menu: Options
	Pan	• Navigation Bar • Shortcut Menu: Pan • Command Prompt: pan or P
	Recent Documents	• Application Menu
	Save	• Quick Access Toolbar • Application Menu • Command Prompt: qsave, <Ctrl>+<S>
	Save As	• Quick Access Toolbar • Application Menu • Command Prompt: save
	Zoom Realtime	• Navigation Bar: Zoom Realtime • Shortcut Menu: Zoom

Command Summary

The Command Summary is located at the end of each chapter. It contains a list of the software commands that are used throughout the chapter, and provides information on where the command is found in the software.

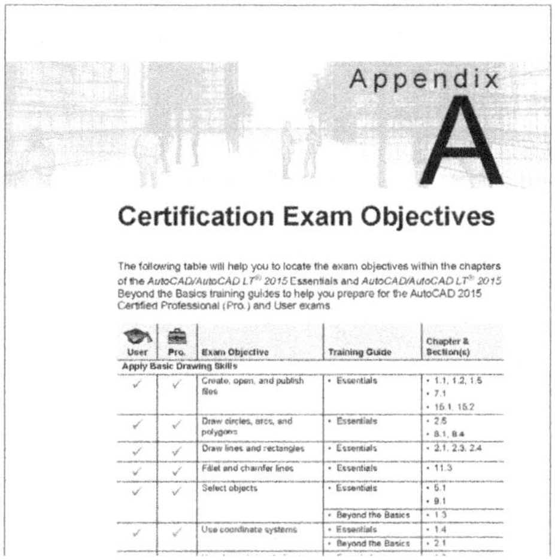
Appendix A

Certification Exam Objectives

The following table will help you to locate the exam objectives within the chapters of the *AutoCAD/AutoCAD LT® 2015* Essentials and *AutoCAD/AutoCAD LT® 2015* Beyond the Basics training guides to help you prepare for the AutoCAD 2015 Certified Professional (Pro.) and User exams.

User	Pro.	Exam Objective	Training Guide	Chapter & Section(s)
Apply Basic Drawing Skills				
✓	✓	Create, open, and publish files	• Essentials	• 1.1, 1.2, 1.5 • 7.1 • 15.1, 15.2
✓	✓	Draw circles, arcs, and polygons	• Essentials	• 2.5 • 8.1, 8.4
✓	✓	Draw lines and rectangles	• Essentials	• 2.1, 2.3, 2.4
✓	✓	Fillet and chamfer lines	• Essentials	• 11.3
✓	✓	Select objects	• Essentials	• 5.1 • 9.1
			• Beyond the Basics	• 1.3
✓	✓	Use coordinate systems	• Essentials	• 1.4
			• Beyond the Basics	• 2.1

Autodesk Certification Exam Appendix

This appendix includes a list of the topics and objectives for the Autodesk Certification exams, and the chapter and section in which the relevant content can be found.

Icons in this Student Guide

The following icons are used to help you quickly and easily find helpful information.

	Indicates items that are new in the Autodesk Revit 2018 software.
	Indicates items that have been enhanced in the Autodesk Revit 2018 software.

Practice Files

To download the practice files for this student guide, use the following steps:

1. Type the URL shown below into the address bar of your Internet browser. The URL must be typed **exactly as shown**. If you are using an ASCENT ebook, you can click on the link to download the file.

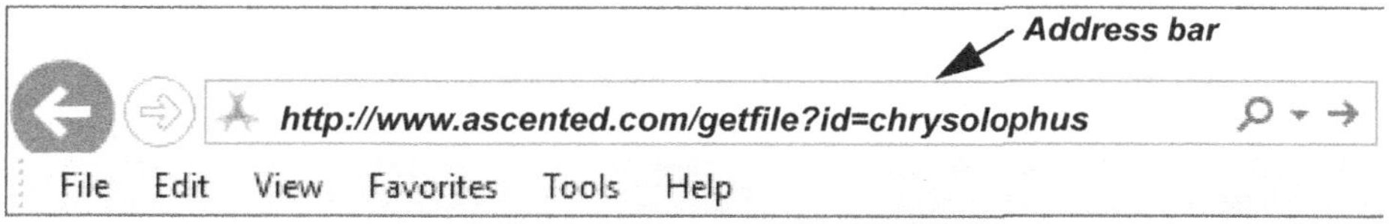

2. Press <Enter> to download the .ZIP file that contains the Practice Files.
3. Once the download is complete, unzip the file to a local folder. The unzipped file contains an .EXE file.
4. Double-click on the .EXE file and follow the instructions to automatically install the Practice Files on the C:\ drive of your computer.

   Do not change the location in which the Practice Files folder is installed. Doing so can cause errors when completing the practices in this student guide.

http://www.ascented.com/getfile?id=chrysolophus

Stay Informed!

Interested in receiving information about upcoming promotional offers, educational events, invitations to complimentary webcasts, and discounts? If so, please visit:

www.ASCENTed.com/updates/

Help us improve our product by completing the following survey:

www.ASCENTed.com/feedback

You can also contact us at: *feedback@ASCENTed.com*

Introduction to BIM and Autodesk Revit

Building Information Modeling (BIM) and the Autodesk® Revit® software work hand in hand to help you create smart, 3D models that are useful at all stages in the building process. Understanding the software interface and terminology enhances your ability to create powerful models and move around in the various views of the model.

Learning Objectives in this Chapter

- Describe the concept and workflow of Building Information Modeling in relation to the Autodesk Revit software.
- Navigate the graphic user interface, including the ribbon (where most of the tools are found), the Properties palette (where you make modifications to element information), and the Project Browser (where you can open various views of the model).
- Open existing projects and start new projects using templates.
- Use viewing commands to move around the model in 2D and 3D views.

1.1 BIM and Autodesk Revit

Building Information Modeling (BIM) is an approach to the entire building life cycle, including design, construction, and facilities management. The BIM process supports the ability to coordinate, update, and share design data with team members across disciplines.

The BIM process is broader than using any one software application, but the Autodesk Revit software is a true BIM product. The Autodesk Revit software enables you to create complete 3D building models that provide considerable information reported through construction documents, and to share these models with other programs for more extensive analysis. The Autodesk Revit software is considered a Parametric Building Modeler:

- *Parametric:* A relationship is established between building elements: when one element changes, other related elements change as well.
- *Building:* The software is designed for working with buildings and the surrounding landscape, as opposed to gears or highways.
- *Modeler:* A project is built in a single file based on the 3D building model, as shown on the left in Figure 1–1. All views, such as plans (as shown on the right in Figure 1–1), elevations, sections, details, construction documents, and reports are generated based on the model.

When a change is made anywhere in the model, all of the views update automatically. For example, if you add an element in a plan view, it displays in all of the other views as well.

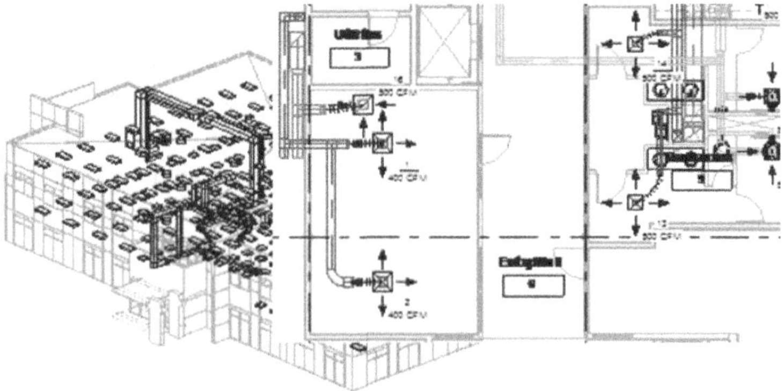

Figure 1–1

- The Autodesk® Revit® software includes tools for architectural, mechanical, electrical, plumbing, and structural design.
- It is important that everyone who is collaborating on a project works in the same version and build of the software.

Workflow and BIM

BIM has changed the process of how a building is planned, budgeted, designed, constructed, and (in some cases) operated and maintained.

In the traditional design process, construction documents are created independently, typically including plans, sections, elevations, details, and notes. Sometimes, a separate 3D model is created in addition to these documents. Changes made in one document, such as the addition of a light fixture in a plan, have to be coordinated with the rest of the documents and schedules in the set, as shown in Figure 1–2.

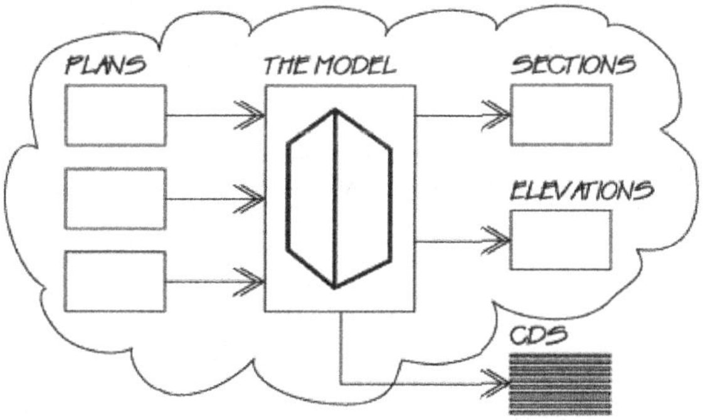

Figure 1–2

In BIM, the design process revolves around the model, as shown in Figure 1–3. Plans, elevations, and sections are simply 2D versions of the 3D model, while and schedules are a report of the information stored in the model. Changes made in one view automatically update in all views and related schedules. Even Construction Documents update automatically with callout tags in sync with the sheet numbers. This is called bidirectional associativity.

By creating complete models and associated views of those models, the Autodesk Revit software takes much of the tediousness out of producing a building design.

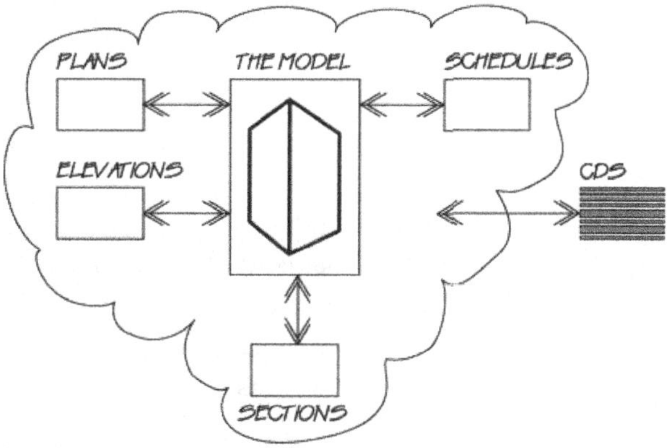

Figure 1–3

Revit Terms

When working in the Autodesk Revit software, it is important to know the typical terms used to describe items. Views and reports display information about the elements that form a project. There are three types of elements: Model, Datum, and View-specific, as shown in Figure 1–4 and described below:

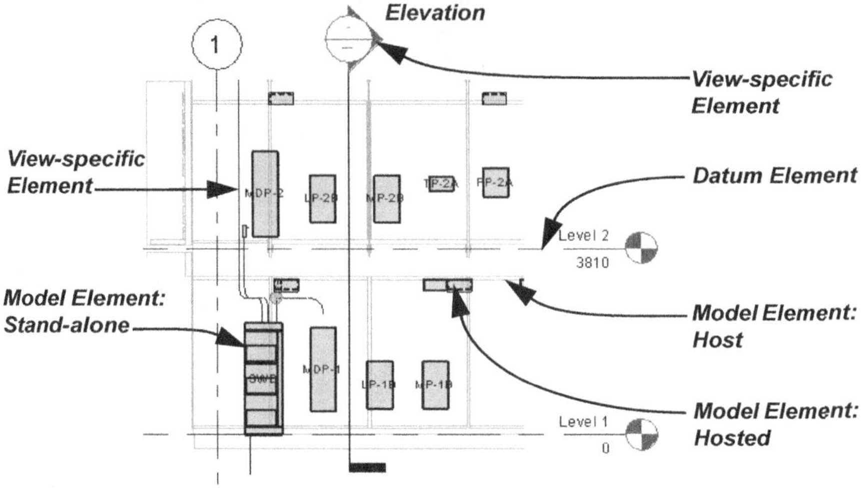

Figure 1–4

Views	Enable you to display and manipulate the model. For example, you can view and work in floor plans, ceiling plans, elevations, sections, schedules, and 3D views. You can change a design from any view. All views are stored in the project.
Reports	Reports, including schedules, gather information from the building model element that can be presented in the construction documents or used for analysis.
Model Elements	Include all parts of a building such as walls, floors, roofs, ceilings, doors, windows, plumbing fixtures, lighting fixtures, mechanical equipment, columns, beams, furniture, plants and many more. • Host elements support other categories of elements. • Hosted elements must be attached to a host element. • Standalone elements do not require hosts.
Datum Elements	Define the project context such as the levels for the floors and other vertical distances, column grids, and reference planes.
View-specific Elements	Only display in the view in which they are placed. The view scale controls their size. These include annotation elements such as dimensions, text, tags, and symbols as well as detail elements such as detail lines, filled regions, and 2D detail components.

- Autodesk Revit elements are "smart": the software recognizes them as walls, columns, plants, ducts, or lighting fixtures. This means that the information stored in their properties automatically updates in schedules, which ensures that views and reports are coordinated across an entire project, and are generated from a single model.

Revit and Construction Documents

In the traditional workflow, the most time-consuming part of the project is the construction documents. With BIM, the base views of those documents (i.e., plans, elevations, sections, and schedules) are produced automatically and update as the model is updated, saving hours of work. The views are then placed on sheets that form the construction document set.

For example, a floor plan is duplicated. Then, in the new view, all but the required categories of elements are hidden or set to halftone and annotations are added. The plan is then placed on a sheet, as shown in Figure 1–5.

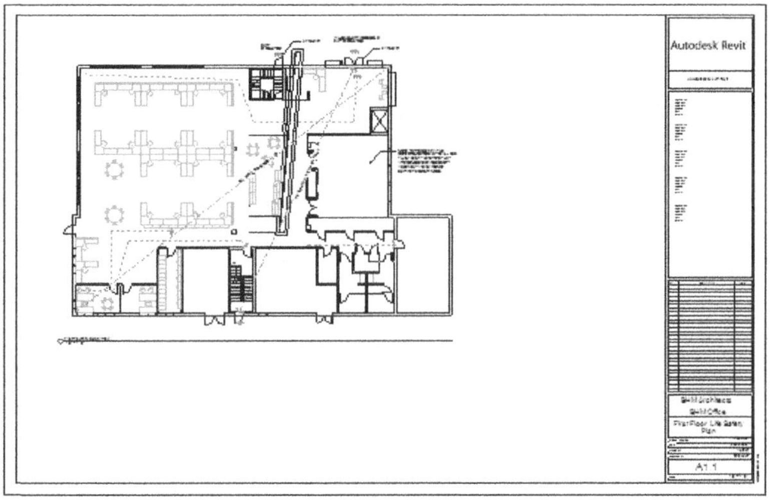

Figure 1–5

- Work can continue on a view and is automatically updated on the sheet.
- Annotating views in the preliminary design phase is often not required. You might be able to wait until you are further along in the project.

1.2 Overview of the Interface

The Autodesk Revit interface is designed for intuitive and efficient access to commands and views. It includes the ribbon, Quick Access Toolbar, Navigation Bar, and Status Bar, which are common to most of the Autodesk® software. It also includes tools that are specific to the Autodesk Revit software, including the Properties Palette, Project Browser, and View Control Bar. The interface is shown in Figure 1–6.

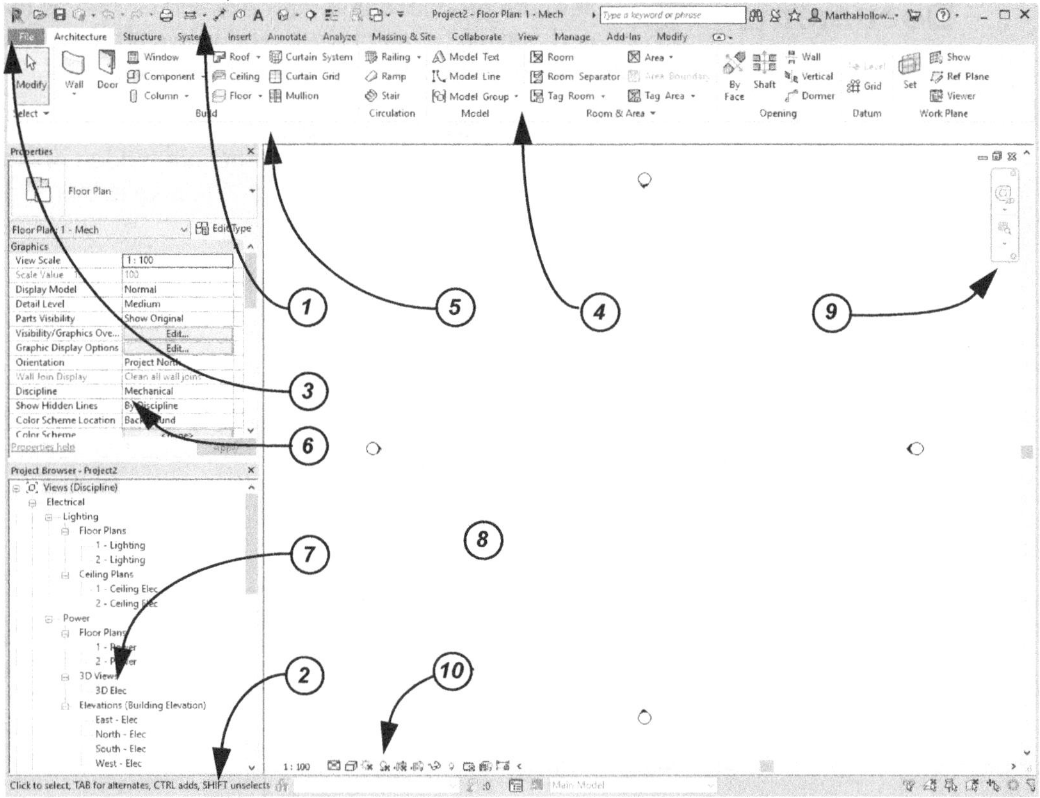

Figure 1–6

1. Quick Access Toolbar	6. Properties Palette
2. Status Bar	7. Project Browser
3. File tab	8. View Window
4. Ribbon	9. Navigation Bar
5. Options Bar	10. View Control Bar

1. Quick Access Toolbar

Enhanced in 2018

The Quick Access Toolbar (shown in Figure 1–7) includes commonly used commands, such as **Open**, **Save**, **Undo**, **Redo,** and **Print**. It also includes frequently used annotation tools, including Measuring tools, **Aligned Dimension**, **Tag by Category**, and **Text**. Viewing tools, including several different 3D Views and **Sections**, are also easily accessed here.

Figure 1–7

Hint: Customizing the Quick Access Toolbar

Right-click on the Quick Access Toolbar to change the docked location of the toolbar to be above or below the ribbon, or to add, relocate, or remove tools on the toolbar. You can also right-click on a tool in the ribbon and select **Add to Quick Access Toolbar**, as shown in Figure 1–8.

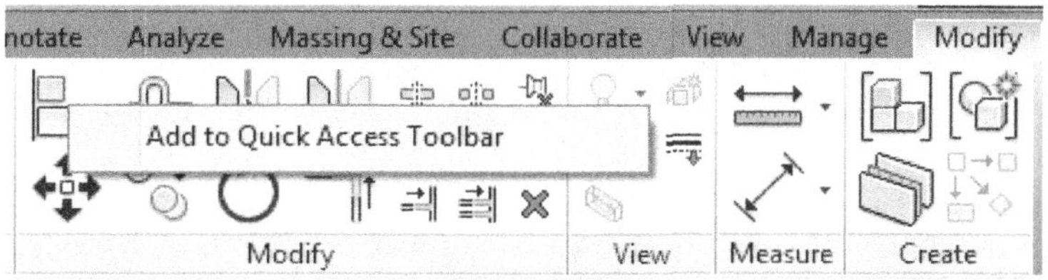

Figure 1–8

The top toolbar also hosts the InfoCenter (as shown in Figure 1–9) which includes a search field to find help on the web as well as access to the Communication Center, Autodesk A360 sign-in, the Autodesk App Store, and other help options.

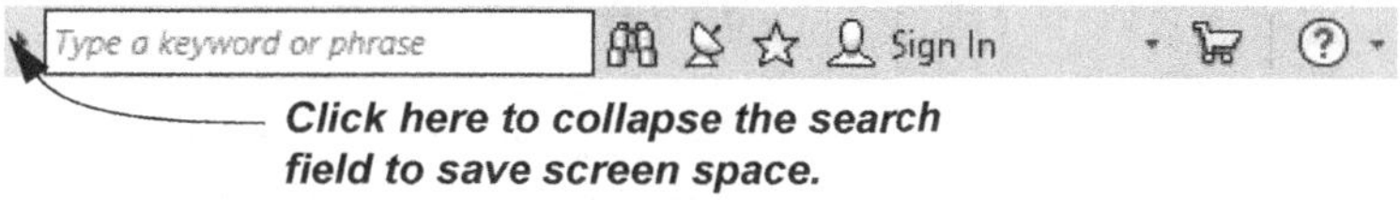

Figure 1–9

2. Status Bar

The Status Bar provides information about the current process, such as the next step for a command, as shown in Figure 1–10.

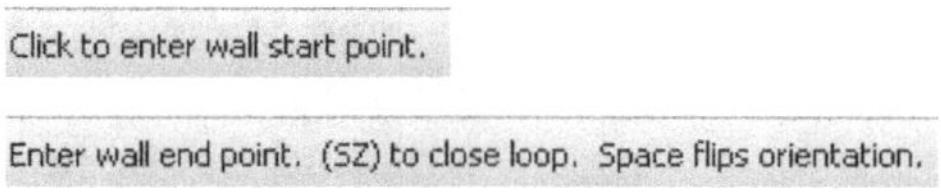

Figure 1–10

- Other options in the Status Bar are related to Worksets and Design Options (advanced tools) as well as selection methods and filters.

Hint: Shortcut Menus

Shortcut menus help you to work smoothly and efficiently by enabling you to quickly access required commands. These menus provide access to basic viewing commands, recently used commands, and the available Browsers, as shown in Figure 1–11. Additional options vary depending on the element or command that you are using.

Figure 1–11

3.File Tab

The *File* tab of the ribbon provides access to file commands, settings, and documents, as shown in Figure 1–12. Hover the cursor over a command to display a list of additional tools.

If you click the primary icon, rather than the arrow, it starts the default command.

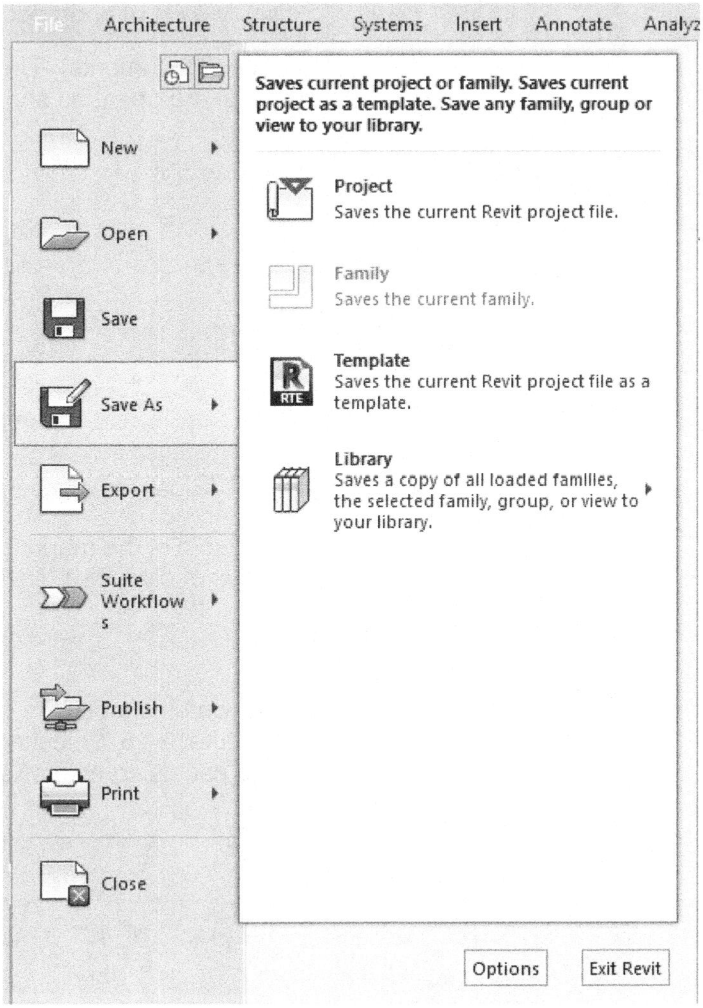

Figure 1–12

- To display a list of recently used documents, click (Recent Documents). The documents can be reordered as shown in Figure 1–13.

Click (Pin) next to a document name to keep it available.

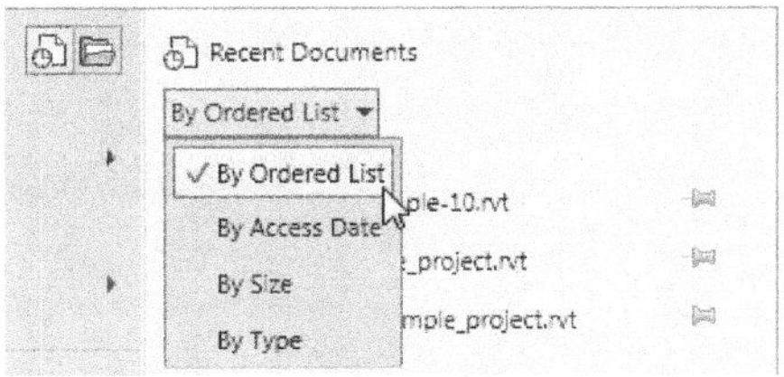

Figure 1–13

You can use the Open Documents list to change between views.

- To display a list of open documents and views, click  (Open Documents). The list displays the documents and views that are open, as shown in Figure 1–14.

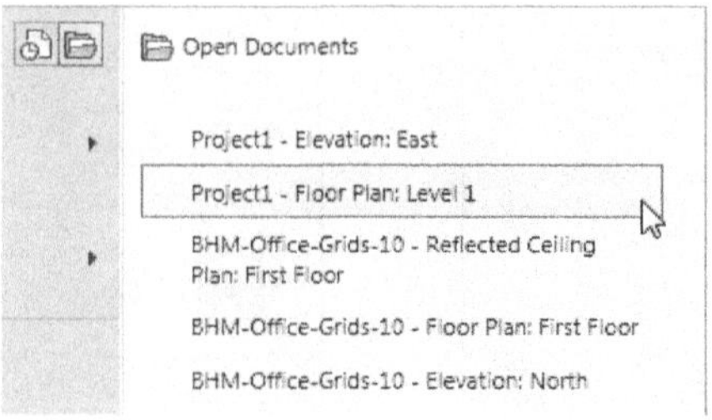

Figure 1–14

- Click  (Close) to close the current project.
- At the bottom of the menu, click **Options** to open the Options dialog box or click **Exit Revi**t to exit the software.

4. Ribbon

The ribbon contains tools in a series of tabs and panels as shown in Figure 1–15. Selecting a tab displays a group of related panels. The panels contain a variety of tools, grouped by task.

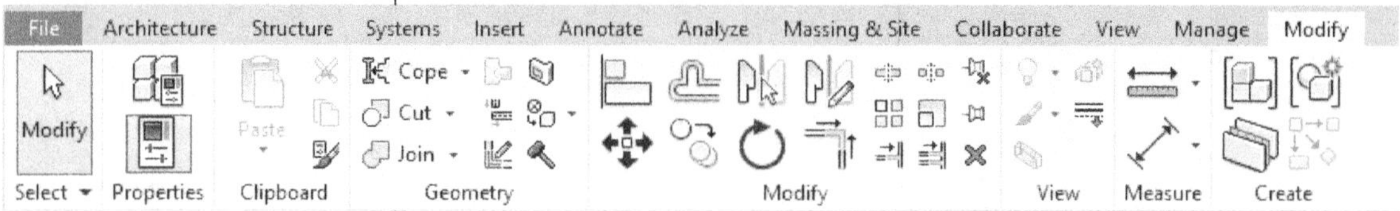

Figure 1–15

When you start a command that creates new elements or you select an element, the ribbon displays the *Modify | contextual* tab. This contains general editing commands and command specific tools, as shown in Figure 1–16.

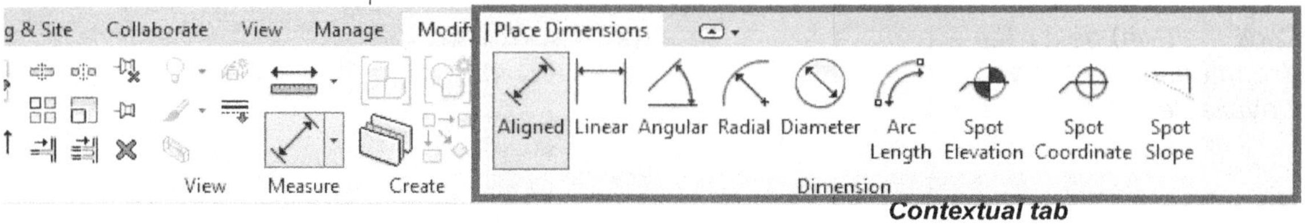

Figure 1–16

- When you hover over a tool on the ribbon, tooltips display the tool's name and a short description. If you continue hovering over the tool, a graphic displays (and sometimes a video), as shown in Figure 1–17.

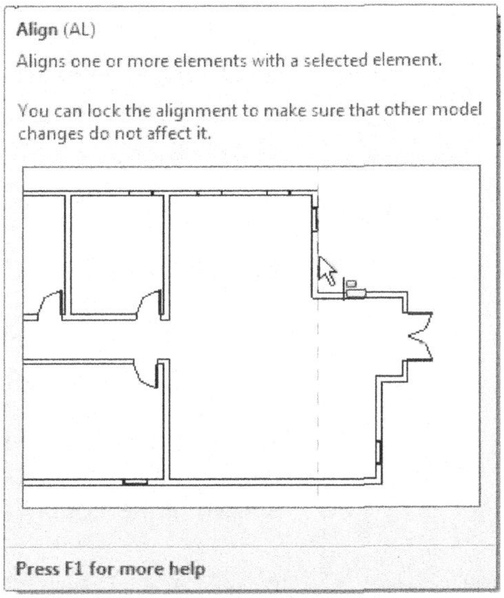

Figure 1–17

- Many commands have shortcut keys. For example, type **AL** for **Align** or **MV** for **Move**. They are listed next to the name of the command in the tooltips. Do not press <Enter> when typing shortcuts.

- To arrange the order in which the ribbon tabs are displayed, select the tab, hold <Ctrl>, and drag it to a new location. The location is remembered when you restart the software.

- Any panel can be dragged by its title into the view window to become a floating panel. Click the **Return Panels to Ribbon** button (as shown in Figure 1–18) to reposition the panel in the ribbon.

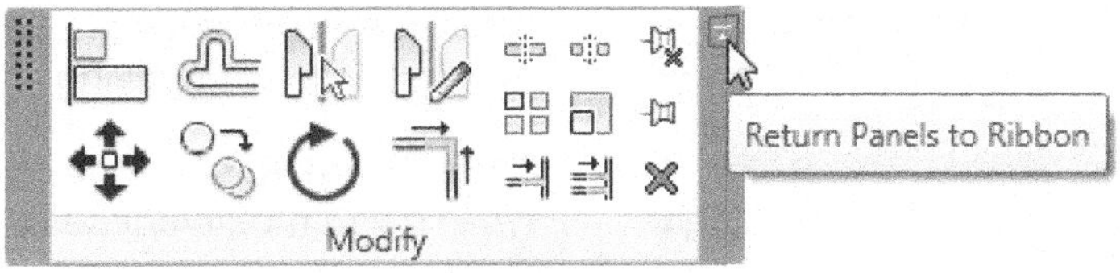

Figure 1–18

Hint: You are always in a command when using the Autodesk Revit software.

When you are finished working with a tool, you typically default back to the **Modify** command. To end a command, use one of the following methods:

- In any tab on the ribbon, click (Modify).
- Press <Esc> once or twice to revert to **Modify**.
- Right-click and select **Cancel...** once or twice.
- Start another command.

5. Options Bar

The Options Bar displays options that are related to the selected command or element. For example, when the **Rotate** command is active it displays options for rotating the selected elements, as shown at the top in Figure 1–19. When the **Place Dimensions** command is active it displays dimension related options, as shown at the bottom in Figure 1–19.

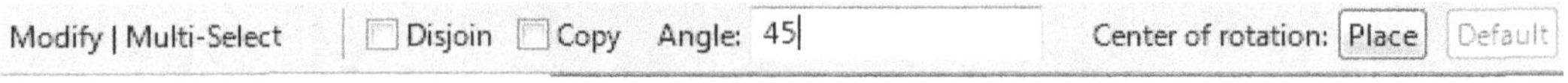

Options Bar for Rotate Command

Options Bar for Dimension Command

Figure 1–19

6. Properties Palette

The Properties palette includes the Type Selector, which enables you to choose the size or style of the element you are adding or modifying. This palette is also where you make changes to information (parameters) about elements or views, as shown in Figure 1–20. There are two types of properties:

- **Instance Properties** are set for the individual element(s) you are creating or modifying.
- **Type Properties** control options for all elements of the same type. If you modify these parameter values, all elements of the selected type change.

*The Properties palette is usually kept open while working on a project to easily permit changes at any time. If it does not display, in the Modify tab>Properties panel click (Properties) or type **PP**.*

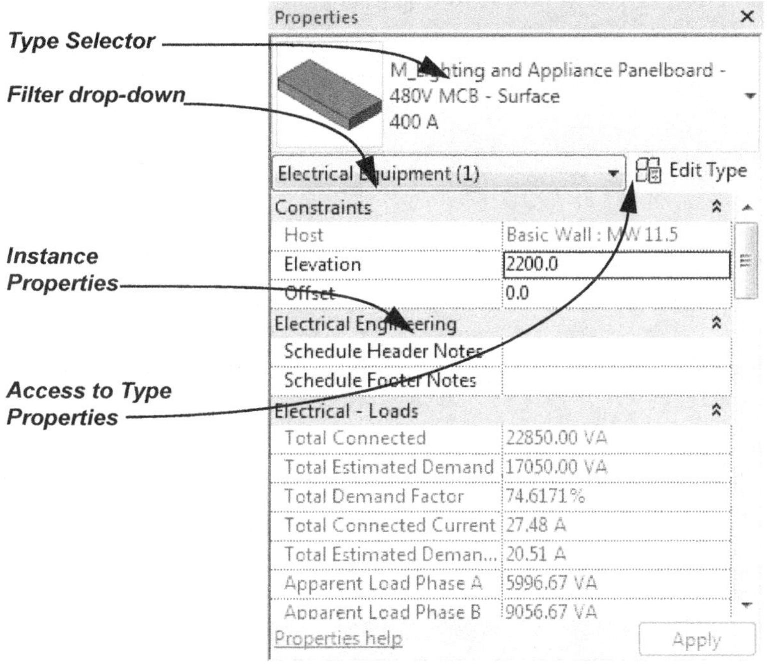

Figure 1–20

Some parameters are only available when you are editing an element. They are grayed out when unavailable.

- Options for the current view display if the **Modify** command is active, but you have not selected an element.
- If a command or element is selected, the options for the associated element display.
- You can save the changes by either moving the cursor off of the palette, or by pressing <Enter>, or by clicking **Apply**.
- When you start a command or select an element, you can set the element type in the Type Selector, as shown in Figure 1–21.

You can limit what shows in the drop-down list by typing in the search box.

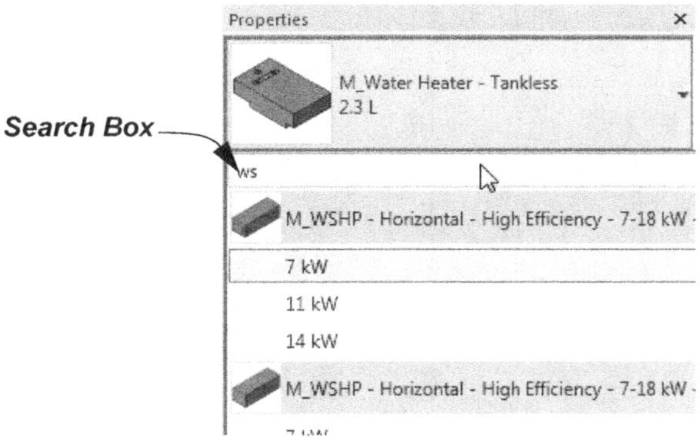

Figure 1–21

- When multiple elements are selected, you can filter the type of elements that display using the drop-down list, as shown in Figure 1–22.

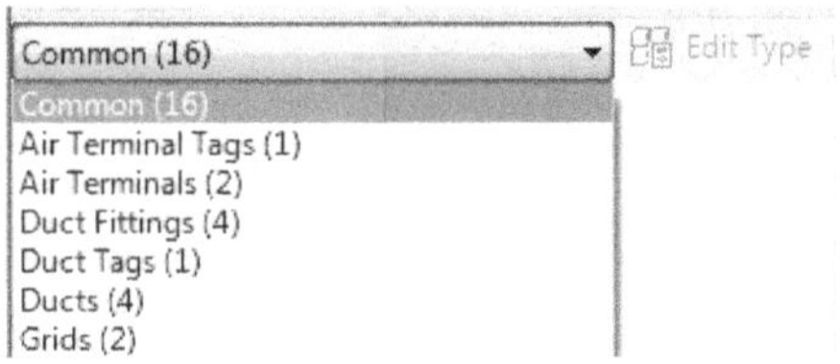

Figure 1–22

- The Properties palette can be placed on a second monitor, or floated, resized, and docked on top of the Project Browser or other dockable palettes, as shown in Figure 1–23. Click the tab to display its associated panel.

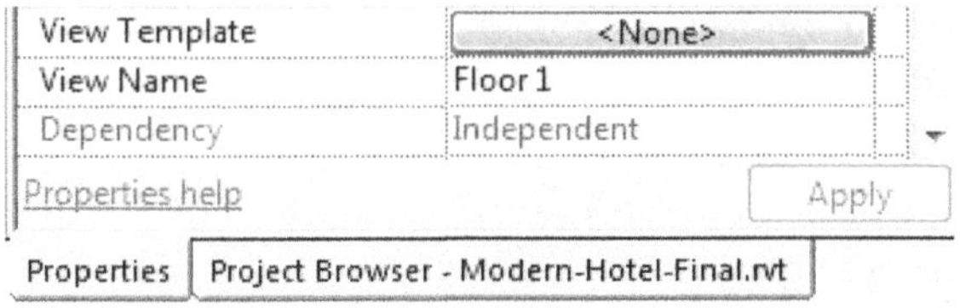

Figure 1–23

7. Project Browser

The Project Browser lists the views that can be opened in the project, as shown in Figure 1–24. This includes all views of the model in which you are working and any additional views that you create, such as floor plans, ceiling plans, 3D views, elevations, sections, etc. It also includes views of schedules, legends, sheets (for plotting), groups, and Autodesk Revit Links.

The Project Browser displays the name of the active project.

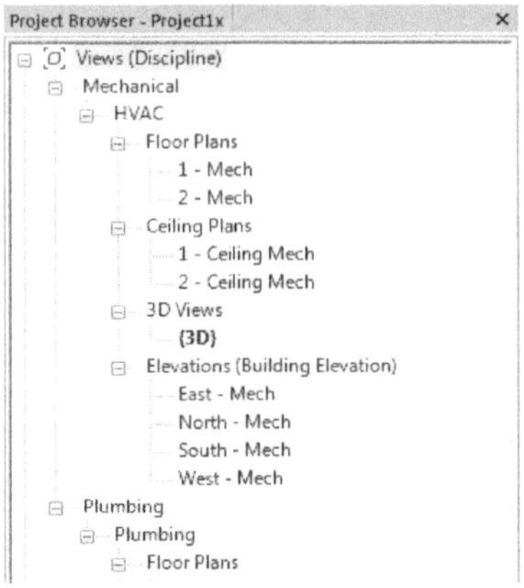

Figure 1–24

- Double-click on an item in the list to open the associated view.
- To display the views associated with a view type, click (Expand) next to the section name. To hide the views in the section, click (Contract).
- Right-click on a view and select **Rename** or press <F2> to rename a view in the Project Browser.
- If you no longer need a view, you can remove it. Right-click on its name in the Project Browser and select **Delete**.
- The Project Browser can be floated, resized, docked on top of the Properties palette, and customized. If the Properties palette and the Project Browser are docked on top of each other, use the appropriate tab to display the required panel.

How To: Search the Project Browser

1. In the Project Browser, right-click on the top level Views node as shown in Figure 1–25.

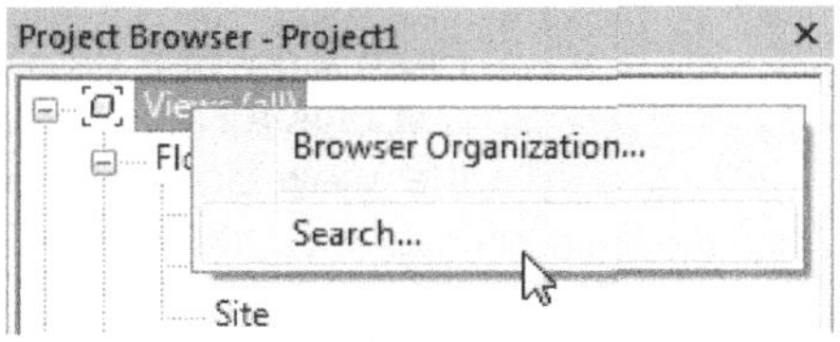

Figure 1–25

2. In the Search in Project Browser dialog box, type the words that you want to find (as shown on the left in Figure 1–26), and click **Next**.
3. In the Project Browser, the first instance of that search displays as shown on the right in Figure 1–26.

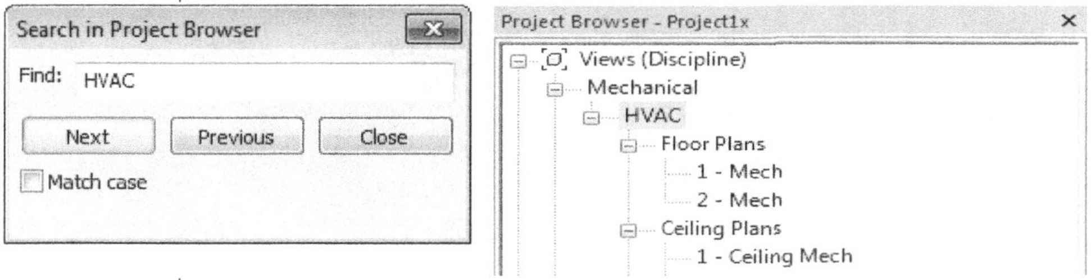

Figure 1–26

4. Continue using **Next** and **Previous** to move through the list.
5. Click **Close** when you are done.

Hint: Setting the Discipline of a View

In the default MEP templates, the Project Browser is set to display views sorted by discipline and sub-discipline. These are set in the Properties of the view, as shown in Figure 1–27.

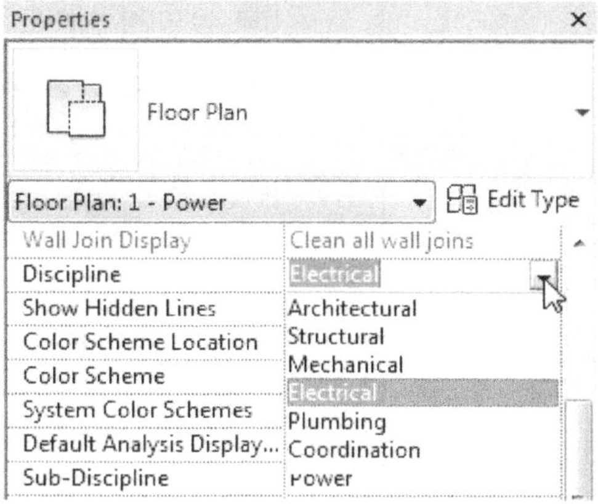

Figure 1–27

8. View Window

Each view of a project opens in its own window. Each view displays a Navigation Bar (for quick access to viewing tools) and the View Control Bar, as shown in Figure 1–28.

In 3D views you can also use the ViewCube to rotate the view.

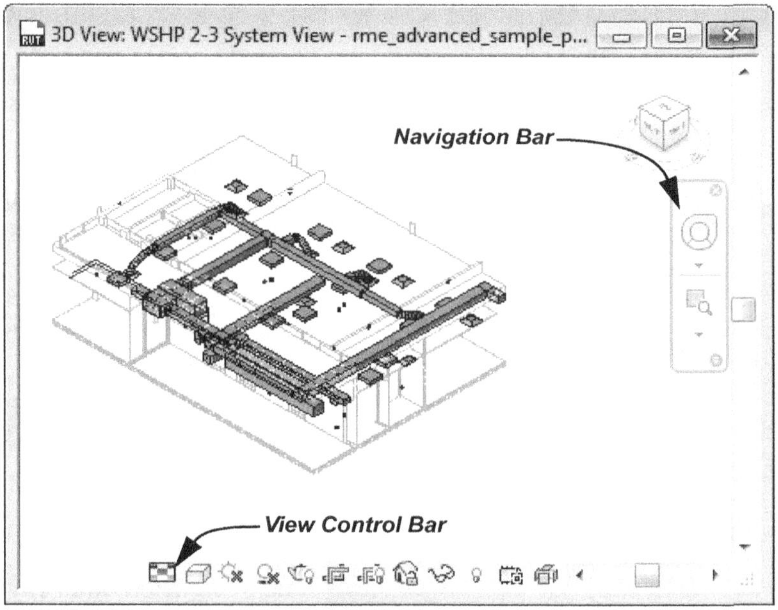

Figure 1–28

- To cycle through multiple views you can use several different methods:
  - Press <Ctrl>+<Tab>
  - Select the view in the Project Browser
  - In the Quick Access Toolbar or *View* tab>Windows panel, expand (Switch Windows) and select the view from the list.
- You can Tile or Cascade views. In the *View* tab>Windows panel, click (Cascade Windows) or (Tile Windows). You can also type the shortcuts **WC** to cascade the windows or **WT** to tile the windows.

9. Navigation Bar

The Navigation Bar enables you to access various viewing commands, as shown in Figure 1–29.

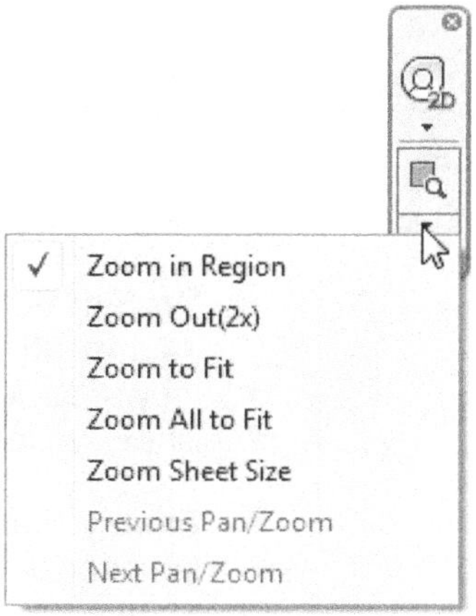

Figure 1–29

10. View Control Bar

The number of options in the View Control Bar change when you are in a 3D view.

The View Control Bar (shown in Figure 1–30), displays at the bottom of each view window. It controls aspects of that view, such as the scale and detail level. It also includes tools that display parts of the view and hide or isolate elements in the view.

Figure 1–30

1.3 Starting Projects

File operations to open existing files, create new files from a template, and save files in the Autodesk Revit software are found in the *File* tab, as shown in Figure 1–31.

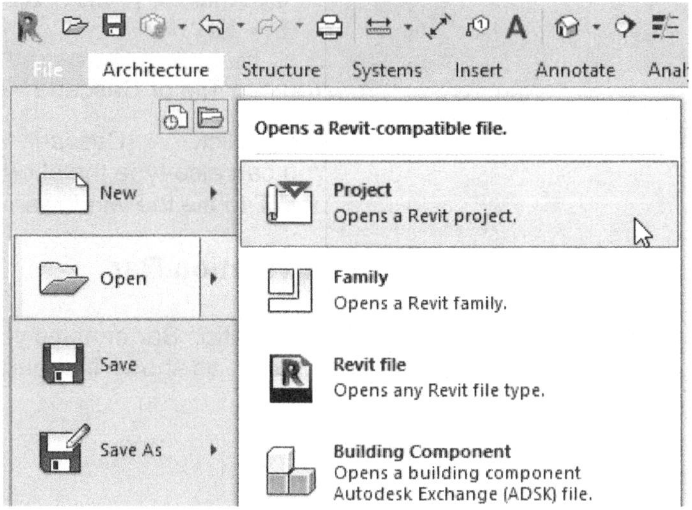

Figure 1–31

There are three main file formats:

- **Project files (.rvt):** These are where you do the majority of your work in the building model by adding elements, creating views, annotating views, and setting up printable sheets. They are initially based on template files.
- **Family files (.rfa):** These are separate components that can be inserted in a project. They include elements that can stand alone (e.g., a table or piece of mechanical equipment) or are items that are hosted in other elements (e.g., a door in a wall or a lighting fixture in a ceiling). Title block and Annotation Symbol files are special types of family files.
- **Template files (.rte):** These are the base files for any new project or family. They are designed to hold standard information and settings for creating new project files. The software includes several templates for various types of projects. You can also create custom templates.

Opening Projects

To open an existing project, in the Quick Access Toolbar or *File* tab click (Open), or press <Ctrl>+<O>. The Open dialog box opens (as shown in Figure 1–32), in which you can navigate to the required folder and select a project file.

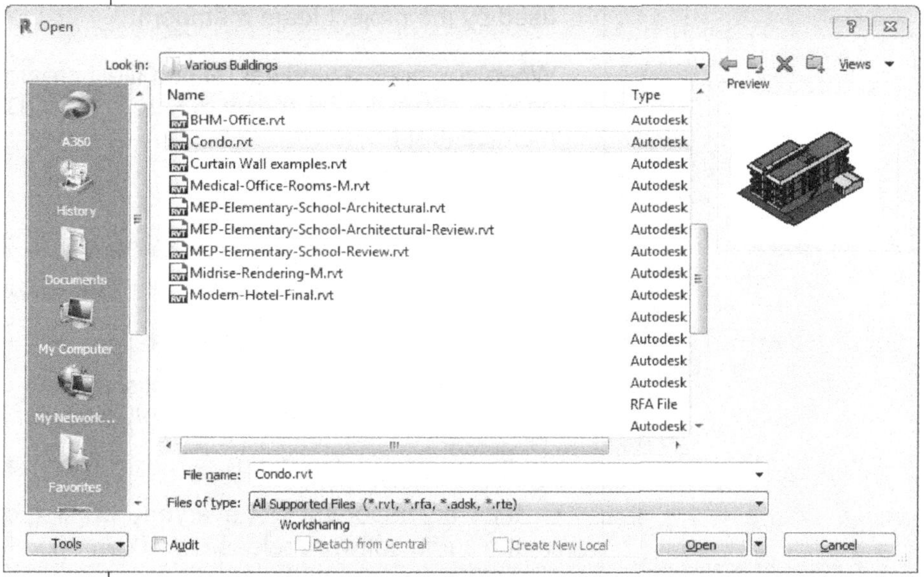

Figure 1–32

- When you first open the Autodesk Revit software, the Startup Screen displays, showing lists of recently used projects and family files as shown in Figure 1–33. This screen also displays if you close all projects.

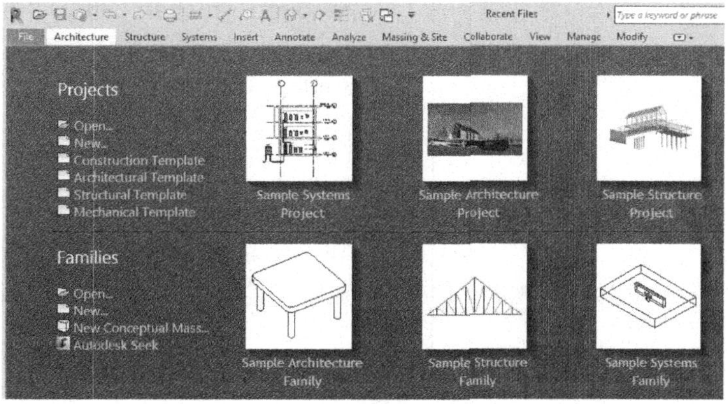

Figure 1–33

- You can select the picture of a recently opened project or use one of the options on the left to open or start a new project using the default templates.

Hint: Opening Workset-Related Files

Worksets are used when the project becomes large enough for multiple people to work on it at the same time. At this point, the project manager creates a central file with multiple worksets (such as element interiors, building shell, and site) that are used by the project team members.

When you open a workset related file it creates a new local file on your computer as shown in Figure 1–34. Do not work in the main central file.

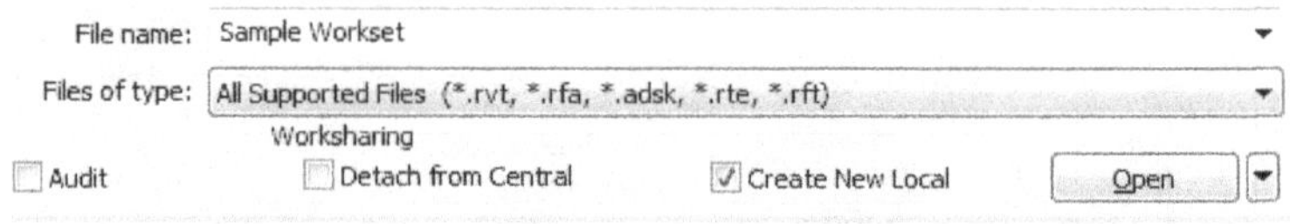

Figure 1–34

- For more information on establishing and using Worksets, refer to the *Autodesk Revit: Collaboration Tools* student guide.

- It is very important that everyone working on a project uses the same software release. You can open files created in earlier versions of the software in comparison to your own, but you cannot open files created in newer versions of the software.
- When you open a file created in an earlier version, the Model Upgrade dialog box (shown in Figure 1–35) indicates the release of a file and the release to which it will be upgraded. If required, you can cancel the upgrade before it completes.

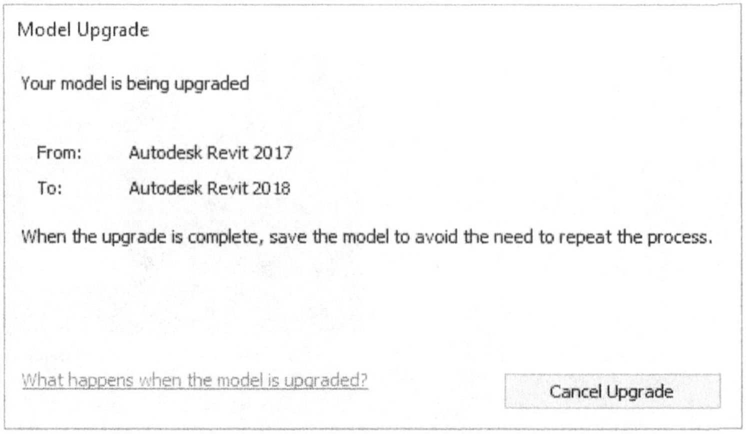

Figure 1–35

Starting New Projects

New projects are based on a template file. The template file includes preset levels, views, and some families, such as wall styles and text styles. Check with your BIM Manager about which template you need to use for your projects. Your company might have more than one based on the types of building that you are designing.

How To: Start a New Project

1. In the *File* tab, expand (New) and click (Project) (as shown in Figure 1–36), or press <Ctrl>+<N>.

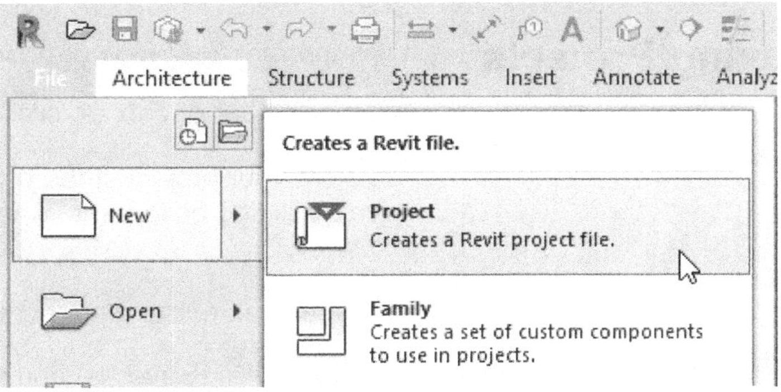

Figure 1–36

2. In the New Project dialog box (shown in Figure 1–37), select the template that you want to use and click **OK**.

The list of Template files is set in the Options dialog box in the File Locations pane. It might vary depending on the installed product and company standards.

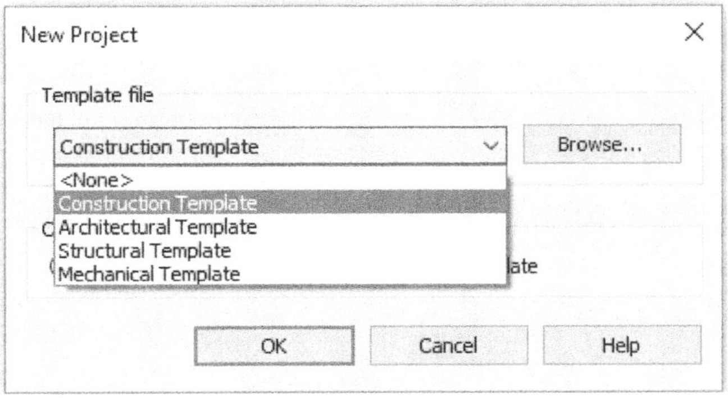

Figure 1–37

- You can select from a list of templates if they have been set up by your BIM Manager.

- You can add (New) to the Quick Access Toolbar. At the end of the Quick Access Toolbar, click (Customize Quick Access Toolbar) and select **New**, as shown in Figure 1–38.

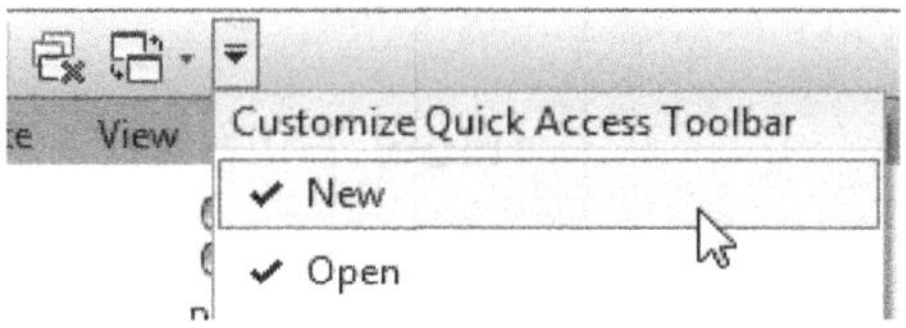

Figure 1–38

Saving Projects

It is important to save your projects frequently. In the Quick Access Toolbar or *File* tab click (Save), or press <Ctrl>+<S > to save your project. If the project has not yet been saved, the Save As dialog box opens, where you can specify a file location and name.

- To save an existing project with a new name, in the *File* tab, expand (Save As) and click (Project).
- If you have not saved in a set amount of time, the software opens the Project Not Saved Recently alert box, as shown in Figure 1–39. Select **Save the project**. If you want to set reminder intervals or not save at this time, select the other options.

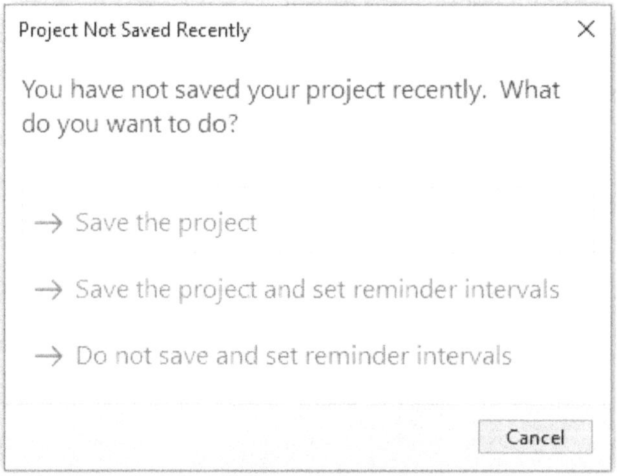

Figure 1–39

- You can set the *Save Reminder interval* to **15** or **30 minutes**, **1**, **2**, or **4 hours**, or to have **No reminders** display. In the *File* tab, click **Options** to open the Options dialog box. In the left pane, select **General** and set the interval as shown in Figure 1–40.

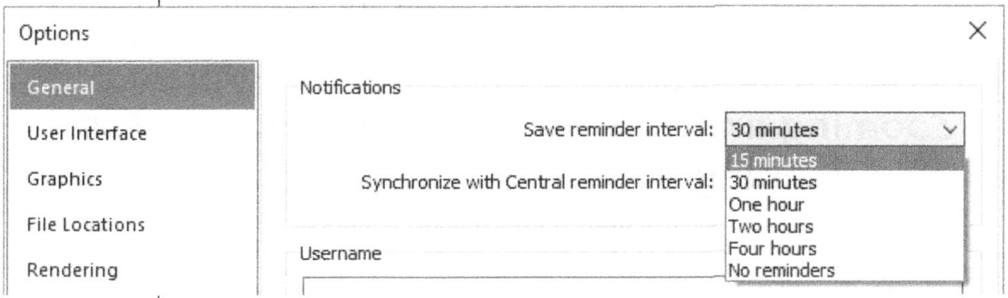

Figure 1–40

Saving Backup Copies

By default, the software saves a backup copy of a project file when you save the project. Backup copies are numbered incrementally (e.g., **My Project.0001.rvt**, **My Project.0002.rvt**, etc.) and are saved in the same folder as the original file. In the Save As dialog box, click **Options...** to control how many backup copies are saved. The default number is three backups. If you exceed this number, the software deletes the oldest backup file.

Hint: Saving Workset-Related Projects

If you use worksets in your project, you need to save the project locally and to the central file. It is recommended to save the local file frequently, just like any other file, and save to the central file every hour or so.

To synchronize your changes with the main file, in the Quick Access Toolbar expand  (Synchronize and Modify Settings) and click  (Synchronize Now). After you save to the central file, save the file locally again.

At the end of the day, or when you are finished with the current session, use  (Synchronize and Modify Settings) to relinquish the files you have been working on to the central file.

- The maximum number of backups for workset-enabled files is set to 20 by default.

1.4 Viewing Commands

Viewing commands are crucial to working efficiently in most drawing and modeling programs and the Autodesk Revit software is no exception. Once in a view, you can use the Zoom controls to navigate in it. You can zoom in and out and pan in any view. There are also special tools for viewing in 3D.

Zooming and Panning

Using The Mouse to Zoom and Pan

Use the mouse wheel (shown in Figure 1–41) as the main method of moving around the models.

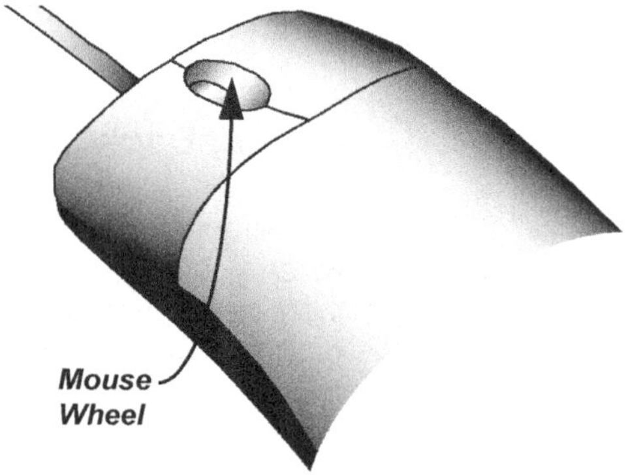

Figure 1–41

- Scroll the wheel on the mouse up to zoom in and down to zoom out.
- Hold the wheel and move the mouse to pan.
- Double-click on the wheel to zoom to the extents of the view.
- In a 3D view, hold <Shift> and the mouse wheel and move the mouse to rotate around the model.

- When you save a model and exit the software, the pan and zoom location of each view is remembered. This is especially important for complex models.

Zoom Controls

A number of additional zoom methods enable you to control the screen display. **Zoom** and **Pan** can be performed at any time while using other commands.

- You can access the **Zoom** commands in the Navigation Bar in the upper right corner of the view (as shown in Figure 1–42). You can also access them from most shortcut menus and by typing the shortcut commands.

 *(2D Wheel) provides cursor-specific access to **Zoom** and **Pan**.*

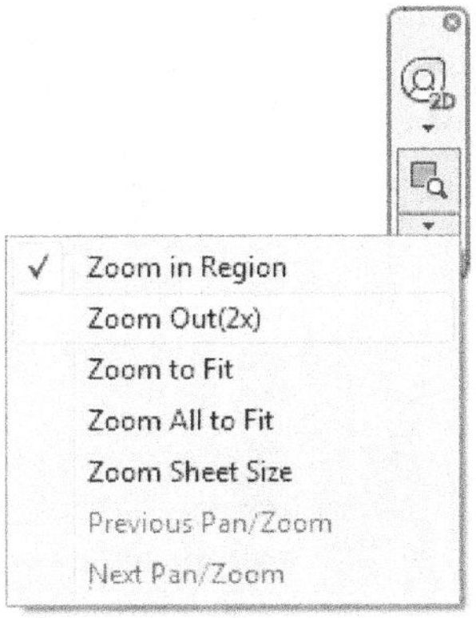

Figure 1–42

Zoom Commands

	**Zoom In Region (ZR)**	Zooms into a region that you define. Drag the cursor or select two points to define the rectangular area you want to zoom into. This is the default command.
	**Zoom Out(2x) (ZO)**	Zooms out to half the current magnification around the center of the elements.
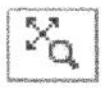	**Zoom To Fit (ZF or ZE)**	Zooms out so that the entire contents of the project only display on the screen in the current view.
	**Zoom All To Fit (ZA)**	Zooms out so that the entire contents of the project display on the screen in all open views.
	**Zoom Sheet Size (ZS)**	Zooms in or out in relation to the sheet size.
N/A	**Previous Pan/Zoom (ZP)**	Steps back one **Zoom** command.
N/A	**Next Pan/Zoom**	Steps forward one **Zoom** command if you have done a **Previous Pan/Zoom**.

Viewing in 3D

Even if you started a project entirely in plan views, you can quickly create 3D views of the model, as shown in Figure 1–43. There are two types of 3D views: isometric views created by the **Default 3D View** command and perspective views created by the **Camera** command.

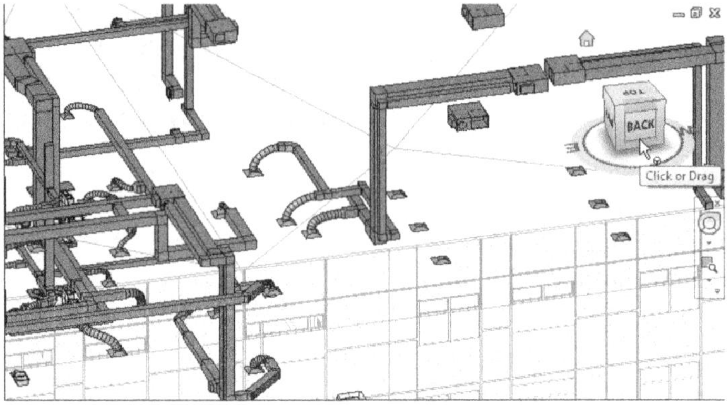

Figure 1–43

Enhanced in **2018**

Working in 3D views helps you visualize the project and position some of the elements correctly. You can create and modify elements in both isometric and perspective 3D views, just as you can in plan views.

- Once you have created a 3D view, you can save it and easily return to it.

How To: Create and Save a 3D Isometric View

You can spin the view to a different angle using the mouse wheel or the middle button of a three-button mouse. Hold <Shift> as you press the wheel or middle button and drag the cursor.

1. In the Quick Access Toolbar or *View* tab>Create panel, click  (Default 3D View). The default 3D Southeast isometric view opens, as shown in Figure 1–44.

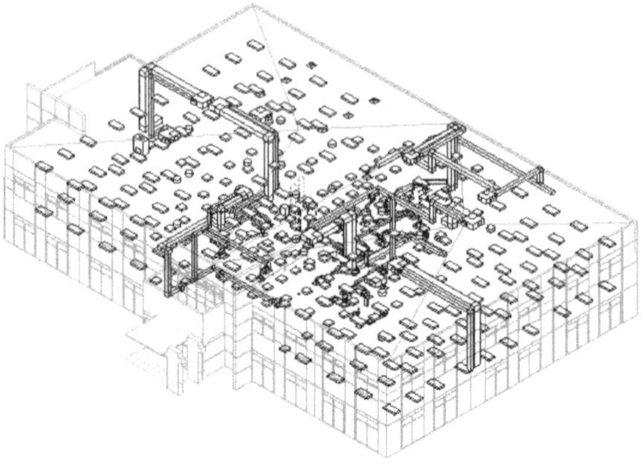

Figure 1–44

2. Modify the view to display the building from other directions.
3. In the Project Browser, right-click on the {3D} view and select **Rename...**
4. Type a new name in the Rename View dialog box, as shown in Figure 1–45, and click **OK**.

All types of views can be renamed.

Figure 1–45

- When changes to the default 3D view are saved and you start another default 3D view, it displays the Southeast isometric view once again. If you modified the default 3D view but did not save it to a new name, the **Default 3D View** command opens the view in the last orientation you specified.

How To: Create a Perspective View

1. Switch to a Floor Plan view.
2. In the Quick Access Toolbar or *View* tab>Create panel, expand (Default 3D View) and click (Camera).
3. Place the camera on the view.
4. Point the camera in the direction in which you want it to shoot by placing the target on the view, as shown in Figure 1–46. The view displays as shown in Figure 1–47.

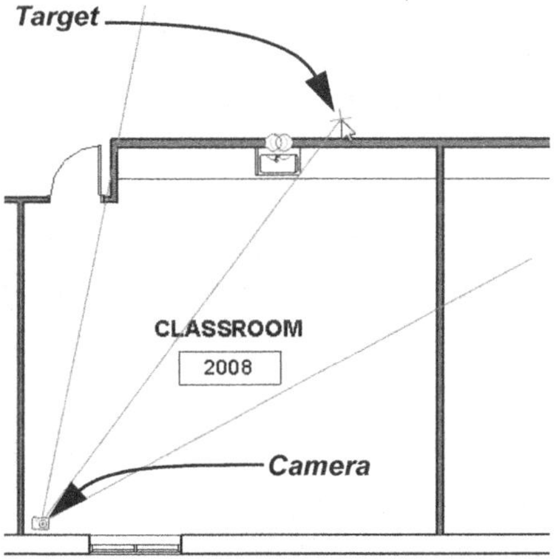

Figure 1–46

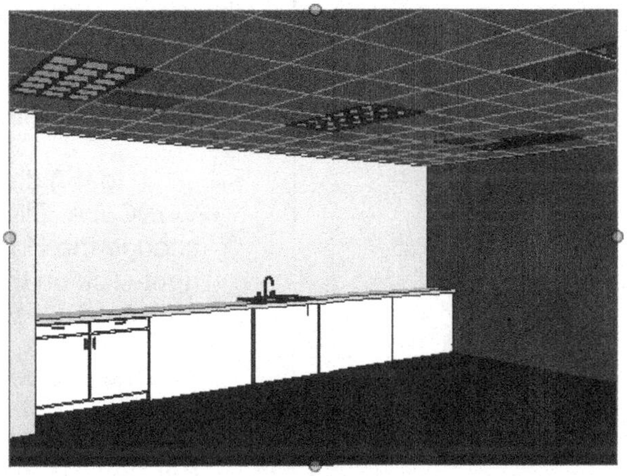

Figure 1–47

- Use the round controls to modify the display size of the view and press <Shift> + the mouse wheel to change the view.

5. In the Properties palette scroll down and adjust the *Eye Elevation* and *Target Elevation* as required.

- If the view is distorted, reset the target so that it is centered in the boundary of the view (called the crop region). In the *Modify | Cameras* tab>Camera panel, click (Reset Target).
- You can modify a view by adding shadows. In the View Control Bar, toggle (Shadows Off) and (Shadows On). Shadows display in any model view, not just in the 3D views.

Hint: Using the ViewCube

The ViewCube provides visual clues as to where you are in a 3D view. It helps you move around the model with quick access to specific views (such as top, front, and right), as well as corner and directional views, as shown in Figure 1–48.

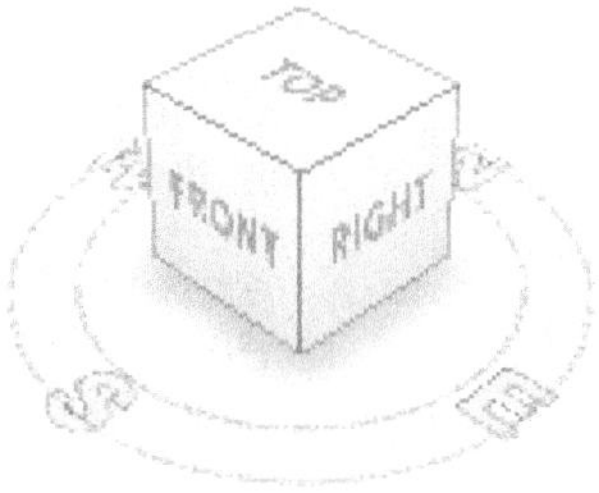

Figure 1–48

Move the cursor over any face of the ViewCube to highlight it. Once a face is highlighted, you can select it to reorient the model. You can also click and drag on the ViewCube to rotate the box, which rotates the model.

- (Home) displays when you roll the cursor over the ViewCube. Click it to return to the view defined as **Home**. To change the Home view, set the view as you want it, right-click on the ViewCube, and select **Set Current View as Home**.
- The ViewCube displays in isometric and perspective views.
- Right-click on the View Cube and click **Toggle to Parallel-3D View** or **Toggle to Perspective-3D View**. You can make more changes to the model in a parallel view.

Visual Styles

Any view can have a visual style applied. The **Visual Style** options found in the View Control Bar (as shown in Figure 1–49), specify the shading of the building model. These options apply to plan, elevation, section, and 3D views.

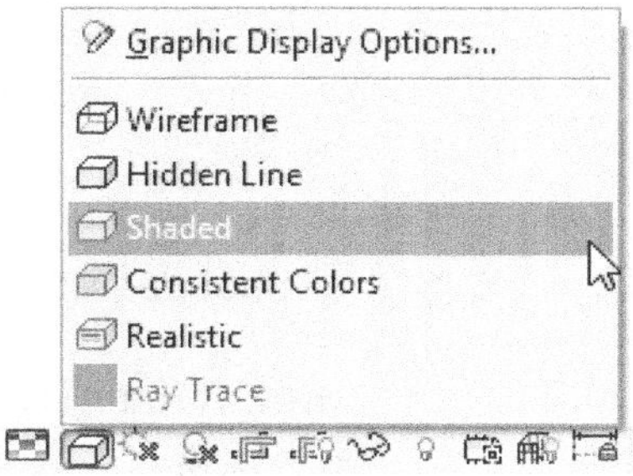

Figure 1–49

- (Wireframe) displays the lines and edges that make up elements, but hides the surfaces. This can be useful when you are dealing with complex intersections.
- (Hidden Line) displays the lines, edges, and surfaces of the elements, but it does not display any colors. This is the most common visual style to use while working on a design.
- (Shaded) and (Consistent Colors) give you a sense of the materials, including transparent glass. An example that uses Consistent Colors is shown in Figure 1–50.

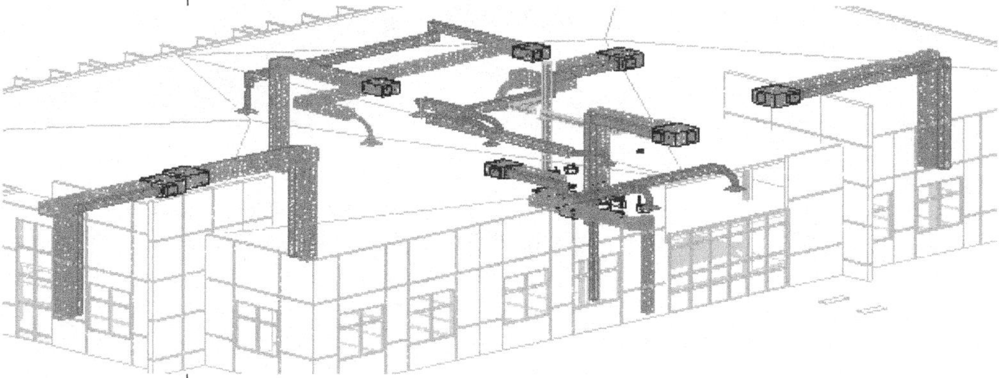

Figure 1–50

- (Realistic) displays what is shown when you render the view, including RPC (Rich Photorealistic Content) components and artificial lights. It takes a lot of computer power to execute this visual style. Therefore, it is better to use the other visual styles most of the time as you are working.

- (Ray Trace) is useful if you have created a 3D view that you want to render. It gradually moves from draft resolution to photorealistic. You can stop the process at any time.

Hint: Rendering

Rendering is a powerful tool which enables you to display a photorealistic view of the model you are working on, such as the example shown in Figure 1–51. This can be used to help clients and designers to understand a building's design in better detail.

Figure 1–51

- In the View Control Bar, click (Show Rendering Dialog) to set up the options. **Show Rendering Dialog** is only available in 3D views.

Practice 1a Open and Review a Project

Practice Objectives

- Navigate the graphic user interface.
- Manipulate 2D and 3D views by zooming and panning.
- Create 3D Isometric and Perspective views.
- Set the Visual Style of a view.

Estimated time for completion: 15 minutes

In this practice you will open a project file, as shown in Figure 1–52 and display each of the various parts of the Autodesk Revit interface. You will open views through the Project Browser, and switch between different views. You will also select elements and display the information about them in the Properties palette. Finally you will create and save 3D views.

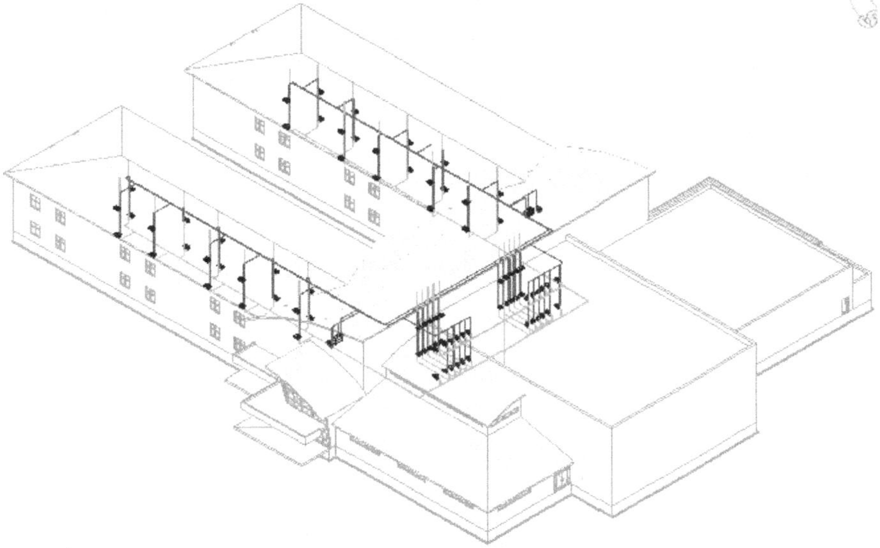

Figure 1–52

Task 1 - Open an Autodesk Revit MEP project and review it.

1. In the *File* tab, expand (Open) and click (Project).
2. In the Open dialog box, navigate to the *Introduction* practice files folder and select **MEP-Elementary-School-Review-M.rvt**.
3. Click **Open**.The project opens in the **3D Plumbing** view, as shown in Figure 1–52 (above).

4. Close any other open projects and views.

5. In the Project Browser, expand **Mechanical>HVAC>Floor Plans** and select **01 Mechanical Plan**, as shown in Figure 1–53.

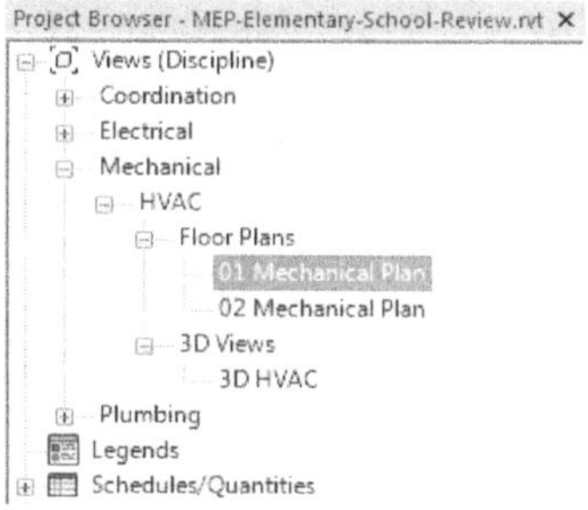

Figure 1–53

6. Double-click on **01 Mechanical Plan**. The applicable view opens as shown in Figure 1–54.

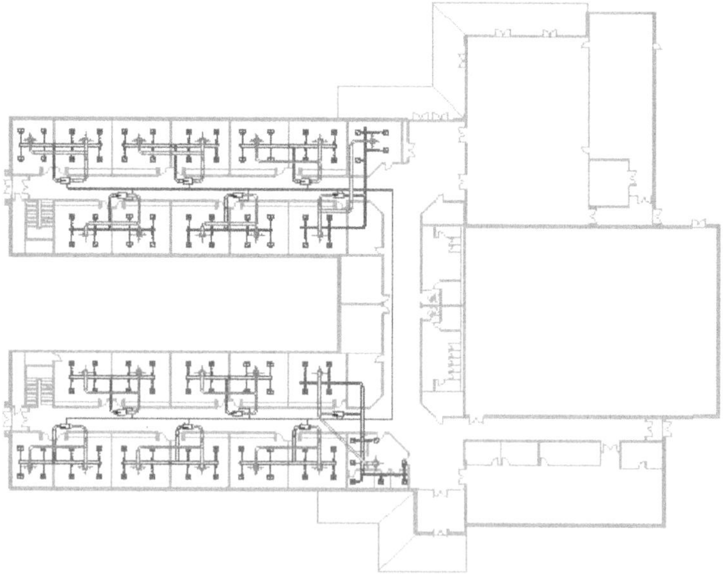

Figure 1–54

7. Use the scroll wheel to zoom and pan around the view.

8. Double-click on the scroll wheel or type **ZF** (Zoom to Fit) to return to the full view.

9. Expand **Plumbing>Plumbing>Floor Plans** and double-click on the **01 Plumbing Plan** view to open it.

10. Expand **Coordination>MEP>Floor Plans** and double-click on **01 Space Planning** to open this view.

11. All of the previous views are still open. In the Quick Access Toolbar (or *View* tab>Windows panel), expand (Switch Windows), as shown in Figure 1–55, and select one of the previous views to which to switch.

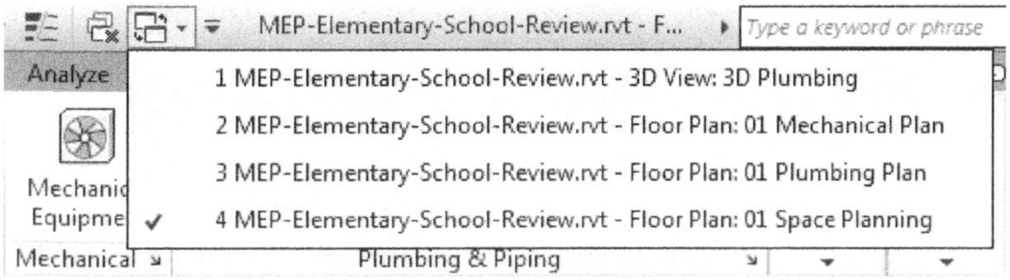

Figure 1–55

12. In the *View* tab>Windows panel, click (Tile) or type **WT** to display all of the open views on the screen at the same time.

13. Type **ZA** (Zoom All to Fit) to have the model display completely within each view window, as shown in Figure 1–56.

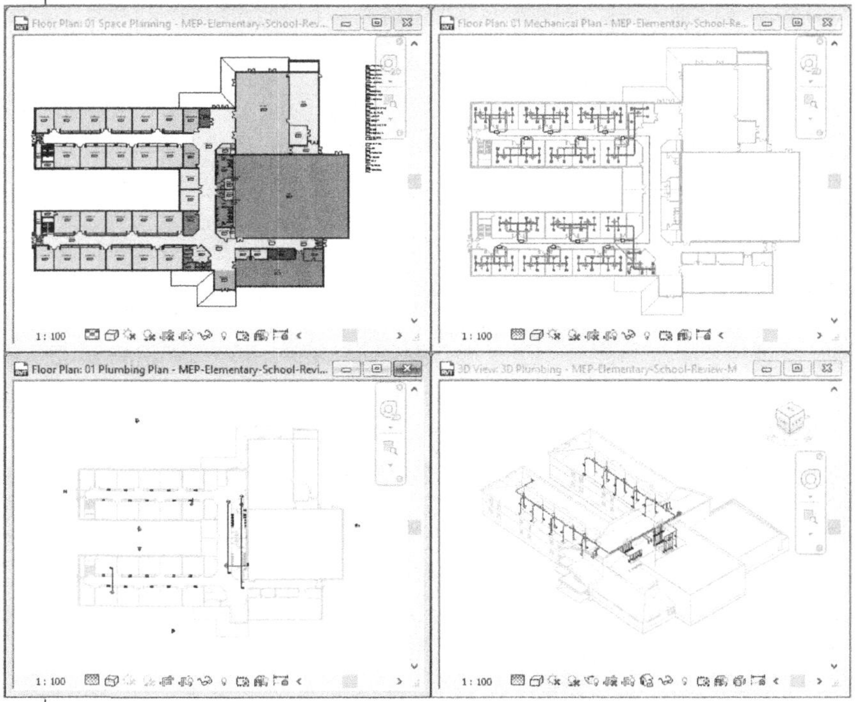

Figure 1–56

14. Click in the open **01 Mechanical Plan** view to make it active.

15. In the upper right corner, click (Maximize), as shown in Figure 1–57, so that this view fills the drawing area. Then use one of the zoom commands so that the model fills the view.

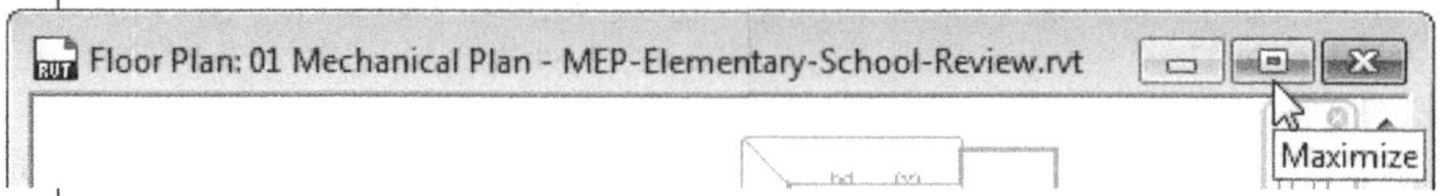

Figure 1–57

16. In the Quick Access Toolbar, click (Close Hidden Windows). Only the current active view is open.

Task 2 - Display the Element Properties.

1. In the **01 Mechanical Plan** view, hover over a duct without selecting it first. The duct highlights and a tooltip displays as shown in Figure 1–58. Information about the element also displays in the Status Bar but not in Properties.

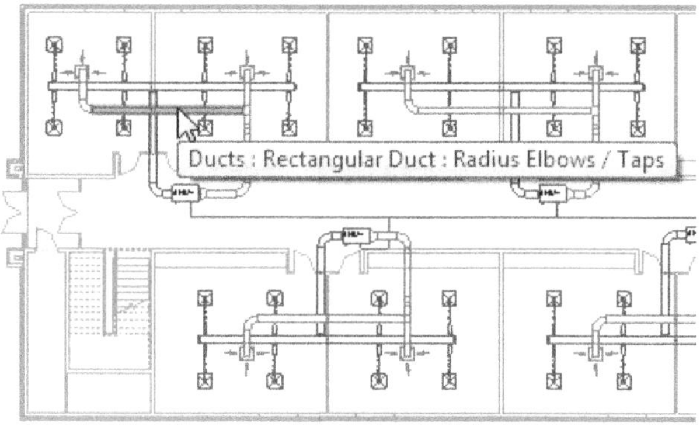

Figure 1–58

2. Click on the duct to select it. The selection color and tabs on the ribbon at the top of the screen change. Properties now displays information about this piece of ductwork, as shown in Figure 1–59.

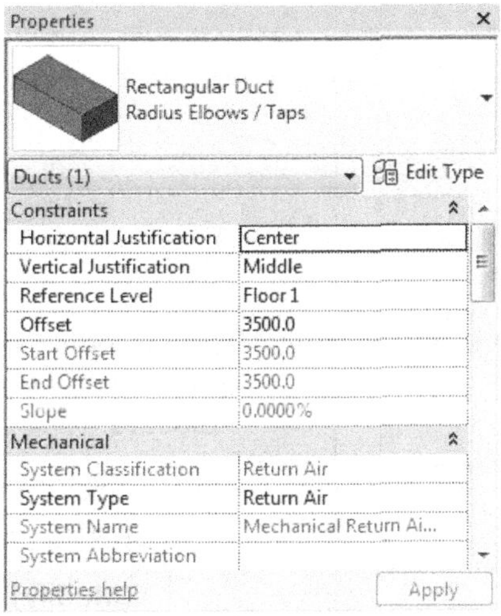

Figure 1–59

3. Hold <Ctrl> and in the view, select another, similar Duct element, as shown in Figure 1–60. Properties now displays that two ducts (Ducts(2)) are selected with the same information.

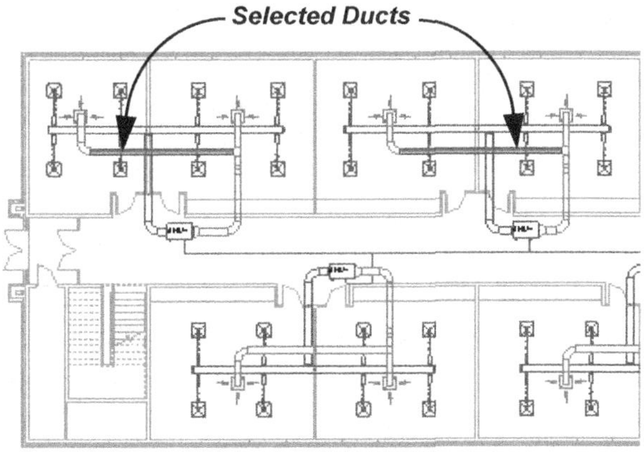

Figure 1–60

4. Hold <Ctrl> and select an air terminal. Properties now displays Common (3) in the Filter drop-down list, because the three selected elements are not of the same type. Therefore they do not share the same type of properties.

5. In Properties, expand the Filter drop-down list and select **Air Terminals**, as shown in Figure 1–61.

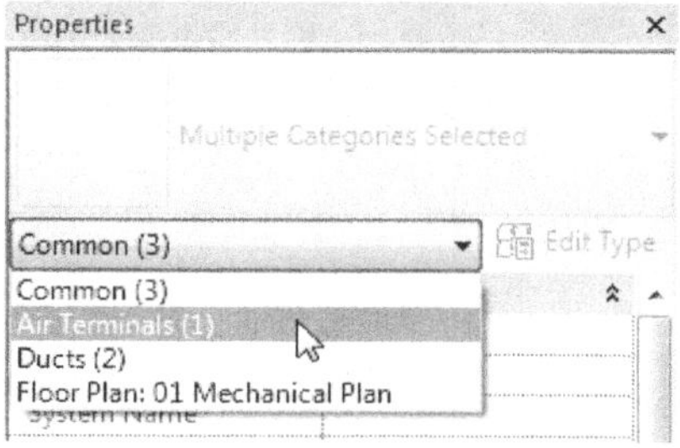

Figure 1–61

6. Only the Air Terminal properties are displayed, but the selection set has not changed. In the view they are all still selected.

7. End the command using one of the following methods:
   - In *Modify | Multi-Select* tab>Select panel, click (Modify).
   - Press <Esc> twice.
   - Click in the view window (without selecting an element).
   - Right-click in the view window and select **Cancel**.

Task 3 - Create 3D Views.

1. In the Quick Access Toolbar, click (Default 3D View).

2. A 3D Isometric view displays, as shown in Figure 1–62.

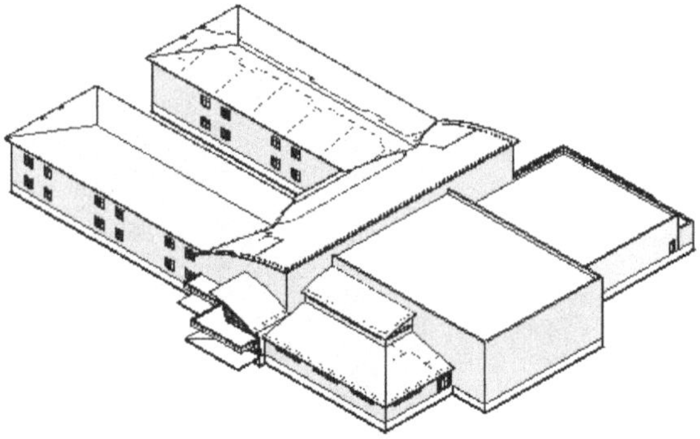

Figure 1–62

3. Press and hold <Shift> and press the middle mouse (scroll) button to orbit the view.

4. In the View Control Bar, select several different Visual Styles to see how they impact the view, as shown in Figure 1–63.

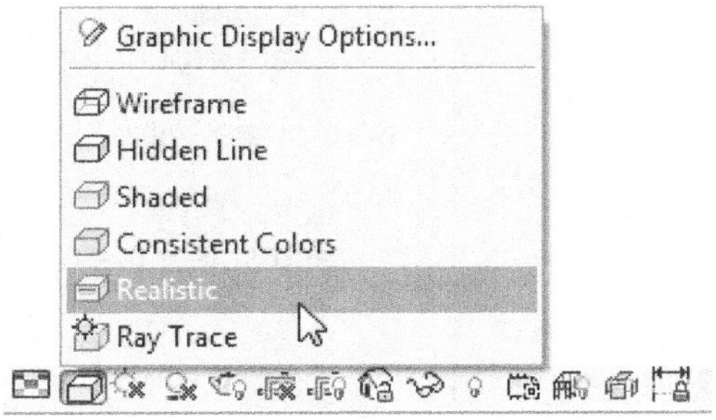

Figure 1–63

5. Select a view and visual style that you like. In the Project Browser, expand Coordination>All>**3D Views**, right-click on **{3D}** and select **Rename**.

6. Name the view **3D Exterior** and click **OK**.

Task 4 - Create a camera view.

1. Switch back to the **01 Mechanical Plan** view.

2. In the Quick Access Toolbar, expand (Default 3D View) and click (Camera).

3. Place the camera and select a point for the target similar to that shown in Figure 1–64.

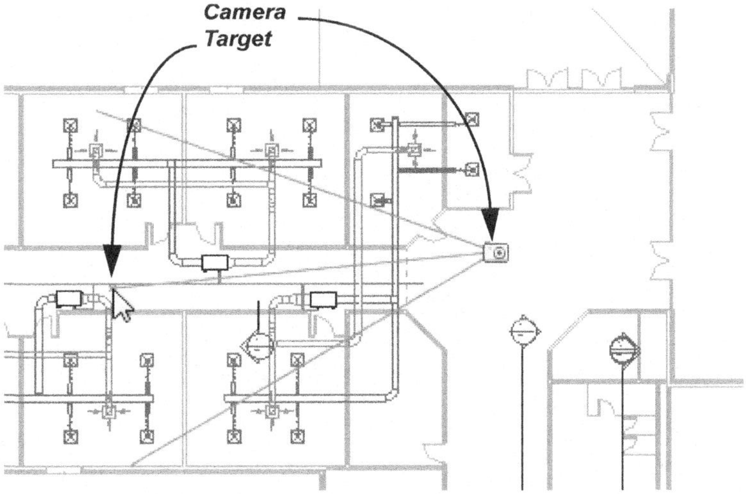

Figure 1–64

4. The new view displays. Use the controls on the outline of the view to resize the view.

5. Click inside the 3D view and use <Shift>+ mouse wheel to rotate around until you get a good view of the ductwork.

6. Set the Visual Style as required.

7. In the Project Browser, expand Mechanical>???>*3D Views* and select the new **3D View 1** as shown in Figure 1–65.

The new view displays in the ??? category because it has not been assigned a Sub-Discipline.

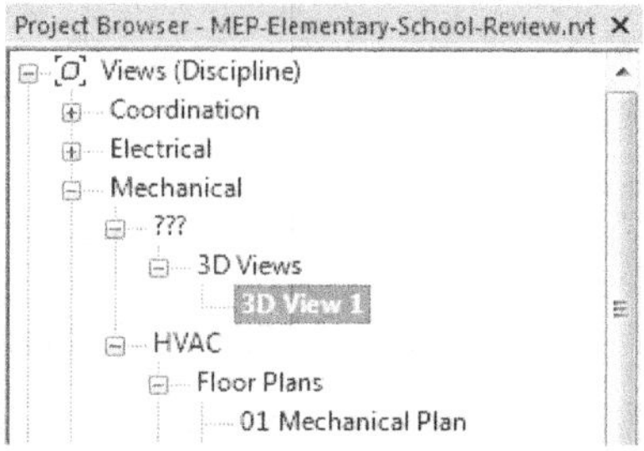

Figure 1–65

8. In Properties, in the *Graphics* area, expand Sub-Discipline and select **HVAC**, as shown in Figure 1–66.

9. Click **Apply**. The view moves to the correct sub-discipline group as shown in Figure 1–67. Rename the view as required.

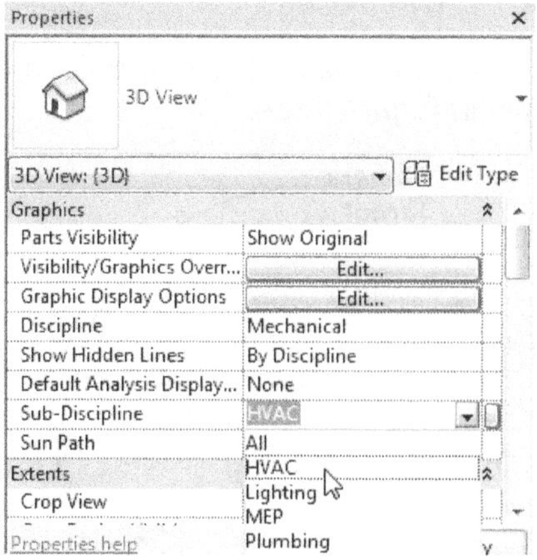

Figure 1–66

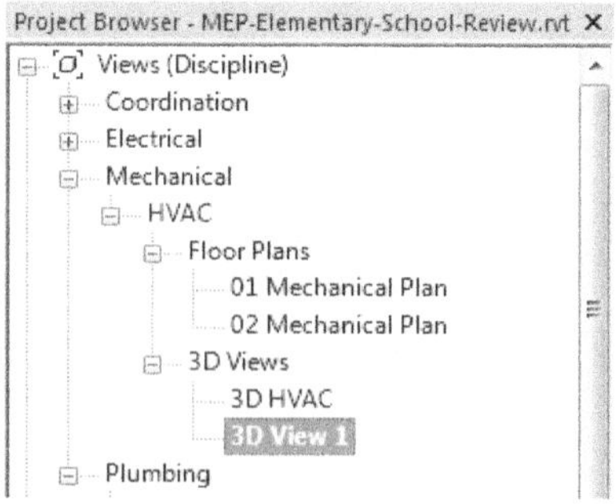

Figure 1–67

10. Save the project.

11. In the *File* tab, click (Close).

Chapter Review Questions

1. When you create a project in the Autodesk Revit software, do you work in 3D (as shown on the left in Figure 1–68) or 2D (as shown on the right in Figure 1–68)?

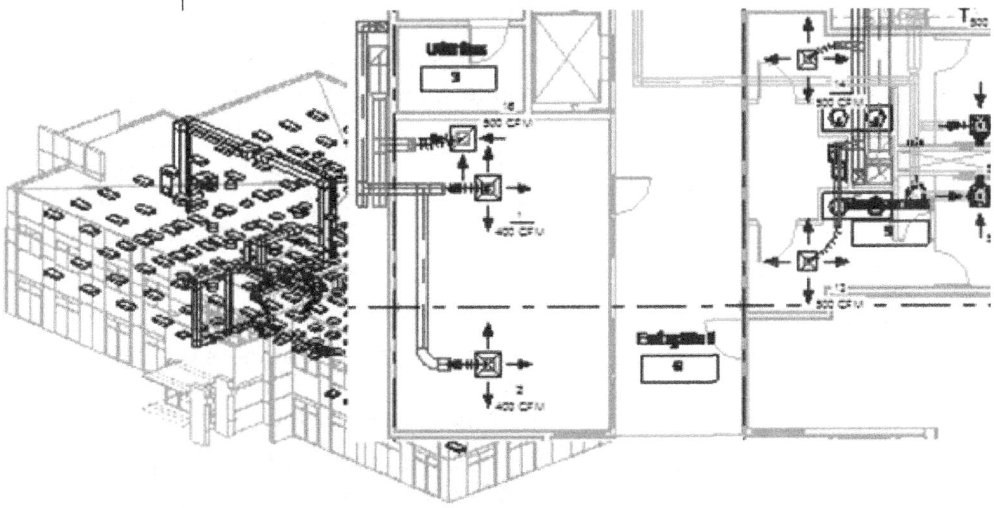

Figure 1–68

   a. You work in 2D in plan views and in 3D in non-plan views.

   b. You work in 3D almost all of the time, even when you are using what looks like a flat view.

   c. You work in 2D or 3D depending on how you toggle the 2D/3D control.

   d. You work in 2D in plan and section views and in 3D in isometric views.

2. What is the purpose of the Project Browser?

   a. It enables you to browse through the building project, similar to a walk through.

   b. It is the interface for managing all of the files that are required to create the complete architectural model of the building.

   c. It manages multiple Autodesk Revit projects as an alternative to using Windows Explorer.

   d. It is used to access and manage the views of the project.

3. Which part(s) of the interface changes according to the command you are using? (Select all that apply.)
    a. Ribbon
    b. View Control Bar
    c. Options Bar
    d. Properties Palette
4. The difference between Type Properties and Properties (the ribbon location is shown in Figure 1–69) is...

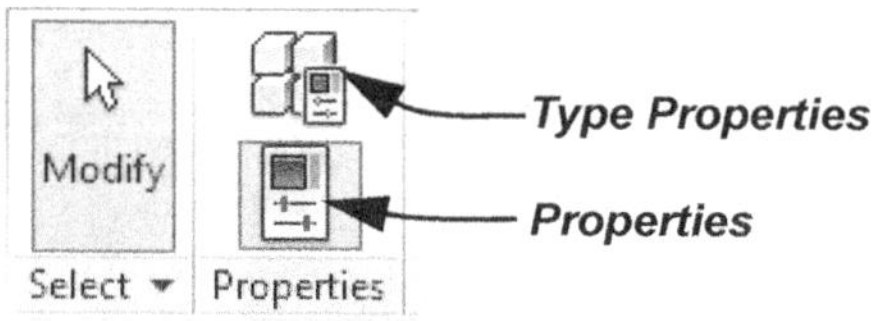

Figure 1–69

    a. Properties stores parameters that apply to the selected individual element(s). Type Properties stores parameters that impact every element of the same type in the project.
    b. Properties stores the location parameters of an element. Type Properties stores the size and identity parameters of an element.
    c. Properties only stores parameters of the view. Type Properties stores parameters of model components.
5. When you start a new project, how do you specify the base information in the new file?
    a. Transfer the base information from an existing project.
    b. Select the right template for the task.
    c. The Autodesk Revit software automatically extracts the base information from imported or linked file(s).
6. What is the main difference between a view made using (Default 3D View) and a view made using (Camera)?
    a. Use Default **3D View** for exterior views and **Camera** for interiors.
    b. **Default 3D View** creates a static image and a **Camera** view is live and always updated.
    c. **Default 3D View** is isometric and a **Camera** view is perspective.
    d. **Default 3D View** is used for the overall building and a **Camera** view is used for looking in tight spaces.

Command Summary

Button	Command	Location
General Tools		
	Modify	• **Ribbon:** All tabs>Select panel • **Shortcut:** MD
	New	• **Quick Access Toolbar** (Optional) • ***File* tab** • **Shortcut:** <Ctrl>+<N>
	Open	• **Quick Access Toolbar** • ***File* tab** • **Shortcut:** <Ctrl>+<O>
	Open Documents	• ***File* tab**
	Properties	• **Ribbon:** *Modify* tab>Properties panel • **Shortcut:** PP
	Recent Documents	• ***File* tab**
	Save	• **Quick Access Toolbar** • ***File* tab** • **Shortcut:** <Ctrl>+<S>
	Synchronize and Modify Settings	• **Quick Access Toolbar**
	Synchronize Now/	• **Quick Access Toolbar**>expand Synchronize and Modify Settings
	Type Properties	• **Ribbon:** *Modify* tab>Properties panel • **Properties palette**
Viewing Tools		
	Camera	• **Quick Access Toolbar**> Expand Default 3D View • **Ribbon:** *View* tab>Create panel> expand Default 3D View
	Default 3D View	• **Quick Access Toolbar** • **Ribbon:** *View* tab>Create panel
	Home	• **ViewCube**
N/A	**Next Pan/Zoom**	• **Navigation Bar** • **Shortcut Menu**
N/A	**Previous Pan/Zoom**	• **Navigation Bar** • **Shortcut Menu** • **Shortcut:** ZP
	Shadows On/Off	• **View Control Bar**

	Show Rendering Dialog/ Render	• **View Control Bar** • **Ribbon:** *View* tab>Graphics panel • **Shortcut:** RR
	Zoom All to Fit	• **Navigation Bar** • **Shortcut:** ZA
	Zoom in Region	• **Navigation Bar** • **Shortcut Menu** • **Shortcut:** ZR
	Zoom Out (2x)	• **Navigation Bar** • **Shortcut Menu** • **Shortcut:** ZO
	Zoom Sheet Size	• **Navigation Bar** • **Shortcut:** ZS
	Zoom to Fit	• **Navigation Bar** • **Shortcut Menu** • **Shortcut:** ZF, ZE
Visual Styles		
	Consistent Colors	• **View Control Bar**:
	Hidden Line	• **View Control Bar** • **Shortcut:** HL
	Ray Trace	• **View Control Bar**:
	Realistic	• **View Control Bar**
	Shaded	• **View Control Bar** • **Shortcut:** SD
	Wireframe	• **View Control Bar** • **Shortcut:** WF

Basic Sketching and Modify Tools

Basic sketching, selecting, and modifying tools are the foundation of working with all types of elements in the Autodesk® Revit® software, including components such as air terminals, plumbing fixtures, and electrical devices. Using these tools with drawing aids helps you to place and modify elements to create accurate building models.

Learning Objectives in this Chapter

- Ease the placement of elements by incorporating drawing aids, such as alignment lines, temporary dimensions, permanent dimensions, and snaps.
- Place Reference Planes as temporary guide lines.
- Insert components such as mechanical equipment, plumbing fixtures, and electrical devices.
- Use techniques to select and filter groups of elements.
- Modify elements using a contextual tab, Properties, temporary dimensions, and controls.
- Move, copy, rotate, and mirror elements and create array copies in linear and radial patterns.

2.1 Using General Sketching Tools

When you start a command, the contextual tab on the ribbon, Options Bar, and Properties palette enable you to set up features for each new element you are placing in the project. As you start modeling, several features called *drawing aids* display, as shown in Figure 2–1. They help you to create designs quickly and accurately.

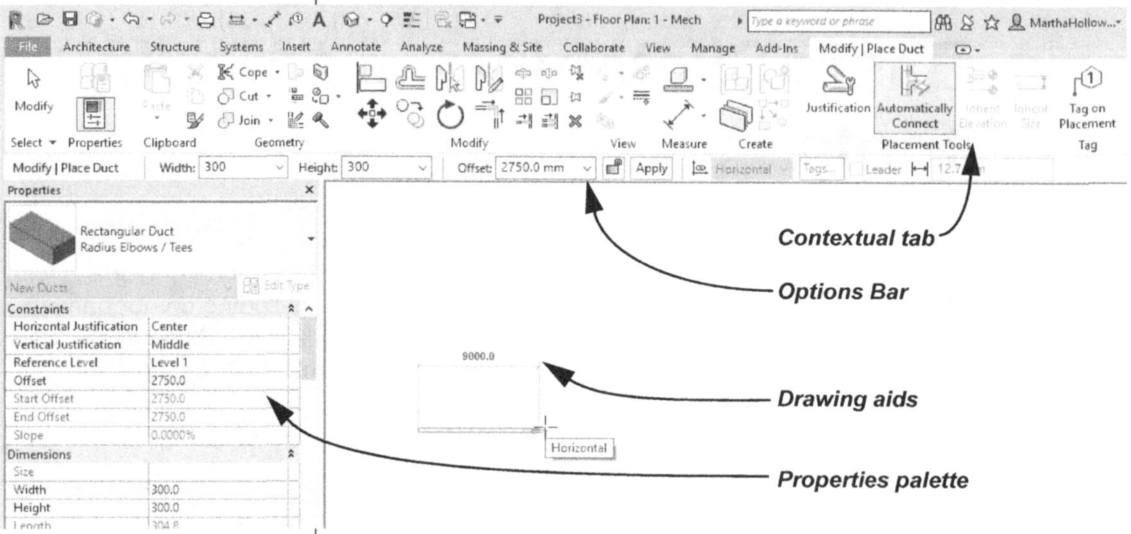

Figure 2–1

- When you model ducts, pipes, cable trays, or conduits or place elements such as air terminals, lighting fixtures or plumbing fixtures, you first need to:
  - Select a type from the Type Selector.
  - Set information in the Options Bar.
  - Check the Contextual tab for other options.

Drawing Aids

As soon as you start sketching or placing elements, several drawing aids display, including:

- Alignment lines
- Temporary dimensions
- Snaps
- Connectors

These aids are available with most drawing and many modification commands, as shown in Figure 2–2.

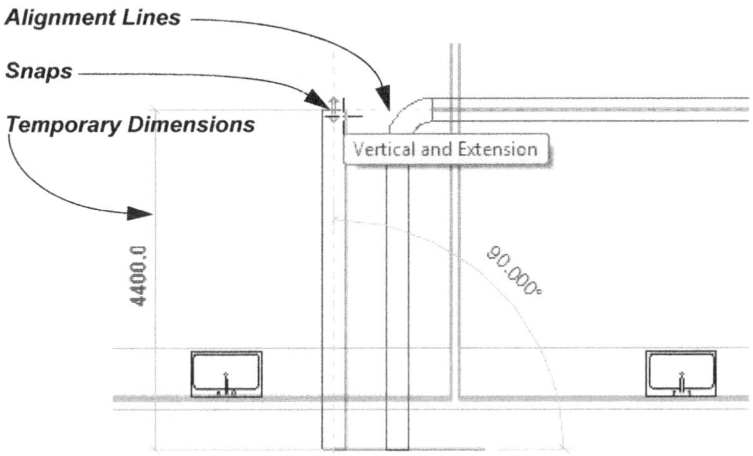

Figure 2–2

Alignment lines display as soon as you move the cursor over nearby elements. They help keep lines horizontal, vertical, or at a specified angle. They also line up with the implied intersections of walls and other elements.

- Hold <Shift> to force the alignments to be orthogonal (90 degree angles only).

Temporary dimensions display to help place elements at the correct length, angle and location.

- You can type in the dimension and then move the cursor until you see the dimension you want, or you can place the element and then modify the dimension as required.

- The length and angle increments shown vary depending on how far in or out the view is zoomed.

Hint: Temporary Dimensions and Permanent Dimensions

Temporary dimensions disappear as soon as you finish adding elements. If you want to make them permanent, select the control shown in Figure 2–3.

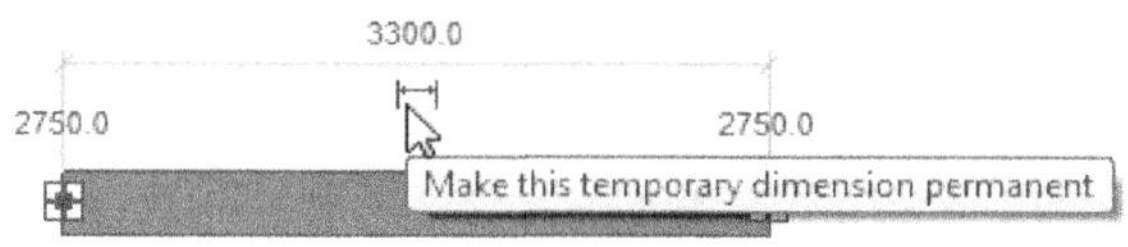

Figure 2–3

Snaps are key points that help you reference existing elements to exact points when drawing, as shown in Figure 2–4.

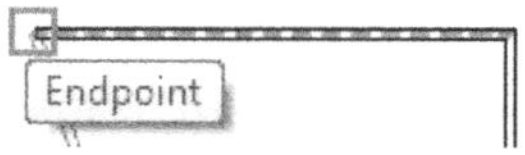

Figure 2–4

- When you move the cursor over an element, the snap symbol displays. Each snap location type displays with a different symbol

Connectors (MEP only) work similar to snaps, but have more intelligence about the size, system, and flow of items (e.g., ducts, pipes, and electrical connections). For example, connectors automatically add fittings to ducts, such as the elbow, transition, and tee shown in Figure 2–5.

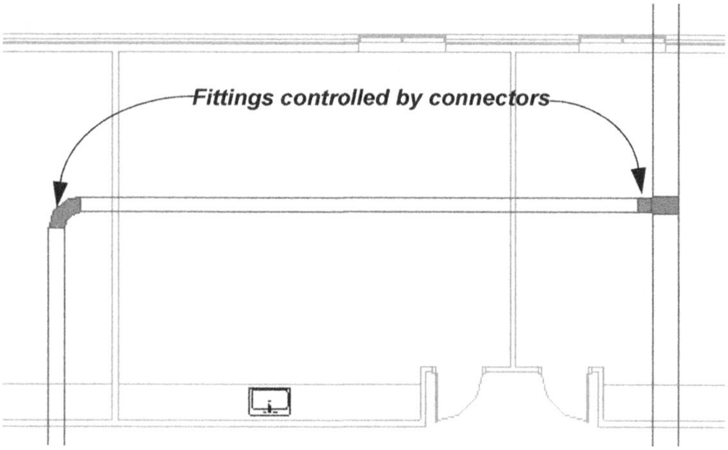

Figure 2–5

Hint: Snap Settings and Overrides

In the *Manage* tab>Settings panel, click (Snaps) to open the Snaps dialog box, which is shown in Figure 2–6. The Snaps dialog box enables you to set which snap points are active, and set the dimension increments displayed for temporary dimensions (both linear and angular).

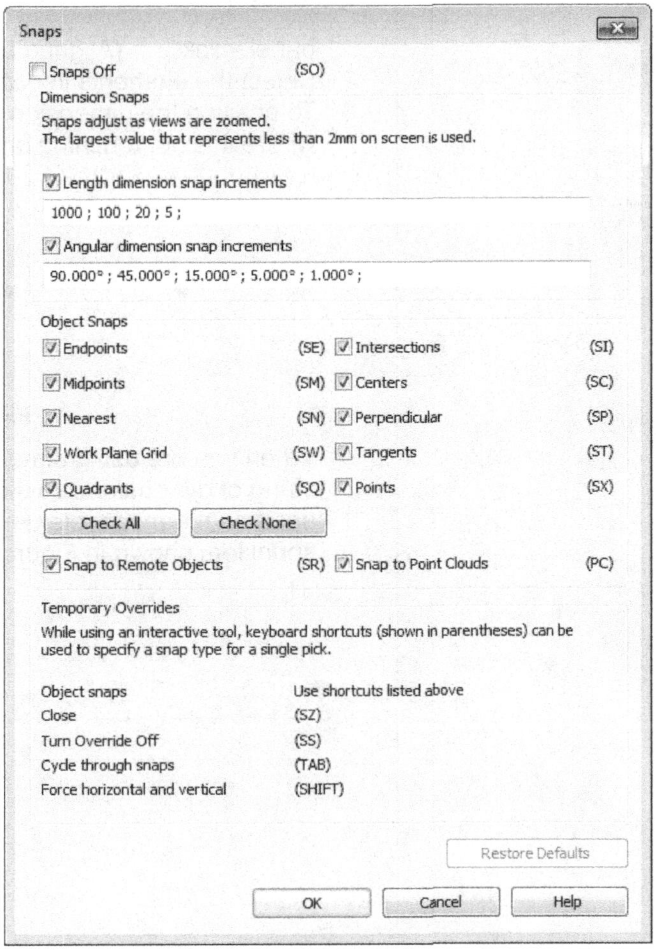

Figure 2–6

- Keyboard shortcuts for each snap can be used to override the automatic snapping. Temporary overrides only affect a single pick, but can be very helpful when there are snaps nearby other than the one you want to use.

Using Dimensions as Drawing Aids

Dimensions are a critical part of construction documents, but they can also help you create elements in your model. There are a variety of dimension types available to you, but the most useful is the **Aligned Dimension** with the *Individual References* option.

How To: Add Aligned Dimensions to Individual References

1. In the Quick Access Toolbar or the *Modify* tab>Measure panel, click (Aligned Dimension). Alternatively, type **DI**.
2. Select the elements in order, as shown in Figure 2–7.
3. To position the dimension string, click a point at a location where it is not touching anything else.

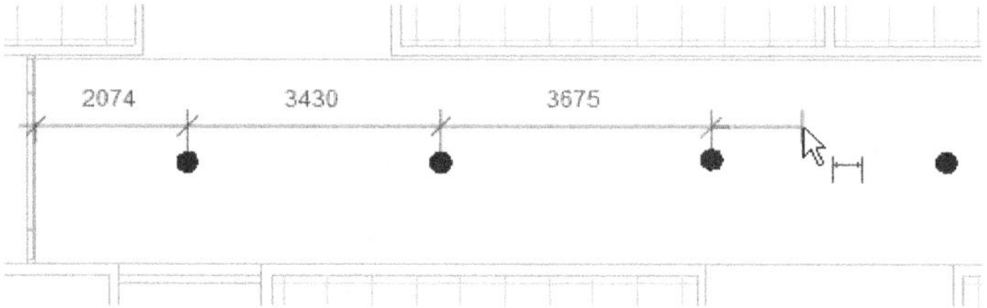

Figure 2–7

- When you are using dimensions in a model, you can set a string of dimensions so that they are equal. Doing this updates the model elements, such as the location of sprinklers shown in Figure 2–8.

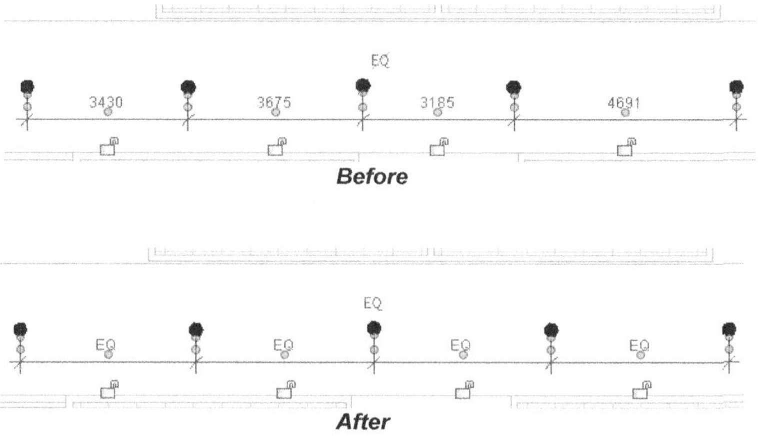

Figure 2–8

Hint: Measuring Tools

When modifying a model, it is useful to know the distance between elements. This can be done with temporary dimensions, or more frequently, by using the measuring tools found in the Quick Access Toolbar or on the *Modify* tab> Measure panel, as shown in Figure 2–9.

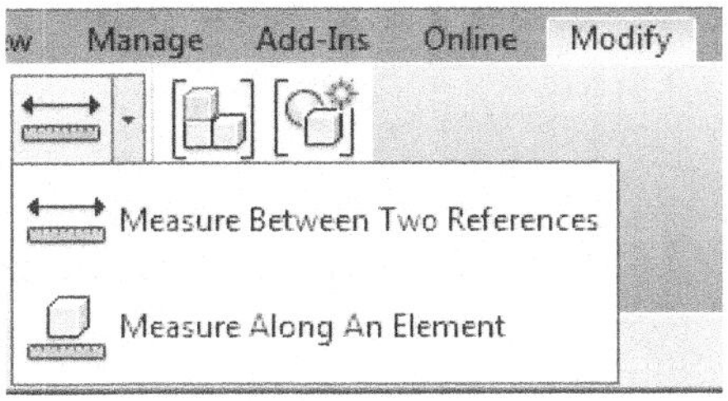

Figure 2–9

- **(Measure Between Two References):** Select two elements and the measurement displays.
- **(Measure Along An Element):** Select the edge of a linear element and the total length displays.

Reference Planes

As you develop designs in the Autodesk Revit software, there are times when you need lines to help you define certain locations. You can draw reference planes (which display as dashed green lines) and snap to them whenever you need to line up elements. For the example shown in Figure 2–10, the lighting fixtures in the reflected ceiling plan are placed using reference planes.

- To insert a reference plane, in the *Architecture, Structure*, or *Systems* tab>Work Plane panel, click (Ref Plane) or type **RP**.

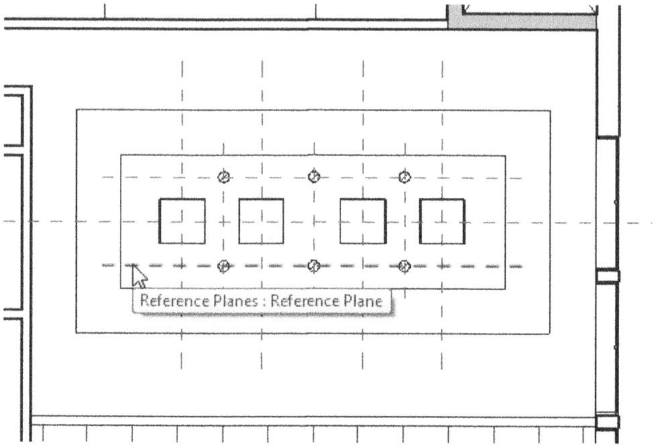

Figure 2–10

- Reference planes display in associated views because they are infinite planes, and not just lines.
- You can name Reference planes by clicking on **<Click to name>** and typing in the text box, as shown in Figure 2–11.

Figure 2–11

- If you sketch a reference pane in Sketch Mode (used with floors and similar elements), it does not display once the sketch is finished.
- Reference planes can have different line styles if they have been defined in the project. In Properties, select a style from the Subcategory list.

2.2 Inserting Components

Components (also known as families) are full 3D elements that can be placed at appropriate locations and heights, and which interact with the building elements around them. For example, a lighting fixture can be designed to be hosted by a face (such as a wall or ceiling), or to stand alone by itself, as shown in Figure 2–12. The Autodesk Revit software includes both architectural components (such as the lamp and wall sconces in Figure 2–12) and MEP components (such as the downlight fixtures) that include connectors.

*Components are located in family files with the extension .RFA. For example, a component family named **Wall Sconce.rfa** can contain several types and sizes.*

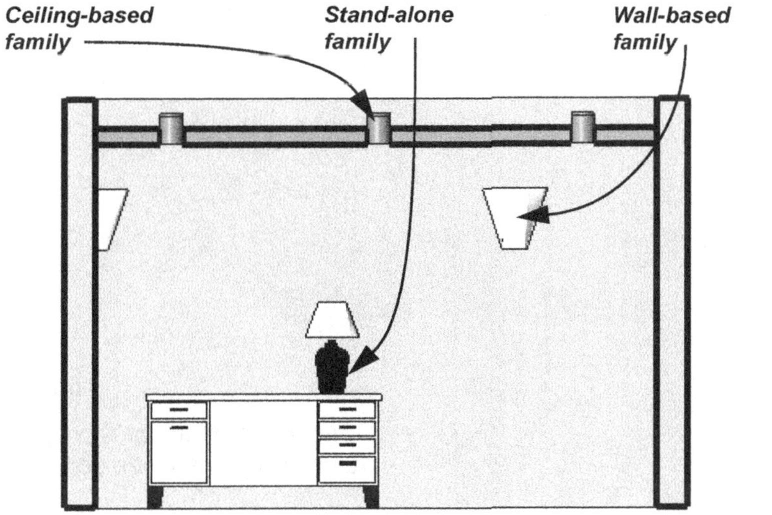

Figure 2–12

Most components are inserted using specific tools, including:

Exact steps for inserting specific components are covered later in this student guide.

Air terminal	Electrical Equipment
Mechanical Equipment	Devices (Data, Fire Alarm, Switches, etc.)
Plumbing Fixture	Lighting Fixtures
Sprinkler	

- Take time to get to know the components that come with the Autodesk Revit software. Their most critical content are the connectors, as you see in for a piece of mechanical equipment in Figure 2–13.

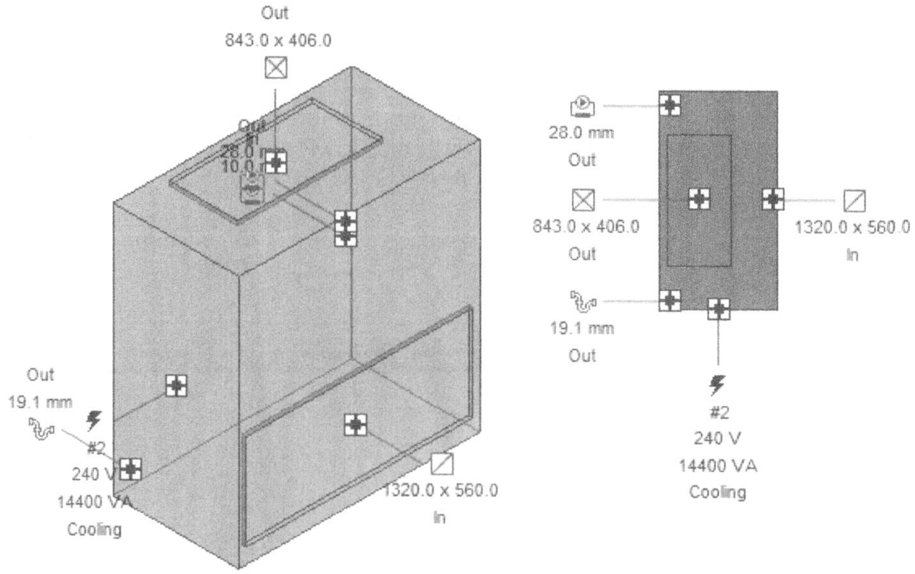

Figure 2–13

- Connectors often contain options to create systems and draw ducts and pipes when you right-click on them.

How To: Insert Components

1. Start the appropriate command.
2. In the Type Selector, select the type/size you want to use, as shown in Figure 2–14.

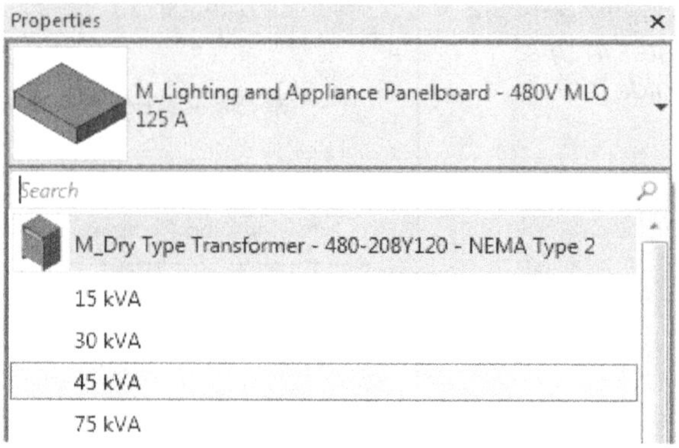

Figure 2–14

3. In the command-specific contextual tab>Tag panel, click  (Tag on Placement) to toggle this option on or off.
4. Proceed as follows, based on the type of component used:

If the component is...	Then...
Not hosted	Set the *Level* and *Offset* in Properties, as shown in Figure 2–15.
Wall hosted	Set the *Elevation* in Properties, as shown in Figure 2–16.
Face hosted	Select the appropriate method in the contextual tab>Placement panel, as shown in Figure 2–17. • Vertical Faces include walls and columns. • Faces include ceilings, beams, and roofs. • Work Planes can be set to levels, faces, and named reference planes.

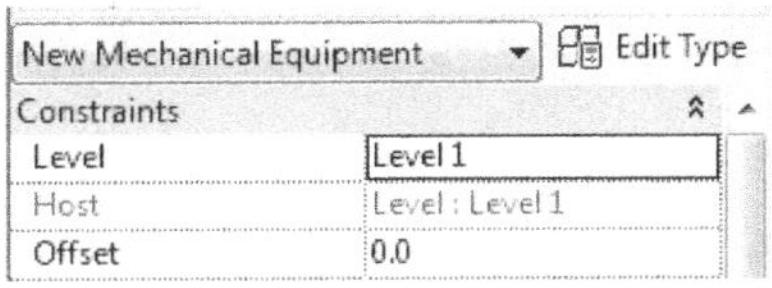

Figure 2–15

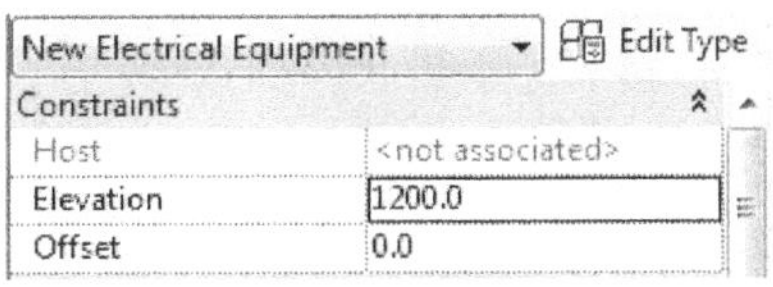

Figure 2–16

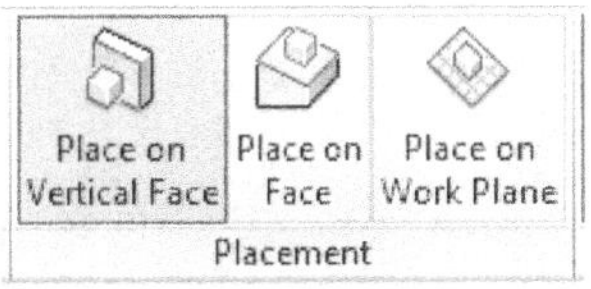

Figure 2–17

5. Place the component in the model.

- A fast way to add components that match those already in your project is to select one, right-click on it, and select **Create Similar**, as shown in Figure 2–18. This starts the appropriate command with the same type selected.

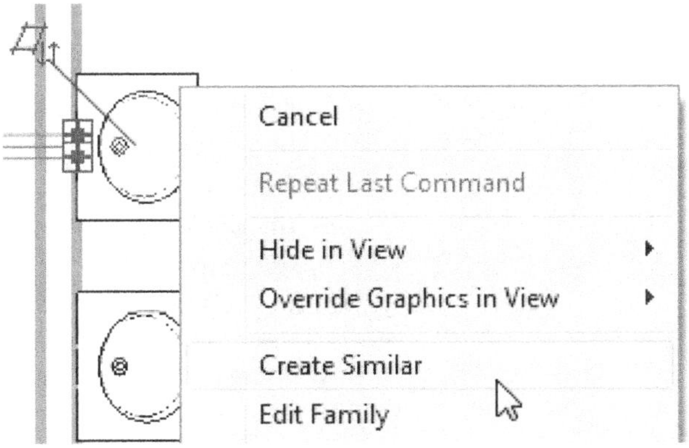

Figure 2–18

Hint: Work Planes

A Work Plane is the surface you sketch on or extrude from. In a plan view, the Work Plane is automatically parallel to the level. In an elevation or 3D view, you must specify the Work Plane before you start sketching

How To: Select a Work Plane

1. Start a command that requires a work plane or, in the *Architecture* tab>Work Plane panel, click (Set).
2. In the Work Plane dialog box, select one of the following options:
   - **Name:** Select an existing level, grid, or named reference plane (as shown in Figure 2–19) and then click **OK**.

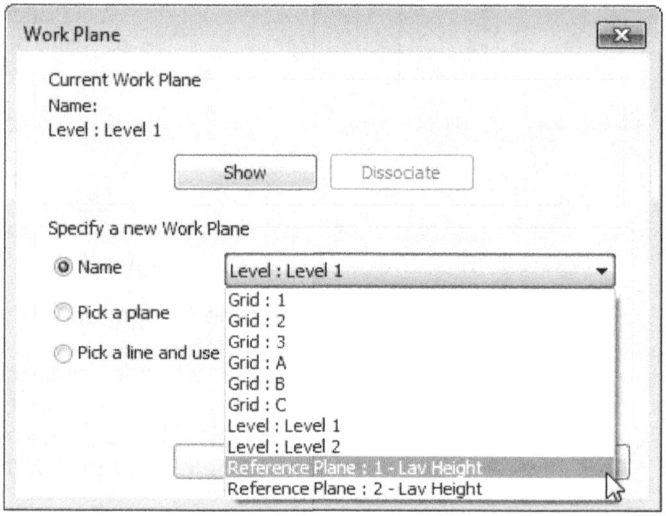

Figure 2–19

   - **Pick a plane:** Click **OK** and select a plane in the view, such as a wall face. Ensure the entire plane is highlighted before you select it.
   - **Pick a line and use the work plane it was sketched in:** Click **OK** and select a model line, such as a room separation line.

If you are in a view in which the sketch cannot be created, the Go To View dialog box opens. Select one of the views and click **Open View**.

Loading Components

You can load additional families into a project. In the *contextual* tab>Mode panel, click (Load Family) and then navigate to the appropriate location for your company. The Autodesk Revit library has MEP-based components available in the following folders: *Cable Tray, Conduit, Duct, Electrical, Fire Protection, Lighting, Mechanical, Pipe,* and *Plumbing.*

How To: Load a Family

1. In the related contextual tab>Mode panel or *Insert* tab>Load from Library panel, click (Load Family).
2. In the Load Family dialog box, locate the folder that contains the family or families you want to load, as shown in Figure 2–20.

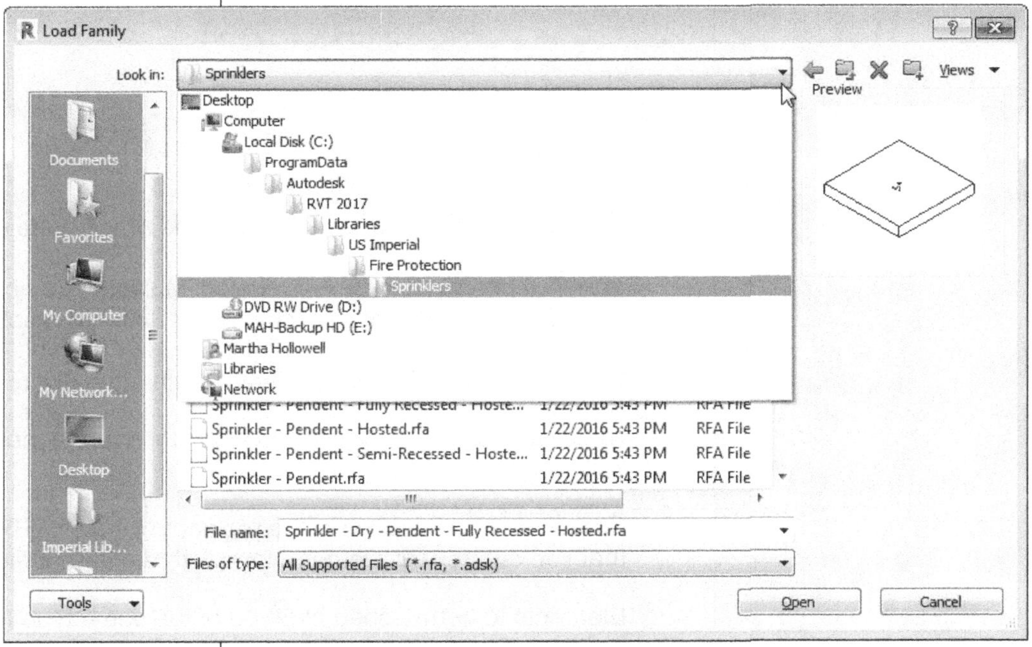

Figure 2–20

3. Select the family or families you want to load. You can hold <Ctrl> to select multiple families.
4. Click **Open**.

Hint: Matching Properties

You can select an existing wall and use it to assign the wall type and instance properties to other walls by using the **Match Type** command. This command also works with all elements that have types.

1. In the *Modify* tab>Clipboard panel, click (Match Type) or type **MA**. The cursor changes to an arrow with a clean paintbrush.
2. Select the source element that you want all of the others to match. The paintbrush changes to look as if it has been dipped in black paint as shown in Figure 2–21.

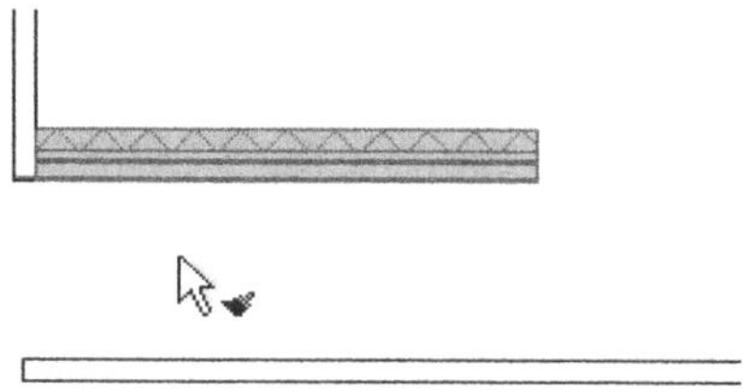

Figure 2–21

3. To select more than one element, in the *Modify | Match Type* tab>Multiple panel, click (Select Multiple). You can then use windows, crossings, <Ctrl>, and <Shift> to create a selection set of elements to change.
4. Select the elements that you want to change. For multiple selections, click (Finish) to apply the type to the selection.

- Click in an empty space in the project to empty the brush so that you can repeat the command with a different element.
- Elements to be matched must be of the same type (e.g., all walls, all doors, etc.).

Practice 2a Insert Components

Practice Objectives

- Load and Insert components.
- Use drawing aids.
- Add and name a reference plan.
- Select a work plane.

Estimated time for completion: 10 minutes

In this practice you will insert a variety of MEP fixtures, including air terminals, plumbing fixtures and lighting fixtures, as shown in Figure 2–22. You will use various drawing aids to help you place the fixtures appropriately.

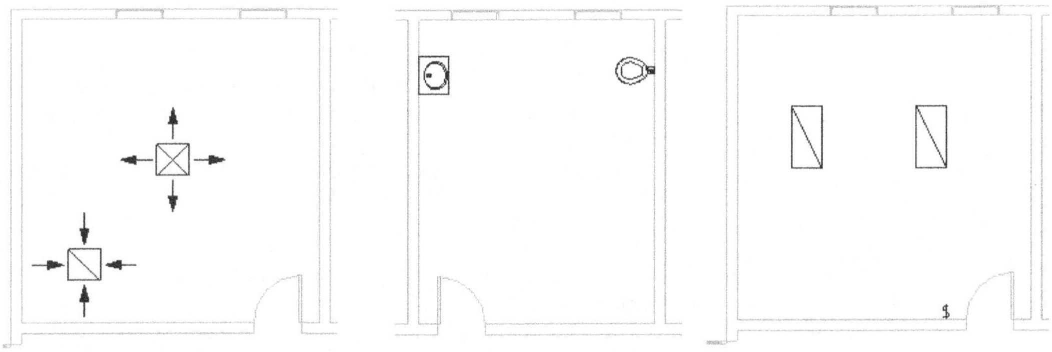

Mechanical ***Plumbing*** ***Electrical***

Figure 2–22

Task 1 - Insert air terminals.

1. In the practice files *Basics* folder, open **Simple-Building-Start-M.rvt.**
2. In the Project Browser, expand the **Mechanical>HVAC> Floor Plans** node. The **1 - Mech** view is highlighted, and you are in a Mechanical floor plan.
3. In the *Systems* tab>HVAC panel, click (Air Terminal).
4. In Properties, note that the default selection is a Supply Diffuser and that the *Level* is **Level 1**. Set the *Offset* to **2500mm**.

5. Click near the center of room **Lab 101**, as shown in Figure 2–23.

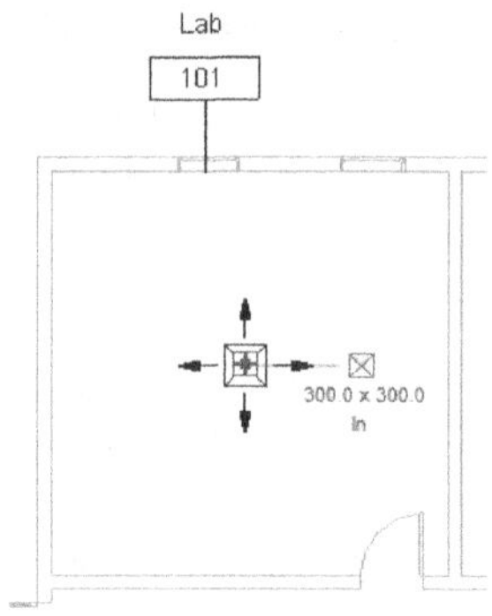

Figure 2–23

6. While still in the Air Terminal command, in the Type Selector, change the *Type* to **M_Return Diffuser: 600 x 600 Face 300x 300 Connection** and set the *Offset* to **2500mm**.

7. Click to place the component in the lower left corner of room **Lab 101**.

8. In the *Systems* tab>Mechanical panel, click (Mechanical Equipment.)

9. In the Type Selector, select **M_Boiler: Standard**.

10. In the **Mech/Elec Room**, move the cursor near the outside wall. Note that the boiler automatically aligns to the wall, as shown in Figure 2–24.

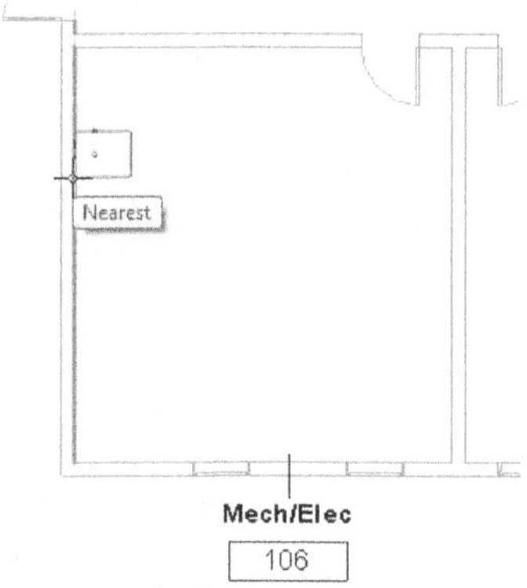

Figure 2–24

11. Click to place the component.

12. Save the project.

Task 2 - Load and place plumbing fixtures.

1. In the Project Browser, expand the Plumbing>Plumbing> Floor Plans node and double-click to open the **1 - Plumbing** view. The air terminals are automatically toggled off because you are in a plumbing view, but the boiler is still displayed because Mechanical Equipment is typically toggled on.
2. In the *Systems* tab>Plumbing & Piping panel, click  (Plumbing Fixture).
3. In the Type Selector, select one of the wall-mounted water closets.
4. Click along one of the walls to place the fixture, as shown in Figure 2–25.

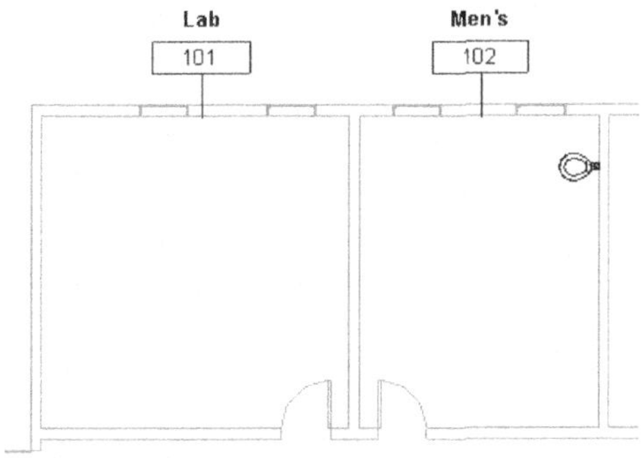

Figure 2–25

5. Return to the Type Selector and review the list. Note that there are sinks, but no lavatories.
6. In the *Modify | Place Plumbing Fixture* tab>Mode panel, click  (Load Family).

This fixture is also available in the Basics practice files folder.

7. In the Load Family dialog box, the Autodesk Revit family library automatically displays. Navigate to the *Plumbing> MEP>Fixtures>Lavatories* folder and select **M_Lavatory - Oval.rfa,** as shown in Figure 2–26.

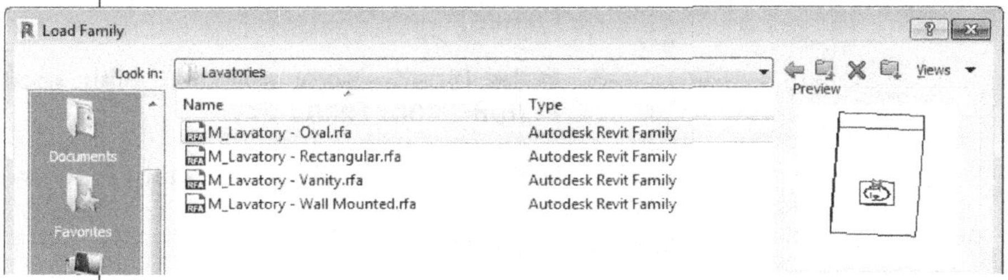

Figure 2–26

8. Click **Open**.

9. In the Type Selector, select **M_Lavatory - Oval: 635mmx510mm - Public**.

10. Place the lavatory against the wall across from the water closet.

11. Click (Modify) and select the new fixture. Drag it up or down until it meets with the alignment line of the WC, as shown in Figure 2–27.

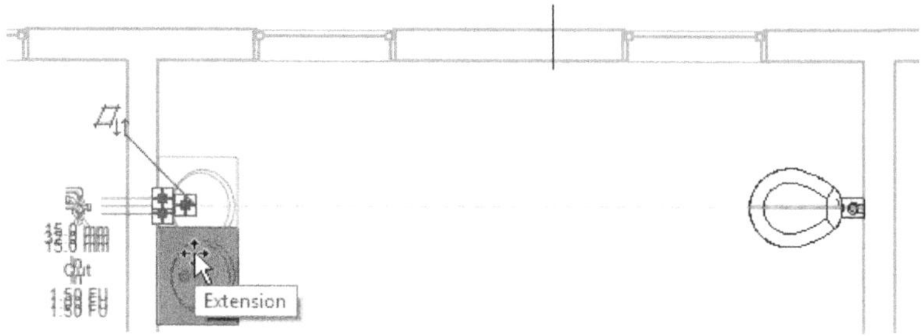

Figure 2–27

12. Click in space to release the selection.

13. Save the project.

Task 3 - Place a lighting fixture and switch.

1. In the Project Browser, expand the Electrical>Lighting> Ceiling Plans node and double-click on **1 - Ceiling Elec** view to open it.
   - Ensure that you are opening the Ceiling Plan so that the ceiling grids display.
   - None of the previous elements that you have added display.

2. In the Systems tab>Electrical panel, click (Lighting Fixture).

3. In the Type Selector, select **M_Plain recessed Lighting Fixture: 600x1200 - 277**.

4. In the *Modify | Place Fixture* tab>Placement panel, click (Place on Face).

5. Move the cursor over the grid. The light snaps to the grid lines, as shown in Figure 2–28.

6. Press <Spacebar> to rotate the fixture. Click to place two fixtures in the room, as shown in Figure 2–29.

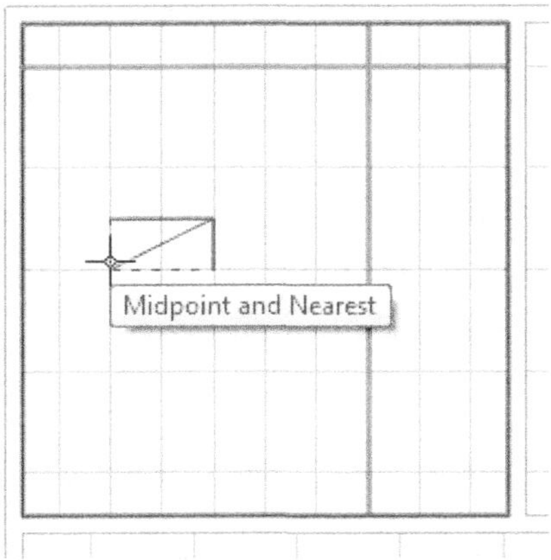

Figure 2–28

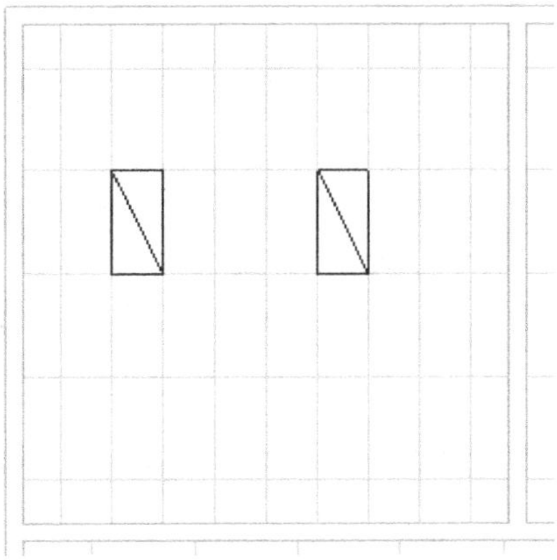

Figure 2–29

7. Open the **Electrical>Lighting>Floor Plans: 1 - Lighting** view. The light fixtures display in this view although you are seeing a plan view.

8. In the *Systems* tab>Electrical panel, expand the Device drop-down list and select (Lighting).

9. In the Type Selector, select **M_Lighting Switches: Single Pole**.

10. In Properties, note that the *Elevation* is set to **1200mm**, a standard height for switches.

11. Place the switch to the left of the door. It displays only as a symbol.

12. Click (Modify) to end the command.

13. Save the project.

2.3 Selecting and Editing Elements

Building design projects typically involve extensive changes to the model. The Autodesk Revit software was designed to make such changes quickly and efficiently. You can change an element using the methods shown in Figure 2–30, and described below:

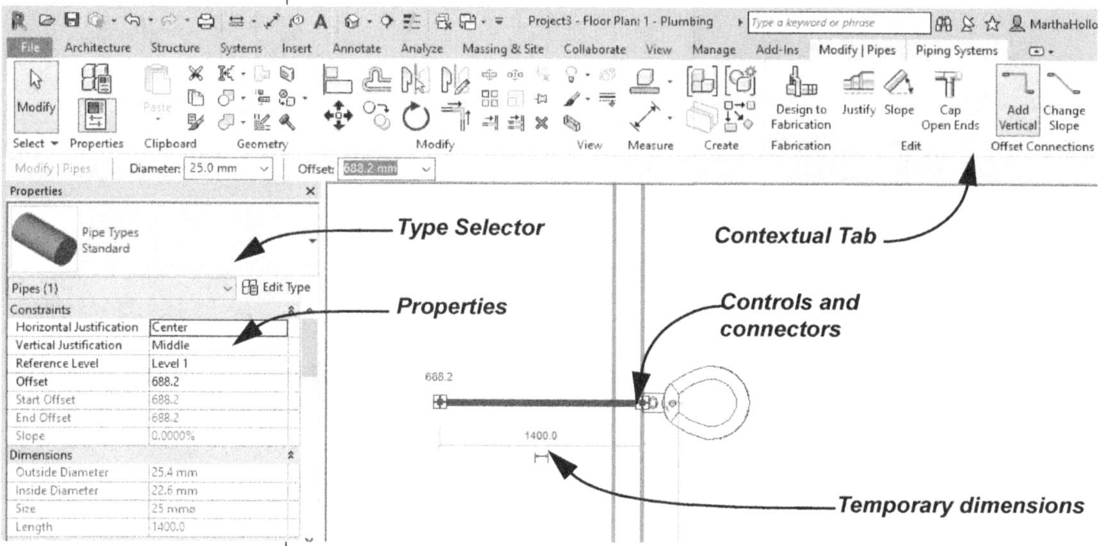

Figure 2–30

- Type Selector enables you to specify a different type. This is frequently used to change the size and/or style of the elements.
- Properties enables you to modify the information (parameters) associated with the selected elements.
- Temporary dimensions enable you to change the element's dimensions or position.
- The contextual tab in the ribbon contains the Modify commands and element-specific tools.
- Controls enable you to drag, flip, lock, and rotate the element.

- Connectors control how related elements attach to another with intelligence about size, needed fittings, and system information. (MEP only)
- Shape handles (not shown) enable you to drag elements to modify their height or length.
- To delete an element, select it and press <Delete>, right-click and select **Delete**, or in the Modify panel, click ✖ (Delete).

Working with Controls and Connectors

When you select an element, various controls and connectors display depending on the element and view. Using controls, you can change an elements length or location, and flip or rotate some elements. MEP connectors also provide information about attachments and enable you to add related elements, as shown for creating pipe from a pipe accessory in Figure 2–31.

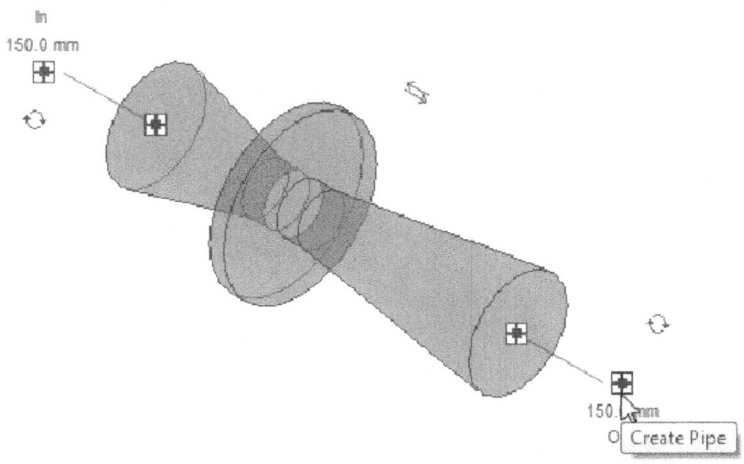

Figure 2–31

- If you hover the cursor over the control or connector, a tooltip displays showing its function.

Hint: Editing Temporary Dimensions

Temporary dimensions automatically link to the closest wall. To change the location, you can drag the *Witness Line* control (as shown in Figure 2–32) to connect to a new reference. You can also click on the control to toggle between justifications in the wall.

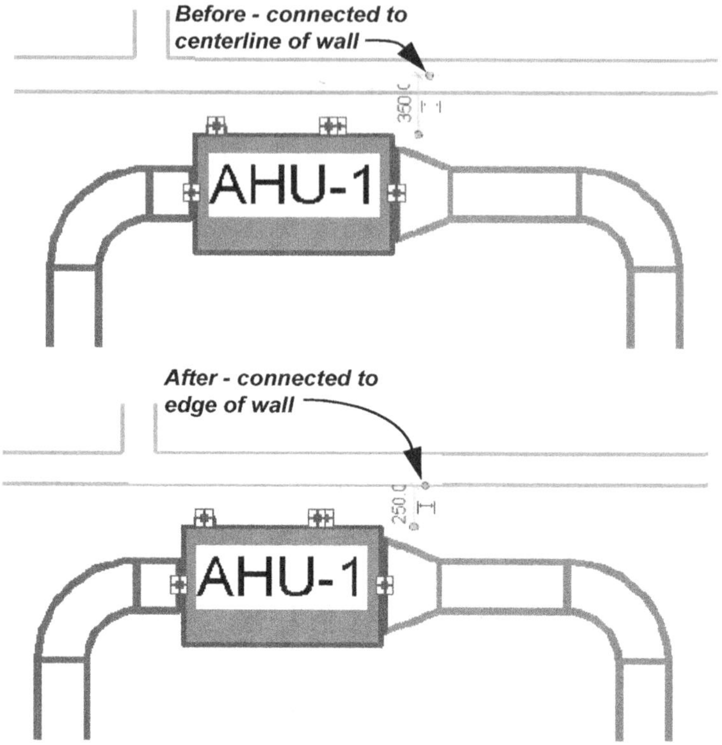

Figure 2–32

- The new location of a temporary dimension for an element is remembered as long as you are in the same session of the software.

Selecting Multiple Elements

- Once you have selected at least one element, hold <Ctrl> and select another item to add it to a selection set.
- To remove an element from a selection set, hold <Shift> and select the element.
- If you click and drag the cursor to *window* around elements, you have two selection options, as shown in Figure 2–33. If you drag from left to right, you only select the elements completely inside the window. If you drag from right to left, you select elements both inside and crossing the window.

Window: Left to Right ***Crossing: Right to Left***

Figure 2–33

- If several elements are on or near each other, press <Tab> to cycle through them before you click. If there are elements that might be linked to each other, such as ductwork, pressing <Tab> selects the chain of elements.
- Press <Ctrl>+<Left Arrow> to reselect the previous selection set. You can also right-click in the drawing window with nothing selected and select **Select Previous**.
- To select all elements of a specific type, right-click on an element and select **Select All Instances>Visible in View** or **In Entire Project**, as shown in Figure 2–34.

You do no have to select an element, just hover over the one you want to select.

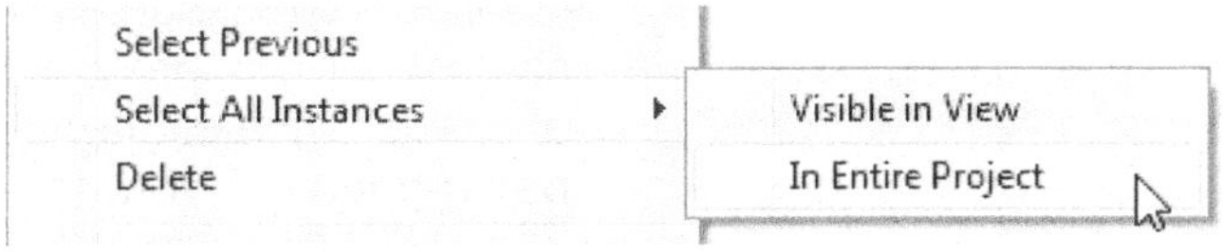

Figure 2–34

Hint: Selection Options

You can control how the software selects specific elements in a project by toggling Selection Options on and off on the Status Bar, as shown in Figure 2–35. Alternatively, in any tab on the ribbon, expand the Select panel's title and select the option.

Figure 2–35

-  **Select links:** When toggled on, you can selected linked drawings or Autodesk Revit models. When it is toggled off you cannot select them when using **Modify** or **Move**.

-  **Select underlay elements:** When toggled on, you can select underlay elements. When toggled off, you cannot select them when using **Modify** or **Move**.

-  **Select pinned elements:** When toggled on, you can selected pinned elements. When toggled off, you cannot select them when using **Modify** or **Move**.

-  **Select elements by face:** When toggled on you can select elements (such as the floors or walls in an elevation) by selecting the interior face or selecting an edge. When toggled off, you can only select elements by selecting an edge.

-  **Drag elements on selection:** When toggled on, you can hover over an element, select it, and drag it to a new location. When toggled off, the Crossing or Box select mode starts when you press and drag, even if you are on top of an element. Once elements have been selected they can still be dragged to a new location.

Filtering Selection Sets

When multiple element categories are selected, the *Multi-Select* contextual tab opens in the ribbon. This gives you access to all of the Modify tools, and the **Filter** command. The **Filter** command enables you to specify the types of elements to select. For example, you might only want to select lighting fixtures, as shown in Figure 2–36.

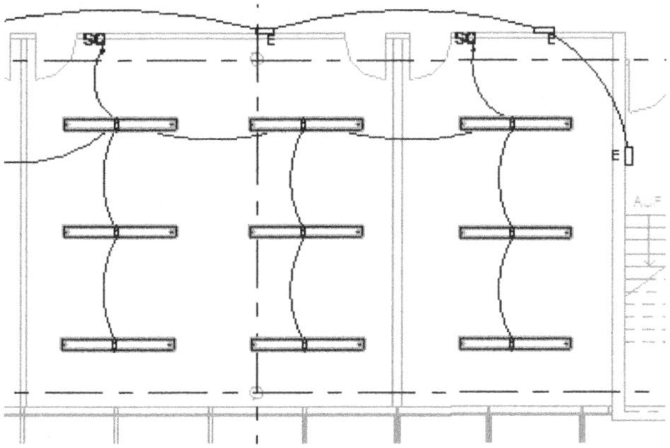

Figure 2–36

How To: Filter a Selection Set

1. Select everything in the required area.
2. in the *Modify | Multi-Select* tab>Selection panel, or in the Status Bar, click (Filter). The Filter dialog box opens, as shown in Figure 2–37.

The Filter dialog box displays all types of elements in the original selection.

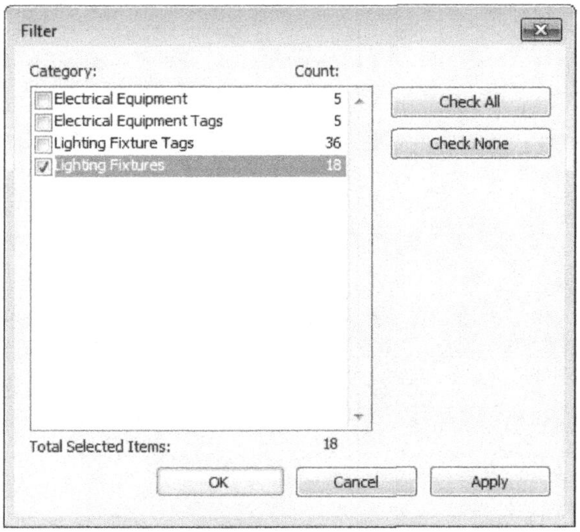

Figure 2–37

3. Click **Check None** to clear all of the options or **Check All** to select all of the options. You can also select or clear individual categories as required.
4. Click **OK**. The selection set is now limited to the elements you specified.

- In the Status Bar, the number of elements selected displays beside the Filter icon, as shown in Figure 2–38. You can also see the number of selected elements in the Properties palette.

Figure 2–38

- Clicking the Filter icon in the Status Bar also opens the Filter dialog box.

Practice 2b Select and Edit Elements

Estimated time for completion: 10 minutes

Practice Objectives

- Use a variety of selection methods.
- Use temporary dimensions and connectors to modify the location of elements.

In this practice you will select lighting fixtures and change the type (as shown in Figure 2–39), as well as test a variety of selection methods and filters. You will then use connectors to modify the location of an air terminal and use **Create Similar** to add additional components. You will also modify the height of the air terminals in Properties.

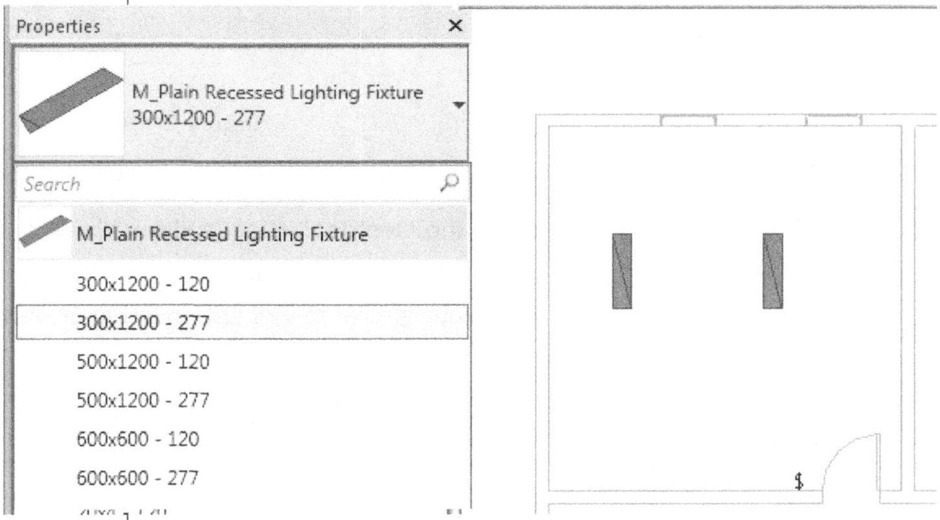

Figure 2–39

Task 1 - Use a variety of selection methods.

1. In the practice files *Basics* folder, open **Simple-Building-Edit-M.rvt**. It opens in the **1 - Lighting** view.
2. Select one of the light fixtures. The connectors and controls are displayed.
3. Hold <Ctrl> and select the other fixture. The connectors no longer display, but you can still modify the fixture type.

4. In the Type Selector, change the type to **M_Plain Recessed Lighting Fixture: 300x1200 - 277**. Both fixtures change, as shown in Figure 2–40.

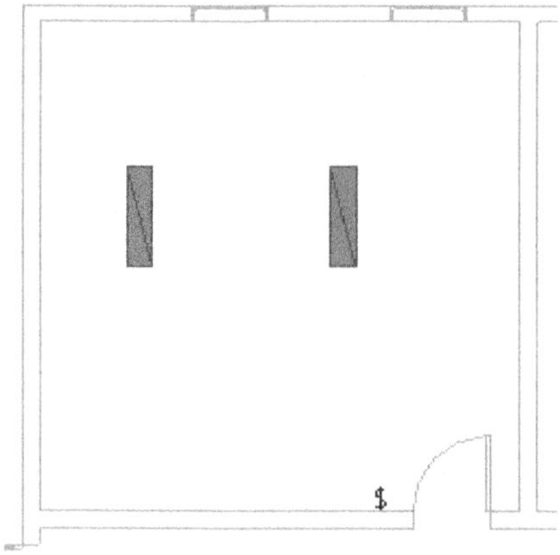

Figure 2–40

5. Click away from any elements to clear the selection.
6. Open the **Mechical>HVAC>Floor Plans:1 - Mech** view.
7. Draw a window from left to right around some of the elements, similar to that shown in Figure 2–41.

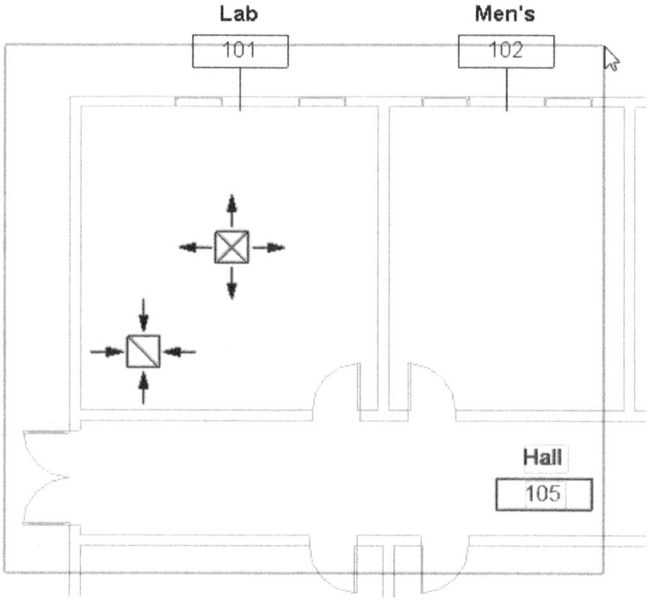

Figure 2–41

8. Note that only the elements completely inside the selection window are selected.

9. Click to clear the selection.

10. Draw a crossing window (i.e., from right to left) around the same area, as shown in Figure 2–42. Note that any elements that the window touches are included in the selection, including the linked architectural model.

You can also toggle (Select Links) in the Status Bar to keep the link from being selected.

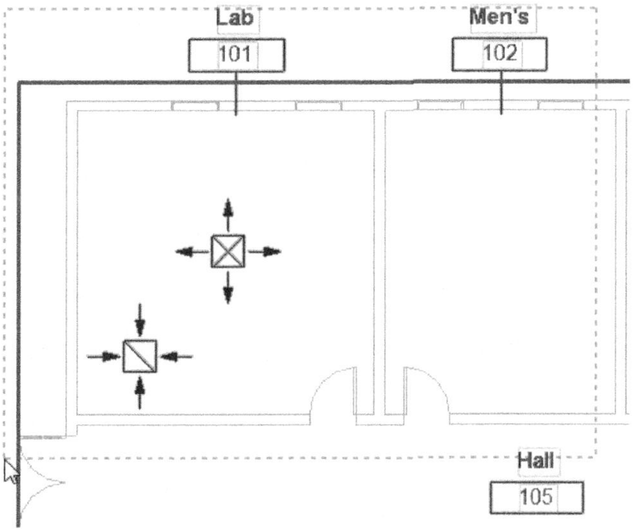

Figure 2–42

11. Hold <Shift> and select the edge of the architectural model. This removes the element from the selection set.

12. In the Status Bar, note the number of items that are selected and click (Filter).

13. In the Filter dialog box, view the categories and clear the check from **Air Terminals**.

14. Click **OK**. Only the room tags are still selected.

15. Press <Esc>. The elements are no longer selected.

16. Select one of the room tags. Right-click and select **Select All Instances>Visible in View**. All of the tags are selected.

17. Click (Modify). The elements are no longer selected.

- Remember these selection methods as you start working in the projects.

Task 2 - Modify elements using controls and properties.

1. Continue working in the **1 - Mech** view.
2. Select, click and drag the supply air terminal to a new location using the alignment lines referencing the return air terminal.
3. Right-click on the control and look at the variety of options you can use, as shown in Figure 2–43.

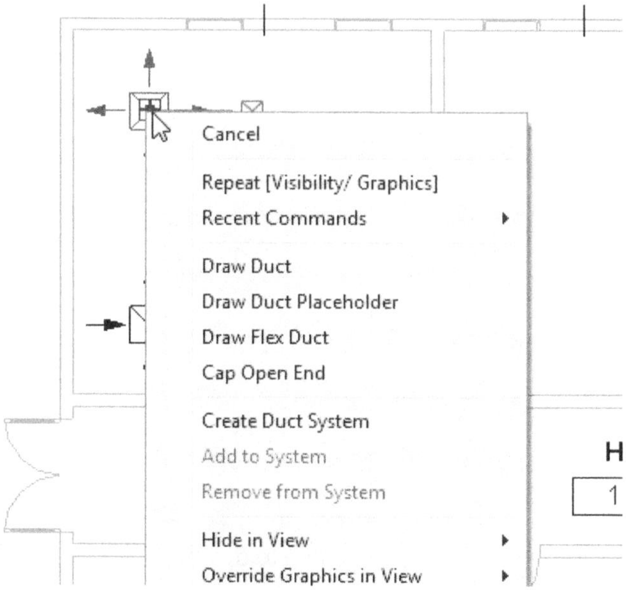

Figure 2–43

4. In the shortcut menu, select **Create Similar**. This starts the **Air Terminal** command using that type. Place two more air terminals in the same room, using alignment lines to place them.
5. Click (Modify) and select all three of the supply air terminals. Note the information in Properties. The *Offset* is set to **0.0** above **Level 1**.
6. Hold <Ctrl> and select the return air terminal. The *Level* and *Offset* are available to change, although two different types of components are selected.

7. Change the *Offset* to **250mm** and click **Apply**. The offset for all of the air terminals is updated, as shown in Figure 2–44.

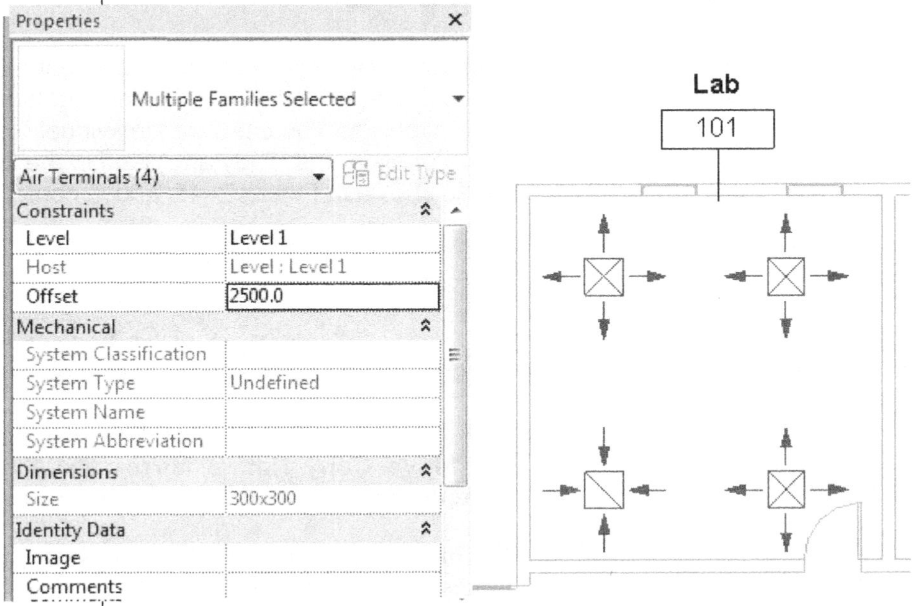

Figure 2–44

8. Click away from any elements to clear the selection.

9. Save the project.

2.4 Working with Basic Modify Tools

The Autodesk Revit software contains controls and temporary dimensions that enable you to edit elements. Additional modifying tools can be used with individual elements or any selection of elements. They are found in the *Modify* tab>Modify panel, as shown in Figure 2–45, and in contextual tabs.

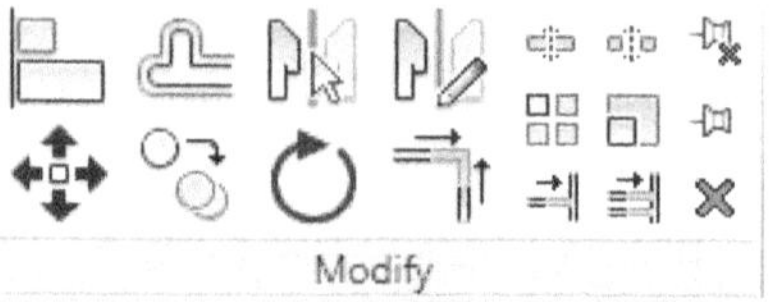

Figure 2–45

- The **Move**, **Copy**, **Rotate**, **Mirror**, and **Array** commands are covered in this topic. Other tools are covered later.
- For most modify commands, you can either select the elements and start the command, or start the command, select the elements, and press <Enter> to finish the selection and move to the next step in the command.

Moving and Copying Elements

The **Move** and **Copy** commands enable you to select the element(s) and move or copy them from one place to another. You can use alignment lines, temporary dimensions, and snaps to help place the elements, as shown in Figure 2–46.

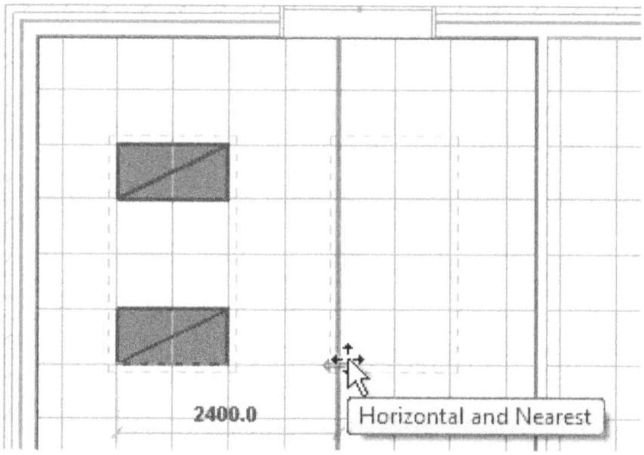

Figure 2–46

Hint: Nudge

Nudge enables you to move elements in short increments. When elements are selected, you can press one of the four arrow keys to move the element in that direction. The distance the element moves depends on how far in or out you are zoomed.

How To: Move or Copy Elements

*You can also use the shortcut for **Move**, **MV** or for **Copy**, **CO**.*

1. Select the elements you want to move or copy.
2. In the Modify panel, click (Move) or (Copy). A dashed boundary box displays around the selected elements.
3. Select a move start point on or near the element.
4. Select a second point. Use alignment lines and temporary dimensions to help place the elements.
5. When you are finished, you can start another modify command using the elements that remain selected, or switch back to **Modify** to end the command.

- If you start the **Move** command and hold <Ctrl>, the elements are copied.

Move/Copy Elements Options

The **Move** and **Copy** commands have several options that display in the Options Bar, as shown in Figure 2–47.

Figure 2–47

Constrain	Restricts the movement of the cursor to horizontal or vertical, or along the axis of an item that is at an angle. This keeps you from selecting a point at an angle by mistake. **Constrain** is off by default.
Disjoin (Move only)	Breaks any connections between the elements being moved and other elements. If **Disjoin** is on, the elements move separately. If it is off, the connected elements also move or stretch. **Disjoin** is off by default.
Multiple (Copy only)	Enables you to make multiple copies of one selection. **Multiple** is off by default.

- These commands only work in the current view, not between views or projects. To copy between views or projects, in the *Modify* tab>Clipboard panel, use (Copy to Clipboard), (Cut to the Clipboard), and (Paste from Clipboard).
- Many tools such as **Move**, **Copy**, and the clipboard commands can be used in perspective views.

Hint: Pinning Elements

If you do not want elements to be moved, you can pin them in place, as shown in Figure 2–48. Select the elements and in the *Modify* tab, in the Modify panel, click (Pin). Pinned elements can be copied, but not moved. If you try to delete a pinned element, a warning dialog displays reminding you that you must unpin the element before the command can be started.

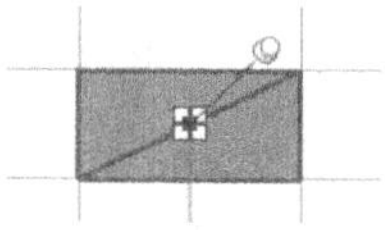

Figure 2–48

Select the element and click (Unpin) or type the shortcut **UP** to free it.

Rotating Elements

The **Rotate** command enables you to rotate selected elements around a center point or origin, as shown in Figure 2–49. You can use alignment lines, temporary dimensions, and snaps to help specify the center of rotation and the angle. You can also create copies of the element as it is being rotated.

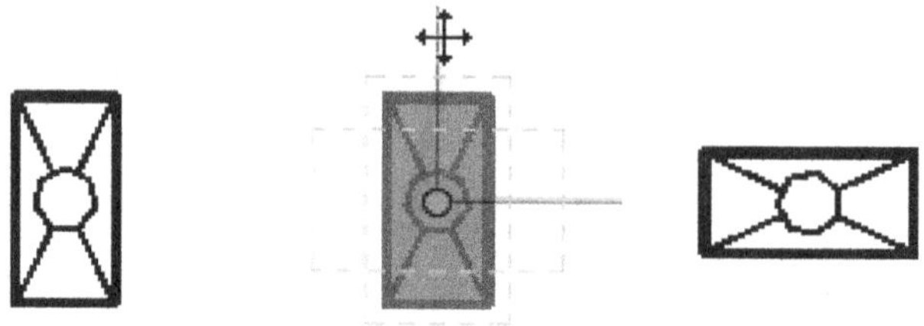

Original ***In process*** ***Completed***

Figure 2–49

How To: Rotate Elements

1. Select the element(s) you want to rotate.
2. In the Modify panel, click (Rotate) or type the shortcut **RO**.
3. The center of rotation is automatically set to the center of the element or group of elements, as shown in Figure 2–50. To change the center of rotation, as shown in Figure 2–51, use the following:

*To start the **Rotate** command with a prompt to select the center of rotation, select the elements first and type **R3**.*

- Drag the (Center of Rotation) control to a new point.
- In the Options Bar, next to **Center of rotation**, click **Place** and use snaps to move it to a new location.
- Press <Spacebar> to select the center of rotation and click to move it to a new location.

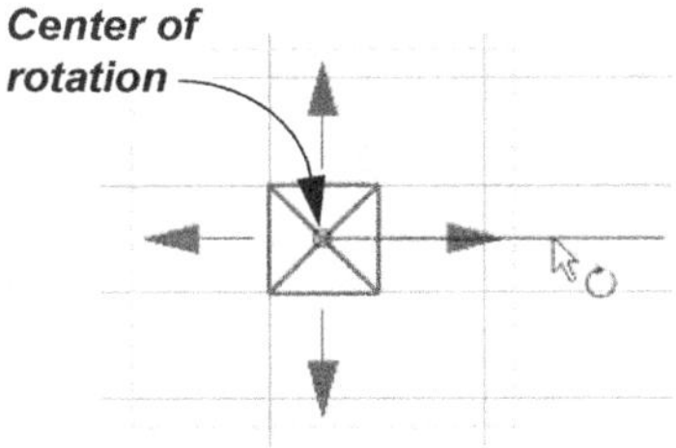

Figure 2–50

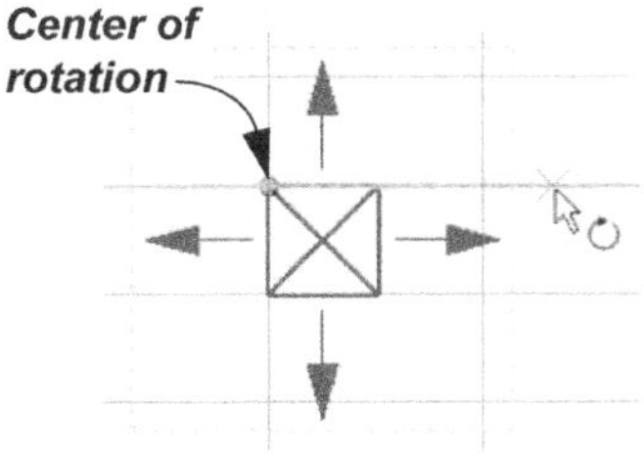

Figure 2–51

4. In the Options Bar, specify if you want to make a Copy (select **Copy**), type an angle in the *Angle* field (as shown in Figure 2–52), and press <Enter>. You can also specify the angle on screen using temporary dimensions.

Figure 2–52

5. The rotated element(s) remain highlighted, enabling you to start another command using the same selection, or click (Modify) to finish.

- The **Disjoin** option breaks any connections between the elements being rotated and other elements. If **Disjoin** is on (selected), the elements rotate separately. If it is off (cleared), the connected elements also move or stretch, as shown for a wall in Figure 2–53. **Disjoin** is toggled off by default.

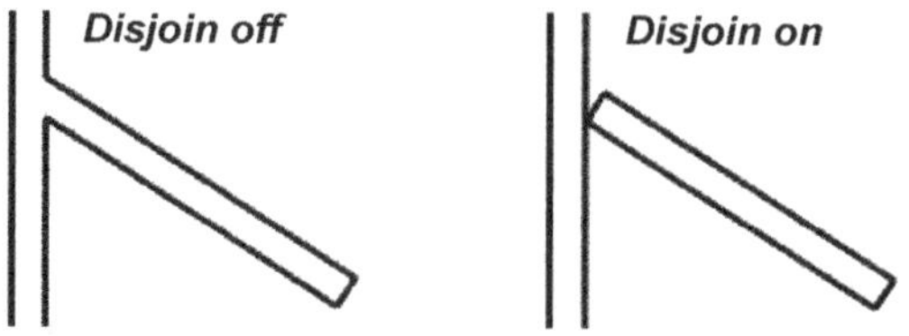

Figure 2–53

- Rotating connected MEP elements can easily cause connection and system problems.

Mirroring Elements

The **Mirror** command enables you to mirror elements about an axis defined by a selected element, as shown in Figure 2–54, or by selected points.

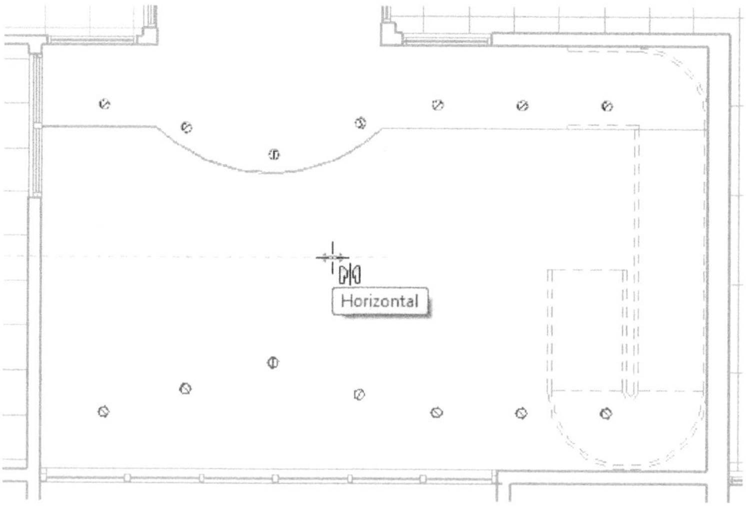

Figure 2–54

How To: Mirror Elements

1. Select the element(s) to mirror.
2. In the Modify panel, select the method you want to use:
   - Click (Mirror - Pick Axis) or type the shortcut **MM**. This prompts you to select an element as the **Axis of Reflection** (mirror line).

- Click (Mirror - Draw Axis) or type the shortcut **DM**. This prompts you to select two points to define the axis about which the elements mirror.

3. The new mirrored element(s) remain highlighted, enabling you to start another command, or return to **Modify** to finish.

- By default, the original elements that were mirrored remain. To delete the original elements, clear the **Copy** option in the Options Bar.

Hint: Scale

The Autodesk Revit software is designed with full-size elements. Therefore, not much can be scaled. However, you can use (Scale) in reference planes, images, and imported files from other programs.

Creating Linear and Radial Arrays

The **Array** command creates multiple copies of selected elements in a linear or radial pattern, as shown in Figure 2–55. For example, you can array a row of columns to create a row of evenly spaced columns on a grid, or array a row of parking spaces. The arrayed elements can be grouped or placed as separate elements.

- A linear array creates a straight line pattern of elements, while a radial array creates a circular pattern around a center point.

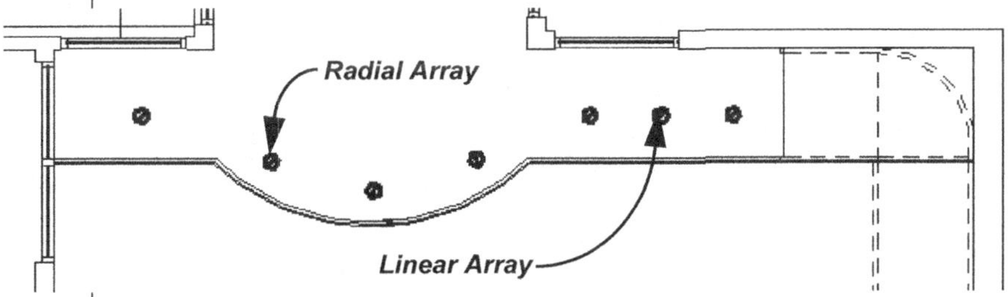

Figure 2–55

How To: Create a Linear Array

1. Select the element(s) to array.
2. In the Modify panel, click (Array) or type the shortcut **AR**.
3. In the Options Bar, click (Linear).
4. Specify the other options as required.

5. Select a start point and an end point to set the spacing and direction of the array. The array is displayed.
6. If the **Group and Associate** option is selected, you are prompted again for the number of items, as shown in Figure 2–56. Type a new number or click on the screen to finish the command.

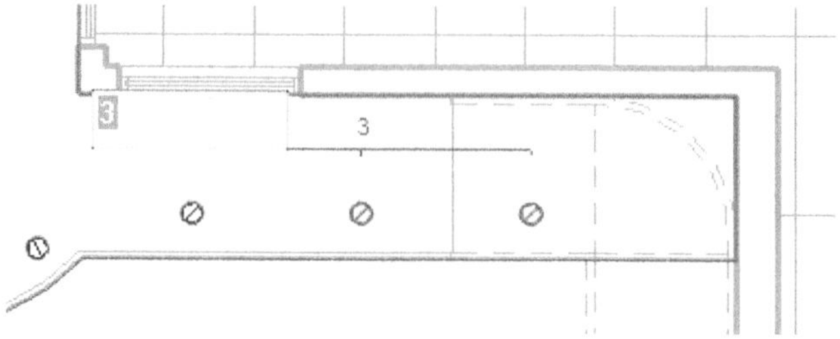

Figure 2–56

- To make a linear array in two directions, you need to array one direction first, select the arrayed elements, and then array them again in the other direction.

Array Options

In the Options Bar, set up the **Array** options for **Linear Array** (top of Figure 2–57) or **Radial Array** (bottom of Figure 2–57).

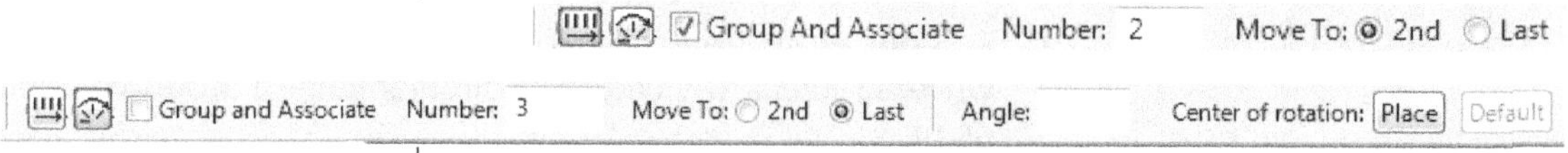

Figure 2–57

Group and Associate	Creates an array group element out of all arrayed elements. Groups can be selected by selecting any elements in the group.
Number	Specifies how many instances you want in the array.
Move To:	**2nd** specifies the distance or angle between the center points of the two elements. **Last** specifies the overall distance or angle of the entire array.
Constrain	Restricts the direction of the array to only vertical or horizontal (Linear only).
Angle	Specifies the angle (Radial only).
Center of rotation	Specifies a location for the origin about which the elements rotate (Radial only).

How To: Create a Radial Array

1. Select the element(s) to array.
2. In the Modify panel, click (Array).
3. In the Options Bar, click (Radial).
4. Drag (Center of Rotation) or in the Options Bar click **Place** to the move the center of rotation to the appropriate location, as shown in Figure 2–58.

*Remember to set the **Center of Rotation** control first, because it is easy to forget to move it before specifying the angle.*

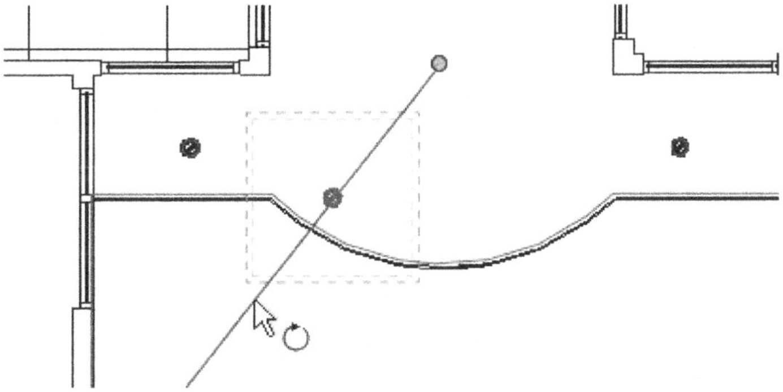

Figure 2–58

5. Specify the other options as required.
6. In the Options Bar, type an angle and press <Enter>, or specify the rotation angle by selecting points on the screen.

Modifying Array Groups

When you select an element in an array that has been grouped, you can change the number of instances in the array, as shown in Figure 2–59. For radial arrays you can also modify the distance to the center.

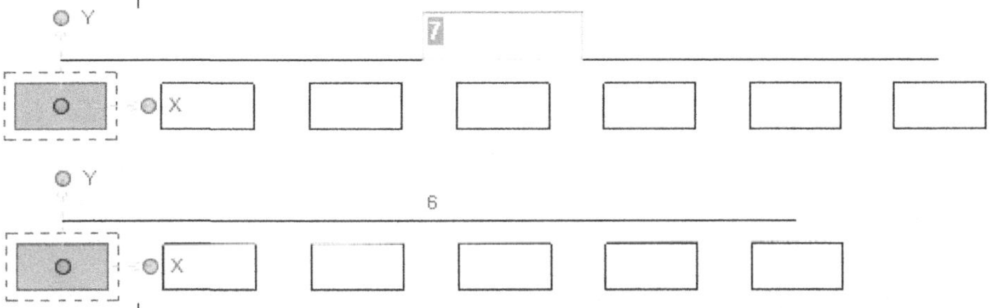

Figure 2–59

- Dashed lines surround the element(s) in a group, and the XY control lets you move the origin point of the group

If you move one of the elements in the array group, the other elements move in response based on the distance and/or angle, as shown in Figure 2–60.

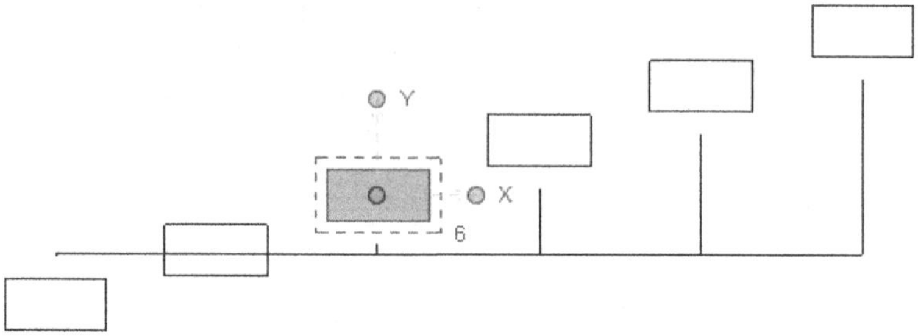

Figure 2–60

- To remove the array constraint on the group, select all of the elements in the array group and, in the *Modify* contextual tab>Group panel, click (Ungroup).
- If you select an individual element in an array and click (Ungroup), the element you selected is removed from the array, while the rest of the elements remain in the array group.

- You can use (Filter) to ensure that you are selecting only **Model Groups**.

Practice 2c Work with Basic Modify Tools

Estimated time for completion: 15 minutes

Practice Objective

- Use basic modify tools, including Move, Copy, Rotate, Mirror, and Array

In this practice you will copy air terminals to several rooms and move some so they fit the room logically. You will array plumbing fixtures in a restroom and then mirror them to the other restroom. Finally, you will rotate lighting fixtures to fit an angled ceiling grid. as shown in Figure 2–61.

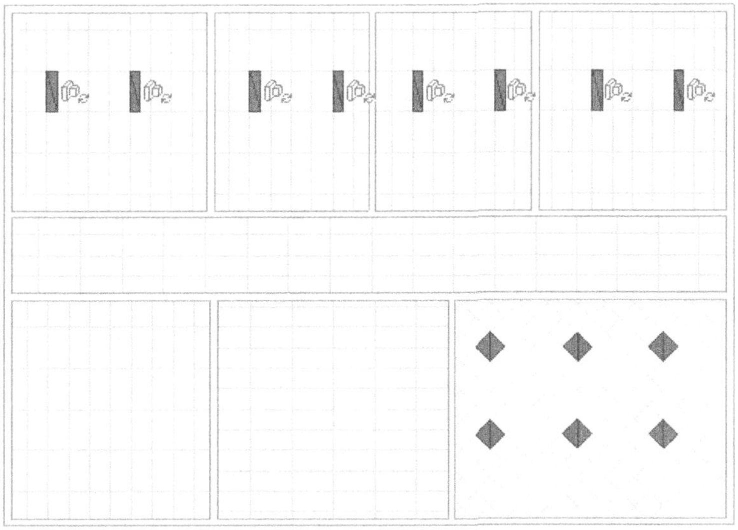

Figure 2–61

Task 1 - Copy elements.

1. In the practice files *Basics* folder open **Simple-Building-Modify-M.rvt**.
2. Open the Mechanical>HVAC>Floor Plans:**1 - Mech** view.
3. Select the four air terminals.
4. In the *Modify | Air Terminals* tab>Modify panel, click  (Copy).

5. In the Options Bar, select **Multiple**.
6. Select the following points, as shown in Figure 2–62:
   - *First point:* **Lab 101**
   - *Second point:* **Lab 104**
   - *Third point:* **Lab 107**

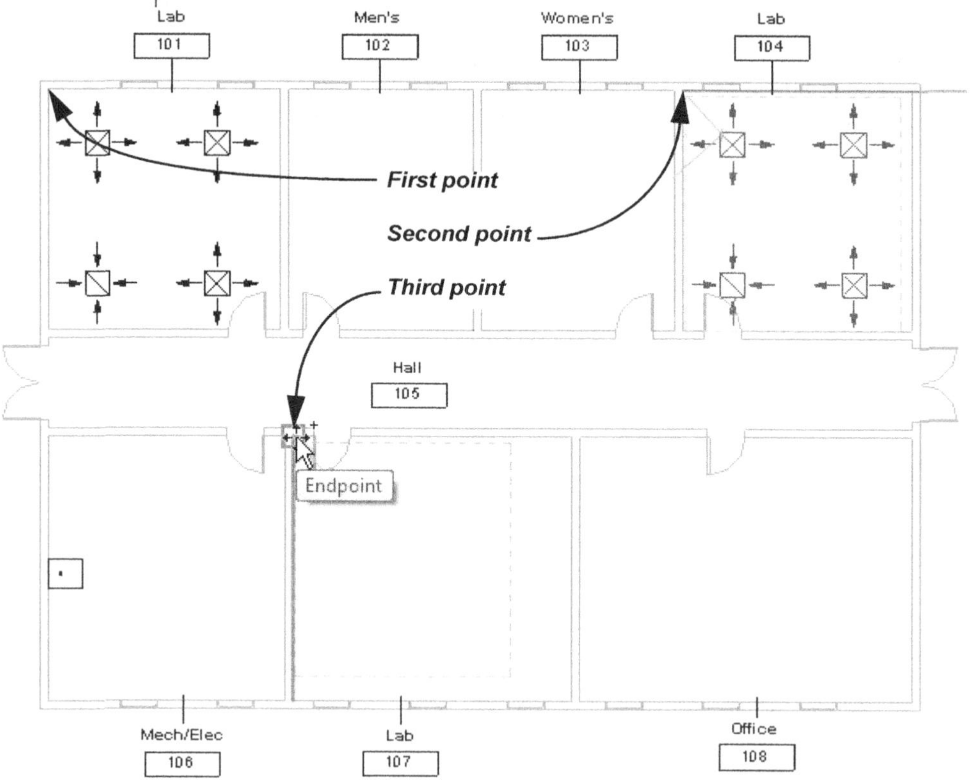

Figure 2–62

7. The air terminals are copied into each room.
8. Click (Modify).
9. In the *Modify* tab>Modify panel, click (Move).
10. As there is no current selection, you need to select the elements to move. In **Lab 107**, select the two air terminals on the right and then press <Enter>.

11. Select a base point on one of the air terminals and then use temporary dimensions to move the air terminals **1200mm**, as shown in Figure 2–63.

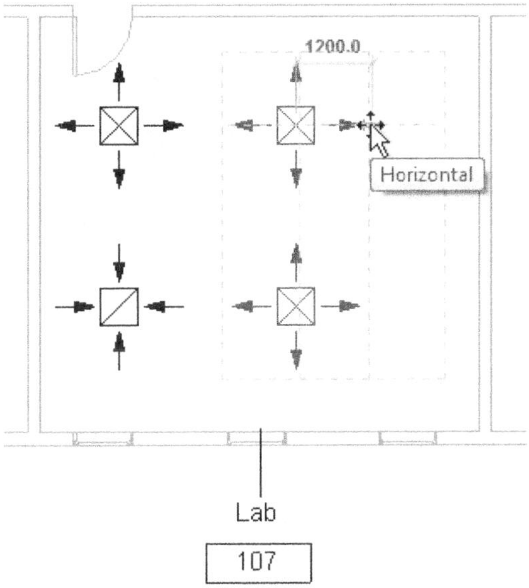

Figure 2–63

12. Save the project.

Task 2 - Array and mirror elements.

1. Open the **Plumbing>Floor Plans: 1 - Plumbing** view.
2. Select the WC and lavatory.
3. In the *Modify | Plumbing Fixtures* tab>Modify panel, click  (Array).
4. In the Options Bar, review the defaults.
5. Pick the first point near one of the fixtures and a second point **900mm** below using temporary dimensions.

6. You are prompted again for the number of elements, as shown in Figure 2–64.

7. Change the number to **4**, and then press <Enter>. The additional fixtures are placed, as shown in Figure 2–65.

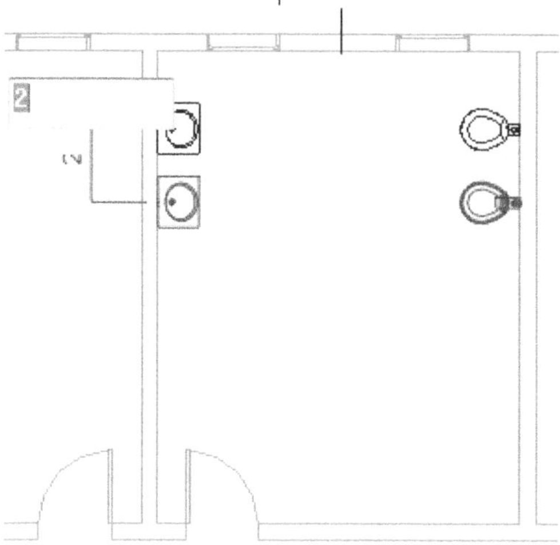

Figure 2–64

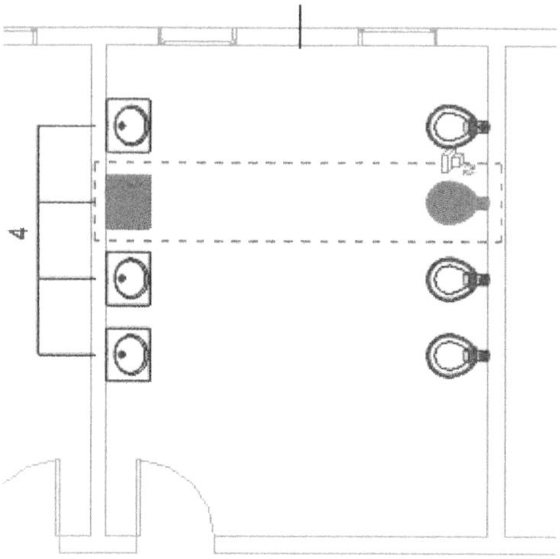

Figure 2–65

8. Click (Modify) and select all of the fixtures. They are grouped together.

9. In the *Modify | Model Groups* tab>Group panel, click (Ungroup). Each element can now be moved separately.

10. Click (Modify) and select the WCs.

11. In the *Modify | Plumbing Fixtures* tab>Modify panel, click (Mirror - Pick Axis).

12. Select the wall between rooms **102** and **103**, as shown in Figure 2–66.

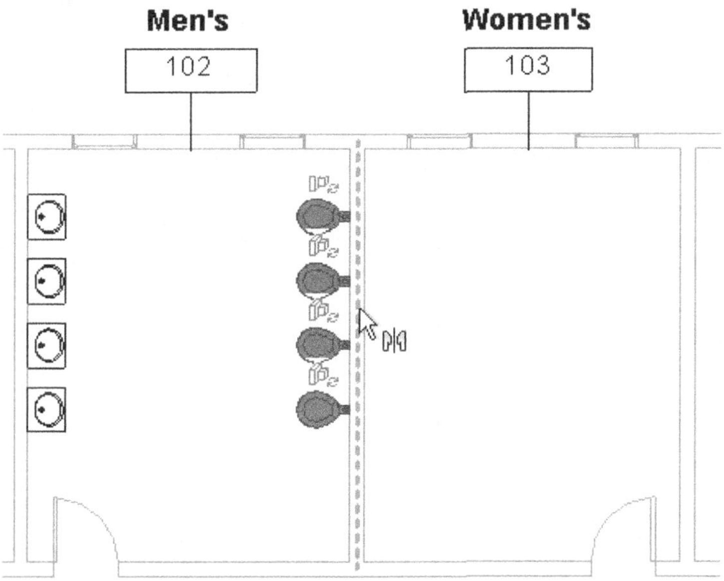

Figure 2–66

Note that mirroring the lavatories reverses the hot and cold water connectors.

13. Select one of the lavatories, right-click and select **Create Similar**.
14. Place the lavatory across from the WC in the Women's room.
15. Click (Modify), select and drag the lavatory into place.
16. With the lavatory still selected, start the **Array** command.
17. In the Options Bar, clear the **Group and Associate** option and set *Number* to **4**.
18. Click a base point on the lavatory, and then click a second point **900mm** below it. Four lavatories are now placed, which do not need to be ungrouped.
19. Select two of the WCs in Room **102**. In the Type selector, change the type to **M_Urinal_Wall Hung 20mm Flush Valve**.
20. Save the project.

Task 3 - Copy and rotate elements.

1. Open the **Electrical>Lighting>Ceiling Plans: 1 - Ceiling Elec** view.
2. Copy the lighting fixtures to the other rooms on the same side of the hall, similar to the example shown in Figure 2–67.

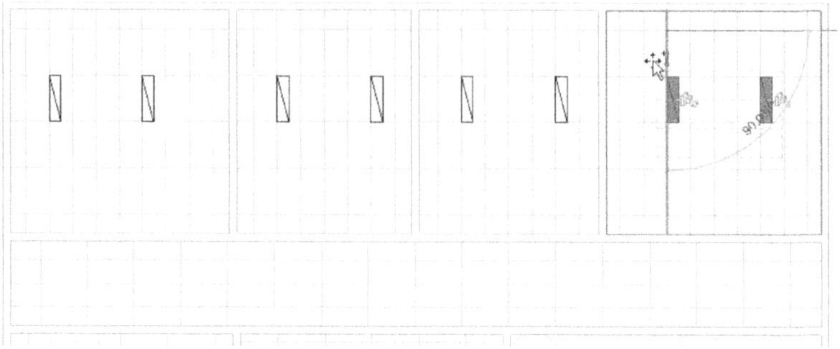

Figure 2–67

3. Add a **M_Plain Recessed Lighting Fixture: 600x600- 277** type lighting fixture to the room with the 45 degree ceiling. (Remember to use **Place on Face**.)
4. Click (Modify) and select the new square lighting fixture.
5. In the *Modify | Lighting Fixtures ta*b>Modify panel, click (Rotate).
6. Drag the center control over to the edge, as shown in Figure 2–68. Click when the cursor displays a horizontal line and then on the nearby 45 degree angled line, as shown in Figure 2–69. The fixture now fits in the grid.

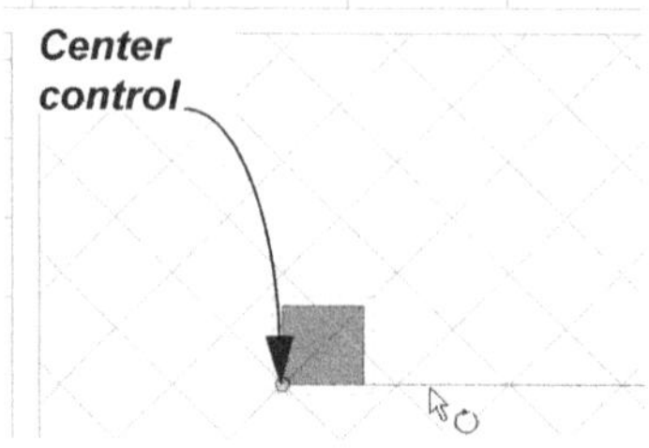

Figure 2–68

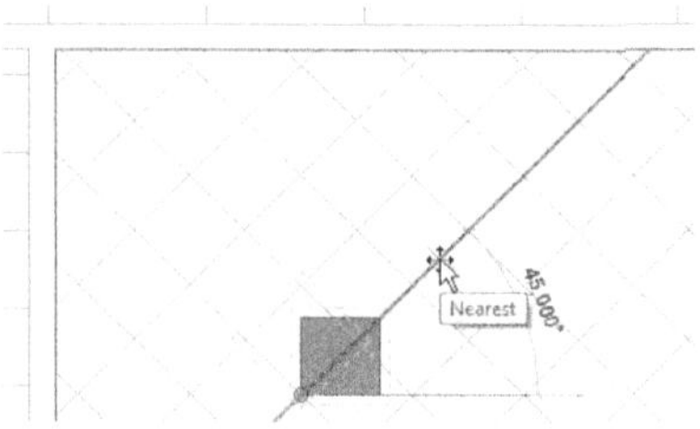

Figure 2–69

7. Copy the fixture to additional places in the room and save the project.

Chapter Review Questions

1. What is the purpose of an alignment line?
   a. Displays when the new element you are placing or drawing is aligned with the grid system.
   b. Indicates that the new element you are placing or drawing is aligned with an existing object.
   c. Displays when the new element you are placing or drawing is aligned with a selected tracking point.
   d. Indicates that the new element is aligned with true north rather than project north.
2. Which of the following commands imports a component (such as the sink shown in Figure 2–70) that is not available in your project?

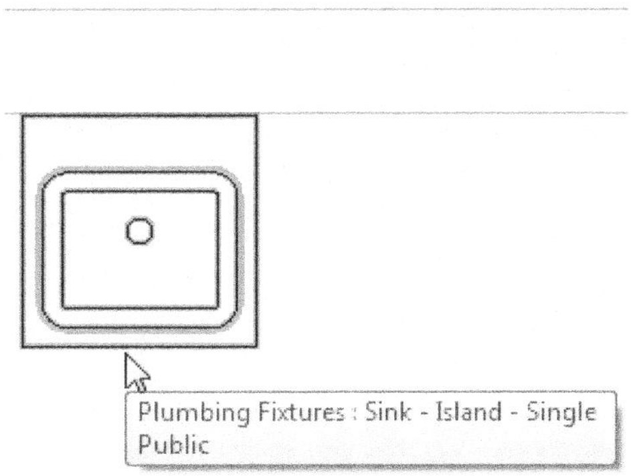

Figure 2–70

   a. **Load Family**
   b. **Load Equipment**
   c. **Load Component**
   d. **Load Fixture**

3. How do you select all Lighting Fixture types, but no other elements in a view?
   a. In the Project Browser, select the *Lighting Fixtures* category.
   b. Select one Lighting Fixture, right-click and select **Select All Instances>Visible in View**.
   c. Select all of the objects in the view and use (Filter) to clear the other categories.
   d. Select one Lighting Fixture and click (Select Multiple) in the ribbon.

4. What are the two methods for starting (Move) or (Copy)?
   a. Start the command first and then select the objects, or select the objects and then start the command.
   b. Start the command from the *Modify* tab, or select the object and then select **Move** or **Copy** from the shortcut menu.
   c. Start the command from the *Modify* tab, or select the objects and select **Auto-Move**.
   d. Use the **Move/Copy** command or **Cut/Copy** and **Paste** using the Clipboard.

5. Where do you change the type for a selected plumbing fixture, as shown in Figure 2–71?

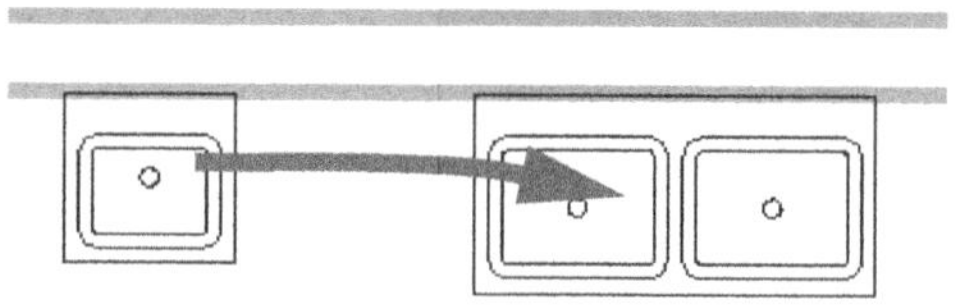

Figure 2–71

   a. In the *Modify | Plumbing Fixtures* tab>Properties panel, click (Type Properties) and select a new type in the dialog box.
   b. In the Options Bar, click **Change Element Type**.
   c. Select the dynamic control next to the selected plumbing fixture and select a new type in the drop-down list.
   d. In Properties, select a new type in the Type Selector drop-down list.

6. Both (Rotate) and (Array) with (Radial) have a center of rotation that defaults to the center of the element or group of elements you have selected. How do you move the center of rotation to another point as shown in Figure 2–72? (Select all that apply.)

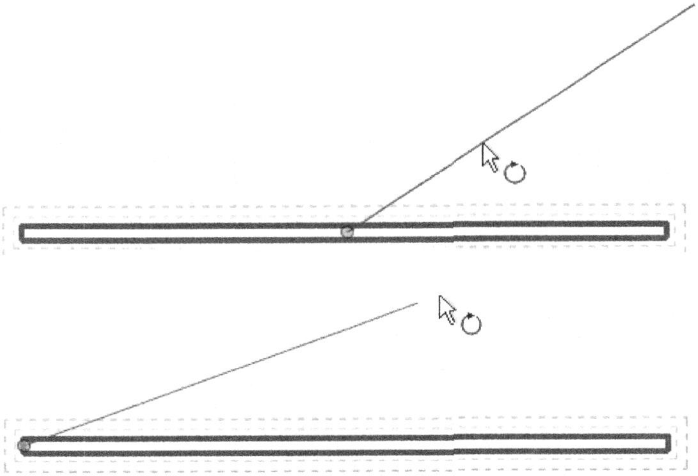

Figure 2–72

a. Select the center of rotation and drag it to a new location.

b. In the Options Bar, click **Place** and select the new point.

c. In the *Modify* tab>Placement panel, click (Center) and select the new point.

d. Right-click and select **Snap Overrides>Centers** and select the new point.

Command Summary

Button	Command	Location
Modify Tools		
	Array	• **Ribbon:** *Modify* tab>Modify panel • **Shortcut:** AR
	Copy	• **Ribbon:** *Modify* tab>Modify panel • **Shortcut:** CO
	Copy to Clipboard	• **Ribbon:** *Modify* tab>Clipboard panel • **Shortcut:** <Ctrl>+<C>
	Delete	• **Ribbon:** *Modify* tab>Modify panel • **Shortcut:** DE
	Mirror - Draw Axis	• **Ribbon:** *Modify* tab>Modify panel • **Shortcut:** DM
	Mirror - Pick Axis	• **Ribbon:** *Modify* tab>Modify panel • **Shortcut:** MM
	Move	• **Ribbon:** *Modify* tab>Modify panel • **Shortcut:** MV
	Paste	• **Ribbon:** *Modify* tab>Clipboard panel • **Shortcut:** <Ctrl>+<V>
	Pin	• **Ribbon:** *Modify* tab>Modify panel • **Shortcut:** PN
	Rotate	• **Ribbon:** *Modify* tab>Modify panel • **Shortcut:** RO
	Scale	• **Ribbon:** *Modify* tab>Modify panel • **Shortcut:** RE
	Unpin	• **Ribbon:** *Modify* tab>Modify panel • **Shortcut:** UP
Select Tools		
	Drag elements on selection	• **Ribbon:** All tabs>Select panel • **Status Bar**
	Filter	• **Ribbon:** *Modify | Multi-Select* tab>Filter panel • **Status Bar**
	Select Elements By Face	• **Ribbon:** All tabs>Select panel • **Status Bar**
	Select Links	• **Ribbon:** All tabs>Select panel • **Status Bar**
	Select Pinned Elements	• **Ribbon:** All tabs>Select panel • **Status Bar**
	Select Underlay Elements	• **Ribbon:** All tabs>Select panel • **Status Bar**

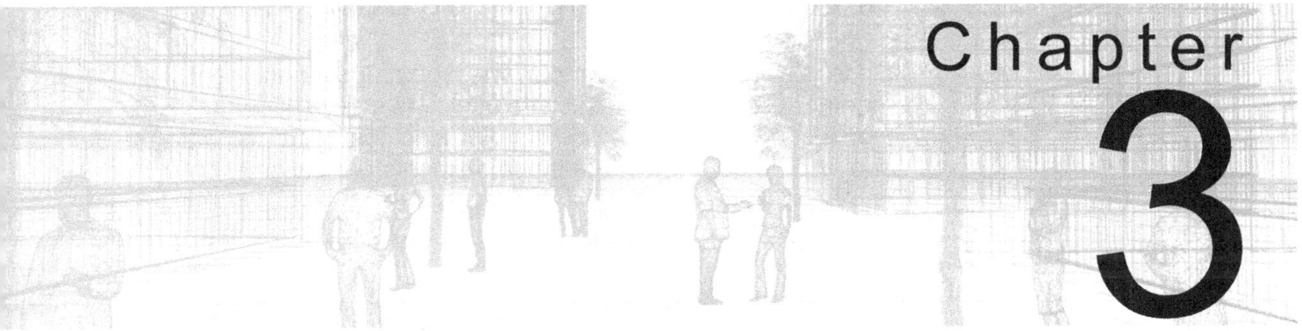

Chapter 3

Basic Systems Tools

Once you have placed components such as air terminals, plumbing fixtures, and lighting fixtures in a project, you need to connect them using ducts, pipes, cable trays, or conduits. As you connect components, you create systems which enable you to test the usefulness of these connections. Systems can be viewed in the Systems Browser.

Learning Objectives in this Chapter

- Connect components using ducts, pipes, cable trays, and conduits.
- Align, trim, and extend elements with the edges of other elements.
- Split linear elements anywhere along their length.
- Offset elements to create duplicates a specific distance away from the original.
- Create MEP Systems.
- Review MEP Systems in the Systems Browser.

In-depth steps for creating these connections are covered later in this student guide.

3.1 Connecting Components

Once you have placed components, you can connect them together using elements such as ducts (as shown in Figure 3–1), pipes, cable trays, and conduits. For electrical systems, wiring can also be generated, but these elements are only symbolic and annotative.

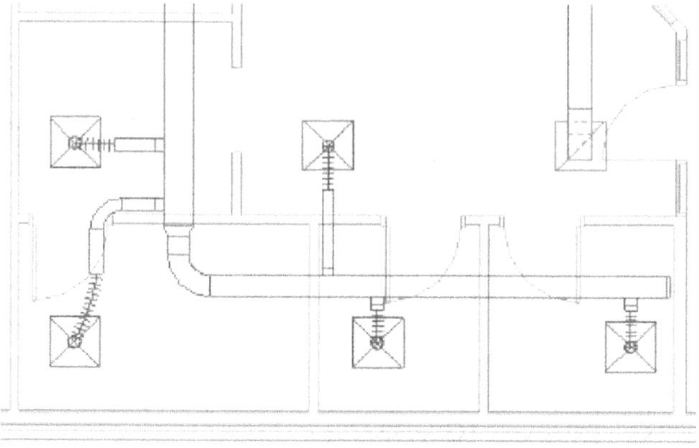

Figure 3–1

- When you draw the connecting elements, the Autodesk® Revit® software calculates the height and size of the opening and applies the appropriate fittings.

There are several ways of drawing connections between components:

- Select a component and click on the connector icon, shown in Figure 3–2.
- Select a component and right-click on a connector to select one of the options, as shown for a plumbing fixture in Figure 3–2.

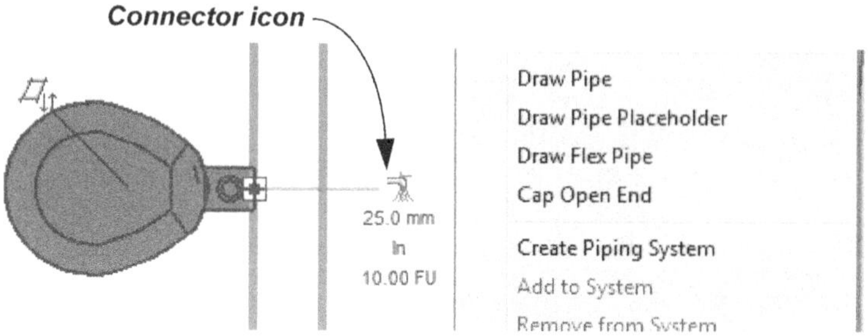

Figure 3–2

- Start the commands from the *Systems* tab>HVAC, Plumbing & Piping, and Electrical panels. Primary tools include:

	**HVAC** Duct and Flex Duct
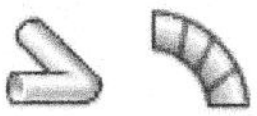	**Plumbing, Hydronic Piping, and Fire Suppression** Pipe and Flex Pipe
	**Electrical** Wire, Cable Tray, and Conduit

- You can also type in the associated shortcut key that displays when you hover over the tool in the ribbon, as shown in Figure 3–3.

Cable tray and conduit are typically placed separately from the components.

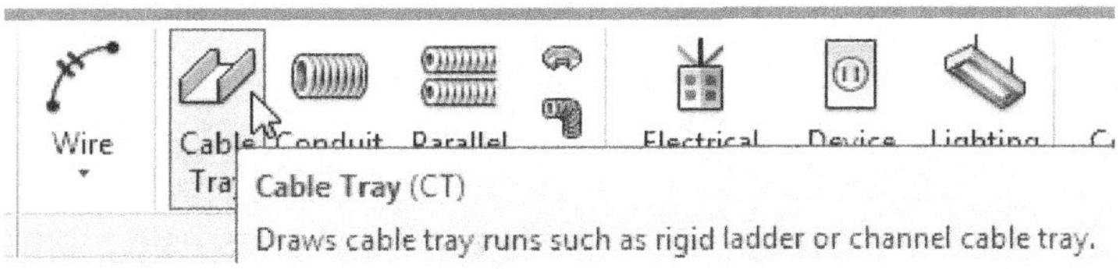

Figure 3–3

How To: Connect Components

1. Select a component and click on the connector icon.
2. In the Type Selector, select the type, as shown in Figure 3–4. For example, you would select a pipe that matches the kind of system you are creating.

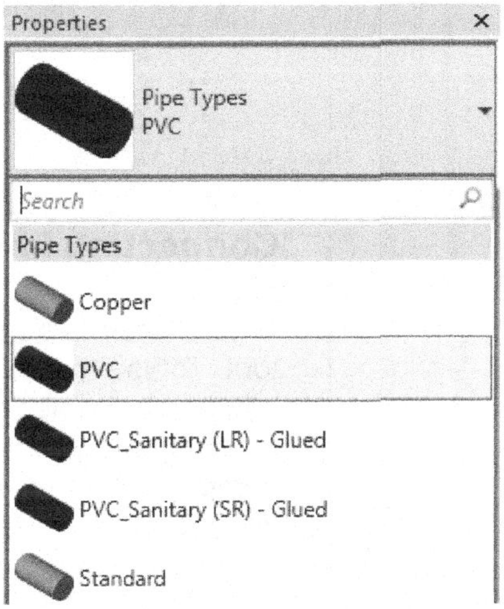

Figure 3–4

3. In the contextual tab, Options Bar, and Properties, specify the required options, as shown in Figure 3–5. The options that are available depend on the type of elements you are using.

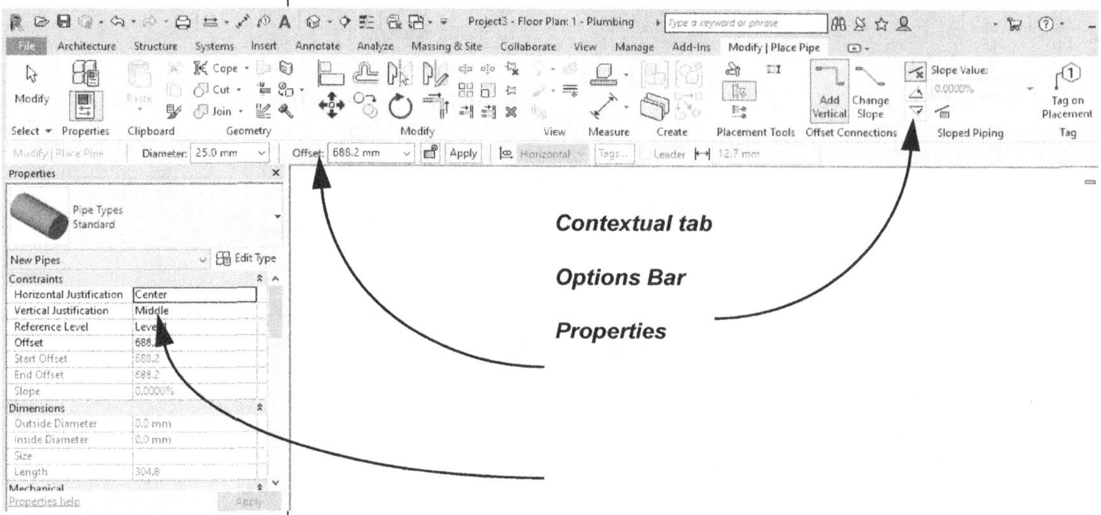

Figure 3–5

4. Draw the objects using temporary dimensions and snaps, as shown in Figure 3–6. Ensure that you are selecting the correct connector or related element. Fittings are automatically applied.

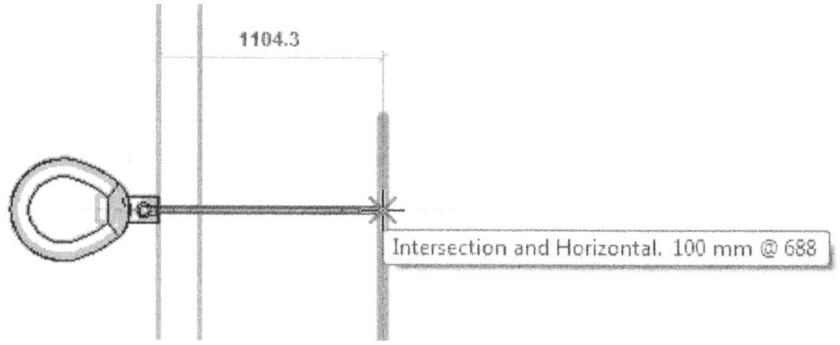

Figure 3–6

Connecting Into

A quick way to generate connections is to use the **Connect Into** tool. To use this tool, you must already have some duct, pipe, conduit, or cable trays in the project, as well as have the components you need to connect. When you select a component, the **Connect Into** option is available in the contextual tab.

- Check your project in a 3D view to ensure that the path is acceptable.

How To: Connect a Component to Existing Connectors

1. Select the component that you want to connect to an existing connector.
2. In the *Modify* | *<contextual>* tab>Layout panel, click  (Connect Into).
3. Select the connector, such as the pipe shown in Figure 3–7.

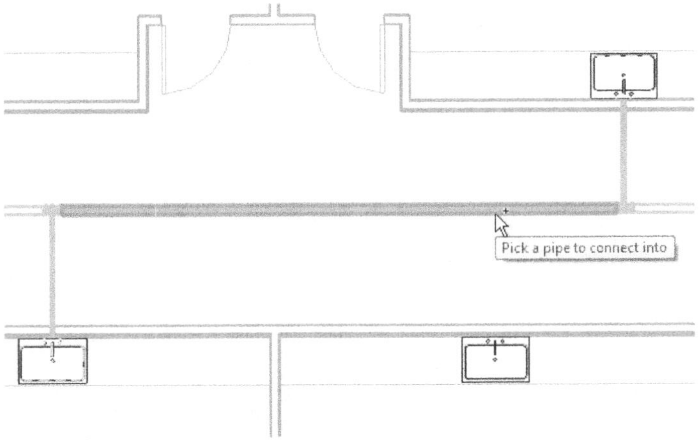

Figure 3–7

- If you select a connector that cannot work with the component, an error is displayed, as shown in Figure 3–8. Click **Cancel** and then try a different connector, or add the connectors separately.
  - This error most often occurs because the offset between two elements is too close for the software to create the connection based on the default fittings.
  - Another cause of this error is that the connector is the wrong system type. The *System Type* can be changed in the Properties of the element, as required.

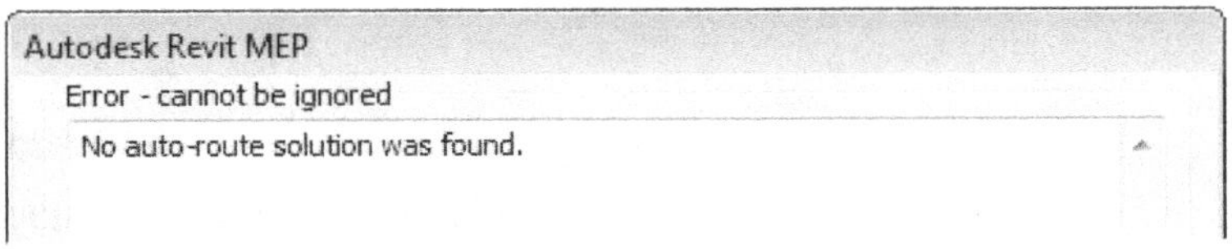

Figure 3–8

- This process automatically connects the component into a system.

Modifying Fittings

Fittings are added automatically when connectors touch each other, turn, or change size. Fittings can be modified using the Type Selector, Properties, Options Bar, or a variety of connectors and controls. For example, when using ducts, an elbow can be changed to a tee connection by clicking a control, as shown in Figure 3–9. You can then add another duct to the newly-opened connector.

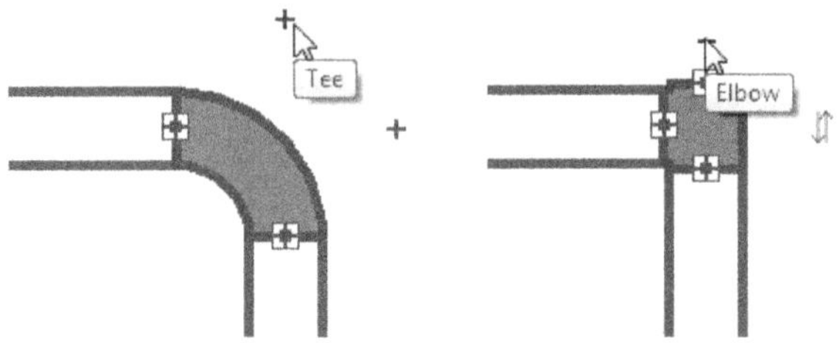

Figure 3–9

Hint: Troubleshooting Errors and Warnings

There are two types of error alerts. Those that you cannot ignore (shown in Figure 3–10) and those that can be ignored but need to be dealt with at a later time (shown in Figure 3–11).

Figure 3–10

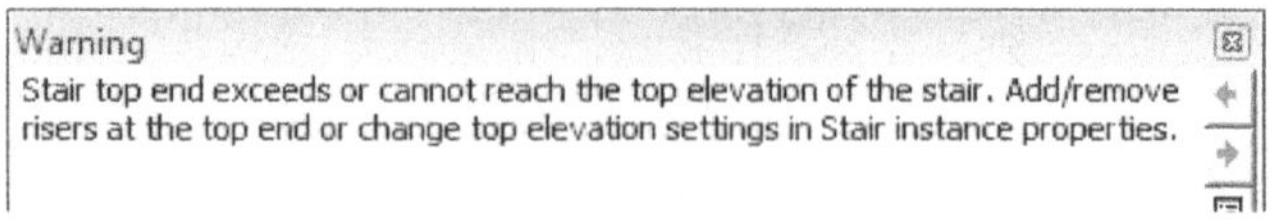

Figure 3–11

- **Errors:** Force you to stop and fix the situation. In some cases, you can resolve the error if it gives you an option, while in other cases, you have to cancel and try again.
- **Warnings**: Display when something is wrong, but you can keep on working. In many cases, you can close the dialog box and fix the issue or wait and do it later.

Testing Connections

A quick way to test the continuity of connectors is to hover the cursor over a linear connection and press <Tab> until the entire system is highlighted. For example, one of the ducts shown in Figure 3–12 is not highlighted because it is not attached to the fitting.

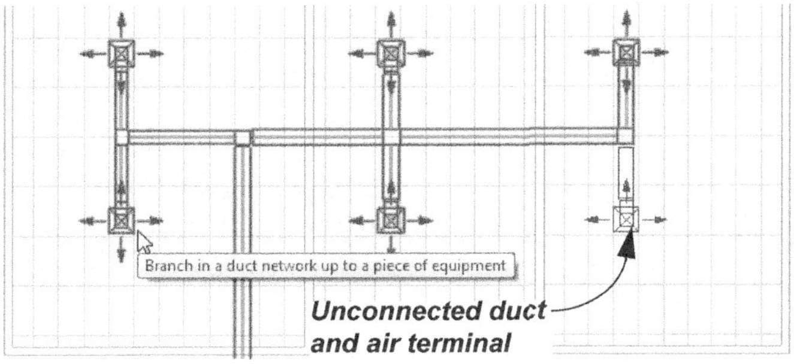

Figure 3–12

Alternatively, you can also display the disconnects using the **Show Disconnects** tool.

How To: Show Disconnects

1. In the *Analyze* tab>Check Systems panel, click (Show Disconnects).
2. In the Show Disconnects Options dialog box, select the types of systems you want to display (as shown in Figure 3–13) and click **OK.**
3. Any disconnects display (Warning), as shown in Figure 3–14.

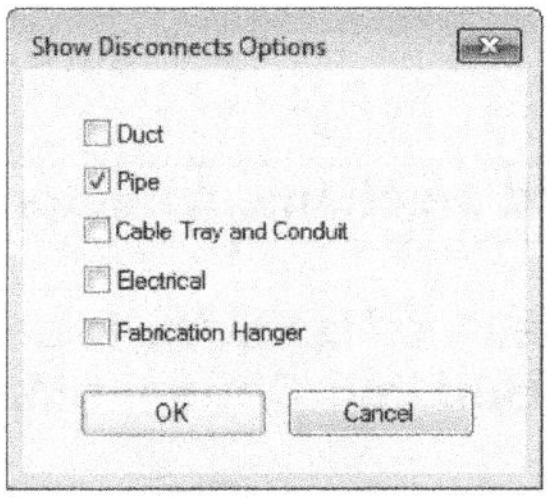

Figure 3–13

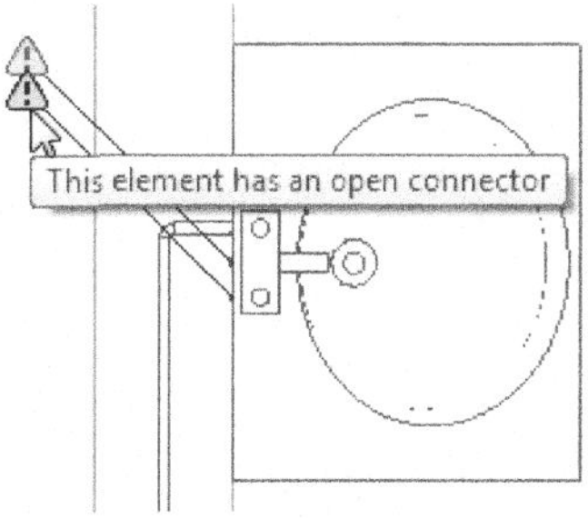

Figure 3–14

- The disconnects continue to display until you either correct the situation or run **Show Disconnects** again and clear all of the selections.
- Hover the cursor over the warning icon to display a tooltip with the warning. You can also click on the icon to open the Warning dialog box.

Practice 3a Connect Components

Estimated time for completion: 15 minutes

Practice Objectives

- Load a component from the Autodesk Revit Library and insert it into the project.
- Draw piping.
- Connect equipment and fixtures to piping.

In this practice you will load and place a hot water heater. You will create piping from a lavatory to the hot water heater. You will then connect the other lavatories into the hot water supply line, as shown in Figure 3–15.

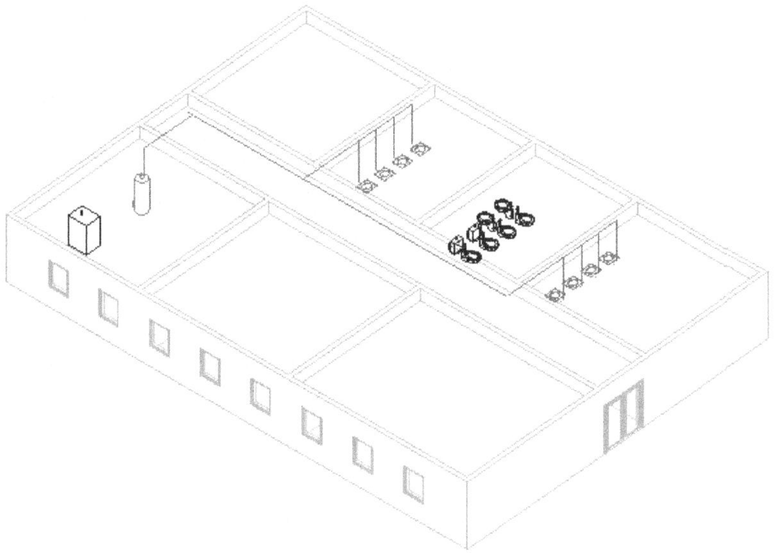

Figure 3–15

Task 1 - Add mechanical equipment.

1. In the practice files *Basic* folder, open **Simple-Building-Connect-M.rvt**.
2. Open the Plumbing>Floor Plans>**1 - Plumbing** view.
3. In the *Systems* tab>Mechanical panel, click (Mechanical Equipment).

4. In the Type Selector, note that there is no hot water heater available.

5. In the *Modify | Place Mechanical Equipment* tab>Mode panel, click  (Load Family).

This fixture is also available in the Basics practice files folder.

6. In the Load Family dialog box, navigate to the *Plumbing> MEP>Equipment>Water Heaters* folder and select **M_Water Heater.rfa**.

7. Click **Open**.

8. Place the Water Heater in the upper-left corner of the Mech/Elec room.

9. Open the Plumbing>3D Views>**3D Plumbing** view.

10. Zoom and rotate the view so you can see water heater.

11. Select the water heater to display the connectors, as shown in Figure 3–16.

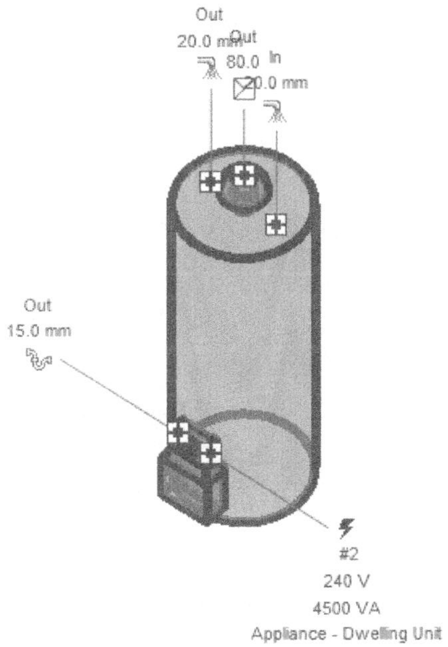

Figure 3–16

12. Return to the **1 - Plumbing** floor plan view. (Hint: press <Ctrl>+<Tab> to switch between open windows.)

13. Rotate the equipment, as shown in Figure 3–17.

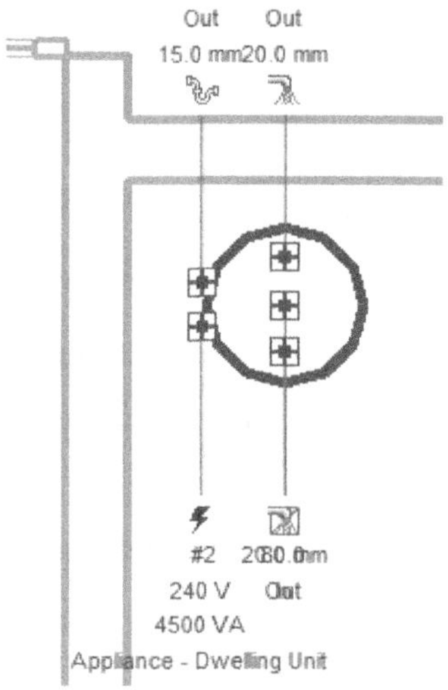

Figure 3–17

14. Save the project.

Task 2 - Connect a plumbing fixture to the hot water heater.

1. Continue working in the **1 - Plumbing** view.
2. Pan and zoom in on the Women's room.
3. Select the sink closest to the window. Zoom so that the three connectors are displayed.
4. Click on the Hot Water connector.
5. In the Options Bar, note that *Diameter* and *Offset* are automatically set to the height of the fixture connector, as shown in Figure 3–18.

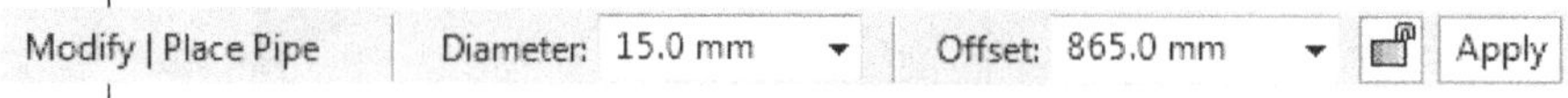

Figure 3–18

6. In the Type Selector, select **Pipe Types: Standard**.
7. If the pipe is too thick, draw the pipe horizontally into the wall. Note that the sink turns red, indicating that it is now part of the Domestic Hot Water system.
8. In the Options Bar, change the *Offset* to**2750mm** and click **Apply**. This sends the pipe directly up, as shown in Figure 3–19.

9. The *Detail Level* of the view is set to **Medium**. In the View Control Bar set the *Detail Level* to (Fine). The pipe now displays full scale (as shown in Figure 3–20), rather than in schematic.

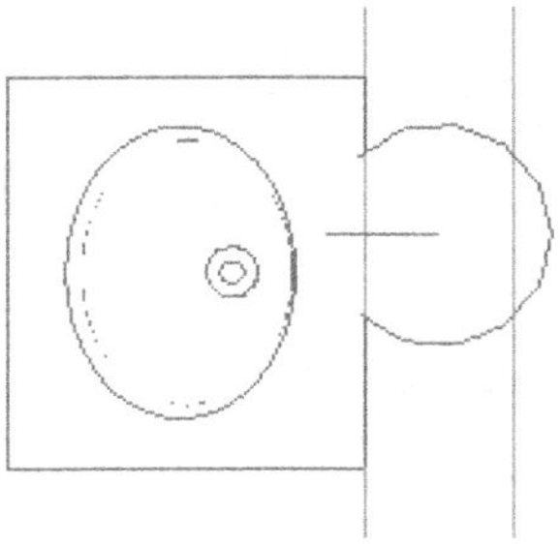

Figure 3–19

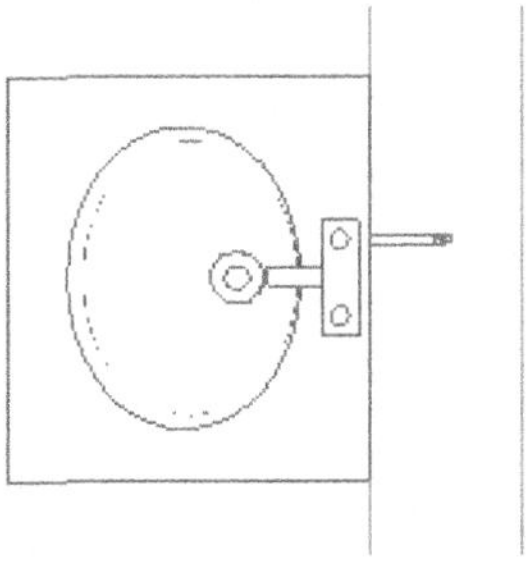

Figure 3–20

10. You are still in the **Pipe** command. Hover over the new pipe and select the connector that is at 2750mm.

11. Draw the pipe down the wall, into the hall, and then down past the hot water heater, as shown in Figure 3–21.

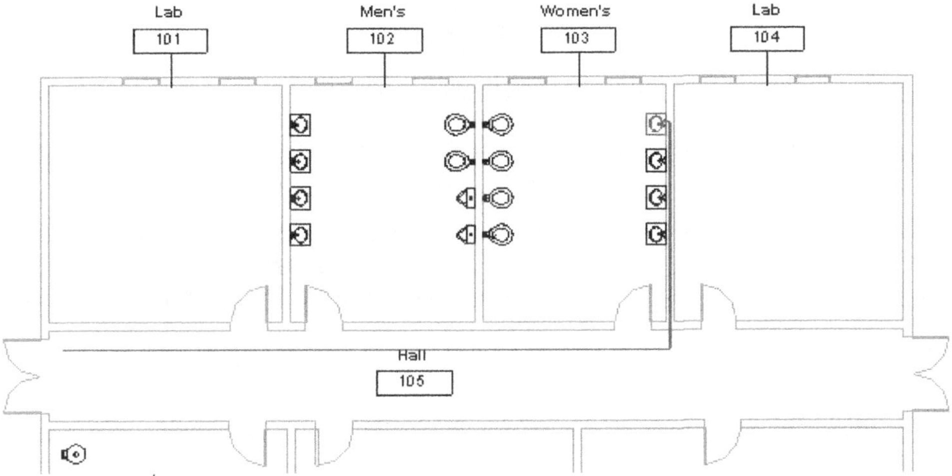

Figure 3–21

12. Click (Modify) and select the hot water heater.

13. In the *Modify | Mechanical Equipment* tab>Layout panel, click (Connect Into).

14. In the Select Connector dialog box select **Connector 2: Domestic Hot Water** (as shown in Figure 3–22) and then click **OK**.

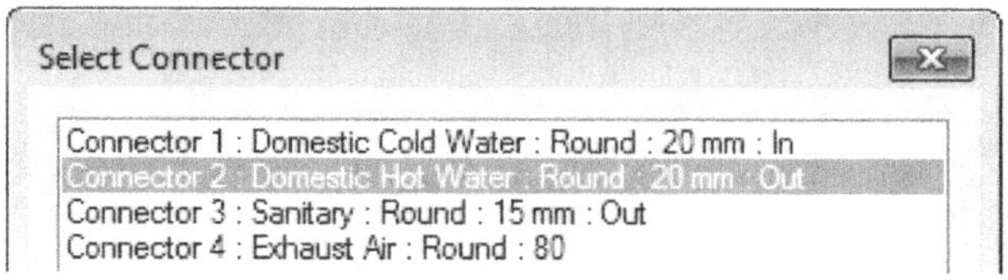

Figure 3–22

15. Select the pipe in the hall. The correct pipe is automatically added. Note that any excess pipe will be corrected later.

16. View the new pipes in the **3D Plumbing** view.

17. Save the Project.

Task 3 - Connect additional fixtures.

1. In the **3D Plumbing** view, select the lavatory in the Men's room that is closest to the window.

2. In the *Modify | Plumbing Fixtures* tab>Layout panel, click  (Connect Into).

3. In the Select Connector dialog box, select the **Domestic Hot Water** connector and then click **OK**.

4. Select the pipe above the hall. Note that the connection is made, but that it is based on the height of the lavatory and not the higher pipe, as shown in Figure 3–23.

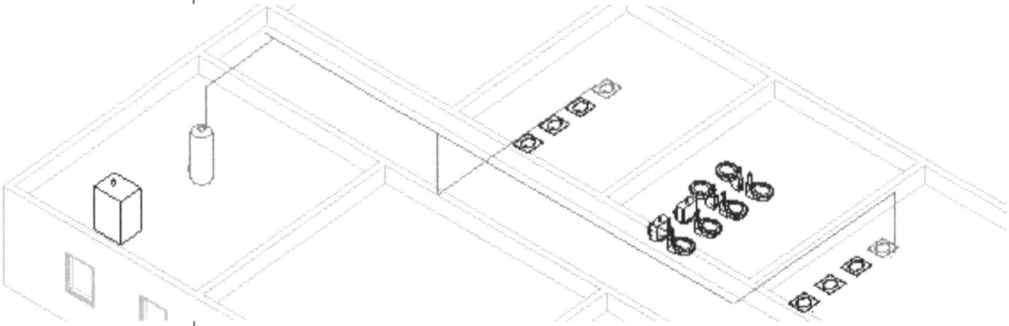

Figure 3–23

5. In the Quick Access Toolbar, click  (Undo).

6. Return to the **1 - Plumbing** view.

7. In the *Systems* tab>Plumbing & Piping panel, click (Pipe). In the Options Bar, set the *Diameter* to **15mm** and the *Offset* to **2750mm**, if it is not already.
8. Draw a pipe down the middle of the wall that does not touch the lavatories, but connects into the horizontal pipe above the hall, as shown in Figure 3–24.

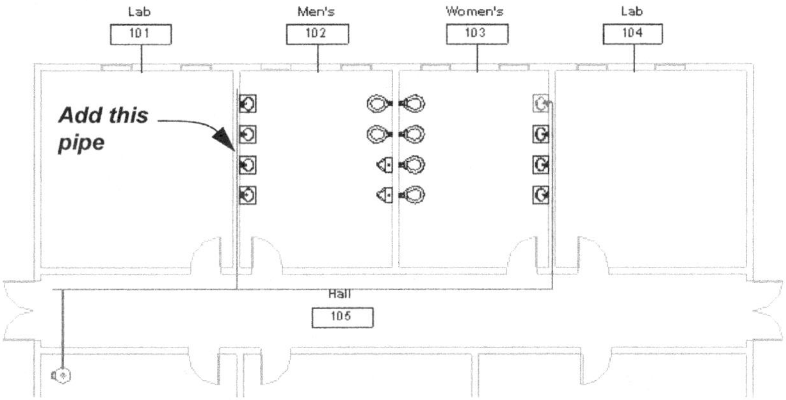

Figure 3–24

9. Click **Modify**.
10. Zoom in and select the new pipe.
11. Drag the end so that it aligns with the lavatory hot water connection, as shown in Figure 3–25.

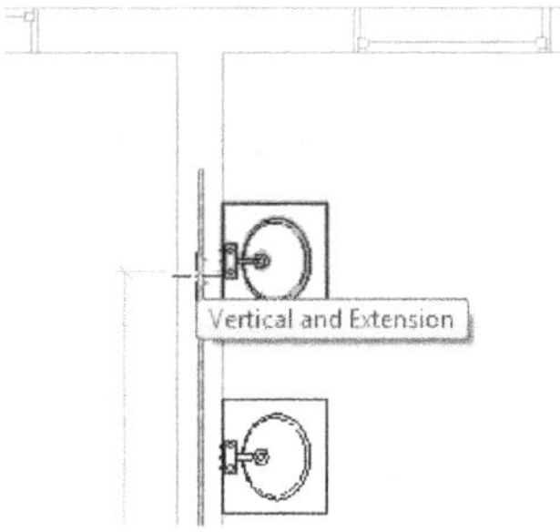

Figure 3–25

12. You can now use **Connect Into** and attach the rest of the lavatories to the appropriate pipe.
13. Open the **3D Plumbing** view. Pan and zoom as required to view the new piping.
14. Save the project.

3.2 Working with Additional Modify Tools

As you work on a project, some additional tools on the *Modify* tab>Modify panel, as shown in Figure 3–26, can help you with placing, modifying, and constraining elements. **Align** can be used with a variety of elements, while **Split Element**, **Trim/Extend**, and **Offset** can only be used with linear elements.

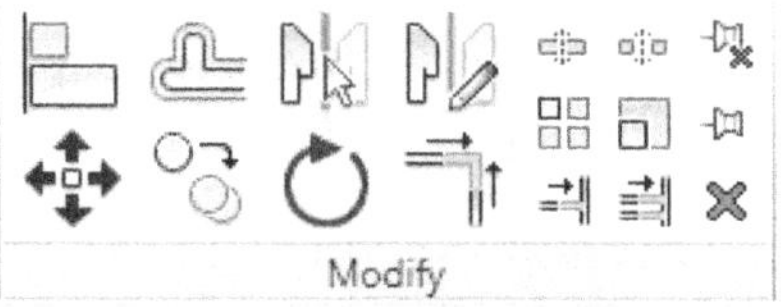

Figure 3–26

Aligning Elements

The **Align** command enables you to line up one element with another. Most Autodesk Revit elements can be aligned. For example, you can line up an air terminal with ceiling grids, as shown in Figure 3–27.

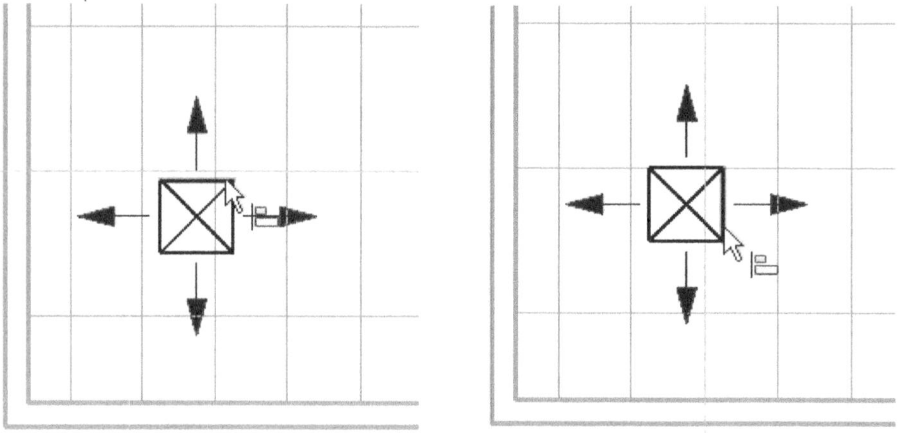

Figure 3–27

How To: Align Elements

1. In the *Modify* tab>Modify panel, click (Align).
2. Select a line or point on the element that is going to remain stationary. For walls, press <Tab> to select the correct wall face.

3. Select a line or point on the element to be aligned. The second element moves into alignment with the first one.

- The **Align** command works in all model views, including parallel and perspective 3D views.
- You can lock alignments so that the elements move together if either one is moved. Once you have created the alignment, a padlock is displayed. Click on the padlock to lock it, as shown in Figure 3–28.

Locking elements enlarges the size of the project file, so use this option carefully.

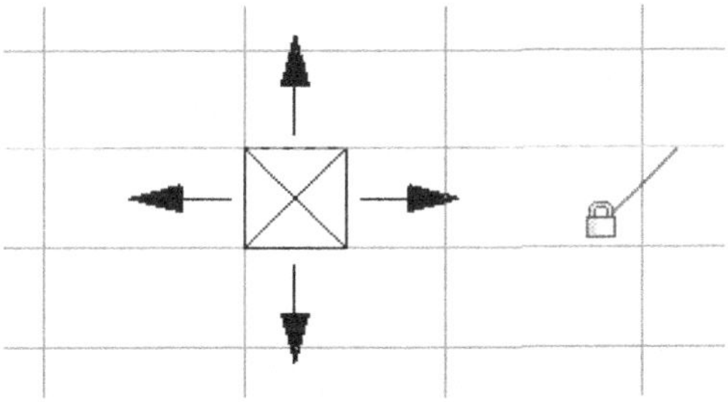

Figure 3–28

- Select **Multiple Alignment** to select multiple elements to align with the first element. You can also hold <Ctrl> to make multiple alignments.
- For walls, you can specify if you want the command to prefer **Wall centerlines**, **Wall faces**, **Center of core**, or **Faces of core**, as shown in Figure 3–29. The core refers to the structural members of a wall as opposed to facing materials, such as sheet rock.

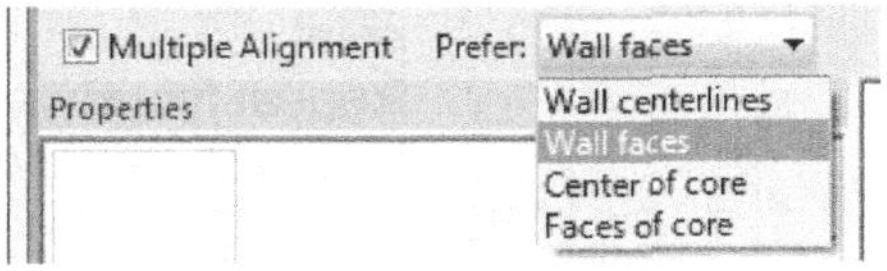

Figure 3–29

Splitting Linear Elements

The **Split** Element command enables you to break a linear element at a specific point. You can use alignment lines, snaps, and temporary dimensions to help place the split point. After you have split the linear element, you can use other editing commands to modify the two parts, or change the type of one part, as shown with walls in Figure 3–30.

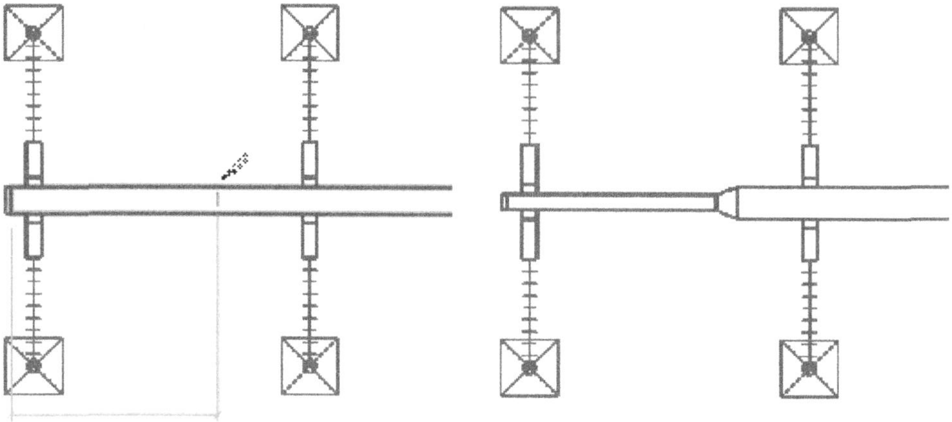

Figure 3–30

How To: Split Linear Elements

1. In the *Modify* tab>Modify panel, click (Split Element) or type the shortcut **SL**.
2. In the Options Bar, select or clear the **Delete Inner Segment** option.
3. Move the cursor to the point you want to split and select the point.
4. Repeat for any additional split locations.
5. Modify the elements that were split, as required.

- The **Delete Inner Segment** option is used when you select two split points along a linear element. When the option is selected, the segment between the two split points is automatically removed.

Trimming and Extending

There are three trim/extend methods that you can use with linear elements: **Trim/Extend to Corner**, **Trim/Extend Single Element**, and **Trim/Extend Multiple Elements**.

- When selecting elements to trim, click the part of the element that you want to keep. The opposite part of the line is then trimmed.

How To: Trim/Extend to Corner

1. In the *Modify* tab>Modify panel, click (Trim/Extend to Corner) or type the shortcut **TR**.
2. Select the first linear element on the side you want to keep.
3. Select the second linear element on the side you want to keep, as shown in Figure 3–31.

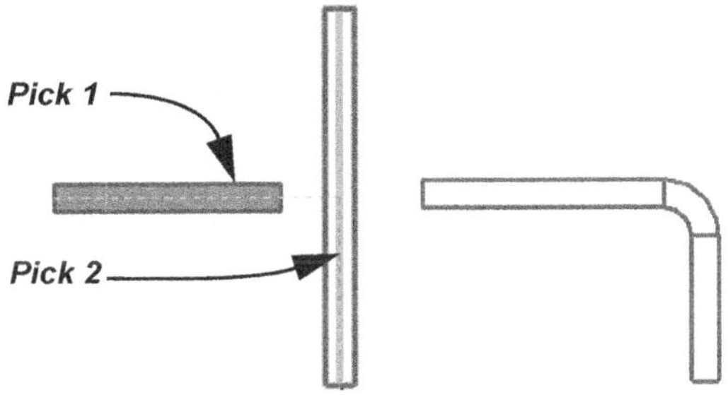

Figure 3–31

How To: Trim/Extend a Single Element

1. In the *Modify* tab>Modify panel, click (Trim/Extend Single Element).
2. Select the cutting or boundary edge.
3. Select the linear element to be trimmed or extended, as shown in Figure 3–32.

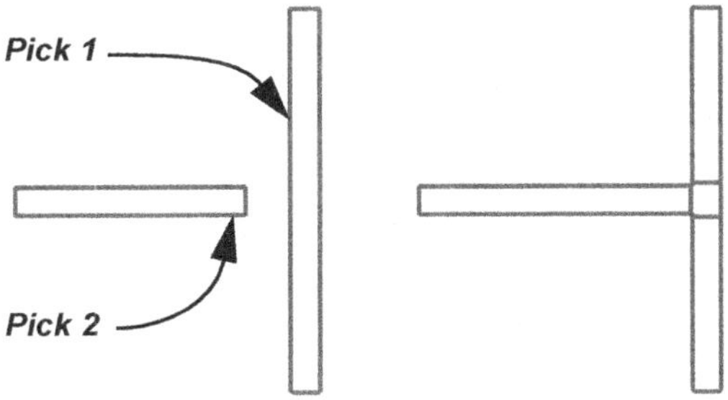

Figure 3–32

How To: Trim/Extend Multiple Elements

1. In the *Modify* tab>Modify panel, click (Trim/Extend Multiple Elements).
2. Select the cutting or boundary edge.

3. Select the linear elements that you want to trim or extend by selecting one at a time, or by using a crossing window, as shown in Figure 3–33. For trimming, select the side you want to keep.

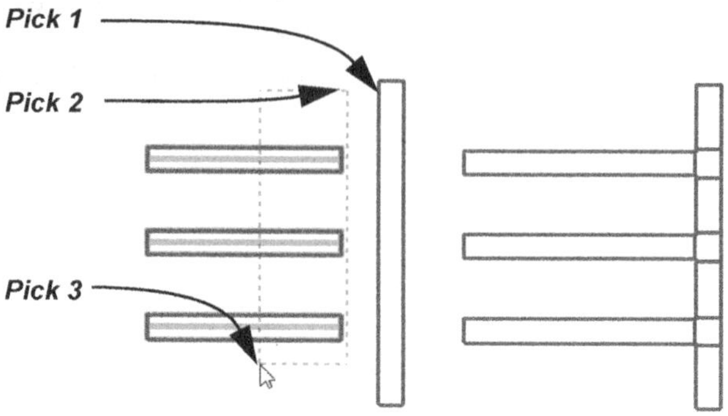

Figure 3–33

- You can click in an empty space to clear the selection and select another cutting edge or boundary.

Offsetting Elements

MEP elements can be offset, but you should typically use other tools to create parallel elements, such as ducts, pipes, and conduits.

The **Offset** command is an easy way of creating parallel copies of linear elements at a specified distance, as shown in Figure 3–34. Walls, beams, braces, and lines are among the elements that can be offset.

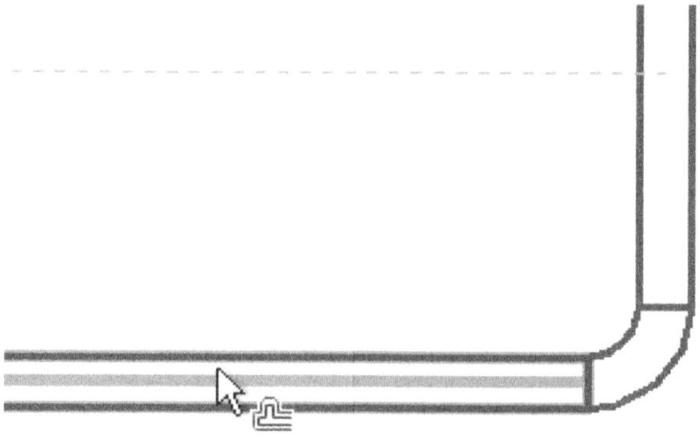

Figure 3–34

The offset distance can be set by typing the distance (**Numerical** method shown in Figure 3–35) or by selecting points on the screen (**Graphical** method).

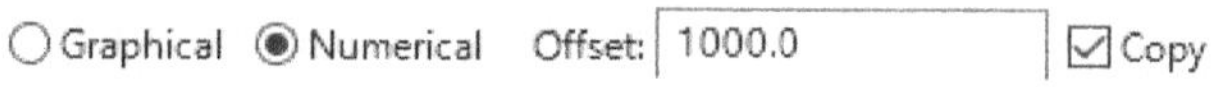

Figure 3–35

How To: Offset using the Numerical Method

*The **Copy** option (which is on by default) makes a copy of the element being offset. If this option is not selected, the **Offset** command moves the element the set offset distance.*

1. In the *Modify* tab>Modify panel, click (Offset) or type the shortcut **OF**.
2. In the Options Bar, select the **Numerical** option.
3. In the Options Bar, type the required distance in the *Offset* field.
4. Move the cursor over the element you want to offset. A dashed line previews the offset location. Move the cursor to flip the sides, as required.
5. Click to create the offset.
6. Repeat Steps 4 and 5 to offset other elements by the same distance, or to change the distance for another offset.

- With the **Numerical** option, you can select multiple connected linear elements for offsetting. Hover the cursor over an element and press <Tab> until the other related elements are highlighted, as shown in Figure 3–36. Select the element to offset all of the elements at the same time.

The offset is from centerline to centerline of elements, such as duct or pipe.

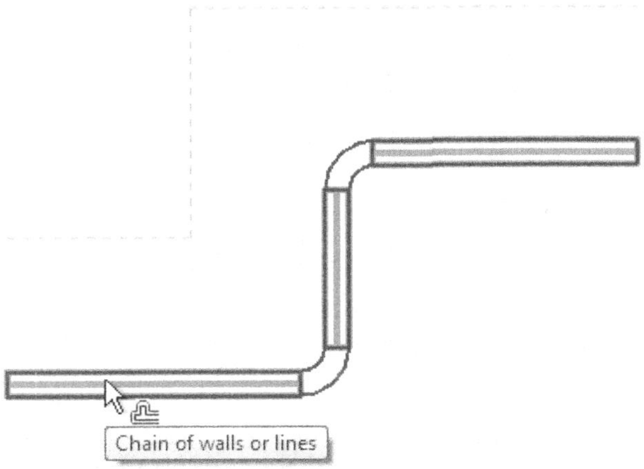

Figure 3–36

How To: Offset using the Graphical Method

1. Start the **Offset** command.
2. In the Options Bar, select the **Graphical** option.
3. Select the linear element to offset.
4. Select two points that define the distance of the offset and which side to apply it. You can type an override in the temporary dimension for the second point.

- Most linear elements connected at a corner automatically trim or extend to meet at the offset distance.

Practice 3b Work with Additional Modify Tools

Practice Objectives

- Show disconnects.
- Use Align, Split, Offset and Trim/Extend.

Estimated time for completion: 15 minutes

In this practice you will discover and delete excess piping and clean it up with modify tools. You will align air terminals to ceiling grids. Finally you will place cable trays and use trim/extend commands to link them. You will also split and resize part of the tray, as shown in Figure 3–37.

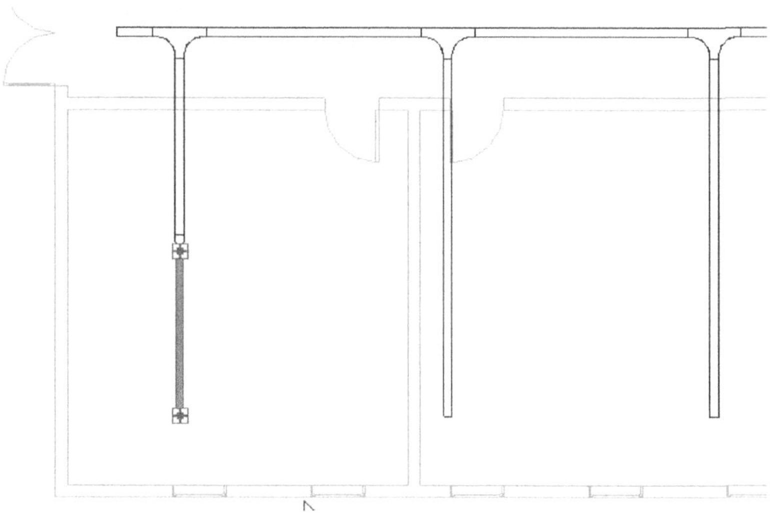

Figure 3–37

Task 1 - Clean up excess piping.

1. In the practice files *Basics* folder, open **Simple-Building-Align-M.rvt**.
2. Open the Plumbing>Floor Plans>**1 - Plumbing** view.
3. Hover the cursor over one of the pipes and press <Tab> until all of the pipes and components are highlighted. Note that everything seems to be correct.
4. In the *Analyze* tab>Check Systems panel, click (Show Disconnects).

5. In the Show Disconnects Options dialog box, select **Pipe** and then click **OK**. A number of disconnects display (as shown in Figure 3–38) because the piping has not been finished.

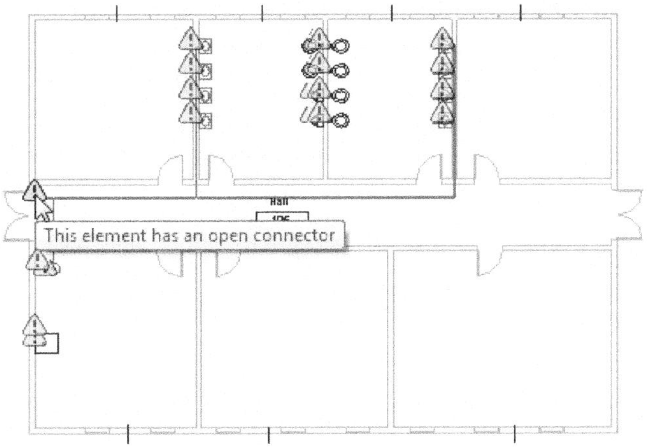

Figure 3–38

6. One open connector (as shown in Figure 3–38) is not related to any of the plumbing fixtures, This is an open pipe that needs to be fixed.

7. Open the Plumbing>3D Views>**3D Plumbing** view.

8. Zoom in on the connection between the hot water heater and the pipe in the hall to display the open connector.

9. Open (Show Disconnects), turn off **Pipes** and close the dialog box.

10. In the View Control Bar, change the *Detail Level* to (Fine) and the Visual Style to (Shaded) to help display the pipes more clearly.

11. Delete the extra pipe and connectors between the pipes, as shown in Figure 3–39.

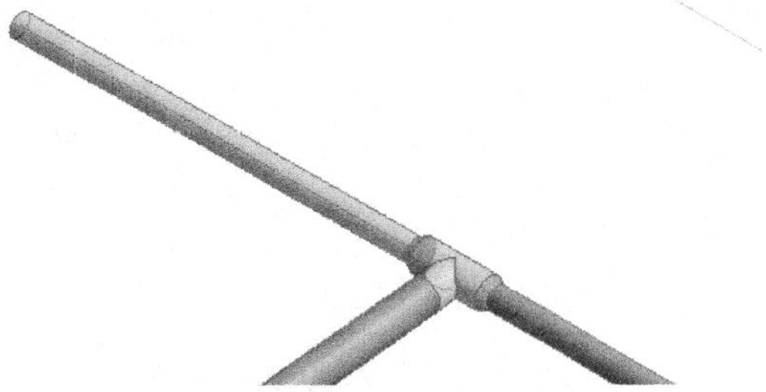

Figure 3–39

12. In the *Modify* tab>Modify panel, click (Trim/Extend to Corner.

13. Select the two pipes, as shown in Figure 3–40. Ensure that you select the smaller pipe first so that the elbow connector uses the size of the larger pipe, as shown in Figure 3–41.

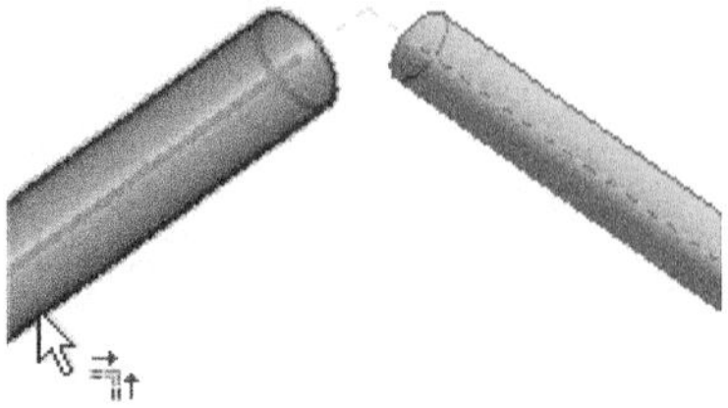

Figure 3–40

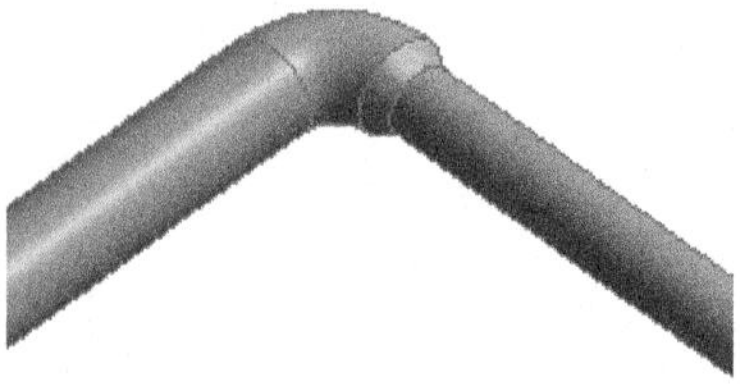

Figure 3–41

14. Type **ZF** to zoom the model to fit the view.

15. Save the project

Task 2 - Align air terminals to ceiling grids.

1. Open the Mechanical>HVAC>Ceiling Plans>**1-Ceiling Mech** view.
2. Zoom in on the lab room in the upper left corner.
3. In the *Modify* tab>Modify panel, click (Align).
4. Select a vertical grid line and then the side of the air terminal, as shown in Figure 3–42.

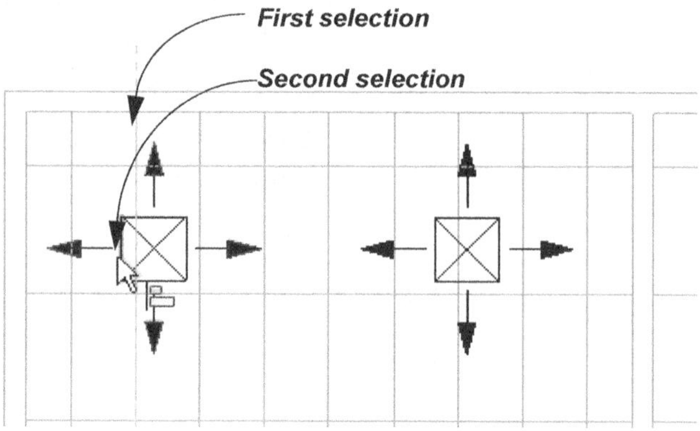

Figure 3–42

5. While still in the **Align** command, in the Options Bar, select **Multiple Alignment**.

6. Without stopping, select the following items in the order listed, as shown in Figure 3–43:
    - Horizontal grid line
    - Horizontal edge of the first air terminal
    - Horizontal edge of the 2nd air terminal

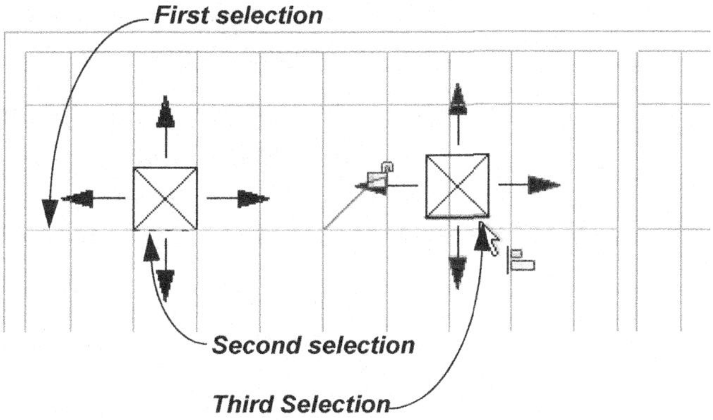

Figure 3–43

7. Press <Esc> once. This keeps you in the command but releases the alignment line.
8. Align the other air terminals to the ceiling grid, as shown in Figure 3–44.

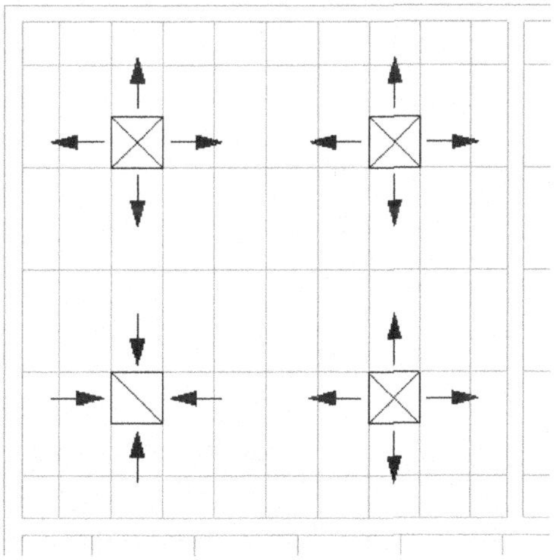

Figure 3–44

9. Use the **Align** tool with or without the multiple alignment (see which works the best for you) to move the air terminals in the other lab rooms.
10. Zoom to fit the view and then save the project.

Task 3 - Draw, modify, and offset cable trays.

1. Open the Electrical>Power>Floor Plans>**1 - Power** view.
2. In the *Systems* tab>Electrical panel, click (Cable Tray).
3. In the Type Selector, select **Cable Tray with Fittings: Trough Cable Tray**.
4. In the Options Bar, set the following options:
   - *Width:* **150mm**
   - *Height:* **50mm**
   - *Offset:* **3000mm**
5. Draw a line of the cable tray down the hall (as shown in Figure 3–45). Press <Esc> to stay in the command, but end the line.

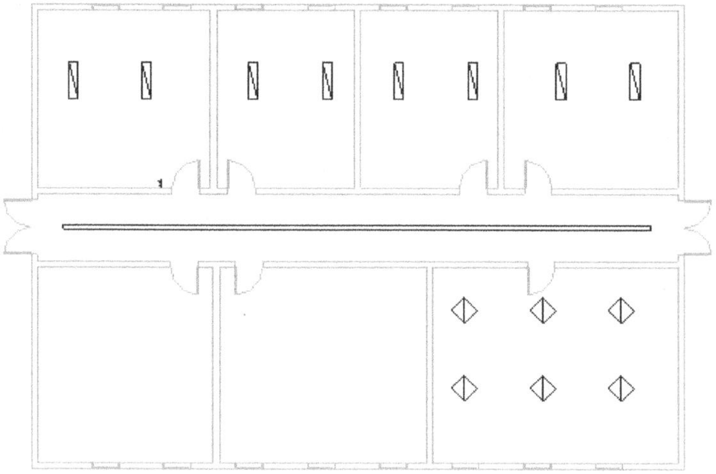

Figure 3–45

6. Draw another cable tray from the Mech/Elec room (lower left) that is perpendicular to and touching the cable tray in the hall.
7. In the *Modify* tab>Modify panel, click (Offset).
8. In the Options Bar, select **Numerical**, set the *Offset* to **4600mm**, and ensure that **Copy** is selected.

9. Hover the cursor over the vertical cable tray and ensure that the alignment line is to the right, as shown in Figure 3–46. Click to create the copy.

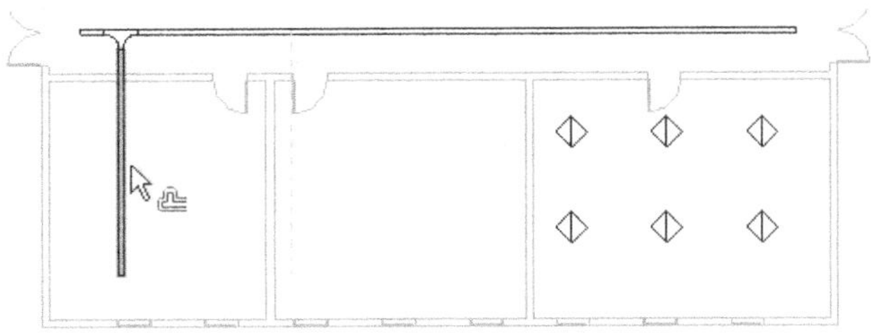

Figure 3–46

10. Select the new cable tray (ensuring that the offset is to the right) and continue until there are five total trays, as shown in Figure 3–47.

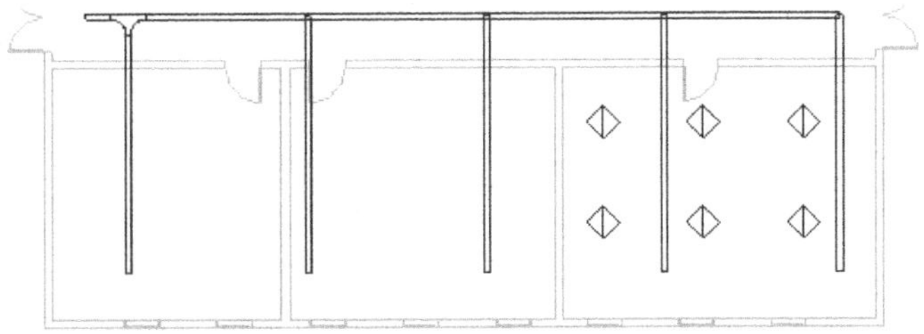

Figure 3–47

11. Click Modify.

12. In the *Modify* tab>Modify panel, click (Trim/Extend Multiple Elements).

13. Select the horizontal cable tray and then draw a crossing window from right to left, as shown in Figure 3–48.

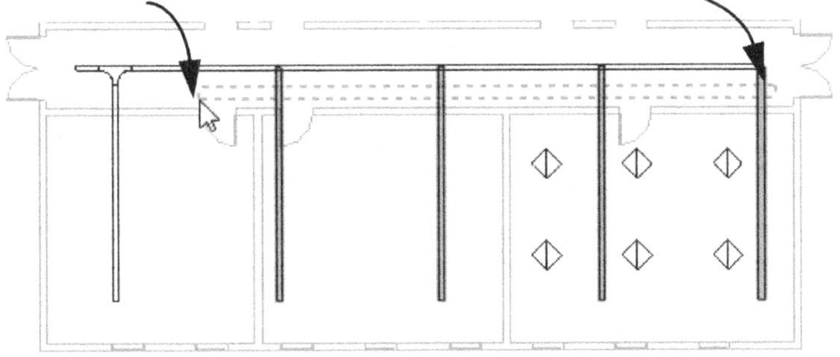

Figure 3–48

14. The cable trays are extended and fittings applied, as shown in Figure 3–49. If the last cable tray does not clean up, use the (Trim/Extend to Corner) command.

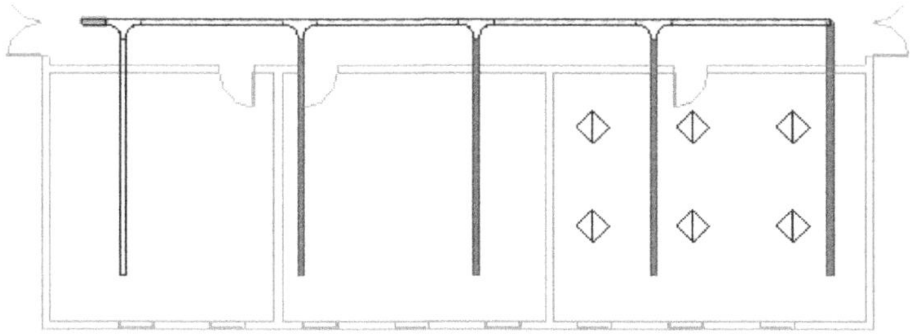

Figure 3–49

15. In the *Modify* tab>Modify panel, click (Split Element).

16. Select the point on the vertical cable tray shown in Figure 3–50. The cable tray is split and fittings are applied.

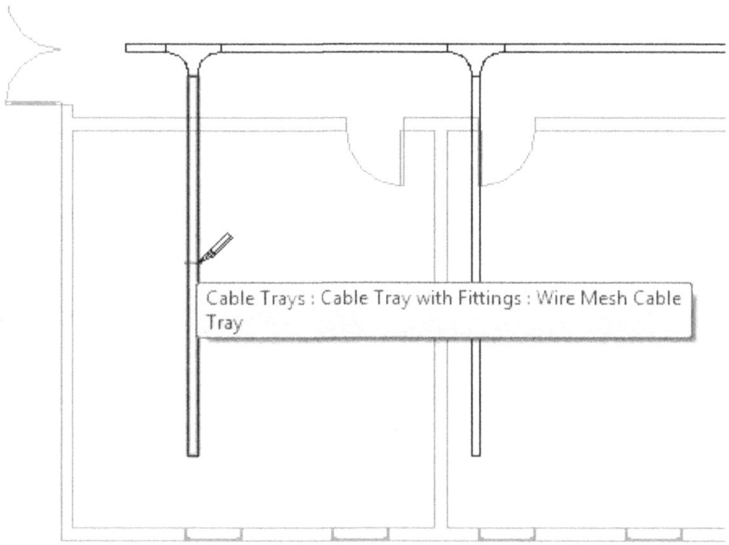

Figure 3–50

17. Select the lower part of the tray. In the Options Bar, change the *Width* to **100mm**. The size changes and the fitting is applied.

18. Save the project.

3.3 Creating Systems - Overview

When you connect components such as air terminals with ducts, or plumbing fixtures with pipes, systems are automatically created. These systems frequently overlap. For example, as a part of a HVAC installation, an air handling unit is connected to supply and return duct systems, as well as hydronic supply and return systems. It is also connected to an electrical system (circuit), as shown in Figure 3–51.

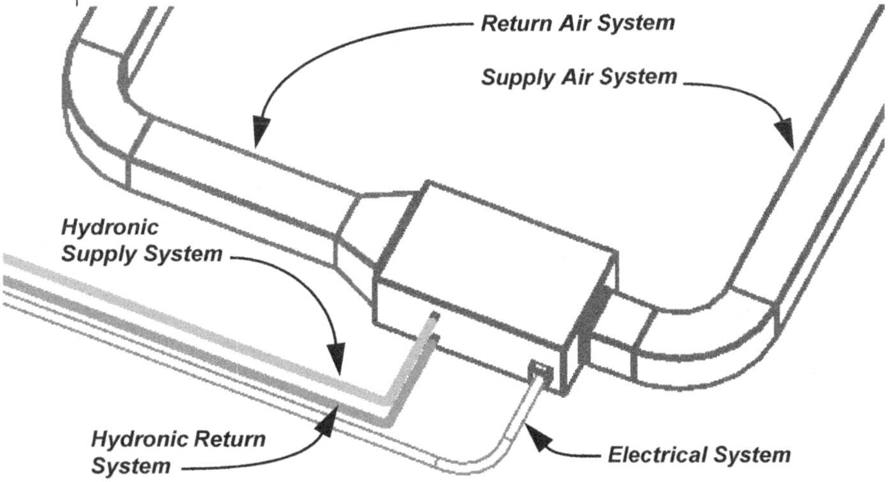

Figure 3–51

- Creating systems correctly is critical for the Autodesk Revit software to understand and calculate flow, pressure, etc.
- While most systems are created automatically as you connect components with duct or pipe, you can create the system first and then connect the components later.
- Electrical systems (such as switches and data) do not have connecting elements and therefore need to be created.

How To: Create a System

The type of systems available depends on the component you select.

1. Select one or more related components. Do not select source equipment at this point.
2. In the *Modify* | *contextual* tab>Create Systems panel, click (Duct), (Power), (Piping), (Data), (Fire Alarm, (Controls) or other system types.

3. For Duct and Piping Systems, you are prompted to select the *System type* and assign a *System name*, as shown in Figure 3–52. Click **OK**.

*If you know you want to add the source equipment or more components to the system at this time, select **Open in System Editor**.*

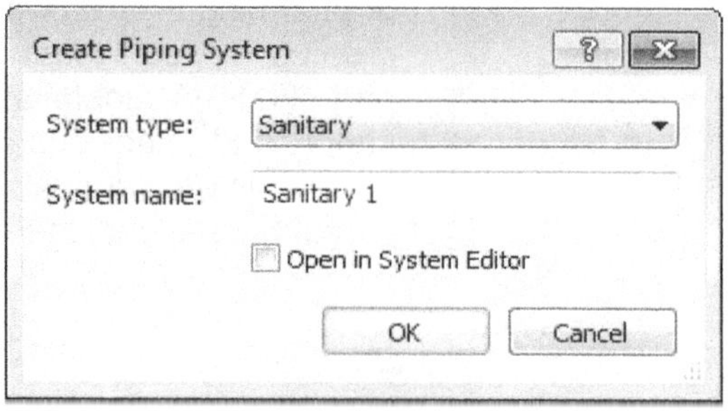

Figure 3–52

4. In the contextual *Modify* tab>System Tools panel, click  (Select Equipment) as shown in Figure 3–53, or, for electrical circuits, click  (Select Panel).

Figure 3–53

- The number of options that display in the *Modify* tab depends on where you are in the system creation.

5. To add additional end components, in the contextual *Modify* tab>System Tools panel, click the **Edit Systems/Circuit** tool. The related contextual tab displays, as shown in Figure 3–54.

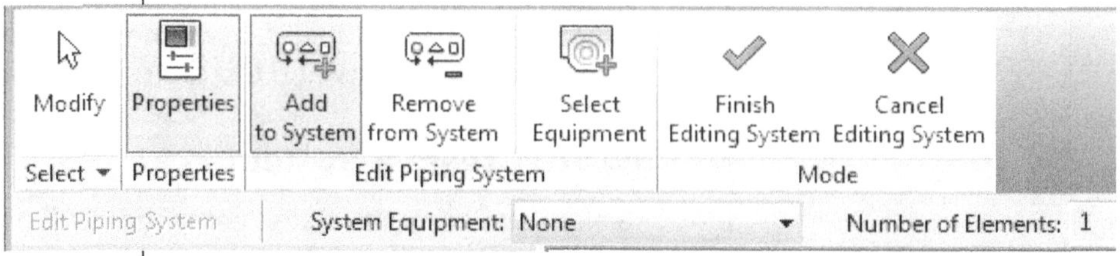

Figure 3–54

- While the icon and name for each system type is different, the processes and locations are still the same.

6. The related **Add to** tool is automatically selected. Click on other components in the model to add them to the system. Remove components from the system using the **Remove from** tool.
7. To add mechanical equipment or an electrical panel to a system, you can use the related **Select** tool or in the Options Bar, select the equipment from a list.
8. When you have completed your selection, click ✓ (Finish Editing System/Circuit).

- You can select systems by hovering over one component and pressing <Tab> until the system displays, as shown in Figure 3–55.

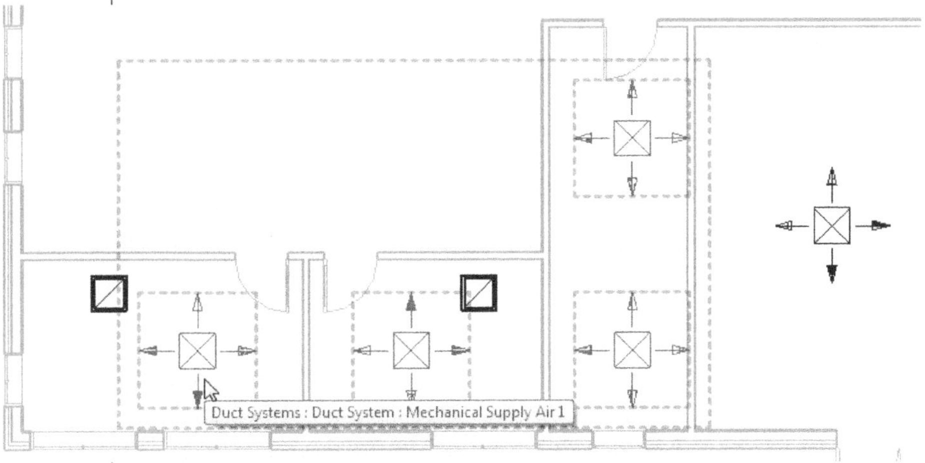

Figure 3–55

- Whenever you select a component that is assigned to a system, you can return to editing the system by clicking on the contextual tabs, as shown for an air handling unit in Figure 3–56.

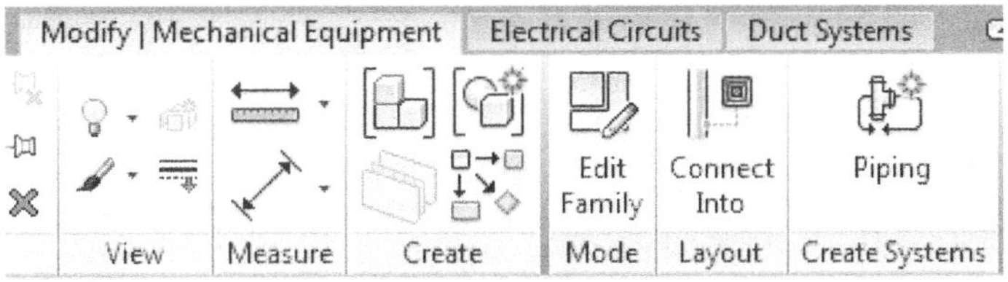

Figure 3–56

Hint: Creating Automatic Layouts

Once you have setup a system you can use the information to generate automatic connections. For example, after you create a system, select the system and click  (Generate Layout) to work through solution types, as shown in Figure 3–57.

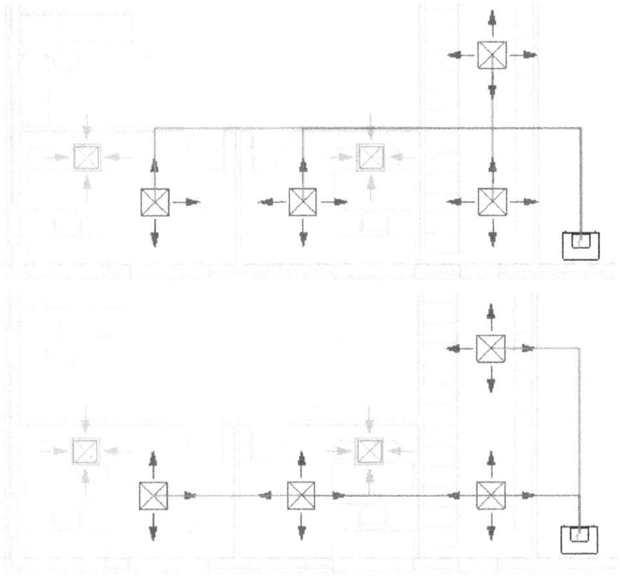

Figure 3–57

- When you have completed the routing, finish the layout and the connecting ducting or piping is automatically created as shown in Figure 3–58.

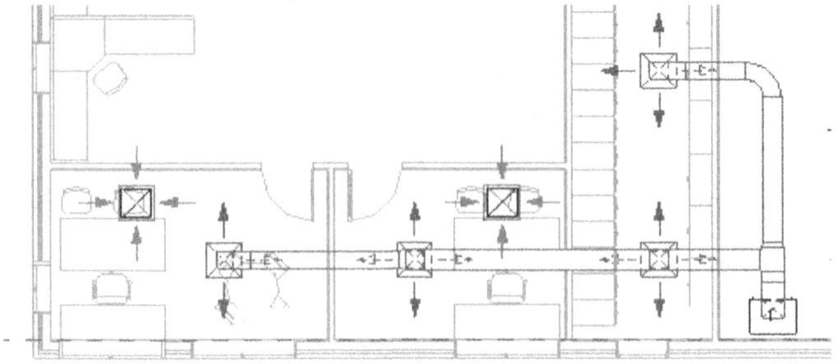

Figure 3–58

- You can use settings to modify the heights and other aspects of the layout.

Using the System Browser

Switch systems do not display in the System Browser as they only denote which fixtures are connected to the switch.

The System Browser, as shown in Figure 3–59, is an important part of determining the relationships between components and the systems they are a part of. It also enables you to identify and select the components, especially those not assigned to a system.

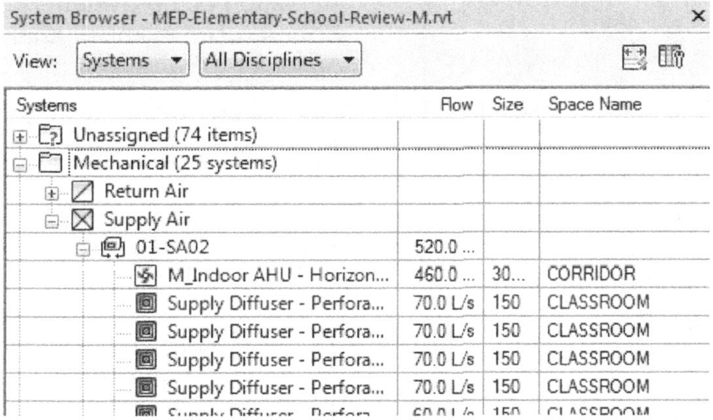

Figure 3–59

- You can open the System Browser using any of the following methods:
  - Press <F9>.
  - In the view, right-click, expand **Browsers**, and select **System Browser**.
  - In the *View* tab>Windows panel, expand (User Interface), and select **System Browser**, as shown in Figure 3–60.

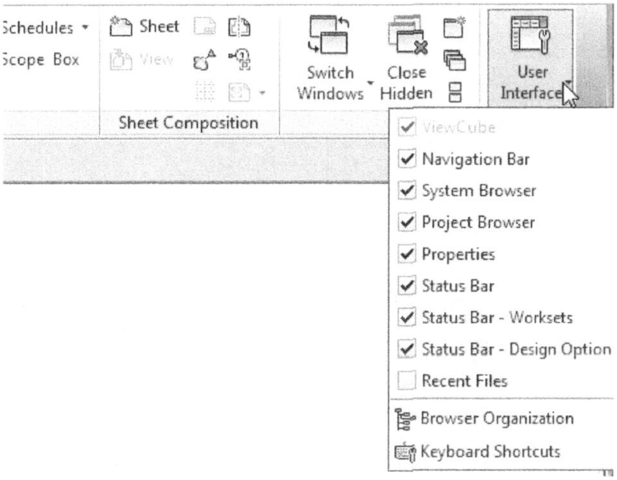

Figure 3–60

- You can float or dock the System Browser to any side of the screen. You can also place it on a second monitor.
- The System Browser can be docked with Properties and the Project Browser to save screen space.
- At the top of the System Browser you can select **Systems** or **Zones** (used in HVAC analysis) to display the appropriate options.
- When working with Systems, select the discipline in which you want to work, as shown in Figure 3–61.

Selecting a discipline limits the display of elements to that specific discipline.

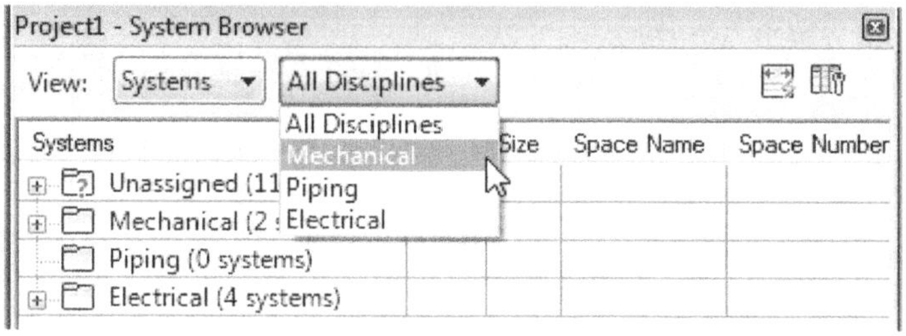

Figure 3–61

- Components that are not in a system, display in the Unassigned list.
- In the System Browser, when you hover the cursor over the system name or select it, or select an individual component, it gets selected in the model as shown in Figure 3–62. It also works the other way when you select the element in the model.

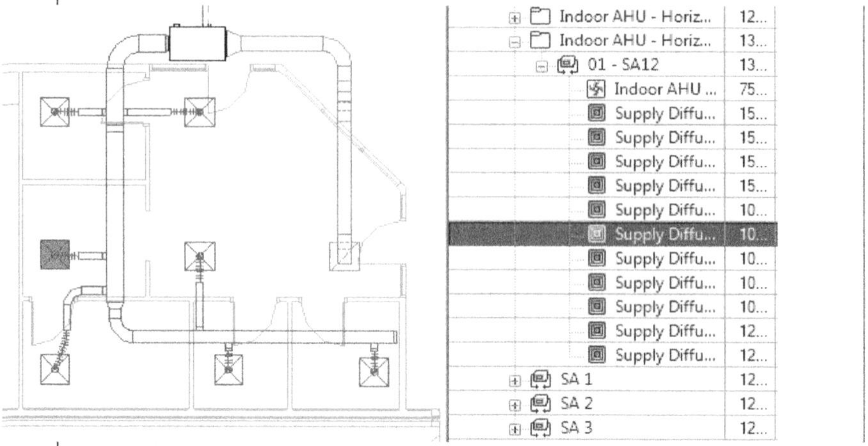

Figure 3–62

- Properties also updates to match the selection, enabling you to modify parameters associated with the elements.
- Hold <Ctrl> or <Shift> to select multiple items in the System Browser.
- If you select a component that is referenced to multiple systems, it is highlighted in each of those systems as shown in Figure 3–63.

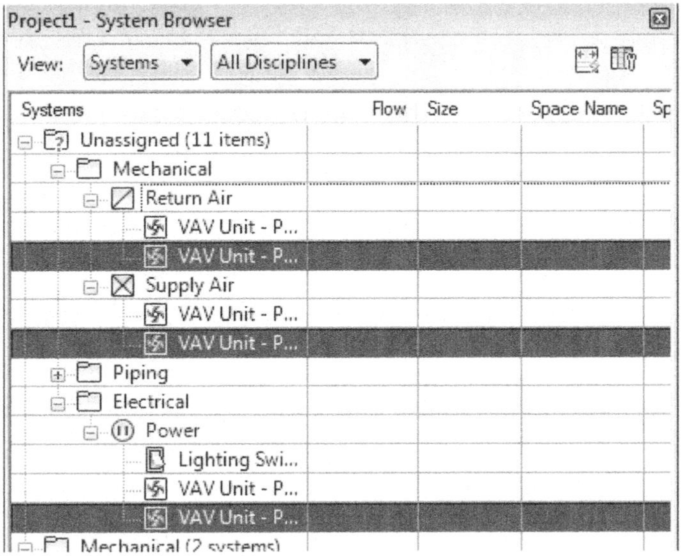

Figure 3–63

- To get a close-up view of a component, select it in the System Browser, right-click and select **Show**. If a view with the component is already open, it zooms into that view. In the Show Element(s) In View dialog box, as shown in Figure 3–64, click **Show** to search for other views.

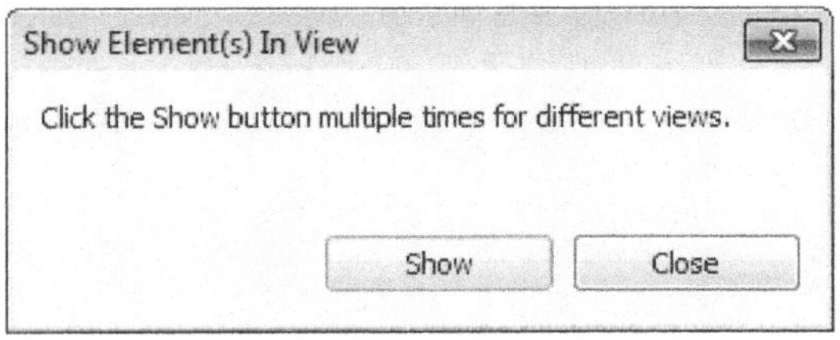

Figure 3–64

- To delete a component through the System Browser, right-click on it and select **Delete**. This deletes it from the project.

Hint: Changing the Display in the System Browser

Two buttons in the System Browser help display what you need to see.

- Click (Autofit all Columns) to change the width of the columns so that the contents fit exactly in the column.
- Click (Column Settings) to open the Column Settings dialog box (shown in Figure 3–65), in which you can select the parameters to display for the various system types.

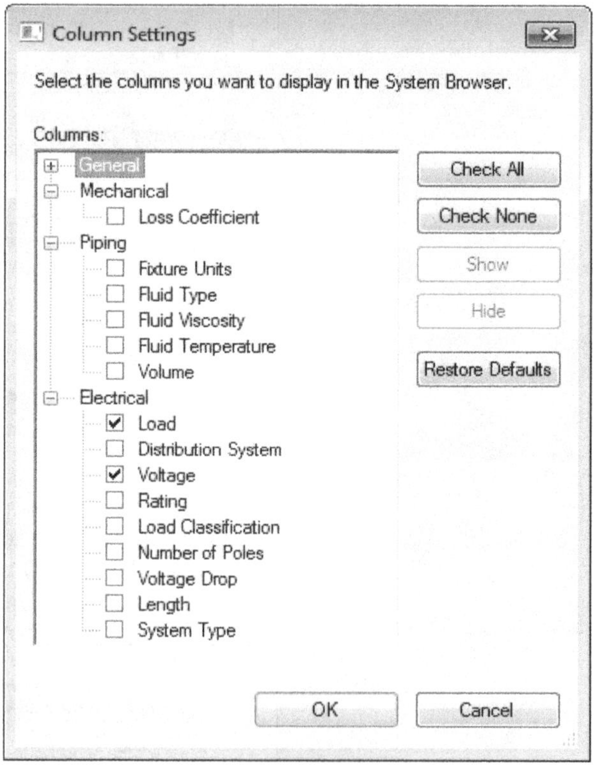

Figure 3–65

Practice 3c View and Create Systems

Practice Objectives

- Create Systems.
- Review and update systems.

Estimated time for completion: 15 minutes

In this practice you will create a supply air system and a switch system. You will then use the System Browser to find elements in the existing hot water system and change the name of the system, as shown in Figure 3–66.

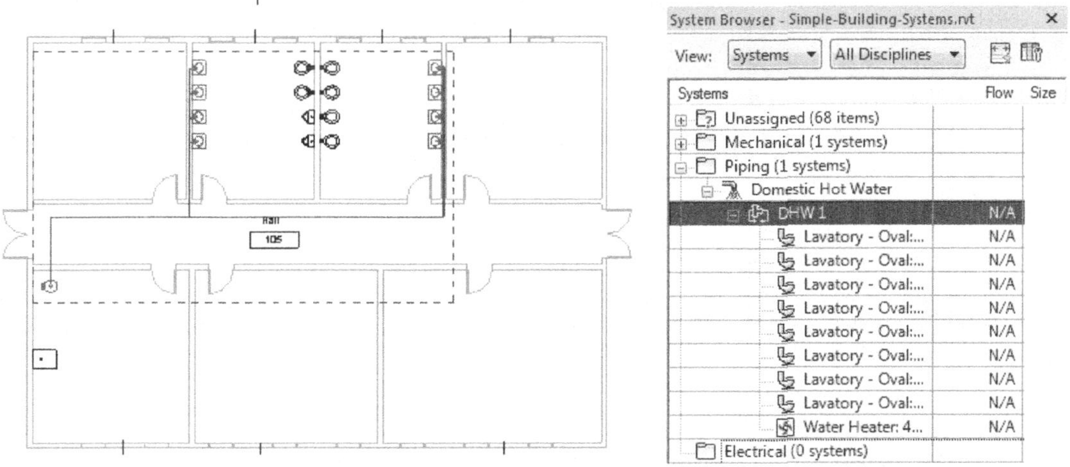

Figure 3–66

Task 1 - Create a supply air system.

1. In the practice files *Basics* folder, open **Simple-Building-Systems-M.rvt**.
2. Open the Mechanical>HVAC>Floor Plans>**1 - Mech** view.
3. In the **Lab 101** room, select one of the supply diffusers.
4. In the *Modify | Air Terminals* tab>Create Systems panel, click (Duct).
5. In the Create Duct System dialog box, verify that the *System* type is set to **Supply Air**. Accept the default name and select **Open in System Editor**, and then click **OK**.

6. The *Edit Duct System* tab displays with **Add to System** already selected, as shown in Figure 3–67.

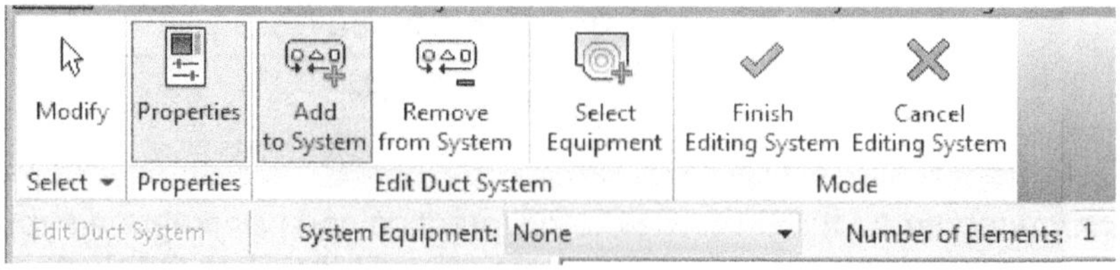

Figure 3–67

7. Hold <Ctr> and select the other air terminals in the room. If you select the return air terminal, a warning displays that you cannot connect to this system.

8. Click  (Finish Editing System). The air terminals are added to the system and turn blue to indicate that it is a supply air system, as shown in Figure 3–68.

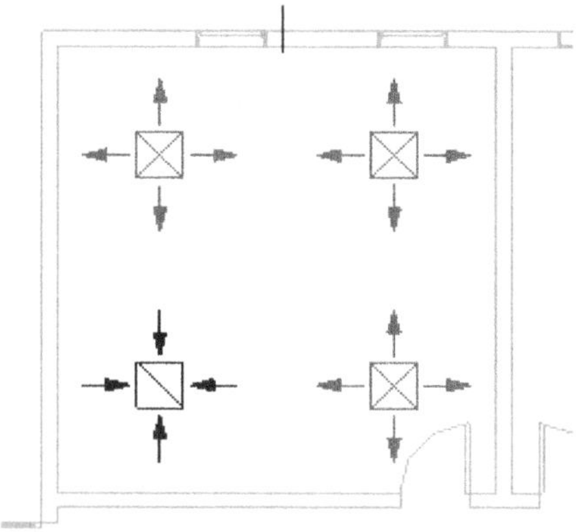

Figure 3–68

9. Save the project.

Task 2 - Create a switch system.

1. Open the Electrical>Lighting>Floor Plans>**1 - Lighting** view.

2. In the *Systems* tab>Electrical panel, expand  (Device), and then select  (Lighting).

3. In the Type Selector, select **M_Lighting Switches: Single Pole**.

4. Add switches near the door to each room, where there is not one already.

5. Select one of the light fixtures in the office (with the rotated lights).

6. Lighting fixtures can be connected to Switch and Power systems. In the *Modify | Lighting Fixtures* tab>Create Systems panel (shown in Figure 3–69), **Power** and **Switch** are the two choices for related systems.

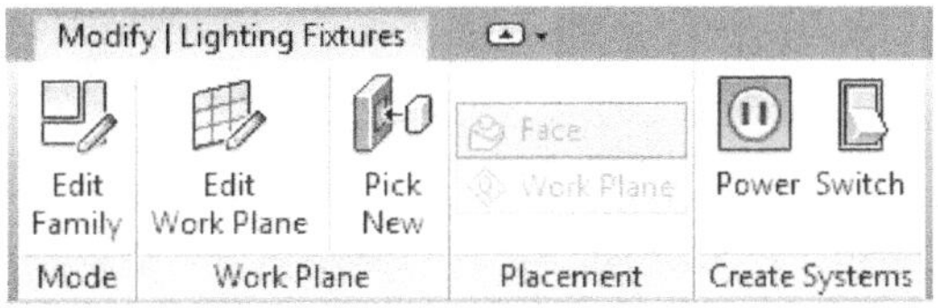

Figure 3–69

7. In the *Modify | Lighting Fixtures* tab>Create Systems panel, click (Switch).

8. In the *Modify | Switch Systems* tab>System Tools panel, click (Select Switch).

9. Select the switch near the door in the same room. A line connecting the lighting fixture to the switch displays, as shown in Figure 3–70.

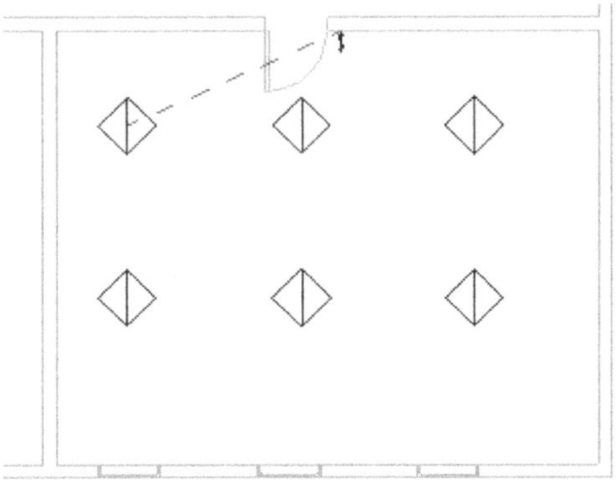

Figure 3–70

10. The new switch system is still selected. In the *Modify | Switch System* tab>System Tools panel, click (Edit Switch System). (Add to System) is automatically selected.

11. Click on the other lighting fixtures in the same room and click (Finish Editing System).

12. Hover over one of the lighting fixtures and press <Tab> until the Switch System displays, as shown in Figure 3–71.

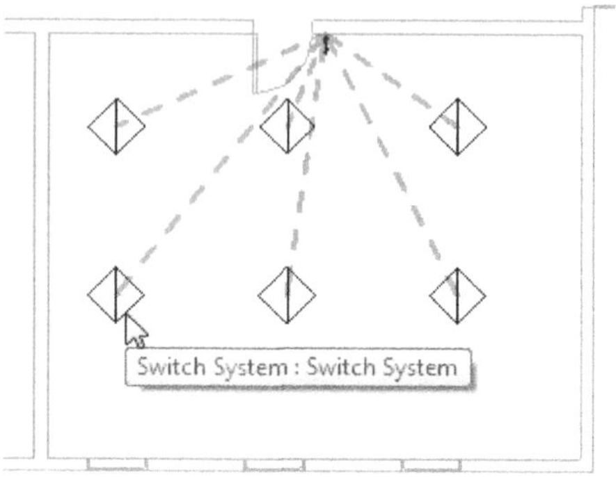

Figure 3–71

13. Move the cursor away from the selection.

14. Add switch systems to each of the other rooms that have lighting fixtures, and then save the project.

Task 3 - Review systems in the System Browser.

1. Open the System Browser by pressing <F9>.

2. Expand the **Mechanical** and **Piping** nodes to display the components that are part of the systems, as shown in Figure 3–72.

There are no electrical systems because switch systems are not included.

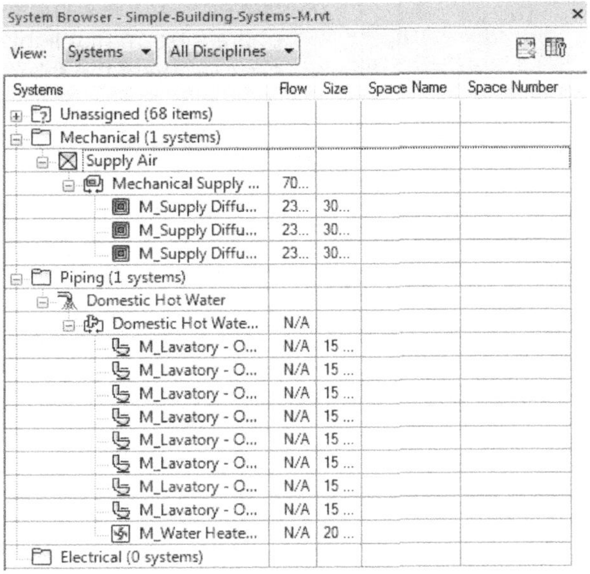

Figure 3–72

3. Select one of the lavatories. Right-click and select **Show**.
4. No open view is available and a warning box displays. Click **OK** to continue and the view opens and zooms in on the selected lavatory, as shown in Figure 3–73. Click **Close**.

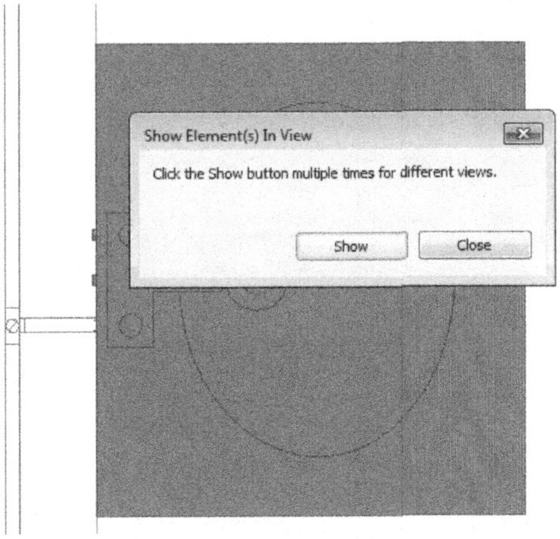

Figure 3–73

5. Zoom out in the view to see the rest of the system.
6. Click **Modify**.

7. Hover over the same lavatory and press <Tab> until the entire system highlights (as shown in Figure 3–74) and then click to select the system.

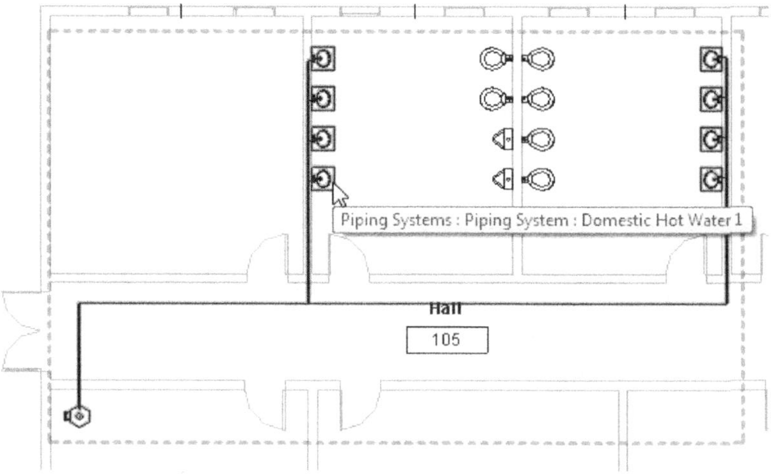

Figure 3–74

8. The system is selected in the System Browser and also in Properties. In Properties, change the *System Name* to **DHW 1,** as shown in Figure 3–75.

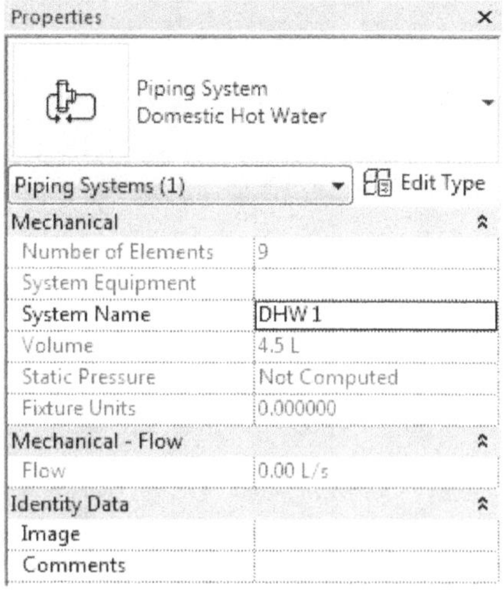

Figure 3–75

9. Click **Apply**, or move the cursor over in the view. The name updates in the System Browser.

10. Save the project.

Chapter Review Questions

1. When you select a Mechanical Equipment component several icons display. What is the purpose of these icons? (Select all that apply.)
    a. They are where ducts, pipes, or electrical circuits connect to the equipment.
    b. You can draw ducts, pipes, or circuits from them.
    c. You can use them to drag and align to other features in the project.
    d. They establish the size or power of the connection.
2. When you draw connecting elements (such as duct or pipe) directly from a component, the connector you select controls the size and elevation.
    a. True
    b. False
3. Which command would you use to break part of a duct so that you can change the duct type?
    a.  (Align)
    b.  (Split)
    c.  (Trim)
    d.  (Offset)

4. Which of the following happens when you select components in the System Browser, as shown in Figure 3–76? (Select all that apply.)

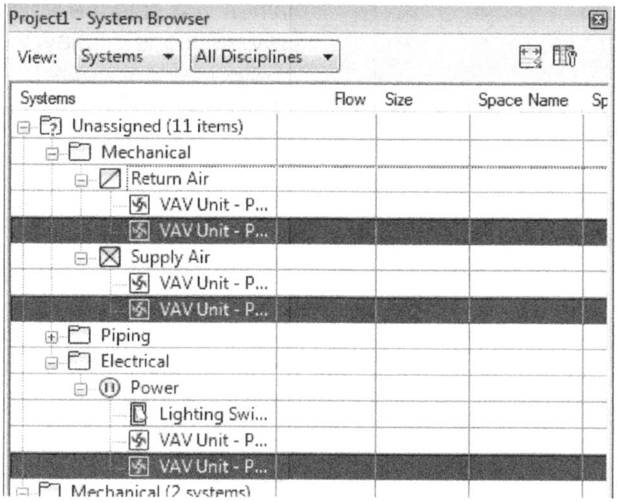

Figure 3–76

a. The components highlight in the current view.

b. The parameters of the components display in Properties.

c. If the components are attached to more than one system they also highlight in the other nodes in the System Browser.

d. The appropriate contextual tab in the ribbon displays.

Command Summary

Button	Command	Location
Connectors		
	**Duct**	• **Ribbon:** *Systems* tab>HVAC panel • **Shortcut:** DT • Right-click on a control: **Draw Duct**
	**Flex Duct**	• **Ribbon:** *Systems* tab>HVAC panel • **Shortcut:** FD • Right-click on a control: **Draw Flex Duct**
	**Flex Pipe**	• **Ribbon:** *Systems* tab>Plumbing & Piping panel • **Shortcut:** FP • Right-click on a control: **Draw Flex Pipe**
	**Pipe**	• **Ribbon:** *Systems* tab>Plumbing & Piping panel • **Shortcut:** PI • Right-click on a control: **Draw Pipe**
	**Cable Tray**	• **Ribbon:** *Systems* tab>Electrical panel • **Shortcut:** CT • Right-click on a control; **Draw Cable Tray**
	**Conduit**	• **Ribbon:** *Systems* tab>Electrical panel • **Shortcut:** CN • Right-click on a control; **Draw Conduit**
	**Wire (Arc)**	• **Ribbon:** *Systems* tab>Electrical panel • **Shortcut:** EW
	**Connect Into**	• **Ribbon:** *Modify* | *<contextual>* tab> Layout panel
	**Show Disconnects**	• **Ribbon**: *Analyze* tab>Check Systems panel
Modify Tools		
	**Align**	• **Ribbon:** *Modify* tab>Modify panel • **Shortcut:** AL
	**Offset**	• **Ribbon:** *Modify* tab>Modify panel • **Shortcut:** OF
	**Split Element**	• **Ribbon:** *Modify* tab>Modify panel • **Shortcut:** SL
	**Trim/Extend Multiple Elements**	• **Ribbon:** *Modify* tab>Modify panel

	**Trim/Extend Single Element**	• **Ribbon:** *Modify* tab>Modify panel
	**Trim/Extend to Corner**	• **Ribbon:** *Modify* tab>Modify panel • **Shortcut:** TR
Systems		
	**Data**	• **Ribbon:** *Modify* | *<contextual>* tab> Create Systems panel • Right-click on a control; **Create Data Circuit**
	**Duct**	• **Ribbon:** *Modify* | *<contextual>* tab> Create Systems panel • Right-click on a control; **Create Duct System**
	**Fire Alarm**	• **Ribbon:** *Modify* | *<contextual>* tab> Create Systems panel • Right-click on a control; **Create Fire Alarm Circuit**
	**Piping**	• **Ribbon:** *Modify* | *<contextual>* tab> Create Systems panel • Right-click on a control; **Create Piping System**
	**Power**	• **Ribbon:** *Modify* | *<contextual>* tab> Create Systems panel • Right-click on a control; **Create Power Circuit**
	**Switch**	• **Ribbon:** *Modify* | *<contextual>* tab> Create Systems panel • Right-click on a control; **Create Switch Circuit**
(varies)	**Add to System**	• **Ribbon**: **Edit System/Circuit tab**> Edit System/Circuit panel
	**Select Equipment**	• **Ribbon:** *Modify* | *<contextual>* tab> System Tools panel • **Ribbon:** *Edit <contextual> System* tab> Edit <contextual> System panel
	**Select Panel**	• **Ribbon:** *Modify* | *<contextual>* tab> System Tools panel • **Ribbon:** *Edit Circuit* tab>Edit Circuit panel
N/A	**System Browser**	• **Ribbon:** *View* tab>Window panel, expand  (User Interface) • **Shortcut:** <F9>

Starting Systems Projects

MEP projects are typically started after an architectural project is underway, and need to use information provided by the architect as the base for the project. You can link Autodesk® Revit® models and then build the systems model around them, copying and monitoring the required information from the architectural model into the systems project.

Learning Objectives in this Chapter

- Link Revit models into the project so that you can design the systems project.
- Add levels to define floor to floor heights and other vertical references.
- Copy and monitor elements from linked Revit models so that you know when changes have been made.
- Batch Copy elements such as air terminals, lighting fixtures, and plumbing fixtures from a linked model.
- Run Coordination Reviews to identify changes between the current project and any linked models.

4.1 Linking in Revit Models

You can link Autodesk Revit architectural or structural models directly into a systems project. A linked model automatically updates if the original file is changed. When the model is linked to the systems project, the architectural and structural elements display in halftone, as shown in Figure 4–1.

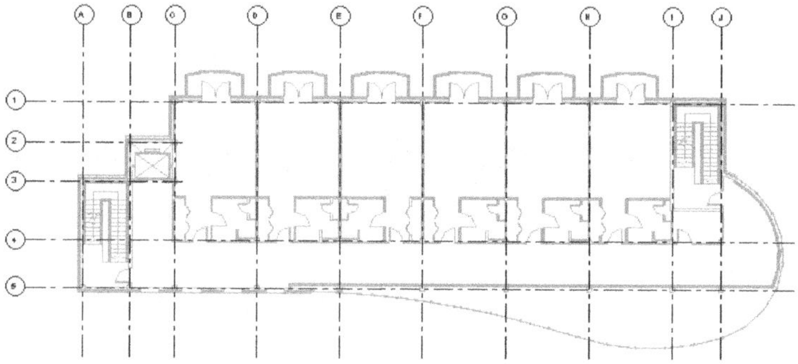

Architectural model linked into a systems project.

Figure 4–1

- Architectural, structural, and MEP models created in the Autodesk Revit software can be linked to each other as long as they are from the same release cycle.
- When you use linked models, clashes between disciplines can be detected and information can be passed between disciplines.

How To: Add a Linked Model to a Host Project

1. In the *Insert* tab>Link panel, click (Link Revit).
2. In the Import/Link RVT dialog box, select the file that you want to link. Before opening the file, set the *Positioning*, as shown in Figure 4–2.

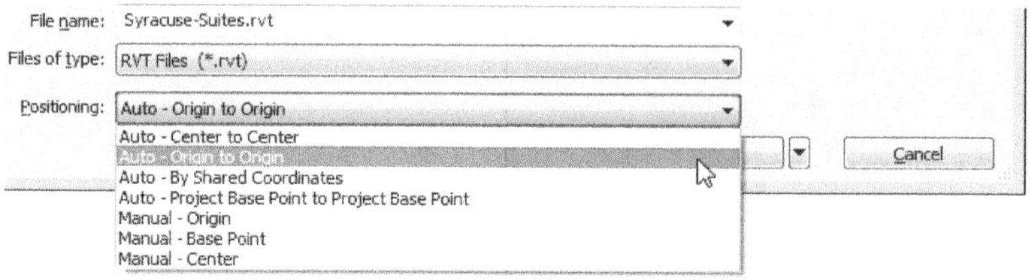

Figure 4–2

3. Click **Open**.

4. Depending on how you decide to position the file, it is automatically placed in the project or you can manually place it with the cursor.

- As the links are loading, do not click on the screen or click any buttons. The more links present in a project, the longer it takes to load.

Hint: Preventing Linked Model from being moved

Once a linked model is in the correct location, you can lock it in place to ensure it does not get moved by mistake, or prevent the linked model from being selected.

- To pin the linked model in place, select it and in the *Modify* tab>Modify panel, click (Pin).
- To prevent pinned elements from being selected, in the Status Bar, click (Select Pinned Elements).
- To toggle off the ability to select links, in the Status Bar, click (Select Links).

If a linked file is moved, you can reposition it to the Project Base Point or Internal Origin. Right-click on it and select the option, as shown in Figure 4–3.

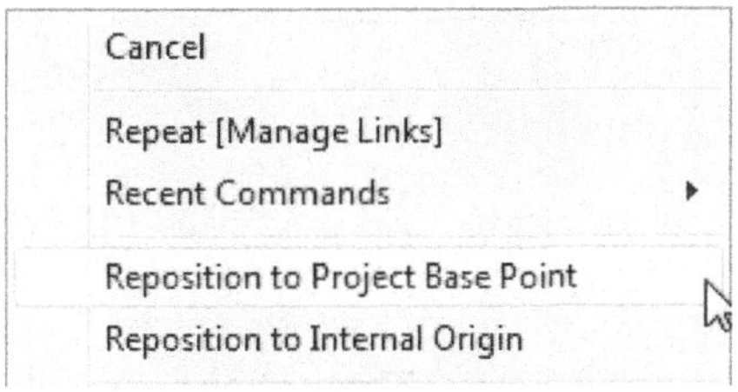

Figure 4–3

Multiple Copies of Linked Models

Copied instances of a linked model are typically used when creating a master project with the same building placed in multiple locations, such as a university campus with six identical student residence halls.

- Linked models can be moved, copied, rotated, arrayed, and mirrored. There is only one linked model, and any copies are additional instances of the link.

- Copies are numbered automatically. You can change their names in Properties when the instance is selected.
- When you have placed a link in a project, you can drag and drop additional copies of the link into the project from the Project Browser>**Revit Links** node, as shown in Figure 4–4.

Figure 4–4

Managing Links

The Manage Links dialog box (shown in Figure 4–5) enables you to reload, unload, add, and remove links, and it also provides access to set other options. To open the Manage Links dialog box, in the *Insert* tab>Link panel, click (Manage Links) or select the link and, in the *Modify | RVT Links* tab> Link panel, click (Manage Links).

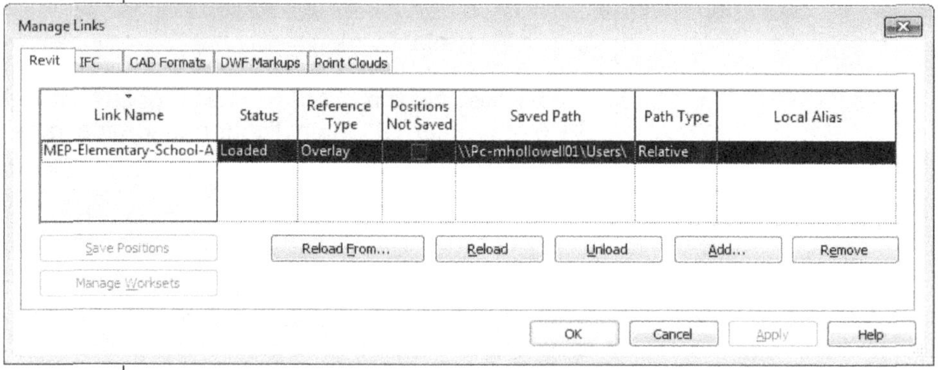

Figure 4–5

The options available in the Manage Links dialog box include the following:

Reload** is also available in the Project Browser. Expand the Revit Links node. Right-click on the Revit Link and select **Reload** or **Reload From...

- **Reload From:** Opens the Add Link dialog box, which enables you to select the file you want to reload. Use this if the linked file location or name has changed.
- **Reload:** Reloads the file without additional prompts.
- **Unload:** Unloads the file so that it the link is kept, but the file is not displayed or calculated in the project. Use **Reload** to restore it.
- **Add:** Opens the Import/Link RVT dialog box which enables you to link additional models into the host project.
- **Remove:** Deletes the link from the file.

Links can be nested into one another. How a link responds when the host project is linked into another project depends on the option in the *Reference Type* column:

- **Overlay**: The nested linked model is not referenced in the new host project.
- **Attach:** The nested linked model displays in the new host project.

The option in the *Path Type* column controls how the location of the link is remembered:

- **Relative**
  - Searches the root folder of the current project.
  - If the file is moved, the software still searches for it.
- **Absolute**
  - Searches the entire file path where the file was originally saved.
  - If the original file is moved, the software is not able to find it.
- Other options control how the linked file interfaces with Worksets and Shared Positioning.

Hint: Visibility Graphics and Linked Files

When you open the Visibility/Graphics dialog box (type **VV** or **VG**), you can modify the graphic overrides for Revit links as shown in Figure 4–6. This can help you clean up the view, or assign a view to build on.

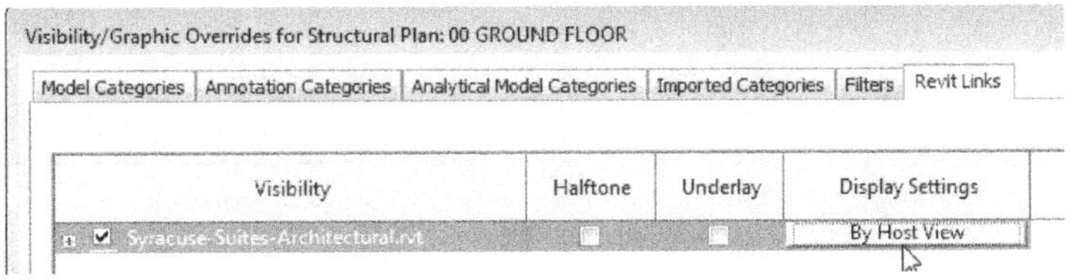

Figure 4–6

The *Display Settings* include:

- **By host view:** The display of the Revit link is based on the view properties of the current view in the host model.
- **By linked view:** The appearance of the Revit link is based on the view properties of the selected linked view and ignores the view properties of the current view.
- **Custom:** You can override all of the graphical elements.

Practice 4a

Start a Systems Project

Estimated time for completion: 5 minutes

Practice Objectives

- Start a new project from a template.
- Link an architectural model into a systems project.

In this practice you will create a new systems project file and link an architectural Autodesk Revit model into it. You will then pin the linked model in place and modify the elevation view marker locations, as shown in Figure 4–7. You will also view the linked model in 3D.

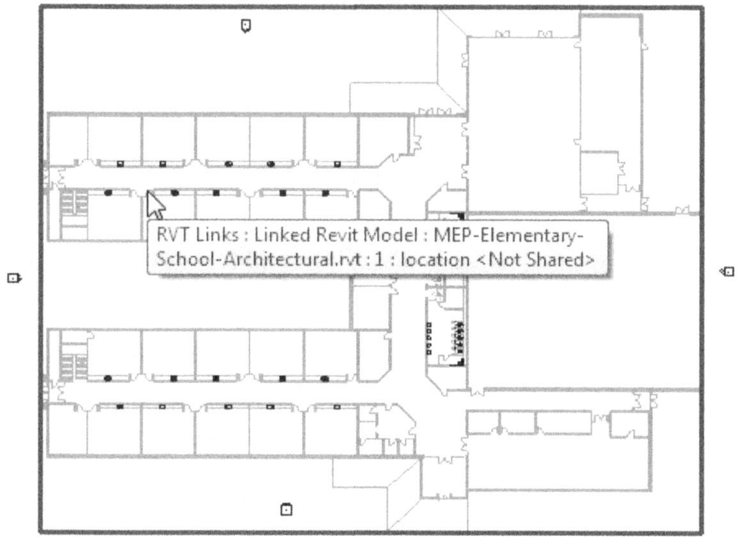

Figure 4–7

Task 1 - Create a new project.

1. In the *File* tab, click (New).
2. In the New Project dialog box, click **Browse...**.
3. In the Choose Template dialog box, select **Systems-Default_Metric.rte**, click **Open**, and then click **OK**.
   - These practices use templates from the US Metric installation of the Autodesk Revit software. The templates are available in the *Metric Templates* practice files folder.
4. Save the project in the practice files *Starting* folder as **MEP-Elementary-School.rvt**.

Task 2 - Link in a architectural model.

1. In the *Insert* tab>Link panel, click (Link Revit).
2. In the Import/Link RVT dialog box, navigate to the practice files *Starting* folder and select **MEP-Elementary-School-Architectural-M.rvt**.
3. Verify that the *Positioning* is set to **Auto - Origin to Origin** and then click **Open**.
4. Type **ZF** (Zoom to Fit). The new building displays in the active view and is linked into the new Revit MEP project.
5. Select the linked model. In the *Modify | RVT Links* tab>Modify panel, click (Pin). The pin icon displays on the linked file as shown in Figure 4–8. This keeps the linked model from being moved by accident.

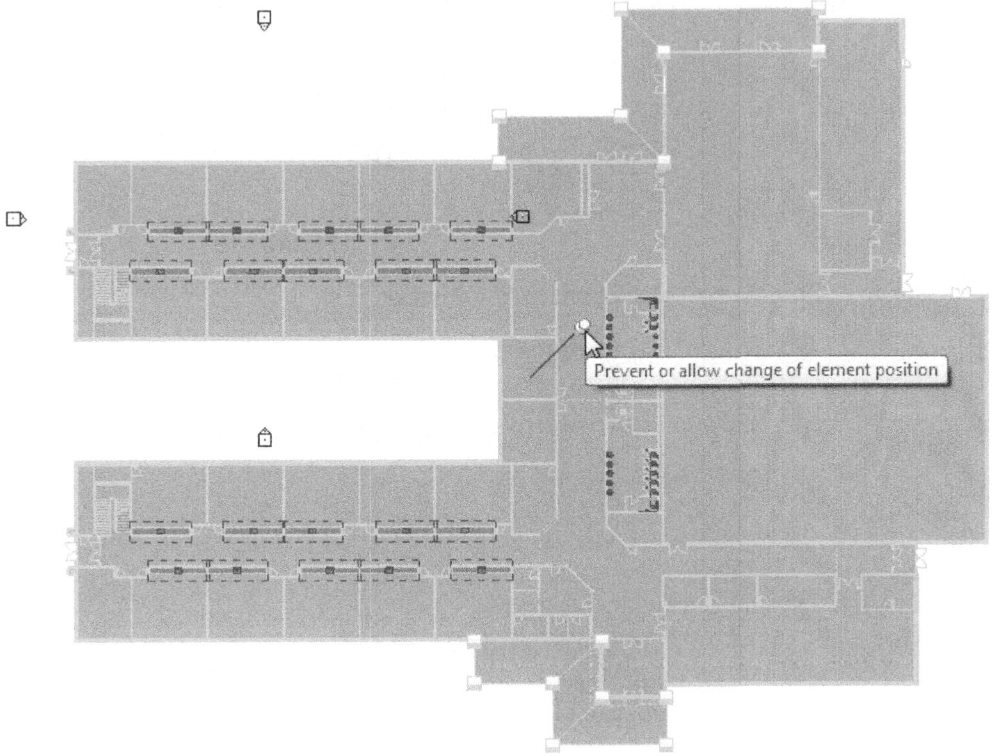

Figure 4–8

6. Click in empty space to clear the selection of the linked model.

7. Move the elevation markers outside of the building, (Hint: Drag a window from left to right around each marker to select both parts.)

8. In the Quick Access Toolbar, click  (Default 3D View.)

9. Zoom in to look at the model. All of the MEP-related elements in the architectural model display in black, while the architectural elements are grayed out, as shown in Figure 4–9.

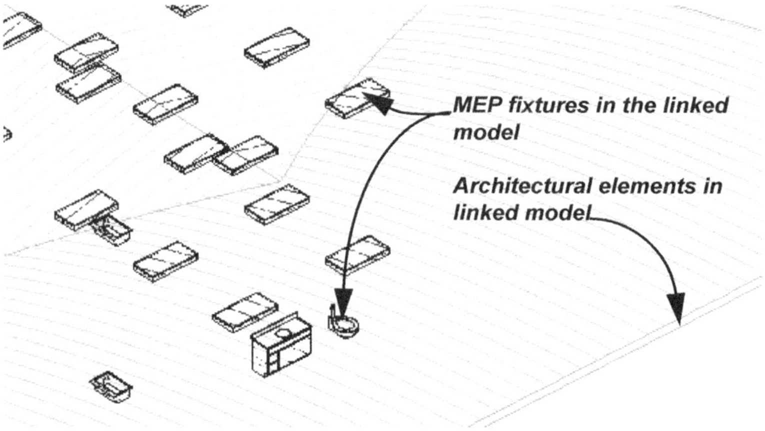

Figure 4–9

10. Zoom to fit the view.

11. Save the project.

4.2 Setting Up Levels

Levels define stories and other vertical heights, as shown in Figure 4–10. The default systems template includes two levels, but you can define as many levels in a project as required. They can go down (for basements) or up.

Floor levels are frequently set by the architect and need to be copied and monitored into the systems model. You can also draw levels directly in a project, as required.

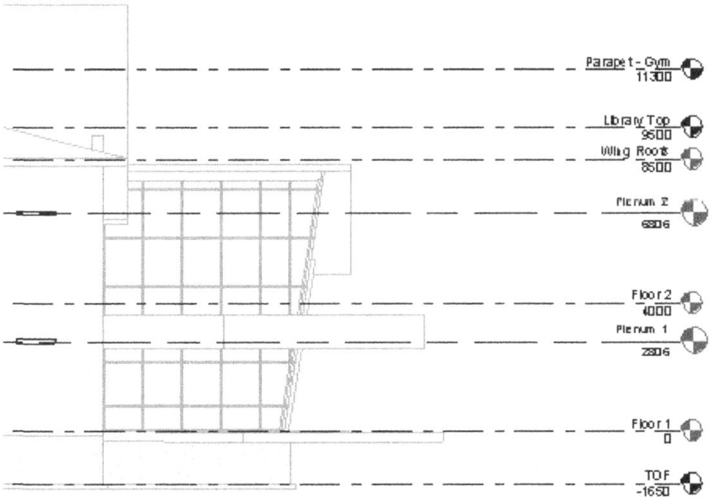

Figure 4–10

- You must be in an elevation or section view to define levels.
- Once you constrain an element to a level it moves with the level when the level is changed.

How To: Create Levels

1. Open an elevation or section view.
2. In the *Architecture* tab>Datum panel, click (Level), or type **LL**.
3. In the Type Selector, set the Level Head type if required.
4. In the Options Bar, select or clear **Make Plan View** as required. You can also click **Plan View Types...** to select the types of views to create when you place the level.
5. In the *Modify | Place Level* tab>Draw panel, click:
   - (Line) to draw a level.
   - (Pick Lines) to select an element using an offset.

   Be careful when you use **Pick Lines** that you do not place levels on top of each other or other elements by mistake.

6. Continue adding levels as required.

- Level names are automatically incremented as you place them so it is helpful to name them in simply (i.e., Floor 1, Floor 2, etc., rather than First Floor, Second Floor, etc.). This also makes it easier to find the view in the Project Browser.

- A fast way to create multiple levels is to use the (Pick Lines) option using an *Offset*. In the Options Bar, specify an *Offset,* select an existing level, and then pick above or below to place the new level, as shown in Figure 4–11.

You specify above or below the offset by hovering the cursor on the required side.

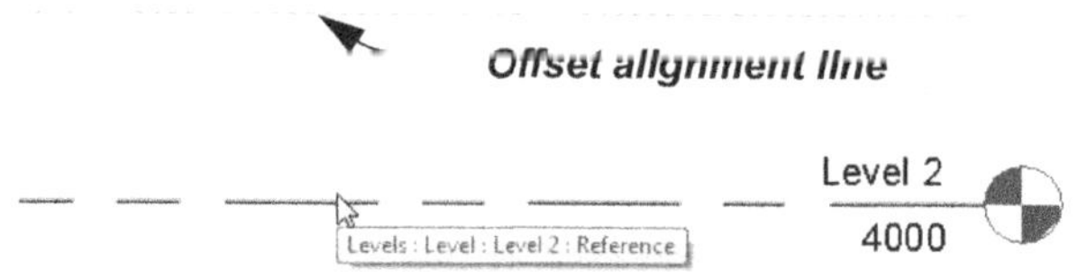

Figure 4–11

- When using the (Line) option, alignments and temporary dimensions help you place the line correctly, as shown in Figure 4–12.

You can sketch the level lines from left to right or right to left depending on where you want the bubble. However, ensure they are all sketched in the same direction.

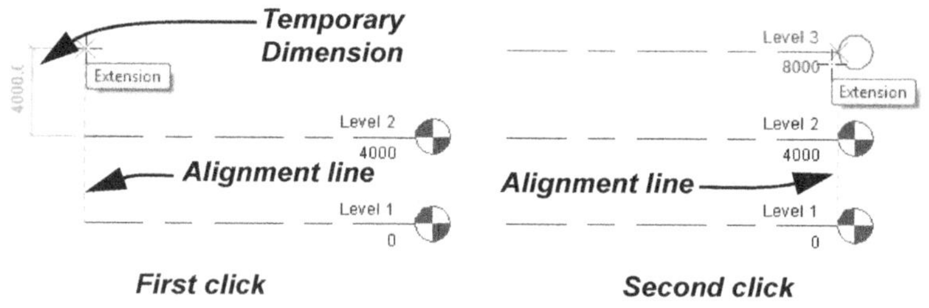

Figure 4–12

- You can also use (Copy) to duplicate level lines. The level names are incremented but a plan view is not created.

- You can change the name or height of a level by selecting the level and then clicking once on the text.

- You can change the length of a level line by dragging the control, as shown in Figure 4–13.

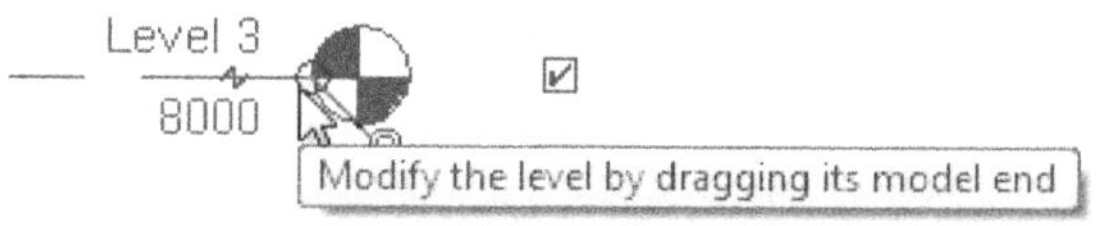

Figure 4–13

Creating Plan Views

By default, when you place a level, plan views for that level are automatically created. If **Make Plan View** was toggled off when adding the level, or if the level was copied, you can create plan views to match the levels.

- Level heads with views are blue and level heads without associated views are black, as shown in Figure 4–14.

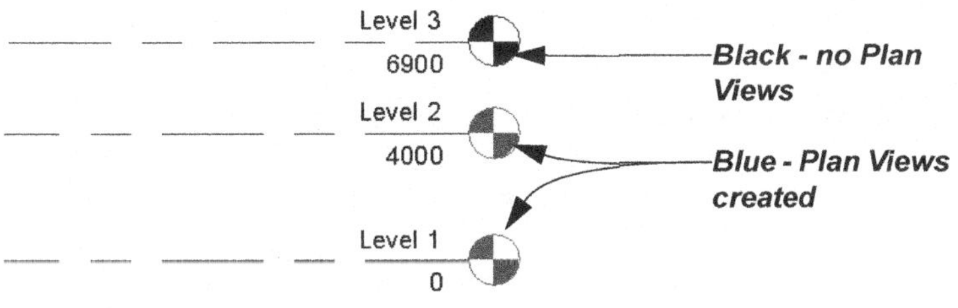

Figure 4–14

- System projects are typically divided into disciplines and sub-disciplines, as shown in Figure 4–15. You can specify the discipline while you are creating the plan view, or after the plan is created in Properties, as shown in Figure 4–16.

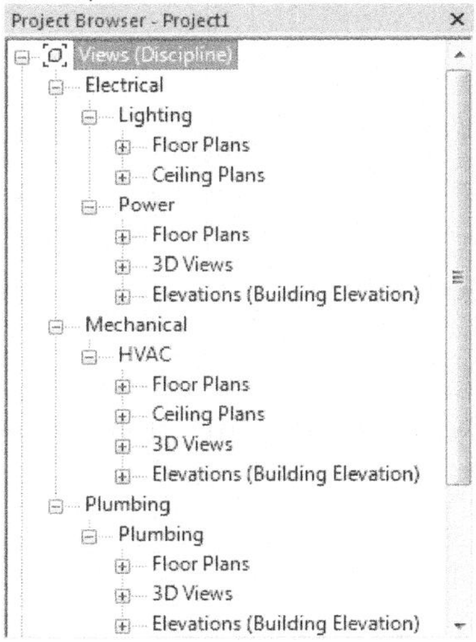

Figure 4–15

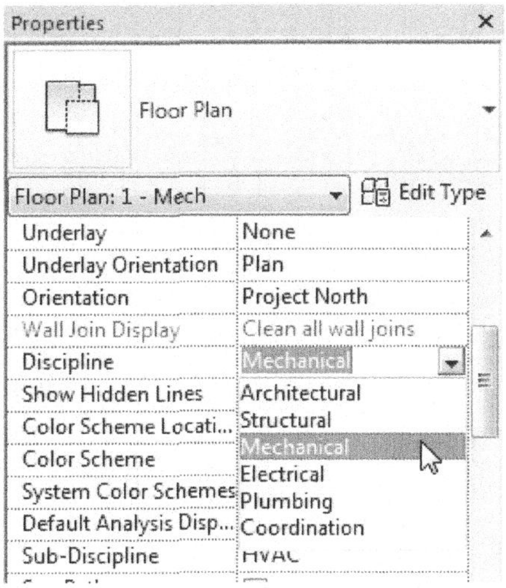

Figure 4–16

How To: Create Plan Views

Hold <Ctrl> or <Shift> to select more than one level.

1. In the *View* tab>Create panel, expand (Plan Views) and select the type of plan view you want to create, as shown in Figure 4–17.
2. To specify the discipline, in the New Plan dialog box, click **Edit Type**.
3. In the Type Properties dialog box, select the button beside *View Template applied to new views*.
4. In the Apply View Template dialog box, select the appropriate view template name. Click **OK** twice.
5. In the New Plan dialog box, select the levels for which you want to create plan views, as shown in Figure 4–18.

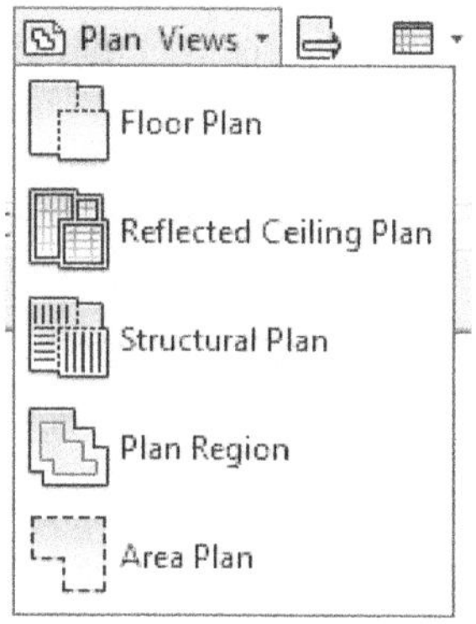

Figure 4–17

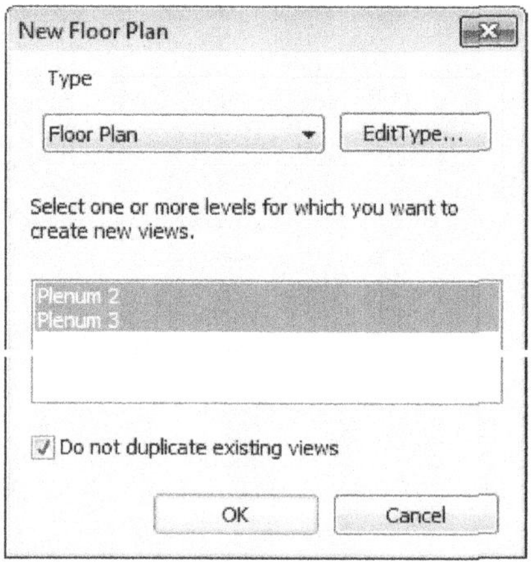

Figure 4–18

6. Click **OK**.

- When **Do not duplicate existing views** is selected, views without the selected plan type display in the list.

4.3 Copying and Monitoring Elements

Once a linked architectural model is in place, the next step is to copy and/or monitor elements that you need from the linked file into the systems project. These elements most often include grids and levels. Other elements commonly include lighting fixtures (as shown in Figure 4–19), plumbing fixtures, mechanical equipment, and sprinklers. A monitoring system keeps track of the copied elements and prompts for updates if something is changed. The (Monitor) icon indicates the monitored elements.

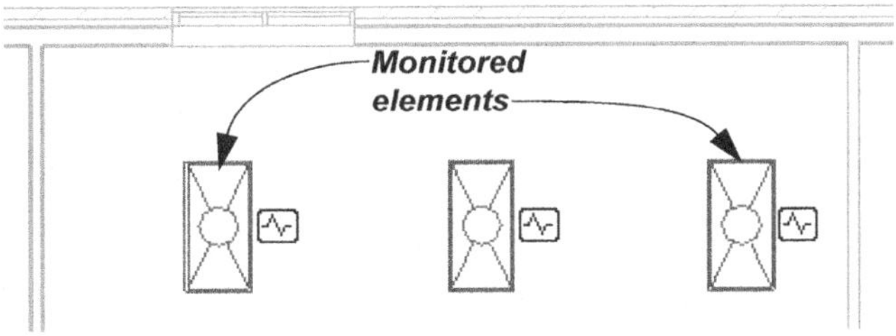

Figure 4–19

- **Copy:** Creates a duplicate of a selected element in the current project and monitors it to a selected element in the linked model or current project.
- **Monitor:** Compares two elements of the same type against each other, either from a linked model to the current project (as shown in Figure 4–20) or in the current project.

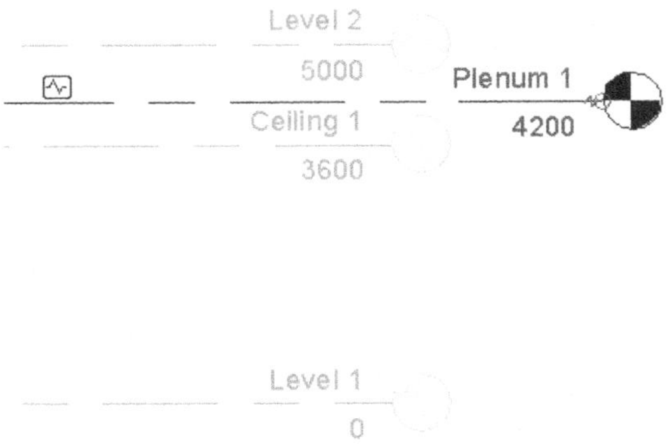

Figure 4–20

How To: Copy and Monitor Elements from a Linked File

1. In the *Collaborate* tab>Coordinate panel, expand (Copy/Monitor) and click (Select Link).
2. Select the link.
3. In the *Copy/Monitor* tab>Tools panel, click (Copy) or (Monitor).
4. If copying from the linked file, select each element that you want to copy. Alternatively, use the **Multiple** option:
   - In the Options Bar, select **Multiple**, as shown in Figure 4–21.

Figure 4–21

   - Hold <Ctrl> and select the elements that you want to copy into your model individually, or use a pick and drag window around multiple elements.
   - In the Options Bar, click **Finish**.

Warnings about duplicated or renamed types might display.

   If monitoring elements in the current project with elements in the linked model, first select the element in the current project, and then select the element in the linked model.

5. Click (Finish) to end the session of Copy/Monitor.

How To: Copy and Monitor Elements in the Current Project.

1. In the *Collaborate* tab>Coordinate panel, expand (Copy/Monitor) and click (Use Current Project).
2. In the *Copy/Monitor* tab>Tools panel, click (Copy) or (Monitor).
3. Select the two elements you want to monitor.
4. Repeat the process for any additional elements.
5. Click (Finish) to end the command.

- The elements do not have to be at the same elevation or location for the software to monitor them.

Practice 4b Copy and Monitor Elements

Practice Objectives

- Modify existing levels.
- Copy and monitor levels.
- Add levels.

Estimated time for completion: 10 minutes

In this practice, you will use **Copy/Monitor** to copy and monitor levels from the architectural model to the MEP project, as shown in Figure 4–22. You will also add levels and then monitor them against other levels.

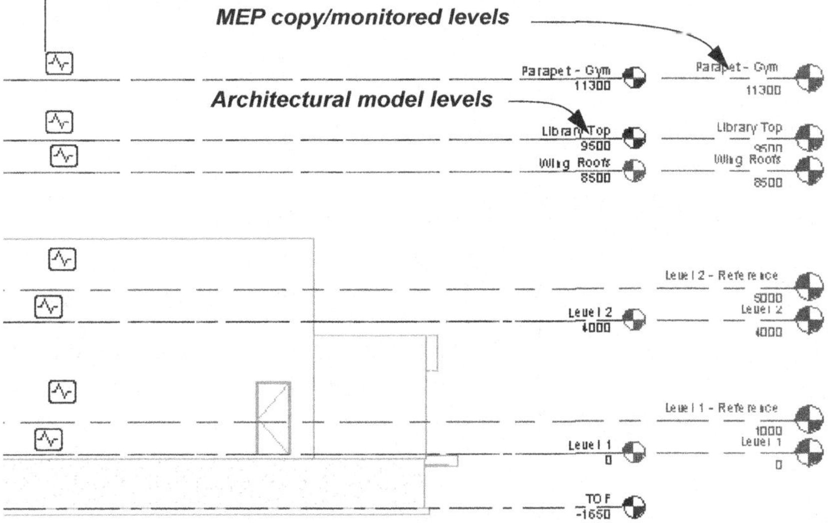

Figure 4–22

Task 1 - Match existing levels to levels in the linked model.

1. In the practice files *Starting* folder, open **MEP-Elementary-School-Levels-M.rvt**.

2. Open the Mechanical>HVAC>**Elevations (Building Elevations): East - Mech** view.

3. There are two levels in the host project. Select the linked architectural model to help you distinguish between them, as shown in Figure 4–23.

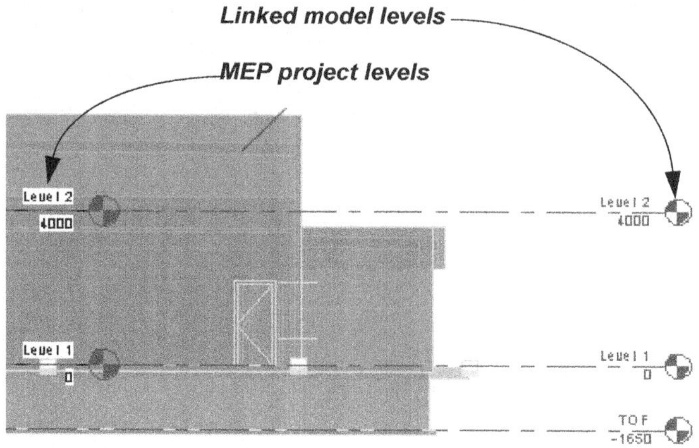

Figure 4–23

4. Click (Modify)

5. In the *Modify* tab>Modify panel, click (Align).

6. In the linked model, select **Level 2** and in the host project, select **Level 2**. The levels are now coincident.

7. Click (Modify) and select one of the level lines in the host project. Select the control and drag it to the side, as shown in Figure 4–24.

If required, press <Tab> to select the level in the host project, and not the linked model.

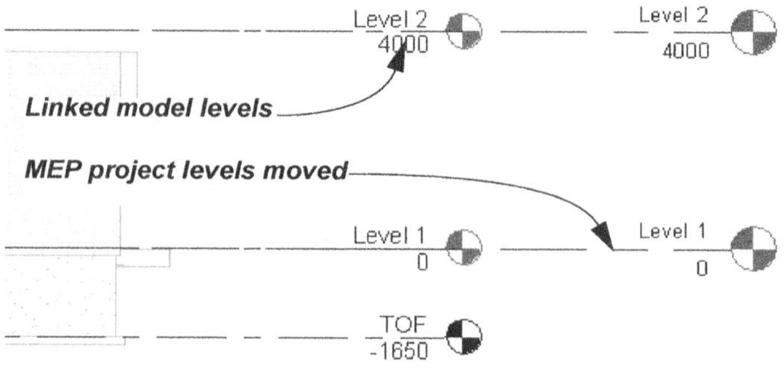

Figure 4–24

8. Click (Modify).

9. Save the project.

Task 2 - Copy and monitor levels.

1. In the *Collaborate* tab>Coordinate panel, expand (Copy/Monitor) and click (Select Link).
2. Select the linked model.
3. In the *Copy/Monitor* tab>Tools panel, click (Monitor).
4. In the host project, select **Level 1**. In the linked model, select **Level 1**. Repeat for **Level 2.**
5. In the Copy/Monitor panel, click (Finish). The levels are now monitored as shown in Figure 4–25.

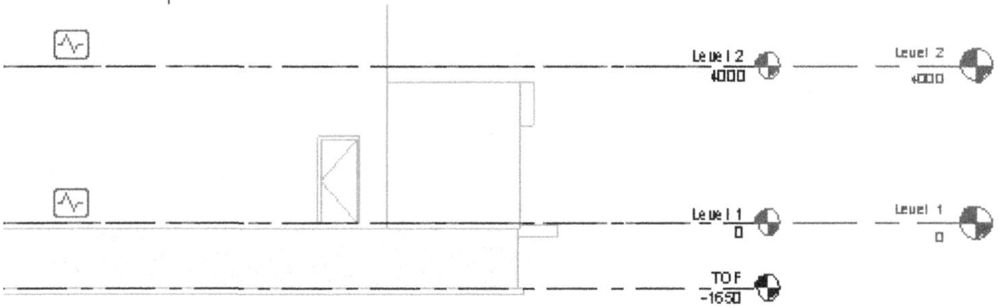

Figure 4–25

6. Select **Level 2** in the host project. Change the *Height* to **5000mm** (use temporary dimensions or change the number below the level name). A Warning box opens as shown in Figure 4–26.

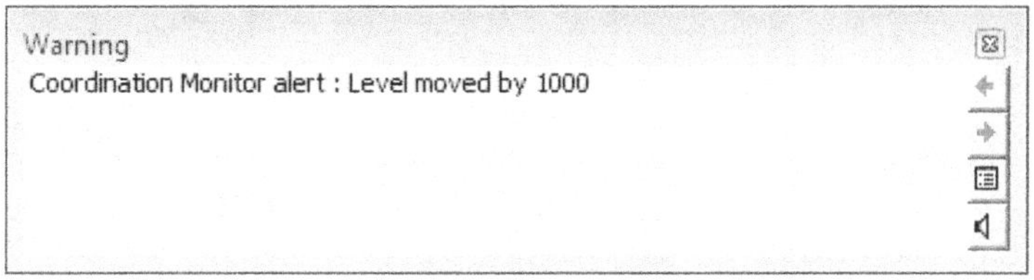

Figure 4–26

7. Close the warning box and undo the level height change.
8. In the *Collaborate* tab>Coordinate panel, expand (Copy/Monitor) and click (Select Link).

9. Select the linked model.

10. In the *Copy/Monitor* tab>Tools panel, click (Copy).

11. Select the top three levels. They are reference levels used to create the heights of spaces. If required, close any alert dialog boxes.

12. In the Copy/Monitor panel, click (Finish).

13. Drag the level bubbles over so that they match with the levels you moved earlier.

14. Save the project.

Task 3 - Add and monitor levels.

1. In the *Architecture* tab>Datum panel, click (Level).

2. In the *Modify | Place Level* tab>Draw panel, click (Pick Lines).

3. In the Options Bar, clear **Make Plan View** and set the *Offset* to **1000mm**.

4. Hover the cursor over **Level 1** and verify that the alignment line for the offset is above the level as shown in Figure 4–27.

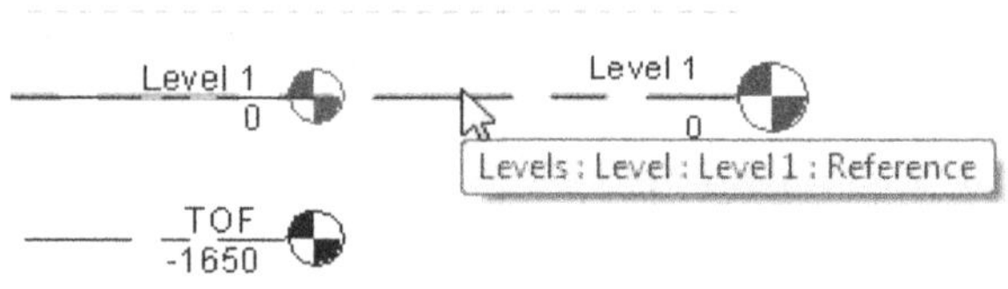

Figure 4–27

5. Click on **Level 1** to place the new level.

6. Repeat with **Level 2** and then click (Modify) to end the command.

7. Click on the name of new level above **Level 1** and change it to **Level 1 - Reference**, as shown in Figure 4–28.

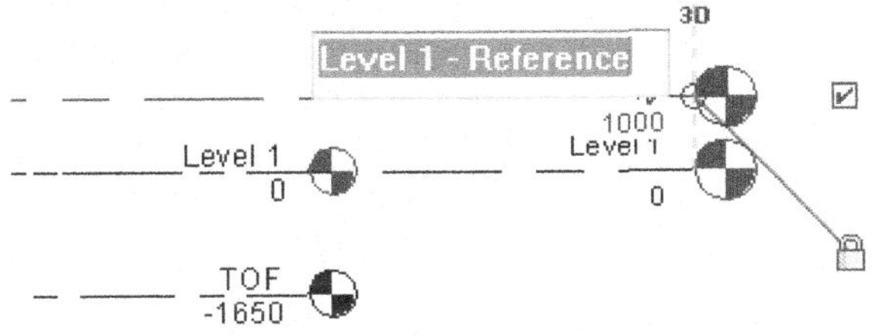

Figure 4–28

8. Repeat with the new level above **Level 2** and name it **Level 2 - Reference**.

9. In the *Collaborate* tab>Coordinate panel, expand (Copy/Monitor) and click (Select Link).

10. Select the linked model.

By monitoring the reference levels to the levels in the linked project, any changes to the linked project (such as a name change) are automatically updated in the reference levels as well.

11. In the *Copy/Monitor* tab>Tools panel, click (Monitor).

12. In the host project, select **Level 1 - Reference**. In the linked model, select **Level 1**. Repeat for **Level 2 - Reference** and **Level 2.**

13. In the Copy/Monitor panel, click (Finish).

14. Zoom out and save the project.

4.4 Batch Copying Fixtures

MEP fixtures can be copied and monitored from linked models. To make the process of copy/monitor more effective, you can set the behavior of various categories as they are copied, as shown in the Coordination Settings dialog box in Figure 4–29. In this dialog box, you can also prepare elements to be batch copy/monitored.

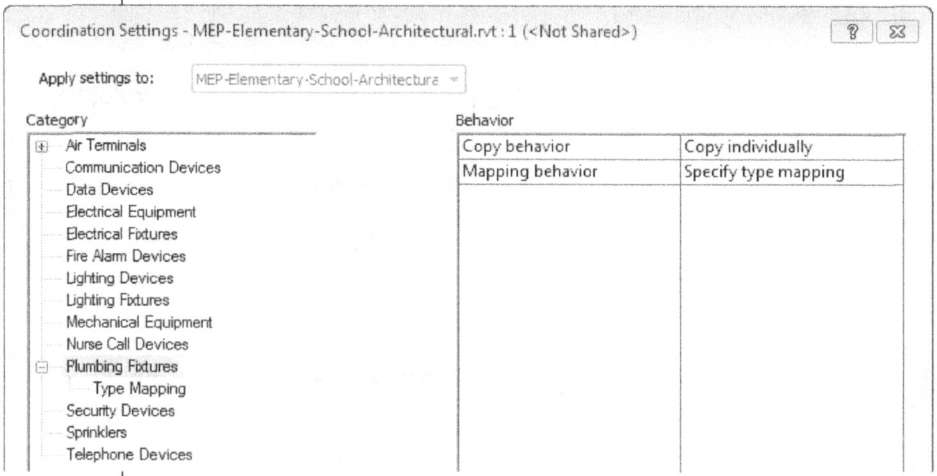

Figure 4–29

- Only Autodesk Revit MEP fixtures in the linked model can be copied and monitored. This process cannot be used for non-MEP elements in the host project.
- If a linked model has nested links you can only copy and monitor fixtures from primary linked model.
- Create the default settings before you start to copy and monitor. This saves you time and reduces errors.

How To: Define Default Coordination Settings

1. In the *Collaborate* tab>Coordinate panel, expand (Copy/Monitor) and click (Select Link).
2. Select the linked model you want to work with.

Coordination Settings are also accessible in the Collaborate tab> Coordinate panel.

3. In the *Copy/Monitor* tab>Tools panel, click (Coordination Settings).
4. In the Coordination Settings dialog box, in the *Category* area, select the type of fixtures you want to modify.

5. In the *Behavior* area, specify the following:

Copy behavior	**Allow batch copy:** You can use the batch copy command on this category. **Copy individually:** You need to select each element in this category you want to copy. **Ignore category:** Prevents you from copying elements from this category.
Mapping behavior	**Copy original:** Copy exact replicas of the fixtures in this category. **Specify type mapping:** Specify the fixtures you want to use in place of the linked models component.

6. If you select **Specify type mapping**, in the *Category* area, select **Type Mapping**. Then you can set up the coordination between the linked model and the host project, as shown in Figure 4–30.

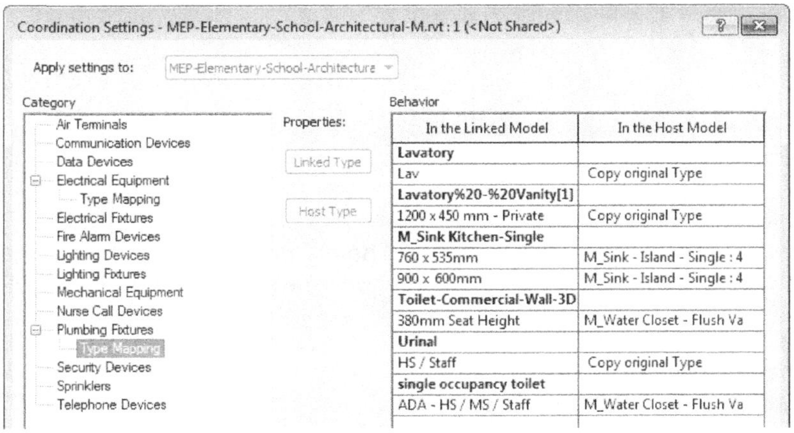

Figure 4–30

7. Click **Save & Close**.

Batch Copying Fixtures

When working with a project in which the architect has placed most of the fixtures and devices, you can use a batch copying process that saves you the time it would take to select each element.

- It is recommended that you set up the Coordination Settings for the linked model before you start the process. However, you can also do this before copying in the fixtures.
- Copy levels first before you copy fixtures into the project.

How To: Batch Copy Fixtures

1. Start the **Copy/Monitor** process and set the **Coordination Settings** for a selected linked model.
2. In the *Copy/Monitor* tab>Tools panel, click (Batch Copy).
3. In the Fixtures Found dialog box shown in Figure 4–31, select **Specify type mapping behavior and copy fixtures** or **Copy the fixtures**.

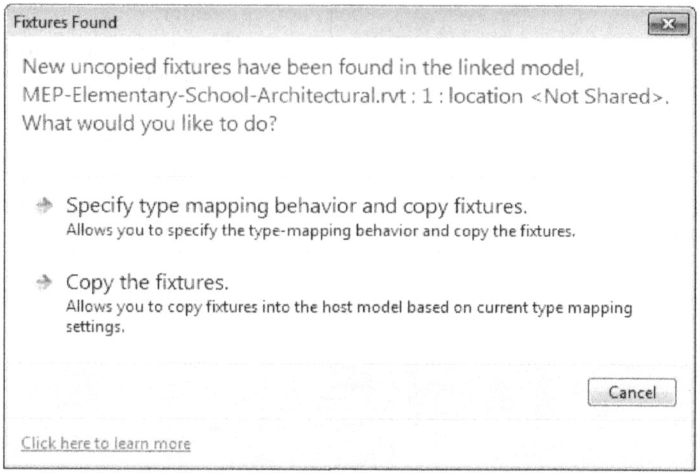

Figure 4–31

4. The elements are copied into the host project and set to be monitored, as shown in Figure 4–32.

If an element of that name already exists in the project, a warning box opens prompting you the copied element has been given a new name.

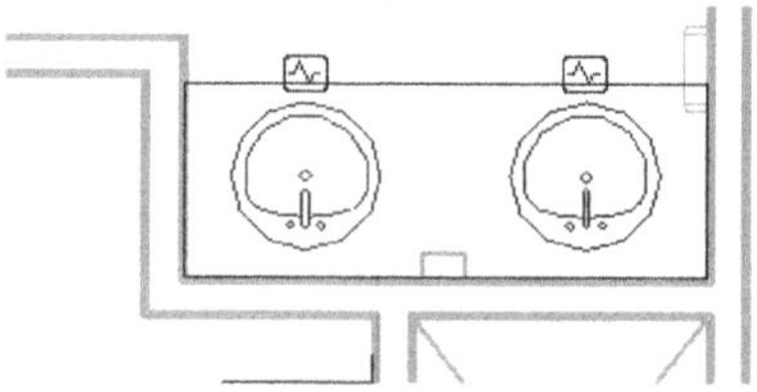

Figure 4–32

- If batch copied elements are added to the linked file, they are copied into the project when it is reloaded or reopened.

Practice 4c Batch Copy Fixtures

Practice Objectives

- Set up the coordination settings.
- Batch copy fixtures from the architectural model.

Estimated time for completion: 10 minutes.

In this practice you will set up coordination settings to select the types of elements you want to copy and monitor. You will then use **Batch Copy** to copy in MEP fixtures for the water closets, as shown in Figure 4–33.

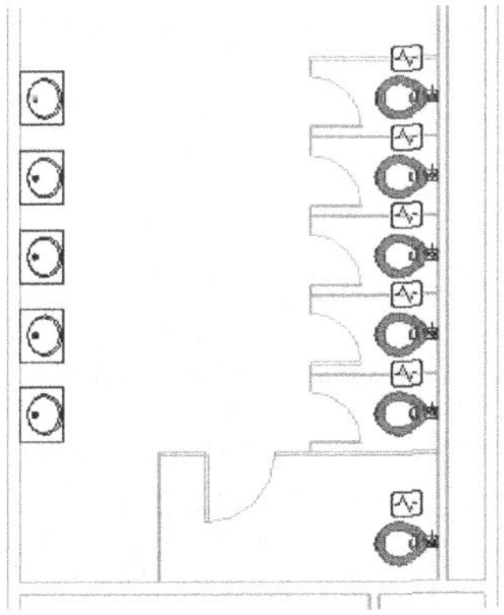

Figure 4–33

Task 1 - Copy and monitor plumbing fixtures.

1. In the practice files *Starting* folder, open the project **MEP-Elementary-School-Batch-M.rvt**.
2. Open the Plumbing>Floor Plans>**1 - Plumbing** view.
3. Plumbing fixtures in the linked model display darker in this view but are not yet copied into the host project.
4. In the *Collaborate* tab>Coordinate panel, expand (Copy/Monitor) and click (Select Link).
5. Select the linked model.
6. In the *Copy/Monitor* tab>Tools panel, click (Coordination Settings).

7. Select the **Plumbing Fixtures** category and set the *Copy behavior* to **Allow batch copy** and the *Mapping behavior* to **Specify type mapping** as shown in Figure 4–34.

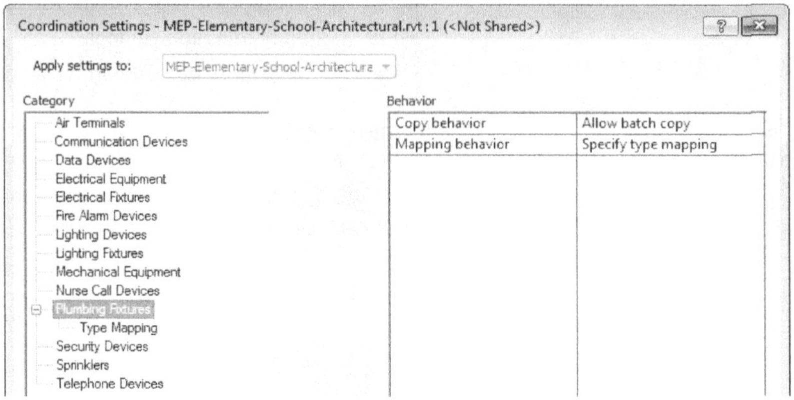

Figure 4–34

8. In the *Category* area, select **Plumbing Fixtures>Type Mapping**.

It is important to select the MEP fixtures because they have connectors. Architectural fixtures typically do not have connectors.

9. In the *Behavior* area, in the *In the Host Model* column, set the following, as shown in Figure 4–35:
   - *M_Lavatory - Oval-A:* **Don't copy this type**
   - *M_Lavatory - Vanity-A:* **Don't copy this type**
   - *M_Sink_Kitchen-Single:* **Don't copy this type**
   - *M_Urinal-Wall Hung-A:* **M_Urinal - Wall Hung: 20 mm Flush Valve**
   - *M_Water Closet Flush Valve - Wall Mounted:* **M_Water Closet - Flush Valve - Wall Mounted: Public - 6.1 Lpf**

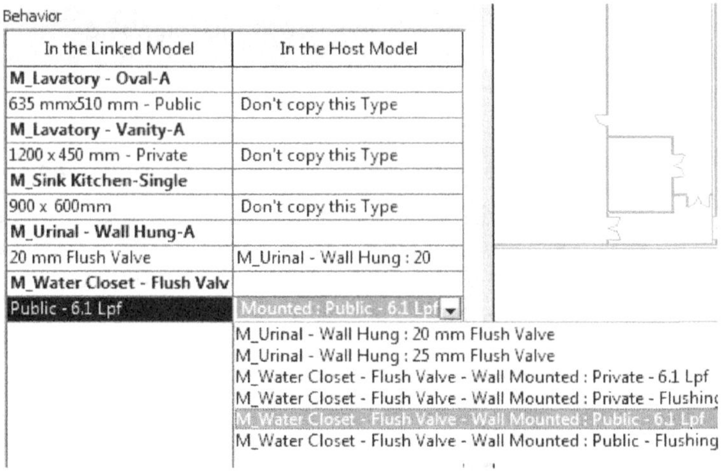

Figure 4–35

10. Click **Save & Close**.

11. In the *Copy/Monitor* tab>Tools panel, click (Batch Copy).

12. In the Fixtures Found dialog box, select **Copy the fixtures**.

13. In the Copy/Monitor panel, click (Finish).

14. Zoom in on one of the restrooms and draw a window around both the lavatories and WCs. Only the WCs are copied into the project, as shown in Figure 4–36.

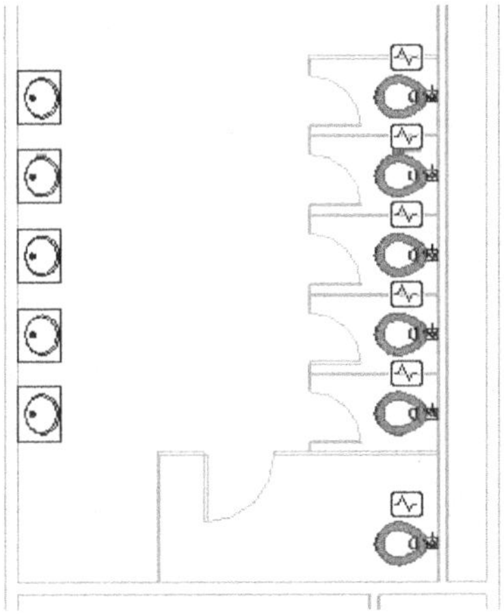

Figure 4–36

15. Zoom out to see the full view.

16. Save and close the project.

4.5 Coordinating Linked Models

Monitoring elements identifies changes in the data and changes in placement. For example, if you move a grid line, a Coordination Monitor alert displays, as shown in Figure 4–37. You can run a Coordination Review to correct or accept these changes.

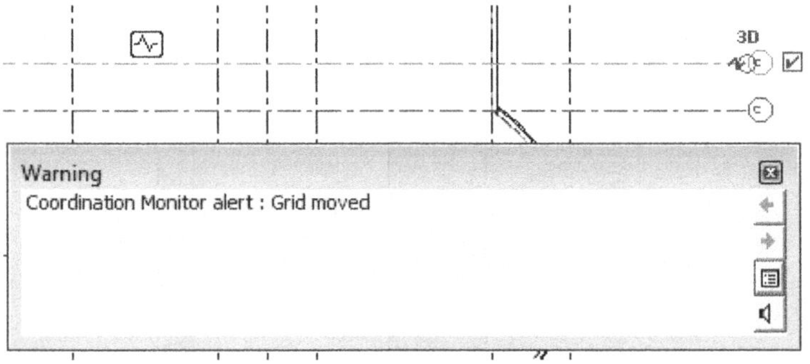

Figure 4–37

- If you open a project with a linked file which contains elements that have been modified and monitored, the Warning shown in Figure 4–38 displays.

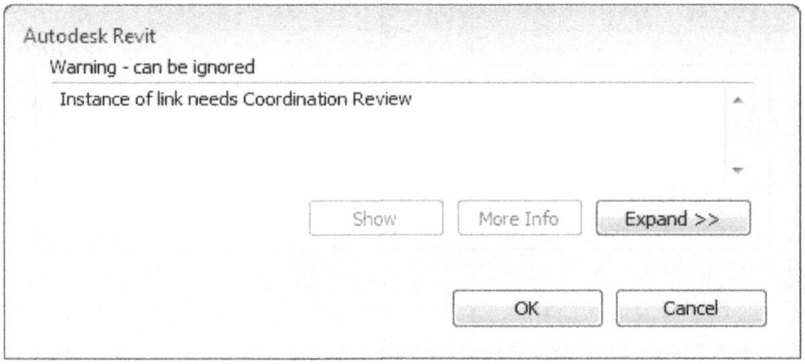

Figure 4–38

- Warnings do not prevent you from making a change, but rather they alert you that the element is monitored and requires further coordination.

- If you no longer want an element to be monitored, select it and in the associated *Modify* tab>Monitor panel, click (Stop Monitoring).

How To: Run a Coordination Review

1. In the *Collaborate* tab>Coordinate panel, expand (Coordination Review) and click (Use Current Project) or (Select Link). The Coordination Review dialog box lists any conflicts detected, as shown in Figure 4–39.
   - If there are no conflicts, the *Message* area is empty.

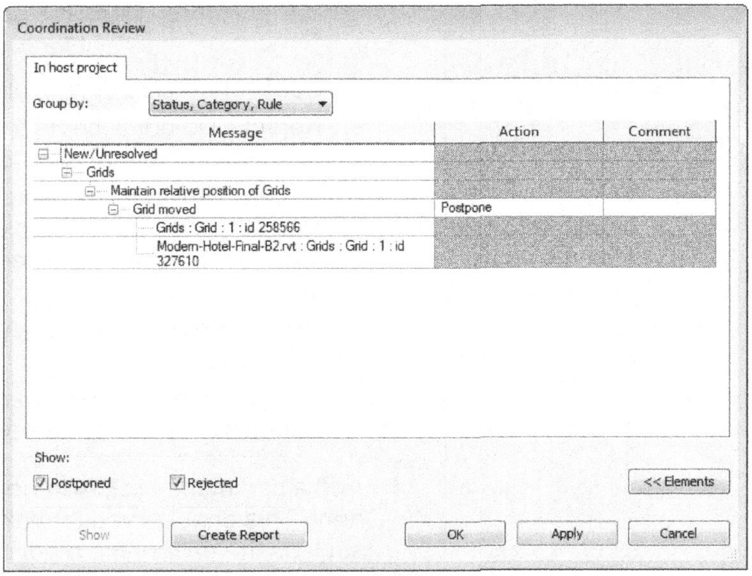

Figure 4–39

2. Use the Group by: drop-down list to group the information by **Status**, **Category**, and **Rule** in a variety of different ways. This is important if you have many elements to review.

3. Select an Action for each conflict related to the elements involved, as shown in Figure 4–40.

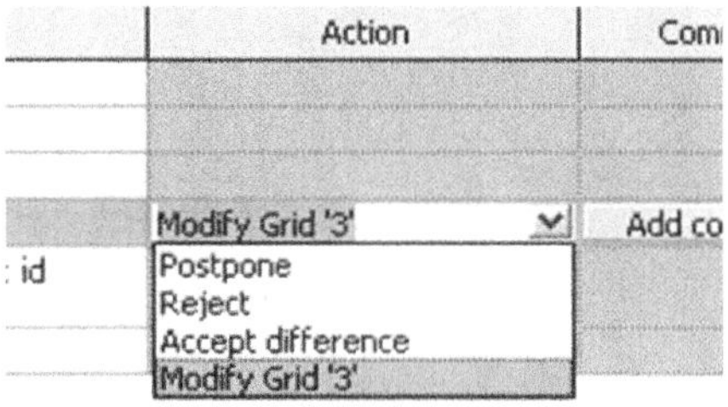

Figure 4–40

- **Postpone** - Do nothing, but leave it to be handled later.
- **Reject** - Do not accept the change. The change needs to be made in the other model.
- **Accept Difference** - Make no change to the monitored element in the current project, but accept the change (such as a distance between the elements) in the monitor status.
- **Rename/Modify/Move** - Apply the change to the monitored element.
- Other options display when special cases occur. See the Autodesk Revit help files for more information.

4. Add a comment, click **Add comment** in the column to the right. This enables you to make a note about the change, such as the date of the modification
5. Select the element names or click **Show** to display any items in conflict. Clicking **Show** changes the view to center the elements in your screen. Selecting the name does not change the view.
6. Click **Create Report** to create an HTML report that you can share with other users, as shown in Figure 4–41.

Revit Coordination Report

In host project

New/Unresolved	Plumbing Fixtures	Maintain relative position of Fixtures	Relative position of two Fixtures changed	Plumbing Fixtures : Sink_Kitchen-Single[1] : Mark 1 : id 734856 MEP-Elementary-School-Architectural.rvt : Plumbing Fixtures : Sink_Kitchen-Single[1] : Mark 80 : id 329165

Figure 4–41

Practice 4d Coordinate Linked Models

Estimated time for completion: 10 minutes

Practice Objectives

- Make a modification to an architectural model.
- Run a Coordination Review.

In this practice you will make a modification to the architectural model, and then open the systems project which prompts you of the change. You will then run a Coordination Review and update the systems project to match the change in the architectural model, as shown in Figure 4–42.

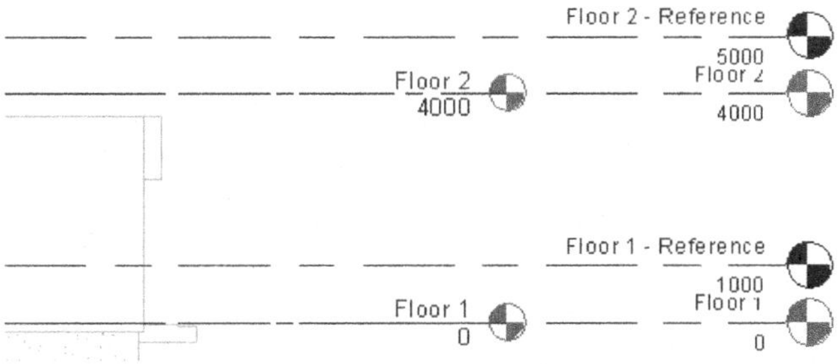

Figure 4–42

Task 1 - Coordinate the architectural and MEP models.

1. Close the previous practice's project if you have not already done so. You cannot open a linked file with it open.
2. In the practice files *Starting* folder, open the project **MEP-Elementary-School-Architectural-M.rvt**. This is the file that is linked into the MEP project.
3. In the Project Browser, open the Elevations (Building Elevation)>Architectural>**East** view.
4. Zoom in on the level names to the right of the elevation.
5. Select **Level 1** and change the *name* to **Floor 1**, as shown in Figure 4–43.

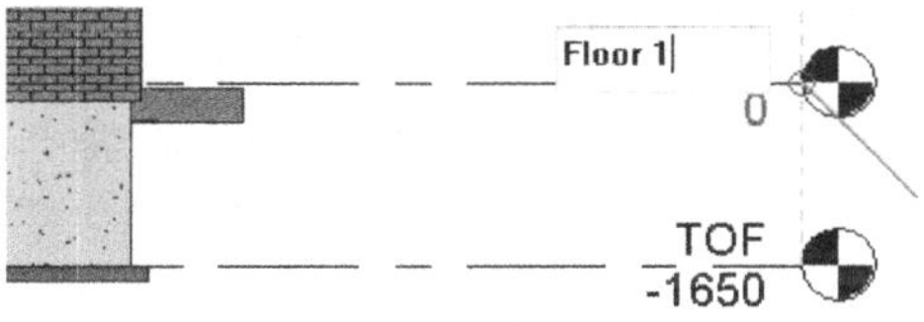

Figure 4–43

6. Repeat with **Level 2** and rename it to **Floor 2**.

7. Save and close the project.

8. In the practice files *Starting* folder, open the project **MEP-Elementary-School-Coordinate-M.rvt**. A Warning box opens, prompting you that the linked model needs a Coordination Review, as shown in Figure 4–44.

Figure 4–44

9. Click **OK**.

10. Open the Mechanical>HVAC>Elevation (Building Elevation): **East - Mech** view and zoom in on the level names. The linked model displays the updated names but the host file has not yet been updated as shown in Figure 4–45.

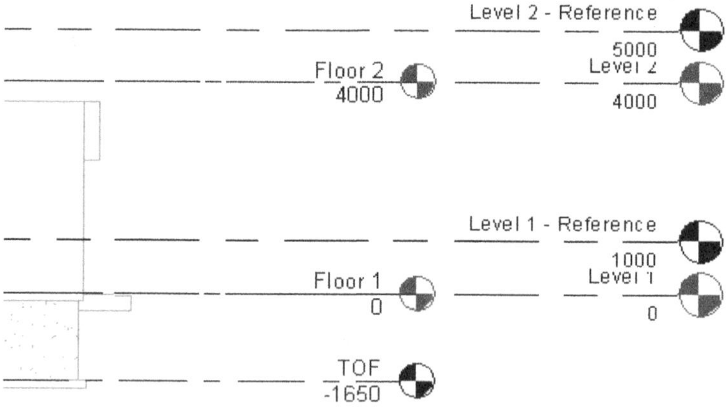

Figure 4–45

11. Select the linked model.

12. In the *Modify | RVT Links* tab>Monitor panel, click (Coordination Review).

13. In the Coordination Review dialog box, expand each of the New/Unresolved>Levels>Maintain Name>*Name changed* categories to display the proposed changes.

14. Select one of the **Name changed** options to display the related levels highlighted in the view as shown in Figure 4–46. In the example, the software recognizes the monitoring connection between **Level 2** in the host project with **Floor 2** in the linked model.

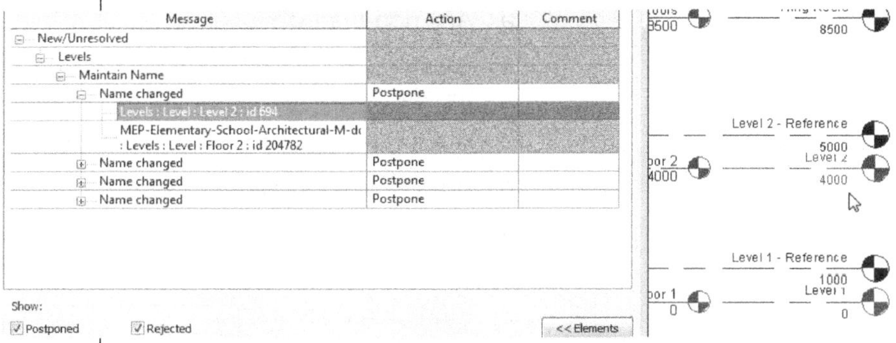

Figure 4–46

15. Next to each N*ame changed* message, expand the list in the *Action* column and select **Rename Element** as shown for Level 2 in Figure 4–47.

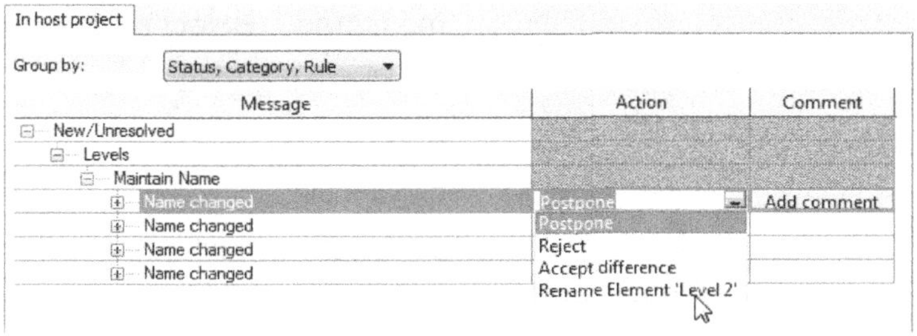

Figure 4–47

16. Click **OK**.

17. The levels in the host project are renamed as shown in Figure 4–48.

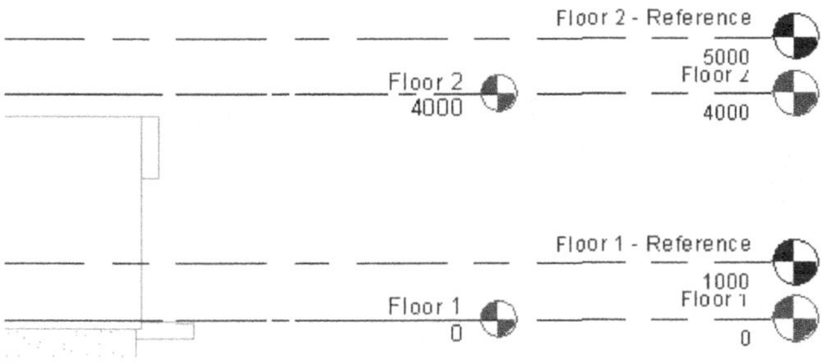

Figure 4–48

18. Save and close the model.

Chapter Review Questions

1. What type of view do you need to be in to add a level to your project?
   a. Any non-plan view.
   b. As this is done using a dialog box, the view does not matter.
   c. Any view except for 3D.
   d. Any section or elevation view.
2. Which of the following elements can be copied and monitored? (Select all that apply.)
   a. Plumbing Fixtures
   b. Levels
   c. Ducts
   d. Electrical Fixtures
3. Which of the following elements can be batch copied and monitored? (Select all that apply.)
   a. Plumbing Fixtures
   b. Levels
   c. Ducts
   d. Electrical Fixtures
4. On which of the following element types can a coordination review with the host project be performed?
   a. CAD link
   b. CAD import
   c. Revit link
   d. Revit import

5. When linking an architectural model into a systems project which of the positioning methods, as shown in Figure 4–49, keeps the model in the same place if the extents of the linked model changes in size?

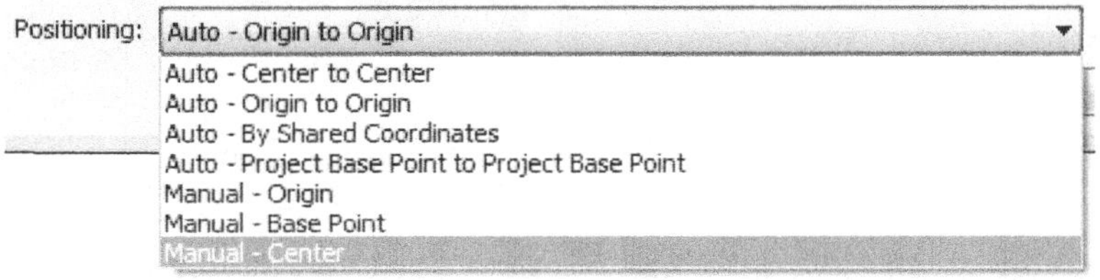

Figure 4–49

   a. Auto - Center-to-Center
   b. Auto - Origin-to-Origin
   c. Manual - Basepoint
   d. Manual - Center

6. How many times can one project file be linked into another project?
   a. Once
   b. It is limited by the size of the link.
   c. As many as you want.

Command Summary

Button	Command	Location
General Tools		
	**Level**	• **Ribbon:** *Architecture* tab>Datum panel • Shortcut: LL
	**Override By Category**	• **Ribbon:** *Modify* tab>View panel, expand Override Graphics in View • **Shortcut Menu:** Override Graphics in View>By Category...
	**Override By Element**	• **Ribbon:** *Modify* tab>View panel, expand Override Graphics in View • **Shortcut Menu:** Override Graphics in View>By Element...
	**Pin**	• **Ribbon:** *Modify* tab>Modify Panel
	**Select Links**	• **Status Bar**
	**Select Pinned Elements**	• **Status Bar**
Linked Revit Files		
	**Coordination Review**	• **Ribbon:** *Collaborate* tab>Coordinate panel
	**Copy (from linked file)**	• **Ribbon:** *Copy/Monitor* tab>Tools panel
	**Copy/Monitor> Select Link**	• **Ribbon:** *Collaborate* tab>Coordinate panel, expand Copy/Monitor
	**Copy/Monitor> Use Current Project**	• **Ribbon:** *Collaborate* tab>Coordinate panel, expand Copy/Monitor
	**Link Revit**	• **Ribbon:** *Insert* tab>Link panel
	**Manage Links**	• **Ribbon:** *Manage* tab>Manage Projects panel or *Insert* tab>Link panel
	**Monitor**	• **Ribbon:** *Copy/Monitor* tab>Tools panel
	**Options (Copy/Monitor)**	• **Ribbon:** *Copy/Monitor* tab>Tools panel

Working with Views

Views are the cornerstone of working with Autodesk® Revit® models as they enable you to see the model in both 2D and 3D. As you are working, you can duplicate and change views to display different information based on the same view of the model. Callouts, elevations, and sections are especially important views for construction documents.

Learning Objectives in this Chapter

- Change the way elements display in different views to show required information and set views for construction documents.
- Duplicate views so that you can modify the display as you are creating the model and for construction documents.
- Create callout views of parts of plans, sections, or elevations for detailing.
- Add building and interior elevations that can be used to demonstrate how a building will be built.
- Create building and wall sections to help you create the model and to include in construction documents.

5.1 Setting the View Display

Views are a powerful tool as they enable you to create multiple versions of a model without having to recreate building elements. For example, you can have views that are specifically used for working on the model, while other views are annotated and used for construction documents. Different disciplines can have different views that show only the features they require, as shown in Figure 5–1. Properties of a view are independent of the properties of other views.

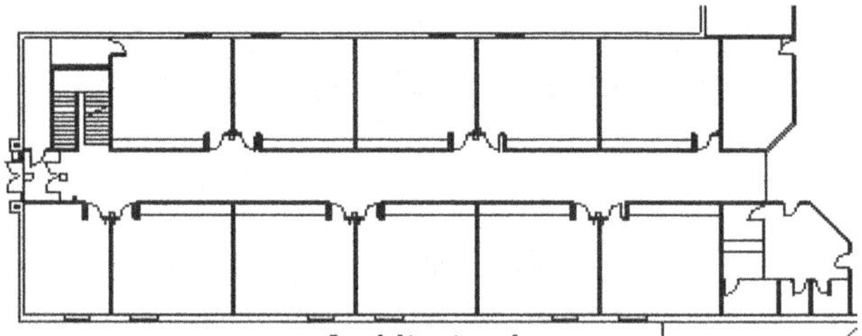

Architectural

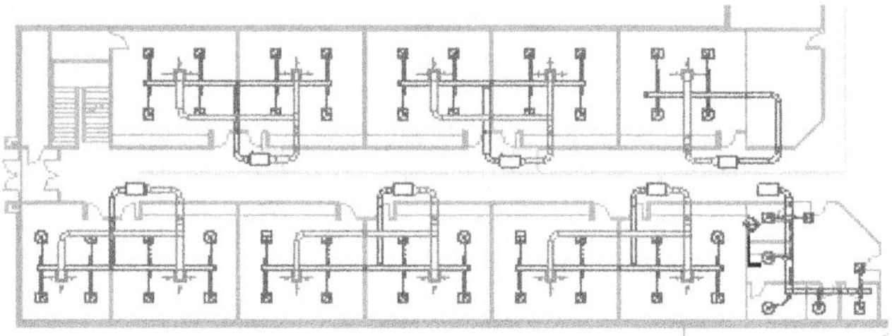

Mechanical

Figure 5–1

The view display can be modified in the following locations:

- View Control Bar
- Properties
- Shortcut menu
- Visibility/Graphic Overrides dialog box

Hiding and Overriding Graphics

Two common ways to customize a view are to:

- Hide individual elements or categories.
- Modify how graphics display for elements or categories (e.g., altering lineweight, color, or pattern).
    - Note that an element is an individual item (i.e., one piece of equipment in a view), while a category includes all instances of a selected element (i.e., all of the equipment in a view).

For example, you can customize the view shown in Figure 5–2 by changing the grid category in a Floor Plan to halftone.

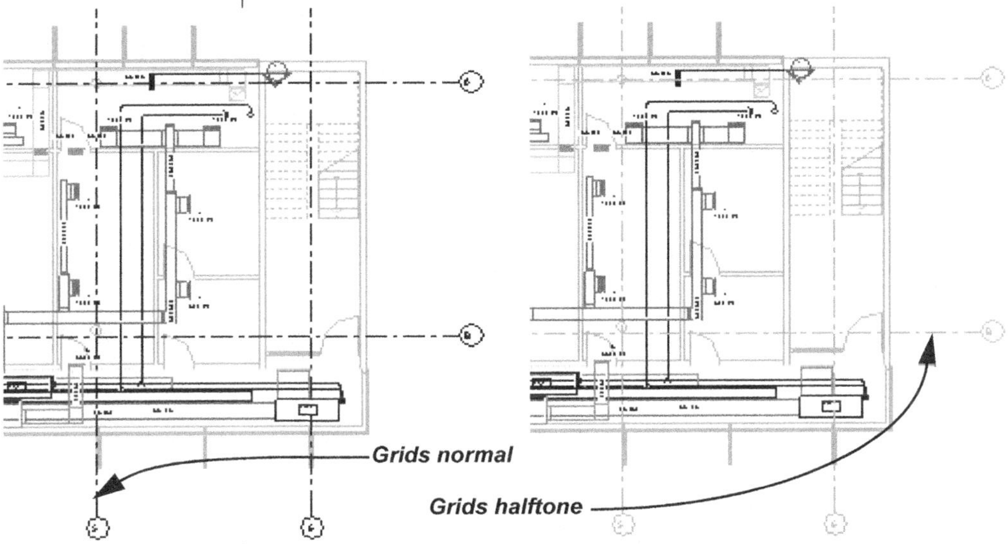

Figure 5–2

How To: Hide Elements or Categories in a view

1. Select the elements or categories you want to hide.
2. Right-click and select **Hide in View>Elements** or **Hide in View>Category**, as shown in Figure 5–3.
3. The elements or categories are hidden in current view only.

A quick way to hide entire categories is to select an element(s) and type ***VH****.*

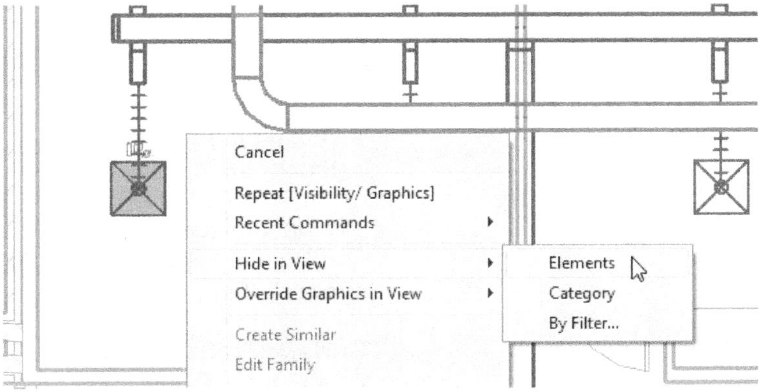

Figure 5–3

How To: Override Graphics of Elements or Categories in a View

The exact options in the dialog box vary depending on the type of elements selected.

1. Select the element(s) you want to modify.
2. Right-click and select **Override Graphics in View>By Element** or **By Category**. The View-Specific Element (or Category) Graphics dialog box opens, as shown in Figure 5–4.

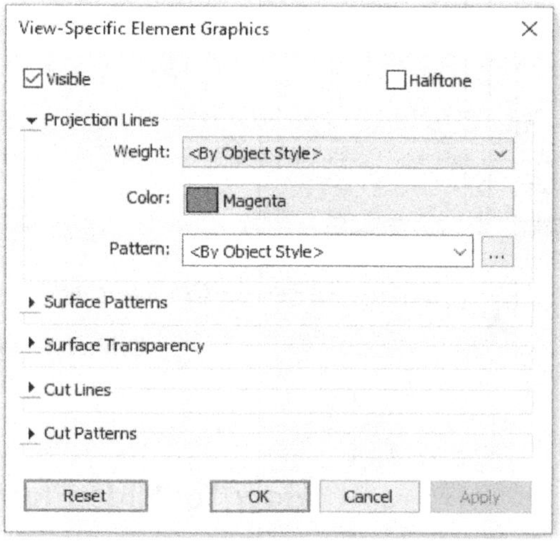

Figure 5–4

3. Select the changes you want to make and click **OK**.

View-Specific Options

- Clearing the **Visible** option is the same as hiding the elements or categories.
- Selecting the **Halftone** option grays out the elements or categories.
- The options for Projection Lines, Surface Patterns, Cut Lines, and Cut Patterns include **Weight**, **Color**, and **Pattern**, as shown in Figure 5–4.
- **Surface Transparency** can be set by moving the slider bar, as shown in Figure 5–5.

Figure 5–5

- The View-Specific Category dialog box includes **Open the Visibility Graphics dialog...**, which opens the full dialog box of options.

The Visibility/Graphic Overrides dialog box

The options in the Visibility/Graphic Overrides dialog box (shown in Figure 5–6) control how every category and sub-category of elements is displayed per view.

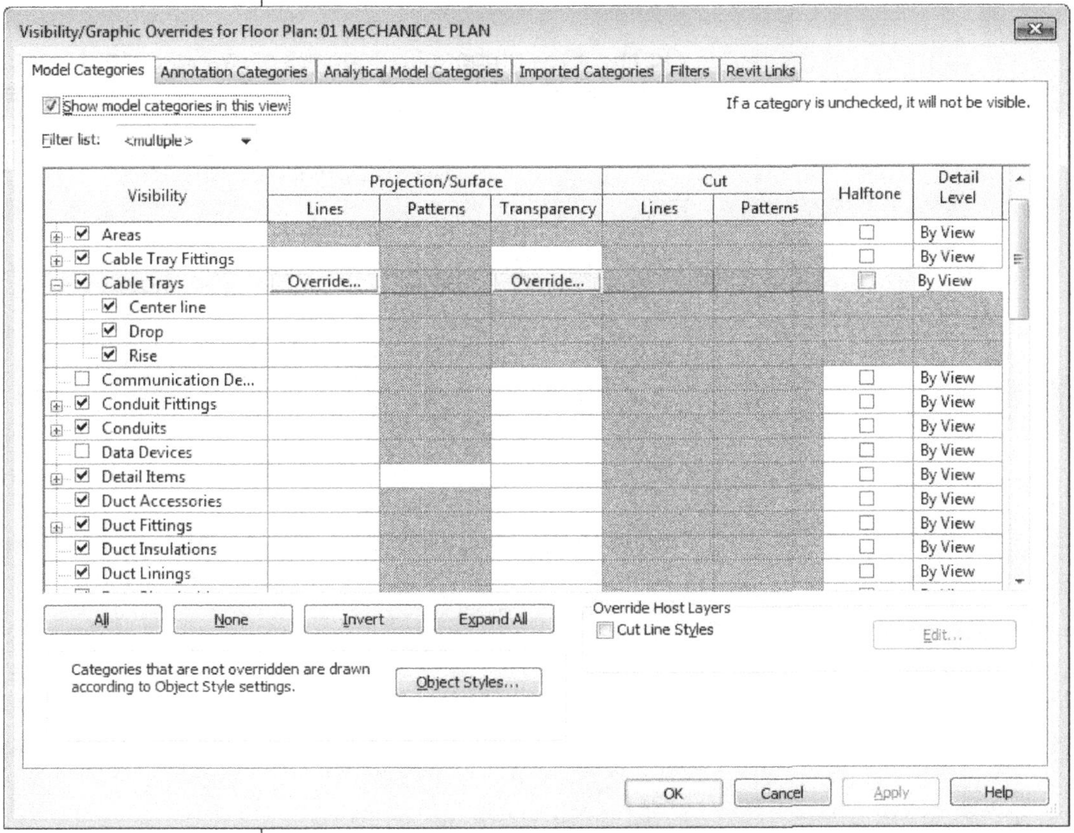

Figure 5–6

To open the Visibility/Graphic Overrides dialog box, type **VV** or **VG**. It is also available in Properties: in the *Graphics* area, beside *Visibility/Graphic Overrides*, click **Edit...**.

- The Visibility/Graphic Overrides are divided into *Model*, *Annotation*, *Analytical Model*, *Imported,* and *Filters* categories.
- Other categories might be available if specific data has been included in the project, including *Design Options*, *Linked Files*, and *Worksets*.
- To limit the number of categories showing in the dialog box select a discipline from the *Filter list,* as shown in Figure 5–7

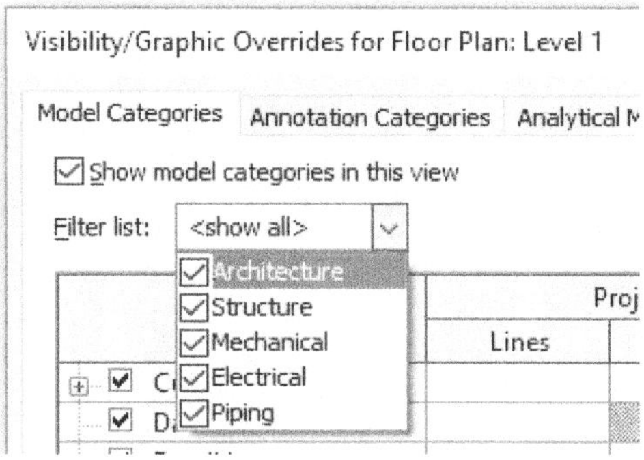

Figure 5–7

- To help you select categories, use the **All**, **None**, and **Invert** buttons. The **Expand All** button displays all of the sub-categories.

Hint: Restoring Hidden Elements or Categories

If you have hidden categories, you can display them using the Visibility/Graphic Overrides dialog box. To display hidden elements, however, you must temporarily reveal the elements first.

1. In the View Control Bar, click (Reveal Hidden Elements). The border and all hidden elements are displayed in magenta, while visible elements in the view are grayed out, as shown in Figure 5–8.

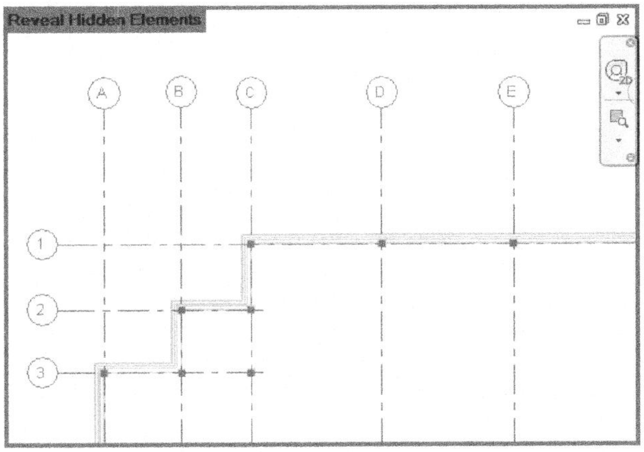

Figure 5–8

2. Select the hidden elements you want to restore, right-click, and select **Unhide in View>Elements** or **Unhide in View>Category**. Alternatively, in the *Modify* | contextual tab>Reveal Hidden Elements panel, click (Unhide Element) or (Unhide Category).
3. When you are finished, in the View Control Bar, click (Close Reveal Hidden Elements) or, in the *Modify* | contextual tab>Reveal Hidden Elements panel click (Toggle Reveal Hidden Elements Mode).

MEP System Filters

Systems in Autodesk Revit MEP are color-coded. For example, supply ducts display in one color and return ducts display in a different color. The system colors display in all views (including 3D views), as shown in Figure 5–9.

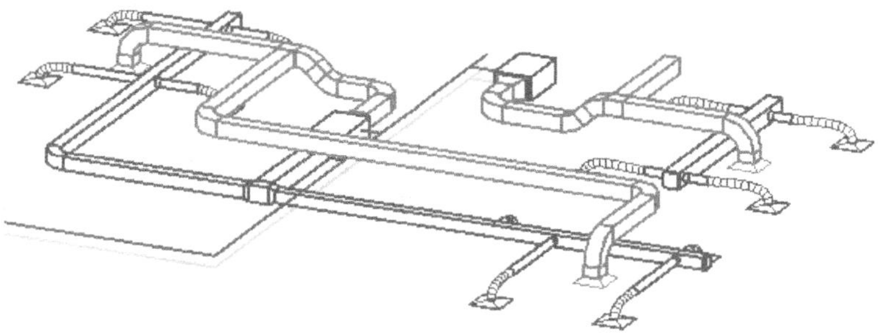

Figure 5–9

You can use filters to display only the systems you want to see in a view. For example, in a section view, you might want to display the sanitary piping only and omit the hot and cold water piping, as shown in Figure 5–10.

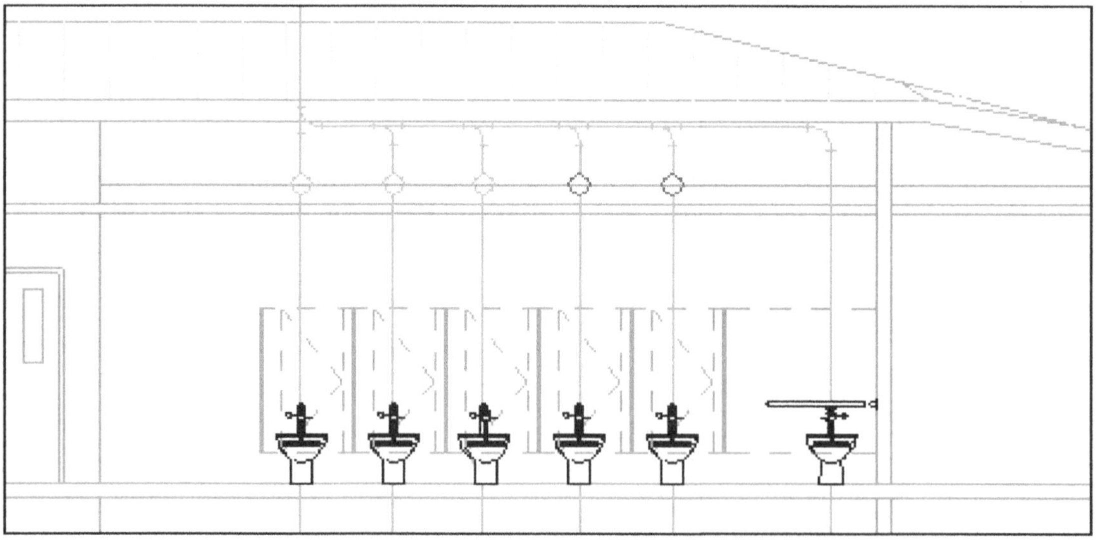

Figure 5–10

- When you create an elevation or section, it uses the basic filters from the original plan view, but some cleanup might be required using Visibility Graphics Overrides.

How To: Apply a View Filter to Override a View

1. Open the Visibility/Graphic Overrides dialog box.
2. In the dialog box, select the *Filters* tab. Some filters might already be available.
3. To add a new filter to this view, click **Add**.
4. In the Add Filters dialog box, as shown in Figure 5–11, select the type of systems you want to modify and click **OK**.

The list might vary depending on the filters that have been set up in the project.

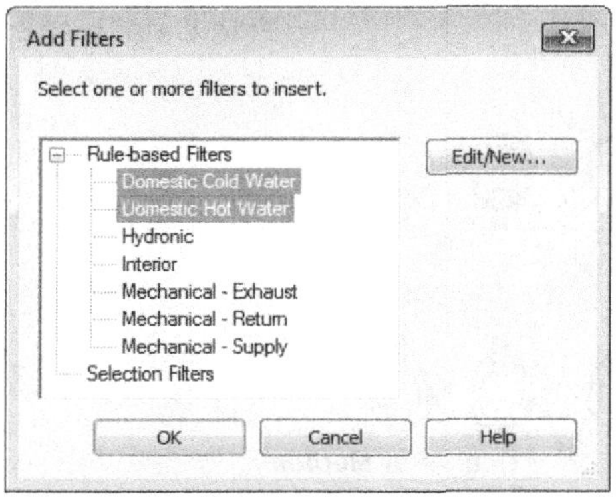

Figure 5–11

5. In the *Filters* tab, select **Visibility** and any other overrides you might want to use. In the example in Figure 5–12, the Domestic Cold and Hot Water have been toggled off while only the Sanitary systems display.

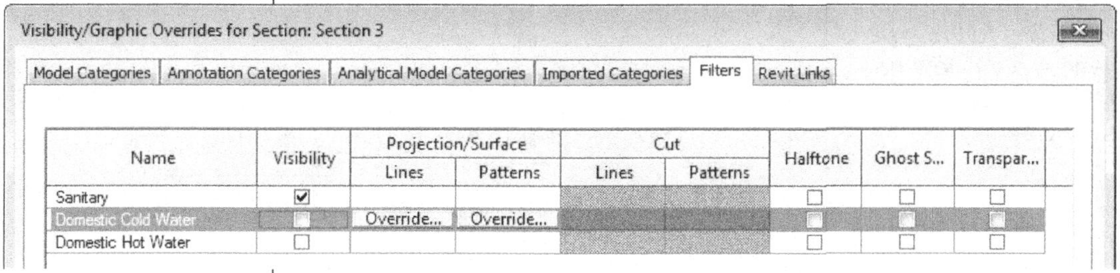

Figure 5–12

6. Click **OK** to close the dialog box.

- To toggle off other elements, such as levels or grids, use the other tabs in the Visibility/Graphics dialog box or use **Hide in View** or **Override Graphics in View**.
- View Filters override system graphics so any colors you set in this dialog box supersede those specified in the System Type.

View Properties

The most basic properties of a view are accessed using the View Control Bar, shown in Figure 5–13. These include the *Scale*, *Detail Level*, and *Visual Style* options. Additional options include temporary overrides and other advanced settings.

Figure 5–13

- The **Detail Level** controls whether you see schematic elements (Coarse or Medium Detail) or full scale elements (Fine Detail), as shown in Figure 5–14.

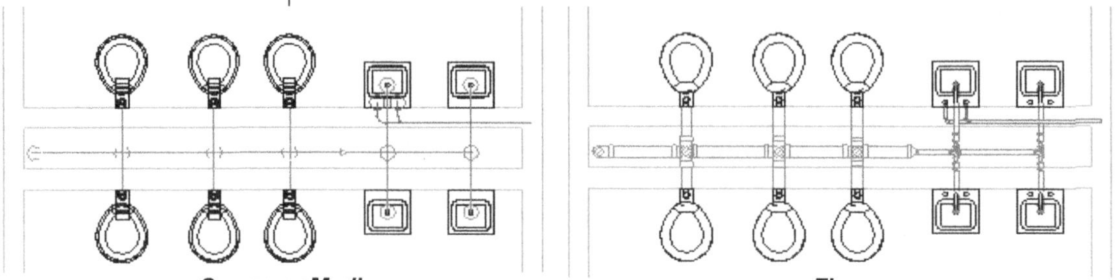

Coarse or Medium ***Fine***

Figure 5–14

Other modifications to views are available in Properties, as shown in Figure 5–15. These properties include *Underlays*, *View Range*, and *Crop Regions*.

The options in Properties vary according to the type of view. A plan view has different properties than a 3D view.

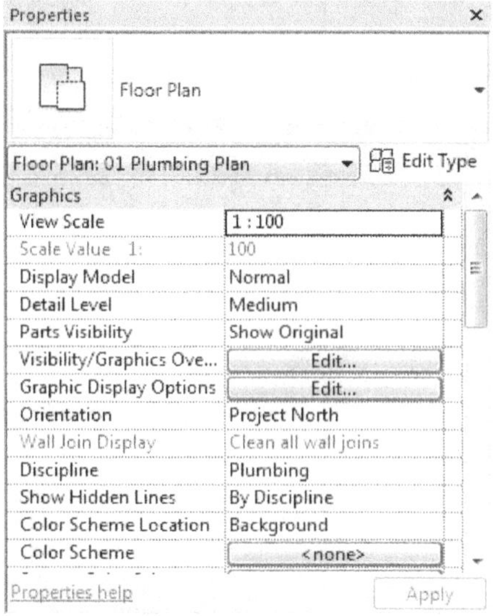

Figure 5–15

Setting an Underlay

Setting an *Underlay* is helpful if you need to display elements on a different level, such as the basement plan shown with an underlay of the first floor plan in Figure 5–16. You can then use the elements to trace over or even copy to the current level of the view.

Underlays are only available in Floor Plan and Ceiling Plan views.

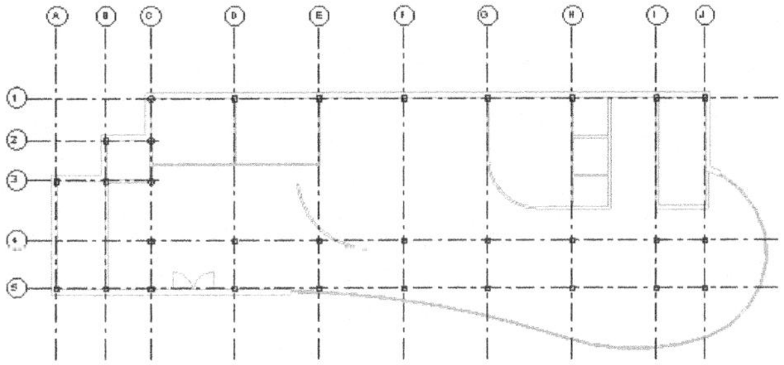

Figure 5–16

In Properties in the *Underlay* area, specify the *Range: Base Level* and the *Range: Top Level*. You can also specify the Underlay Orientation to **Look down** or **Look up** as shown in Figure 5–17.

Underlay	
Range: Base Level	Floor 2
Range: Top Level	Floor 3
Underlay Orientation	Look down

Figure 5–17

- To prevent moving elements in the underlay by mistake, in the Select panel, expand the panel title, and clear **Select underlay elements**. You can also toggle this on/off using  (Select Underlay Elements) in the Status Bar.

How To: Set the View Range

1. In Properties, in the *Extents* area, beside *View Range*, select **Edit...** or type **VR**.
2. In the View Range dialog box, as shown in Figure 5–18, modify the Levels and Offsets for the *Primary Range* and *View Depth*.
   - Click **Show>>** to display the Sample View Range graphics and key to the various options.
3. Click **OK**.

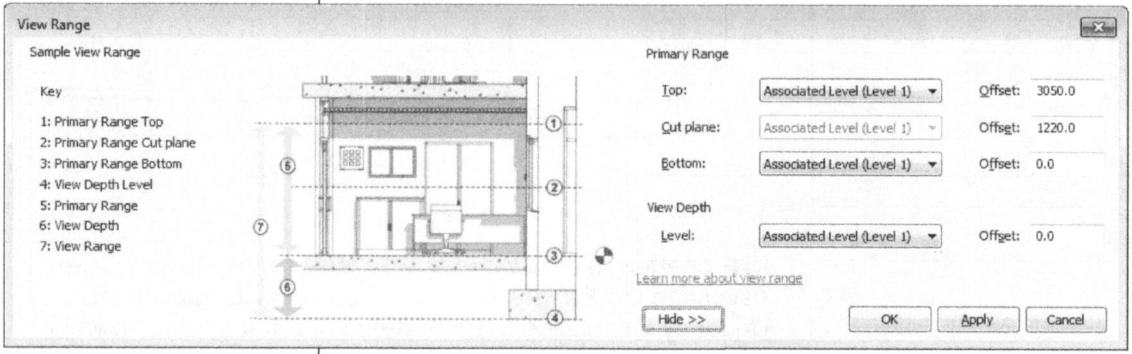

Figure 5–18

- If the settings used cannot be represented graphically, a warning displays stating the inconsistency.

- A Reflected Ceiling Plan (RCP) is created as if the ceiling is reflected by a mirror on the floor so that the ceiling is the same orientation as the floor plan. The cutline is placed just below the ceiling to ensure that any windows and doors below do not display.

Plan Regions

When you have a plan view with multiple levels of floors or ceilings, you can create plan regions that enable you to set a different view range for part of a view, as shown in Figure 5–19 for a set of clerestory windows.

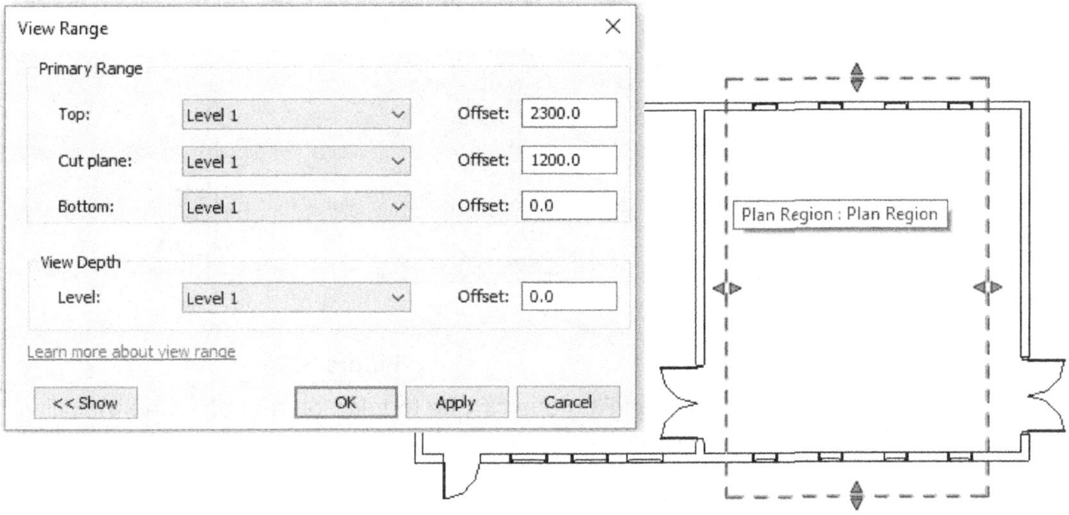

Figure 5–19

How To: Create Plan Regions

1. In a plan view, in the *View* tab>Create panel, expand (Plan Views) and select (Plan Region).
2. In the *Modify | Create Plan Region Boundary* tab>Draw panel, select a draw tool and create the boundary for the plan region.
   - The boundary must be closed and cannot overlap other plan region boundaries, but the boundaries can be side by side.
3. Click (Finish Edit Mode).
4. In the *Modify | Plan Region* tab>Region panel, click (View Range).
5. In the View Range dialog box, specify the offsets for the plan region and click **OK**. The plan region is applied to the selected area.

- Plan regions can be copied to the clipboard and then pasted into other plan views.
- You can use shape handles to resize plan region boundaries without having to edit the boundary.

- If a plan region is above a door, the door swing displays, but the door opening does not display. as shown in Figure 5–20.

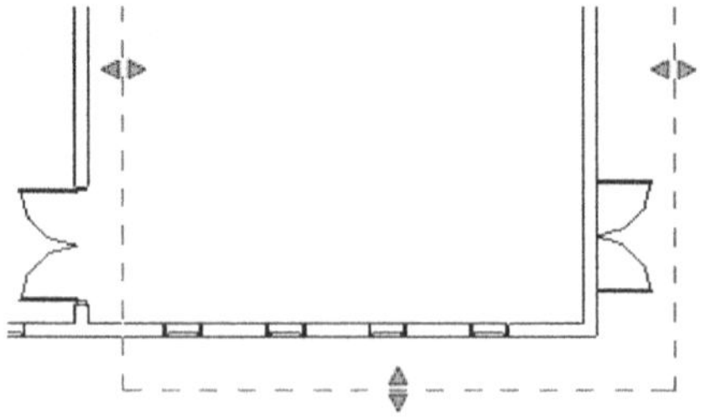

Figure 5–20

- Plan Regions can be toggled on and off in the Visibility/ Graphic Overrides dialog box on the *Annotation Categories* tab. If they are displayed, the plan regions are included when printing and exporting.

Hint: Depth Clipping and Far Clipping

Depth Clipping, shown in Figure 5–21, is a viewing option which sets how sloped walls are displayed if the *View Range* of a plan is set to a limited view.

Far Clipping (shown in Figure 5–22) is available for section and elevation views.

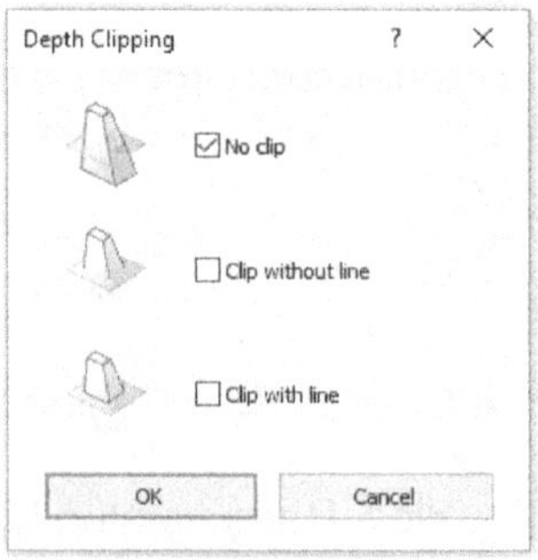

Figure 5–21

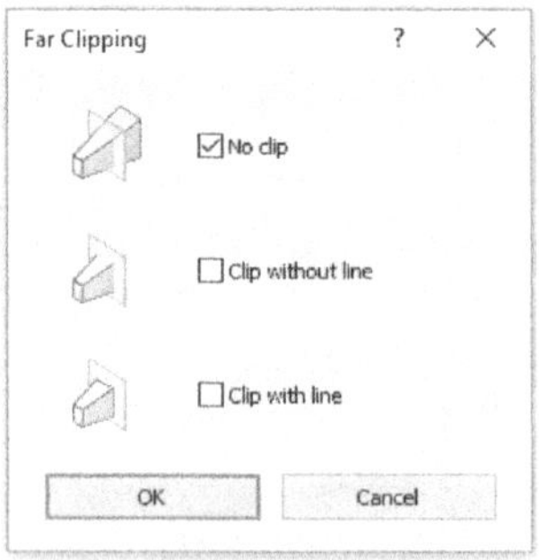

Figure 5–22

- An additional Graphic Display Option enables you to specify *Depth Cueing*, so that items that are in the distance will be made lighter.

Crop Regions

Plans, sections, and elevations can all be modified by changing how much of the model is displayed in a view. One way to do this is to set the Crop Region. If there are dimensions, tags, or text near the required crop region, you can also use the Annotation Crop Region to include these, as shown in Figure 5–23.

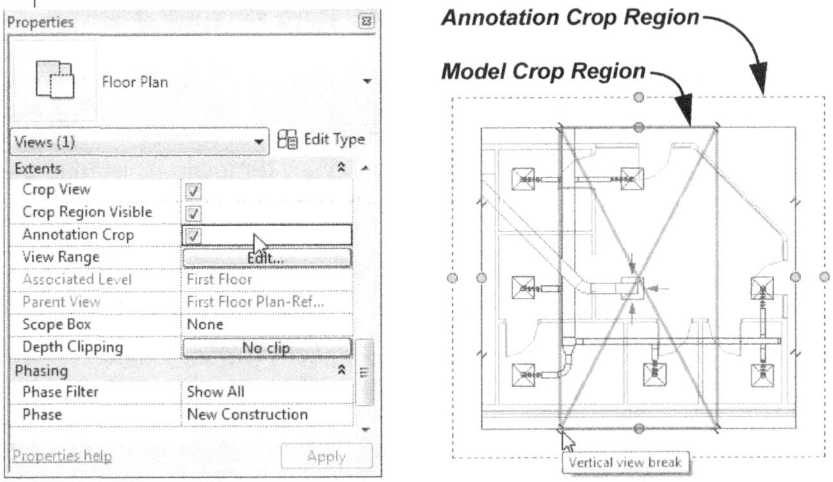

Figure 5–23

Zoom out if you do not see the crop region when you set it to be displayed.

- The crop region must be displayed to modify the size of the view. In the View Control Bar, click (Show Crop Region) Alternatively, in Properties, in the *Extents* area, select **Crop Region Visible**. **Annotation Crop** is also available in this area.
- Resize the crop region using the control on each side of the region.

Breaking the crop region is typically used with sections or details.

- Click (Break Line) control to split the view into two regions, horizontally or vertically. Each part of the view can then be modified in size to display what is required and be moved independently.
- It is a best practice to hide a crop region before placing a view on a sheet. In the View Control Bar, click (Hide Crop Region).

Using View Templates

A powerful way to use views effectively is to set up a view and then save it as a View Template. You can apply view templates to views individually, or though the Properties palette. Setting the View Template using the Properties palette helps to ensure that you do not accidentally modify the view while interacting with it.

How To: Create a View Template from a View

1. Set up a view, as required.
2. In the Project Browser, right-click on the view and select **Create View Template from View**.
3. In the New View Template dialog box, type in a name and then click **OK**.
4. The new view template is listed in the View Templates dialog box. Make any required modifications.
5. Click **OK**.

How To: Specify a View Template for a View

1. In the Project Browser, select the view or views to which you want to apply a view template.
2. In Properties, scroll down to the *Identity Data* section and click the button beside *View Template*.
3. In the Apply View Template dialog box, select the view template from the list, as shown in Figure 5–24.

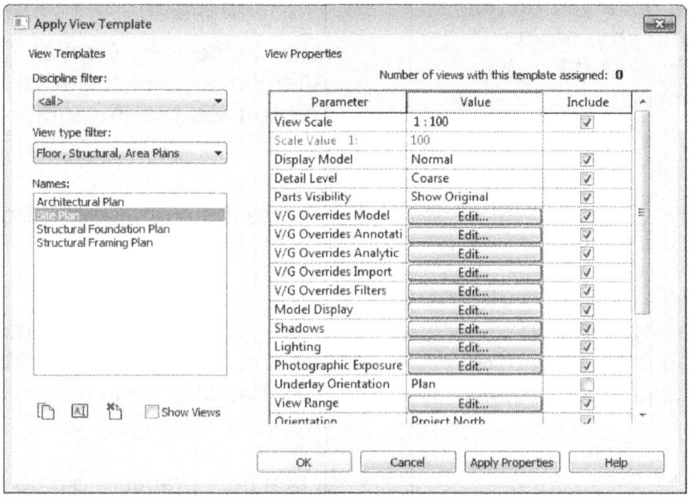

Figure 5–24

4. Click **OK**.

- In the View Control Bar, use  (Temporary View Properties) to temporarily apply a view template to a view.

5.2 Duplicating Views

Once you have created a model, you do not have to recreate the elements at different scales or copy them so that they can be used on more than one sheet. Instead, you can duplicate the required views and modify them to suit your needs.

Duplication Types

Duplicate creates a copy of the view that only includes the building elements, as shown in Figure 5–25. Annotation and detailing are not copied into the new view. Building model elements automatically change in all views, but view-specific changes made to the new view are not reflected in the original view.

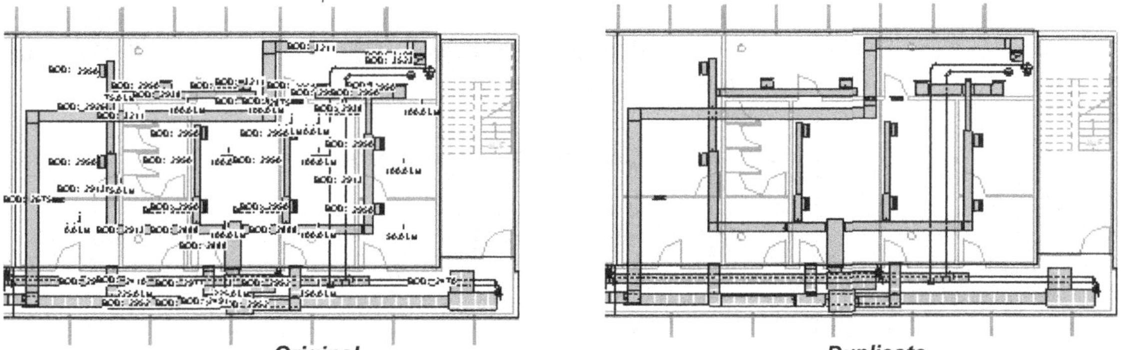

Original ***Duplicate***

Figure 5–25

Duplicate with Detailing creates a copy of the view and includes all annotation and detail elements (such as tags), as shown in Figure 5–26. Any annotation or view-specific elements created in the new view are not reflected in the original view.

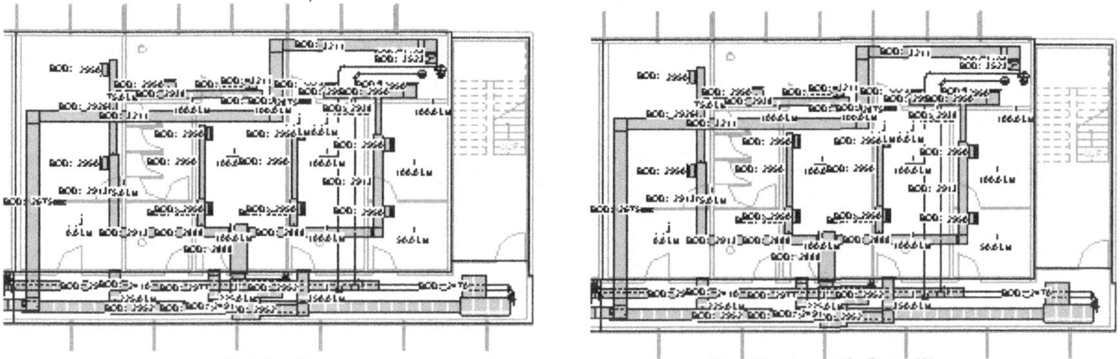

Original ***Duplicate with Detailing***

Figure 5–26

Duplicate as a Dependent creates a copy of the view and links it to the original (parent) view, as shown in the Project Browser in Figure 5–27. View-specific changes made to the overall view, such as changing the *Scale*, are also reflected in the dependent (child) views and vice-versa.

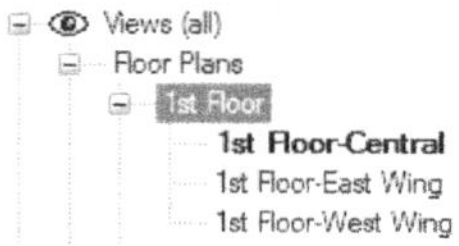

Figure 5–27

- Use dependent views when the building model is so large that you need to split the building onto separate sheets, while ensuring that the views are all same scale.

- If you want to separate a dependent view from the original view, right-click on the dependent view and select **Convert to independent view**.

How To: Create Duplicate Views

Most types of views can be duplicated.

1. Open the view you want to duplicate.
2. In the *View* tab>Create panel, expand **Duplicate View** and select the type of duplicate view you want to create, as shown in Figure 5–28.

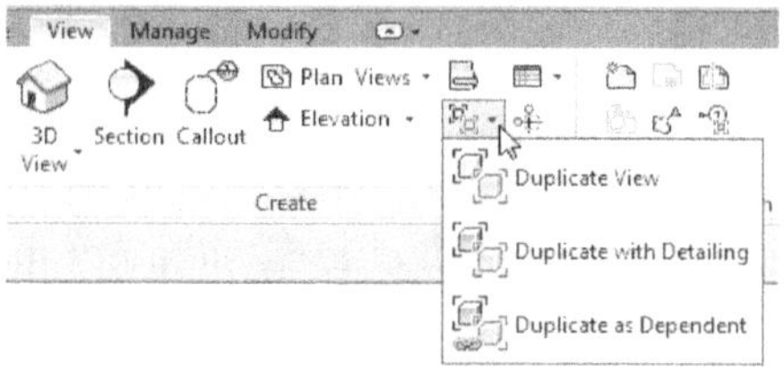

Figure 5–28

3. Alternatively, you can right-click on a view in the Project Browser and select the type of duplicate that you want to use, as shown in Figure 5–29.

Figure 5–29

You can also press <F2> to start the ***Rename*** *command.*

- To rename a view, right-click on the new view in the Project Browser and select **Rename**. In the Rename View dialog box, type in the new name.

Practice 5a Duplicate Views and Set the View Display

Practice Objectives

- Duplicate a view.
- Apply view filters.
- Modify the view display using the Visibility/Graphic Overrides dialog box.

Estimated time for completion: 5 minutes

In this practice you will duplicate views and modify them using filters and Visibility/Graphic Overrides. There is a task for each of the major disciplines: Mechanical, Electrical, and Plumbing. You will change a 3D plumbing view that displays sanitary systems to also display the hot and cold water systems, as shown in Figure 5–30.

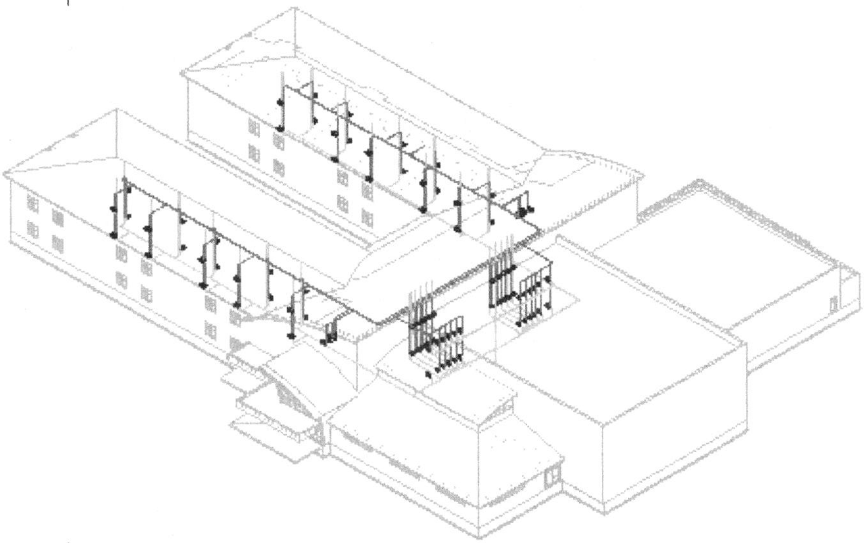

Figure 5–30

Task 1 - Duplicate and modify a view: Mechanical.

1. In the *Views* practice files folder, open **MEP-Elementary-School-Views-M.rvt**.
2. In the Project Browser, right-click on the **3D Plumbing** view and select **Duplicate View>Duplicate**.
3. Right-click on the new view name and select **Rename**.
4. In the Rename View dialog box type **3D HVAC**. Click **OK**.

5. The 3D HVAC view is still in the **Plumbing** sub-category of the Project Browser. In Properties, change the *Discipline* to **Mechanical** and the *Sub-Discipline* to **HVAC**, as shown in Figure 5–31.

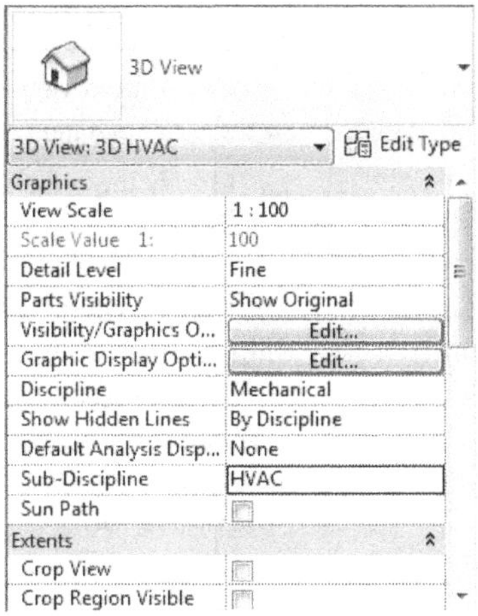

Figure 5–31

6. Open the Visibility/Graphic Overrides dialog box and set the filters to display only **Mechanical - Supply** and **Mechanical - Return**. Click **OK**.

7. The ductwork now displays, but the plumbing fixtures still display.

8. Select one of the plumbing fixtures and type **VH** (for Hide category in view). Now only the HVAC systems display, as shown in Figure 5–32.

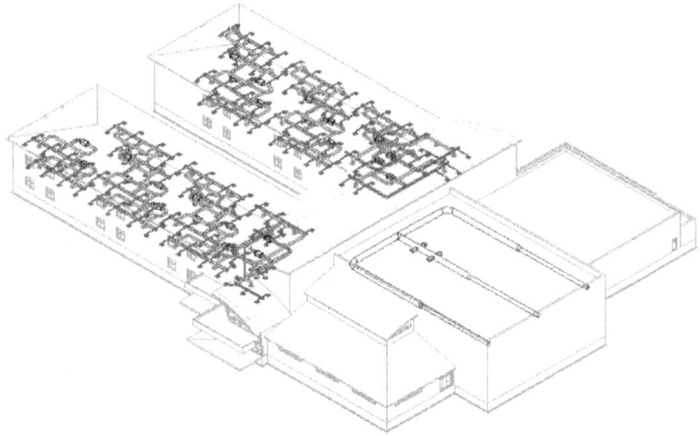

Figure 5–32

9. Save the project.

Task 2 - Duplicate and modify a view: Electrical.

1. In the *Views* practice files folder, open **MEP-Elementary-School-Views-M.rvt**.
2. In the Project Browser, right-click on the **3D HVAC** view and select **Duplicate View>Duplicate**.
3. Right-click on the new view name and select **Rename**.
4. In the Rename View dialog box. type **3D Electrical** and then click **OK**.
5. Note that the new view is still in the **HVAC** sub-category of the Project Browser. In Properties, change the *Discipline* to **Electrical** and the *Sub-Discipline* to **Lighting**, as shown in Figure 5–33.

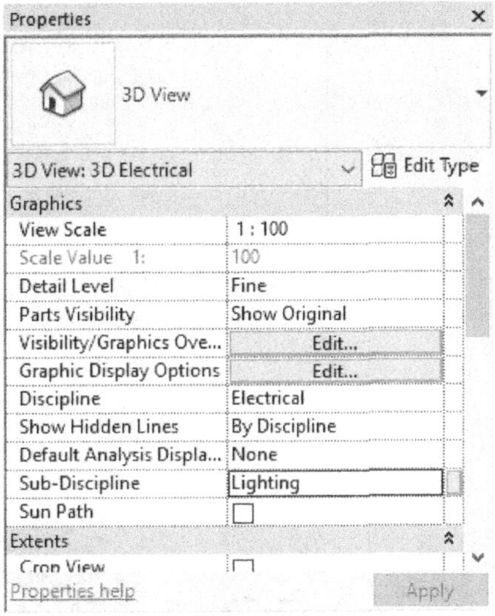

Figure 5–33

6. Open the Visibility/Graphic Overrides dialog box and toggle off the display of all filters. Click **OK**. Note that no systems display in the view.

7. Open the Visibility/Graphic Overrides dialog box again. On the *Model Categories* tab, set the *Filter list* to display only **Electrical**. Then, select the information shown in Figure 5–34.

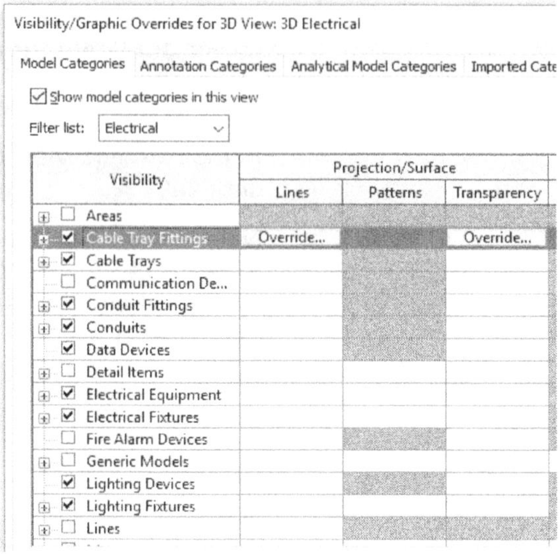

Figure 5–34

8. Click **OK**. Note that the lighting fixtures and electrical equipment now display, but that no cable trays or conduits have been added yet, as shown in Figure 5–35.

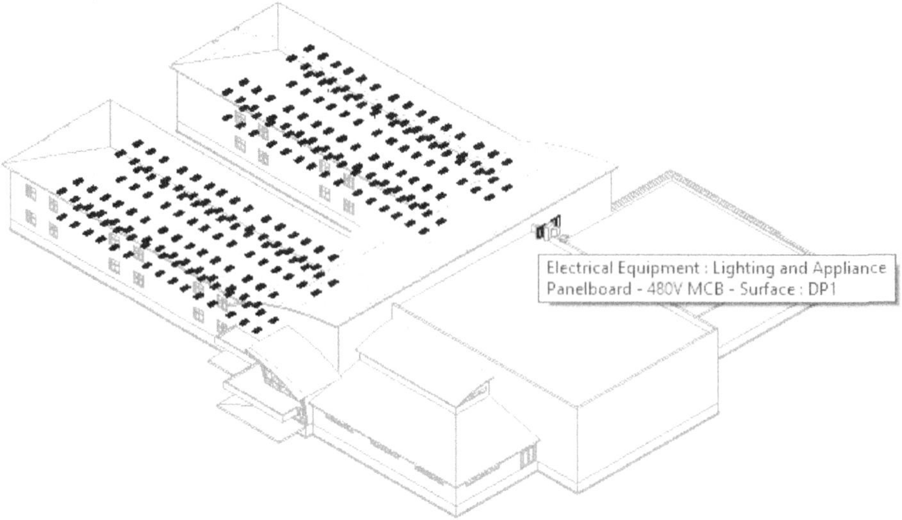

Figure 5–35

9. Save the project.

Task 3 - Apply view filters: Plumbing.

1. In the *Views* practice files folder, open **MEP-Elementary-School-Views-M.rvt**.

2. Open the Plumbing>Plumbing>**3D Plumbing** view. Note that this view displays only the sanitary piping.

3. Type **VV** to open the Visibility/Graphic Overrides dialog box, and then select the *Filters* tab.

4. In the *Visibility* column, select **Domestic Cold Water** and **Domestic Hot Water,** as shown in Figure 5–36. Click **OK**.

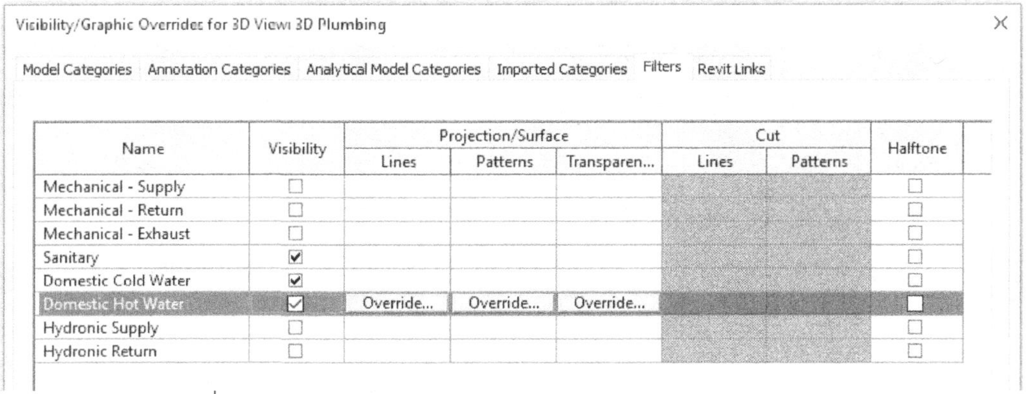

Figure 5–36

5. Note that the rest of the plumbing system elements now display, as shown in Figure 5–37.

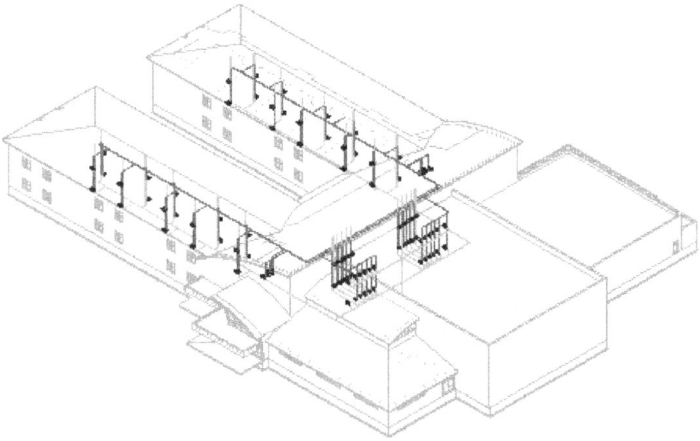

Figure 5–37

6. Save the project.

5.3 Adding Callout Views

Callouts are details of plan, elevation, or section views. When you place a callout in a view, as shown in Figure 5–38, it automatically creates a new view clipped to the boundary of the callout, as shown in Figure 5–39. If you change the size of the callout box in the original view, it automatically updates the callout view and vice-versa. You can create rectangular or sketched callout boundaries.

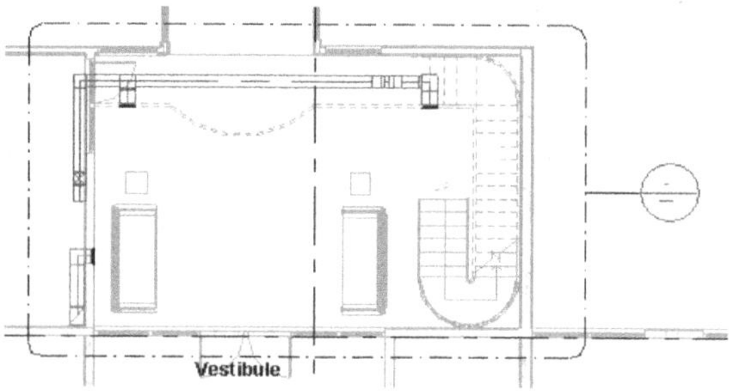

Callout in a view

Figure 5–38

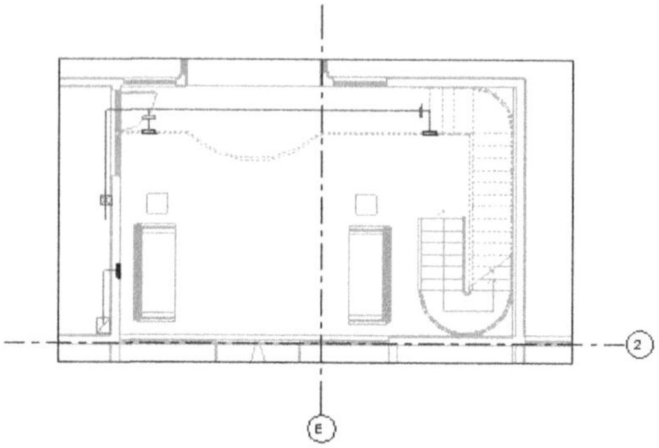

Callout view

Figure 5–39

How To: Create a Rectangular Callout

1. In the *View tab>Create panel,* click (**Callout**).
2. Select points for two opposite corners to define the callout box around the area you want to detail.
3. Select the callout and use the shape handles to modify the location of the bubble and any other edges that might need changing.
4. In the Project Browser, rename the callout.

How To: Create a Sketched Callout

1. In the *View tab>Create panel,* expand (Callout), and click (Sketch).
2. Sketch the shape of the callout using the tools in the *Modify | Edit Profile* tab>Draw panel, as shown in Figure 5–40.

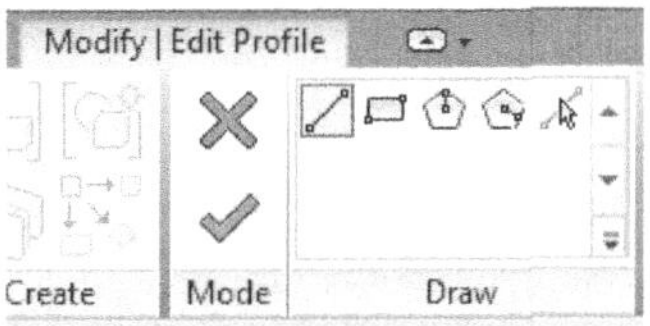

Figure 5–40

3. Click (Finish) to complete the boundary.
4. Select the callout and use the shape handles to modify the location of the bubble and any other edges that might need to be changed.
5. In the Project Browser, rename the callout

- To open the callout view, double-click on its name in the Project Browser or double-click on the callout bubble (ensure that the callout is not selected before you double-click on it).

Modifying Callouts

The callout bubble displays numbers when the view is placed on a sheet.

In the original view where the callout is created, you can use the shape handles to modify the callout boundary and bubble location, as shown in Figure 5–41.

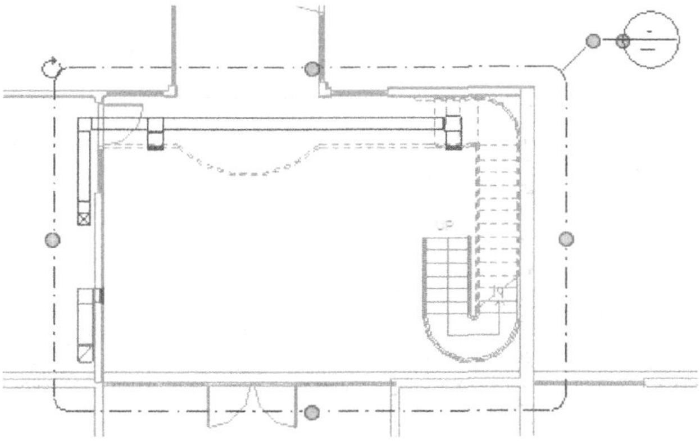

Figure 5–41

- You can rotate the callout box by dragging the (Rotate) control or by right-clicking on edge of callout and selecting **Rotate**.

In the callout view, you can modify the crop region with shape handles and view breaks, as shown in Figure 5–42.

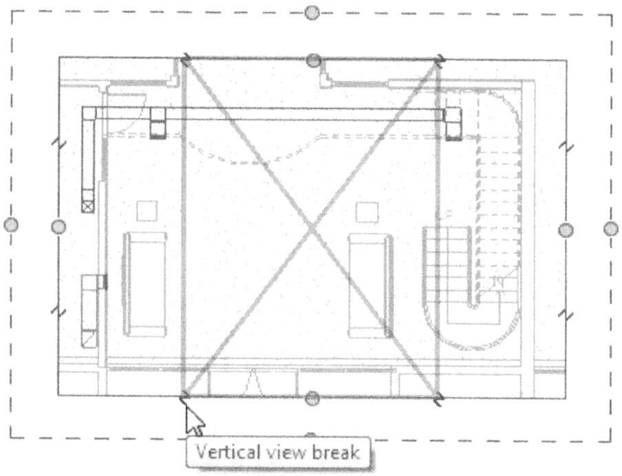

Figure 5–42

- If you want to edit the crop region to reshape the boundary of the view, select the crop region and, in the *Modify | Floor Plan* tab>Mode panel, click (Edit Crop).
- If you want to return a modified crop region to the original rectangular configuration, click (Reset Crop).
- You can also resize the crop region and the annotation crop region using the Crop Region Size dialog box as shown in Figure 5–43. In the *Modify | Floor Plan* tab>Crop panel, click (Size Crop) to open the dialog box.

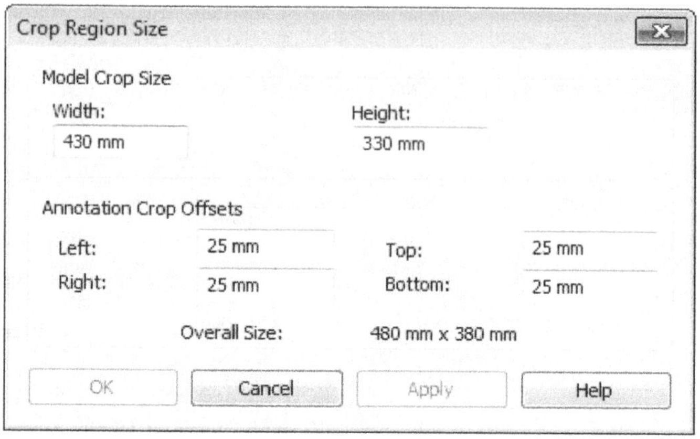

Figure 5–43

Practice 5b Add Callout Views

Practice Objective

- Create callout views.

Estimated time for completion: 10 minutes

In this practice you will create a callout view of one wing of the building. In the new callout view, you will then create an additional callout view, as shown for electrical in Figure 5–44. Choose the task specific for your discipline: Mechanical, Electrical, or Plumbing.

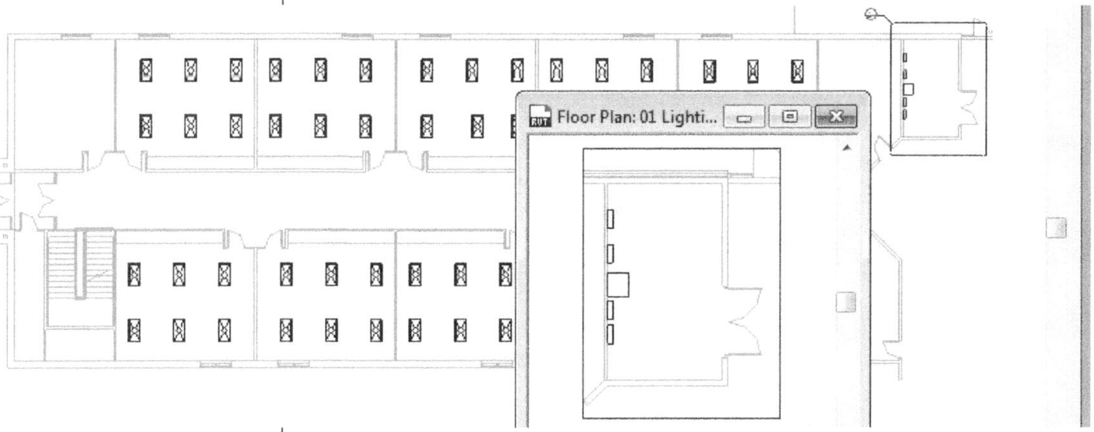

Figure 5–44

Task 1 - Add callout views: Mechanical.

1. In the *Views* practice files folder, open **MEP-Elementary-School-Callout-M.rvt**.
2. Open the Mechanical>HVAC>Floor Plans>**01 Mechanical Plan** view.
3. In the *View* tab>Create panel, expand (Callout) and select (Sketch).

4. Sketch a boundary similar to that shown in Figure 5–45.

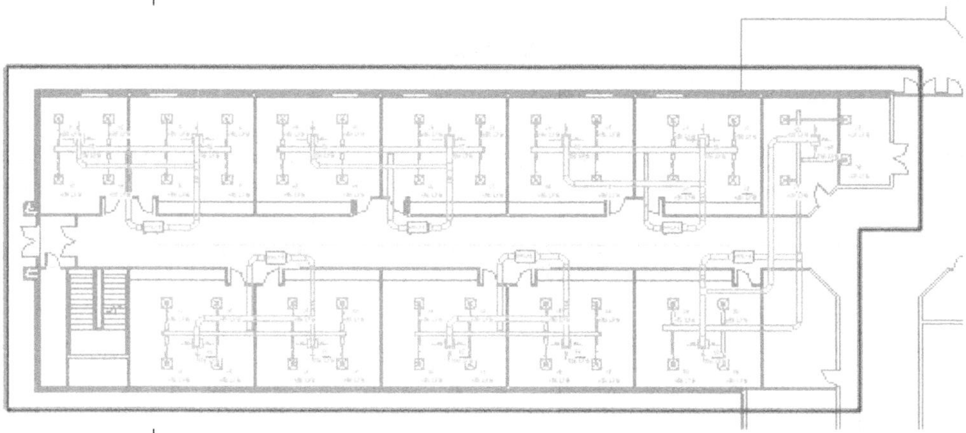

Figure 5–45

5. Click (Finish Edit Mode). Use the controls to move the bubble as shown in Figure 5–46.

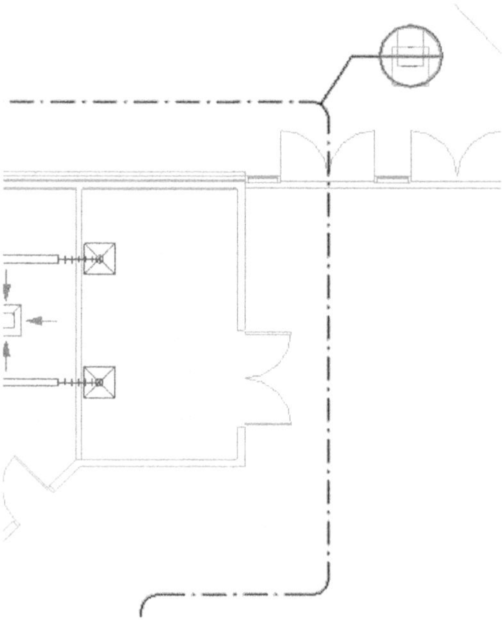

Figure 5–46

6. In the Project Browser, double-click on the new callout view to open it. Rename the callout **01 Mechanical Plan-Area A**.

7. In the View Control Bar, notice that the *Scale* is automatically increased to be two times the previous view.

8. In the View Control Bar, click (Hide Crop Region).

9. In the *View* tab>Create panel, click (Callout).

10. Draw a callout box around one set of two classrooms and move the bubble as shown in Figure 5–47.

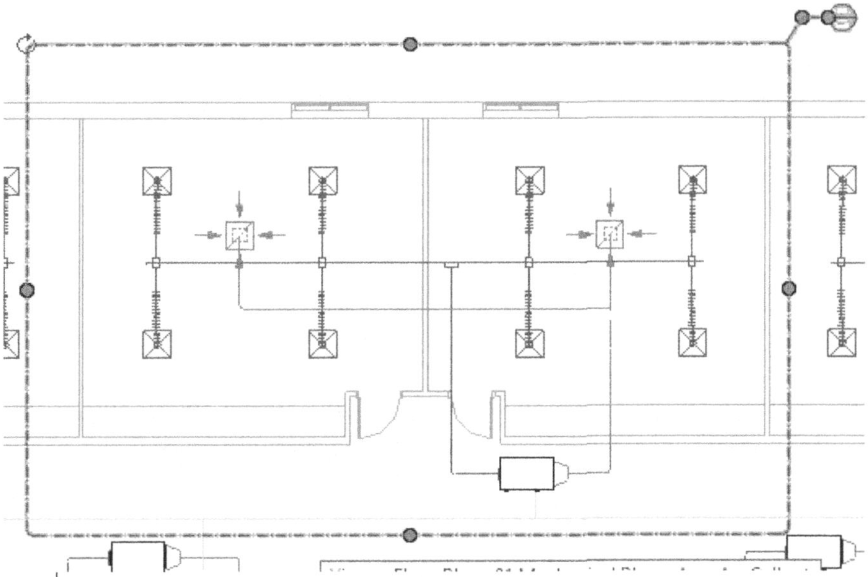

Figure 5–47

11. In the Project Browser, rename the new callout **Typical Classroom Mechanical**. Open the view and you can see that the scale was doubled again from the previous callout view.

12. Reopen the **01 Mechanical Plan** view. Note that the larger callout displays, but the callout in the larger callout does not.

13. Save the project.

Task 2 - Add callout views: Electrical.

1. In the *practice files Views* folder, open **MEP-Elementary-School-Callout-M.rvt**.

2. Open the Electrical>Lighting>Floor Plans>**01 Lighting Plan** view.

3. In the *View* tab>Create panel, expand (Callout) and select (Sketch).
4. Sketch a boundary similar to that shown in Figure 5–48.

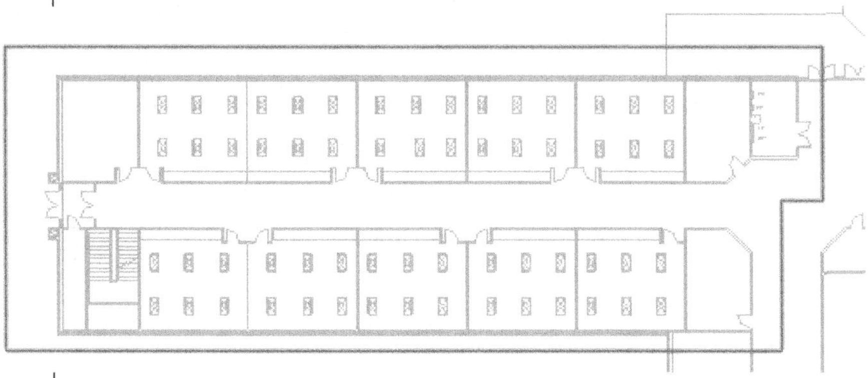

Figure 5–48

5. Click (Finish Edit Mode). Use the controls to move the bubble as shown in Figure 5–49.

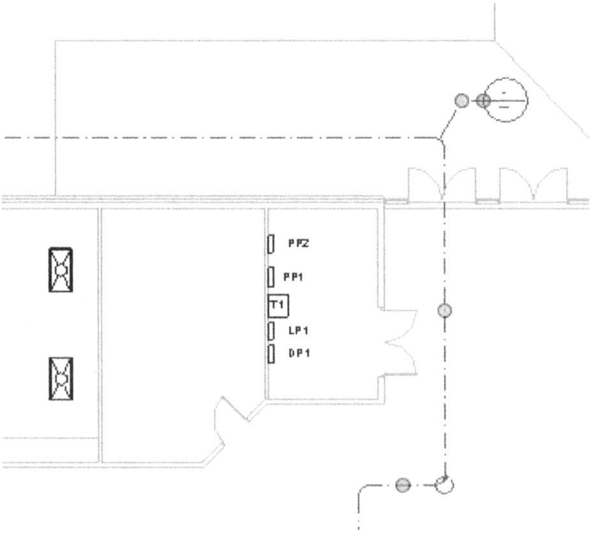

Figure 5–49

6. In the Project Browser, double-click on the new callout view to open it. Rename the callout **01 Lighting Plan-Area A**.
7. In the View Control Bar, notice that the *Scale* is automatically increased to two times the previous view.

8. In the View Control Bar, click (Hide Crop Region).

9. In the *View* tab>Create panel, click (Callout).

10. Draw a callout box around the electrical room and move the bubble as shown in Figure 5–50.

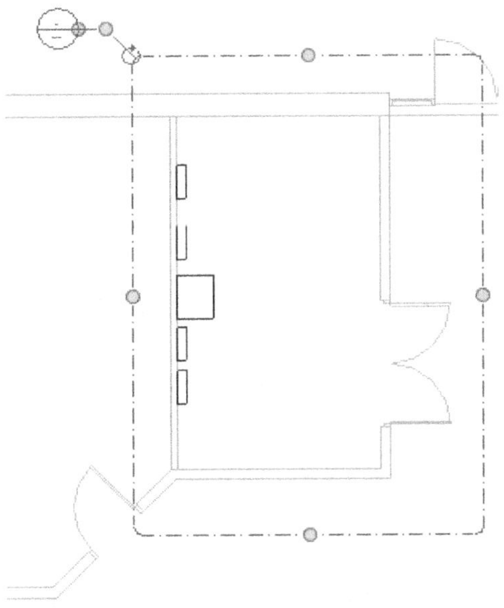

Figure 5–50

11. Open the view and note that the scale was doubled again from the previous callout view.

12. In the Project Browser, rename the new callout **01 Electrical Room**.

13. Right-click on the view name and select **Apply Template Properties**.

14. In the Apply View Template dialog box, select P**ower Plan** and click **OK**. The view moves to the **Power** node.

15. Note that the view scale is changed by the view template. Change *Scale* to **1:100**, which works best for this size of plan.

16. Reopen the **01 Lighting Plan** view. The larger callout displays, but the callout in the larger callout does not.

17. Save the project.

Task 3 - Add callout views: Plumbing.

1. In the *Views* practice files folder, open **MEP-Elementary-School-Callout-M.rvt**.
2. Open the Plumbing>Plumbing>Floor Plans>**01 Plumbing Plan** view.
3. In the *View* tab>Create panel, expand (Callout) and select (Sketch).
4. Sketch a boundary similar to that shown in Figure 5–51.

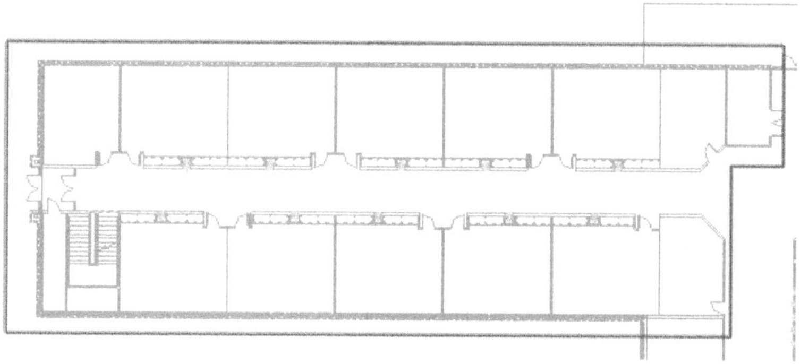

Figure 5–51

5. Click (Finish Edit Mode). Use the controls to move the bubble as shown in Figure 5–52.

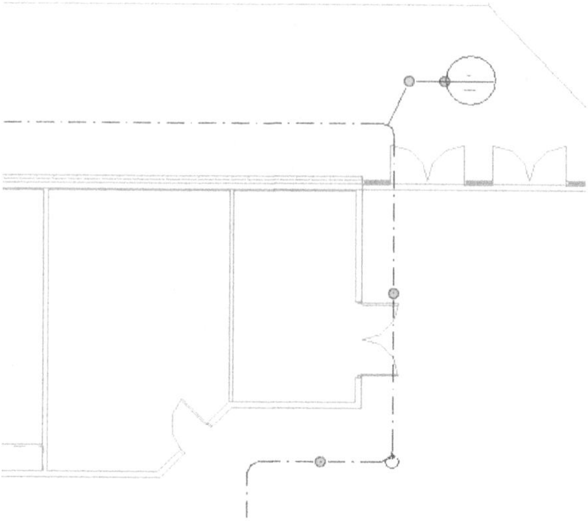

Figure 5–52

6. In the Project Browser, double-click on the new callout view to open it. Rename the callout **01 Plumbing Plan-Area A**.
7. In the View Control Bar, note that the *Scale* is automatically increased to two times the previous view.
8. In the View Control Bar, click  (Hide Crop Region).
9. In the *View* tab>Create panel, click  (Callout).
10. Draw a callout box around one of the classroom sinks and move the bubble, as shown in Figure 5–53.

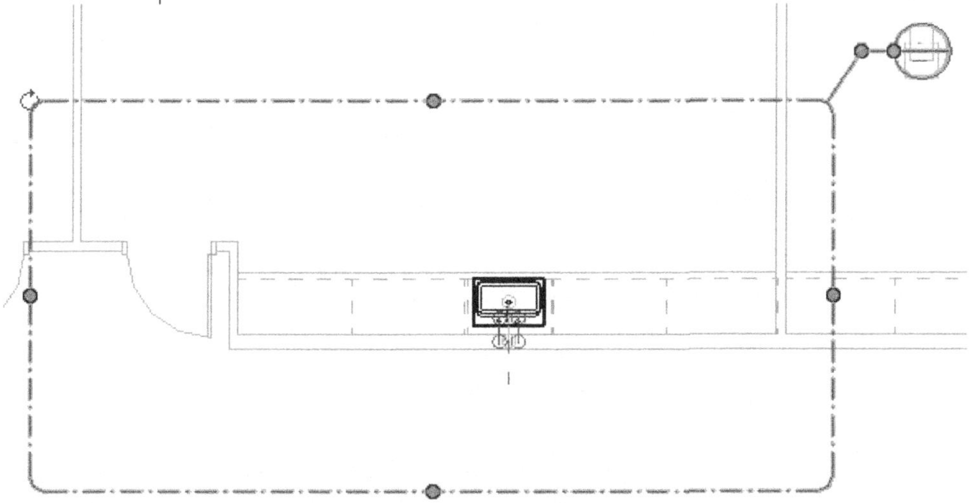

Figure 5–53

11. In the Project Browser, rename the new callout **Typical Classroom Plumbing**. Open the view and note that the scale was doubled again from the previous callout view.
12. Reopen the **01 Plumbing Plan** view. The larger callout displays, but the callout in the larger callout does not.
13. Save the project.

5.4 Creating Elevations and Sections

Elevations and sections are critical elements of construction documents and can assist you as you are working on a model. Any changes made in one of these views (such as the section in Figure 5–54), changes the entire model and any changes made to the project model are also displayed in the elevations and sections.

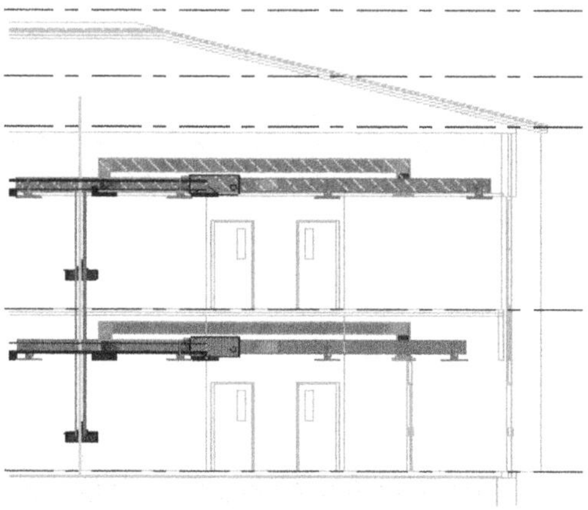

Figure 5–54

- In the Project Browser, elevations are separated by elevation type and sections are separated by section type as shown in Figure 5–55.

To give the elevation or section a new name, right-click on it in the Project Browser and select ***Rename...***

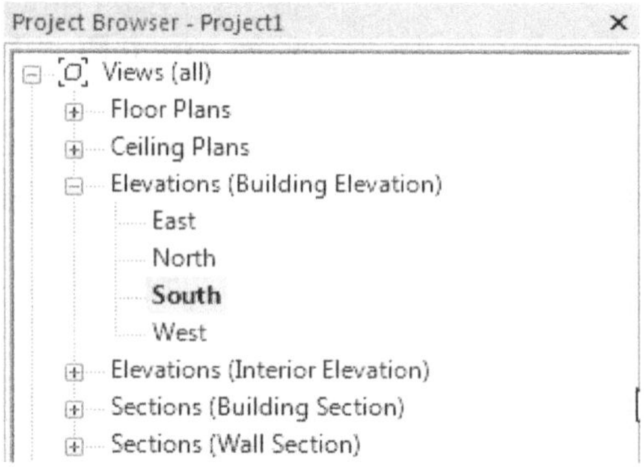

Figure 5–55

- To open an elevation or section view, double-click on the marker arrow or on its name in the Project Browser.

Elevations

Elevations are *face-on* views of the interiors and exteriors of a building. Four Exterior Elevation views are defined in the default template: **North**, **South**, **East**, and **West**. You can create additional building elevation views at other angles or interior elevation views, as shown in Figure 5–56.

When you add an elevation or section to a sheet, the detail and sheet number are automatically added to the view title.

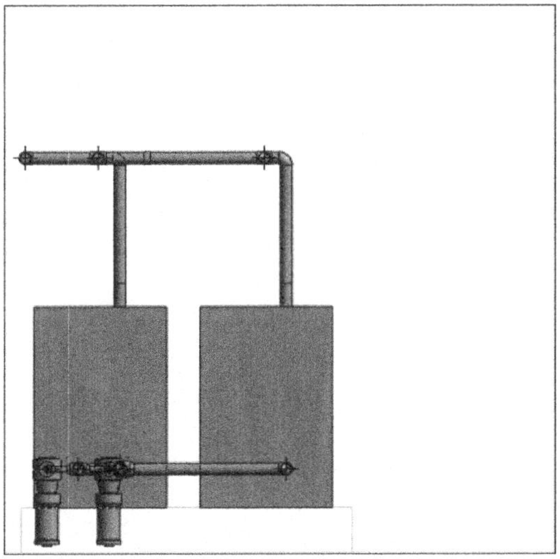

Figure 5–56

- Elevations must be created in plan views.

How To: Create an Elevation

The software remembers the last elevation type used, so you can click the top button if you want to use the same elevation command.

1. In the *View* tab>Create panel, expand (Elevation) and click (Elevation).
2. In the Type Selector, select the elevation type. Two types come with the templates: **Building Elevation** and **Interior Elevation**.
3. Move the cursor near one of the walls that defines the elevation. The marker follows the angle of the wall.
4. Click to place the marker.

- The length, width, and height of an elevation are defined by the walls and ceiling/floor at which the elevation marker is pointing.
- When creating interior elevations, ensure that the floor or ceiling above is in place before creating the elevation or you will need to modify the elevation crop region so that the elevation markers do not show on all floors.

Sections

Sections can be created in plan, elevation, and other section views.

Sections are slices through a model. You can create a section through an entire building, as shown in Figure 5–57, or through one wall for a detail.

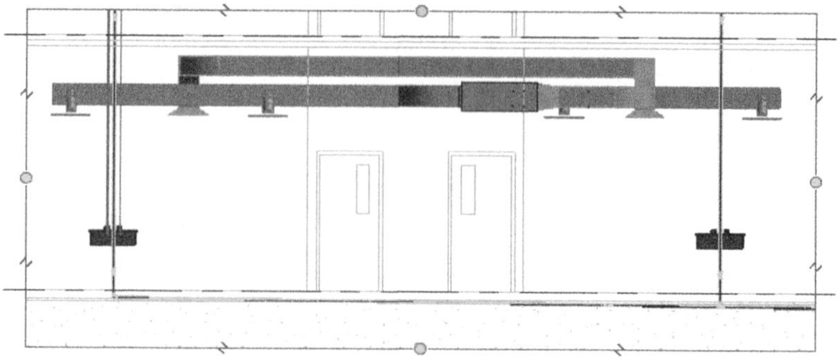

Figure 5–57

How To: Create a Section

1. In the *View* tab>Create panel or in the Quick Access Toolbar, click  (Section).
2. In the Type Selector, select **Section: Building Section** or **Section: Wall Section.** If you want a section in a Drafting view select **Detail View: Detail.**
3. In the view, select a point where you want to locate the bubble and arrowhead.
4. Select the other end point that describes the section.
5. The shape controls display. You can flip the arrow and change the size of the cutting plane, as well as the location of the bubble and flag.

Hint: Selection Box

You can modify a 3D view to display parts of a building, as shown in Figure 5–58.

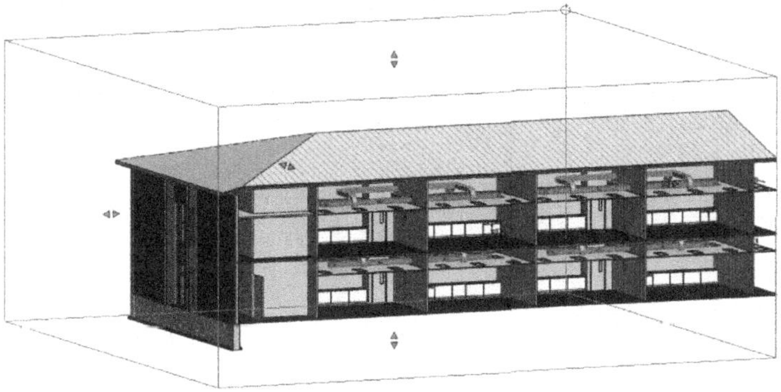

Figure 5–58

1. In a 3D view, select the elements you want to isolate. In the example shown in Figure 5–58, the front wall was selected.
2. In the *Modify* tab>View panel click  (Selection Box) or type **BX**.
3. The view is limited to a box around the selected item(s).
4. Use the controls of the Section Box to modify the size of the box to show exactly what you want.

- To toggle off a section box and restore the full model, in the view's Properties, in the *Extents* area, clear the check from **Section Box**.

Modifying Elevations and Sections

There are two parts to modifying elevations and sections:

- To modify the view (as shown in Figure 5–59), use the controls to modify the size or create view breaks.
- To modify the markers (as shown in Figure 5–60), use the controls to change the length and depth of elevations and sections. There are other specific type options as well.

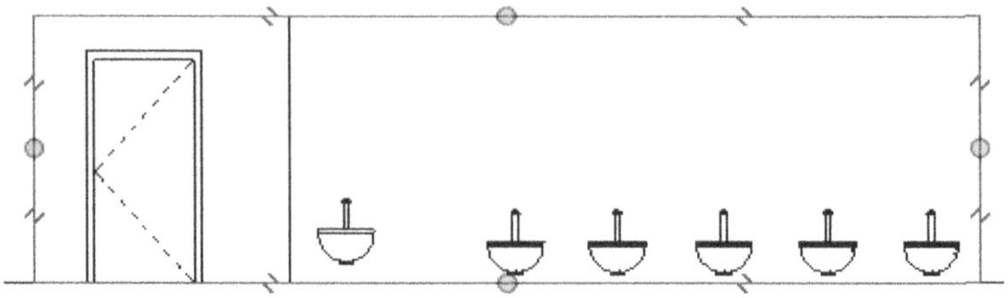

Figure 5–59

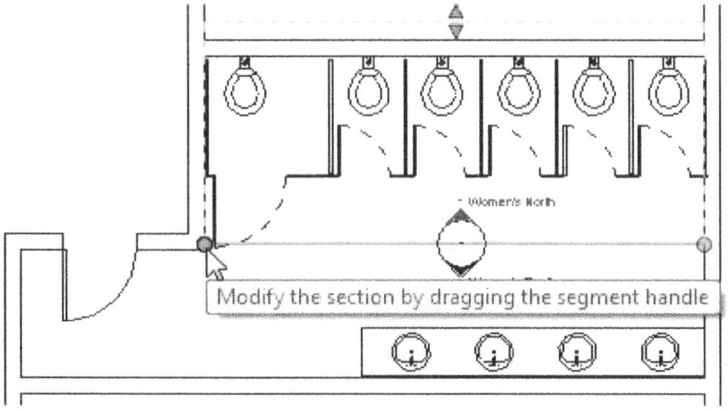

Figure 5–60

Modifying Elevation Markers

When you modify elevation markers, you can specify the length and depth of the clip plane, as shown in Figure 5–61.

- Select the arrowhead of the elevation marker (not the circle portion) to display the clip plane.
- Drag the round shape handles to lengthen or shorten the elevation.
- Drag the  (Arrow) controls to adjust the depth of the elevation.

To display additional interior elevations from one marker, select the circle portion (not the arrowhead) and place a checkmark in the directions that you want to display, as shown in Figure 5–61.

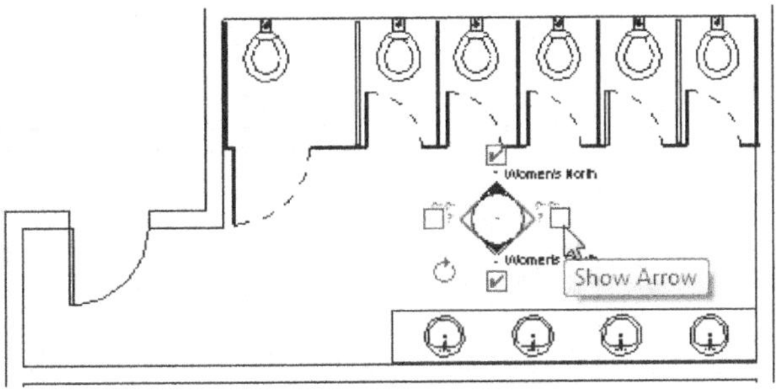

Figure 5–61

- Use the (Rotate) control to angle the marker (i.e., for a room with angled walls).

Modifying Section Markers

When you modify section markers, various shape handles and controls enable you to modify a section, as shown in Figure 5–62.

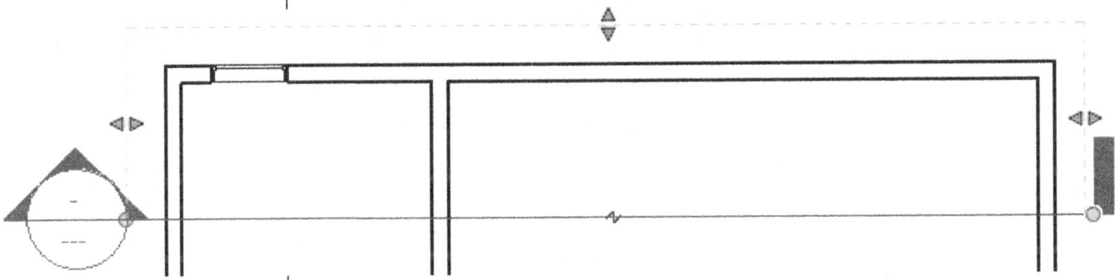

Figure 5–62

- Drag the (Arrow) controls to change the length and depth of the cut plane.
- Drag the circular controls at either end of the section line to change the location of the arrow or flag without changing the cut boundary.
- Click (Flip) to change the direction of the arrowhead, which also flips the entire section.
- Click (Cycle Section Head/Tail) to switch between an arrowhead, flag, or nothing on each end of the section.

- Click (Gaps in Segments) to create an opening in section lines, as shown in Figure 5–63. Select it again to restore the full section cut.

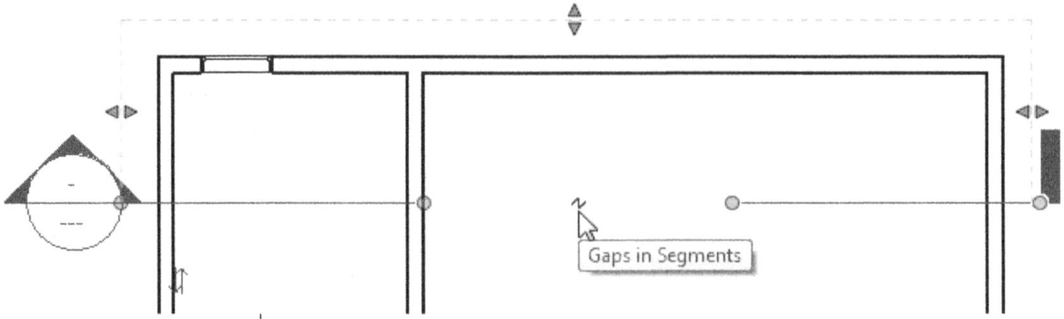

Figure 5–63

How To: Add a Jog to a Section Line

1. Select the section line you want to modify.
2. In the *Modify | Views* tab> Section panel, click (Split Segment).
3. Select the point along the line where you want to create the split, as shown in Figure 5–64.
4. Specify the location of the split line, as shown in Figure 5–65.

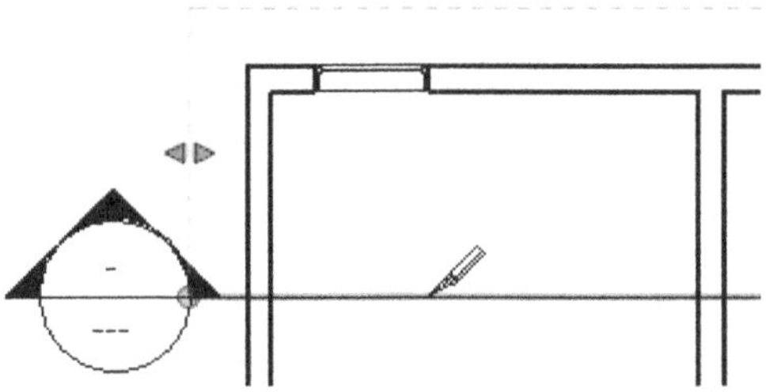

Figure 5–64

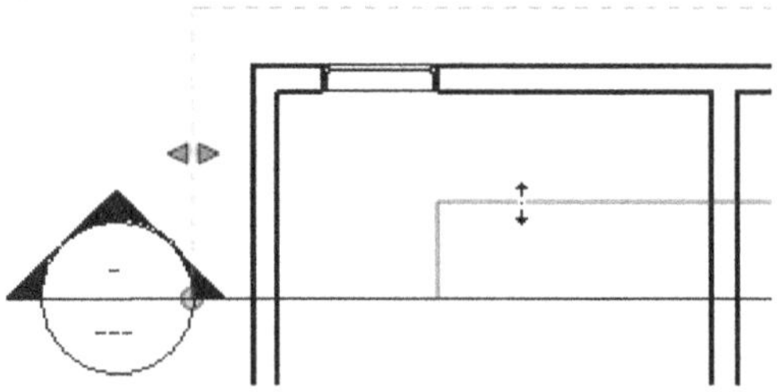

Figure 5–65

- If you need to adjust the location of any segment on the section line, modify it and drag the shape handles along each segment of the line, as shown in Figure 5–66.

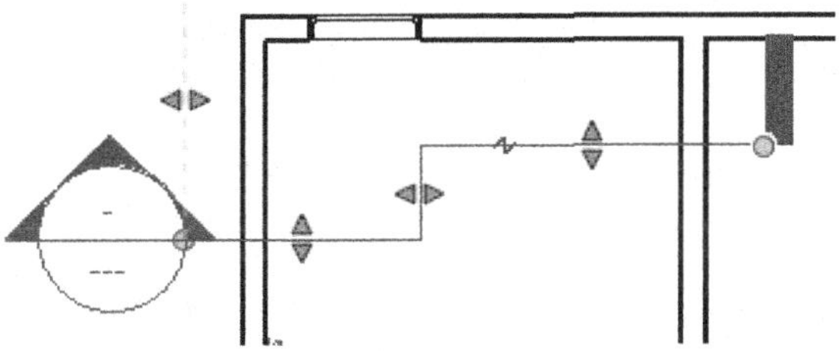

Figure 5–66

To bring a split section line back into place, use a shape handle to drag the jogged line until it is at the same level with the rest of the line.

Hint: Using Thin Lines

The software automatically applies line weights to views, as shown for a section on the left in Figure 5–67. If a line weight seems heavy or obscures your work on the elements, toggle off the line weights. In the Quick Access Toolbar or in the *View* tab>Graphics panel, click (Thin Lines) or type **TL**. The lines display with the same weight, as shown on the right in Figure 5–67.

Thin Lines Off ***Thin Lines On***

Figure 5–67

- The Thin Line setting is remembered until you change it, even if you shut down and restart the software.

Practice 5c Create Elevations and Sections

Practice Objectives

- Create interior elevations.
- Add building sections.

Estimated time for completion: 10 minutes

In this practice you will create interior elevations, as shown for a plumbing view in Figure 5–68. You will also add several building sections. Complete the task specific for your discipline: Mechanical, Electrical, or Plumbing.

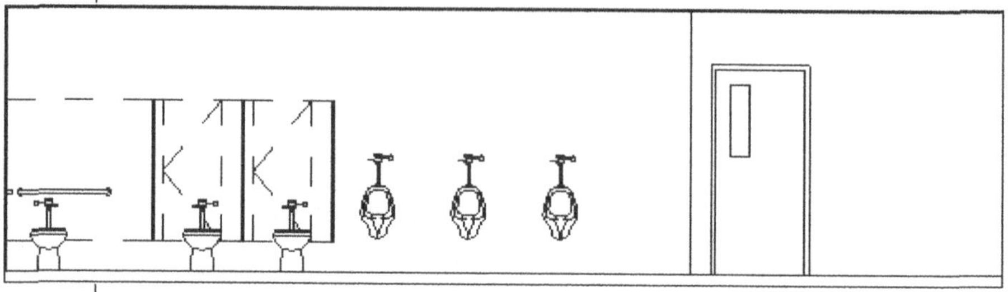

Figure 5–68

Task 1 - Add building sections: Mechanical.

1. In the *Views* practice files folder, open **MEP-Elementary-School-Elevations-M.rvt**.
2. Open the Mechanical>HVAC>FloorPlans> **01 Mechanical Plan** view.
3. In the *View* tab>Create panel, click (Section).
4. In the Type Selector, select **Section: Building Section**.
5. Draw a section through the north wing, as shown in Figure 5–69.

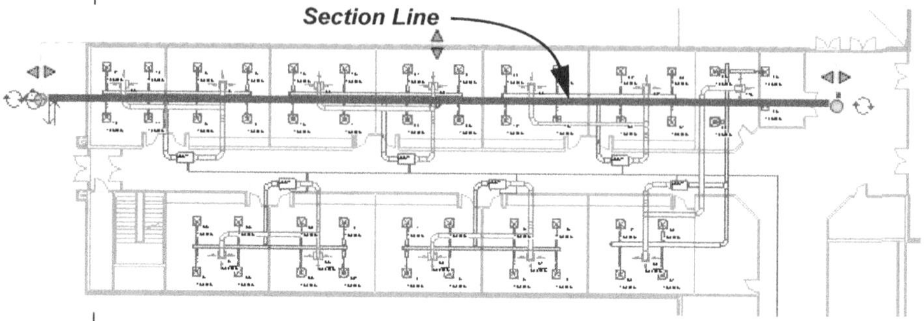

Figure 5–69

6. Press <Esc> and then double-click on the arrow of the section marker to open the section view.
7. Expand the crop region so that the first floor and the full height of the roof is displayed, as shown in Figure 5–70.

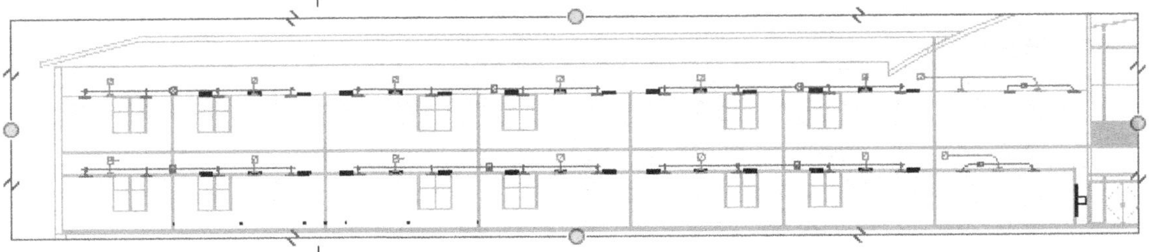

Figure 5–70

8. In the Project Browser, expand Mechanical>???> Sections (Building Section) and rename the new section **North Wing - HVAC**.
9. Right-click on the new section and select **Apply Template Properties**.
10. In the Apply View Template dialog box, select **Mechanical Section** and click **OK**.
11. In the plan view, draw several other sections.
12. In the Project Browser, rename the sections and apply the **Mechanical Section** view template as required.
13. Save the project.

Task 2 - Add interior elevations: Electrical.

1. In the *Views* practice files folder, open **MEP-Elementary-School-Elevations-M.rvt**.
2. Open the Electrical>Power>Floor Plans>**01 Electrical Room** view.
3. Set the *Scale* to **1:50**.
4. In the *View* tab>Create panel, click (Elevation).
5. In the Type Selector, select **Elevation: Interior Elevation**.
6. Place an elevation marker facing the wall of electrical equipment.

7. Click (Modify).

8. Select the circle part of the elevation marker and check the box facing the bottom of the view, as shown in Figure 5–71.

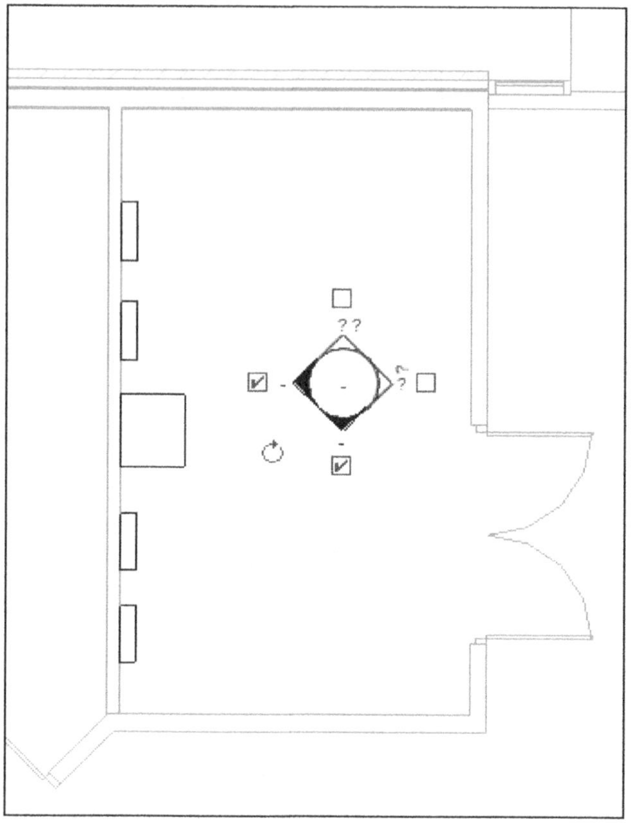

Figure 5–71

9. Press <Esc> to release the selection.

10. Select one of the arrows and zoom out to see the full length and depth of the section.

Note that the elevation does not automatically reflect the size of the room because it cannot read the location of the walls in the linked model.

11. Drag the ends back to the electrical room and modify the depth as required, as shown in Figure 5–72.

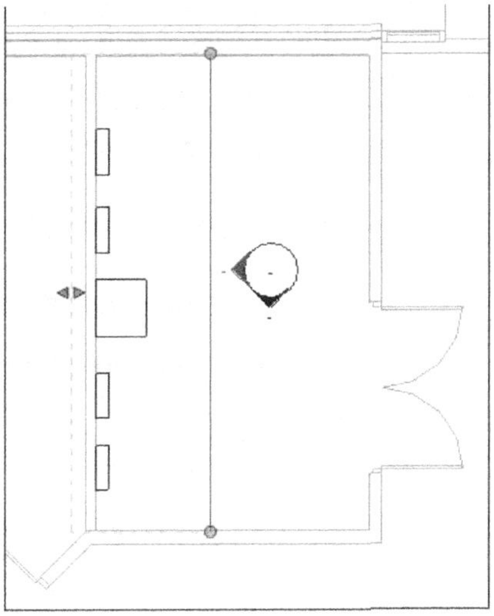

Figure 5–72

12. Repeat with the other direction.

13. In the Project Browser apply the **Electrical Section** view template to the elevation views.

14. Rename the elevation view as **Electrical Room - South Elevation** and **Electrical Room - West Elevation**, as shown in Figure 5–73.

15. Open the section views and adjust the crop regions, as shown in Figure 5–73.

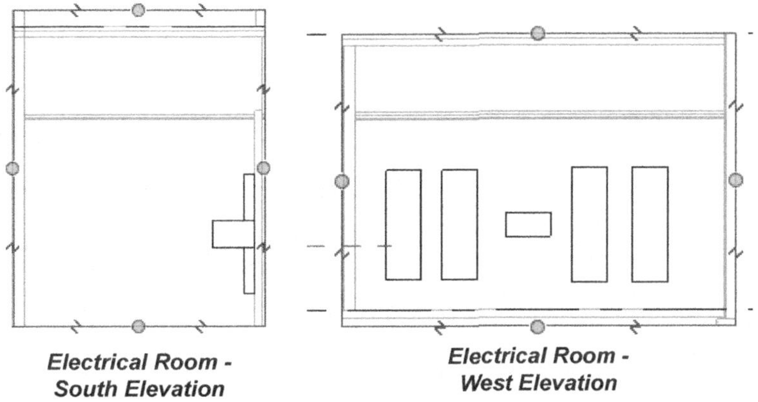

Figure 5–73

16. Save the project.

Task 3 - Add interior elevations: Plumbing.

1. In the practice files *Views* folder, open **MEP-Elementary-School-Elevations-M.rvt**.
2. Open the Plumbing>Plumbing>Floor Plans>**01 Plumbing Plan** view.
3. Zoom in on the restrooms near the gym.
4. In the *View* tab>Create panel, click (Elevation).
5. In the Type Selector, select **Elevation: Interior Elevation**.
6. Place an elevation facing the wall of sinks in one of the restrooms.
7. Click (Modify).
8. Select the circle part of the elevation marker and check the box on the opposite side, as shown in Figure 5–74.

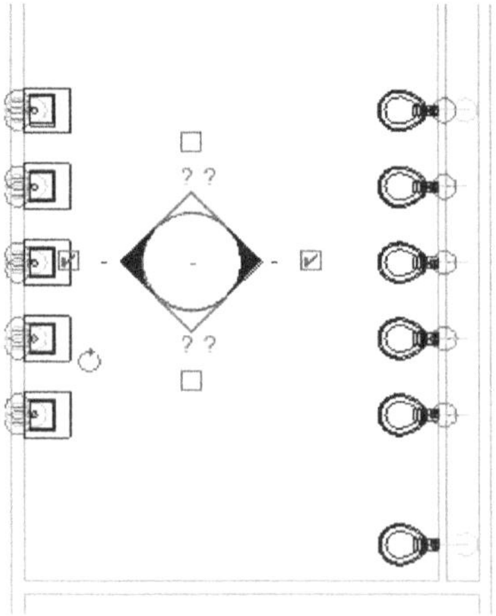

Figure 5–74

9. Press <Esc> to release the selection.
10. Select one of the arrows and zoom out to see the full length and depth of the section.

The elevation does not reflect the size of the room automatically because it cannot read the location of the walls in the linked model.

11. Drag the ends back to the restroom and modify the depth as required as shown in Figure 5–75.

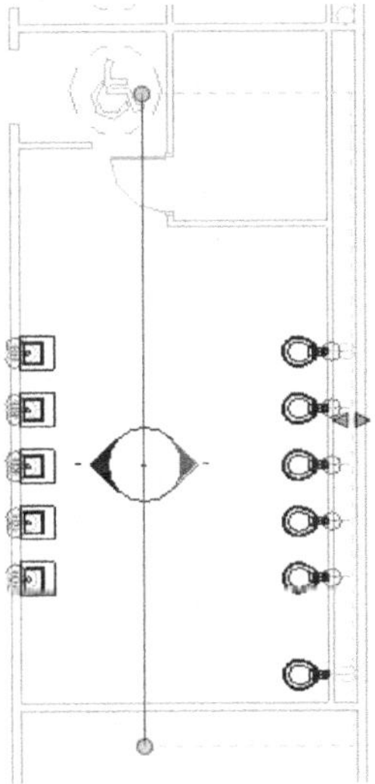

Figure 5–75

12. Repeat with the other direction.

Task 4 - Modify elevation views: Plumbing.

1. Double-click on the arrow pointing toward the water closets to open the corresponding view. The elevation cannot find the ceiling of the linked model so it selects the extents of the building model, as shown in Figure 5–76.

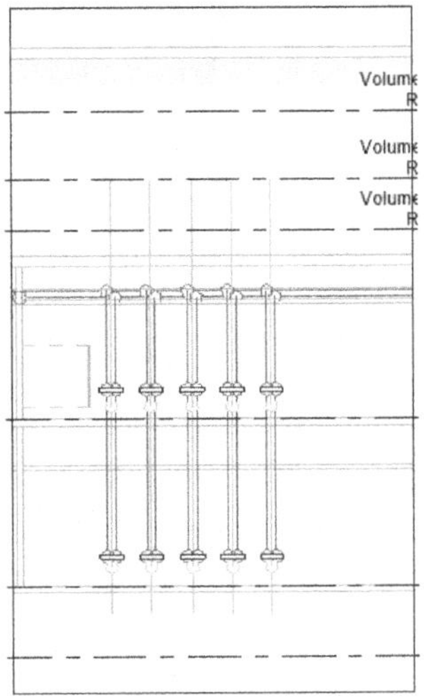

Figure 5–76

2. Select the crop region and resize the view so that only the lower floor restroom is displayed.

3. Return to plan view and open the arrow in the other direction. Repeat the process of resizing the crop region as shown in Figure 5–77.

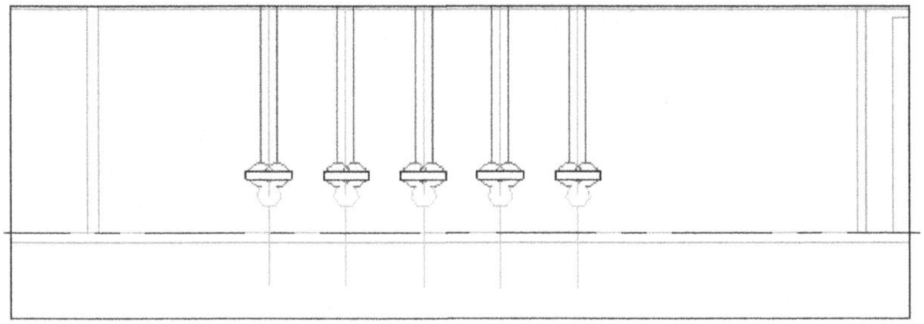

Figure 5–77

4. Return to plan view.

5. Select the entire elevation marker (the circle and both arrows).

6. Hold <Ctrl> and drag a copy of the marker up to the other restroom.

7. Open each of the new elevation views and modify the crop regions as required. The example in Figure 5–78 was lengthened to display the full sanitary line.

By setting up one elevation and then copying it to a location, you can save some steps.

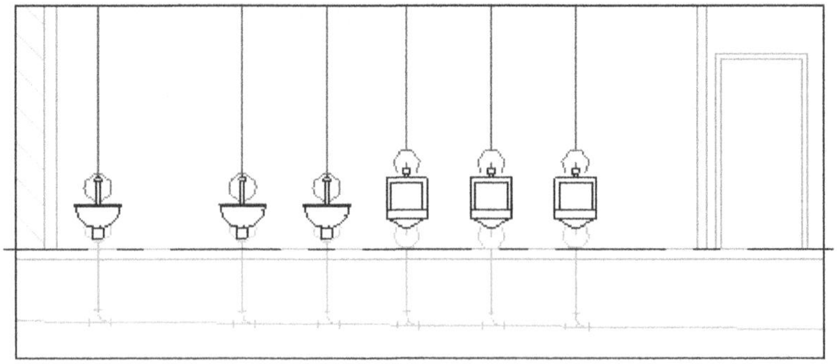

Figure 5–78

8. In the Project Browser expand Plumbing>???>**Elevations (Interior Elevation)**. Note that the four new elevations have generic names and are in an unknown sub-category, as shown in Figure 5–79.

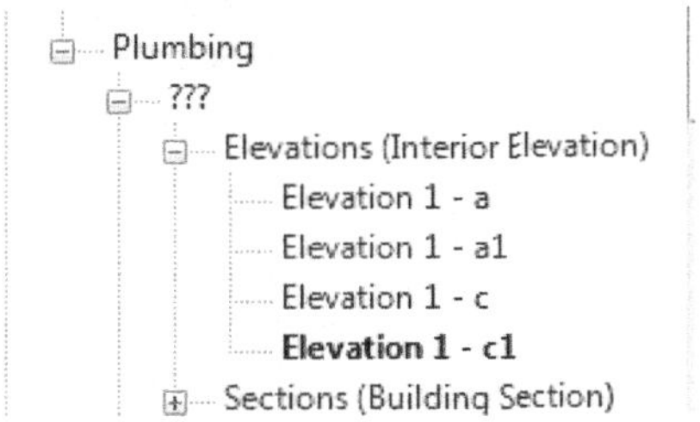

Figure 5–79

9. Right-click on the open elevation and give it a new title. For example, the elevation in Figure 5–78 would be **01 Men's East Elevation**.

10. Once you have finished renaming each of the elevations, hold <Ctrl> and select each of the new elevations.

11. In Properties, change the *Sub-Discipline* to **Plumbing**.

12. In the Project Browser, note that the elevations are now in the Plumbing sub-category, as shown in Figure 5–80.

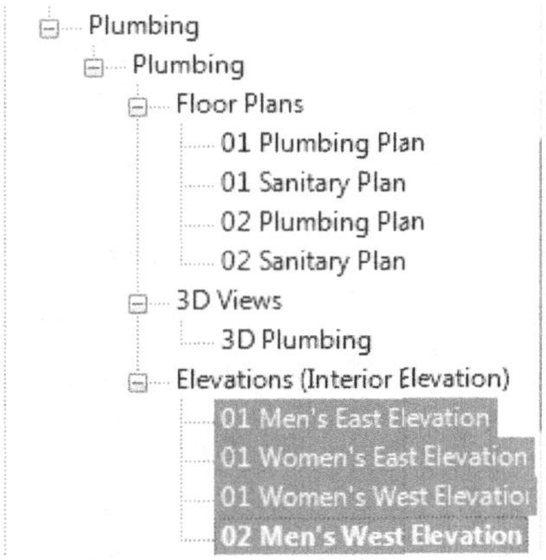

Figure 5–80

13. Save the project.

Chapter Review Questions

1. Which of the following commands shown in Figure 5–81, creates a view that results in an independent view displaying the same model geometry and containing a copy of the annotation?

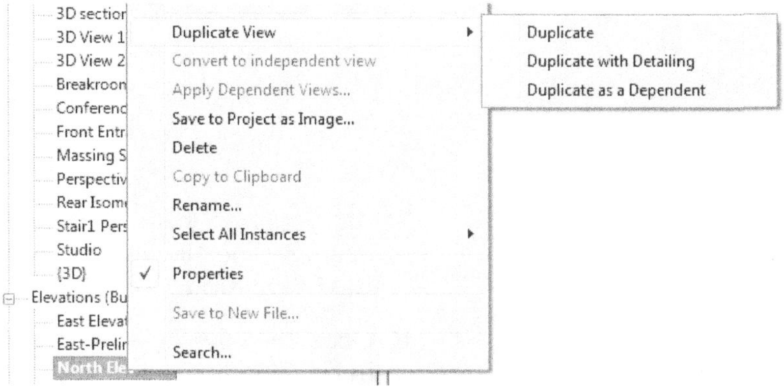

Figure 5–81

   a. Duplicate
   b. Duplicate with Detailing
   c. Duplicate as a Dependent

2. Which of the following is true about the Visibility Graphic Overrides dialog box?
   a. Changes made in the dialog box only affect the current view.
   b. It can only be used to toggle categories on and off.
   c. It can be used to toggle individual elements on and off.
   d. It can be used to change the color of individual elements.

3. The purpose of callouts is to create a...
   a. Boundary around part of the model that needs revising, similar to a revision cloud.
   b. View of part of the model for export to the AutoCAD® software for further detailing.
   c. View of part of the model that is linked to the main view from which it is taken.
   d. 2D view of part of the model.

4. You placed dimensions in a view and some of them display and others do not (as shown on the left in Figure 5–82) but you were expecting the view to display as shown on the right in Figure 5–82. To display the missing dimensions you need to modify the...

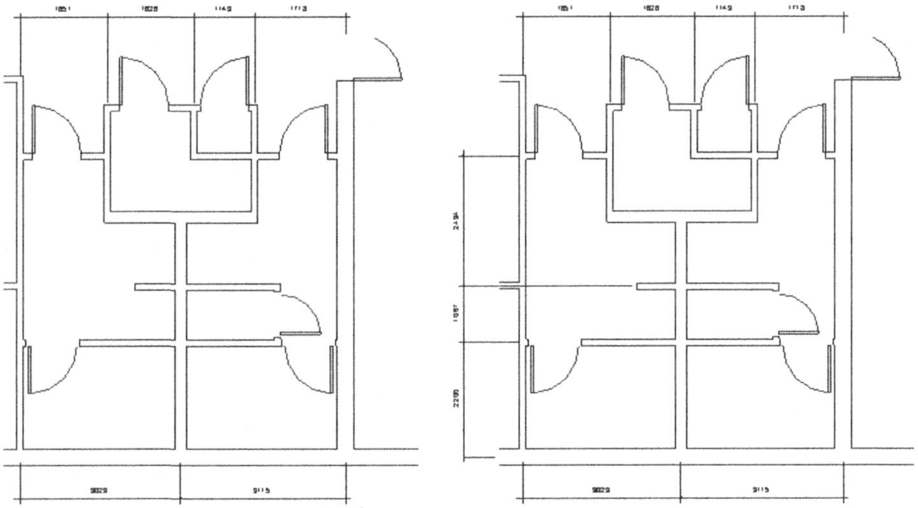

Figure 5–82

   a. Dimension Settings
   b. Dimension Type
   c. Visibility Graphic Overrides
   d. Annotation Crop Region

5. How do you create multiple interior elevations in one room?
   a. Using the **Interior Elevation** command, place the elevation marker.
   b. Using the **Elevation** command, place the first marker, select it and select the appropriate Show Arrow boxes.
   c. Using the **Interior Elevation** command, place an elevation marker for each wall of the room you want to display.
   d. Using the **Elevation** command, select a Multiple Elevation marker type, and place the elevation marker.

6. How do you create a jog in a building section, such as that shown in Figure 5–83?

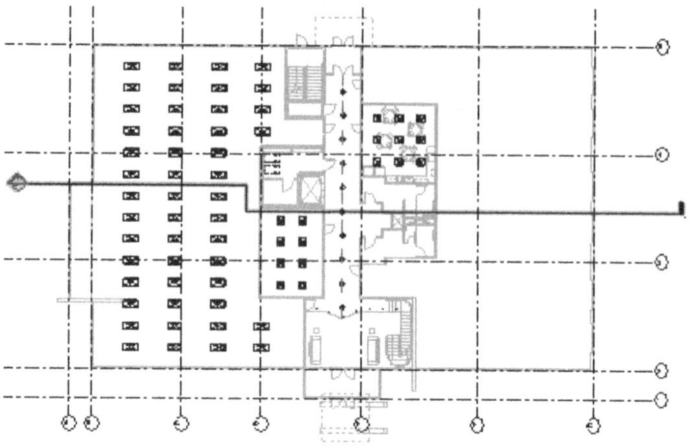

Figure 5–83

   a. Use the **Split Element** tool in the *Modify* tab>Modify panel.

   b. Select the building section and then click **Split Segment** in the contextual tab.

   c. Select the building section and click the blue control in the middle of the section line.

   d. Draw two separate sections, and use the **Section Jog** tool to combine them into a jogged section.

Command Summary

Button	Command	Location
Views		
	**Elevation**	• **Ribbon:** *View* tab>Create panel> expand Elevation
	**Callout: Rectangle**	• **Ribbon:** *View* tab>Create panel> expand Callout
	**Callout: Sketch**	• **Ribbon:** *View* tab>Create panel> expand Callout
	**Duplicate**	• **Ribbon:** *View* tab>Create panel> expand Duplicate View • **Right-click:** (*on a view in the Project Browser*) expand Duplicate View
	**Duplicate as Dependent**	• **Ribbon:** *View* tab>Create panel> expand Duplicate View • **Right-click:** (*on a view in the Project Browser*) expand Duplicate View
	**Duplicate with Detailing**	• **Ribbon:** *View* tab>Create panel> expand Duplicate View • **Right-click:** (*on a view in the Project Browser*) Duplicate View
	**Plan Region**	• **Ribbon:** *View* tab>Create panel> expand Plan Views
	**Section**	• **Ribbon:** *View* tab>Create panel • **Quick Access Toolbar**
	**Split Segment**	• **Ribbon:** (*when the elevation or section marker is selected*) *Modify | Views* tab>Section panel
Crop Views		
	**Crop View**	• **View Control Bar** • **View Properties:** Crop View (*check*)
	**Do Not Crop View**	• **View Control Bar** • **View Properties:** Crop View (*clear*)
	**Edit Crop**	• **Ribbon:** (*when the crop region of a callout, elevation, or section view is selected*) *Modify | Views* tab>Mode panel
	**Hide Crop Region**	• **View Control Bar** • **View Properties:** Crop Region Visible (*clear*)
	**Reset Crop**	• **Ribbon:** (*when the crop region of a callout, elevation or section view is selected*) *Modify | Views* tab>Mode panel

	Show Crop Region	• **View Control Bar** • **View Properties:** Crop Region Visible (*check*)
	Size Crop	• **Ribbon:** (*when the crop region of a callout, elevation or section view is selected*) *Modify* | *Views* tab>Mode panel
View Display		
	Hide in View	• **Ribbon:** *Modify* tab>View Graphics panel>Hide>Elements *or* By Category • **Right-click:** *(when an element is selected)* Hide in View>Elements *or* Category
	Override Graphics in View	• **Ribbon:** *Modify* tab>View Graphics panel>Hide>Elements *or* By Category • **Right-click:** *(when an element is selected)* Override Graphics in View>By Element *or* By Category • **Shortcut:** *(category only)* VV or VG
	Reveal Hidden Elements	• **View Control Bar**
	Temporary Hide/Isolate	• **View Control Bar**
	Temporary View Properties	• **View Control Bar**

Chapter 6

Setting Up Spaces

Spaces are used with most MEP disciplines to identify rooms and room numbers from the linked architectural model, however they also include information about the 3D surroundings. Spaces are critical as the basis for analyzing heating and cooling loads and calculating light levels.

Learning Objectives in this Chapter

- Prepare a model so that you can add spaces.
- Create spaces individually or automatically.
- Add space separation lines to further divide spaces.
- Select spaces and modify them graphically and in Properties.
- Set up spaces for specific situations, including shafts, sliver spaces, cavities, and plenums.

6.1 Preparing a Model for Spaces

The Space element is a critical component in the process of establishing heating and cooling loads. Spaces are also used to calculate the light levels based on the number and types of lighting fixtures in a room. Spaces identify each room in a building providing area, perimeter, and volume information about each space, and information used in Electrical, Mechanical, and Energy Analysis, as shown in Properties in Figure 6–1.

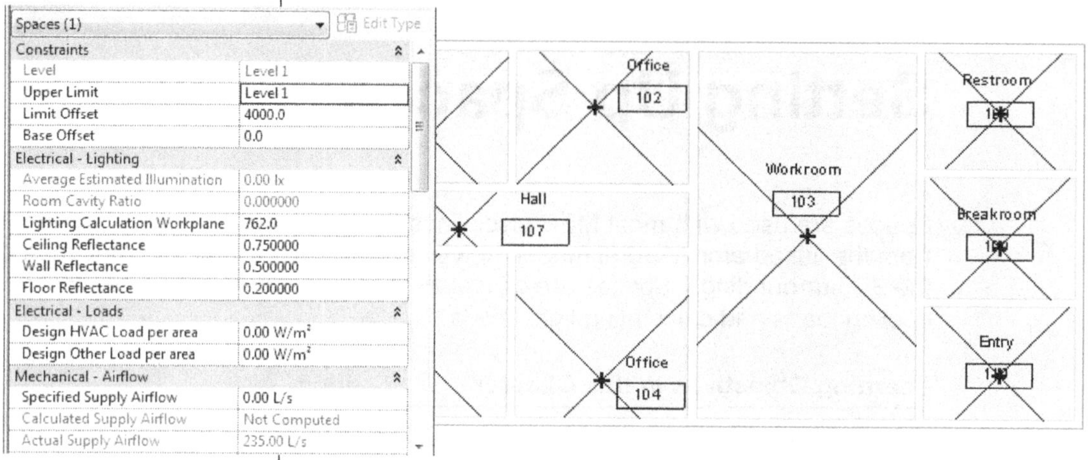

Figure 6–1

- Spaces are similar to rooms created in Autodesk® Revit® architectural models. However, they contain more information for heating and cooling loads analysis and electrical lighting analysis.
- In MEP projects, you need to add spaces not only to occupiable rooms but to shafts, chases, plenums, and other enclosed areas that would not normally be assigned a room by the architect.

Before adding spaces to a project, you must:

- Set up the room bounding status of linked models so that the spaces identify elements such as walls and ceilings.
- Turn on the area and volume computations so that the spaces will read the volume of the room correctly.
- Create views that display the spaces to make the process of adding and modifying spaces easier.

How To: Set a Linked Model to Room Bounding

1. Select the linked model.
2. In Properties, click (Edit Type).
3. In the Type Properties dialog box, select the value for **Room Bounding**, as shown in Figure 6–2. Click **OK**.

Room bounding elements, whether in a linked model or the host project include: walls, roofs, floors, ceilings, columns, curtain systems, and room or space separation lines.

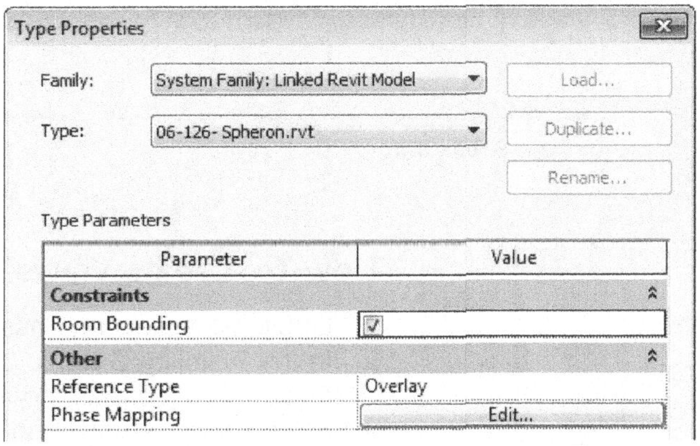

Figure 6–2

How To: Set Area and Volume Computations

1. In the *Analyze* tab>Spaces & Zones panel, expand the panel title and click (Area and Volume Computations).
2. In the Area and Volume Computations dialog box, select **Area and Volumes** and **At wall finish**, as shown in Figure 6–3.

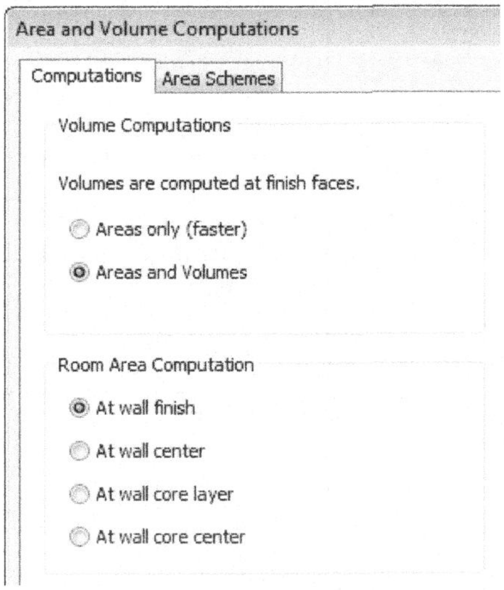

Figure 6–3

3. Click **OK**. As you add spaces, they fill the volume bounding area appropriately, as shown in Figure 6–4.

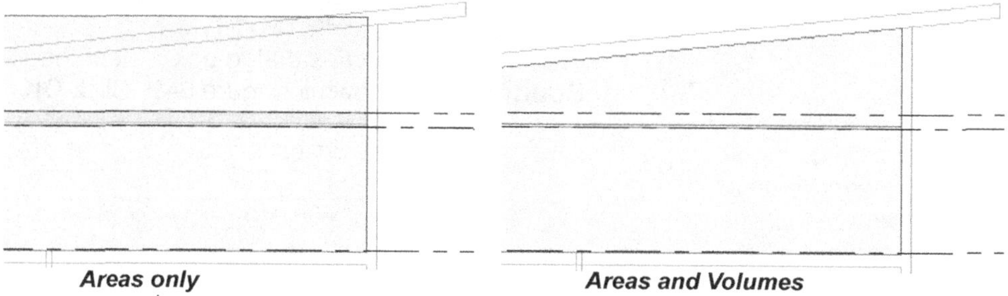

Areas only *Areas and Volumes*

Figure 6–4

How To: Create Views for Spaces

1. Duplicate a view and assign it to the *Coordination* discipline.
2. In the Visibility/Graphic Overrides dialog box, in the *Model Categories* tab, expand *Spaces* and select **Interior** and/or **Reference**, as shown in Figure 6–5 and Figure 6–6.

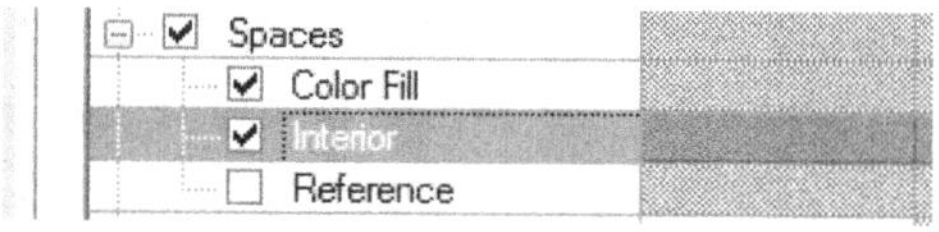

Figure 6–5

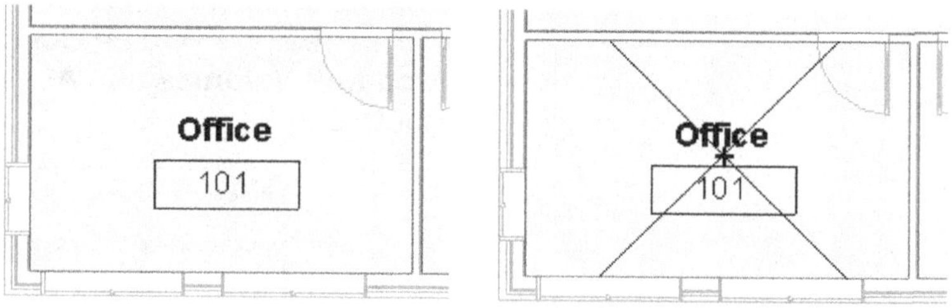

Interior Fill *Interior Fill and Reference Line*

Figure 6–6

3. Toggle off any other categories that are not required in the view.

6.2 Adding Spaces

Once you have set up views for the spaces, you can start applying them to the model, as shown in Figure 6–7. You can do this quickly by automatically filling each space, and then applying space names from a linked architectural model. You can also add spaces individually and divide them using Space Separators.

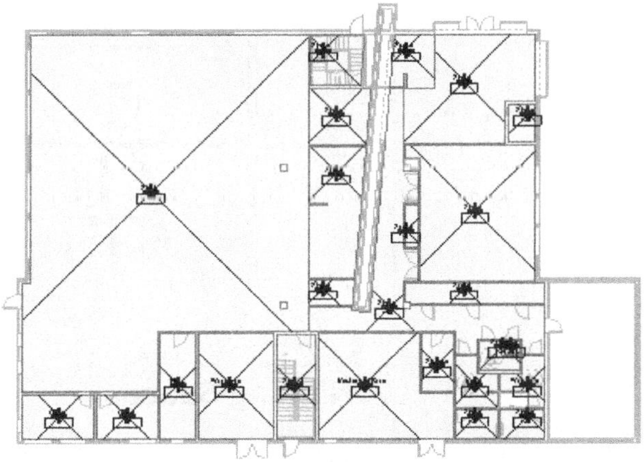

Figure 6–7

How To: Place Spaces Automatically

1. In the *Analyze* tab>Spaces & Zones panel, click (Space).
2. If you want to include a tag as you place the space, in the *Modify | Place Space* tab>Tag panel, click (Tag on Placement).
3. In the Options Bar, you can set the *Orientation* of the tag and the *Leader*, if required.
4. In the Options Bar, set the *Upper Limit* and *Offset* (which controls the volume calculations), and set the height of the space, as shown in Figure 6–8.

Figure 6–8

- If you want elements (such as ceilings) to control the height of the space, set the *Upper Limit* to the level above and the *Offset* to **0**.

5. In the *Modify | Place Space* tab>Spaces panel, click (Place Spaces Automatically).

6. An alert box opens, prompting you about the number of spaces that were created. Click **Close**.
7. Spaces are added in each bounded area and a tag is placed if that option is selected in the ribbon.

- To help you understand the volume of the spaces as you create them, it helps to have a section view open, as shown in Figure 6–9.

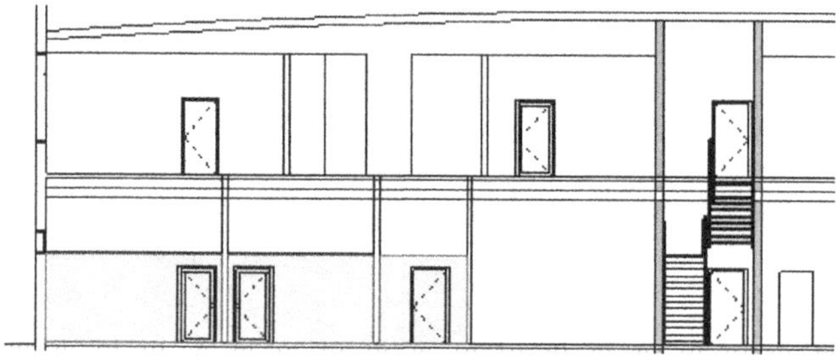

Figure 6–9

Naming Spaces

New in 2018

Spaces are named and numbered as they are placed, but they are probably not the names or numbers that are most useful to you. Typically, you want the spaces to relate to the room names and numbers that were used in the architectural model. If a linked architectural model includes rooms, the associated *Room Name* and *Number* are displayed in the space's Properties (as shown in Figure 6–10), and can be set to match using the **Space Naming** command, which automatically updates space names based on the corresponding architectural model's room name.

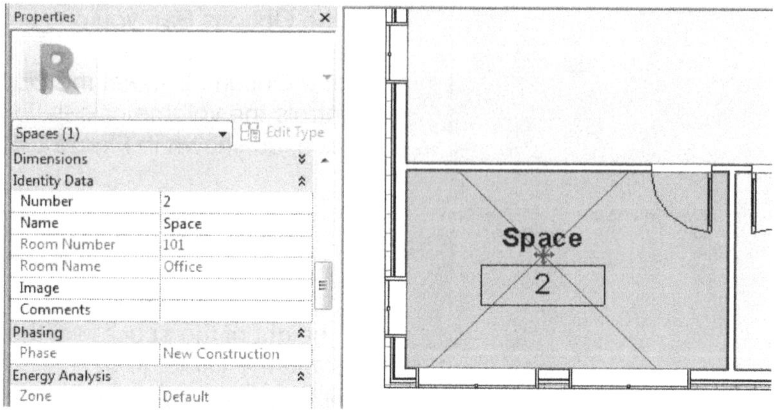

Figure 6–10

How To: Run the Space Naming Command

1. Add spaces to the model.
2. In the *Analyze* tab>Spaces & Zones panel, click (Space Naming).
3. In the Space Naming dialog box (shown in Figure 6–11), select the Options and Selection for the spaces you want named and then click **OK**.

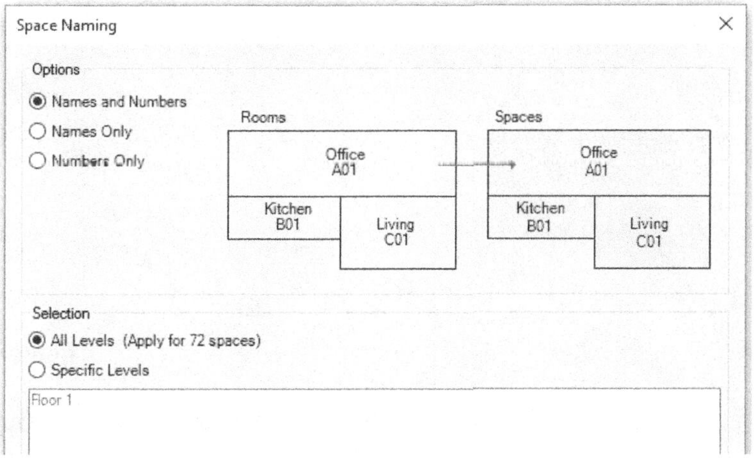

Figure 6–11

- Some spaces (such as plenums, cavities, and chases) are specific to MEP projects and are not named in the linked architectural model. Select the space(s) and change the name and number in Properties, or select the tag name or number to modify it, as shown in Figure 6–12.

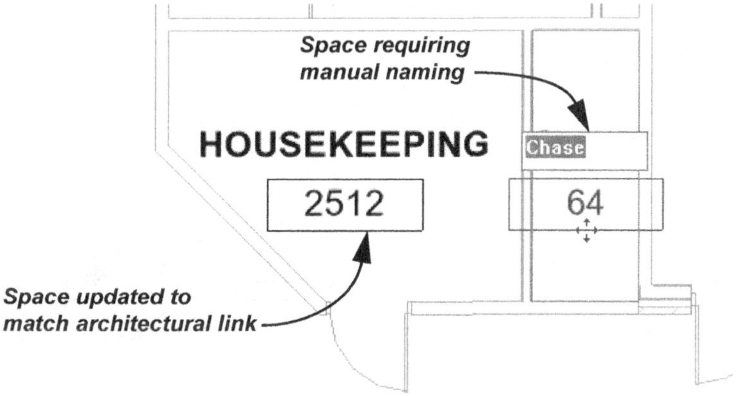

Figure 6–12

- If room names and numbers are changed in the linked architectural model, run the Space Naming tool again to update them.

Creating Individual Spaces

While most of the spaces you need can be created using the **Place Spaces Automatically** tool, you can also add individual spaces by selecting boundaries and by using Space Separators to sub-divide spaces. For example, in a lobby, there might be an area open to above that does not have a wall that defines the change in space height. Draw a space separation boundary as shown in Figure 6–13.

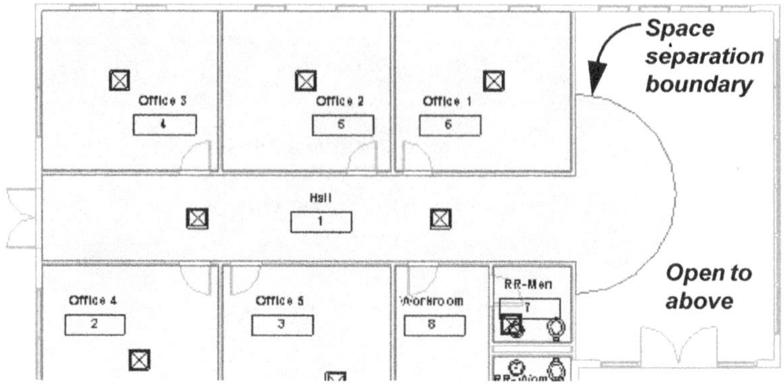

Figure 6–13

How To: Create Spaces by Selecting Boundaries

1. In the *Analyze* tab>Spaces & Zones panel, click (Space).
2. Specify tagging and other options.
3. Move the cursor into a boundary area and click to place the space. Continue adding spaces, as shown in Figure 6–14.

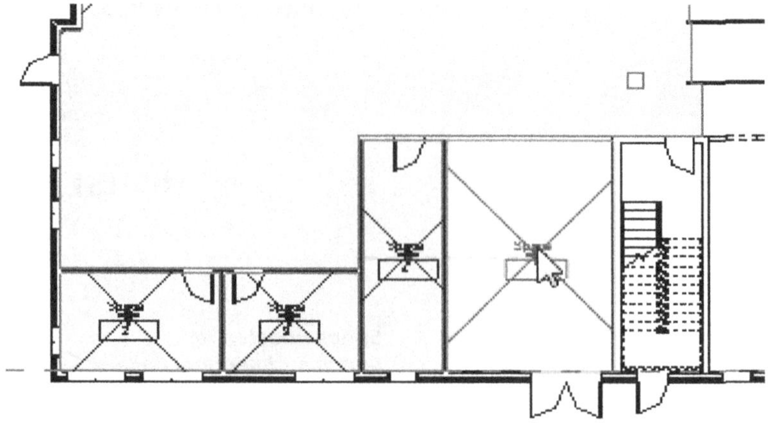

Figure 6–14

How To: Create Space Separation Boundaries

1. In the *Analyze* tab>Spaces & Zones panel, click (Space Separator).
2. In the *Modify | Place Space Separation* tab>Draw panel, use the sketch tools to draw the edges of the boundary.
3. Use (Space) to add spaces in the areas bounded by the separation lines.

- You can edit space separation lines by splitting, trimming, etc.

Space Properties

You can modify the properties of a space by selecting it and using Properties, as shown in Figure 6–15, including:

- **Constraints:** Includes *Upper Limit* and *Limit Offset*, which displays the height of the space.
- **Electrical - Lighting**
- **Electrical - Loads**
- **Mechanical - Flow**
- **Energy Analysis**
- **Identity Data:** Includes the *Space Name* and *Space Number*.

This information is critical to setup before doing Heating and Cooling Loads and Lighting analysis.

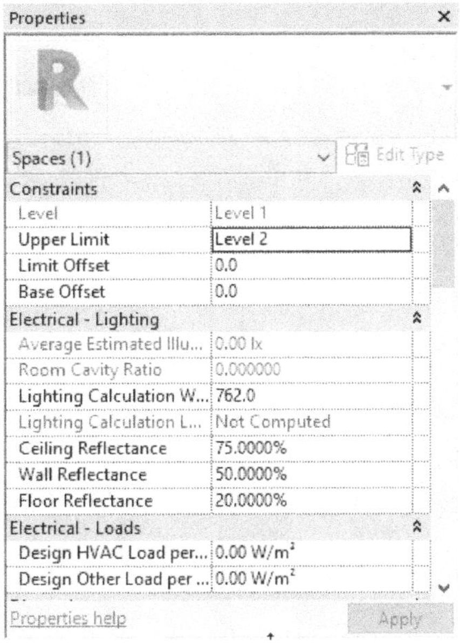

Figure 6–15

- To select a space, hover the cursor over it until you see the crossing line, as shown in Figure 6–16. Click on the reference point to select the space.

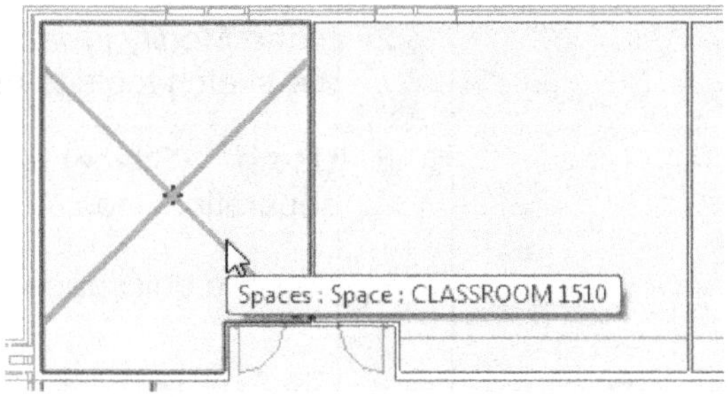

Figure 6–16

Practice 6a Add Spaces

Estimated time for completion: 10 minutes

Practice Objectives

- Set up the model to add spaces.
- Rename spaces to match rooms in a linked architectural model.
- Add spaces and space separator lines.

In this practice you will set up a project by setting the linked model to Room Bounding, setting the area and volume computations, and creating a view where you can add spaces. You will also create a view template of that view to be used in similar views. You will then automatically add spaces and rename them to match the linked architectural model, as shown in Figure 6–17.

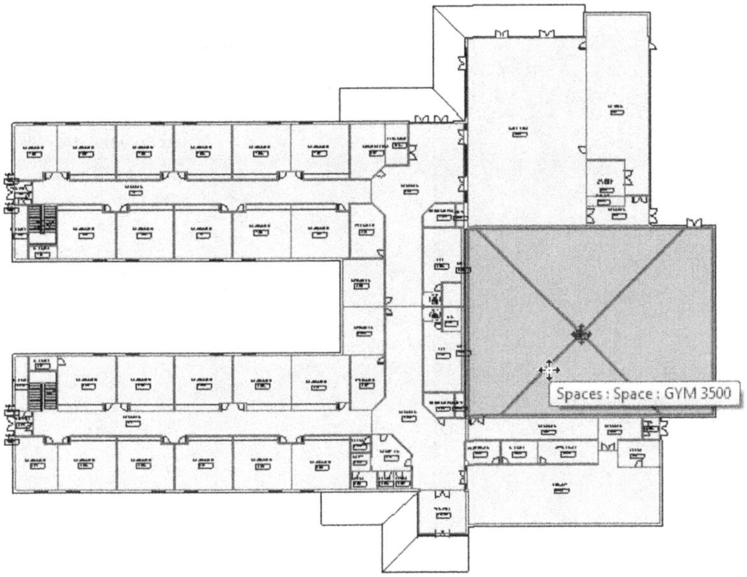

Figure 6–17

Task 1 - Set up a view in which you will define spaces.

1. In the practice files *Spaces* folder, open **MEP-Elementary-School-Spaces-M.rvt**.
2. Select the linked model.
3. In Properties, click (Edit Type).

4. In the Type Properties dialog box, select **Room Bounding** and click **OK**.
5. In the *Analyze* tab, expand the Spaces & Zones panel and click (Area and Volume Computations).
6. In the Area and Volume Computations dialog box, select **Areas and Volumes** and click **OK**.
7. In the Project Browser, expand Coordination>All>Floor Plans. Select the **Floor 1** view, right-click and select **Duplicate View>Duplicate**.
8. Rename the new view as **01 Space Plan**.
9. In Properties, change the *Sub-Discipline* to **MEP**.
   - Note that you want the *Discipline* to remain **Coordination** but *Sub-Discipline* to be **MEP** (rather than **All**), as spaces are used in multiple disciplines.
10. The new view moves to the MEP node as shown in Figure 6–18.

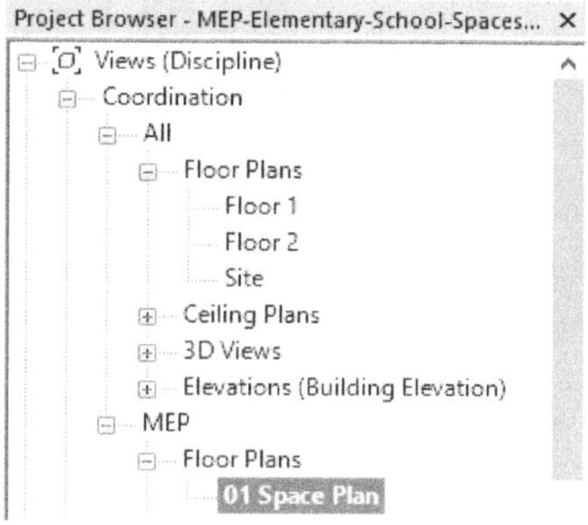

Figure 6–18

11. No spaces display in this view. Type **VG** to open the Visibility/Graphics dialog box.
12. In the *Model Categories* tab, scroll down and select **Spaces**. Expand the **Spaces** node, select **Interior** and click **OK**. Note that no spaces are placed yet.
13. In the Project Browser, right-click on the **01 Space Plan** view and select **Create View Template from View...**

14. In the New View Template dialog box, type **Space Plan** and click **OK**.
15. In the View Templates dialog box, beside the **View Scale** parameter, clear the checkmark from the *Include* column and click **OK**. Note that when you apply this view template, it does not change the scale of the view.
16. Duplicate the Coordination>All>Floor Plans> **Floor 2** view and rename it **02 Space Plan**.
17. Right-click on the new **02 Space Plan** view and select **Apply Template Properties**.
18. In the Apply View Template dialog box, select **Space Plan** and click **OK**. The view moves to the MEP *Sub-Discipline* and the view is ready to have spaces applied.
19. Save the project.

Task 2 - Add spaces.

1. Open the **01 Space Plan** view.
2. In the *Analyze* tab>Spaces & Zones panel, click (Space).
3. In the Options Bar, set the *Upper Limit* to **Floor 2** and the *Offset* to **0.**
4. In the *Modify* | *Place Space* tab>Tag panel, verify that (Tag on Placement) is selected.
5. In the Spaces panel, click (Place Spaces Automatically). The spaces are created as shown in Figure 6–19. Click **Close**.

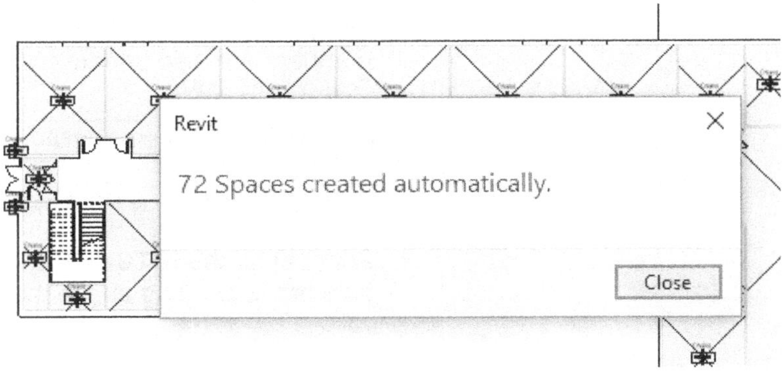

Figure 6–19

6. Zoom in to see the names of the spaces. Note that they are all named the same with numbers starting in the 1000's.

7. Open the **02 Space Plan** view and place spaces on the second floor with an *Upper Limit* of **Floor 2** and *an Offset* of **4000mm**.

8. Return to the **01 Space Plan** view.

9. In the *Analyze* tab>Spaces & Zones panel, click (Space Naming).

10. In the Space Naming dialog box, accept the default settings for **Names and Numbers** and **All Levels** and click **OK**. Most of the spaces are updated as shown in Figure 6–20.

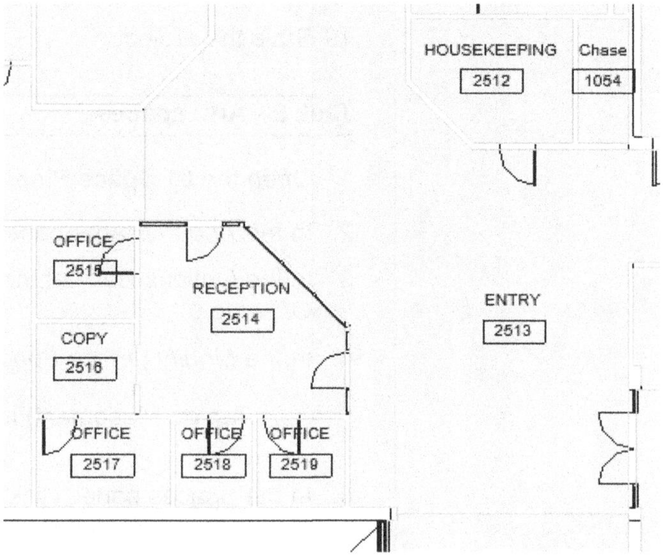

Figure 6–20

11. Open the **02 Space Plan** view. Most of the space names and numbers are also updated.

Task 3 - Add a space separation line and new space.

1. Open the **01 Space Plan** view.

2. Zoom in on the **KITCHEN STORAGE** space in the top right side of the building above the gym.

3. In the *Analyze* tab>Spaces & Zones panel, click (Space Separator).

4. Draw a line across part of the storage area, as shown in Figure 6–21. Press <Esc> twice to end the command.

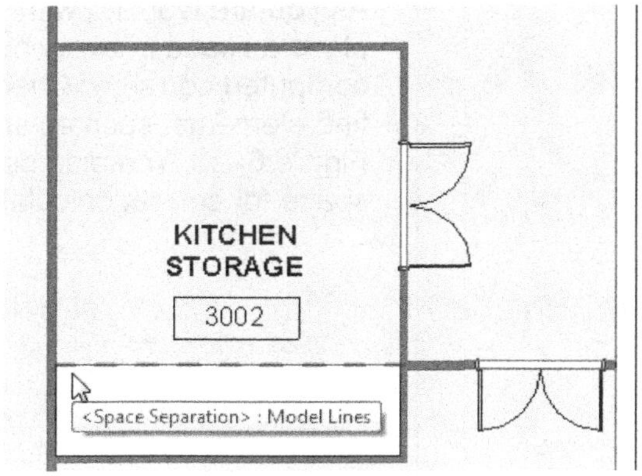

Figure 6–21

5. In the *Analyze* tab>Spaces & Zones panel, click  (Space) and click inside the empty area.

6. Click **Modify** and select the space tag. Double-click on the name and rename it **PANTRY**. Double-click on the number and enter **3003**, as shown in Figure 6–22.

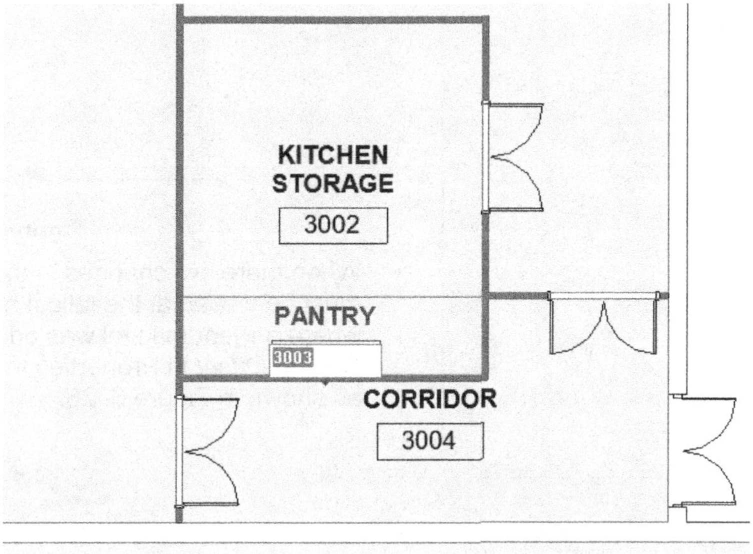

Figure 6–22

7. Zoom out to fit the view.

8. Save the project.

6.3 Working with Spaces

As you are working with spaces in a project, it is important to place a space in every open area so that the energy analysis is computed correctly. Check the project in plan and in section to find elements, such as shafts and plenum spaces as shown in Figure 6–23. You also need to set up the properties of each space for correct calculation.

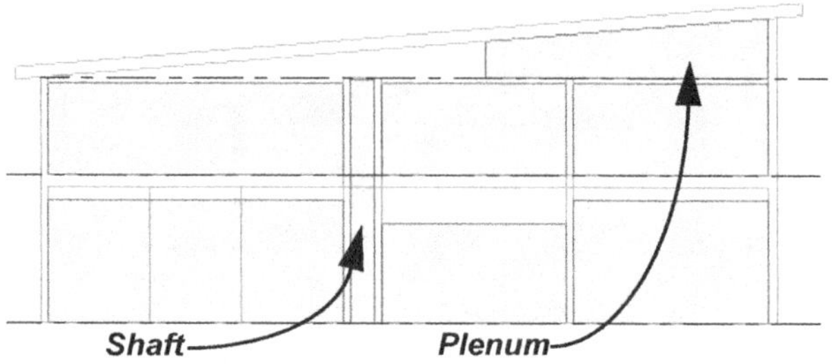

Figure 6–23

- You can change the height of a space in properties or visually in a section using controls and temporary dimensions, as shown in Figure 6–24.

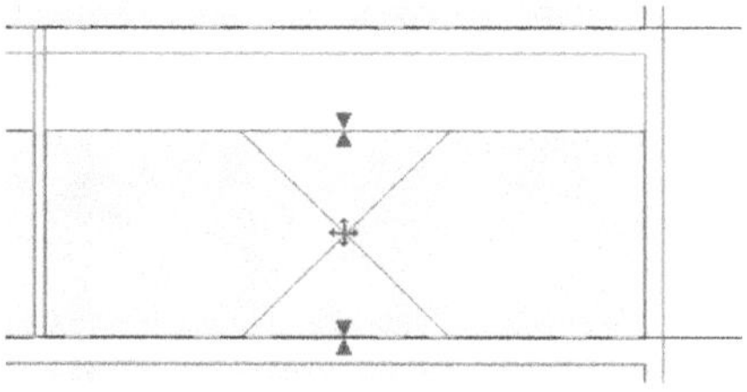

Figure 6–24

- When there are changes in the height of an area, the space must be placed at the tallest height as shown in Figure 6–25, where a Plenum level was added. You can then change the *Bottom Offset* in Properties to have the space extend down, as shown in Figure 6–26.

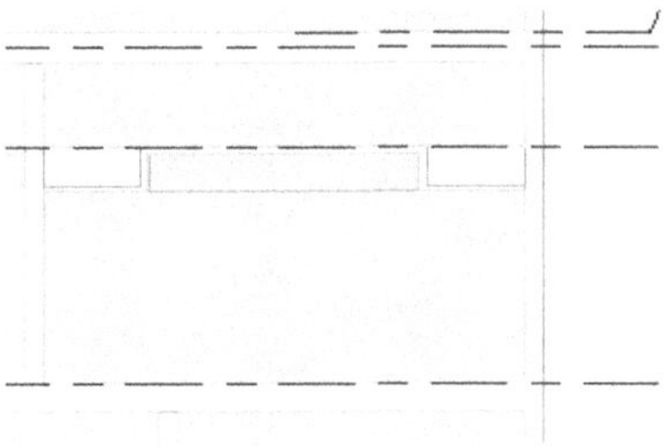

Figure 6–25

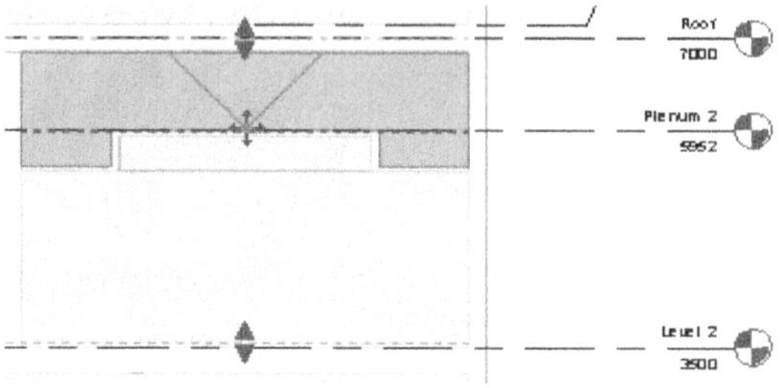

Figure 6–26

Special Space Situations

There are several situations in which you need to make modifications to spaces or the surrounding bounding areas to have them read correctly when analysis is done. These include shafts, sliver spaces, cavities, and plenum spaces.

Shafts and Interior/Exterior Bounding Elements

It is critical to place a space in every area in a building before you try to analyze the heating and cooling load because any wall that is not bounded by another space is considered an exterior wall. In the example shown in Figure 6–27, there are several spaces that have not been added, including a shaft, an elevator shaft, and a room. The open spaces are considered exterior rather than interior spaces.

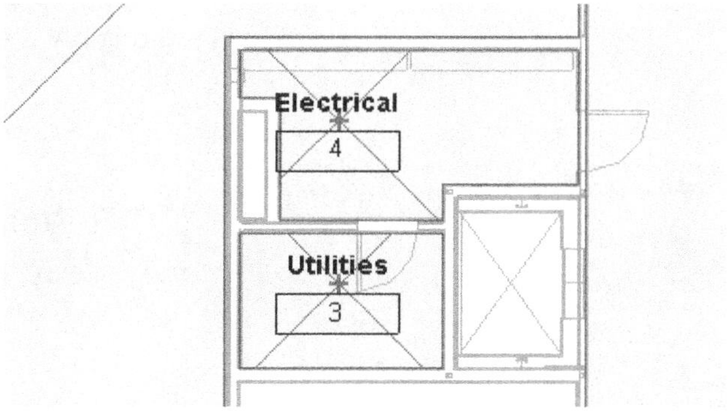

Figure 6–27

- Wall type functions can be specified in the Type Parameters as shown in Figure 6–28. **Interior** and **Core-shaft** *Function* types are considered interior whether they have a space on the other side of the wall or not.

When space boundary objects are contained in linked projects it might be required to coordinate these settings with the project Architect or Structural Engineer.

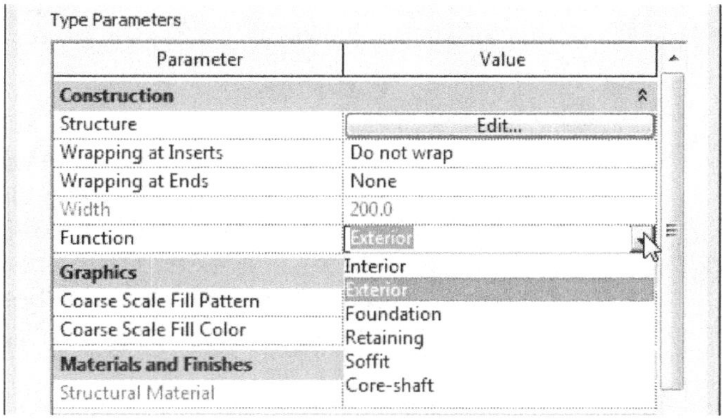

Figure 6–28

- Floor types can also have a *Function* of **Interior** or **Exterior**.

Sliver Spaces

This is useful when the boundary objects have not been set to define core, soffit, interior, or exterior options.

Sliver spaces are shafts or other thin vertical spaces that have parallel walls with spaces on all sides and meet a Sliver Space Tolerance setup in Energy Settings. The default is **300mm**. You cannot place a space in such areas.

- To define the Sliver Space Tolerance, in the *Manage* tab> Settings panel, click (Project Information) and click **Edit..**. next to the **Energy Settings** parameter.
- Instead of changing the Sliver Space Tolerance, which could cause problems elsewhere in your project, you can clear the Room Bounding status in the wall properties as shown in Figure 6–29. If there is a linked model this must be done directly in the original file.

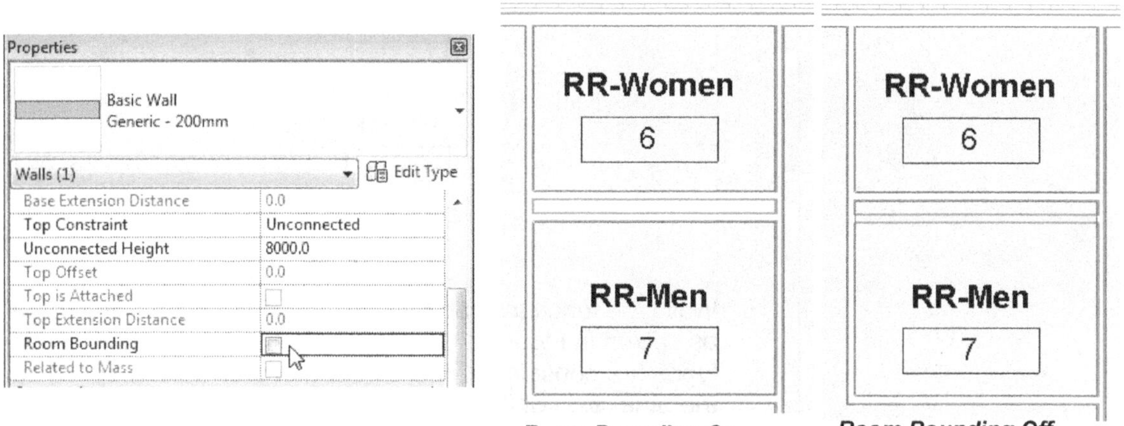

Room Bounding On ***Room Bounding Off***

Figure 6–29

Cavities

Cavities are small areas in which the walls are asymmetrical, such as a curved or triangular space that defines an odd shaped room, as shown in Figure 6–30. Typically, walls that define such spaces only extend to the ceiling or just above the ceiling. If you can add a space, do so. Check the area in section to verify that the entire space has been filled.

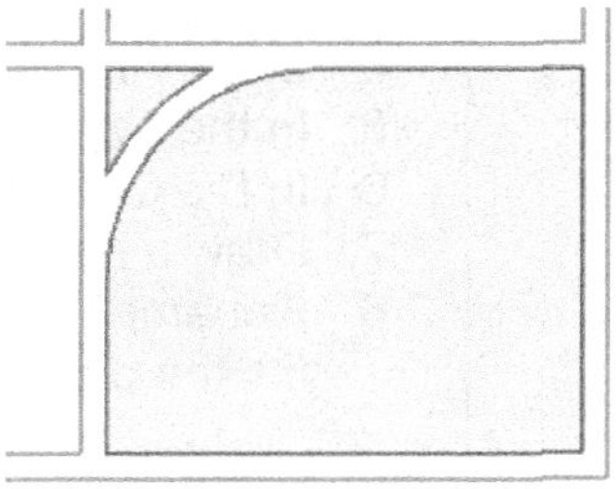

Figure 6–30

Plenum Spaces

Plenum spaces are the areas between ceilings and the floor above, typically where ducts, piping, and electrical lines are run. Plenum areas need to have spaces added to them as shown in Figure 6–31.

In Properties, plenum spaces can have the Plenum box checked, which automatically clears and grays out **Occupiable** *and sets Condition Type to Unconditioned.*

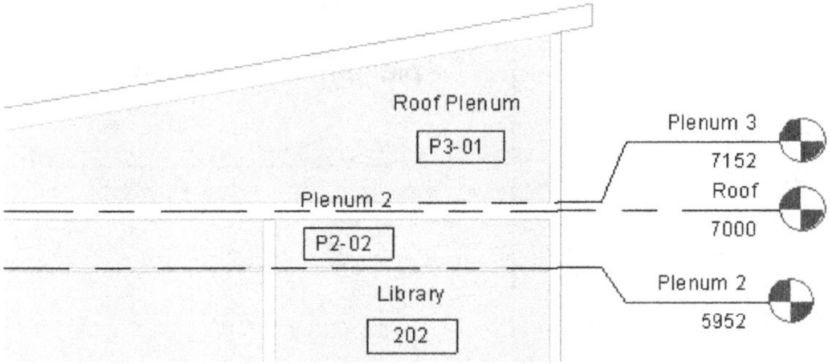

Figure 6–31

How To: Create Spaces in a Plenum

1. Place spaces in the existing areas.
2. In a plan view, create a section that cuts through the area in which the plenum runs.
3. In the section, verify that all of the spaces are touching the ceilings, as shown in Figure 6–32. (Typically, set the space **Upper Limit** to the level above to have the space automatically stop at a boundary, such as a ceiling.)

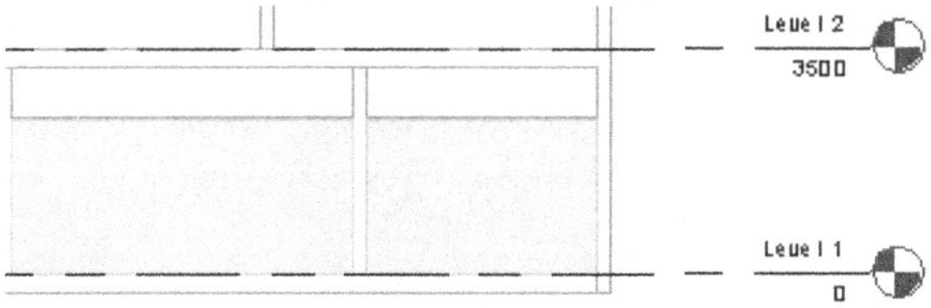

Figure 6–32

4. In the *Architecture* tab>Datum panel, click (Level).
5. In the Type Selector, select **Level: Plenum**.
6. In the Options Bar, select **Make Plan View**.
7. Draw a new level at the height of the ceiling.
8. Rename the level and any associated views with a name that fits the project, such as **Plenum 1** shown in Figure 6–33.

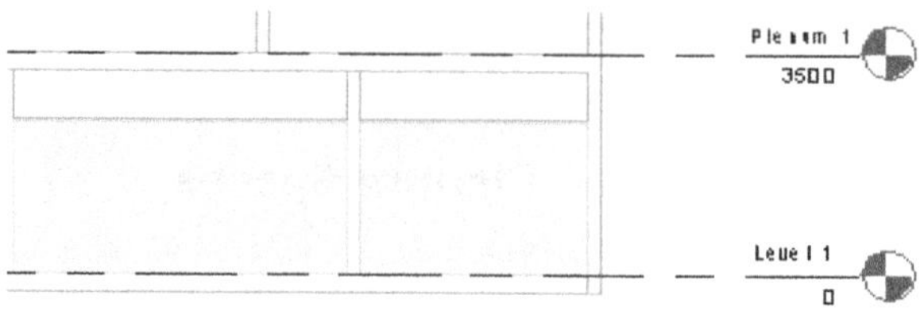

Figure 6–33

9. Open the new floor plan.
10. In Properties, edit the View Range and set the *cut plane offset* to a value that fits the height of the plenum.
11. In the plan view, place the spaces. They should fill the plenum area as shown in Figure 6–34.

In this example, one wall touches the ceiling and another goes up to the floor above to indicate how the space in the plenum is divided.

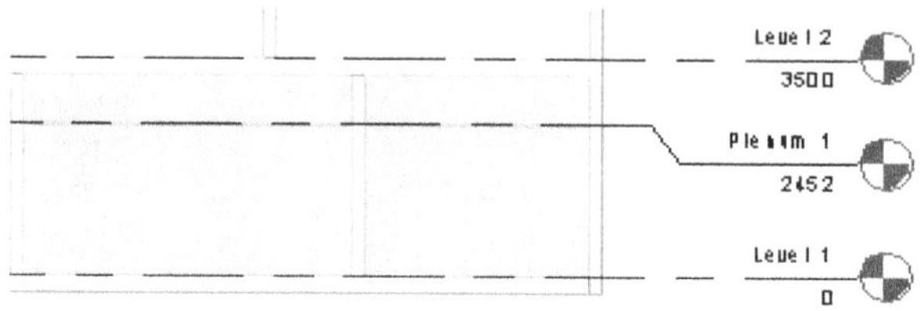

Figure 6–34

12. Repeat as required for all other plenum areas.

Practice 6b Work with Spaces

Practice Objective

- Modify spaces.

Estimated time for completion: 15 minutes

In this practice you will modify the heights of spaces in the gym and cafeteria areas. You will also create a plenum level and add plenum spaces, as shown in Figure 6–35. You will investigate an overlap of spaces and add space separation lines to correct it.

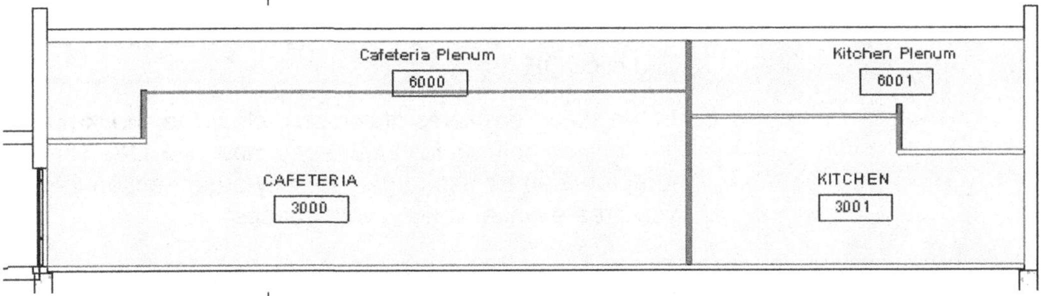

Figure 6–35

Task 1 - Modify the heights of spaces.

1. In the project files *Spaces* folder, open **MEP-Elementary-School-Spaces-Modify-M.rvt**. This project file includes additional space elements for the practice.
2. Draw a section across the part of the gym that extends beyond the rest of the building, as shown in Figure 6–36.

Draw the section so it does not display the far wall. This makes it easier to just display the gym and its space.

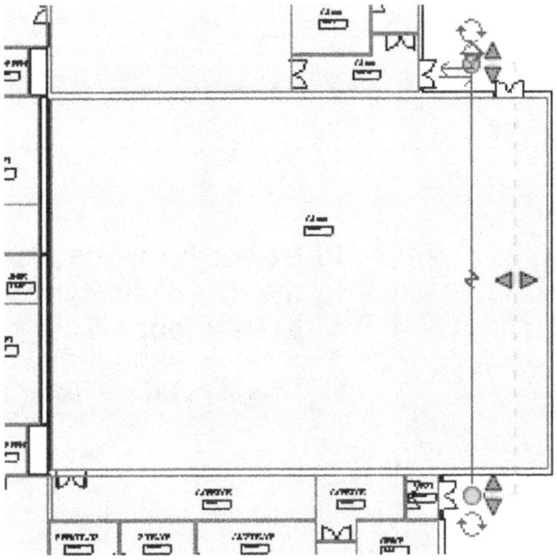

Figure 6–36

3. Click **Modify** and then double-click on the arrow of the section marker to open the section.

4. In Properties, set the *Sub-Discipline* to **MEP** and the *View Name* to **Gym Section.**

5. In the Visibility/Graphics Overrides dialog box, in the *Model Categories* tab, select the **Spaces>Interior** category.

6. In the Project Browser, right-click on the Coordination> MEP>Section (Building Section): **Gym Section** section view and select **Create View Template from View**.

7. In the New View Template dialog box, type **Space Section** and click **OK**.

8. In the View Templates dialog box, clear the checkmark from the *Include* column for *View Scale* and click **OK**. This template can be used again for any other section views that you create while working with spaces.

9. The space height in the gym is too low, as shown in Figure 6–37.

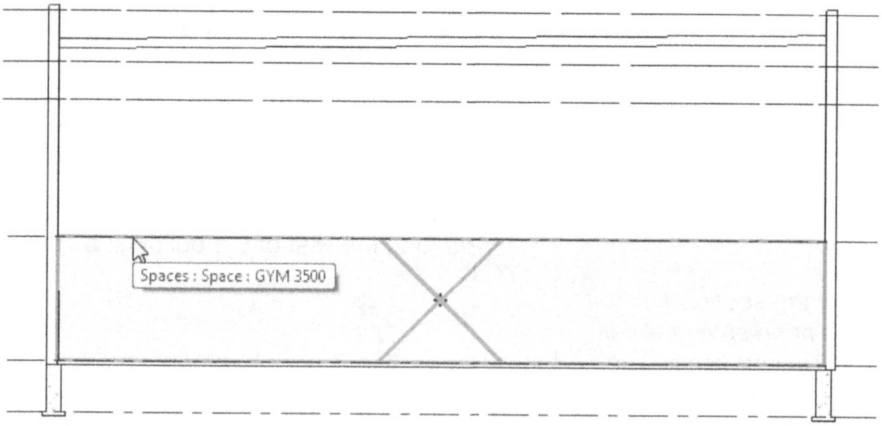

Figure 6–37

10. Select the space. Use the controls to extend the space above the roof of the gym or, in Properties, change the *Upper Limit* to **Reference 3**.

11. Press <Ctrl>+<Tab> to return to the **01 Space Plan** view.

12. Draw a section across the end of the Cafeteria and Kitchen as shown in Figure 6–38.

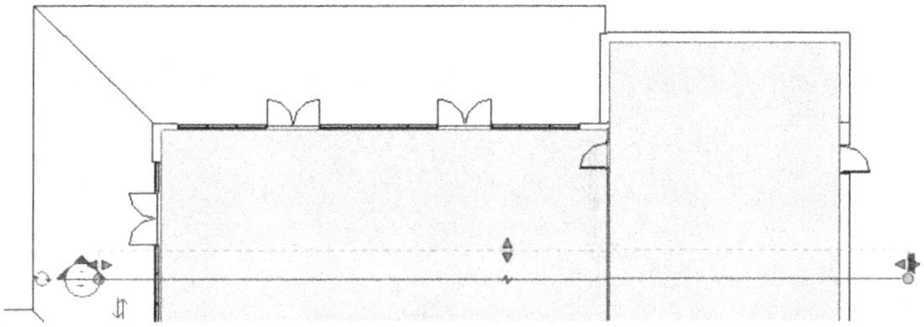

Figure 6–38

13. Click in empty space to clear the selection and then double-click on the arrow of the section marker to open the section.

When a View Template is specified in Properties, you cannot make changes to many of the view properties.

14. In Properties, in the *Identity Data* area click the button next to *View Template.* In the Apply View Template dialog box, select **Space Section** and click **OK**. The view inherits the settings of the View Template that you created earlier.

15. Change the name of the view to **Cafeteria Section**.

16. You can see that the Kitchen space (to the right in Figure 6–39) fills the height correctly but the Cafeteria (to the left in Figure 6–39) does not.

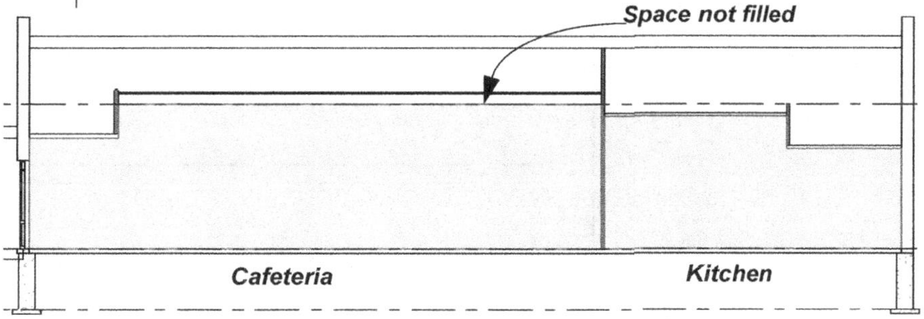

Figure 6–39

17. Select the Cafeteria space. In Properties, change *Upper Limit* to **Floor 2** and *Limit Offset* to **1000mm**, as shown in Figure 6–40.

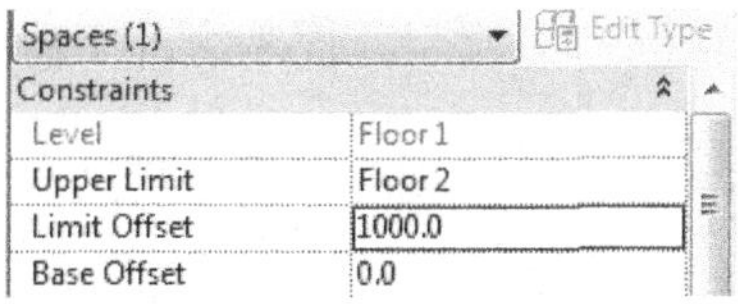

Figure 6–40

18. The space is now filled in correctly as shown in Figure 6–41.

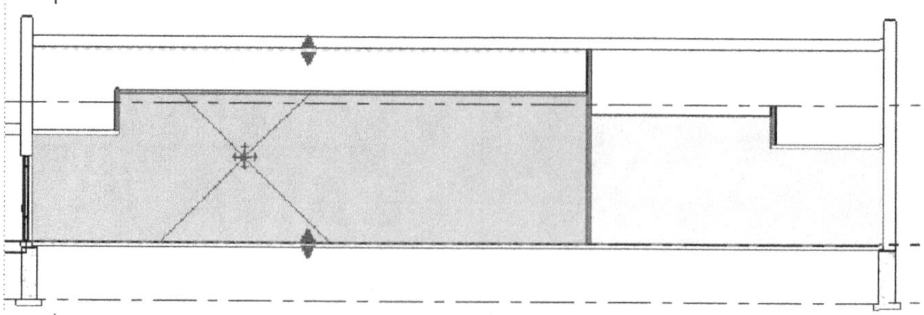

Figure 6–41

19. Save the project.

Task 2 - Add Plenum Spaces above the cafeteria and kitchen.

Ensure you select the Plenum Level type, as it can cause problems if it is drawn on a building story level.

1. In the *Architecture* tab>Datum panel, click (Level).
2. In the Type Selector, select **Level: Plenum** and, in Properties, clear the **Building Story** option.
3. Draw a level line **4350mm** above the First Floor and rename it as **Cafeteria Plenum** as shown in Figure 6–42. When prompted, rename the associated views.

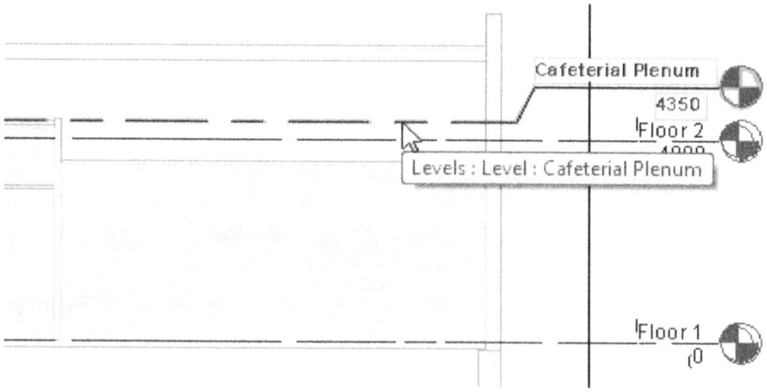

Figure 6–42

4. Double-click on the **Cafeteria Plenum** level head to open the floor plan view.
5. In Properties, apply the *View Template* **Space Plan** to this view.

6. In the *Analyze* tab>Spaces & Zones panel, click (Space).
7. Add spaces to the Cafeteria and Kitchen areas, as shown in Figure 6–43.

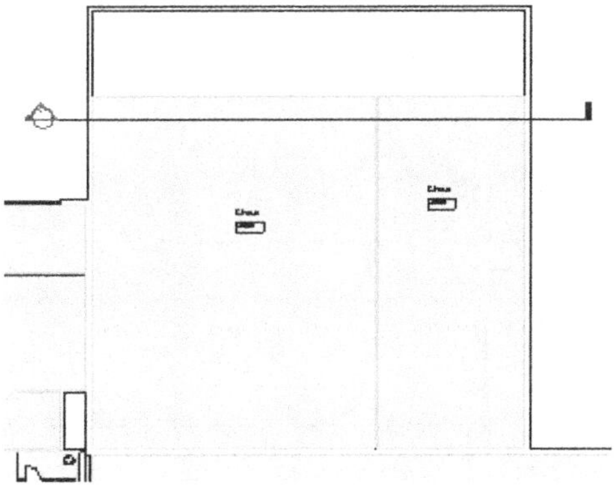

Figure 6–43

8. Click **Modify**.
9. Change the space name and number over the cafeteria to **Cafeteria Plenum** and **6000**. Change the space name and number over the kitchen to **Kitchen Plenum** and **6001**.
10. Switch to the Cafeteria section. The height of the space is appropriate but the depth of some parts is not as shown in Figure 6–44.

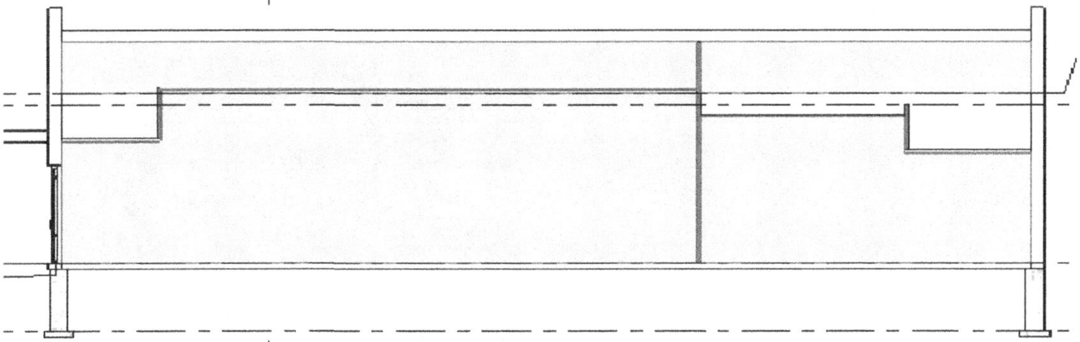

Figure 6–44

11. Select the Cafeteria Plenum space. In Properties, change the *Base Offset* to (negative) **-1000mm**. The space expands down but not all of the way. Change the *Base Offset* to (negative) **-1500mm**. The space expands down to fill the plenum area.

12. Select the Kitchen Plenum space. This time use the Drag controls to extend the space below the lowest ceiling. The section should display as shown in Figure 6–45.

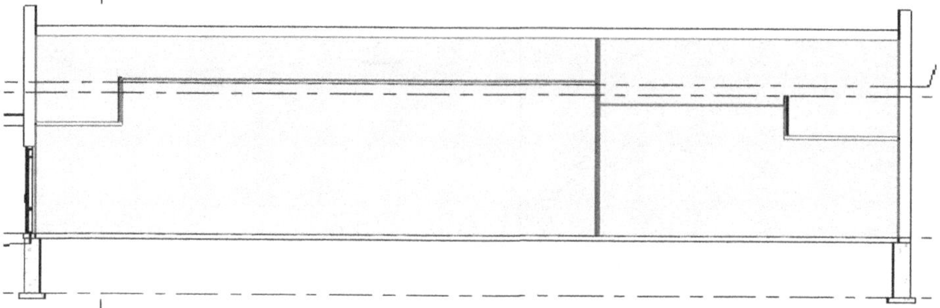

Figure 6–45

13. Save the project.

Task 3 - Correct an issue where spaces overlap.

1. Return to the **01 Space Plan** view.

2. Zoom in on the office area and select the **RECEPTION** space, as shown in Figure 6–46.

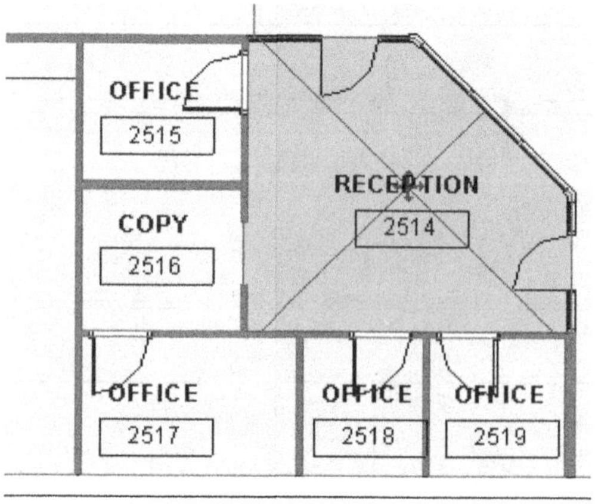

Figure 6–46

This option displays if there is a problem with the selected space.

3. In the *Modify | Spaces* tab>Warnings panel, click (Show Related Warnings).

4. In the dialog box, expand the warnings as shown in Figure 6–47. The issue is with the reception space on the first floor and the plenum space above.

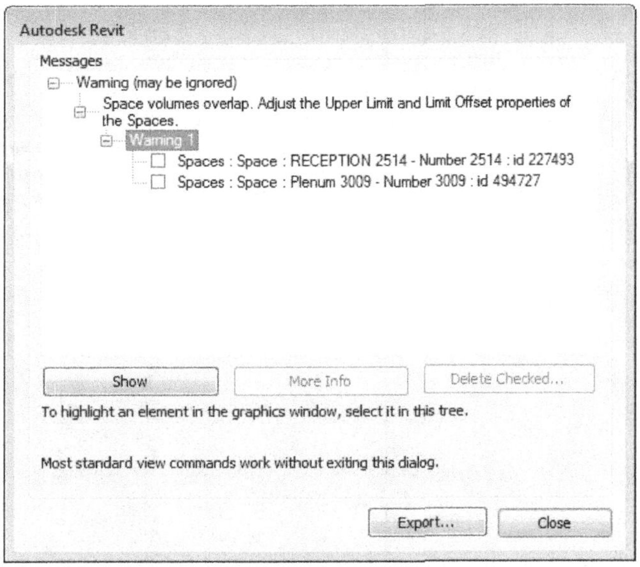

Figure 6–47

5. In **Warning 1**, select the plenum space and click **Show**. Read any alerts and continue. The view zooms in and displays the problems, as shown in Figure 6–48.

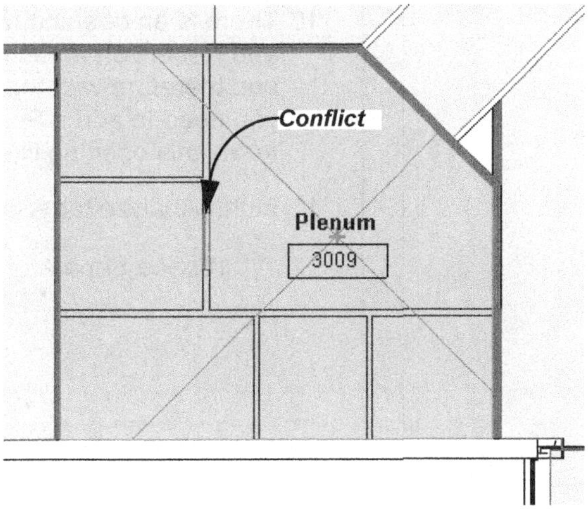

Figure 6–48

6. Close the dialog box.
7. Draw a short section through this area. Open the section and apply the **Space Section** view template to it.
8. When you select the copy space you can see how it extends into the plenum area as shown in Figure 6–49 but you cannot tell why.

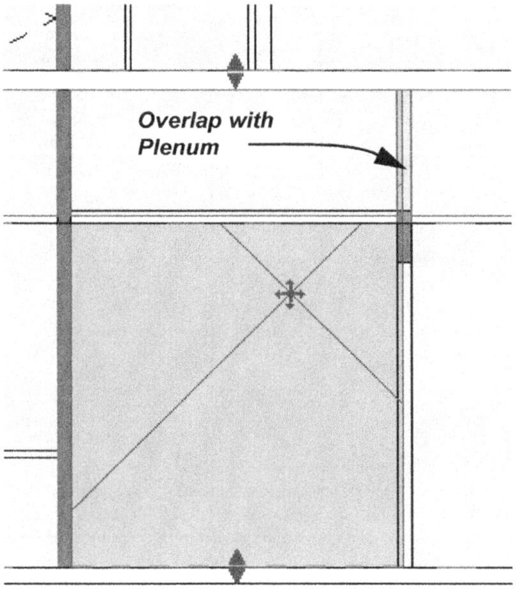

Figure 6–49

9. Open the **01 Space Plan** view.
10. There is an opening rather than a door between the Copy and Reception areas. This is creating an issue with the wall and therefore with the plenum space. To solve this problem you need to add a Space Separator so that the software treats this opening like any other door.
11. In the *Analyze* tab>Spaces and Zones panel, click  (Space Separator).

12. In the Options Bar, clear **Chain** and draw two lines on each side of the framed opening as shown in Figure 6–50.

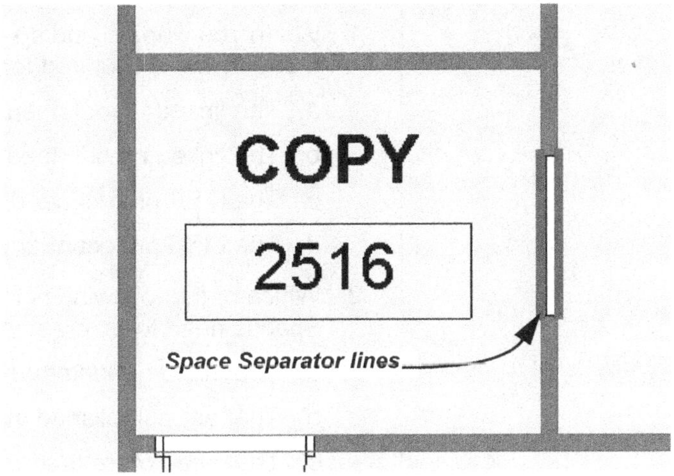

Figure 6–50

13. Select the Reception space again. The Warning no longer displays.

14. Display the related section and the **01 Plenum** plan view. None of the overlaps exist.

15. Open the **01 Space Plan** view.

16. Zoom out and save the project.

Chapter Review Questions

1. When you want to add spaces to a project that uses a linked model, what is required for the spaces to work as expected?
   a. The linked model needs to have rooms.
   b. The linked model needs to be set to Room Bounding.
   c. The MEP project needs to be set to Room Bounding.
   d. The MEP project needs to have rooms.
2. Which of the following is true to get an accurate analysis? Spaces need to be created in all rooms...
   a. That have heating and cooling.
   b. That are established in the architectural drawing.
   c. That span more than one level.
   d. As well as shafts, plenums, and other non-occupied spaces.
3. If you do not see spaces in the view you are working in, as shown on the top in Figure 6–51, what is required to display them as shown on the bottom in Figure 6–51?

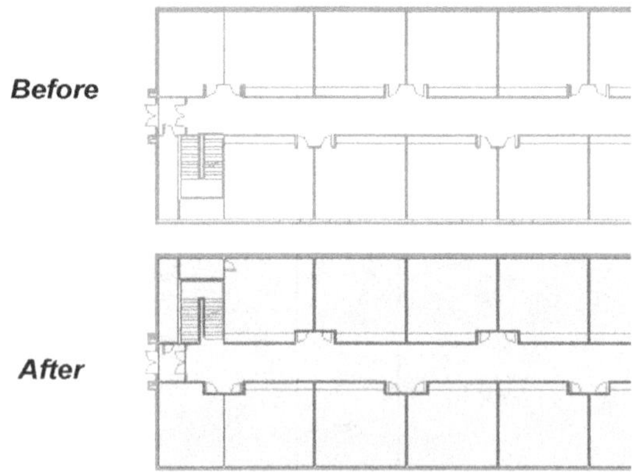

Figure 6–51

   a. Open the Visibility/Graphics dialog box and toggle on the **Interior** option under *Spaces*.
   b. Before placing spaces, set the *Space Visibility* to **Interior** in the Option Bar.
   c. In Properties, select **Space View**.
   d. In the View Control Bar, toggle on **Spaces**.

4. If a space is not reaching the ceiling, as shown in a section in Figure 6–52, which of the following methods can you use to fix the issue? (Select all that apply.)

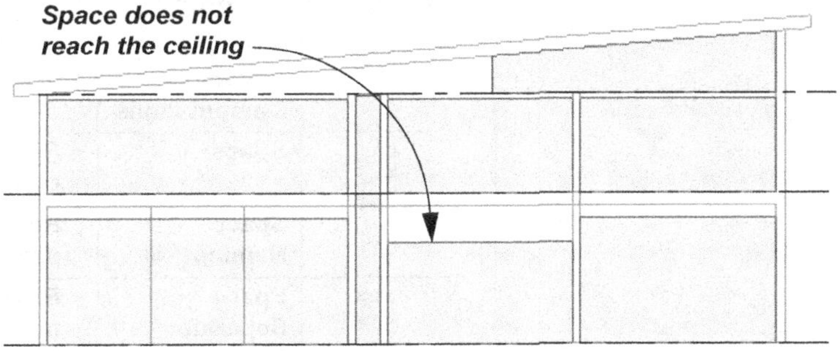

Figure 6–52

   a. Change the height of the room because the space reflects room size.
   b. Select the space and use the controls to move the top edge above the ceiling.
   c. Change the *Space Settings* to **Height by Ceiling**.
   d. Verify that the ceiling is set to **Room Bounding**.

5. When you have a space that is not defined entirely by walls, such as a balcony in a 2-story lobby, how do you control the size of the space?
   a. Sketch the boundaries of the space.
   b. Add space separation lines.
   c. Modify the size in Properties.
   d. Change the Room Bounding status of the other walls.

Command Summary

Button	Command	Location
	**Area and Volume Computations**	• **Ribbon:** *Analyze* tab>Spaces & Zones panel>expand the panel title
	**Space**	• **Ribbon:** *Analyze* tab>Spaces & Zones panel
	**Space Naming**	• **Ribbon:** *Analyze* tab>Spaces & Zones panel
	**Space Separator**	• **Ribbon:** *Analyze* tab>Spaces & Zones panel
	**Space Tag**	• **Ribbon:** *Analyze* tab>Spaces & Zones panel or *Annotate* tab>Tag panel

Chapter 7

Heating and Cooling Loads Analysis

To prepare a project so that you can run a Heating and Cooling Loads analysis involves grouping spaces into zones that are heated and cooled in the same manner. Creating color schemes that graphically indicate the various zones is helpful. When you start the Heading and Cooling Loads tool, you must specify the building type, location, and other options before you can calculate the energy demands of the model.

Learning Objectives in this Chapter

- Add zones to connect spaces for analysis.
- Use the System Browser with zones.
- Apply color schemes and color fill legends for spaces and zones.
- Prepare a project for heating and cooling loads analysis.
- Run a Heating and Cooling Loads analysis.

7.1 Creating Zones

After creating spaces, the next step in preparing to compute heating and cooling loads is to divide the building into zones, as shown in Figure 7–1. Each zone consists of similar spaces that would be heated and cooled in the same manner.

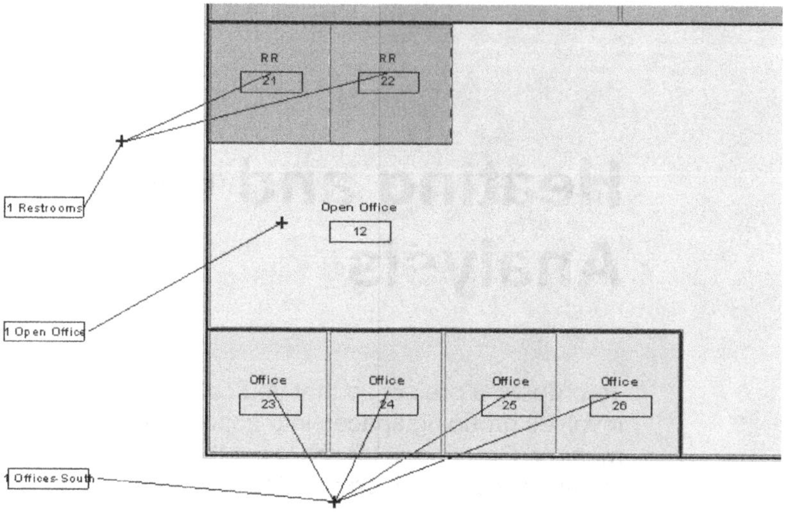

Figure 7–1

- There is always one **Default** zone in a project. All spaces are automatically attached to that zone when they are created.
- While you can add zones into a template, you usually add spaces first, then create zones and add spaces to the zones.
- You can create zones in plan and section views.

How To: Add Zones

You can set up a view template for zones in the same way as you set up one for spaces.

1. Open a plan view that contains the spaces you want to work with. If you have a zone that stretches across two levels, open a section view as well.
2. For each view, open the Visibility/Graphic Overrides dialog box, expand **HVAC Zones**, and select all of the options, as shown in Figure 7–2.

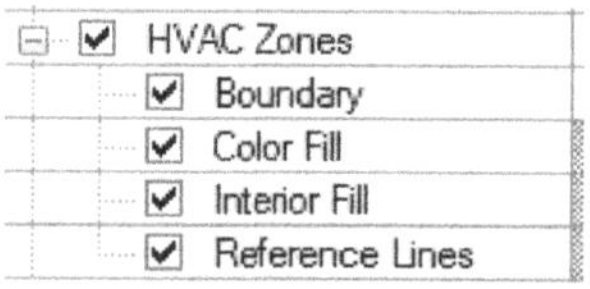

Figure 7–2

3. In the *Analyze* tab>Spaces & Zones panel, click (Zone).
4. In Properties, under *Identity Data*, type a name for the Zone. By default, the zones are numbered incrementally.
5. In the *Edit Zone* tab (shown in Figure 7–3), ensure that (Add Space) is automatically selected.

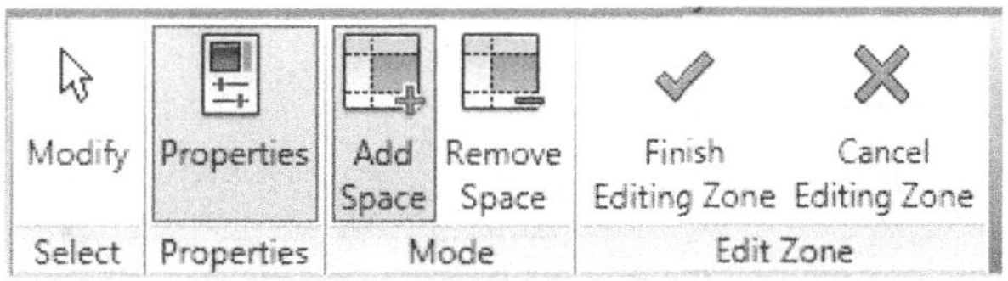

Figure 7–3

6. Select the spaces that you want to add to the zone.
7. Click (Finish Editing Zone).

- Another quick way to add a zone is to select the spaces first, then in the *Analyze* tab>Spaces & Zones panel, click (Zone). The spaces are automatically added to the zone.
- To edit an existing zone, select one of the zone lines, then in the *Modify | HVAC Zones* tab>Zone panel, click (Edit Zone). The *Edit Zone* tab displays which enables you to add more spaces.
- Click (Remove Space) to detach a space from the zone or modify the zone properties.
- Zones do not automatically have a tag placed, but it is helpful to display these as you are working, as shown in Figure 7–4.

  In the *Annotate* tab>Tag panel, click (Tag by Category) and select on the zone(s) that you want to tag.

You can change the name of a zone by changing the tag or in Properties. Zone tags are found in the library in the Annotations> Mechanical folder.

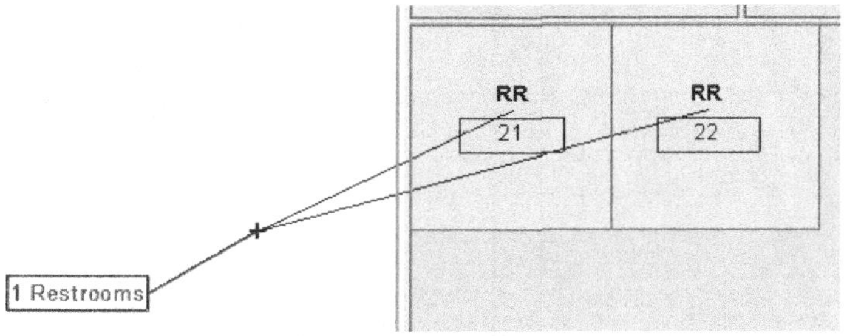

Figure 7–4

Using the System Browser with Zones

The System Browser is a useful tool when working with spaces and zones. When you select a space in the System Browser, it displays in the project, as shown in Figure 7–5. The selected zone or space is automatically made active in the Properties. This enables you to modify names for spaces and zones and assign information, such as electrical loads and mechanical airflow.

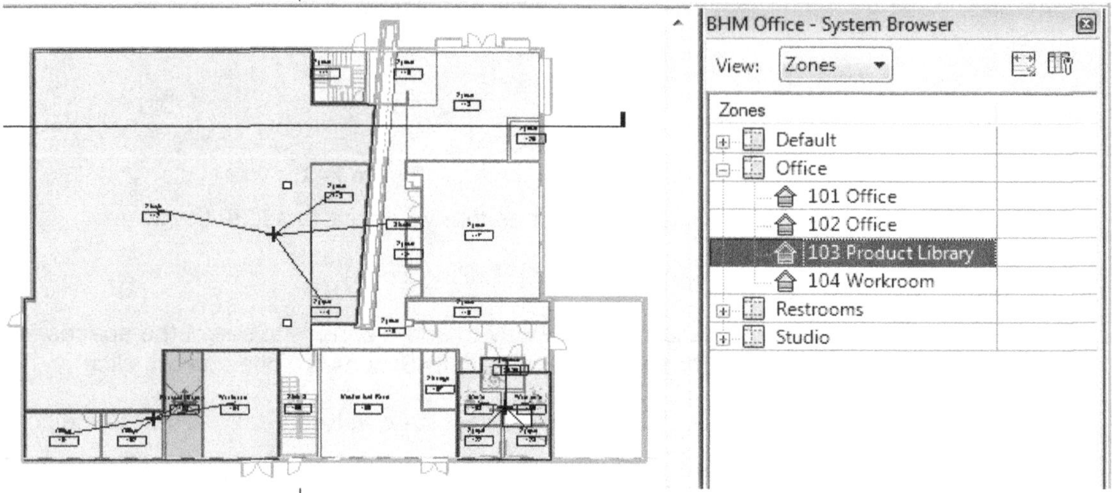

Figure 7–5

How To: Use the System Browser with Zones

1. In the *Analyze* tab>System Browser panel, click (System Browser).
2. If the zones are not displayed, expand the View drop-down list and select **Zones** as shown in Figure 7–6.

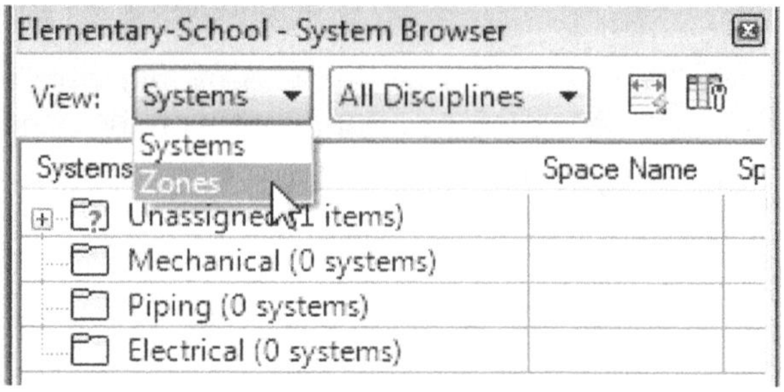

Figure 7–6

3. All of the spaces are listed under the **Default** zone (as shown in Figure 7–7) until they are added to a specific zone.

   - Each space displays an icon showing its status: (Occupiable), (Not Occupiable), and (Space not placed).
   - As new zones are added, the spaces are moved into the new zones.

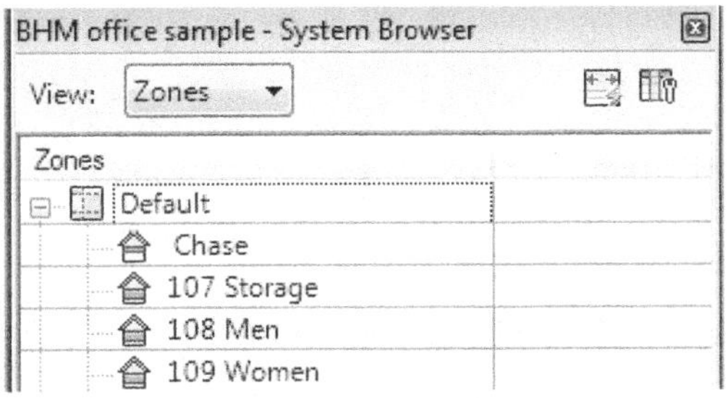

Figure 7–7

4. Select a space or a zone. It is highlighted in the project and becomes active in the Properties.

- You can select more than one space or zone at a time using <Ctrl> and <Shift>.
- In the System Browser, if you right-click on a space or zone and select **Show**, the software zooms in on the selected elements. If there is more than one view in which the space can be displayed, the Show Element(s) in View dialog box opens, as shown in Figure 7–8.

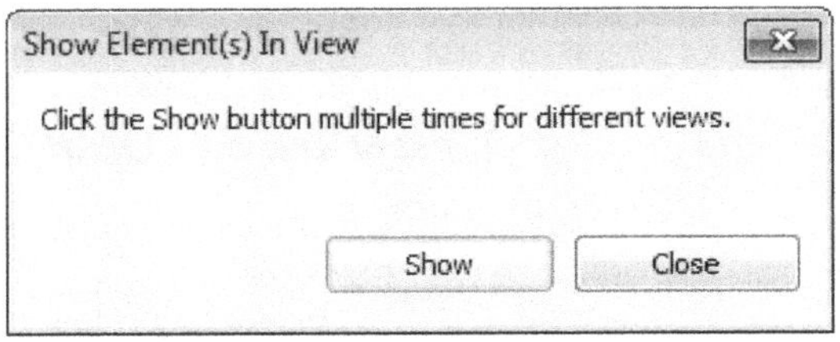

Figure 7–8

- If you place spaces and then delete them, they remain in the project. To delete a space entirely, in the System Browser, right-click on the space name and select **Delete**.
  - You can also delete spaces in a space schedule view.

7.2 Applying Color Schemes

When working with Zones and Spaces, it is useful to have a view that displays color coding for individual zones, spaces, or rooms, as shown for zones in Figure 7–9. You can include a color fill legend in the same view to clarify the use of the colors.

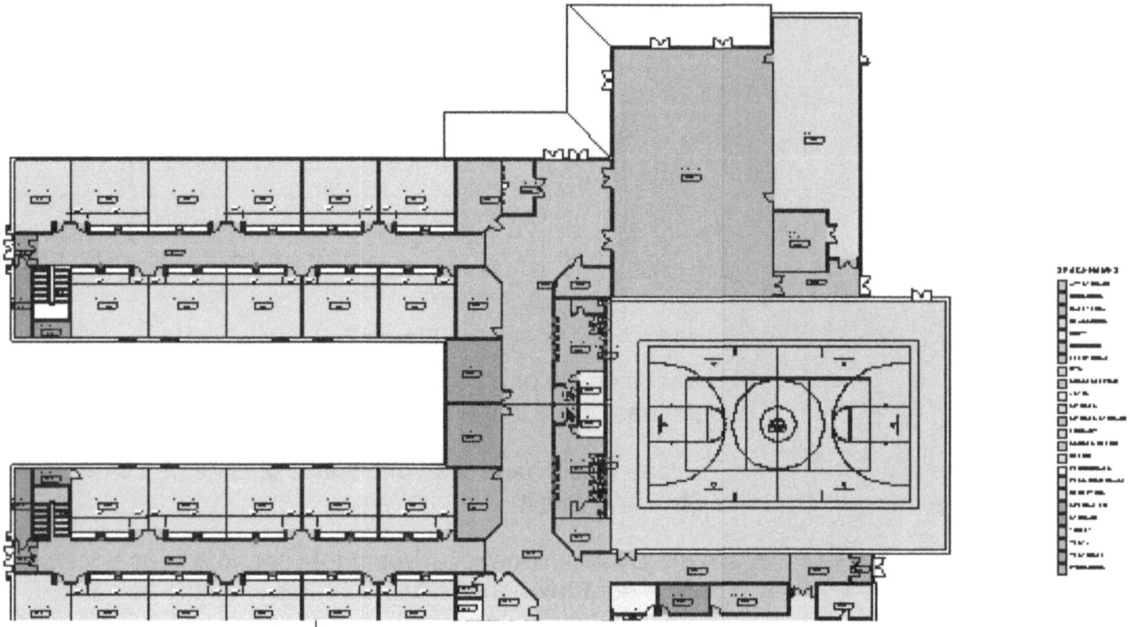

Figure 7–9

- Color schemes are controlled by a view property. Therefore, you should create a view for each color diagram that you want to include.

How To: Set Up a Color Scheme in a View

1. Create or duplicate a view that you want to use for the color scheme.
2. In Properties, click the button next to the **Color Scheme** parameter, as shown in Figure 7–10.

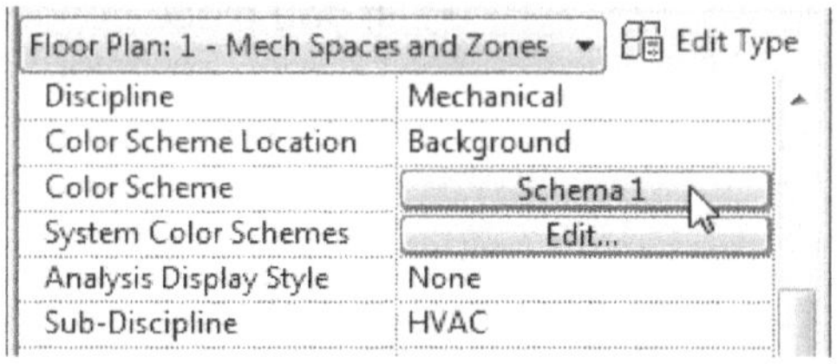

Figure 7–10

3. In the Edit Color Scheme dialog box, in the *Schemes* area, select a **Category**.

4. Select a scheme in the list. In the example shown in Figure 7–11, **Space Names** is selected.

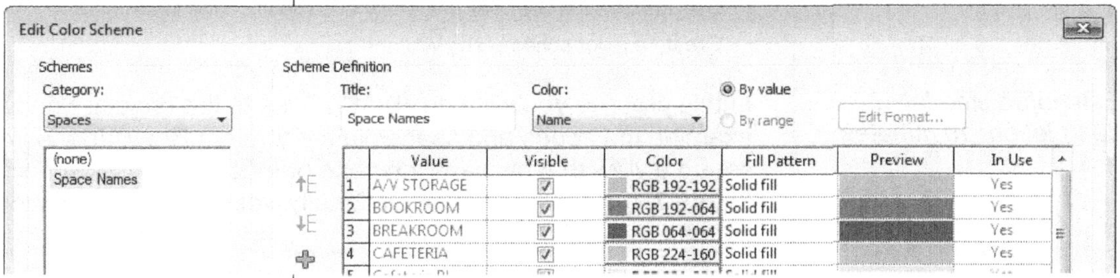

Figure 7–11

5. Click **OK**. The new color scheme displays in the view.

- The color fill of the scheme can display in the background or foreground of the view. In Properties, set the *Color Scheme Location*. This impacts how components display and whether or not the color fill stops at the walls.

- You can add a legend that matches the Color Scheme, as shown in Figure 7–12. In the *Analyze* tab>Color Fill panel, click (Color Fill Legend), and place the legend where you want it.

The Type Properties for the Color Fill Legend control the appearance of the legend, including the swatch size and text styles.

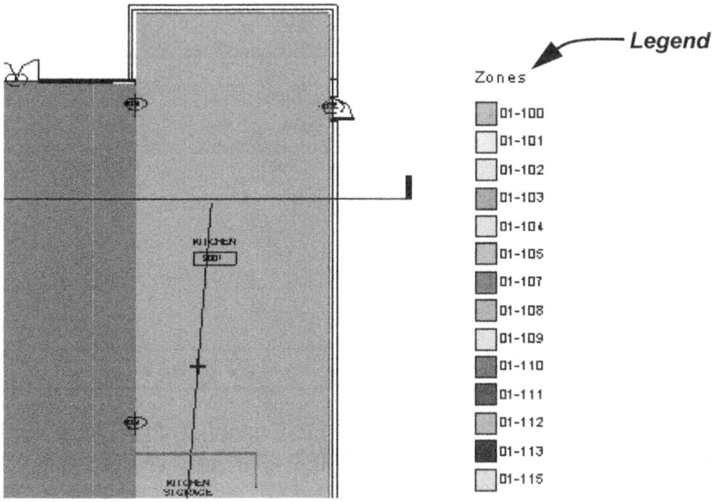

Figure 7–12

- If you change the **Color Scheme** in the View Properties dialog box, it also updates in the associated legend.

Practice 7a Create Zones

Estimated time for completion: 10 minutes

Practice Objectives

- Add zones.
- Use the System Browser to identify and modify zone information.
- Create a color scheme showing the zones.

In this practice you will add HVAC zones to the project. You will examine the zones and spaces in the System Browser and you set up a view that displays the zone names by color as shown in Figure 7–13 with zone tags. Optionally, you can create additional zones.

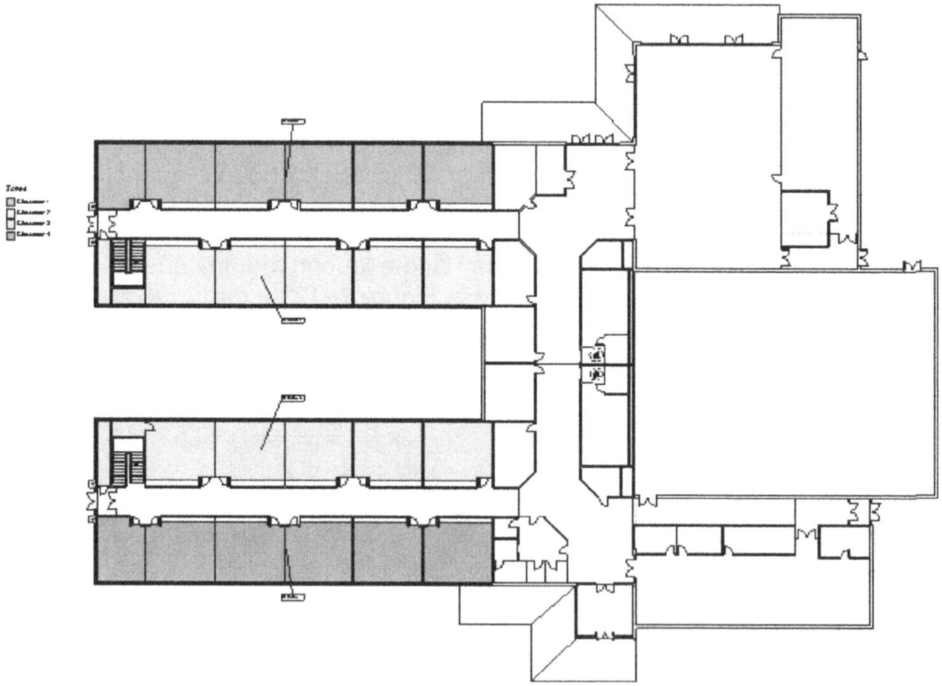

Figure 7–13

Task 1 - Add zones.

1. In the practice files *Analysis* folder, open **MEP-Elementary-School-Zones-M.rvt**.
2. Duplicate the Coordination>MEP>Floor Plans>**01 Space Plan** view
3. Rename it to **01 Zones**.

4. Select one of the section markers and type **VH** to hide the category in the view.
5. Open the Visibility/Graphics Overrides dialog box and set the following:
   - **HVAC Zones**: select **Interior Fill** and **Reference Lines**
   - **Spaces:** clear **Interior Fill** and **Color Fill**

You can still select the spaces, but the interior fill does not display.

6. In the *Analyze* tab>Spaces & Zones panel, click (Zone).
7. In the *Edit Zone* tab, verify that (Add Space) is selected.
8. Select the spaces across the top group of Classrooms, so the zone displays as shown in Figure 7–14.

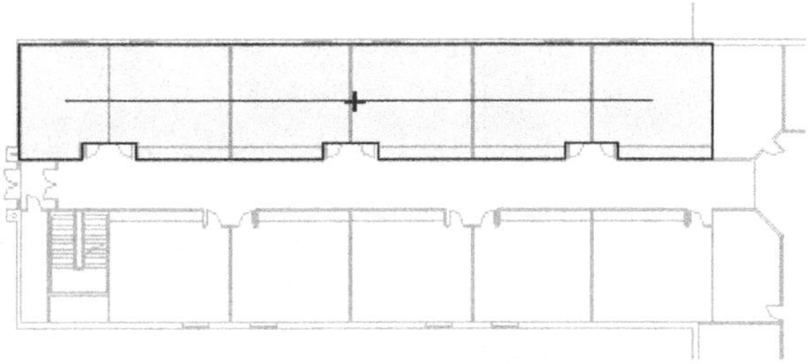

Figure 7–14

9. In Properties, change the *Name* to **Classroom 1**.
10. In the *Edit Zone* tab>Edit Zone panel, click (Finish Editing Zone).
11. Add another zone to the Classrooms and Storage Areas on the other side of the hall as shown in Figure 7–15.

The name of the zone automatically increments as each zone is added.

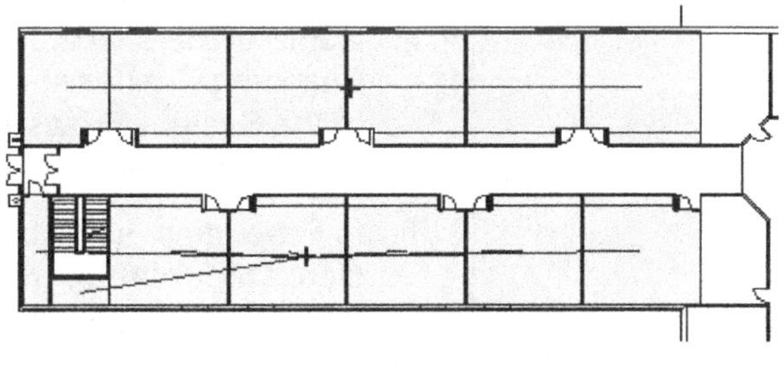

Figure 7–15

12. Add zones to the two classroom groups in the other wing.
13. In the *Annotate* tab>Tags panel, click (Tag by Category), and select each zone to place a tag.
14. Save the project.

Task 2 - Use the System Browser.

1. Press **<F9>** to open the System Browser, if it is not already open.

2. In the System Browser, set the view so it displays **Zones**. It should display as shown in Figure 7–16.

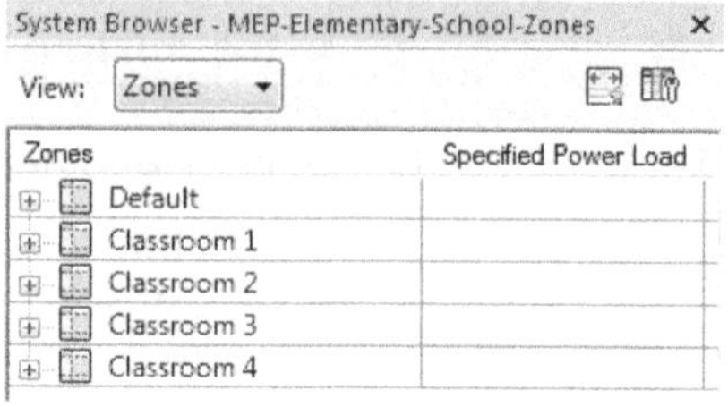

Figure 7–16

3. Expand the Default node. Note that there are a lot of spaces that are not placed in zones. There are also two different types of icons for spaces: occupied and unoccupied, as shown in Figure 7–17.

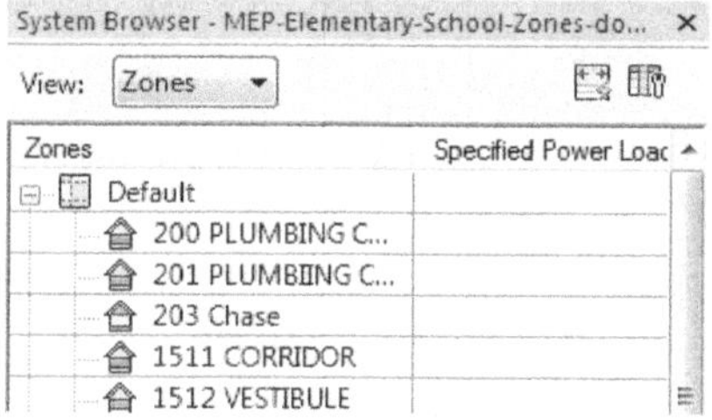

Figure 7–17

4. Some of the spaces that should be unoccupied, such as the Plumbing Chases shown in Figure 7–17, are not set correctly. In the System Browser, hold <Ctrl> and select the two plumbing chases.

5. In Properties, scroll down to the *Energy Analysis* area and clear **Occupiable**. Repeat this for other chases or plenums that might not be correctly.

6. As you scroll through the spaces, note that some display  (Space Not Placed). Right-click on them and click **Delete**.

7. In the System Browser, in the default zone, right-click on one of the plenums and select **Show**. (Open additional views as necessary) The view changes to display the location of the plenum, such as the one shown in Figure 7–18. Close the Show Element(s) in View dialog box.

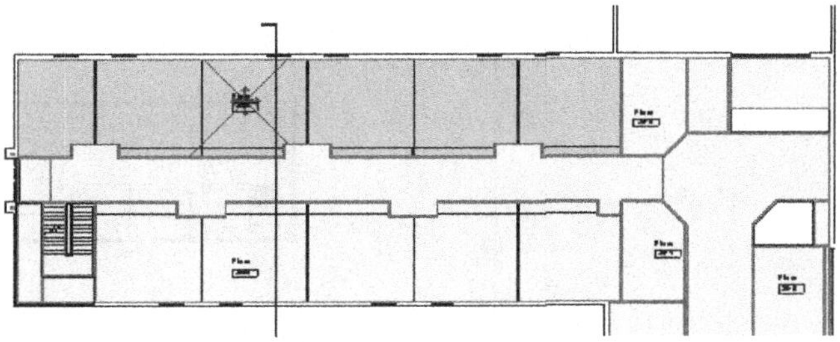

Figure 7–18

8. Click in space to release the selection.

9. Close the System Browser.

10. Save the project.

Task 3 - Add a color scheme.

1. Open the **01 Zones** view. Close any hidden windows (in the Quick Access Toolbar, click (Close Hidden Windows)).
2. In Properties, in the *Graphics* area, click the button next to *Color Scheme*.
3. In the Edit Color Scheme dialog box, in the *Schemes* area, change the *Category* to **HVAC Zones**.
4. Select the default **Schema 1**. The Scheme Definition automatically populates by zone name as shown in Figure 7–19.

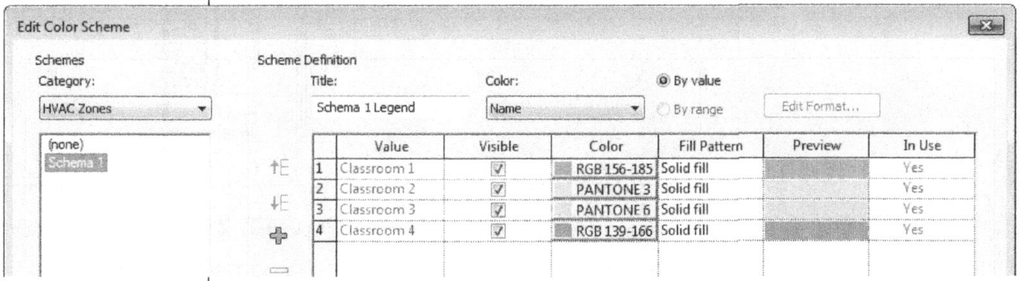

Figure 7–19

5. In the *Schemes* area, click (Rename). In the Rename dialog box, type **Zones** and then click **OK**.

Your zone colors might vary.

6. In the *Scheme Definition* area, in the *Title* field, type **Zones Legend**.
7. Click **OK**. The color scheme is applied to the view. The display will be similar to that shown in Figure 7–20.

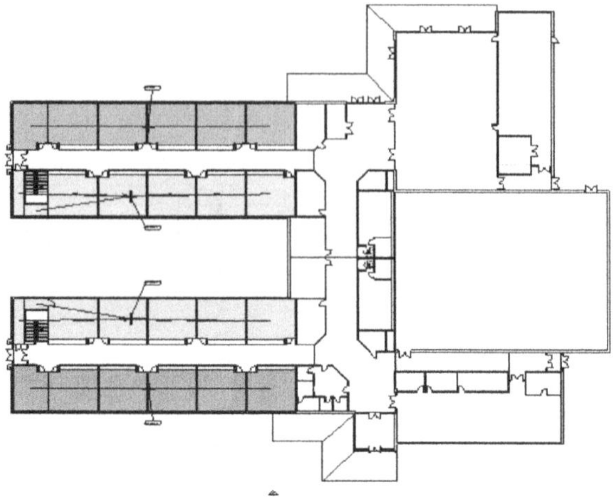

Figure 7–20

8. In the *Analyze* tab>Color Fill panel, click (Color Fill Legend) and place the legend near the classrooms, as shown in Figure 7–21.

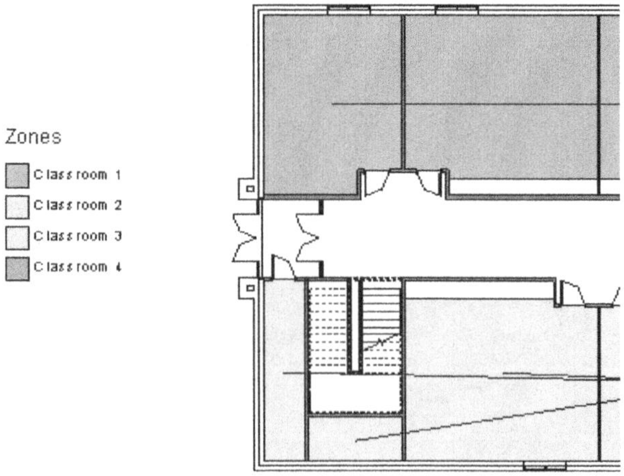

Figure 7–21

9. In the Visibility/Graphics dialog box, expand HVAC Zones and clear **Reference Lines**. This can make the color fill easier to read.
10. Save the project.

Task 4 - Optional: Add additional zones.

1. Add the zones listed below and shown in Figure 7–22.
   - (1) The classroom zones (created in previous steps).
   - (2) All of the corridors plus the Electrical Room.
   - (3) All of the vestibules.
   - (4) Nurse's Office, Bookroom, Special Ed rooms, and Workroom.
   - (5) Reception, Offices, and Copy Room.
   - (6) Library and associated rooms.
   - (7) Gym.
   - (8) Cafeteria.
   - (9) Kitchen and Kitchen Storage.
   - (10) Restrooms.
   - (11) Housekeeping, Janitor, and associated chases.

Note: This figure uses different shades for clarity.

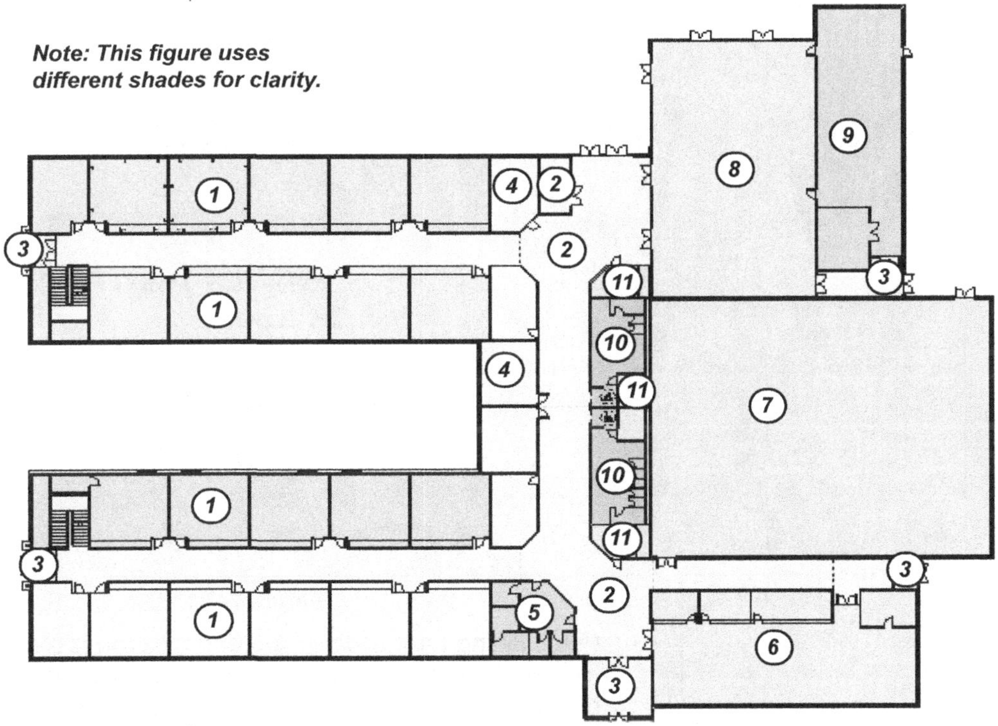

Figure 7–22

2. In the *Annotate* tab>Tags panel, click (Tag by Category), and select each zone to place a tag.

3. Save the project.

7.3 Analyzing the Heating and Cooling Loads

Additional cloud-based tools for Energy Optimization are included with a subscription.

Using the power of BIM technology in the Autodesk Revit software, the information you set in spaces, zones, and other energy analysis parameters is used as the basis of the loads analysis for the project. Use the **Heating and Cooling Loads** tool to set up important information, including the type and location of the building, as well as to verify the spaces and zones (as shown in Figure 7–23), before calculating a Loads Report.

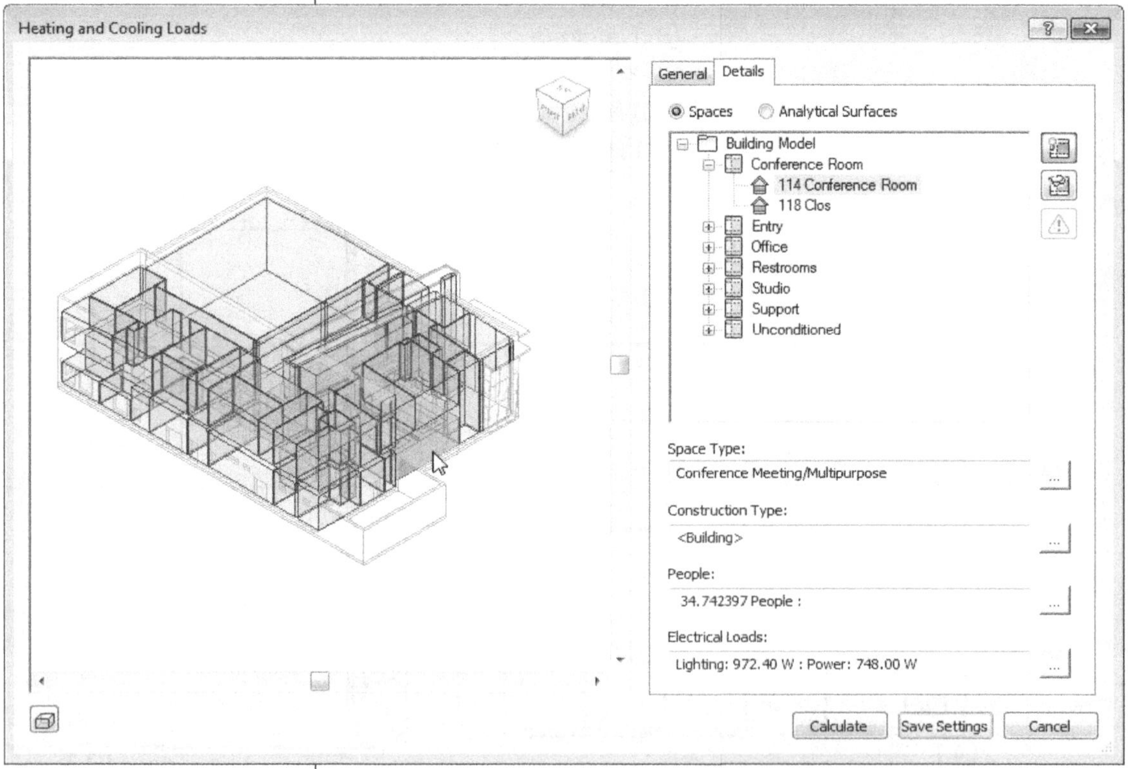

Figure 7–23

- Establishing the building type and location is a critical step because a multi-story office in a tropical climate has different heating and cooling requirements than a warehouse in a cold climate.

How To: Set up a Heating and Cooling Loads Analysis

1. In the *Analyze* tab>Reports & Schedules panel, click (Heating and Cooling Loads).
2. The Heating and Cooling Loads dialog box opens as shown in Figure 7–23. It contains a 3D view of the space volumes and displays information in the *General* and *Details* tabs.
3. In the *General* tab, verify or apply the parameters, as shown in Figure 7–24 and listed in the table below.

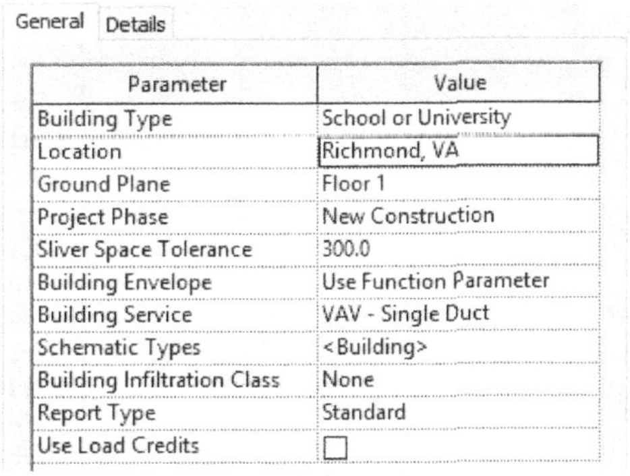

Parameter	Value
Building Type	School or University
Location	Richmond, VA
Ground Plane	Floor 1
Project Phase	New Construction
Sliver Space Tolerance	300.0
Building Envelope	Use Function Parameter
Building Service	VAV - Single Duct
Schematic Types	<Building>
Building Infiltration Class	None
Report Type	Standard
Use Load Credits	☐

Figure 7–24

4. Click **Save Settings** to set the information in the General tab.

<table>
<tr><td>Building Type</td><td>Select from a list of building types that are set up in the program. You can also add and modify building types</td></tr>
<tr><td>Location</td><td>Specify the geographic location for the building using the Location Weather and Site dialog box.
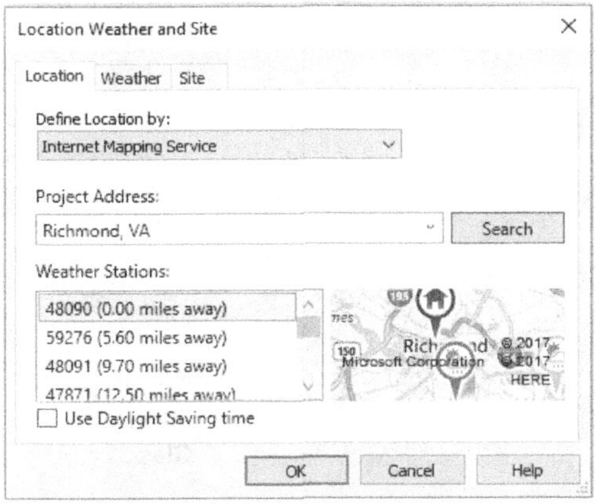

• This dialog box is also available from the ribbon. In the Manage tab> Project Location panel or Analysis tab>Energy Optimization panel, click (Location).</td></tr>
</table>

Ground Plane	Specify the level that correlates with the ground plane of the project. Levels below the ground plane are processed as being underground.
Project Phase	Select the phase for the state of the project you are analyzing.
Sliver Space Tolerance	Specify the size for areas considered sliver spaces.
Building Envelope	Specify the method used to calculate the building envelope. • **Use Function Parameter:** The default option, which uses the function parameter of walls, floors, and building pads to determine interior and exterior spaces. • **Identify Exterior Elements:** Uses ray-casting and flood-fill algorithms to determine interior and exterior spaces. An additional parameter, **Analytical Grid Cell Size**, determines the size of 3D grid cubes that divide the building for processing.
Building Service	Specify the type of heating and cooling system used by the building.
Schematic Types	Specify overrides for material and insulation. Select **<Building>** and then click **...** to open the Schematic Types dialog box .

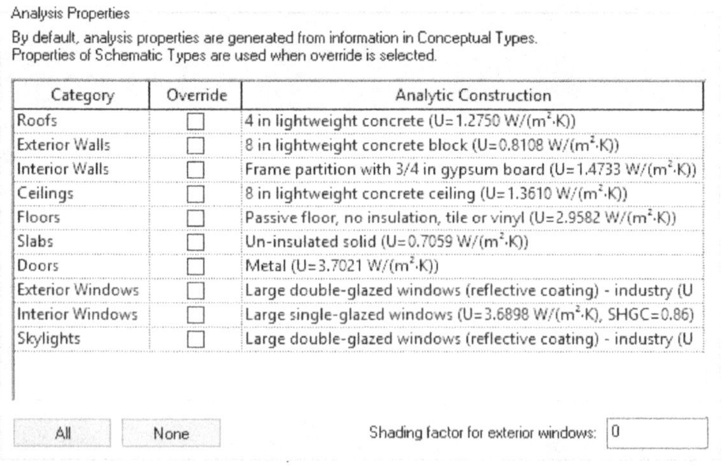

Building Infiltration Class	Select from the list to specify the estimated outdoor air from leaks in the building envelope based on tightly constructed walls. • **Loose** • **Medium** • **Tight** • **None:** Infiltration is excluded from the calculations.

Report Type	Specify the level of information provided by the calculations: **Simple**, **Standard**, **Detailed**.
Use Load Credits	Enables negative loads that leaves a zone through a partition into another zone.

How To: Review and Update Spaces and Zones

1. Open the Heating and Cooling Loads dialog box.
2. Select the *Details* tab and expand the levels to display the spaces for each level. Icons next to the space name indicate whether the space has been able to be calculated and if it is occupiable or not, as shown in Figure 7–25.
   - Add spaces to zones other than the default zone. The default zone is calculated, but might not work correctly as spaces in the default zone can be far apart.

In this example there are still some spaces left in the Default Zone. You should stop the process and return to the System Browser to establish zones for the spaces and remove extra spaces.

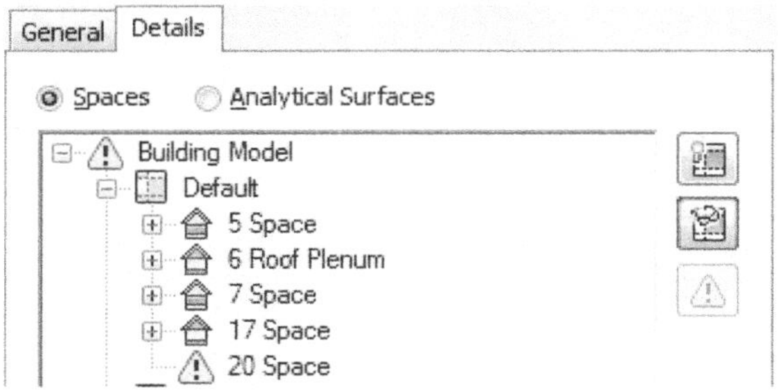

Figure 7–25

3. To display an error, select the room name and click (Show Related Warnings). The Warning box opens as shown in Figure 7–26, indicating the cause of the warning.

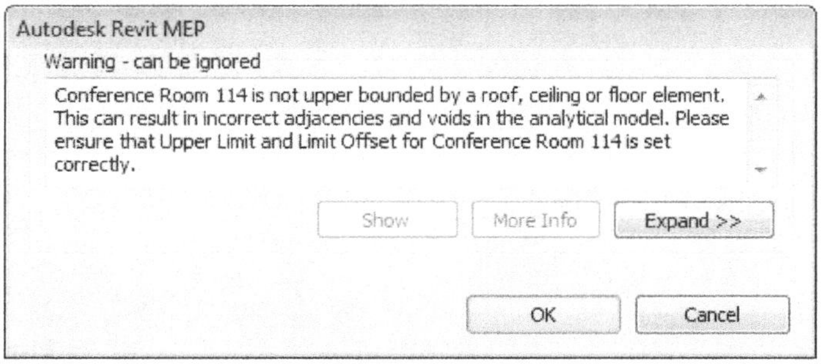

Figure 7–26

4. To display visual information about the space, select the space name and click  (Highlight) to highlight the space in the 3D view. You can also click  (Isolate) to turn off the display of all of the other spaces in the 3D view.
   - Click the icons again to turn them off.
5. Select **Analytical Surfaces** to display the surface calculation planes, as shown in Figure 7–27.

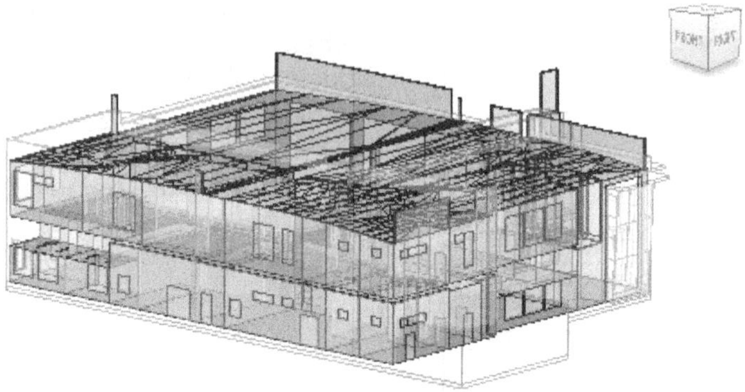

Figure 7–27

   - You can use the cursor or the ViewCube to zoom, pan, and rotate around the model in the dialog box.
6. If you need to make changes to the model, click **Save Settings** to save any changes you have made and return to the model.
7. When you are ready to run the report, click **Calculate**. The Loads Report displays and is also available in the Project Browser. Expand **Reports>Loads Reports** and select the one you need as shown in Figure 7–28.

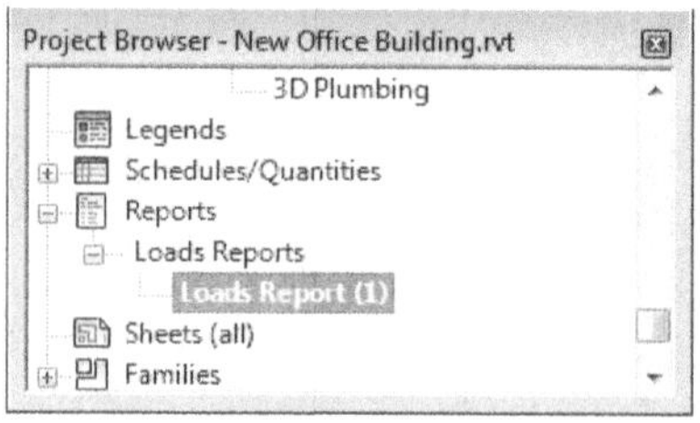

Figure 7–28

   - The name of the report can be changed in Properties when the report is selected in the Project Browser.

- The Loads Report (shown in Figure 7–29), includes summaries for the Project, Building, and each Zone.

Project Summary

Location and Weather	
Project	Project Name
Address	
Calculation Time	Monday, June 03, 2013
Report Type	Standard
Latitude	42.39°
Longitude	-71.24°
Summer Dry Bulb	34 °C
Summer Wet Bulb	26 °C
Winter Dry Bulb	-14 °C
Mean Daily Range	6 °C

Building Summary

Inputs	
Building Type	School or University
Area (m²)	5,864
Volume (m³)	25,253.50
Calculated Results	
Peak Cooling Total Load (W)	**603,272**
Peak Cooling Month and Hour	July 2:00 PM
Peak Cooling Sensible Load (W)	534,527
Peak Cooling Latent Load (W)	68,745
Maximum Cooling Capacity (W)	603,272
Peak Cooling Airflow (L/s)	40,259.9
Peak Heating Load (W)	**346,656**
Peak Heating Airflow (L/s)	18,302.4
Checksums	
Cooling Load Density (W/m²)	102.87
Cooling Flow Density (L/(s·m²))	6.87
Cooling Flow / Load (L/(s·kW))	66.74
Cooling Area / Load (m²/kW)	9.72
Heating Load Density (W/m²)	59.11
Heating Flow Density (L/(s·m²))	3.12

Zone Summary - Default

Inputs	
Area (m²)	6,087
Volume (m³)	25,253.50
Cooling Setpoint	23 °C
Heating Setpoint	21 °C
Supply Air Temperature	12 °C
Number of People	1467

Figure 7–29

Practice 7b Heating and Cooling Analysis

Estimated time for completion: 20 minutes

Practice Objectives

- Prepare a project for energy analysis with Energy Settings.
- Review the details of zones and spaces in the Heating and Coolings Loads dialog box and fix any warnings.

In this practice you will run the Heating and Cooling Loads tool and review the details of the zones and spaces in the project. You will identify problems, as shown in Figure 7–30, return to the model to solve them and then rerun the software and calculate the analysis.

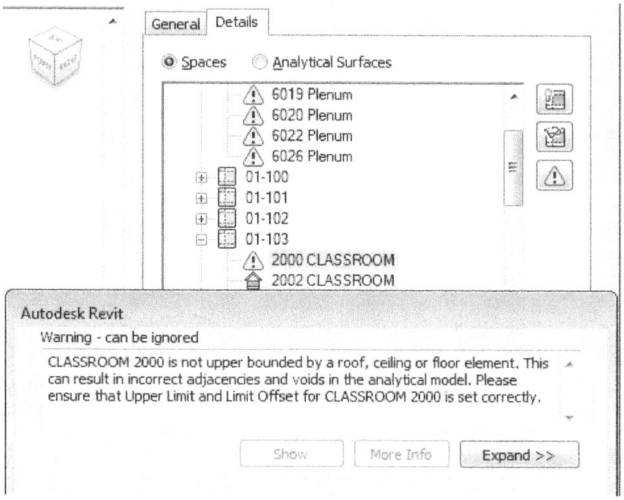

Figure 7–30

Task 1 - Prepare the project for energy analysis.

1. In the practice files *Analysis* folder, open **MEP-Elementary-School-Analysis-M.rvt**.
2. In the *Analyze* tab>Reports & Schedules panel, click  (Heating and Cooling Loads).
3. In the *General* tab, set the following parameter values, and shown in Figure 7–31:
   - *Building Type:* **School or University**
   - *Location*: Your hometown
   - *Building Service:* **VAV - Dual Duct**

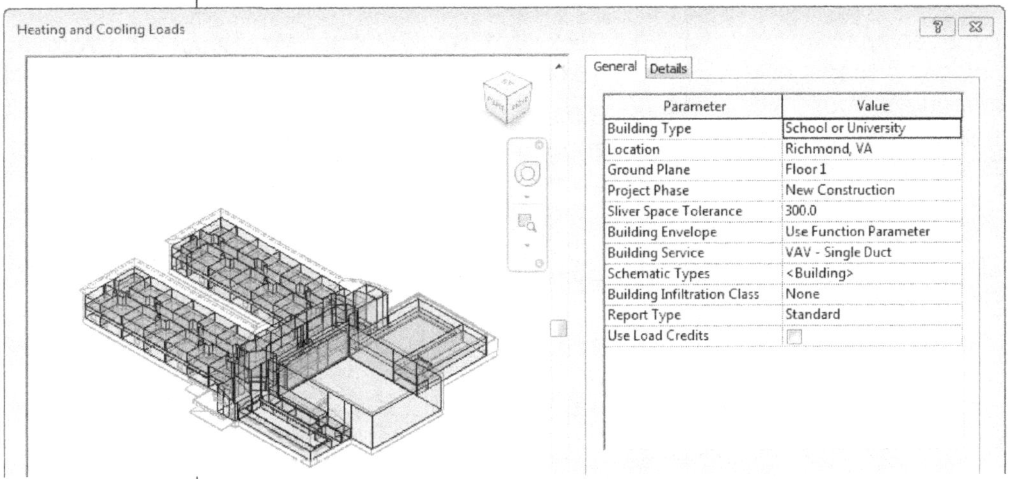

Figure 7–31

4. Click **Save Settings**.
5. Save the project.

Task 2 - Test the project.

1. Reopen the Heating and Cooling Loads dialog box and select the *Details* tab.
2. Several issues need to be resolved before you can calculate the loads starting with a Warning at the top of the building model, as shown in Figure 7–32.

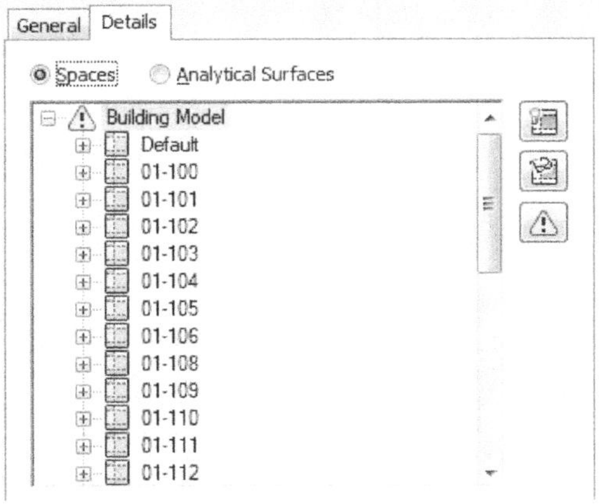

Figure 7–32

If your company includes a space schedule in your templates you can use it as mentioned in the Warning. You can also delete empty spaces in the Zone view of the System Manager.

3. Click (Show Related Warnings). The Warning indicates that there are undefined spaces in the model. Click **Cancel**.
4. Expand the Default zone. There are several spaces in this zone that need to be modified and moved to other zones, as shown in Figure 7–33.

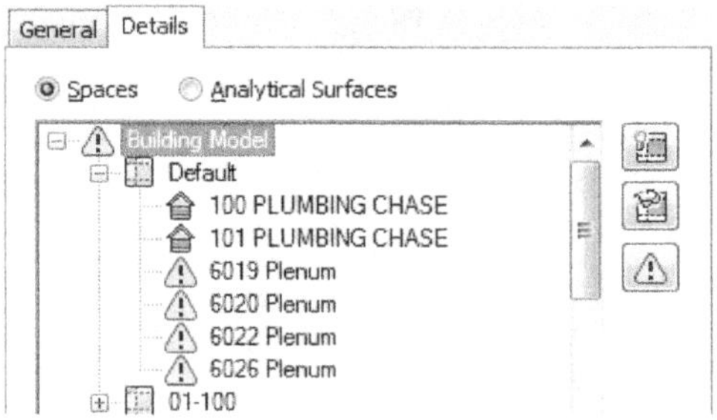

Figure 7–33

5. Select **100 Plumbing Chase**. The information about the space indicates that there are People and Electrical Loads associated with this space when they should not be, as shown in Figure 7–34. This is also indicated by the (Occupiable) icon beside the space name.

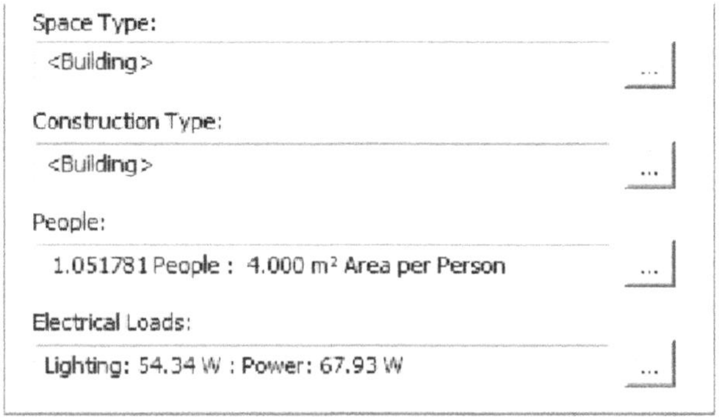

Figure 7–34

6. Use (Highlight) and/or (Isolate) to identify the plumbing chase locations. For example, you might want to select both chases and isolate them first as shown in Figure 7–35. Then switch to **Highlight** to indicate their location in the building. They are hard to identify because they are very thin.

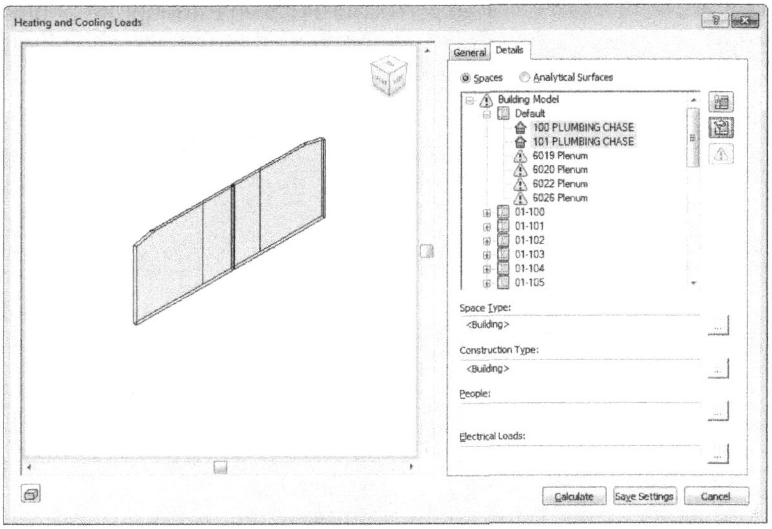

Figure 7–35

7. Toggle off **Highlight** and **Isolate**.

8. Select the four plenum spaces by holding <Ctrl> as you select.

9. Click  (Show Related Warnings). These spaces have not been placed and are ignored in the energy analysis as shown in Figure 7–36.

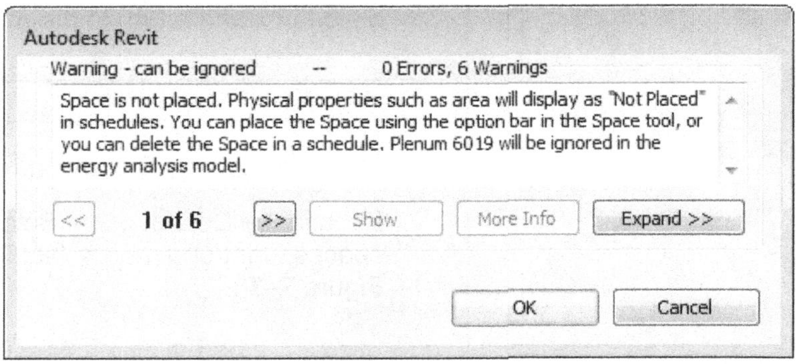

Figure 7–36

10. Scroll down through the zones to check for other problems, such as the one shown in Figure 7–37. Write down this zone and the space number so you can correct it in the model.

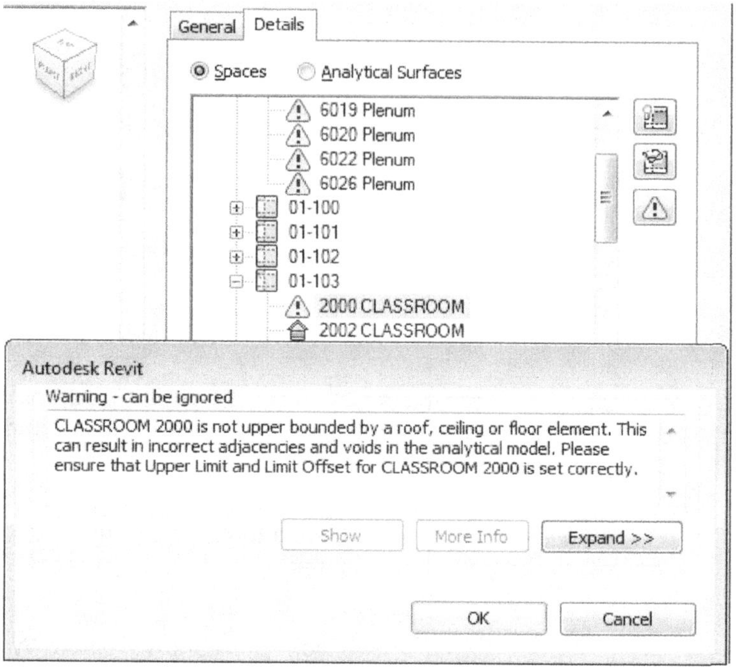

Figure 7–37

11. Click **Save Settings** to close the Heating and Cooling Loads dialog box and return to the model so that it can be modified.

Task 3 - Modify the model.

1. Open the System Browser (press <F9>) in the Zones view.
2. Expand the Default zone. Select the four unplaced plenum spaces, right-click and select **Delete**, as shown in Figure 7–38.

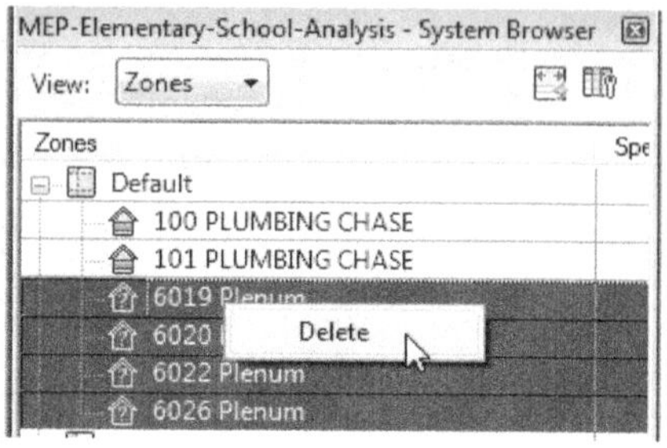

Figure 7–38

3. When prompted to delete the spaces, click **OK**.
   - If they do not get deleted, in the Project Browser, open the Schedules/Quantities>**SPACE SCHEDULE** view. The unplaced spaces display at the top of the view. Select them, right-click and select **Delete Row** and click **OK**. Return to the previous view.
4. In the System Browser in the *Default* zone, select both of the plumbing chase spaces.

*If you want see it is in the project, right-click and select **Show**. The view zooms in to the location with the space selected.*

5. In Properties, scroll down to the *Energy Analysis* area, clear **Occupiable** and click **Apply**. The icons in the System Browser change as shown in Figure 7–39.

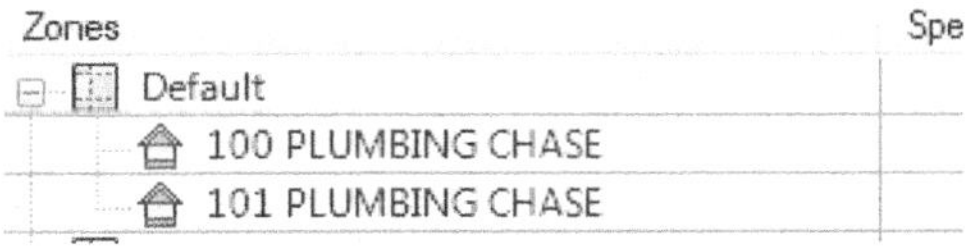

Figure 7–39

6. These two chases need to be added to the same zone as the other chases nearby. Hover the cursor over **Chase 104** and press <Tab> until the Zone lines highlight as shown in Figure 7–40. Click to select the zone.

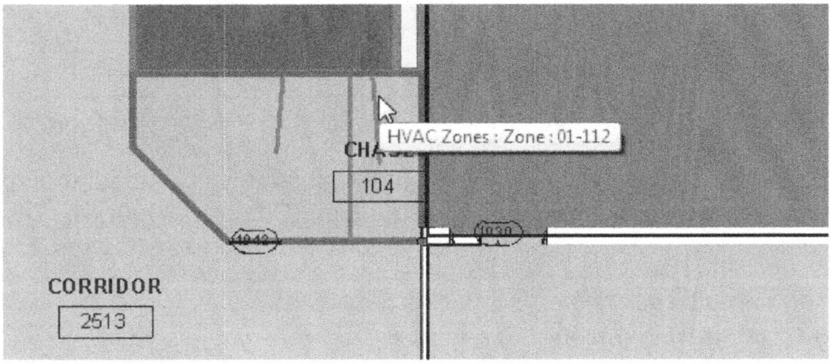

Figure 7–40

7. In the *Modify | HVAC Zones* tab>Zone panel, click (Edit Zone).
8. In the *Edit Zone* tab>Mode panel, click (Add Space).
9. Zoom in as required and select the two plumbing chase spaces. They should change to the color of the selected zone. Click (Finish Editing Zone).
10. In the System Browser, there should no longer be any spaces in the default zone.

Task 4 - Fix a space.

1. In the Systems Browser, find Zone **01-103** Space **2000 Classroom**. This had a problem with HVAC Loads, but does not display any warnings in the Systems Browser.

2. Right-click on the space and select **Show**. The view zooms in on the space but there are no warnings that anything is wrong.

3. Double-click on the nearby section arrow to open the section. The space does not extend up to the ceiling as it should, as shown in Figure 7–41.

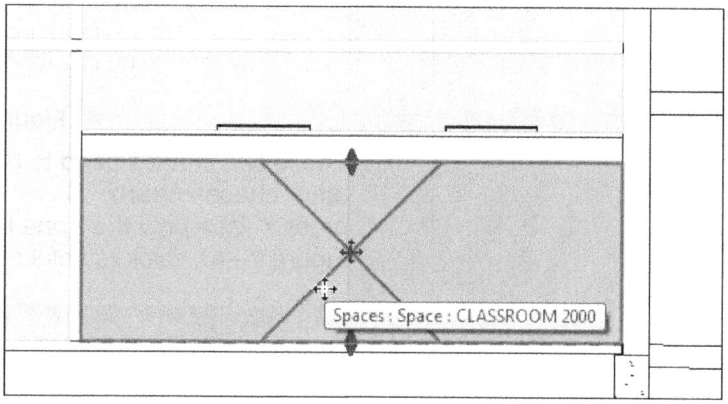

Figure 7–41

4. In the section view, select the space. In Properties, change the *Limit Offset* to **3000mm**. The space now extends up to touch the ceiling as shown in Figure 7–42.

You can also use the drag controls to modify the height of the space.

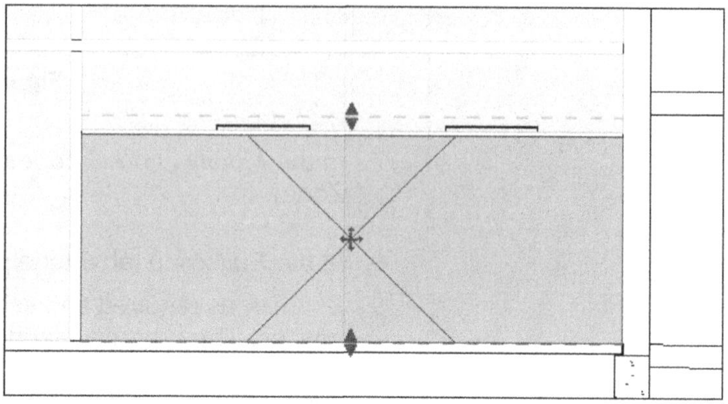

Figure 7–42

5. Return to the **01 Zones** plan.

6. Zoom out to display the entire plan.

7. Save the project.

Task 5 - Run the Heating and Cooling Loads.

1. Type **LO** (the shortcut key) or in the *Analyze* tab>Reports & Schedules panel, click  (Heating and Cooling Loads).

2. In the Heating and Cooling Loads dialog box, in the *Details* tab, expand the zones. The problems have been taken care of as shown in Figure 7–43.

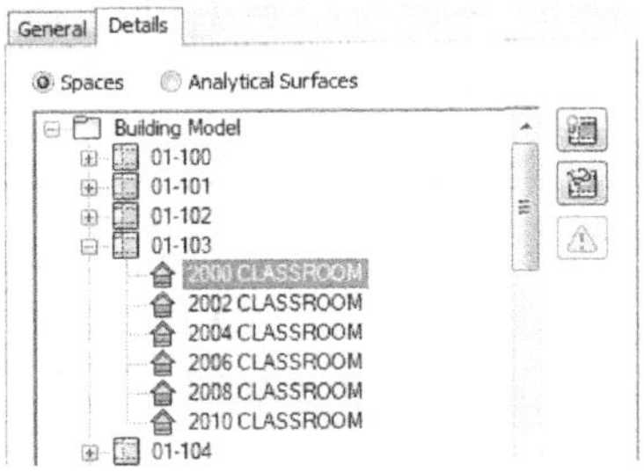

Figure 7–43

3. Click **Calculate**. The progress displays in the Status bar as shown in Figure 7–44. This takes time.

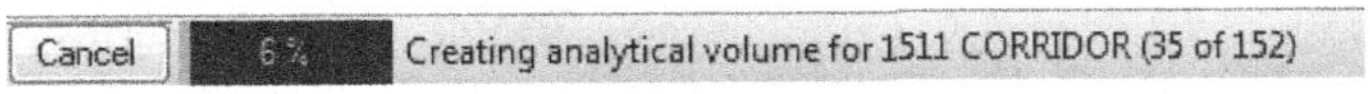

Figure 7–44

4. Review the Loads analysis document as shown in part in Figure 7–45.

Building Summary

Inputs	
Building Type	School or University
Area (m²)	6,071
Volume (m³)	26,260.58
Calculated Results	
Peak Cooling Total Load (W)	**509,133**
Peak Cooling Month and Hour	July 2:00 PM
Peak Cooling Sensible Load (W)	437,963
Peak Cooling Latent Load (W)	71,170
Maximum Cooling Capacity (W)	516,737
Peak Cooling Airflow (L/s)	33,449.6
Peak Heating Load (W)	**224,094**
Peak Heating Airflow (L/s)	12,882.6

Figure 7–45

5. Save the project.

Chapter Review Questions

1. You want to modify a view so that colors for the various zones display as shown in Figure 7–46. How do you apply the colors to the view?

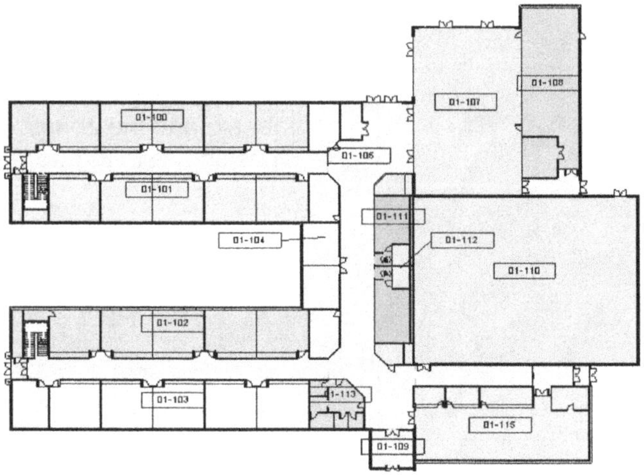

Figure 7–46

   a. Modify the color scheme in Visibility/Graphics.
   b. Assign a color scheme in Properties.
   c. Toggle on **Color Schemes** in the View Control Bar.
   d. Add a Color Fill Legend.

2. Zones (shown in Figure 7–47) are formed of spaces that can be heated and cooled in the same manner.

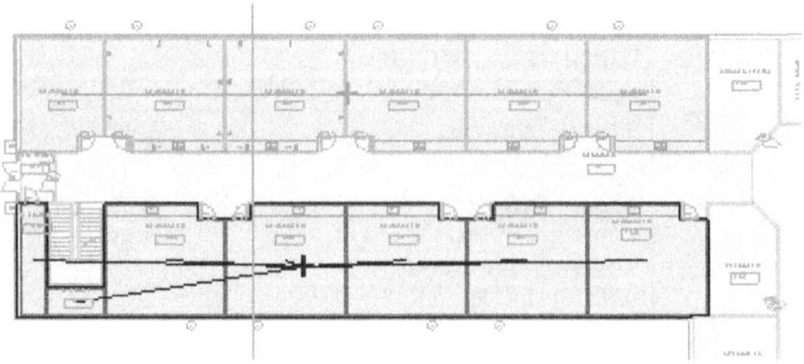

Figure 7–47

   a. True
   b. False

3. Which of the following are Energy Settings that impact Energy Analysis? (Select all that apply.)
    a. Geographic location of the building.
    b. Exterior wall construction.
    c. Number of spaces in the model.
    d. Plenum heights.

4. In the System Browser, in the Zones view, displays next to the name of the space. It indicates that the space...
    a. occupancy has not been defined.
    b. does not have an upper boundary.
    c. has not been placed.
    d. is not part of a zone.

5. When running the Heating and Cooling Loads analysis, the *Details* tab indicates that there are still spaces listed under Default, as shown in Figure 7–48. What needs to be done?

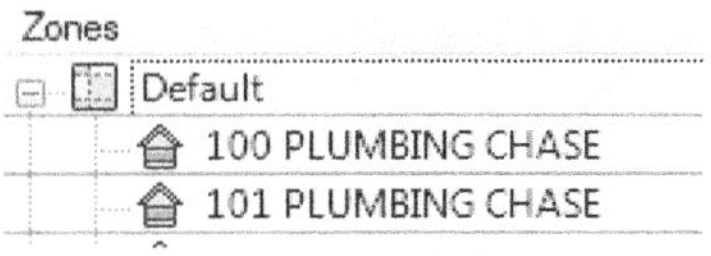

Figure 7–48

    a. Delete those spaces from the model.
    b. Verify the height of the spaces.
    c. Move the spaces to another zone.
    d. Change the status of the spaces to unoccupied.

6. To get an accurate energy analysis, all areas in the project need to be set up with...
    a. Light fixtures
    b. Spaces
    c. Heating equipment
    d. Sun shade devices

Command Summary

Button	Command	Location
	**Color Fill Legend**	• **Ribbon:** *Analyze* tab>Color Fill panel
	**Heating and Cooling Loads**	• **Ribbon:** *Analyze* tab>Reports & Schedules panel
	**System Browser**	• **Ribbon:** *View* tab>Windows panel, expand User Interface • **Shortcut:** <F9>
	**Zone**	• **Ribbon:** *Analyze* tab>Spaces & Zones panel

Chapter 8

HVAC Networks

HVAC networks consist of components that include mechanical equipment, air terminals, ducts. and pipes. The process of combining these components and ensuring they work correctly is a significant part of developing an HVAC project.

Learning Objectives in this Chapter

- Add HVAC components including mechanical equipment and air terminals.
- Add ducts and pipes to connect HVAC components.
- Modify ducts and pipes.

8.1 Adding Mechanical Equipment and Air Terminals

When beginning an HVAC system in a project, you typically start with mechanical equipment and air terminals, and then network them together using ducts, as shown in Figure 8–1. You also add hydronic piping connecting mechanical equipment.

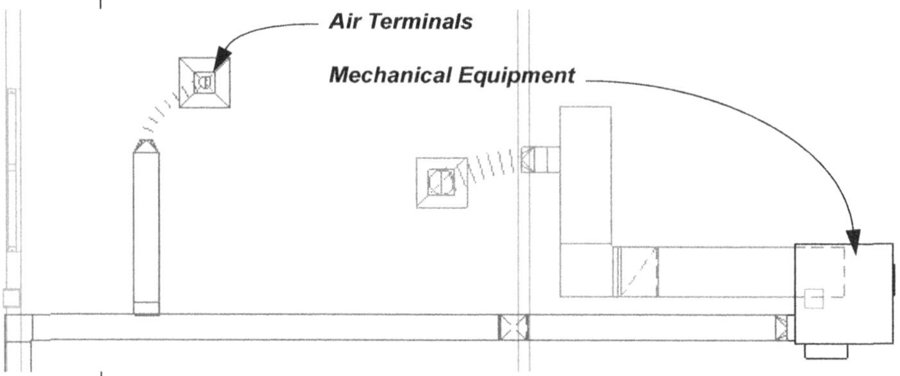

Figure 8–1

Mechanical Equipment

Mechanical Equipment includes various air handling units, such as fan coil units or variable air volume units. Mechanical equipment families are managed in Properties and have connectors, as shown in Figure 8–2.

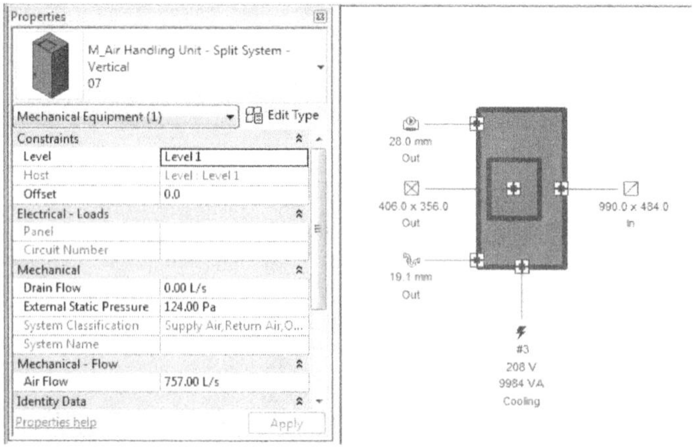

Figure 8–2

- Mechanical equipment might also include connections for hydronic piping and electrical power.

- Depending on the component, Mechanical Equipment can be placed in plan, elevation, and 3D views.

How To: Place Mechanical Equipment

1. In the *Systems* tab>Mechanical panel, click (Mechanical Equipment), or type **ME**.
2. In the Type Selector, select a mechanical equipment type.
3. In Properties, set any other values, such as the *Level* and *Offset,* if it is not hosted.
4. In the Options Bar, specify if you want to be able to rotate the equipment after placement.
5. Place the equipment in the model by clicking at the required location in the model view.

- You can use other objects in the model to align the element and press <Spacebar> to rotate it before placing it.
- Additional boilers, radiators, VAV units and more can be loaded from the Autodesk® Revit® Library in the *Mechanical> MEP* subfolders.

Hint: Tagging Mechanical Equipment and Air Terminals

Both air terminals and mechanical equipment can be tagged, as shown in Figure 8–3.

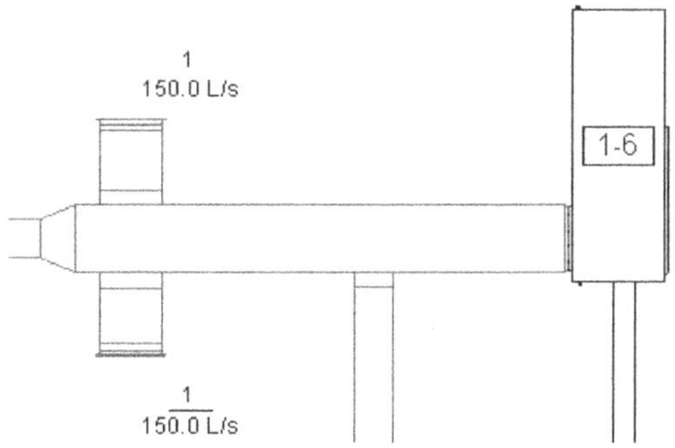

Figure 8–3

- When you are adding the elements, in the *Modify | contextual* tab>Tag panel, toggle (Tag on Placement) on or off as required.
- To add tags later, in the *Annotate* tab>Tag panel, click (Tag by Category) and select the elements to tag.

Air Terminals

Air terminals can be used in supply, return, or exhaust air systems, as shown in Figure 8–4. You can place individual air terminals or batch copy them from a linked model.

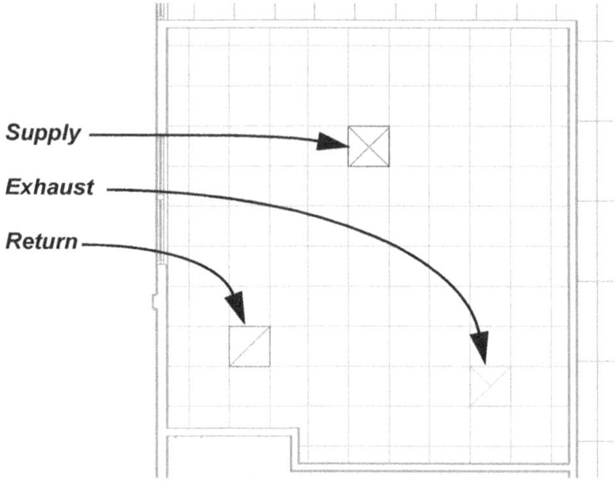

Figure 8–4

- Often, air terminals are placed on a host, such as a ceiling. Therefore when placing an air terminal, use a reflected ceiling plan view.
- Some air terminal types can also be placed directly on ducts.
- Air terminals display regardless of the cut plane of the view.
- The flow of each air terminal in a space is summed, so that total air flow in a space can be easily checked against the Specified Airflow and Calculated Airflow in a schedule.

How To: Place an Air Terminal

1. In the *Systems* tab>HVAC panel, click (Air Terminal) or type **AT**.
2. In the Type Selector, select an air terminal type.
   - If the Air terminal is not hosted, in Properties, set the *Level* and *Offset*.
   - If the air terminal type is hosted, in the *Modify | Place Air Terminal* tab>Placement panel, select the type of placement to a face or a plane.

	Place on Vertical Face	Places air terminal on a vertical face, such as a wall.

	Place on Face	Places the air terminal on a defined face, such as the ceiling grid.
	Place on Work Plane	Places the air terminal on a defined plane such as a level or ceiling in a linked architectural model.

3. In Properties, set the *Flow* and other parameters.
4. Place the air terminal in the model by clicking at the required location in the model view.
5. Continue to place additional air terminals, as shown in Figure 8–5, or click (Modify) to exit the command.

Use other objects in the model, such as the ceiling grid or previously placed air terminals, to line up the air terminal.

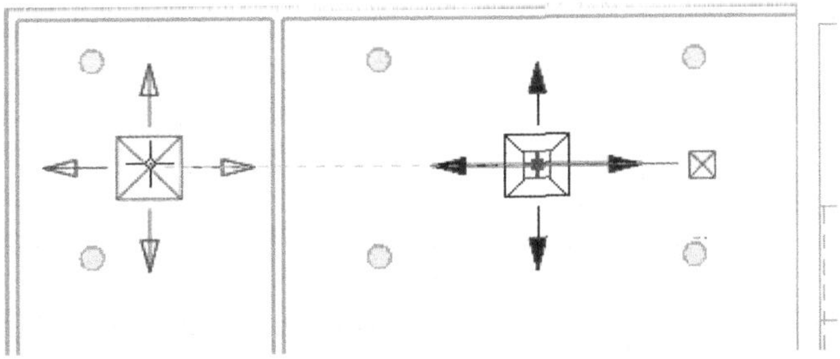

Figure 8–5

- After any air terminal is initially placed, you can modify it in any view and use the standard modify tools to move, align, and rotate it.
- If the air terminal you want does not exist in your project, you can load one from the Library>*Mechanical>MEP>Air-Side Components>Air Terminals* folder. Some air terminal types prompt you to select sizes as shown in Figure 8–6.

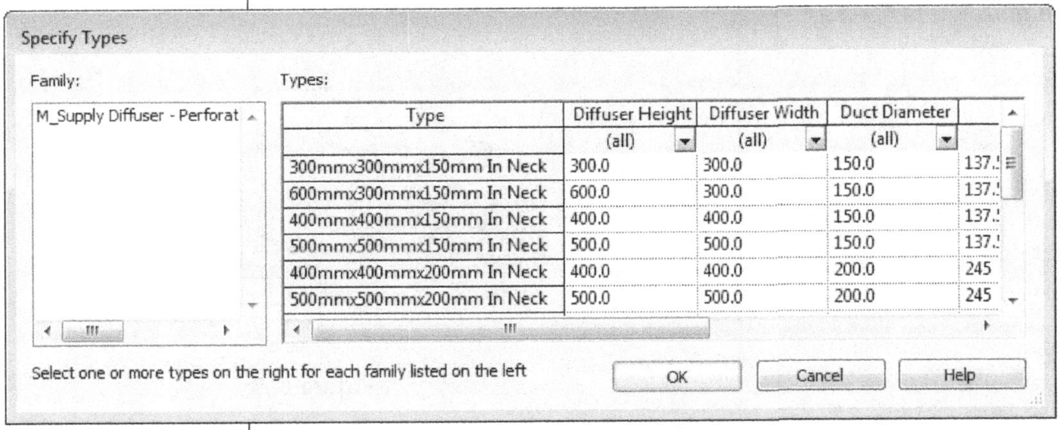

Figure 8–6

Some firms add reference planes and place the hosted families on them instead of in the ceiling. This gives them control over the height of the families. If the architect moves the ceilings up or down, the engineer adjusts the height of the reference plane to match.

- Air terminals that are hosted by a ceiling in a linked model (as shown in Figure 8–7), move automatically with any changes that the architects make to the ceiling height. This can be an advantage of using hosted fixtures.

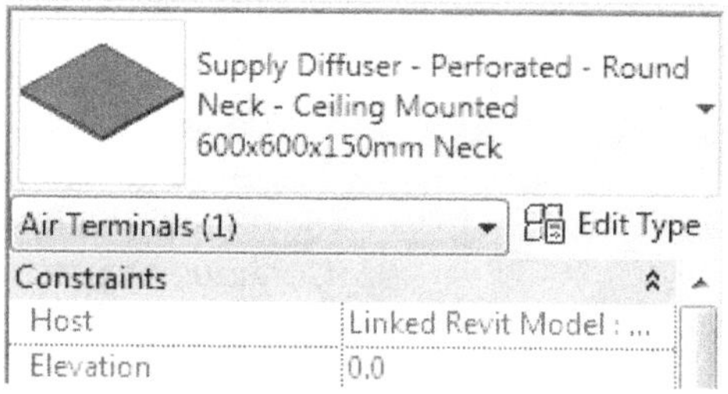

Figure 8–7

- If the architect deletes the ceiling and puts a new one in the linked model, the hosted air terminals are orphaned and do not move with changes in the ceiling height. A warning box opens when you reload the linked model or reopen the MEP project, as shown in Figure 8–8. Use the **Coordination Monitoring** tools to address the issue.

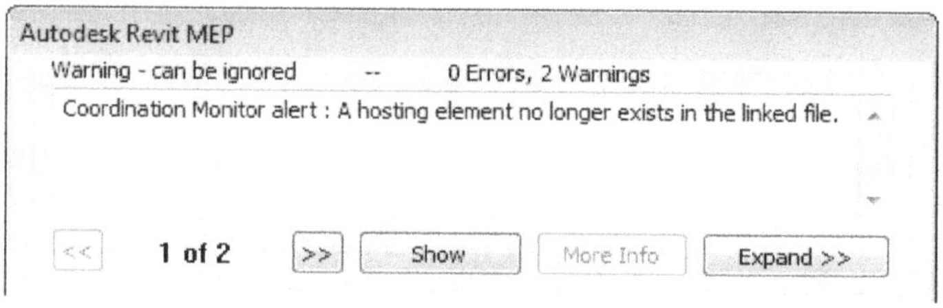

Figure 8–8

- When using a non-hosted air terminal it is placed at a specified height above the level of the current view, as shown in Figure 8–9. It is not modified if the linked architectural model is modified.

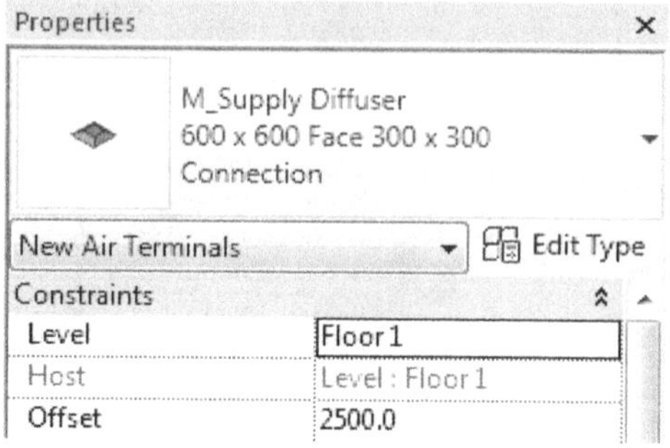

Figure 8–9

How To: Place an Air Terminal on a Duct

1. Have a duct in place. If it is a round or oval duct, verify the diameter before selecting the air terminal.
2. Start the **Air Terminal** command.
3. In the Type Selector, select the required air terminal. There are different types for curved and rectangular duct faces. Curved face air terminals are created by duct diameter as shown in Figure 8–10.

Ensure that you are selecting an air terminal that matches the system type of the duct.

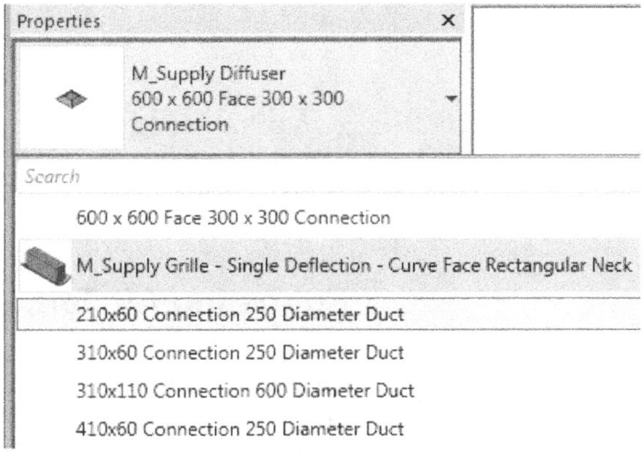

Figure 8–10

4. In the *Modify | Place Air Terminal* tab>Layout panel, verify that (Air Terminal on Duct) is toggled on.
5. Move the cursor over to the duct where you want to place the air terminal. The air terminal automatically rotates to the face you are closest to, as shown in Figure 8–11.

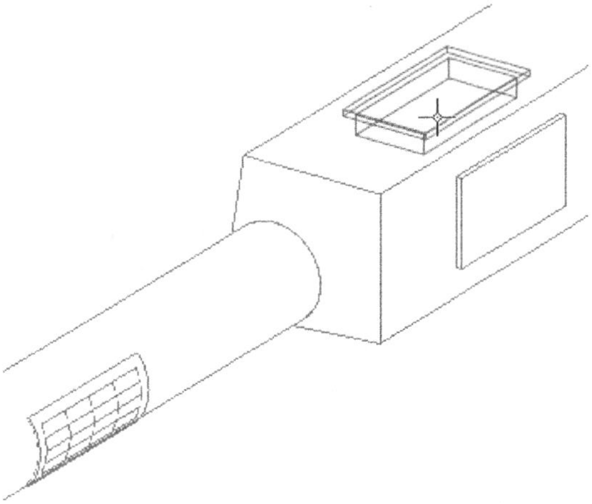

Figure 8–11

6. Click to place the air terminal.

Copying Air Terminals

If you have air terminals in a project with similar parameters including the type, elevation, and flow, you can place one and then copy it to the other locations. This works with independently placed air terminals and those placed directly on ducts, as shown in Figure 8–12.

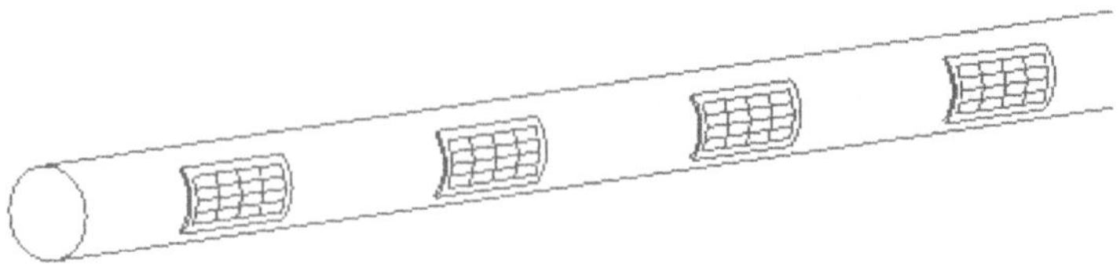

Figure 8–12

Rehosting Air Terminals

While working with linked models, if air terminals are copied from one ceiling to other ceilings of the same height, the copied air terminals are hosted by their respective new ceilings. However, if the ceilings are a different height than the ceiling that hosts the original air terminal, the copied fixtures are not associated with the ceiling. They end up at the same elevation as the original air terminal, as shown in Figure 8–13. Therefore, you need to rehost the air terminal.

If the ceilings are in the host project you are not permitted to copy a hosted air terminal from one ceiling to another.

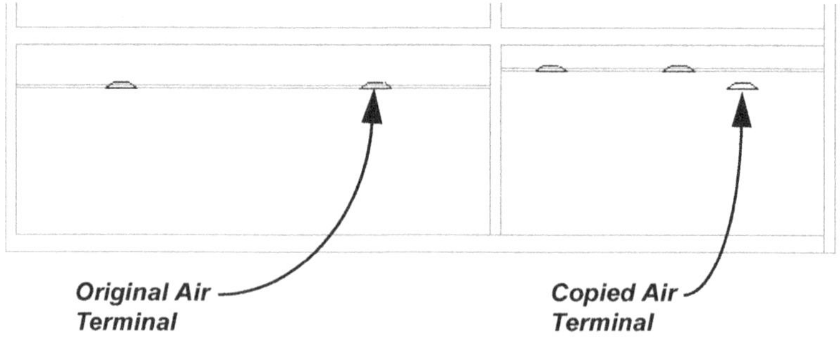

Figure 8–13

How To: Rehost an Air Terminal

1. Copy the air terminals as required.
2. Select the one(s) that need to be rehosted to a different ceiling.
3. In the *Modify | Air Terminals* tab>Work Plane panel, click (Pick New).
4. In the Placement panel, click (Face).
5. Select the ceiling to which you want the air terminal(s) hosted.

- This needs to be done in the reflected ceiling plan view for ceiling hosted fixtures.
- Occasionally, the location of a light fixture or air terminal is such that the software assigns its electrical/mechanical values to the wrong space. This results in faulty heating and cooling load calculations and incorrect space values. To correct this, use a family that has the **Room Calculation Point** turned on. The point is displayed in the project when a fixture is selected, as shown in Figure 8–14. However, the point cannot be manipulated and its visibility is only for review purposes.

Not all air terminals or light fixtures have this feature turned on by default. It must be added in the Family Parameters of the component.

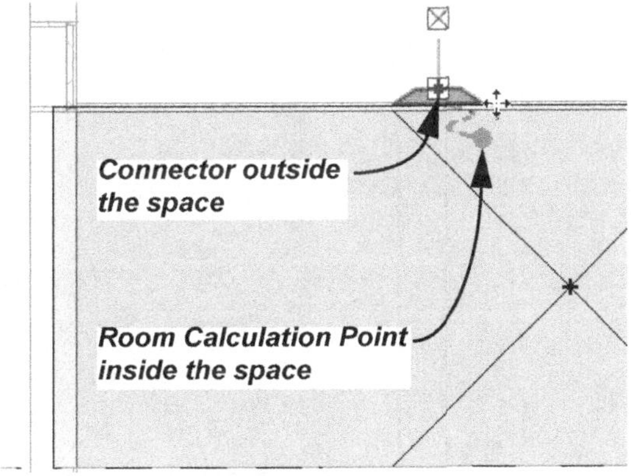

Figure 8–14

Practice 8a

Add Mechanical Equipment and Air Terminals

Estimated time for completion: 10 minutes

Practice Objectives

- Place mechanical equipment.
- Place air terminals.

In this practice you will add Air Handling Units (AHUs) in the hallway at a specified height. You will then place supply and return air terminals on the face of a ceiling. You will align the air terminals to the ceiling grid and copy the air terminals as required to create the layout shown in Figure 8–15.

Figure 8–15

Task 1 - Add mechanical equipment.

1. In the practice files *HVAC* folder, open **MEP-Elementary-School-HVAC-M.rvt**.
2. Open the Mechanical>HVAC>Floor Plans>**01 Mechanical Plan** view. There are some existing HVAC systems and open locations where you will add components, as shown in Figure 8–16.

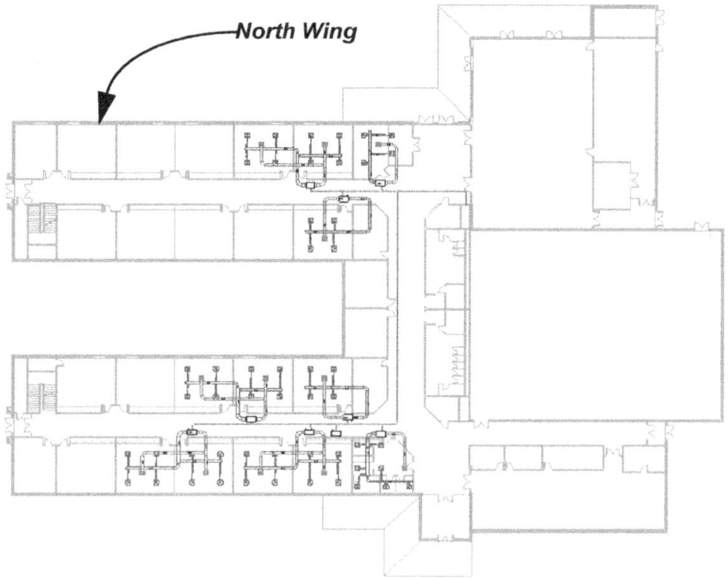

Figure 8–16

3. Zoom in on the north wing, shown in Figure 8–16.

4. In the *Systems* tab>Mechanical panel, click (Mechanical Equipment).

5. In the Type Selector, select **M_Indoor AHU - Horizontal - Chilled Water Coil: Unit Size 24** and then set the *Offset* to **2850mm**.

6. Place the AHU so that the connectors are facing the hallway, as shown in Figure 8–17.

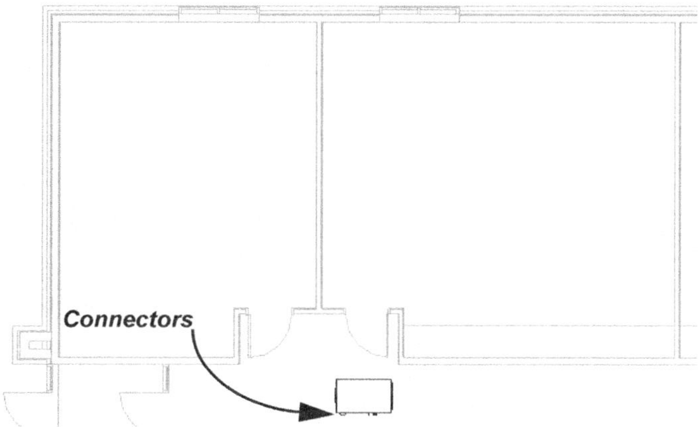

Figure 8–17

7. While still in placement mode, press <Spacebar> until the equipment is rotated 180 degrees. Place another AHU outside of the classroom doors on the opposite side of the hall, as shown in Figure 8–18.

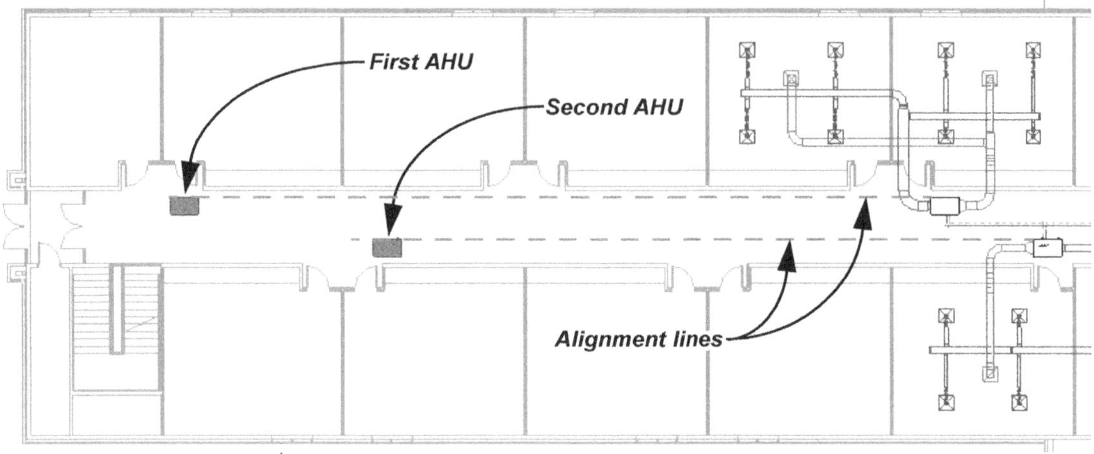

Figure 8–18

8. Click **Modify**.

9. In the *Modify* tab>Modify panel, click (Align).

10. Select the inside edge of the existing AHU and then the new AHU, as shown in Figure 8–18. Repeat this on the other side of the hall.

11. Save the project.

Task 2 - Add air terminals.

1. Open the Mechanical>HVAC>Ceiling Plans>**01 Mechanical - Ceiling** view. In this view you can see the locations of the ceiling grid and light fixtures provided in the architectural project.

2. In the *Systems* tab>HVAC panel, click (Air Terminal).

3. In the Type Selector, select **M_Supply Diffuser - Round Neck - Ceiling Mounted: 600x600x150 In Neck,** as shown in Figure 8–19.

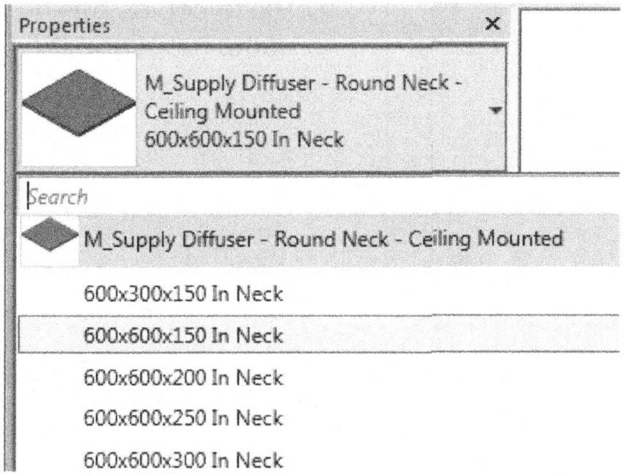

Figure 8–19

4. In Properties, set *Flow* to **70 L/s**.
5. In the *Modify | Place Component* tab>Placement panel, click (Place on Face).
6. Move the cursor into the project. As the cursor passes over a ceiling, the ceiling highlights. Place the air terminal near one of the lighting fixtures, as shown in Figure 8–20.

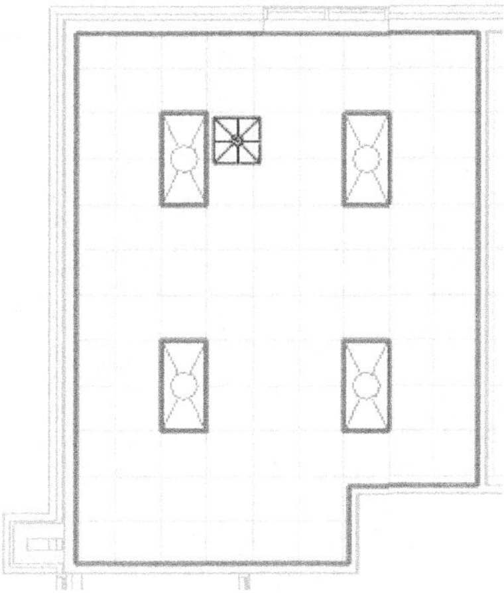

Figure 8–20

7. Type **AL** to start the **Align** command. Align the air terminal to the grid.
8. Type **CO** to start the **Copy** command. Select the air terminal and press <Enter>.
9. In the Options Bar, select **Multiple**.

10. Place copies beside each of the other lighting fixtures in the same room and the room beside it, as shown in Figure 8–21.

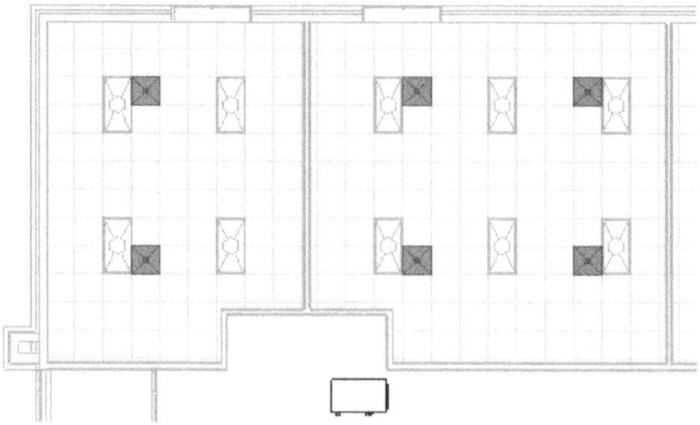

Figure 8–21

11. Zoom out so that one of the existing systems in the same hallway displays.
12. Select one of the return diffusers, right-click and select **Create Similar**. The Air Terminal command is started with the correct type and properties automatically applied.
13. In the *Modify | Place Component* tab>Placement panel, click  (Place on Face).
14. Place two return diffusers in the rooms, as shown in Figure 8–22. Align them to the ceiling grid.

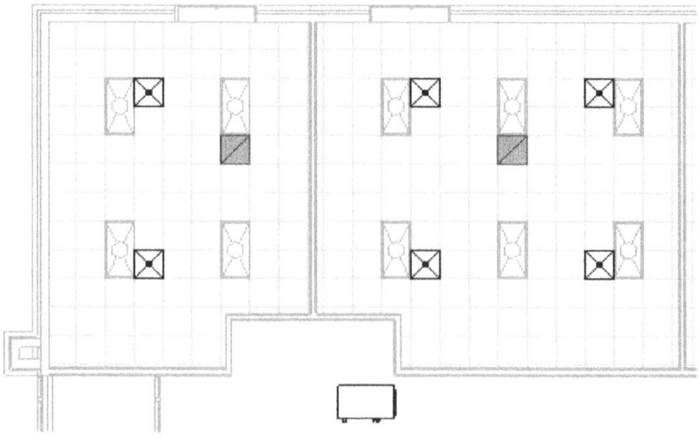

Figure 8–22

15. Copy the air terminals and diffusers to the two rooms across the hall. Align them to the ceiling grid.
16. Save the project.

8.2 Adding Ducts and Pipes

Ducts connect mechanical equipment to air terminals and pipes connect mechanical equipment to the hydronic supply, as shown in Figure 8–23. There are various shapes and sizes that can be used both for regular and flex duct and pipe. By using connectors in the equipment and the air terminals, you can quickly attach the ducts and pipes and have the software automatically calculate any differences in height.

Fittings are automatically added in some cases. You can also modify fittings and add others.

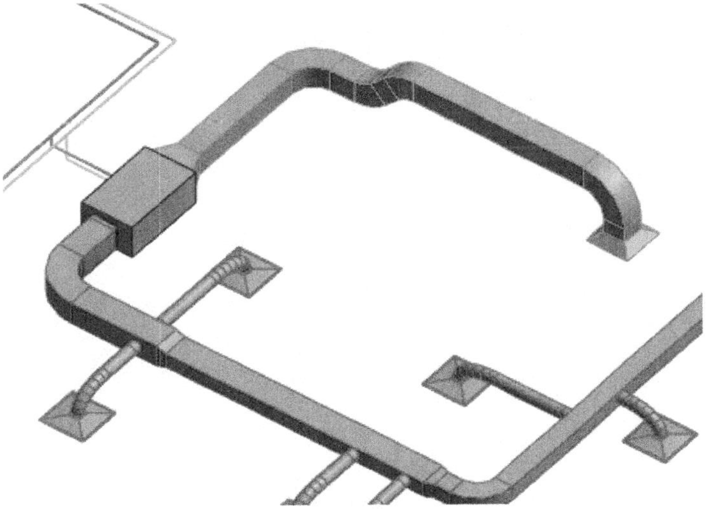

Figure 8–23

- Ducts and pipes can be drawn in plan, elevation/section, and 3D views.
- To get the ducts and pipes at the right height, it is recommended to start it from the Mechanical Equipment.
- Fittings between changes of height or size are automatically applied as you model the elements, as shown in Figure 8–24.

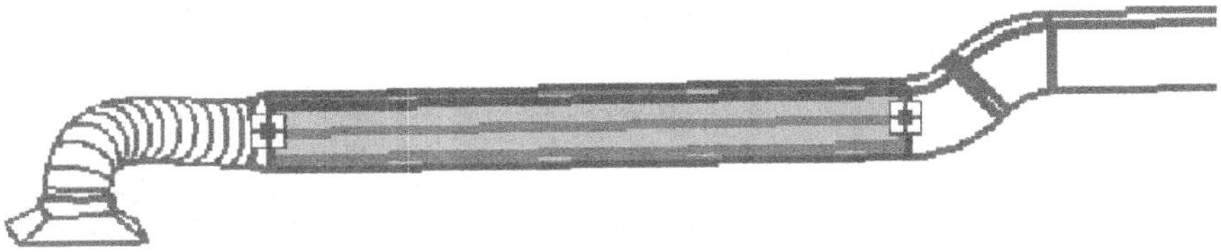

Figure 8–24

- If you need to lay the runs, but the type and size has not yet been determined, create Duct or Pipe Placeholders and convert them to standard ducts or pipes at a later stage.

Mechanical Settings

Before you add ducts or pipes, review and modify the Mechanical Settings to suit your project or office standards. These settings control the angles at which the ducts and pipes can be drawn (as shown in Figure 8–25), and the default types, offsets, sizes, and Pressure Drop calculation method.

- In the *Systems* tab>Mechanical panel, click (Mechanical Settings), or type **MS**, to open the Mechanical Settings dialog box.

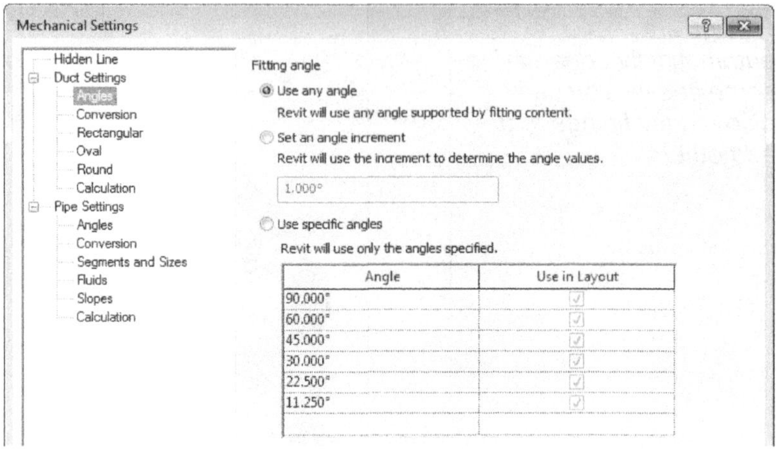

Figure 8–25

Hidden Line	Specify the size and type of hidden lines that show when ducts or pipe cross over each other.
Angles	Specify at what angles fittings are applied for both duct and pipe.
Conversion	Specify how the ducts or pipe work when using the Generate Layout tool. (These are also available in that command.)
Rectangular, Oval, and Round	Specify the sizes that can be used when placing ducts. (Duct only.)
Segments and Sizes	Specify the sizes and other properties for piping by material type. (Pipe only.)
Fluids	Specify the temperature, viscosity, and density of fluids by fluid type. (Pipe only.)
Slopes	Specify slope values for piping runs. (Pipe only.)
Calculation	Specify the duct or pipe pressure drop for straight sections. You can select from a variety of calculation methods.

- Duct and Pipe Settings are set by project and can be included in templates or imported into a project from another project using **Transfer Project Standards**.
- If you are working with hydronic piping, you need to set up the analysis process in **Mechanical Settings** on the *Pipe Settings>Calculation >Hydronic Networks* tab. Select **Enable analysis for closed loop hydronic piping networks**.

Enhanced in 2018

Adding Ducts and Pipes

The process of adding various types of duct or pipe is essentially the same whether you are drawing standard, flex, or placeholder elements.

There are several ways to start the commands:

1. In the *Systems* tab>HVAC or Plumbing & Piping panels, click the required command:

Duct (DT)	Pipe (PI)
Duct Placeholder	Pipe Placeholder
Flex Duct (FD)	Flex Pipe (FP)

2. Select the element, hover the cursor over a connector icon, and then select the command, as shown in Figure 8–26.
3. Select the element, right-click on a connector, and then select the command name, as shown in Figure 8–27.

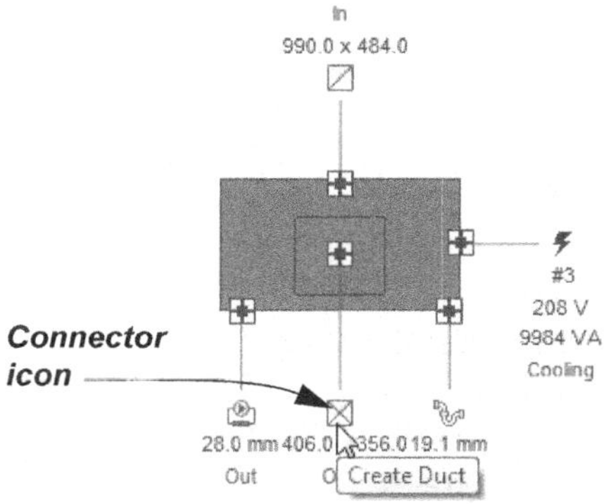

Figure 8–26

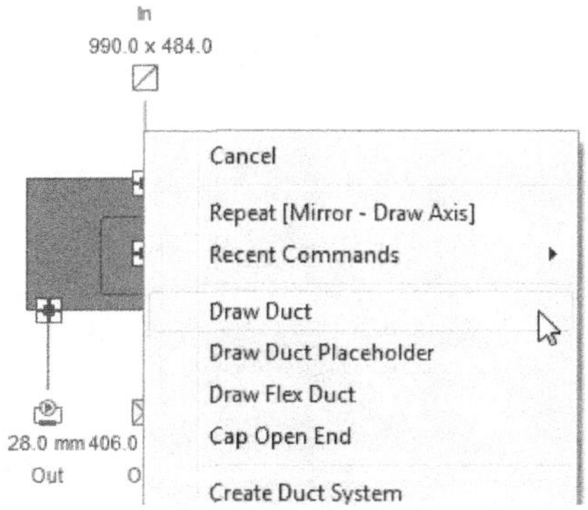

Figure 8–27

How To: Draw Duct and Pipe

You can limit the number of options that display by typing part of the name in the search box.

1. Start the command using one of the options outlined above.
2. In the Type Selector, select a type as shown for ducts in Figure 8–28.

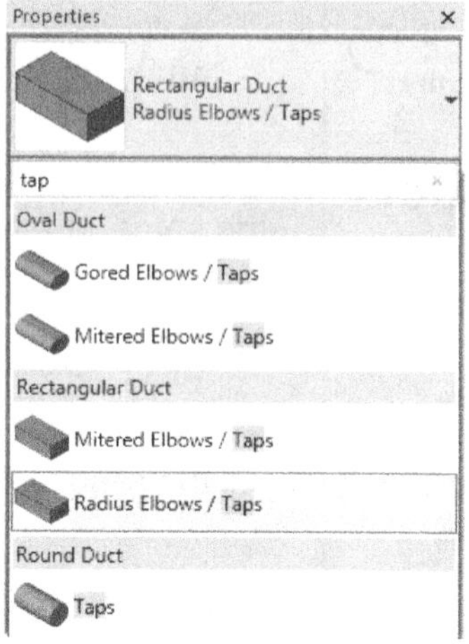

Figure 8–28

3. If you are drawing ducts or pipes without selecting an existing connector, in Properties, specify the *System Type* (as shown in Figure 8–29) before you start drawing the elements.

Drawing from existing connectors automatically applies the System Type.

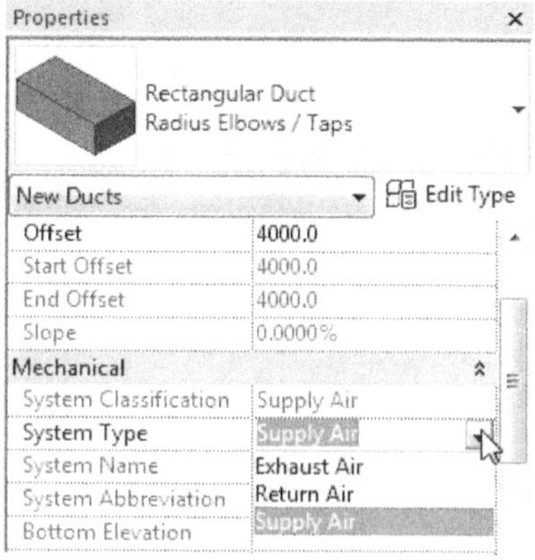

Figure 8–29

4. In the Options Bar set the *Width*, *Height* (or *Diameter* for round ducts and pipes), and *Offset,* as shown in Figure 8–30. If you started from a connector, the default sizes and offset match the parameters of the selected connector.

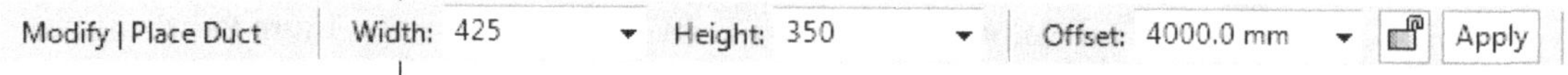

Figure 8–30

5. In the ribbon, set up the various placement tools, as outlined in the next section.
6. Draw the elements using temporary dimensions, snaps, and alignments to locate each point along the path as shown in Figure 8–31.

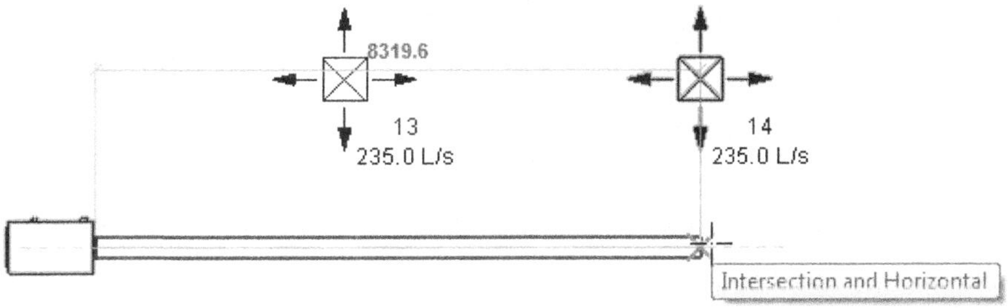

Figure 8–31

7. Press <Esc> once to stay in the command, but have a new start location.

- When snapping to another element with connectors, ensure that you select the point snap on the end of the other element to create the connection, as shown in Figure 8–32.

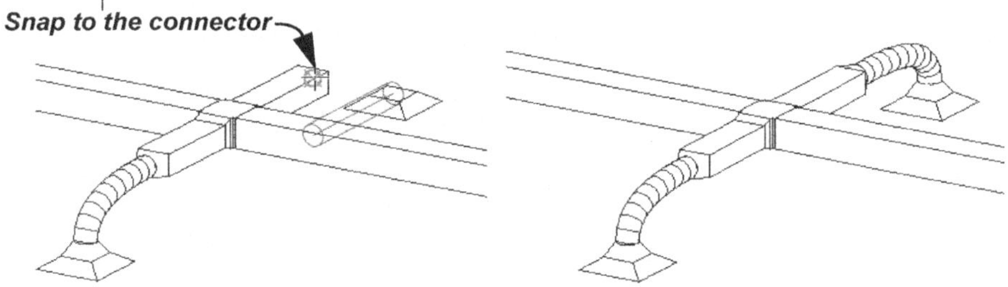

Figure 8–32

Duct and Pipe Placement Tools

	**Automatically Connect (on/off)**	On by default. Ducts and pipes connect to other ones and automatically place all of the required fittings. To draw a duct or pipe that remains at the original elevation, toggle this option off. • Even if **Automatically Connect** is not toggled on, when you snap to a connector any changes in height and size are applied with the appropriate fittings.
	**Justification**	Opens the Justification Setting dialog box, which enables you to set the default settings for the *Horizontal Justification, Horizontal Offset,* and *Vertical Justification.*

	**Inherit Elevation (on/off)**	If the tool is toggled on and you start modeling a duct or pipe by snapping to an existing one, the new duct or pipe takes on the elevation of the existing one regardless of what is specified, as shown in Figure 8–33.
	**Inherit Size (on/off)**	If the tool is toggled on and you start modeling duct or pipe by snapping to an existing one, the new duct or pipe takes on the size of the existing one regardless of what is specified, as shown in Figure 8–33.

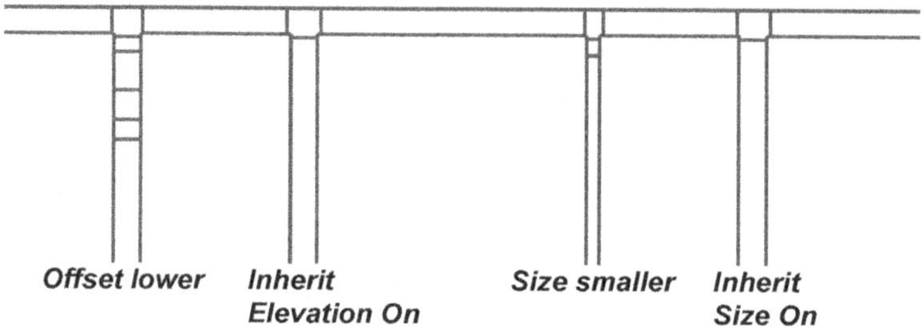

Figure 8–33

- If you already have some ducts or pipes in the project, you can use  (Connect Into). This option displays in the contextual tab when you select a component.

- To display centerlines for round ducts or pipe, in the Visibility/ Graphics Overrides dialog box, turn on the *Centerline* subcategory for duct and duct fittings, as shown in Figure 8–34.

*Centerlines display in plan and elevation views set to the **Wireframe** or **Hidden Line** visual style.*

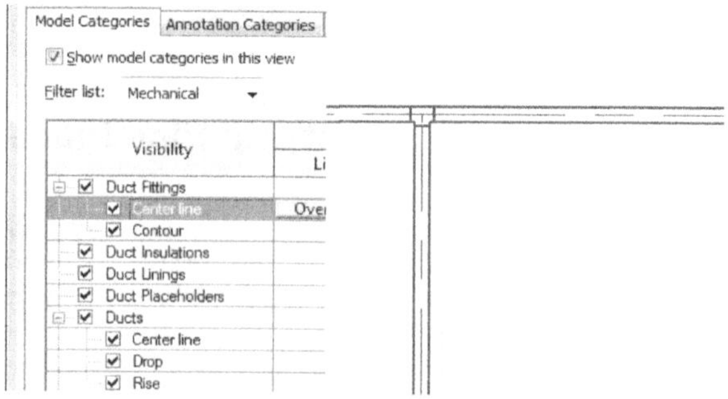

Figure 8–34

Creating Parallel Pipes

You can also press <Spacebar> to inherit the elevation and the size of the duct or pipe you snap to.

The **Parallel Pipes** tool facilitates the creation of piping runs parallel to an existing run, as shown in Figure 8–35. This can save time because only one run needs to be laid out, and the tool generates parallel runs for you.

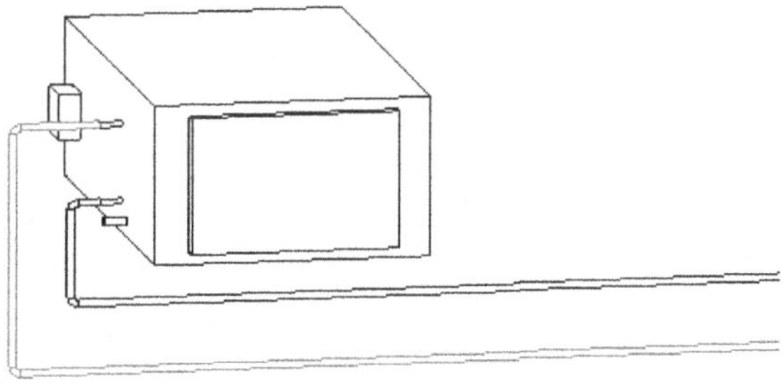

Figure 8–35

- The **Parallel Pipes** tool creates an exact duplicate of the selected pipe, including the *System Type*. You can change the *System Type* in Properties before connecting other pipes into it.

- It might be easier to draw the parallel pipes directly from the fixtures so that they use the correct system type. Also, you might have to modify connectors to get the pipe in the correct place.

- Parallel pipes can be created in plan, section, elevation, and 3D views.

How To: Create Parallel Pipe Runs

1. Create an initial single run of pipe or use an existing pipe run, as required.
2. In the *Systems* tab>Plumbing & Piping panel, click  (Parallel Pipes).
3. In the *Modify | Place Parallel Pipes* tab>Parallel Pipes panel, set the options as shown in Figure 8–36.

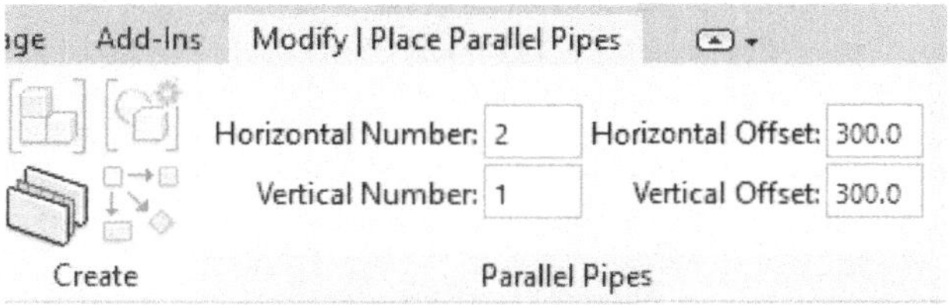

Figure 8–36

4. Hover the cursor over the existing piping (as shown in Figure 8–37) and press <Tab> to select the existing run.

If you do not select the entire run, parallel pipes are only created for the single piece of existing pipe.

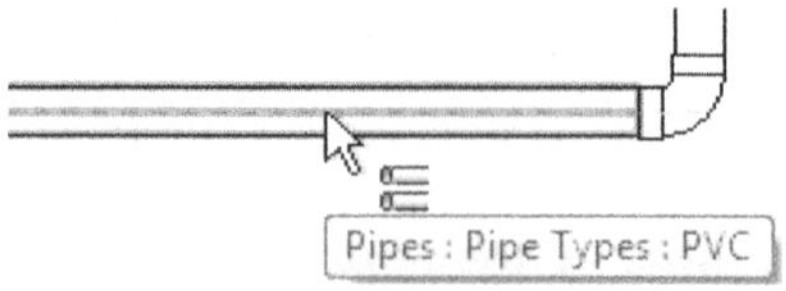

Figure 8–37

5. When the preview displays, click to create the parallel runs. The preview varies depending on which side of the existing run you hover the cursor.

Parallel Pipe Creation Options

Horizontal Number	The total number of parallel pipe runs in the horizontal direction.
Horizontal Offset	The distance between parallel pipe runs in the horizontal direction.
Vertical Number	The total number of parallel pipe runs in the vertical direction.
Vertical Offset	The distance between parallel pipe runs in the vertical direction.

- In section and elevation views, horizontal refers to parallel to the view (visually up, down, left, or right from the original conduit). Vertical creates parallel conduit runs perpendicular to the view, in the direction of the user.

New in 2018

Hint: Analytical Hydronic Piping

In the early stages of a project you might not want to create all of the exact connections between hydronic piping and mechanical equipment, but you still want to be able to calculate flow and pressure drop. To do this, you can add analytical connections, as shown in Figure 8–38.

Select mechanical equipment or hydronic piping, and then in the *Modify* contextual tab>Create panel, click (Analytical Connections). Then select the pipe or equipment you want to connect into.

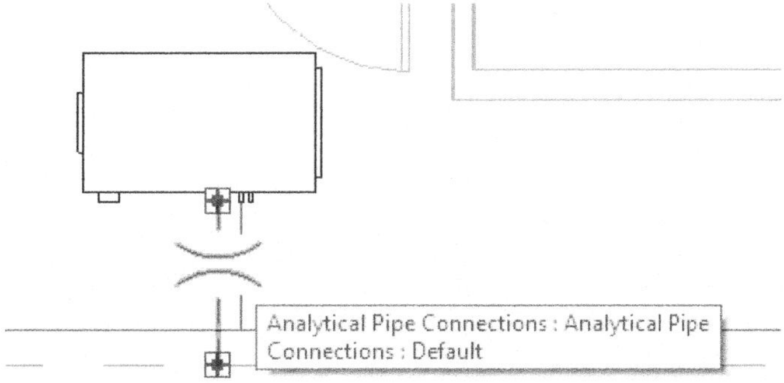

Figure 8–38

- Assign the **Pressure Drop** (which is 0 by default) in the Type Properties of the analytical connection element.

Practice 8b Add Ducts and Pipes

Practice Objectives

- Add Ductwork.
- Add hydronic piping.

Estimated time for completion:10 minutes

In this practice you will draw ducts from mechanical equipment connectors and from air terminals using flex duct. You will also add hydronic piping from the mechanical equipment using connectors and the **Connect Into** tool. The completed project is shown in Figure 8–39.

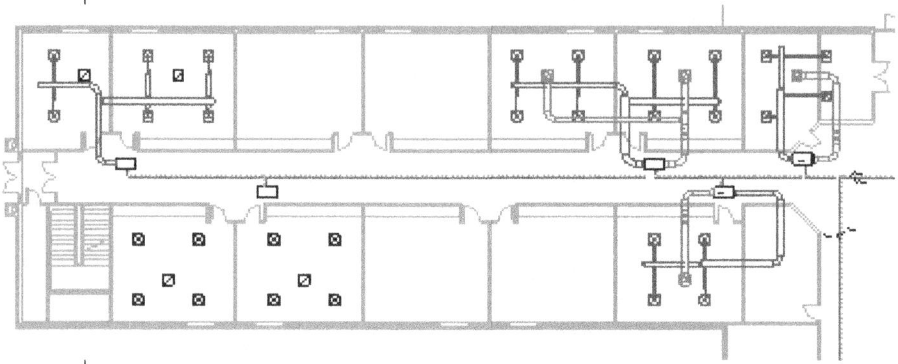

Figure 8–39

Task 1 - Add ducts

1. In the practice files *HVAC* folder, open the project **MEP-Elementary-School-Ducts-M.rvt**.
2. Open the Mechanical>HVAC>Floor Plans>**01 Mechanical Plan** view and zoom in on the area with the new air terminals.
3. Select the Air Handling Unit (AHU) in the hallway. On the left side, click **Create Duct**, as shown in Figure 8–40.

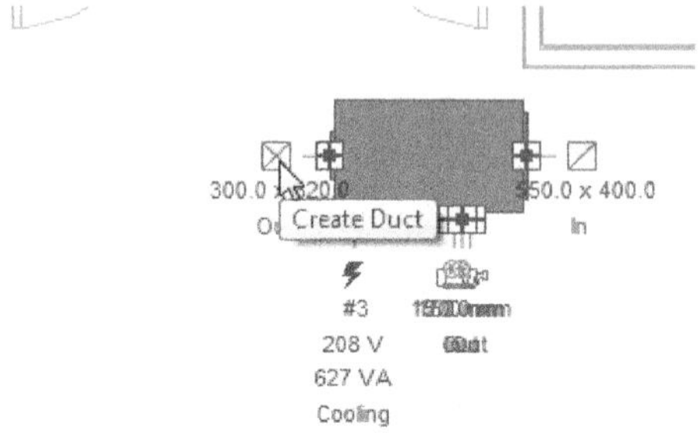

Figure 8–40

4. In the Type Selector, select **Rectangular Duct: Radius Elbow / Taps**.

5. Draw the duct into the room on the left, as shown in Figure 8–41. Press <Esc> once and then draw duct from the main vertical line over into the other room.

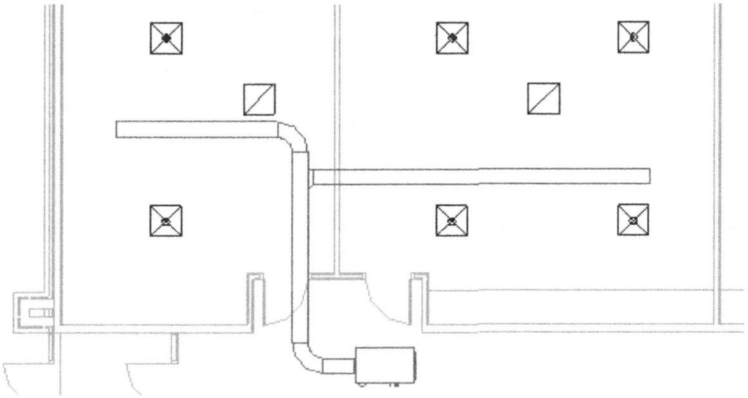

Figure 8–41

6. In the *Systems* tab>HVAC panel, click (Duct).

7. In the Type Selector, select R**ound Duct: Taps / Long Radius.**

8. In the *Modify* | *Place Duct* tab>Placement Tools panel, click (Inherit Elevation).

9. In the Options Bar, set *Diameter* to **150mm**.

10. Select a point on the duct where it is aligned to the air terminal (as shown in Figure 8–42), and draw it about halfway to the air terminal (as shown in Figure 8–43).

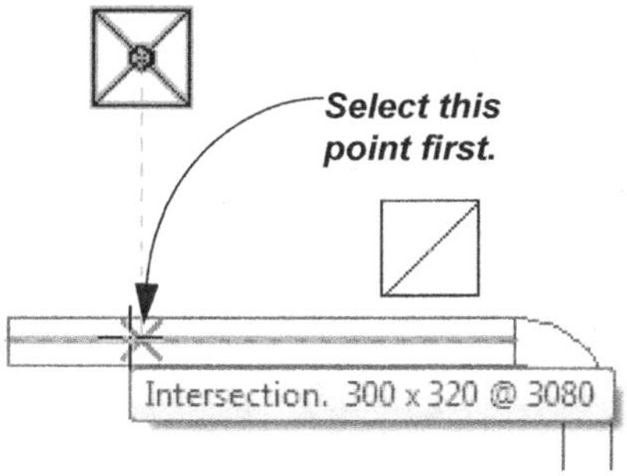

Figure 8–42

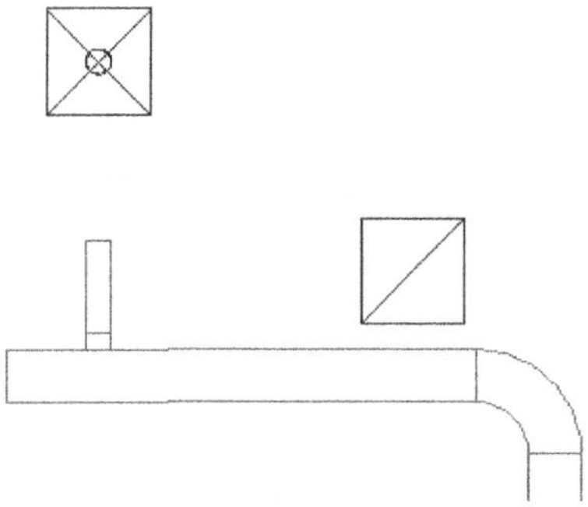

Figure 8–43

11. Click **Modify**.

12. Select the Air Terminal, right-click on it, and then select **Draw Flex Duct**.

13. Draw the flex duct from the air terminal to the new duct, ensuring that you select the point connectors shown in Figure 8–44. As soon as you connect the duct, the air terminal turns blue. It is now attached to the supply air system.

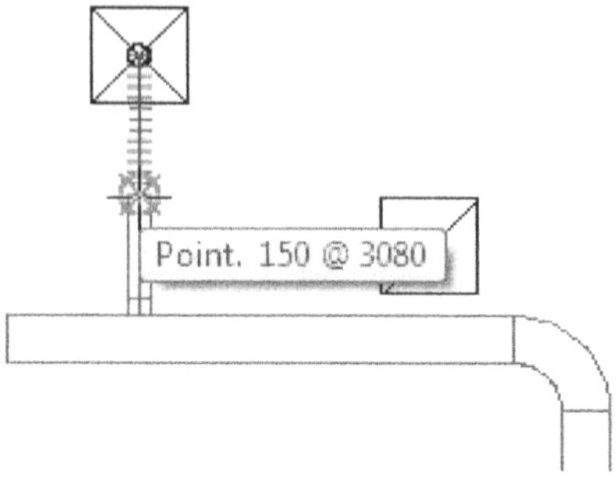

Figure 8–44

14. Repeat the process to connect the other air terminals to the ducts. The final system should look similar to Figure 8–45.

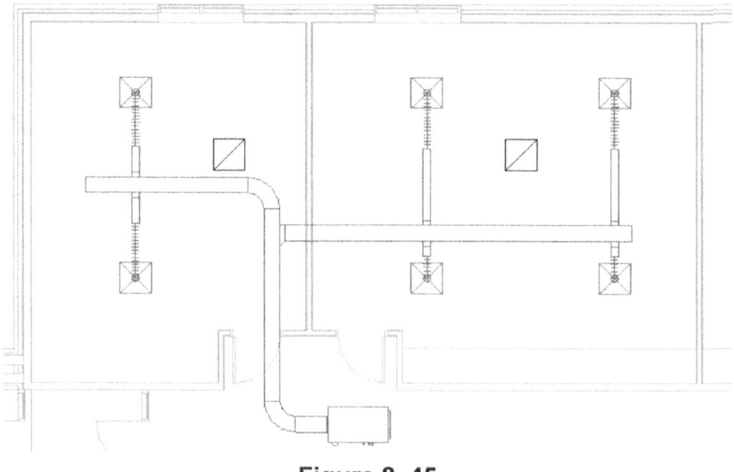

Figure 8–45

15. Save the project.

Task 2 - Draw pipe.

1. Select the AHU and zoom in so that the three pipe outlets clearly display, as shown in Figure 8–46.

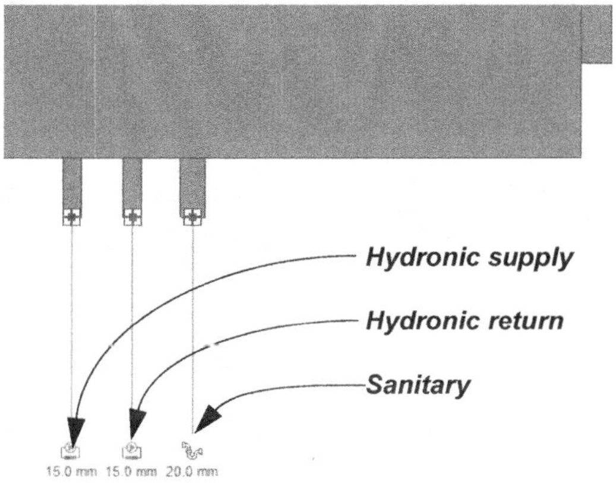

Figure 8–46

2. Select the **Hydronic Supply** icon to start the **Draw Pipe** command.
3. In the Type Selector, select **Pipe Types: Standard**.
4. Draw the pipe down from the AHU, and continue drawing the pipe down the hallway until it is near but not touching existing pipe (as shown in Figure 8–47), zooming out as required.

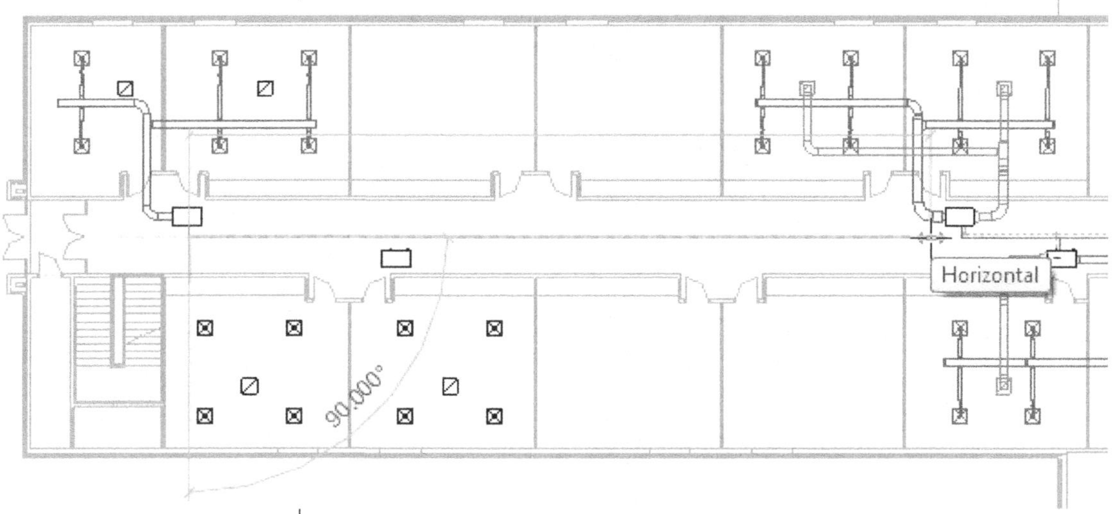

Figure 8–47

5. Press <Esc> and use the **Align** command to align the pipe with existing hydronic supply pipe. (You will modify the connections in the next practice.)
6. Repeat the process with the Hydronic Return pipe, which displays with a dashed line style.
7. Zoom in on and select the other AHU in the hallway.
8. In the *Modify | Mechanical Equipment* tab>Layout panel, click  (Connect Into).
9. In the Select Connector dialog box, select the **Hydronic Return** connector and click **OK**.
10. Select the Hydronic Return pipe (the dashed line).
11. Repeat the process with the Hydronic Supply connector and pipe, as shown in Figure 8–48.

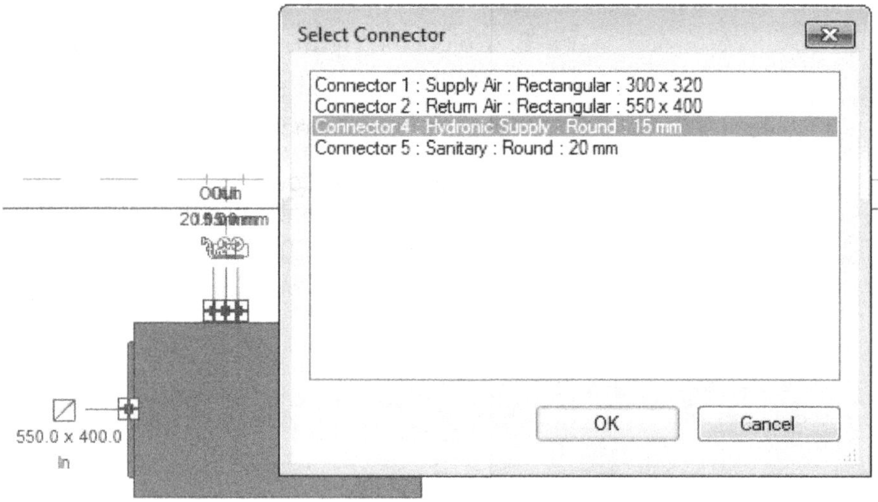

Figure 8–48

12. Zoom out to fit the model in the view.
13. Save the project.

Task 3 - (Optional) Add Return Air Ducts

Add return air ducts to the same area where you added the supply air ducts. You can also add ducts to the air terminals across the hall.

8.3 Modifying Ducts and Pipes

Ducts and pipes can be modified using a variety of standard modifying tools and other specialty tools, such as duct/pipe sizing, converting placeholders, changing rigid ducts/pipes to flexible ones, adding insulation and lining, and modifying the justification of ducts/pipes.

For example, the elbow fitting in Figure 8–49 is too large. In Figure 8–50, the size has changed, a fitting automatically applied, and another fitting added to create the appropriate layout.

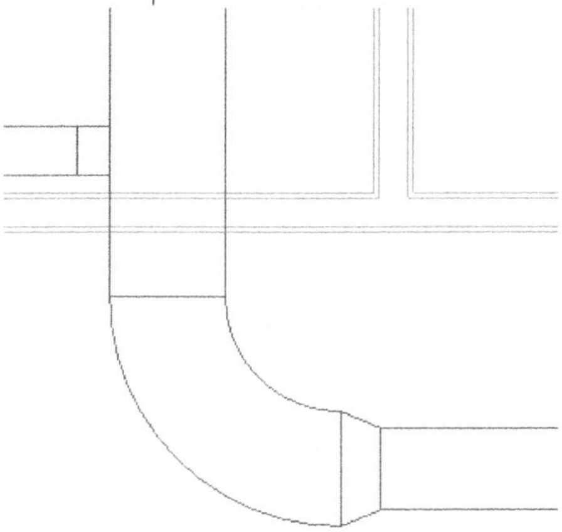

Figure 8–49

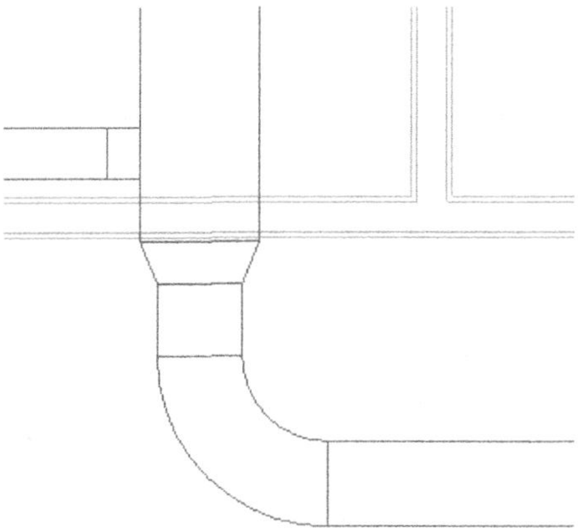

Figure 8–50

Using Standard Modify Tools

- You can modify ducts and pipes using universal methods by making changes in:
    - Properties
    - Options Bar
    - Temporary Dimensions
    - Controls
    - Connectors
- You can also use modify tools (e.g., **Move**, **Rotate**, **Split, Trim/Extend**, and **Align**) to help you place the ducts and pipes at the correct locations.

Adding Fittings & Accessories

Many fittings are automatically applied as you draw ducts and pipes. However, you might want to modify or add new fittings or accessories, such as a Butterfly Valve (shown in Figure 8–51), fire damper, filter, or smoke detector, and place it at an appropriate connector.

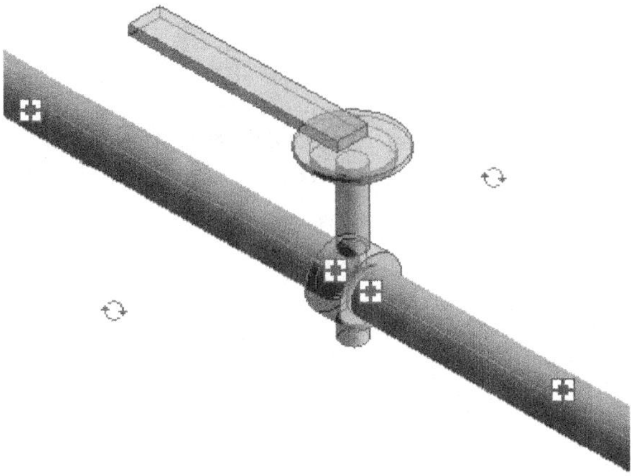

Figure 8–51

How To: Add Fittings and Accessories

1. In the *Systems* tab>HVAC or Plumbing & Piping panel, select the appropriate command:

    Duct Fitting (DF)

    Duct Accessory (DA)

    Pipe Fitting (PF)

    Pipe Accessory (PA)

2. In the Type Selector, select the type of fitting or accessory you want to use.
3. Hover the cursor over the duct or pipe. Only usable locations are highlighted.
4. Click on the required location. The fitting or accessory resizes to fit the element on which it is placed.

- Additional fittings and accessories can be loaded from the library. Ensure that you start the correct command for the element you want to load. You cannot load fittings when you have started the **Accessories** command.

Modifying Fittings

Whether added automatically or manually, fittings can be modified using the Type Selector, Properties, the Options Bar, and a variety of connectors and controls. For example, an Elbow can be changed to a Tee by clicking a control, as shown in Figure 8–52.

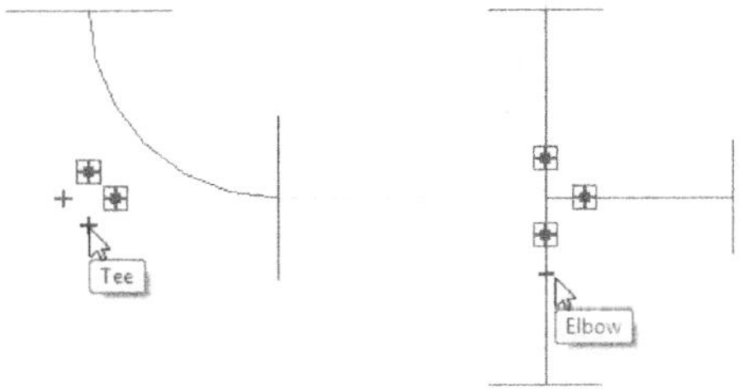

Figure 8–52

Capping Open Ends

You can cap the open end of a duct or pipe by right-clicking on the end control and selecting **Cap Open End**, as shown in Figure 8–53.

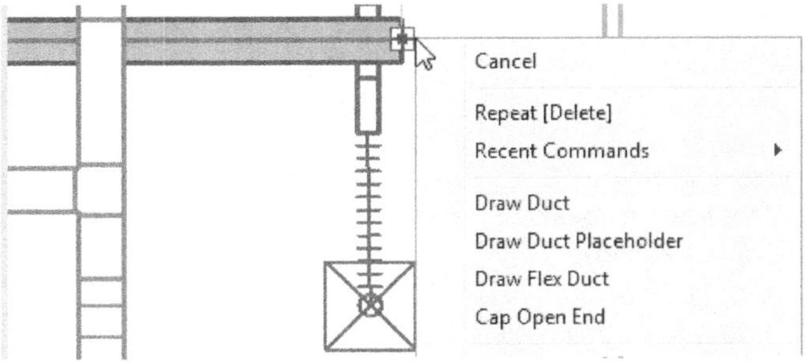

Figure 8–53

Alternatively, if you have more than one opening on the ends of a run, in the *Modify* contextual tab>Edit panel, click (Cap Open Ends). The caps are applied (as shown in Figure 8–54) and a warning displays telling you the number of caps applied.

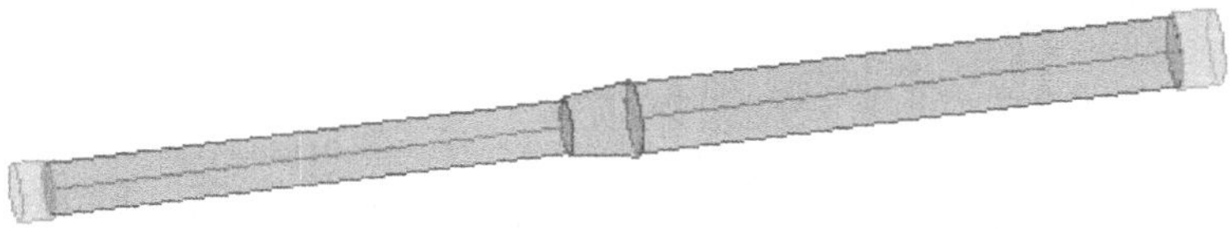

Figure 8–54

Duct and Pipe Sizing

It is easiest to draw ducts or pipes using the default sizes provided by the opening sizes of the equipment, or as preset in the Mechanical Settings. However, these sizes are often incorrect for the system being used. The **Duct/Pipe Sizing** tool uses a specified sizing method and constraints to determine how to correctly size the pipes or ducts, as shown in Figure 8–55.

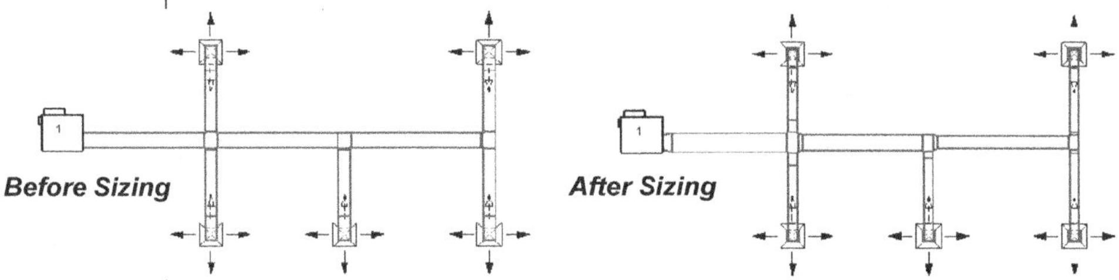

Figure 8–55

- If you select only one duct or pipe, it analyzes just that one set of connections. Select the entire system to ensure that all of the connections are analyzed.

How To: Size Ducts and Pipes

1. Select all of the components in a duct or pipe system.
2. In the *Modify* | *Multi-Select* tab>Analysis panel, click  (Duct/Pipe Sizing).
3. In the Duct Sizing dialog box, set the *Sizing Method* and *Constraints* as required, as shown in Figure 8–56.

*The most common method for low pressure duct work is **Friction**. Ducts and pipes should be sized according to company design standards.*

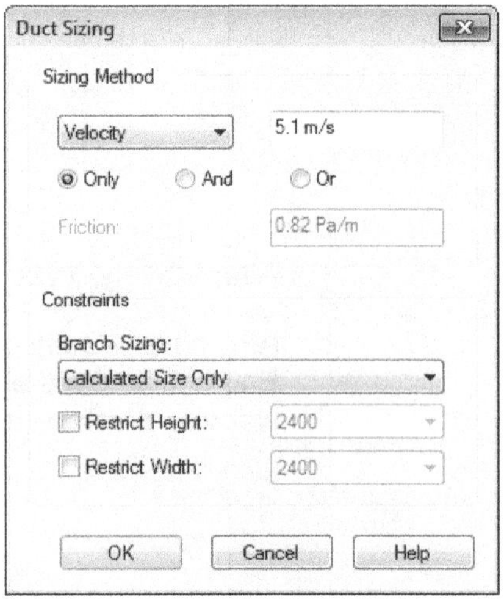

Figure 8–56

4. Click **OK**.

- Once you make a change to the system, you need to run the software again. For example, the L/s was changed on two the air terminals shown in Figure 8–57.

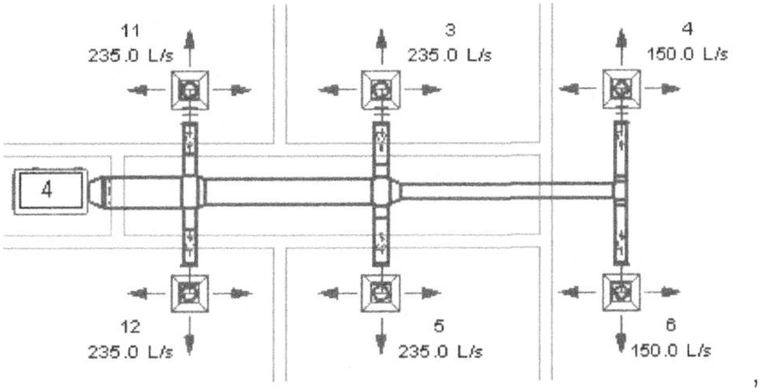

Figure 8–57

- You can also modify duct or pipe sizes on your own to create the most appropriate layout for your methodology. A helpful tool to separate lengths of duct or pipe before you change the size is  (Split Element).

Converting Ducts and Pipes

After placing ducts or pipes, you can change the type of the entire run (including fittings). If the definition of a type has been changed, you can reapply the type to existing runs. You can also convert placeholders to standard ducts/pipes and, (for ducts only) rigid duct to flex duct when connected to an air terminal.

How To: Change the Type of Duct/Pipe Runs

1. Select the duct/pipe run and filter out everything except the related duct/pipe, accessories, and fittings.
2. In the *Modify | Multi-Select* tab>Edit panel, click  (Change Type).
3. In the Type Selector, select a new type of run. For the example shown in Figure 8–58, the type **Rectangular Duct: Radius Elbows / Tees** was changed to the type **Round Duct: Taps**.

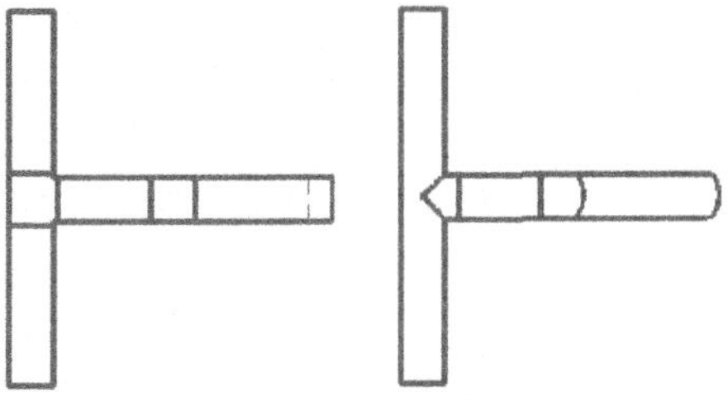

Figure 8–58

How To: Reapply the Type to Runs

1. Select a single duct/pipe run. You can select different runs, but they must be all of the same type and same system. If you select runs in different systems, the software prompts you to select one system to which to reapply the type.
2. Filter out everything except ducts/pipes, fittings, and accessories.
3. In the *Modify* | *Multi-Select* tab>Edit panel, click (Reapply Type).

How To: Convert Placeholders to Duct/Pipe

1. Select the duct/pipe placeholder(s).
2. In the *Modify* | *contextual* tab>Edit panel, click (Convert Placeholder).
3. The placeholders are changed into the duct/pipe type, including the appropriate fittings, as shown for pipes in Figure 8–59.

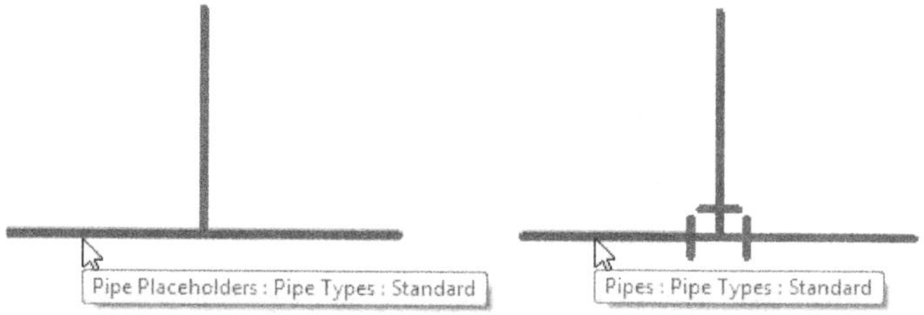

Figure 8–59

How To: Convert Rigid Duct to Flex Duct

1. In the *Systems* tab>HVAC panel, click (Convert to Flex Duct) or type **CV**.
2. In the Options Bar set the *Max Length*.
3. Select the air terminal connected to the rigid duct. The duct is converted as shown in Figure 8–60.

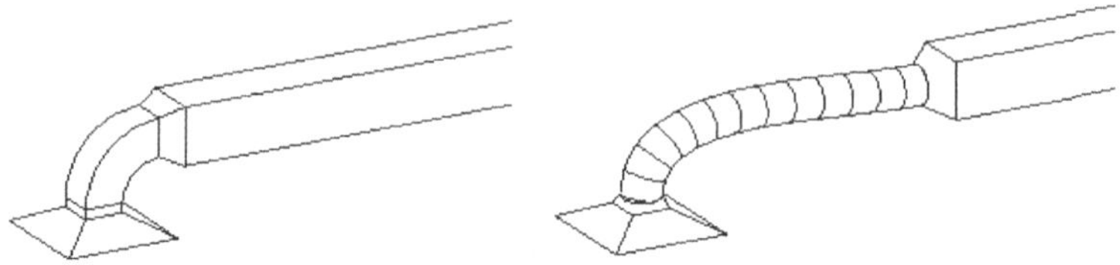

Figure 8–60

- This command only works if the rigid duct is connected to an air terminal.

Adding Insulation and Lining

You can add insulation to ducts and pipes and add lining to ducts. This information displays as a thin line outside of the duct/pipe for insulation and a dashed line inside the duct for lining, as shown in Figure 8–61.

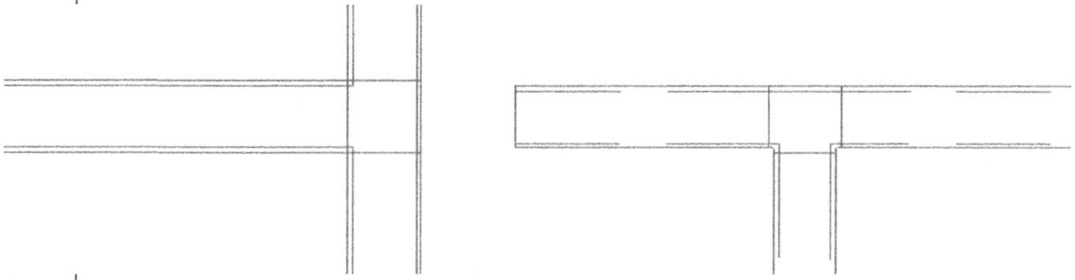

Figure 8–61

- Accessories can also be insulated, as shown in Figure 8–62.

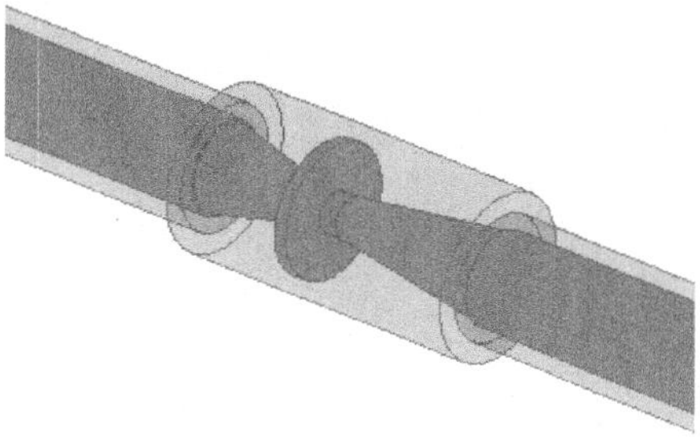

Figure 8–62

How To: Add Insulation or Lining

1. Select the duct/pipe run that you want to insulate, or the duct run you want to line. You can select more than one system at a time for these commands.
2. Use (Filter) to select only the ducts/pipes, fittings, and accessories.
3. In the *Modify* | *contextual* tab>Duct or Pipe Insulation panel or Duct Lining panel, select the appropriate command:
   - Add Insulation (Duct)
   - Add Lining (Duct)
   - Add Insulation (Pipe)

4. In the associated dialog box, select a *Insulation Type* and set the *Thickness*, as shown for Duct Insulation in Figure 8–63. Click **OK**.

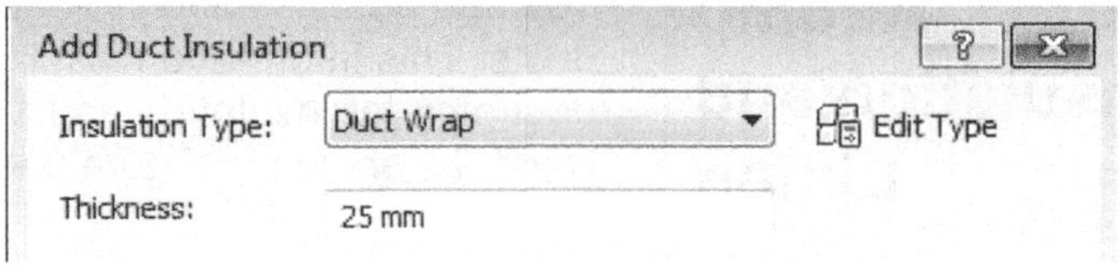

Figure 8–63

> **Hint: Using Thin Lines**
>
> Line thickness can negatively impact the display of elements, such as insulation or lining. To toggle lineweight on or off, in the Quick Access Toolbar, click (Thin Lines) or type **TL**.

- To modify the insulation, select the insulated duct or pipe and, in the contextual ribbon, select one of the following commands. When editing, change the *Type* in the Type Selector and/or change the *Thickness* in Properties.
  - Edit Insulation (Duct)
  - Edit Lining (Duct)
  - Remove Insulation (Duct)
  - Remove Lining (Duct)
  - Edit Insulation (Pipe)
  - Remove Insulation (Pipe)

Modifying the Justification

If a duct/pipe run has different sized duct/pipe, you can modify the justification, as shown in Figure 8–64.

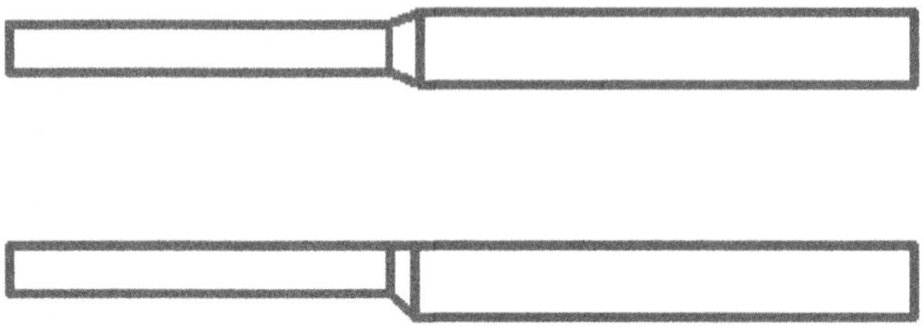

Figure 8–64

How To: Modify Justifications

1. Select the duct/pipe run.
2. In the *Modify | Multi-Select* tab>Edit panel, click (Justify).
3. To specify the point on the duct that you want to justify around, in the *Justification Editor* tab>Justify panel, click (Control Point) to cycle between the end point references.
   - The alignment location displays as an arrow, as shown in Figure 8–65.

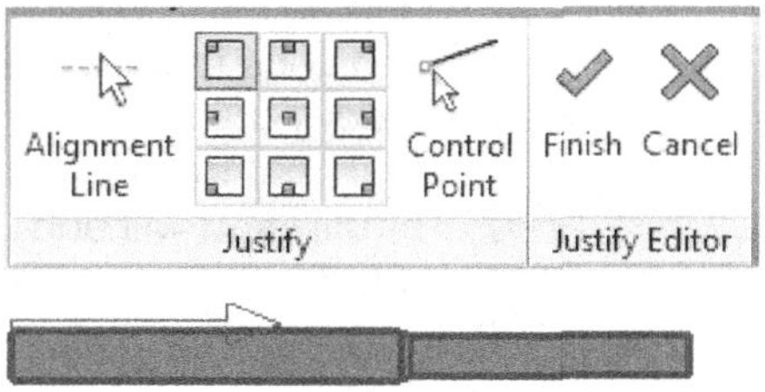

Figure 8–65

4. To indicate the required alignment, either click one of the nine alignment buttons in the Justify panel, or in a 3D view, use (Alignment Line) to select the required dashed line, as shown in Figure 8–66.

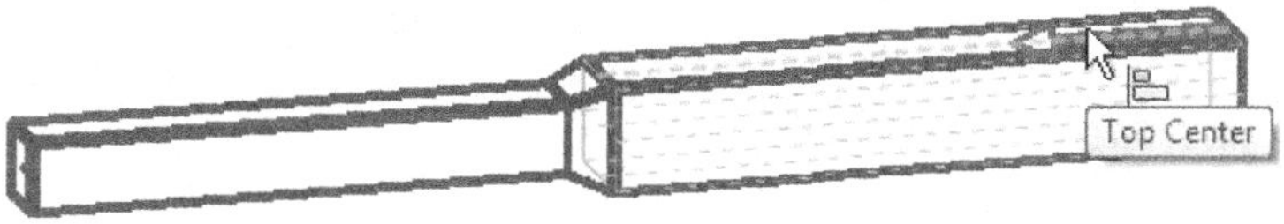

Figure 8–66

Practice 8c Modify Ducts and Pipes

Practice Objectives

- Change pipe types.
- Modify pipe fittings.
- Cap open duct ends.
- Use the Duct/Pipe Sizing tool.
- Add lining to ducts.

Estimated time for completion: 20 minutes

In this practice you will change a run of pipes from one type to another. You will view the pipes in 3D, modify fittings, and make revisions to the pipes to match existing pipes. You will also modify ducts by capping open ends, using the **Duct/Pipe Sizing** tool, and modifying the duct fittings, as shown in Figure 8–67. Finally you will add lining to all of the duct networks in the project.

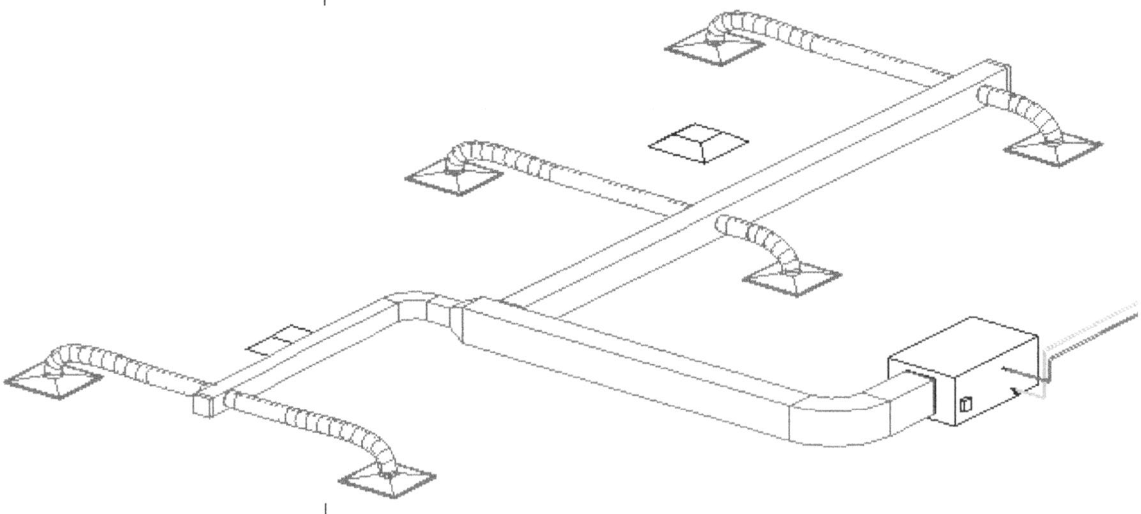

Figure 8–67

Task 1 - Modify the type of pipes.

1. In the practice files *HVAC* folder, open **MEP-Elementary-School-HVAC-Modify-M.rvt**.

2. In the **01 Mechanical Plan** view, zoom in on the area near **AHU 3**, as shown in Figure 8–68. Note that the pipes are not connected.

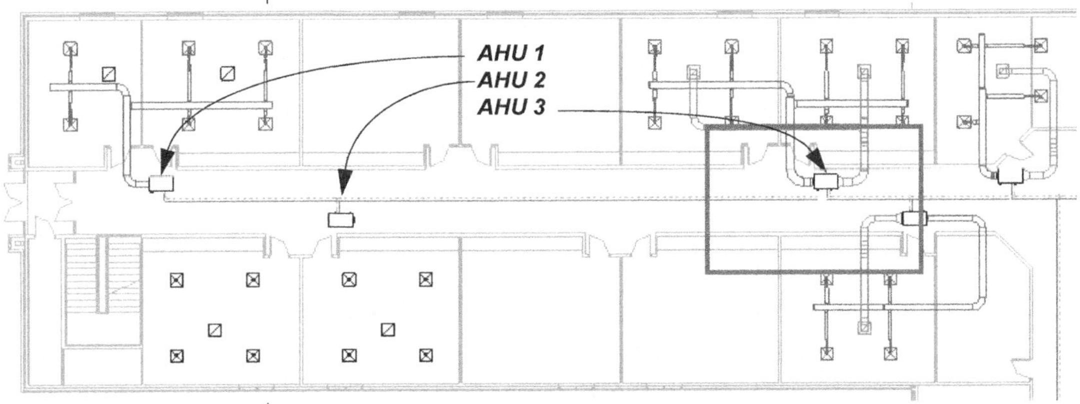

Figure 8–68

3. Hover the cursor over one of the pipes on the left and then over one of the pipes on the right. Note that they are two different types, as shown in Figure 8–69.

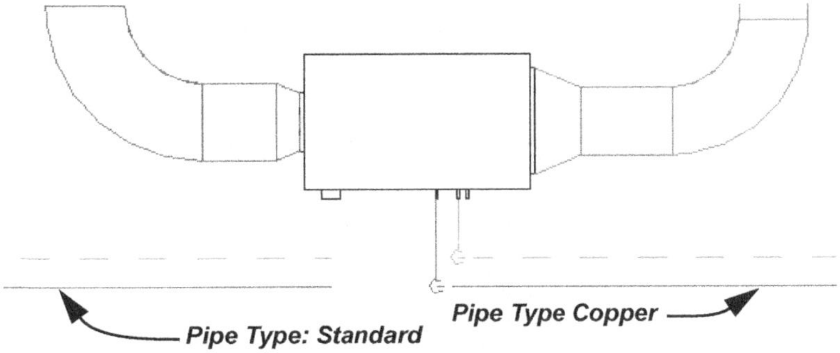

Figure 8–69

4. Zoom out to see the entire piping layout.

5. Hover the cursor over one of the pipes on the left and press <Tab> until the entire pipe run is highlighted (as shown in Figure 8–70) and then select it.

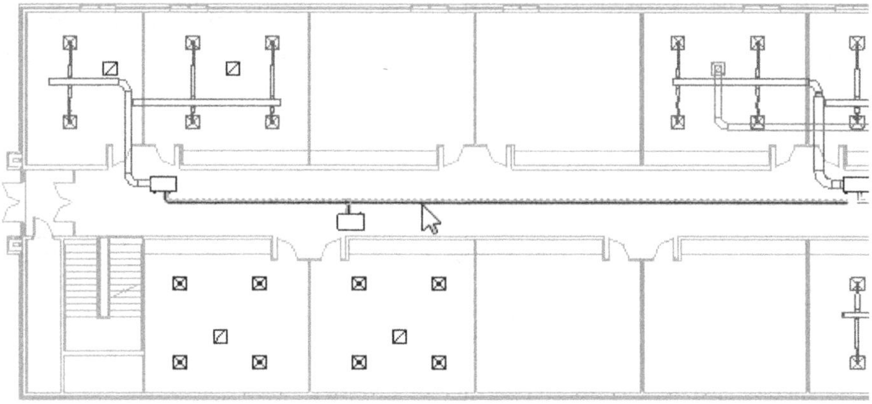

Figure 8–70

6. In the *Modify* | *Multi-Select* tab>Edit panel, click (Change Type).
7. In the Type Selector, change the type to **Pipe Types: Copper**.
8. Repeat the process with the pipes running parallel.
9. Save the project.

Task 2 - Modify fittings.

1. Open the Mechancial>HVAC>3D Views: **3D Mechanical** view.
    - The Hydronic Return system color has been changed for clarity in this view.
2. Select the linked model, in the View Control Bar, click (Temporary Hide/Isolate) and then select **Hide Element**.

If you align the pipes while they are connected to the mechanical equipment the AHUs will also move.

3. Zoom in on **AHU 3**. Note that the pipes are not connected and are at different heights, as shown in Figure 8–71.

4. Delete the pipes shown in Figure 8–71.

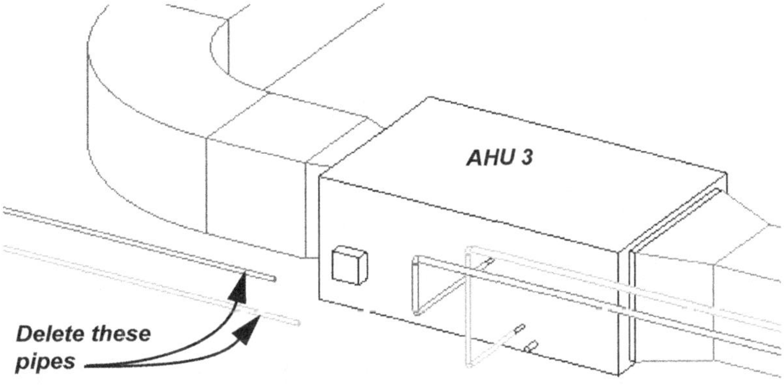

Figure 8–71

5. Select the elbow connector on each of the top pipes and click the **Tee** icon, as shown in Figure 8–72.

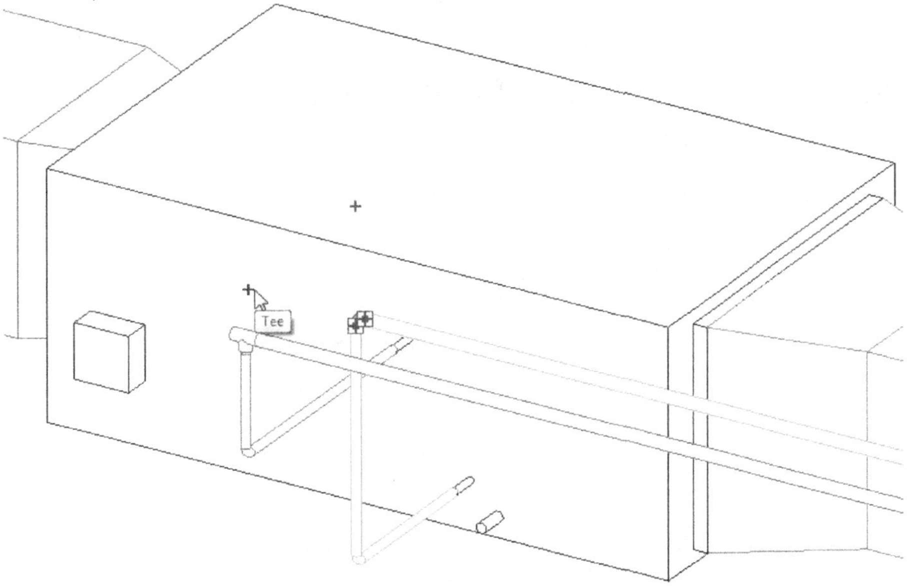

Figure 8–72

6. Switch back to the plan view. Remember that you can press <Ctrl>+<Tab> to cycle through the open views.

7. Delete the rest of the horizontal pipes created earlier. Zoom in on **AHU 1** and **AHU 2** and delete the orphaned fittings, as shown in Figure 8–73.

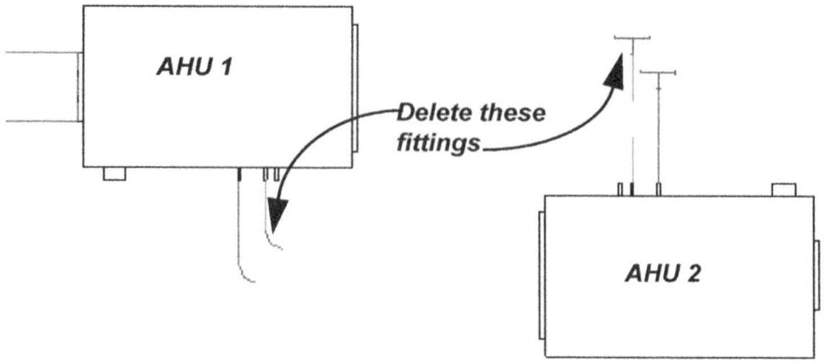

Figure 8–73

8. Zoom or pan back over to **AHU3**.
9. Change the *Display Level* to **Fine** to improve the display of the connectors.
10. Select the Tee fitting, right-click on the open connector, and then select **Draw Pipe**.
11. Draw the pipe down the hall past **AHU 1**.
12. Repeat the process with the other pipe.
13. Zoom in on **AHU 1**.
14. In the *Modify* tab>Modify panel, click (Trim/Extend to Corner).
15. Select the pipe coming from the **AHU** and then the horizontal pipe. Repeat with the second pipe as shown in Figure 8–74.

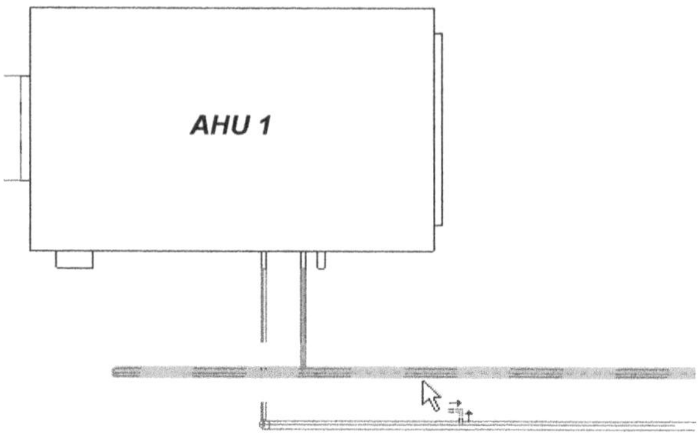

Figure 8–74

16. Pan over to **AHU 2** and use the (Trim/Extend Single) command to clean up the intersection between the horizontal and vertical pipes.
17. Return to the 3D Mechanical view to see the revised pipe layout, as shown in Figure 8–75.

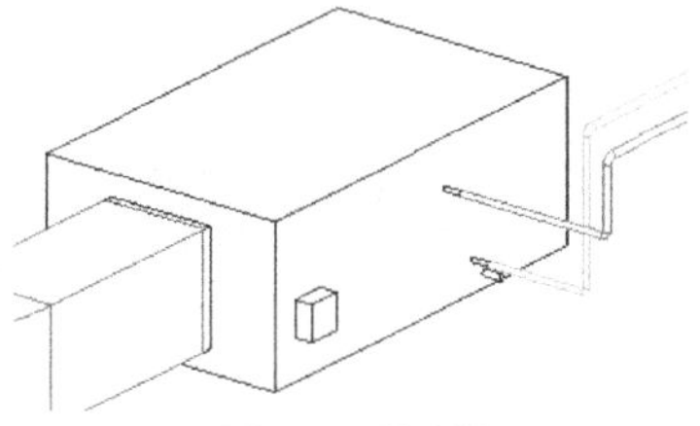

Figure 8–75

18. Save the project.

Task 3 - Cap open duct ends.

1. Continue working in the **3D Mechanical** view.
2. Zoom in on the supply duct system connected to **AHU 1**.
3. In the *Analyze* tab>Check Systems panel, click (Show Disconnects).
4. In the Show Disconnects Options dialog box, select **Duct** and click **OK**.
5. Warnings display indicating the end of the duct where there is an open connector, as shown in Figure 8–76.

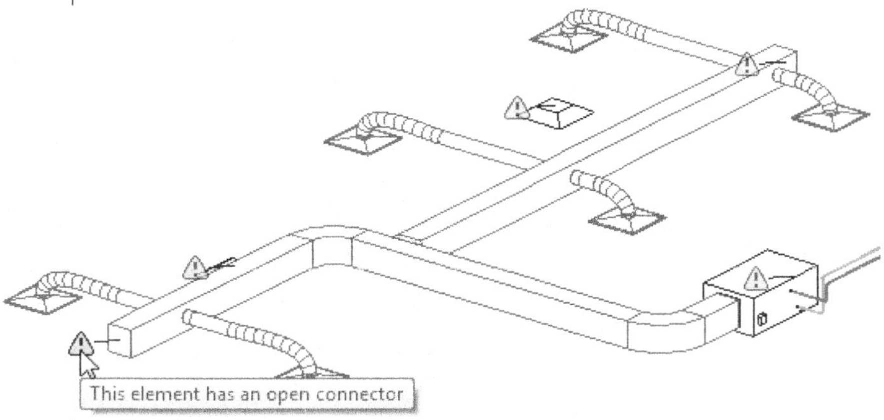

Figure 8–76

6. Right-click on the end of that duct and select **Cap Open End**.
7. The duct is capped and the warning does not display.
8. Repeat the process on the end of the other open duct.
9. Open the Show Disconnects Options dialog box. Turn off the **Duct** option and click **OK**.
10. Save the project.

Task 4 - Resize the ducts.

1. Continue working in the **3D Mechanical** view.
2. Select all of the supply ducts and air terminals coming from **AHU1** by hovering the cursor over one duct and pressing <Tab> until the full network displays.
3. In the **Modify | Multi-Select** tab>Analysis panel, click  (Duct/Pipe Sizing).
4. In the Duct Sizing dialog box, accept the defaults and click **OK**. The ducts resize, as shown in Figure 8–77.

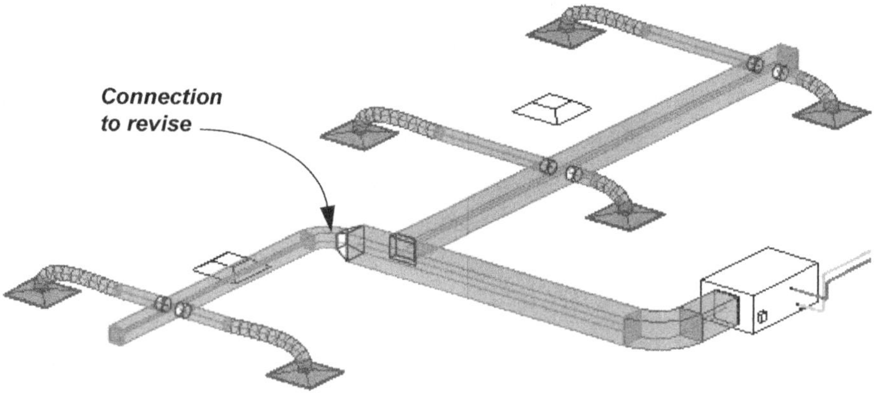

Figure 8–77

5. One of the connections needs to be revised, as shown in Figure 8–77.
6. Open the **01 Mechanical Plan** view and zoom in on the supply duct network.

7. Delete the fitting shown in Figure 8–78.
8. Select the open end of the vertical duct and drag it closer to the intersection with the horizontal duct on the right.
9. Right-click on the open end of the elbow and select **Draw Duct**. Draw the duct until it connects to the vertical duct. The appropriate fitting is reapplied, as shown in Figure 8–79.

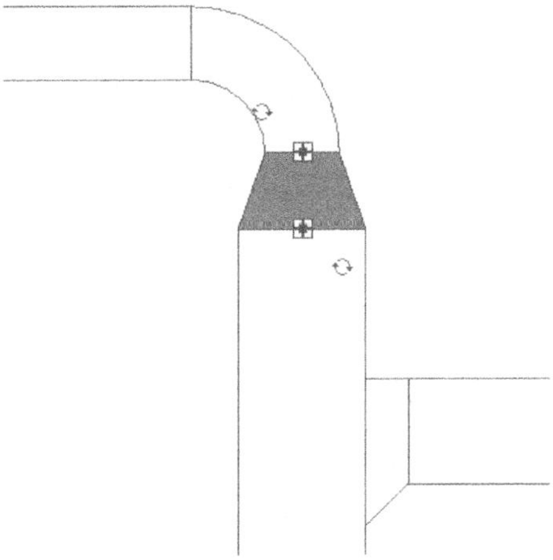

Figure 8–78

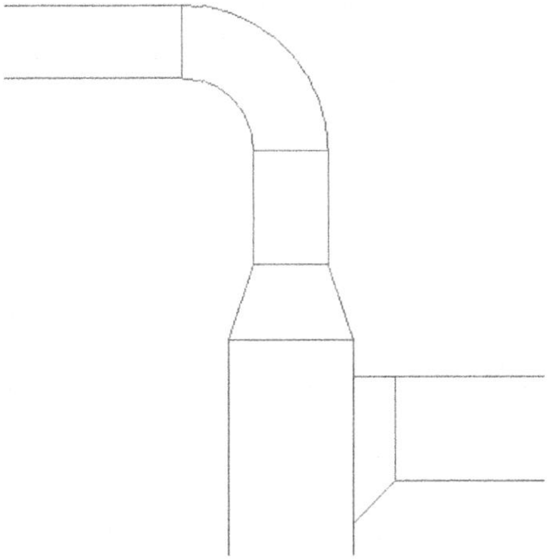

Figure 8–79

10. (Optional) Make additional adjustments to the ducts, including shortening the horizontal ducts past the final air terminals.
11. Zoom to fit everything in the view.
12. Save the project.

Task 5 - Add duct lining.

1. Continue working in the **01 Mechanical Plan** view.
2. Draw a window around all of the elements in the view.
3. In the Status Bar or in the *Modify* | *Multi-Select* tab>Selection panel, click (Filter).
4. In the Filter dialog box, clear everything except **Ducts**, **Duct Fittings**, and **Flex Ducts**. Click **OK**.

If required, in the Quick Access Toolbar, click (Thin Lines).

5. In the *Modify | Multi-Select* tab>Duct Lining panel, click (Add Lining).
6. In the Add Duct Lining dialog box, set the *Thickness* to **15mm** and click **OK**.
7. Zoom in and see the lining applied to the ducts, as shown in Figure 8–80.

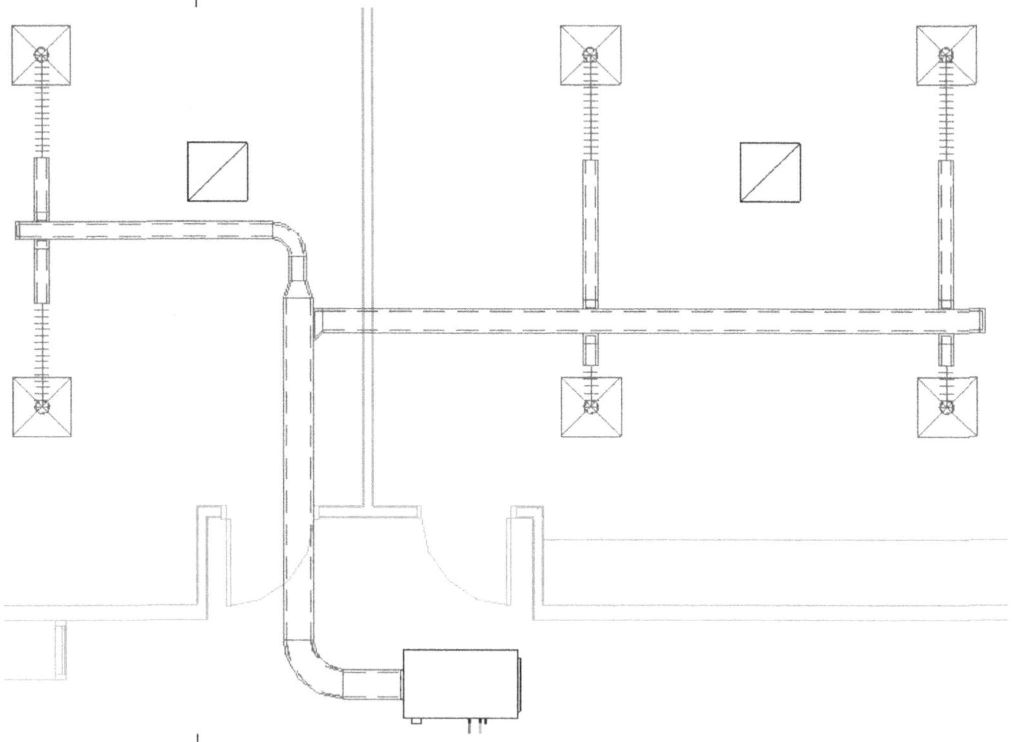

Figure 8–80

8. Zoom out.
9. Reset the **Temporary Hide/Isolate**.
10. Save the project.

Chapter Review Questions

1. Where do you specify the *Flow* of an air terminal, such as that shown in Figure 8–81? (Select all that apply.)

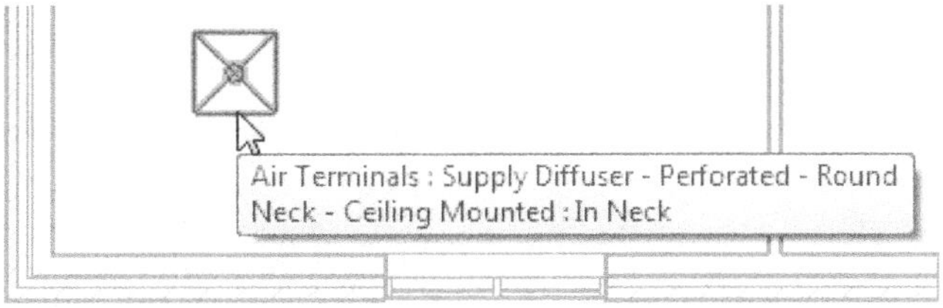

Figure 8–81

   a. In the Ribbon
   b. In the Options Bar
   c. In the Air Flow Dialog Box
   d. In the Properties
   e. In the Air Terminal tag

2. Which method enables you to move an air terminal hosted by a ceiling that has been copied, as shown in Figure 8–82, up to a different ceiling height?

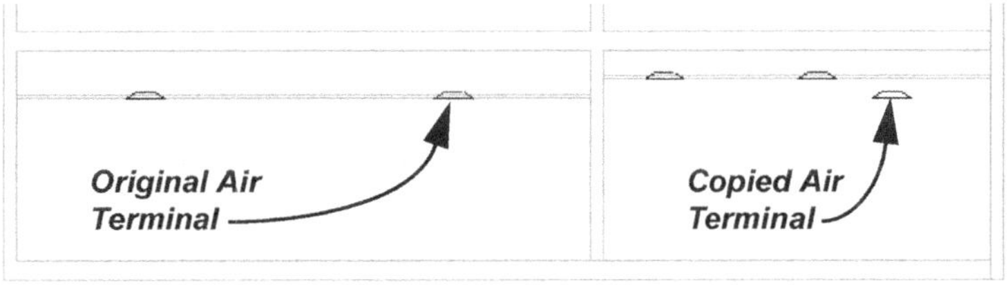

Figure 8–82

   a. Move
   b. Pick New Host
   c. Change the elevation in Properties
   d. Copied air terminals cannot be moved off the original plane.

3. The size of the duct drawn from a control on mechanical equipment must remain the same size as the opening on the equipment until it intersects with another duct.

   a. True
   b. False

4. How do you change an elbow fitting to a tee fitting?
   a. Delete the elbow and place a tee instead.
   b. Select the elbow and use the Type Selector to select a tee fitting instead.
   c. Select the elbow and click **+** (Plus).
   d. Select the elbow and click **Convert to Tee** in the ribbon.
5. When adding pipe accessories, such as the Butterfly Valve shown in Figure 8–83, you are first required to:

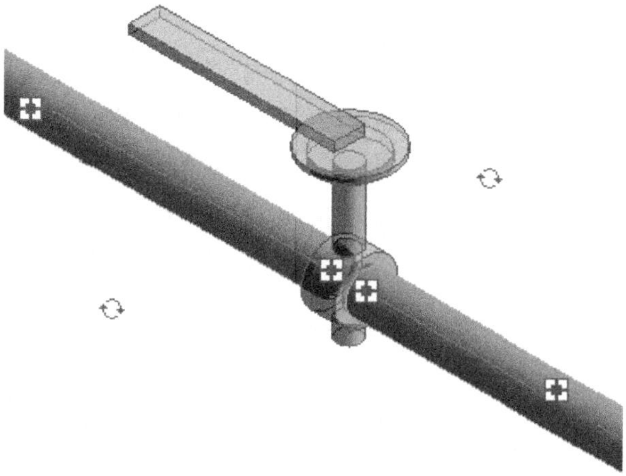

Figure 8–83

   a. Split the pipe using (Split Element).
   b. Split the pipe using (Split with Gap).
   c. Place the accessory nearby and then move it in place.
   d. Do nothing extra, just place the accessory on the pipe.

6. When can you convert a rigid duct to a flexible duct, such as that shown in Figure 8–84?

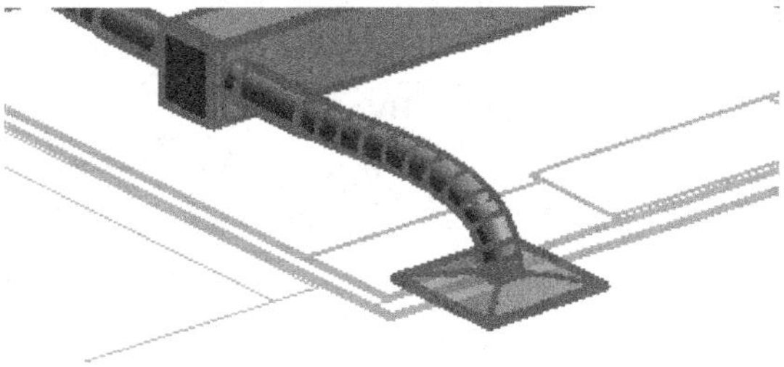

Figure 8–84

   a. When the rigid duct is round.
   b. When the air terminal is already connected by a rigid duct.
   c. When creating a system and sizing the ducting.
   d. When the **Allow Conversion** parameter is selected in the rigid duct's instance properties.

7. Which of the following commands can be used when modifying pipe? (Select all that apply.)
   a. **Change Type**
   b. **Reapply Type**
   c. **Add Insulation**
   d. **Edit Lining**
   e. **Modify Justification**
   f. **Modify Material**
   g. **Change Offset**

8. Parallel pipe runs are created automatically at the correct distance from equipment, as shown in Figure 8–85.

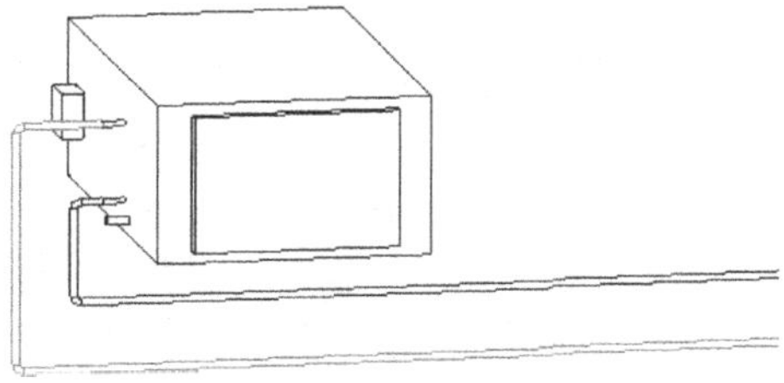

Figure 8–85

   a. True
   b. False

Command Summary

Button	Command	Location
HVAC Tools		
	**Air Terminal**	• **Ribbon:** *Systems* tab>HVAC panel • **Shortcut:** AT
	**Air Terminal on Duct**	• **Ribbon:** *Modify* | *Place Air Terminal* tab>Layout panel
	**Analytical Connections**	• **Ribbon:** *Modify* | *Mechanical Equipment* (or *Modify* | *Pipes*) tab>Create panel
	**Cap Open Ends**	• **Ribbon:** *Modify* | *contextual* tab>Edit panel
	**Duct**	• **Ribbon:** *Systems* tab>HVAC panel • **Shortcut:** DT
	**Duct Accessory**	• **Ribbon:** *Systems* tab>HVAC panel • **Shortcut:** DA
	**Duct Fitting**	• **Ribbon:** *Systems* tab>HVAC panel • **Shortcut:** DF
	**Duct Placeholder**	• **Ribbon:** *Systems* tab>HVAC panel
	**Flex Duct**	• **Ribbon:** *Systems* tab>HVAC panel • **Shortcut:** FD
	**Flex Pipe**	• **Ribbon:** *Systems* tab>Plumbing & Piping panel • **Shortcut:** FP
	**Pipe**	• **Ribbon:** *Systems* tab>Plumbing & Piping panel • **Shortcut:** PI
	**Pipe Accessory**	• **Ribbon:** *Systems* tab>Plumbing & Piping panel • **Shortcut:** PA
	**Pipe Fitting**	• **Ribbon:** *Systems* tab>Plumbing & Piping panel • **Shortcut:** PF
	**Pipe Placeholder**	• **Ribbon:** *Systems* tab>Plumbing & Piping panel
	**Mechanical Equipment**	• **Ribbon:** *Systems* tab>Mechanical panel • **Shortcut:** ME

	Mechanical Settings	• **Ribbon:** *Systems* tab>HVAC or Mechanical panel title • **Shortcut:** MS
Duct Modification		
	Add Insulation	• **Ribbon:** (*with Ducts and Duct Fittings selected*) *Modify* | *Multi-Select* tab>Duct Insulation panel
	Add Lining	• **Ribbon:** (*with Ducts and Duct Fittings selected*) *Modify* | *Multi-Select* tab> Duct Lining panel
	Change Type	• **Ribbon:** (*with Ducts and Duct Fittings selected*) *Modify* | *Multi-Select* tab>Edit panel
	Convert to Flex Duct	• **Ribbon:** *Systems* tab>HVAC panel • **Shortcut:** CV
	Edit Insulation	• **Ribbon:** (*with Ducts and Duct Fittings that have Insulation selected*) *Modify* | *Multi-Select* tab>Duct Insulation panel
	Edit Lining	• **Ribbon:** (*with Ducts and Duct Fittings that have Lining selected*) *Modify* | *Multi-Select* tab>Duct Lining panel
	Inherit Elevation	• **Ribbon:** *Modify* | *Place Duct* tab>Placement Tools panel
	Inherit Size	• **Ribbon:** *Modify* | *Place Duct* tab>Placement Tools panel
	Justification (Settings)	• **Ribbon:** *Modify* | *Place Duct* tab>Placement Tools panel
	Justify	• **Ribbon:** (*with Ducts and Duct Fittings selected*) *Modify* | *Multi-Select* tab> Edit panel
	Remove Insulation	• **Ribbon:** (*with Ducts and Duct Fittings that have Insulation selected*) *Modify* | *Multi-Select* tab>Duct Insulation panel
	Remove Lining	• **Ribbon:** (*with Ducts and Duct Fittings that have Lining selected*) *Modify* | *Multi-Select* tab>Duct Lining panel
Pipe Modification		
	Add Insulation	• **Ribbon:** (*with one or more Pipes selected*) *Modify* | *Pipe* tab>Edit panel or (*with Pipes and Pipe Fittings selected*) *Modify* | *Multi-Select* tab>Edit panel
	Change Type	• **Ribbon:** (*with one or more Pipes selected*) *Modify* | *Pipe* tab>Edit panel or (*with Pipes and Pipe Fittings selected*) *Modify* | *Multi-Select* tab>Edit panel

	**Convert Placeholder**	• **Ribbon:** *Modify* | *Pipe Placeholders* tab>Edit panel
	**Edit Insulation**	• **Ribbon:** (*with one or more Pipes selected*) *Modify* | *Pipe* tab>Edit panel or (*with Pipes and Pipe Fittings selected*) *Modify* | *Multi-Select* tab>Edit panel
	**Inherit Elevation**	• **Ribbon:** *Modify* | *Place Pipe* tab>Placement Tools panel
	**Inherit Size**	• **Ribbon:** *Modify* | *Place Pipe* tab>Placement Tools panel
	**Justification (Settings)**	• **Ribbon:** *Modify* | *Place Pipe* tab>Placement Tools panel
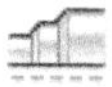	**Justify**	• **Ribbon:** (*with one or more Pipes selected*) *Modify* | *Pipe* tab>Edit panel or (*with Pipes and Pipe Fittings selected*) *Modify* | *Multi-Select* tab>Edit panel
	**Remove Insulation**	• **Ribbon:** (*with one or more Pipes selected*) *Modify* | *Pipe* tab>Edit panel or (*with Pipes and Pipe Fittings selected*) *Modify* | *Multi-Select* tab>Edit panel

Chapter 9

Plumbing Networks

Plumbing networks consist of pipes which connect plumbing fixtures and mechanical equipment. The process of putting these together and ensuring they work correctly is a significant part of developing a plumbing project. Frequently, fire protection is included in the plumbing design. Fire Protection networks include wet and dry sprinklers with the associated piping

Learning Objectives in this Chapter

- Add plumbing fixtures and mechanical equipment.
- Add pipes to connect plumbing fixtures and equipment.
- Modify pipes and fittings.
- Add sprinklers and piping for fire protection systems.

9.1 Adding Plumbing Fixtures and Equipment

When you start to create plumbing systems in a project, you typically start by adding plumbing fixtures (and sometimes mechanical equipment) and then network them together using pipes, as shown in Figure 9–1.

Figure 9–1

Mechanical Equipment

Mechanical Equipment for plumbing includes various water heaters, pumps, and water filters. Mechanical equipment families are set up through Properties and have connectors, as shown in Figure 9–2.

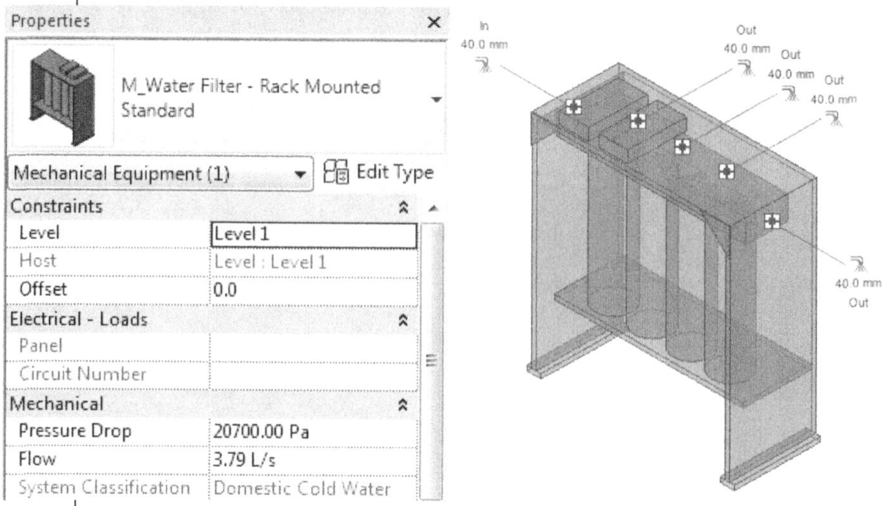

Figure 9–2

- Depending on the component, mechanical equipment can be placed in plan, elevation, and 3D views.

How To: Place Mechanical Equipment

1. In the *Systems* tab>Mechanical panel, click  (Mechanical Equipment) or type **ME**.
2. In the Type Selector, select a mechanical equipment type.
3. In Properties, set any other values such as the *Level* and *Offset* if the equipment is not hosted.
4. In the Options Bar, specify if you want to be able to rotate the equipment after placement.
5. Place the mechanical equipment in the model by clicking at the required location in the model view

- You can use other objects in the model to align the element, or press <Spacebar> to rotate it before placing it.

- Plumbing-based mechanical equipment can be loaded from the Autodesk® Revit® library in the *Mechanical>MEP>Water-side Components* folder (as shown in Figure 9–3) and the *Mechanical>MEP>Equipment* folder.

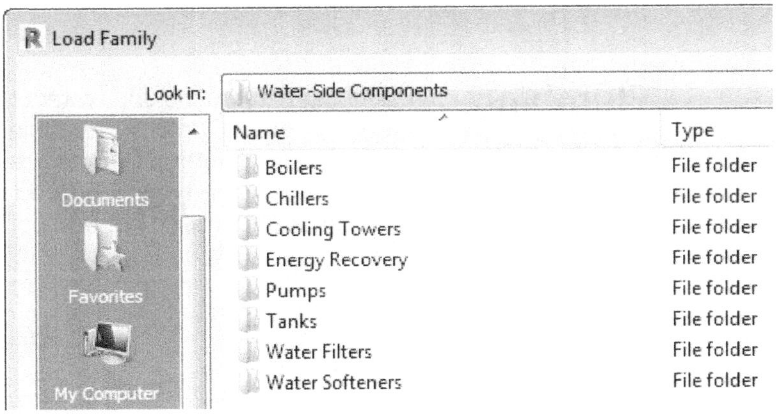

Figure 9–3

Hint: Tagging Equipment and Fixtures

You can tag both plumbing fixtures and mechanical equipment, as shown in Figure 9–4.

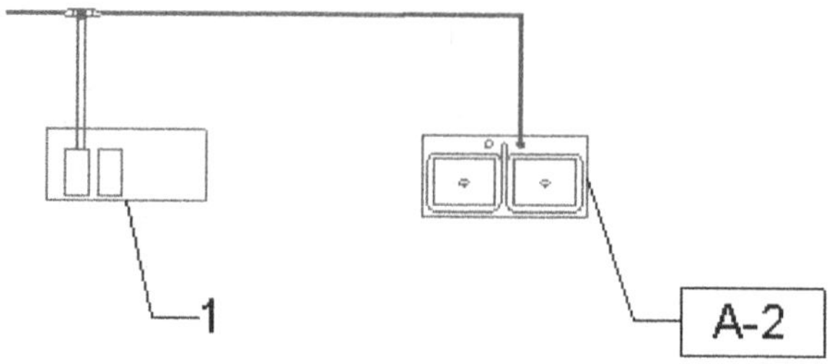

Figure 9–4

- When you are adding plumbing elements, in the *Modify | contextual* tab>Tag panel, toggle (Tag on Placement) on or off as required.
- To add a tag to an existing element, in the *Annotate* tab>Tag panel, click (Tag by Category) and select the elements to tag.

Plumbing Fixtures

Plumbing fixtures include water closets, sinks, lavatories, bathtubs, drains, drinking fountains and many more. Some examples of plumbing fixtures are shown in Figure 9–5. Depending on the type of fixture, there are connectors for sanitary and domestic hot and cold water pipes.

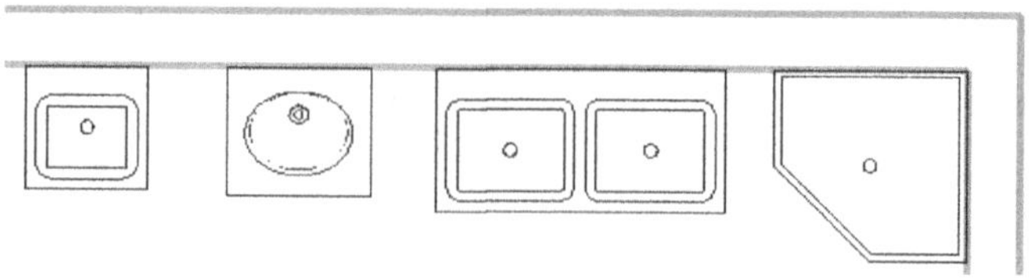

Figure 9–5

- Plumbing fixtures can also be copy/monitored into projects from linked architectural models.

How To: Place Plumbing Fixtures

1. In the *Systems* tab>Plumbing & Piping panel, click (Plumbing Fixture) or type **PX**.
2. In the Type Selector, select a plumbing fixture type.
3. Proceed as follows:

If the fixture is...	Then...
Not hosted	In Properties, set any required values (e.g., *Level*, etc.).
Hosted	In the *Modify | Place Plumbing Fixture* tab>Placement panel, select the type of placement for the specific fixture. The default placement type is (Place on Vertical Face), as shown in Figure 9–6.

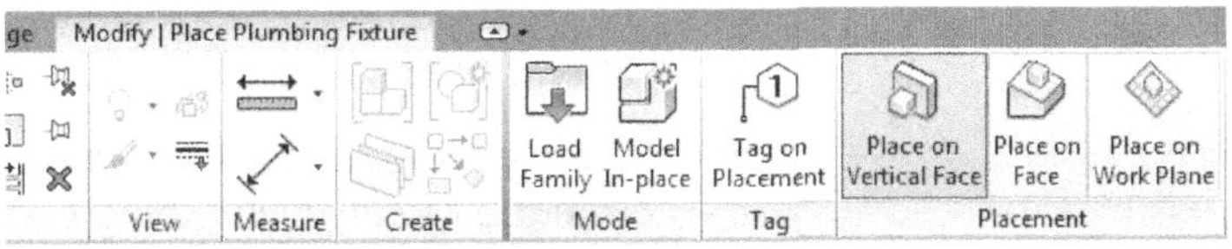

Figure 9–6

4. Place the fixture in the model by clicking on the required location in the model view.

- Press <Spacebar> to rotate the fixture before placing it.
- Additional plumbing fixtures can be loaded from the Autodesk Revit Library in the */Plumbing/MEP/Fixtures* subfolder.
- If you have plumbing fixtures in a project with similar parameters, you can place one and then copy or array it to the other locations. as shown in Figure 9–7.

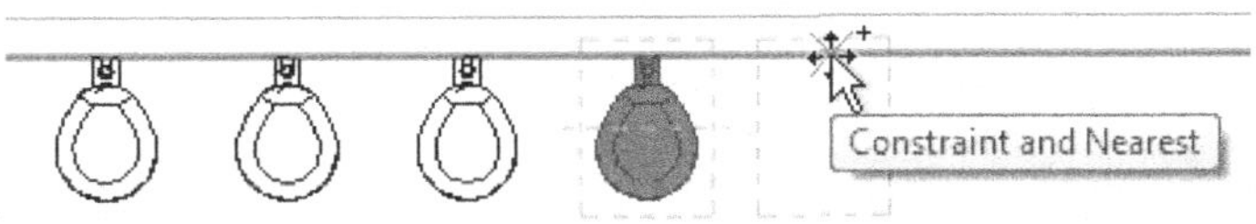

Figure 9–7

- When mirroring fixtures, note that the location of hot and cold water taps in lavatories and sinks can change.

Rehosting Fixtures

If you want to move a wall or face-based fixture to a different location, you might need to rehost the fixture. as shown in Figure 9–8.

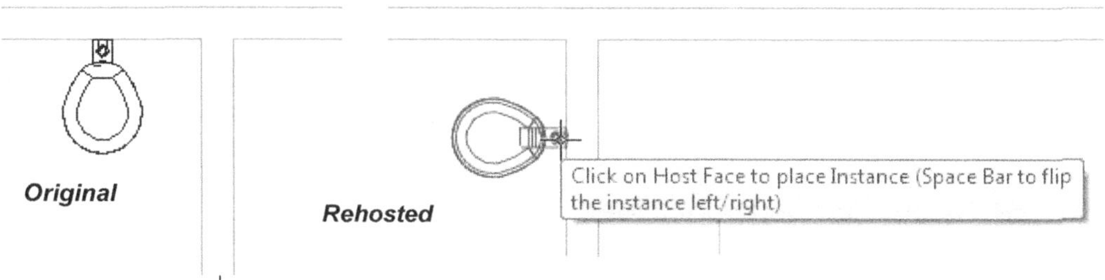

Figure 9–8

How To: Rehost Plumbing Fixtures

1. Select the fixture that needs to be rehosted.
2. In the *Modify | Plumbing Fixtures* tab>Work Plane panel, click (Pick New).
3. In the Placement panel, select the type of placement required by the fixture:
   - **Vertical Face**
   - **Face**
   - **Work Plane**
4. Select the element to which you want the fixture hosted.

Practice 9a Add Plumbing Fixtures and Equipment

Estimated time for completion: 10 minutes

Practice Objective

- Add plumbing fixtures and equipment.

In this practice you will copy/monitor lavatories from a linked model. You will also load and place a plumbing fixture and hot water heaters, as shown in Figure 9–9. Optionally, you can also place floor drains in the restrooms and kitchen area.

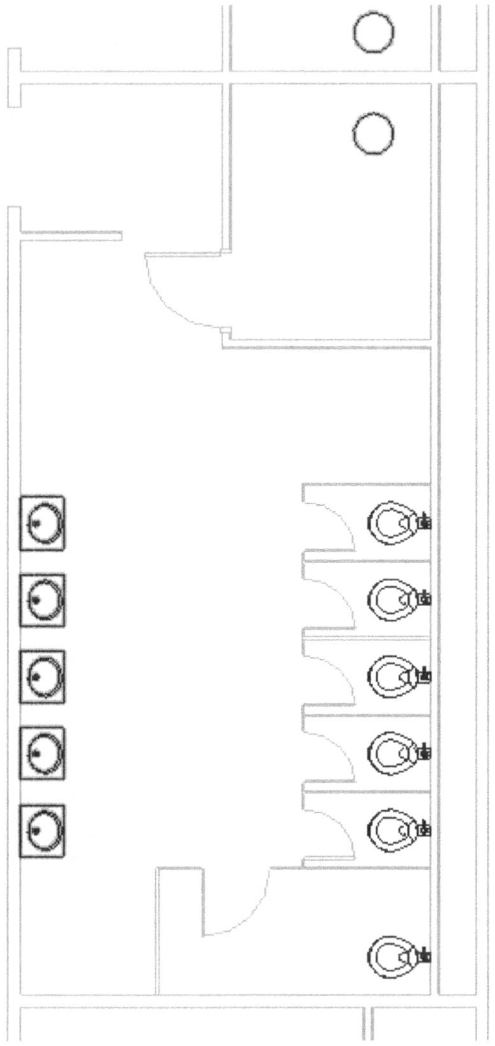

Figure 9–9

Task 1 - Copy/Monitor plumbing fixtures.

1. In the practice files *Plumbing* folder, open **MEP-Elementary-School-Plumbing-M.rvt.**

2. In the Plumbing>Floor Plans:**1 - Plumbing** view, note that some of the water closets have already be placed in the project through copy/monitor, while the lavatories have not, as shown in Figure 9–10.

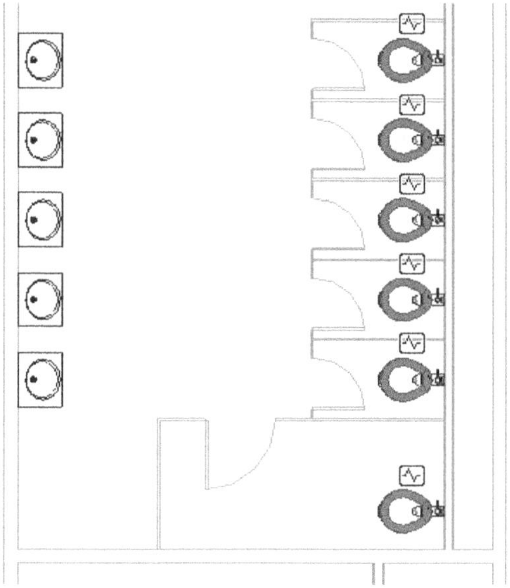

Figure 9–10

3. In the *Collaborate* tab>Coordinate panel, expand  (Copy/Monitor) and click  (Select Link).

4. Select the linked model.

5. In the *Copy/Monitor* tab>Tools panel, click  (Coordination Settings).

6. In the Coordination Settings dialog box, expand **Plumbing Fixtures** and select **Type Mapping**. Several elements were set so that they did not get copied in, as shown in Figure 9–11.

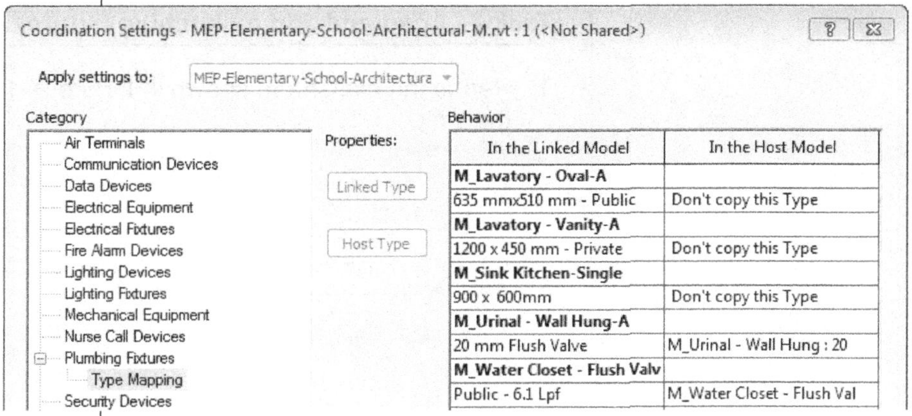

Figure 9–11

7. Beside the option for *M_Lavatory-Oval-A*, select **M_Lavatory-Oval: 635mmx510mm - Public**. This is an MEP-based fixture with connectors for pipes included.

8. Click **Copy**.

9. In the *Copy/Monitor* tab>Copy/Monitor panel, click (Finish).

10. The lavatories in the restrooms have now been copied and monitored into the project (as shown in Figure 9–12), but the sinks in the classrooms have not.

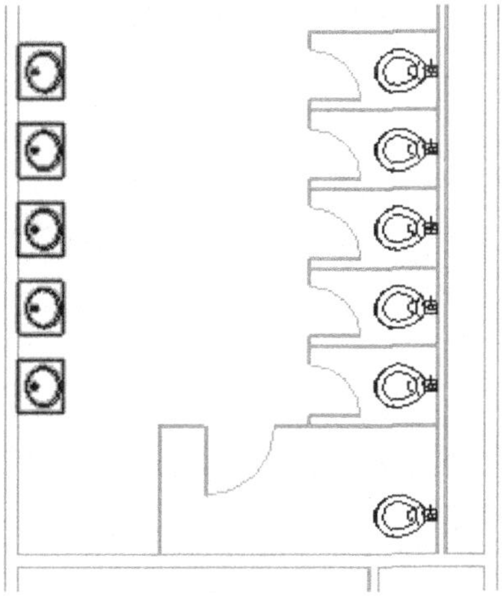

Figure 9–12

11. Save the project.

Task 2 - Load and add a plumbing fixture.

1. Pan to the classroom shown in Figure 9–13 and zoom in on the sink.

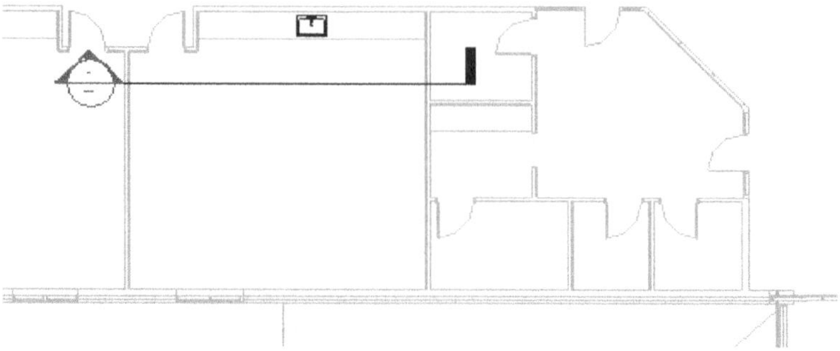

Figure 9–13

2. In the *Systems* tab>Plumbing & Piping panel, click  (Plumbing Fixture).

3. Expand the Type Selector list and in the search box type **kit**. A short list of plumbing fixtures display that have Kitchen in the name, as shown in Figure 9–14.

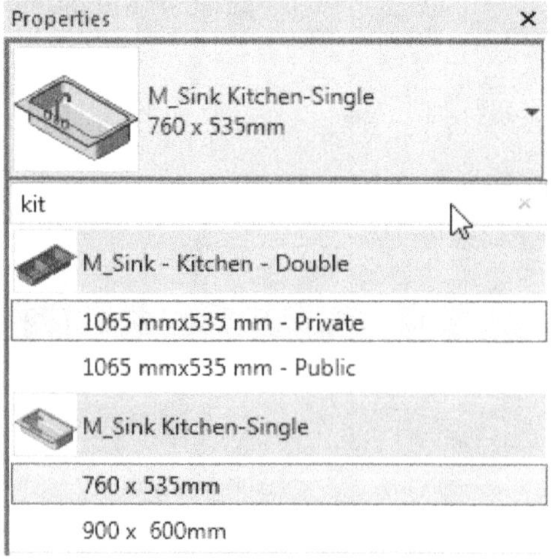

Figure 9–14

4. Select **M_Sink Kitchen-Single: 900 x 600mm** and place it directly on top of the sink in the linked model.

5. Click **Modify** and select the new sink. Note that the sink does not include connectors for piping, as shown in Figure 9–15.

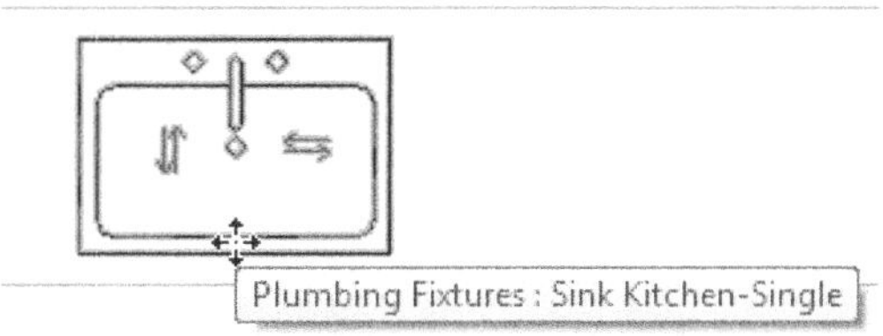

Figure 9–15

This is a method of loading families without starting a command.

6. In the *Insert* tab>Load from Library panel, click (Load Family).

7. In the Load Family dialog box, navigate to the practice files *Plumbing* folder (not the Autodesk Revit library folder) and select **M_Sink_Kitchen-Single-MEP.rfa**. This is a custom sink that matches the architectural sink, but which includes MEP connectors.

8. In the view, select the sink. In the Type Selector, change the type to **M_Sink Kitchen-Single: 900 x 600mm** . The fixture updates with connectors, as shown in Figure 9–16.

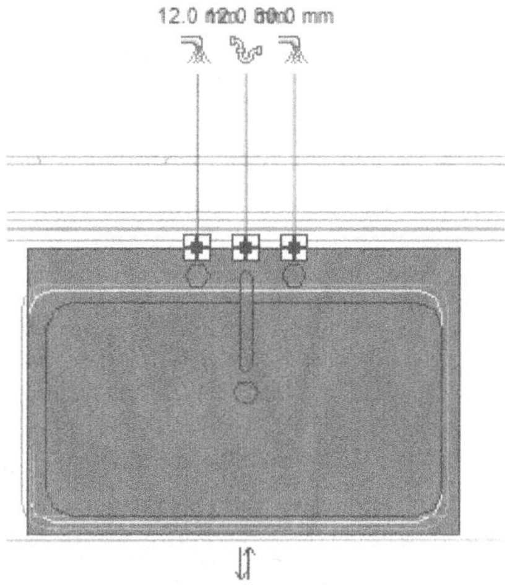

Figure 9–16

9. With the sink still selected, right-click and select **Create Similar**.

10. Place a copy of the sink across the hall, as shown in Figure 9–17. Press <Spacebar> to rotate the sink to the correct orientation before placing it so that it is aligned with the fixture in the linked architectural model.

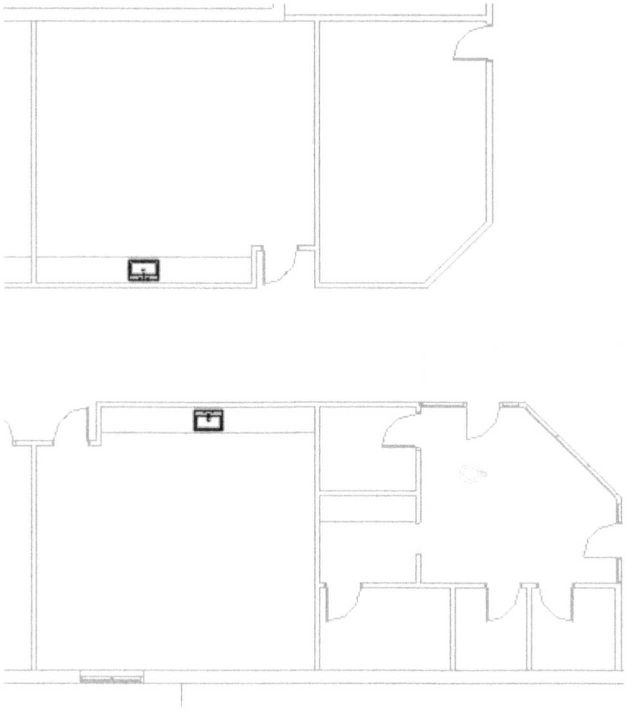

Figure 9–17

11. Click **Modify** and select both of the sinks.

12. In the *Modify | Plumbing Fixtures* tab>Clipboard panel, click (Copy to Clipboard).

13. In the Clipboard panel, expand (Paste) and select (Paste Aligned to Selected Levels).

14. In the Select Levels dialog box, select **Level 2** and then click **OK**.

15. Open the **2 - Plumbing** view. Note that copies of the sinks are placed on Level 2 directly above the selected sinks.

16. Return to the **1 - Plumbing** view and zoom out to see the entire building.

17. Save the project.

Task 3 - Add water heaters.

This family is also available in the Plumbing practice files folder.

1. In the **1 - Plumbing** view, zoom in on the janitor's closets between the restrooms.
2. In the *Systems* Tab>Mechanical panel, click (Mechanical Equipment).
3. In the Autodesk Revit library, navigate to the *Plumbing>MEP>Equipment>Water Heaters* folder and load the family **M_Water Heater.rfa**.
4. In the Type Selector, select **M_Water Heater: 152 L**.
5. Place a water heater in the janitor's closet in each restroom. Rotate the components so that the Sanitary connector faces the wall, as shown in Figure 9–18.

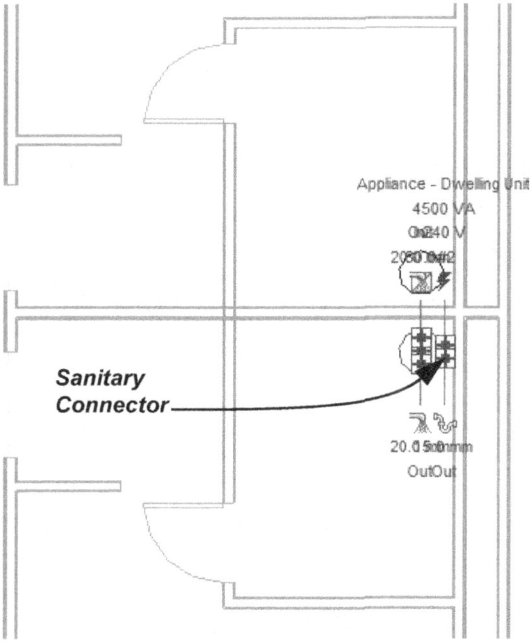

Figure 9–18

6. Zoom out to fit the view.
7. Save the project.

Task 4 - Add floor drains.

1. For additional practice, add drains to the restrooms and kitchen, as shown in Figure 9–19.
   - Work in the Plumbing>Drainage>Floor Plans> **1 - Drainage** view.
   - Use the plumbing fixture **M_Floor Drain - Round: 125 mm Strainer - 80 mm Drain**.
   - Place the drain on the work plane.

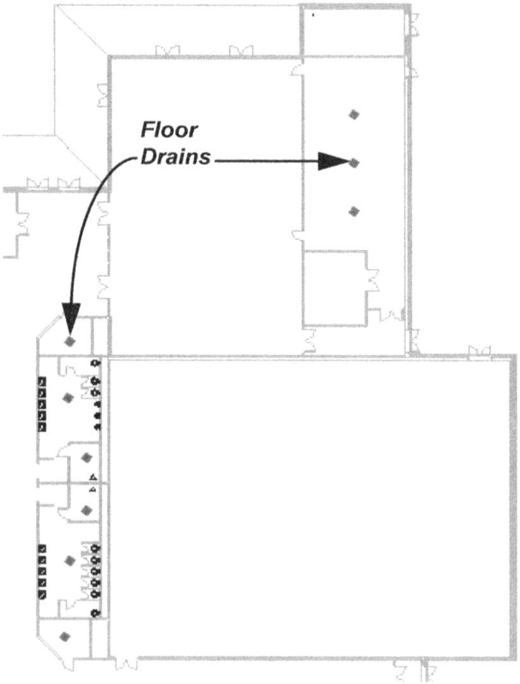

Figure 9–19

2. Save the project.

9.2 Adding Plumbing Pipes

Fittings are automatically added in some cases, but you can also add and modify fittings.

Check sanitary pipe fittings in particular to ensure that they are pointing the right way.

Plumbing Systems include sanitary, domestic hot water, and domestic cold water, as shown in Figure 9–20. The pipes in a system connect plumbing fixtures together and indicate how the network is laid out. You can draw the pipes independently or using connectors in the fixtures.

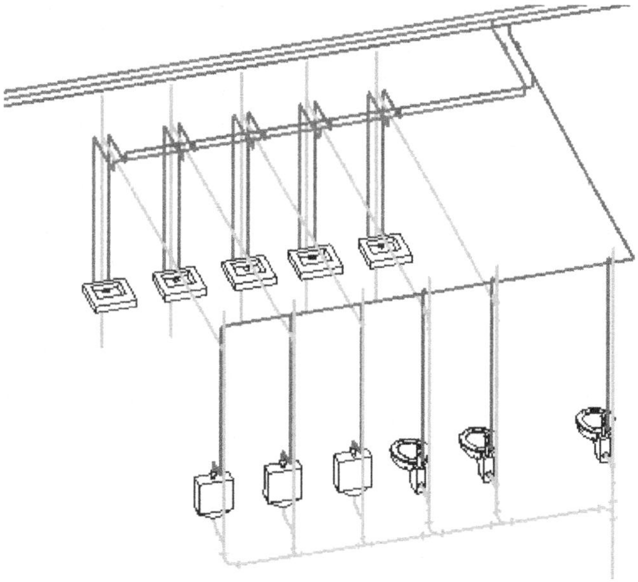

Figure 9–20

- Pipes can be drawn in plan, elevation/section, and 3D views.
- To get the pipes at the right height, it is recommended to start from the connectors in the plumbing fixtures.
- Fittings between changes of height or size are automatically applied as you model the elements, as shown in Figure 9–21.

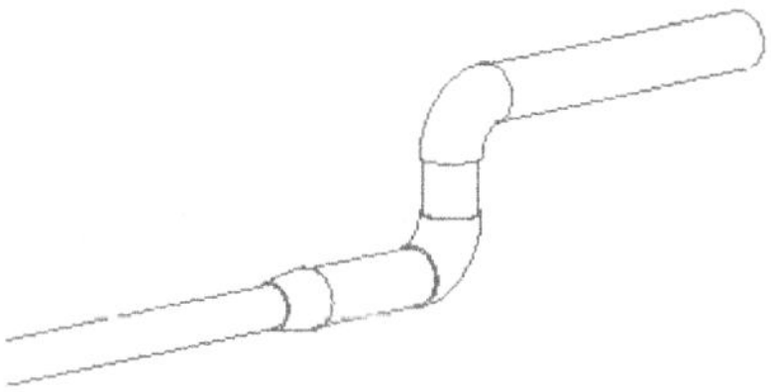

Figure 9–21

- If you need to lay the runs, but the type and size has not yet been determined, create Placeholders and convert them to standard pipes at a later stage.

Mechanical Settings

Before you add pipes, review and modify the Mechanical Settings to suit your project or office standards. These settings control the angles at which the pipes can be drawn (as shown in Figure 9–22), the default types, offsets, sizes, slopes, and the Pressure Drop calculation method.

- In the *Systems* tab>Mechanical panel, click (Mechanical Settings) or type **MS** to open the Mechanical Settings dialog box.

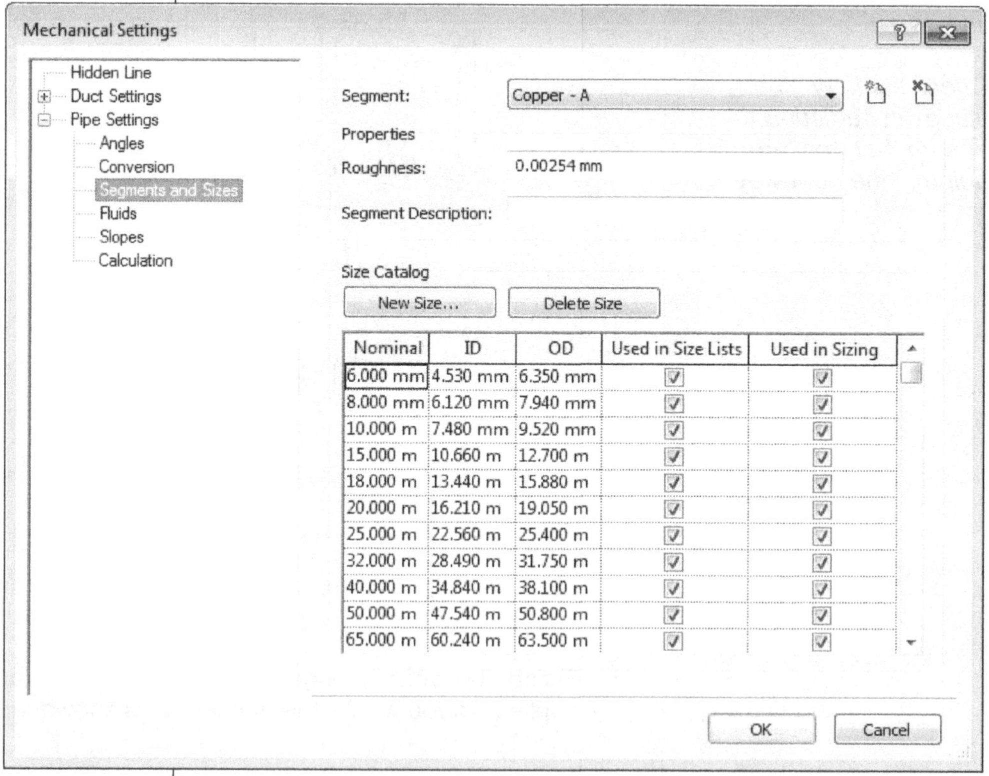

Figure 9–22

Hidden Line	Specify the size and type of hidden lines that show when pipes cross over each other.
Angles	Specify at what angles fittings are applied for pipe runs.
Conversion	Specify how the pipes work when using the Generate Layout tool. (These are also available in that command.)
Segments and Sizes	Specify the sizes and other properties for piping by material type.

Fluids	Specify the temperature, viscosity, and density of fluids by fluid type.
Slopes	Specify slope values for piping runs.
Calculation	Specify the pipe pressure drop for straight sections. You can select from a variety of calculation methods.

- Mechanical Settings are set by project and can be included in templates or imported into a project from another one using **Transfer Project Standards**.

Adding Pipes

The process of adding standard, flex, or placeholder pipes is essentially the same. There are several ways to start the commands:

1. In the *Systems* tab>Plumbing & Piping panel, click the appropriate command or type the shortcut:

    Pipe (PI)

    Pipe Placeholder

    Flex Pipe (FP)

2. Select the element, hover the cursor over a connector icon, and then select the command, as shown in Figure 9–23.

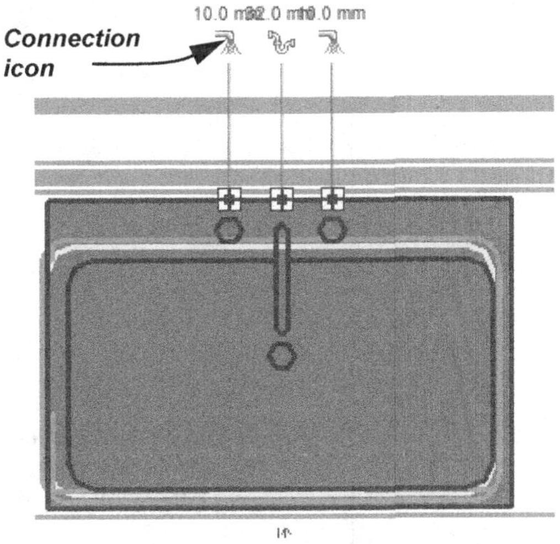

Figure 9–23

3. Select the element, right-click on a connector, and then select the command name.

How To: Add Pipe

1. Start the (Pipe), (Pipe Placeholder), or (Flex Pipe) command
2. In the Type Selector, select a pipe type as shown in Figure 9–24.

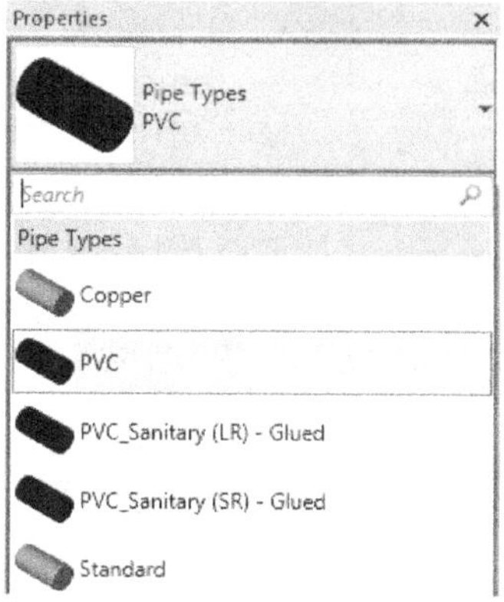

Figure 9–24

3. If you are drawing pipes without selecting an existing connector, in Properties, specify the *System Type* (as shown in Figure 9–25) before you start drawing the elements.

Drawing from existing connectors automatically applies the System Type.

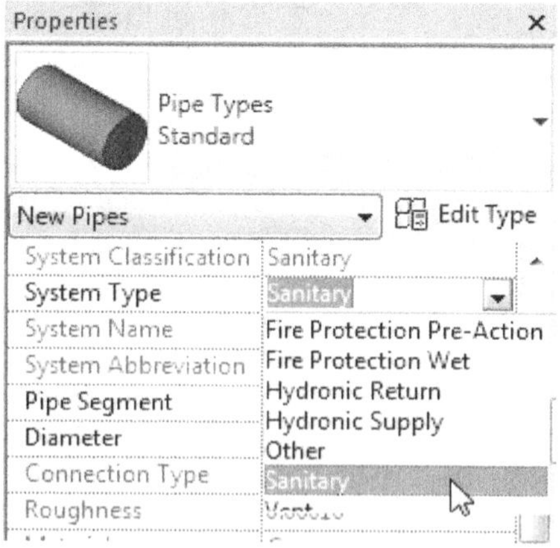

Figure 9–25

4. In the Options Bar, set the *Diameter* and *Offset*, as shown in Figure 9–26. If you started from a connector, the default size and offset match the parameters of the selected connector.

Figure 9–26

5. In the ribbon, set up the various placement tools, as outlined below.
6. Press <Esc> once to stay in the command but begin a new start location.

Pipe Placement Tools

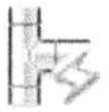	**Automatically Connect (on/off)**	On by default. Pipes connect to other pipes and automatically place all of the required fittings. Toggle this option off, if you want to draw a pipe that remains at the original elevation. • Even if **Automatically Connect** is not toggled on, when you snap to a connector any changes in height and size are applied with the appropriate fittings.
	**Justification**	Opens the Justification Setting dialog box, which enables you to set the default settings for the *Horizontal Justification, Horizontal Offset,* and *Vertical Justification.*
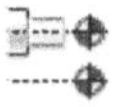	**Inherit Elevation (on/off)**	If the tool is toggled on and you start modeling a pipe by snapping to an existing one, the new pipe takes on the elevation of the existing one regardless of what is specified, as shown in Figure 9–27.
	**Inherit Size (on/off)**	If the tool is toggled on and you start modeling pipe by snapping to an existing one, the new pipe takes on the size of the existing one regardless of what is specified, as shown in Figure 9–27.

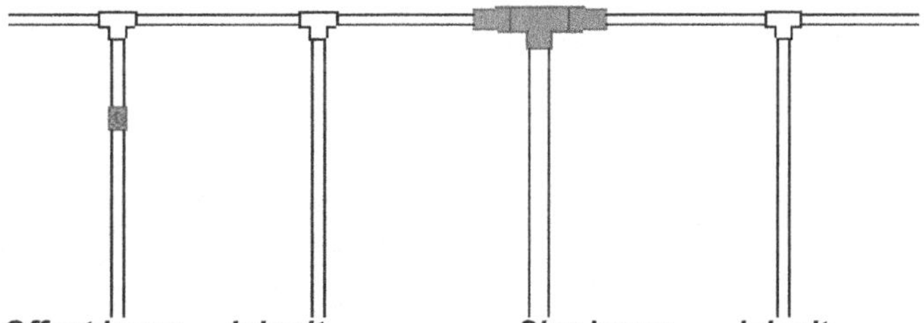

Figure 9–27

- If you already have some pipes in the project, you can use  (Connect Into). This option displays in the contextual tab when you select a component.

- To display centerlines for pipe, in the Visibility/Graphics Overrides dialog box, turn on the *Centerline* subcategory for pipes and pipe fittings, as shown in Figure 9–28.

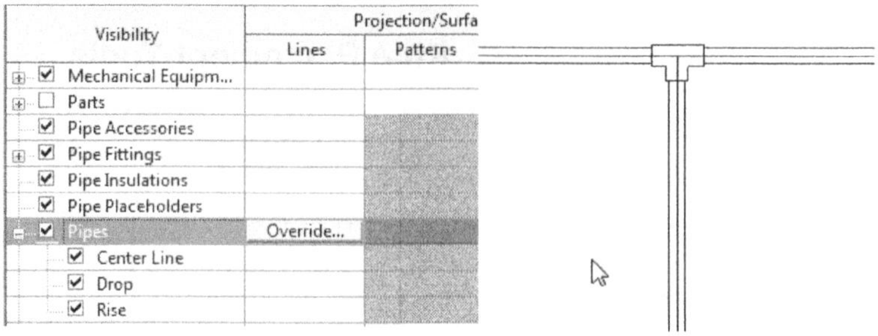

Figure 9–28

- Centerlines display in plan and elevation views set to the **Wireframe** or **Hidden Line** visual style.

Sloped Piping

When drawing pipes with a slope, it helps to identify the direction that *drains to daylight* (the point in the system where it attaches to the exterior drainage pipes). Then, start drawing the pipes from the top most fixture in the system as shown in Figure 9–29.

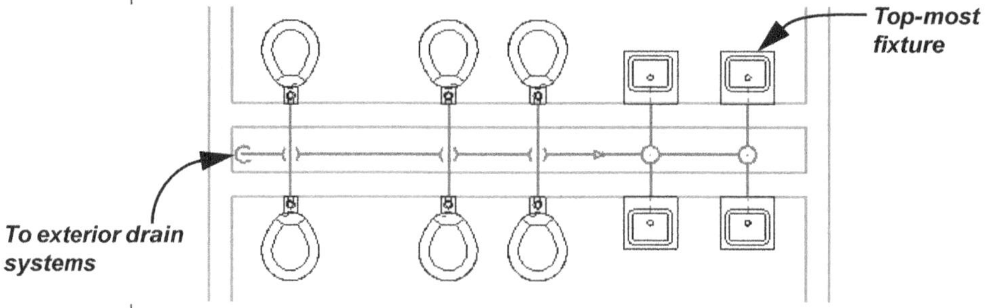

Figure 9–29

- As you are drawing pipes with slopes, you can set the information in the *Modify | Place Pipe* tab>Sloped Piping panel as shown in Figure 9–30. You can change the direction of the slope, the slope value, and turn the slope off or specify that it be ignored when connecting.

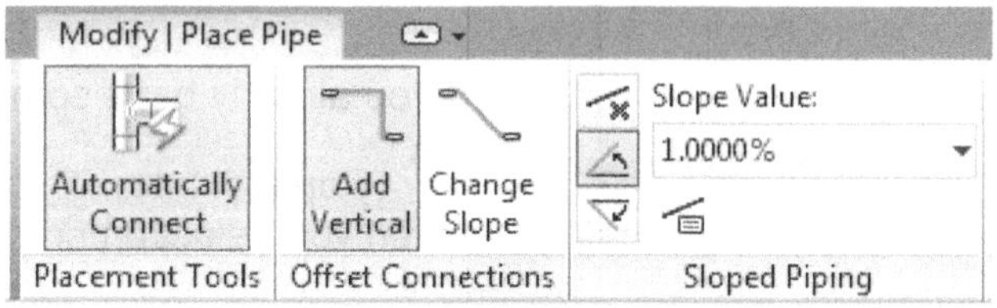

Figure 9–30

- In the Sloped Piping panel, toggle on (Show Slope Tooltip) to see the exact information of the offsets and slope as you draw, as shown in Figure 9–31.

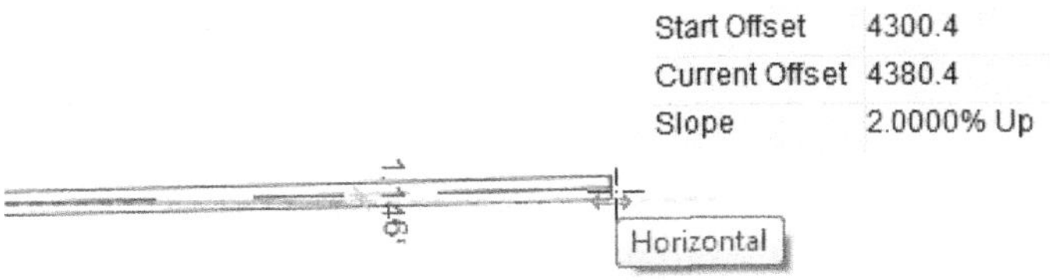

Figure 9–31

Creating Parallel Pipes

The **Parallel Pipes** tool helps you create piping runs that are parallel to an existing run, as shown in Figure 9–32. This can save time because only one run needs to be laid out, and the tool generates the parallel runs for you.

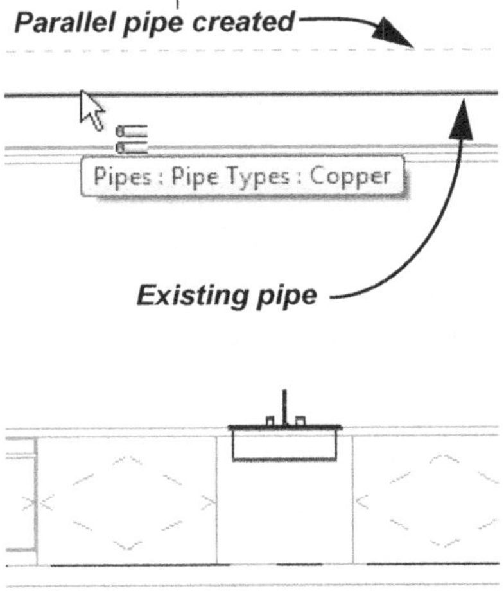

Figure 9–32

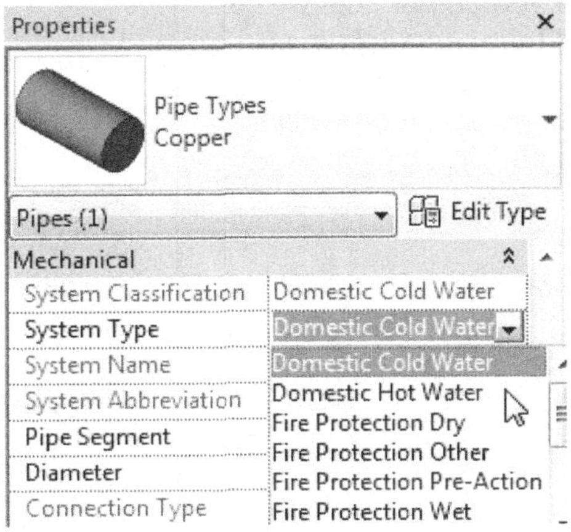

Figure 9–33

- The **Parallel Pipes** tool creates an exact duplicate of the selected pipe, including the system type. You can change the System Type in Properties (as shown in Figure 9–33) before connecting other pipes into it.
- It might be easier to draw the parallel pipes directly from the fixtures so that the pipe takes on the correct system type. Also, you might have to modify connectors to get the pipe in the correct place.
- Parallel pipes can be created in plan, section, elevation, and 3D views.

How To: Create Parallel Pipe Runs

1. Create an initial pipe run, or use an existing pipe run.
2. In the *Systems* tab>Plumbing & Piping panel, click  (Parallel Pipes).
3. In the *Modify | Place Parallel Pipes* tab>Parallel Pipes panel, set the required options, as shown in Figure 9–34.

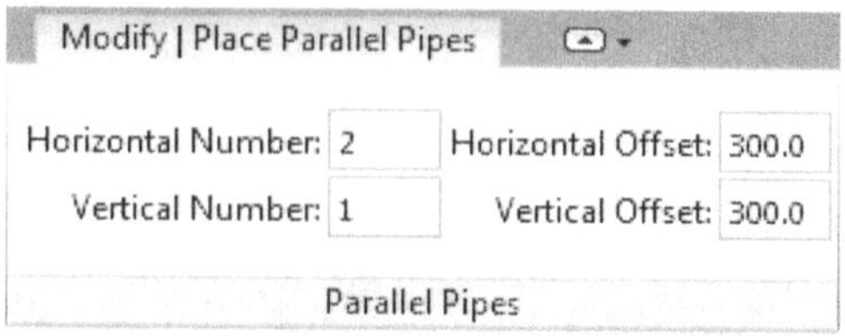

Figure 9–34

4. Hover the cursor over the existing piping (as shown in Figure 9–35) and press <Tab> to select the existing run.

If you do not press <Tab>, parallel pipes are only created for the single piece of existing pipe.

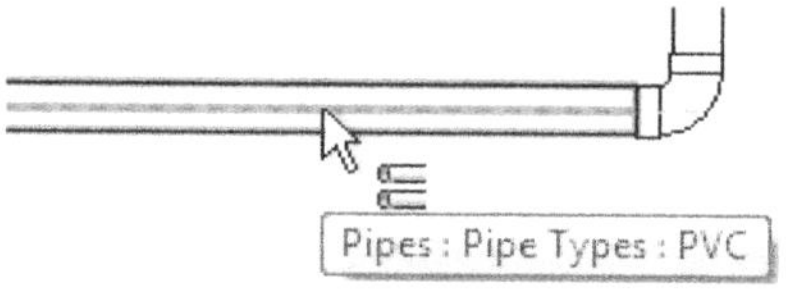

Figure 9–35

5. When the preview displays as required, click to create the parallel runs. The preview varies depending on which side of the existing run you hover the cursor.

Parallel Pipe Creation Options

Horizontal Number	The total number of parallel pipe runs, in the horizontal direction.
Horizontal Offset	The distance between parallel pipe runs, in the horizontal direction.
Vertical Number	The total number of parallel pipe runs, in the vertical direction.
Vertical Offset	The distance between parallel pipe runs, in the vertical direction.

- In section and elevation views, horizontal refers to parallel to the view (visually up, down, left, or right from the original conduit). Vertical creates parallel conduit runs perpendicular to the view, in the direction of the user.

Practice 9b Add Plumbing Pipes

Practice Objectives

- Set Mechanical Settings.
- Add pipes.
- Change the size and height of the pipes as you draw them.
- Create sloped pipes.

Estimated time for completion: 10 minutes

In this practice you will draw cold water mains from the origin point to the classroom wing, changing the diameter and offset of the pipes as you draw them. You will connect water heaters into the mains and then draw hot water pipes from the water heater to the classroom wing. Finally, you will draw sloped sanitary piping from floor drains, as shown in Figure 9–36.

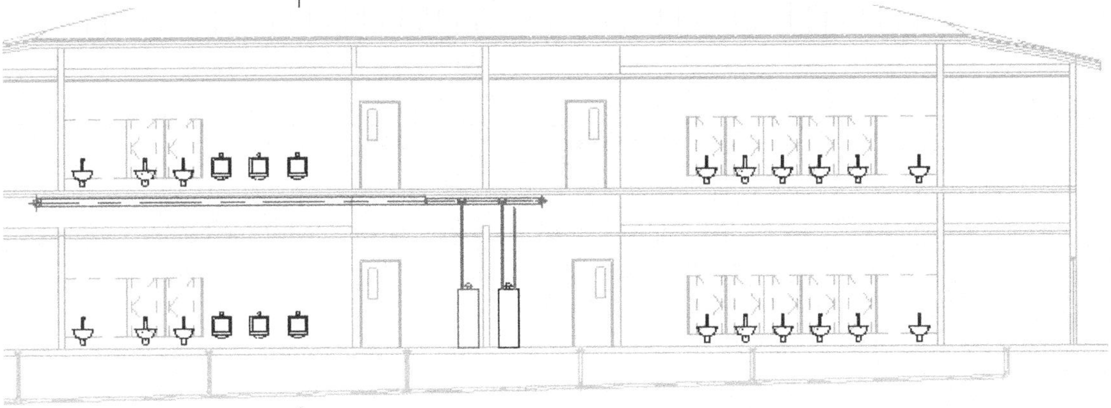

Figure 9–36

Task 1 - Set mechanical settings.

1. In the practice files *Plumbing* folder, open the project **MEP-Elementary-School-Piping-M.rvt**.
2. In the *Systems* tab>Mechanical panel title bar, click ↘ (Mechanical Settings).
3. In the Mechanical Settings dialog box, in *Pipe Settings,* select **Angles**.

4. In the right pane, select **Use specific angles** and clear the checks from 22.500° and 11.250°, as shown in Figure 9–37. This limits the angles you can use to draw the piping to industry specific fittings.

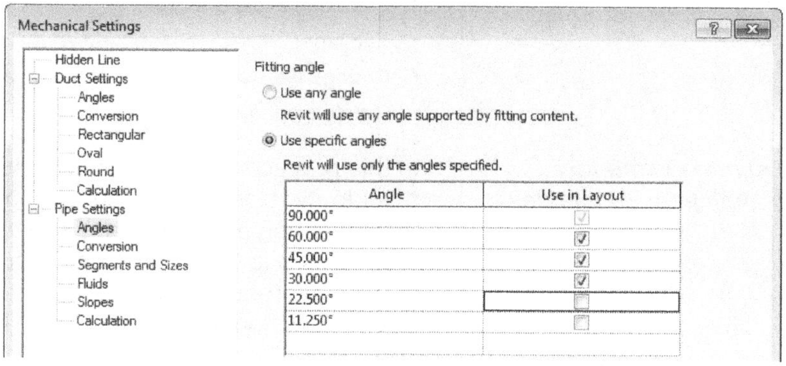

Figure 9–37

5. Click **OK**.

Task 2 - Run cold water mains

In this task you will model cold water mains following the path shown in Figure 9–38. You will change the diameter and offset of the pipes as you progress.

The piping lines in this graphics is enhanced for clarity.

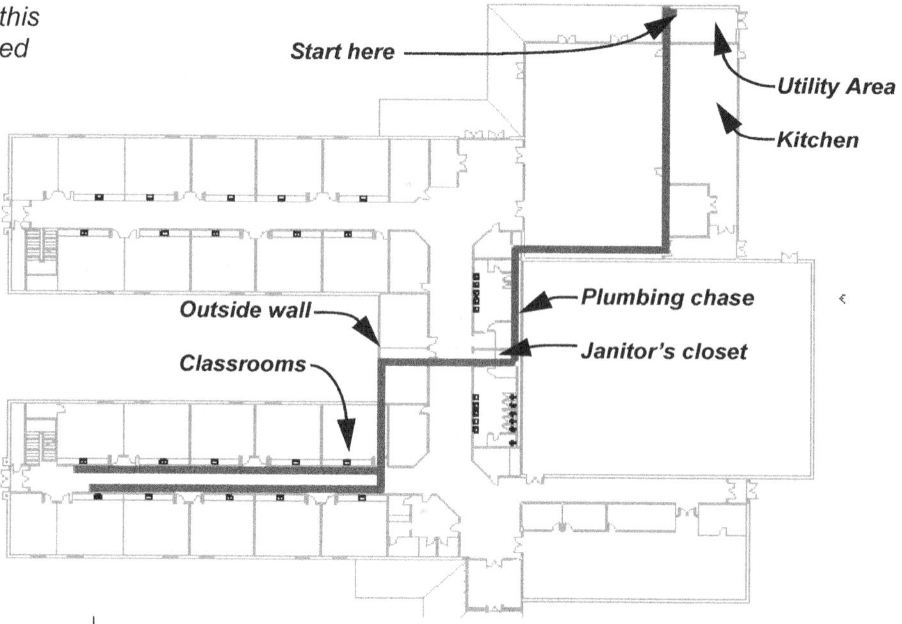

Figure 9–38

1. Open the Plumbing>Plumbing>Floor Plans>**1 - Plumbing** view.
2. Review the path of the piping shown in Figure 9–38
3. In Properties, in the *Underlay* area, set the *Range: Base Level* to **Level 2**. This will display the piping as it is being drawn above the first level.
4. Zoom in on the utility area outside the kitchen. There is a water main connector available as shown in Figure 9–39.

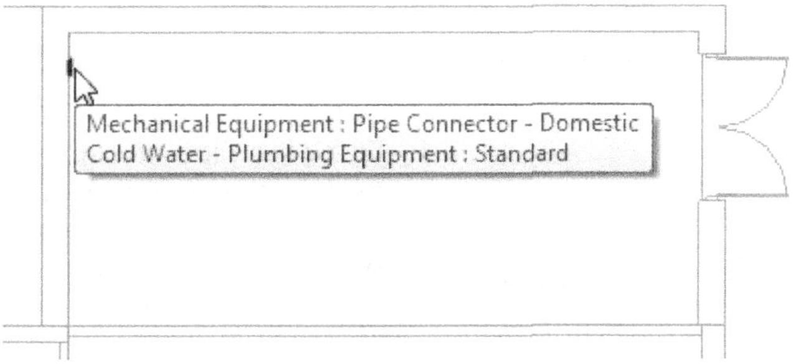

Figure 9–39

5. Right-click on the connector and select **Draw Pipe**.
6. In the Type Selector, select **Pipe Types: Copper**.
7. Note that the following is automatically set based on the information stored in the connector:
   - In Properties, *System Type* is set to **Domestic Cold Water.**
   - In the Options Bar, *Diameter* is set to **200mm** and *Offset* to **200mm**.
8. Draw the pipe to the right a short distance. In the Options Bar, change the *Offset* to **3650mm** and press <Enter>.

9. Continue drawing the pipe down the side of the kitchen, as shown in Figure 9–40.

Figure 9–40

10. Draw the pipe around the restrooms in the plumbing chase, and then across the hall to the exterior wall of the building. In the Options Bar, change the *Diameter* and *Offset* at the points shown in Figure 9–41.

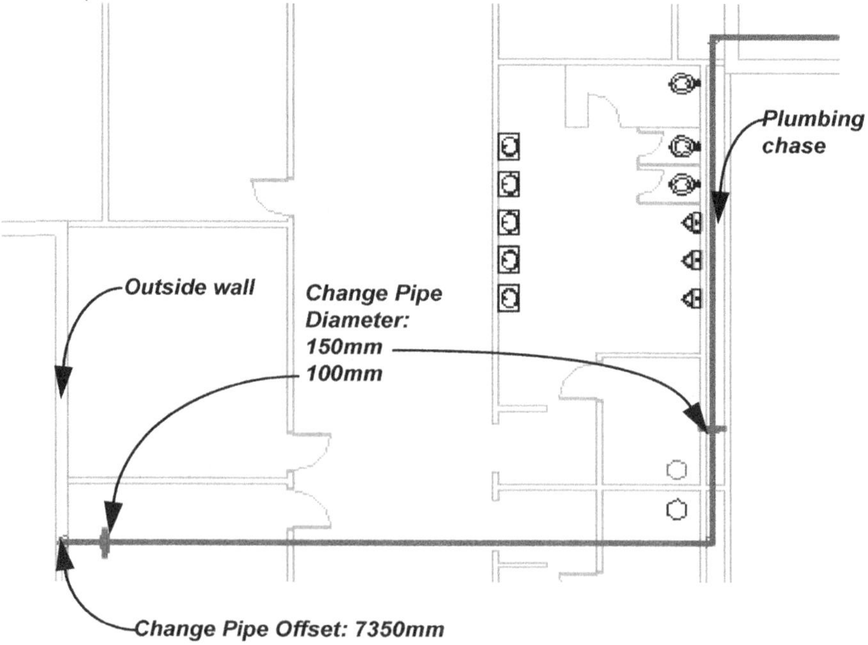

Figure 9–41

11. Continue drawing the pipe down the hall of the classroom wing until it is past the last sink.

12. Press <Esc> once to stop the pipe run but stay in the command.

13. Draw a pipe run starting from the last sink on the other side of the hall until it ties into the vertical pipe, as shown in Figure 9–42.

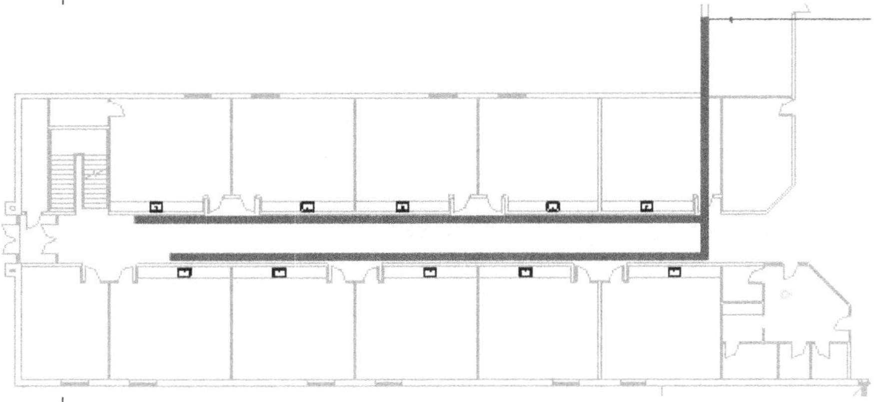

Figure 9–42

14. Click **Modify**.

15. Zoom in on the water heaters.

16. Select one of the water heaters. In the *Modify | Mechanical Equipment* tab>Layout panel, click  (Connect Into).

17. In the Select Connector dialog box, select the Cold Water connector and click **OK**.

18. Select the cold water main.

19. Repeat Steps 16 and 17 with the other water heater. The pipes are connected as shown in Figure 9–43

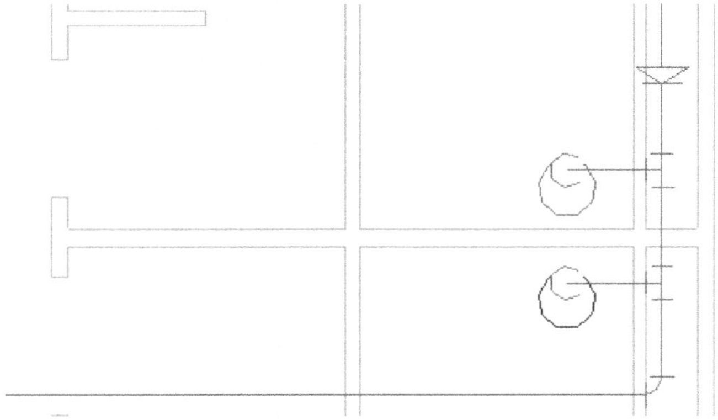

Figure 9–43

20. Save the project.

Task 3 - Add hot water lines.

1. Continue working zoomed in to the water heaters.
2. Select the water heater closest to the south wing of the building.
3. Click on the hot water connector to start the **Create Pipe** command.
4. In the Options Bar, change *Offset* to **3500mm** and press <Enter>.
5. Continue drawing the pipe following the path of the cold water pipes, changing the *Offset* to **7150mm** at the point shown in Figure 9–44.

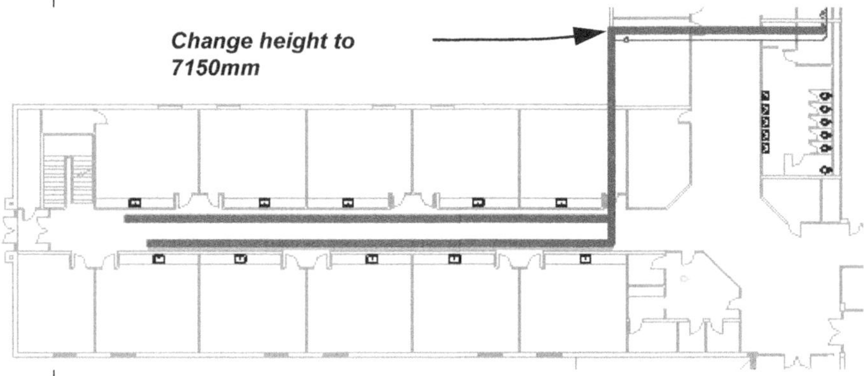

Figure 9–44

- When you draw the second horizontal pipe, ensure that the extra pipe connects to the hot water pipe and not the cold water pipe. Press <Tab> to cycle through the options. In the Status Bar, you want to see Pipe Type Copper 20mm @7150.
- If you need to make changes to the pipe on the second floor, open the **2 - Plumbing** view.

6. Save the project.

Task 4 - Draw sloped pipes for drains.

1. Open the Plumbing>Plumbing>Sections (Building Section): **Restroom Section** view. Note that the floor drains display.
2. Select the floor drain on the right and click the Sanitary connector to start the **Draw Pipe** command.
3. In the Type Selector, select **Pipe Types: Standard**. (This type acts as a placeholder until a later practice.)
4. In the *Modify* | *Place Pipe* tab>Sloped Piping panel, select  (Slope Down) and set the *Slope Value* to **1.000%**.
5. Draw the pipe down and then over to the left as shown in Figure 9–45.

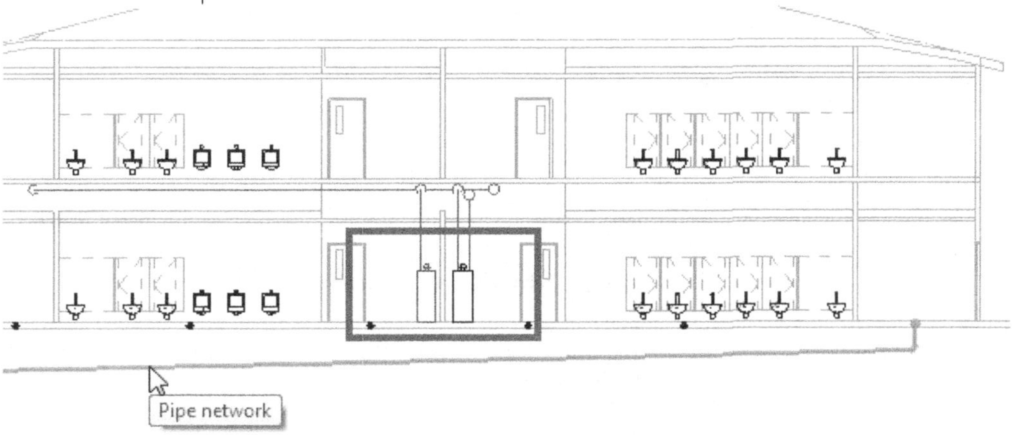

Figure 9–45

6. Draw pipe from each of the other floor drains into the sloped pipe.
   - Note that the floor drains that are near the hot water heaters are not in direct line with the rest of the floor drains. You might need to adjust the slope of the lateral pipes in a section view or using a selection box in a 3D view.
7. Save the project.

9.3 Modifying Plumbing Pipes

Plumbing pipes can be modified using a variety of standard and specialty tools, such as converting placeholders, changing rigid pipes to flexible ones, adding insulation, and modifying the justification of pipes.

For the example shown in Figure 9–46, the fittings are incorrect for sanitary systems. In Figure 9–47, these have been changed to create the appropriate layout.

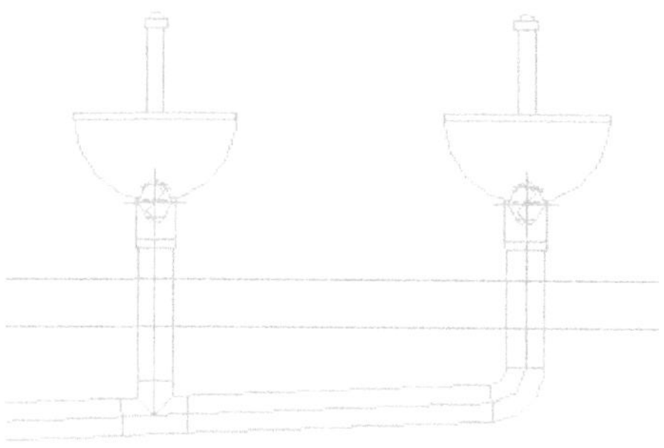

Figure 9–46

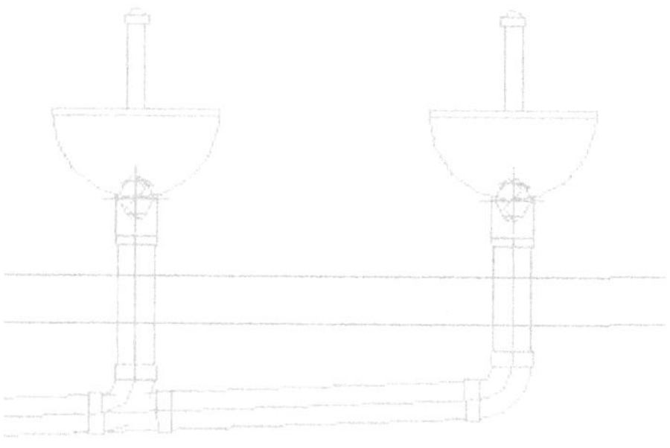

Figure 9–47

Using Standard Modify Tools

You can modify pipes using universal methods by making changes in:

- Properties
- Options Bar
- Temporary Dimensions
- Controls
- Connectors

- You can also use modify tools, such as **Move**, **Rotate**, **Split Trim/Extend**, and **Align**, to help you place the pipes at the required locations.

Pipe Fittings & Accessories

One of the challenges about working with plumbing is specifying the correct pipe fitting or accessory and verifying that it is working as expected. For example, if a fitting is facing the wrong direction, you can use (Flip) to switch it, as shown in Figure 9–48.

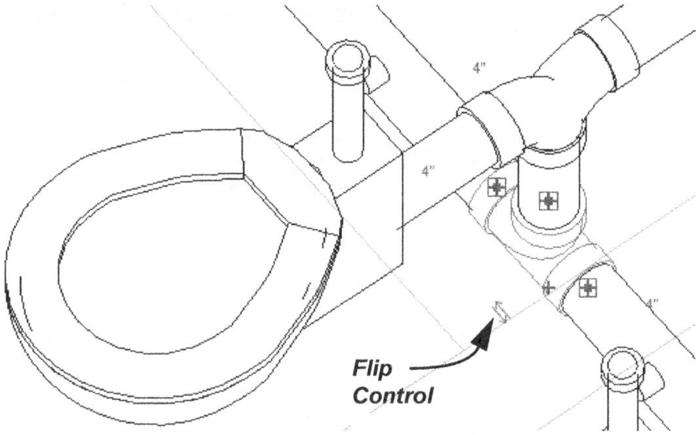

Figure 9–48

- Check various views to verify that you have correctly attached the plumbing fittings to the pipes.
- Some pipe fittings are specified in the Routing Preferences in the Type Properties of the pipe but others have to be added separately. Accessories are always added later.
- Additional fittings and accessories can be loaded from the library. Ensure you start the correct command for the element you want to load. You cannot load fittings when you have started the accessories command.
- Pipe fittings can be loaded from the Library in the *Pipe>Fittings* subfolder. Select the folder for the type of pipe you are using, such as **PVC**, as shown in Figure 9–49. Pipe accessories are in the *Pipe>Accessories* subfolder.

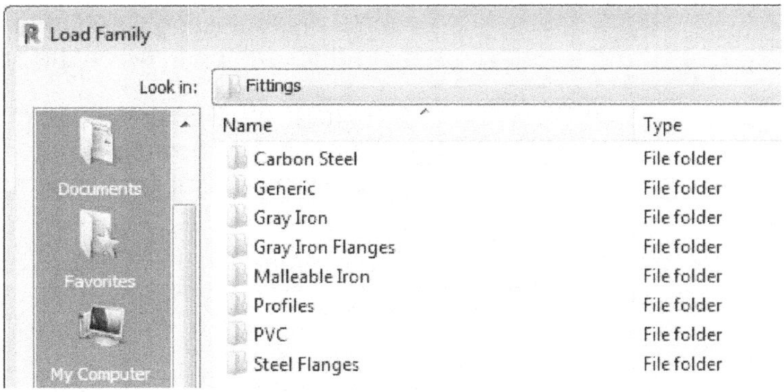

Figure 9–49

How To: Add a Pipe Fitting or Accessory

1. In the *Systems* tab>Plumbing & Piping panel, select the appropriate command:

    Pipe Fitting (PF)

    Pipe Accessory (PA)

2. In the Type Selector, select the fitting or accessory you want to use.
3. Click on the pipe where you want the fitting.
4. In some cases, the fitting might be pointing in the wrong direction, as shown in the left in Figure 9–50. Click  (Rotate) until it points in the required direction.

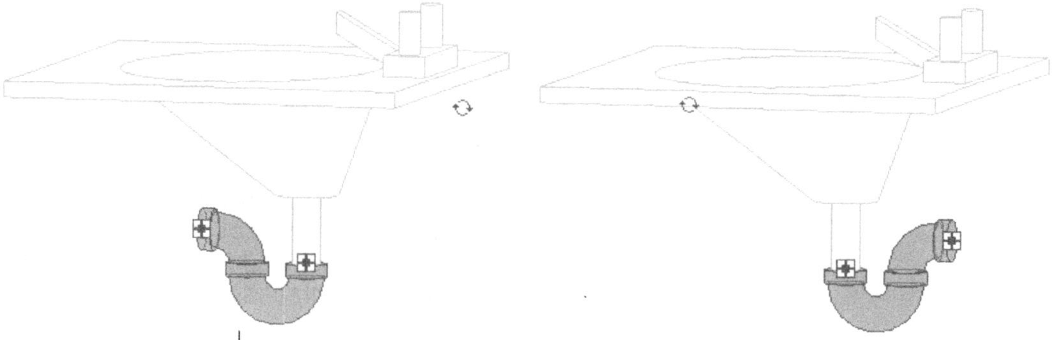

Figure 9–50

Capping Open Ends

You can cap the open end of a pipe by right-clicking on the end control and selecting **Cap Open End**. Alternatively, if you have more than one opening on the ends of a run, in the *Modify* contextual tab>Edit panel, click  (Cap Open Ends). The caps are applied (as shown in Figure 9–51) and a warning displays telling you the number of caps applied.

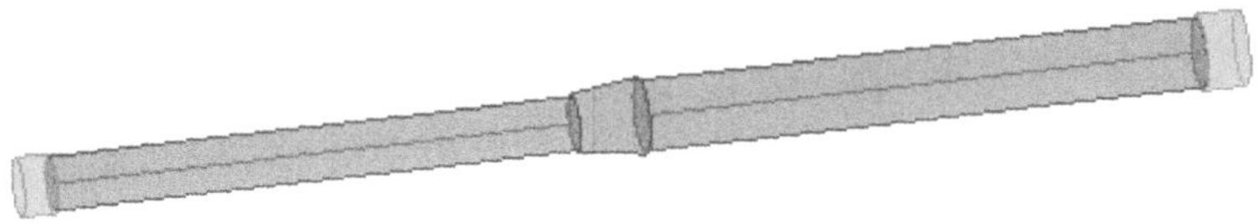

Figure 9–51

Changing the Slope

To change the slope of a pipe, select it and modify the *Edit Slope* control, as shown in Figure 9–52. You can also click (Slope) to open the Slope Editor. The controls are available in plan or section/elevation views.

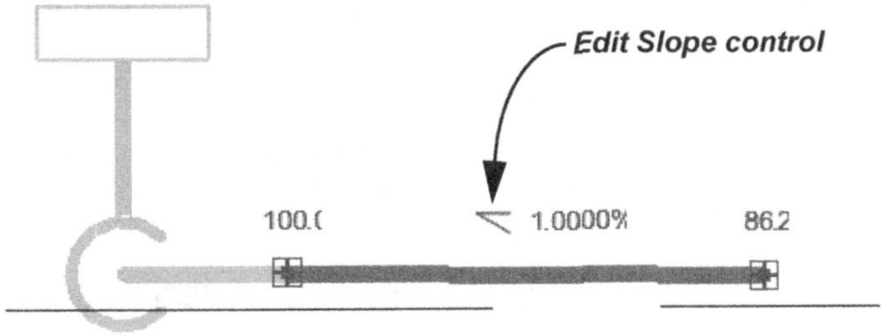

Figure 9–52

- You can change the size of the pipe in the Options Bar or Properties. The offset of the pipe ends can be changed using Properties or the *Edit Start/End Offset* controls.

Converting Pipes

After placing pipes, you can change the type of the entire run (including fittings). If the definition of a type has been changed, you can reapply the type to existing runs. You can also convert placeholders to standard pipes.

How To: Change the Type of Pipe Runs

1. Select the pipe run and filter out everything except the related pipe, accessories, and fittings.
2. In the *Modify | Multi-Select* tab>Edit panel, click (Change Type).
3. In the Type Selector, select a new type of run. For the example shown in Figure 9–53, the type **Standard** was changed to **PVC - DWV**.

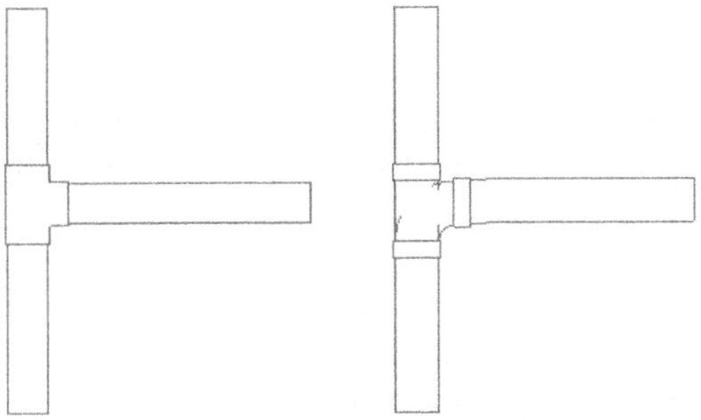

Figure 9–53

How To: Reapply a Type to Pipe Runs

1. Select a single pipe run.
   - You can select different runs, but they must all be of the same type and system. If you select runs in different systems, the software prompts you to select one system to which to reapply the type.
2. Filter out everything except pipes, fittings, and accessories.
3. In the *Modify | Multi-Select* tab>Edit panel, click (Reapply Type).

How To: Convert Placeholders to Pipe

1. Select the pipe placeholder(s).
2. In the *Modify | contextual* tab>Edit panel, click (Convert Placeholder).
3. The placeholders are changed into the pipe type and includes the appropriate fittings, as shown in Figure 9–54.

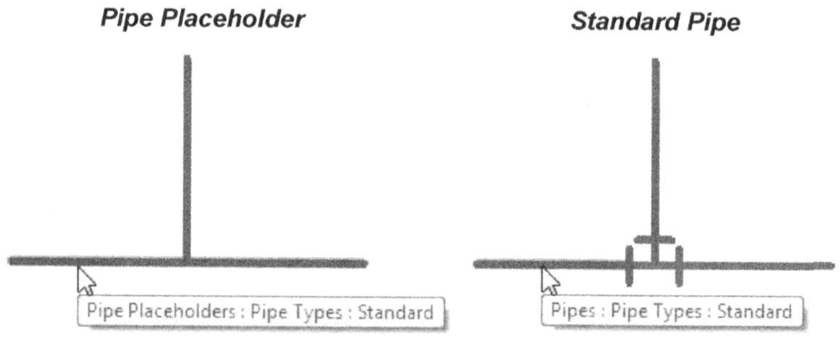

Figure 9–54

Adding Insulation

You can add insulation to pipes which displays in plan as a thin line outside of the pipe. Accessories can also be insulated, as shown in Figure 9–55.

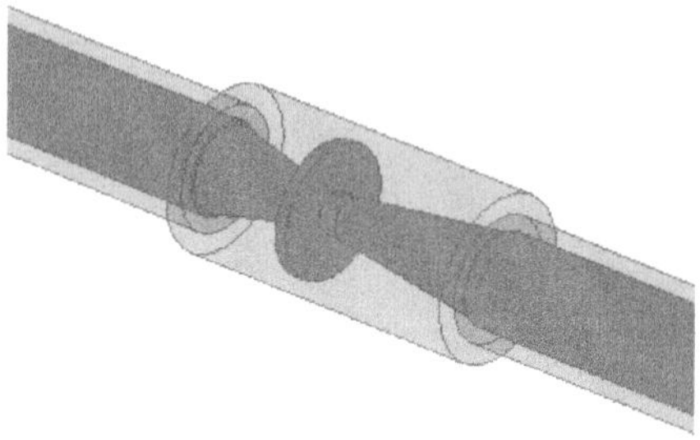

Figure 9–55

How To: Add Insulation

1. Select the pipe run that you want to insulate. You can select more than one system at a time for this command.
2. Use (Filter) to select only the pipes, pipe fittings, and pipe accessories.
3. In the *Modify | contextual* tab>Pipe Insulation panel, click (Add Insulation).
4. In the Add Pipe Insulation dialog box, select a *Insulation Type* and set the *Thickness,* as shown in Figure 9–56. Click **OK**.

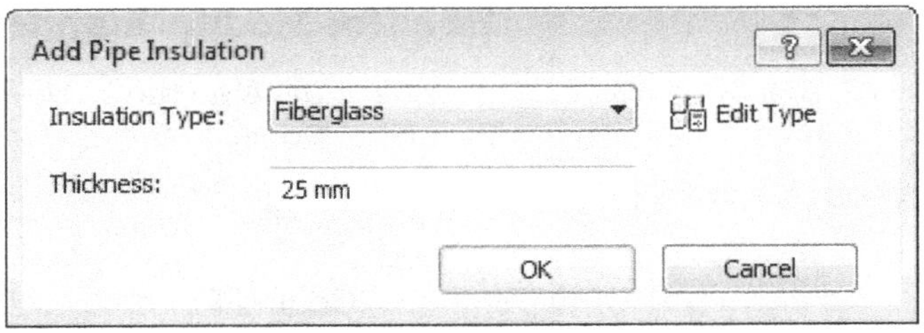

Figure 9–56

Hint: Using Thin Lines

Line thickness can negatively impact the display of elements, such as insulation or lining. To toggle lineweight on or off, in the Quick Access Toolbar, click (Thin Lines) or type **TL**.

- To modify the insulation, select the insulated pipe and, in the contextual ribbon, select one of the following commands. When editing, change the type in the Type Selector and/or change the thickness in Properties.

  Edit Insulation (Pipe)

  Remove Insulation (Pipe)

Modifying the Justification

If a pipe run has different sized pipe, you can modify the justification, as shown in Figure 9–57.

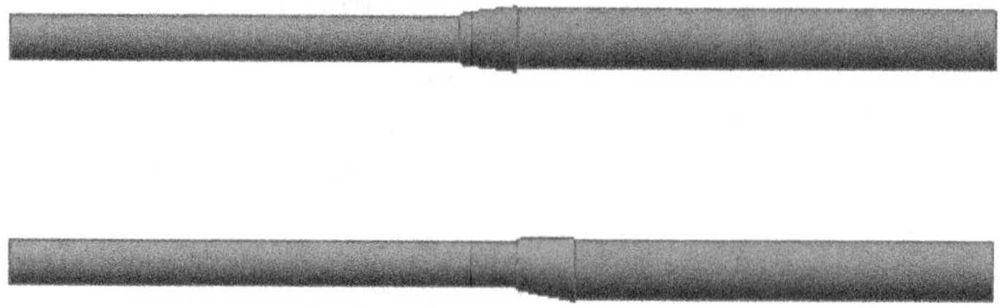

Figure 9–57

How To: Modify Justifications

1. Select the pipe run.
2. In the *Modify | Multi-Select* tab>Edit panel, click (Justify).
3. To specify the point on the pipe that you want to justify around, in the *Justification Editor* tab>Justify panel, click (Control Point) to cycle between the end point references.
   - The alignment location displays as an arrow, as shown in Figure 9–58.

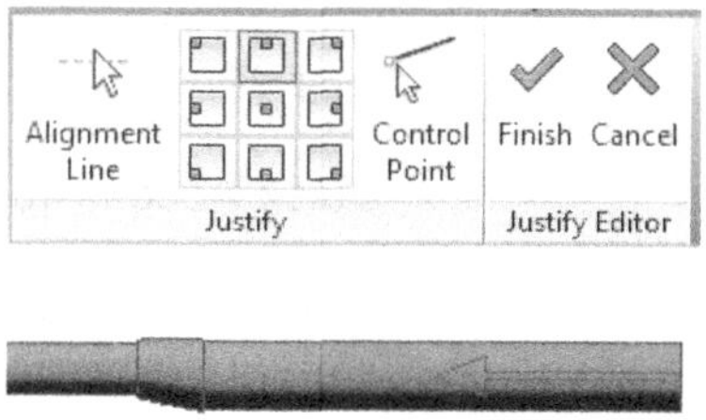

Figure 9–58

4. To indicate the required alignment, either click one of the nine alignment buttons in the Justify panel, or in a 3D view, use (Alignment Line) to select the required dashed line, as shown in Figure 9–59.

Figure 9–59

Practice 9c Modify Plumbing Pipes

Practice Objectives

- Change the type of pipe runs.
- Modify locations and sizes of pipes.
- Connect fixtures to pipes.
- Modify pipe fittings.

Estimated time for completion: 15 minutes

In this practice you will change the type of a piping run to the correct sanitary type. You will modify the size and location of pipes. You will connect two classroom sinks to the cold and hot water mains and then copy the sinks and piping along the hall. Finally, you will modify connections where the copies did not clean up automatically, as shown in Figure 9–60.

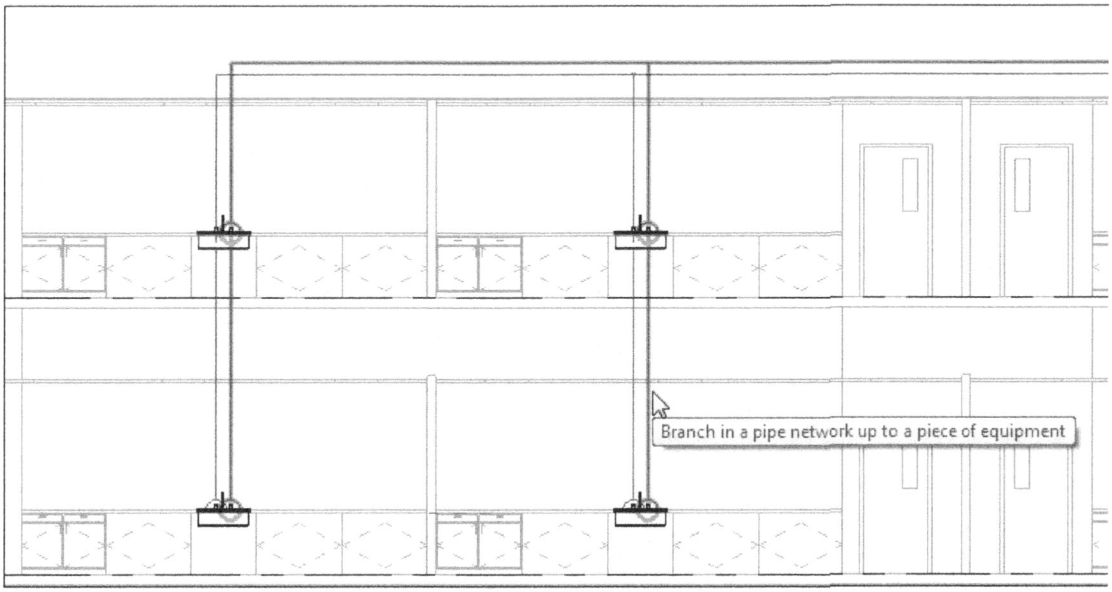

Figure 9–60

Task 1 - Change the type of pipe and verify fittings.

1. In the practice files *Plumbing* folder, open **MEP-Elementary-School-Modify-Piping-M.rvt**.
2. Open the Plumbing>Plumbing>Sections (Building Section): **Restroom Section** view.
3. Zoom in on one of the piping intersections and highlight the fitting. As shown in Figure 9–61, this is not the correct type of fitting for a sanitary system.

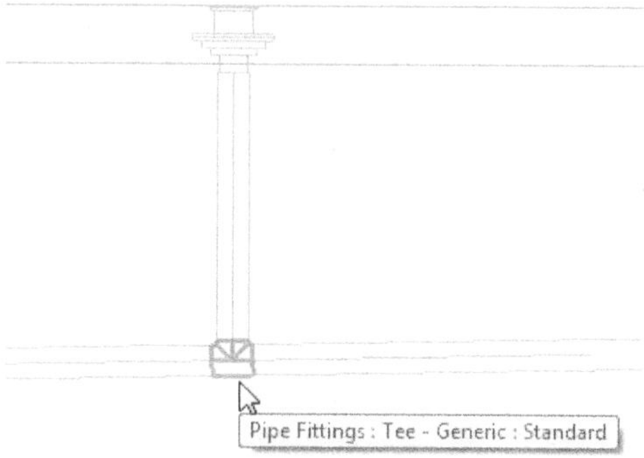

Figure 9–61

4. Zoom out to see the full view.
5. Hover the cursor over one of the sanitary sloped pipes and press <Tab> until everything in the line is selected (do not select the system.
6. In the *Modify | Multi-Select* tab>Selection panel, click (Filter).
7. In the Filter dialog box, clear the check beside **Plumbing Fixtures** and then click **OK**. Note that:
   - The ribbon tabs have now changed because only pipes and pipe fittings are selected.
   - The Type Selector is grayed out. You cannot make changes to the pipe type here.
8. In the *Modify | Multi-Select tab*>Edit panel, click (Change Type).
9. In the Type Selector, select **Pipe Types: PVC - DWV**.
10. Zoom back in and check the fitting. It is now the correct type, as shown in Figure 9–62.

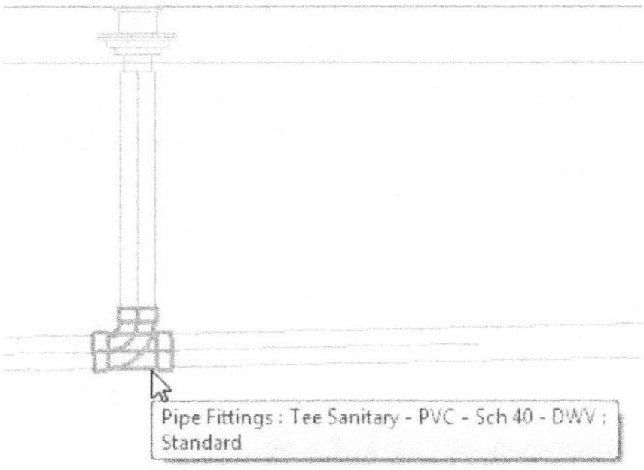

Figure 9–62

11. Save the project.

Task 2 - Modify location and size of piping.

1. Open the Plumbing>Plumbing>Floor Plans:**2 - Plumbing** view.
2. Zoom in on the sinks at the beginning of the hall in the south classroom wing.
3. Change the *Detail Level* to **Fine** to display the pipe sizes clearly.
4. Select one of the hot water pipes (zoom in) and drag slightly to the left, as shown in Figure 9–63.
5. Select the cold water horizontal pipes in the classroom wing. Note that they are larger in diameter than they need to be, as shown in Figure 9–63.
6. In the Options Bar, change the *Diameter* to **25mm**. New step down fittings are applied, as shown in Figure 9–64.

Figure 9–63

Figure 9–64

7. Change the *Detail Level* to **Coarse**.

8. The Piping needs to be moved out of the hall. Select one of the horizontal cold water pipes and drag it into the wall. Repeat with all of the others, as shown in Figure 9–65.

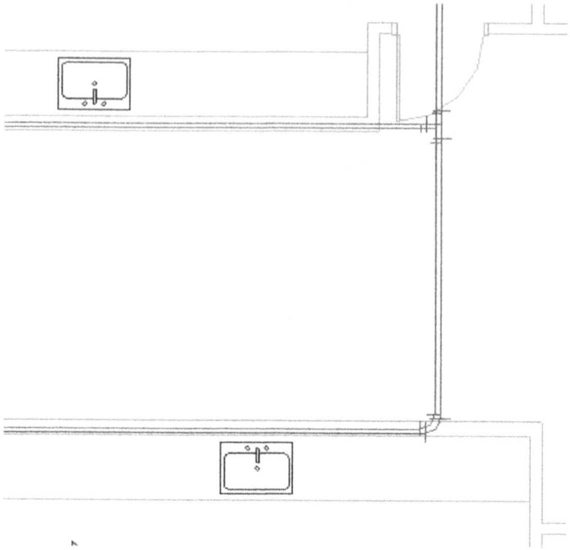

Figure 9–65

- Zoom in as required to place the pipes inside the wall.

9. Save the project.

Task 3 - Connect the sinks into the piping.

At this point there are only four sinks in the classroom wing: two on the first floor and two directly above on the second floor. In this task you will attach piping to the sinks. In the next task you will copy the entire set of four sinks and related piping to the rest of the locations.

1. Return to the **1 - Plumbing** view.

2. Use the **Connect Into** command to connect the sinks to the Hot and cold water pipes, as shown in Figure 9–66.

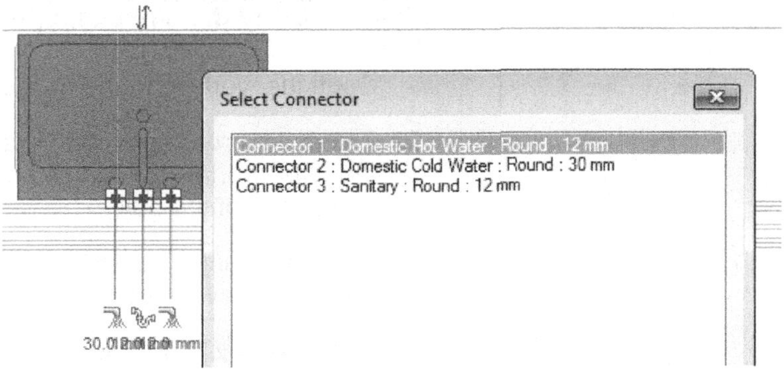

Figure 9–66

3. Open the Plumbing>Plumbing>Sections (Building Section)> **Classroom Section** view.

4. Select the crop region and drag the top control up until you can see the second floor.

5. Select the second floor sink and use the **Connect Into** command to connect to the vertical pipes, as shown in Figure 9–67.

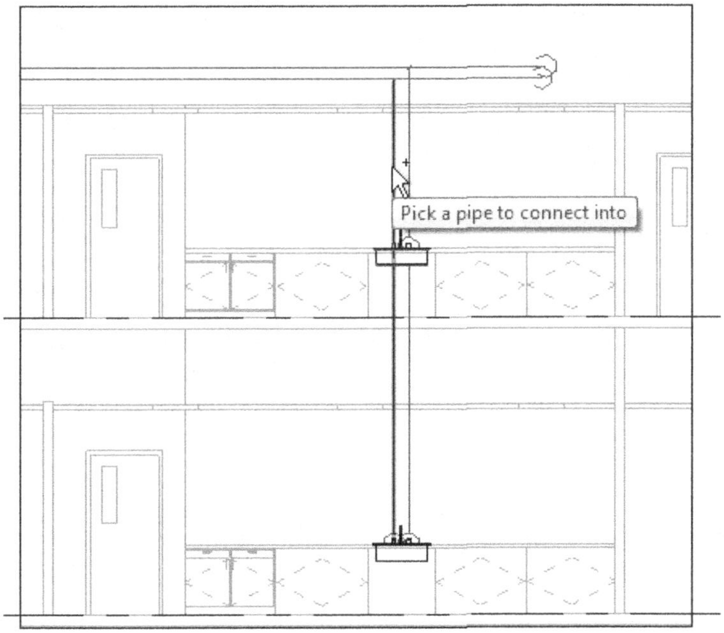

Figure 9–67

6. Save the project.

Task 4 - Copy the sinks and piping to other locations.

1. Continue working in the **Classroom Section** view.
2. Select the crop region and drag the left side control farther to the lefts so that you can see the rest of the sinks along the same side of the hall.
3. Select the sinks, vertical pipes, and associated connectors (use a window selection),
4. In the *Modify* | *Multi-Select* tab>Modify panel, click (Copy).
5. In the Options Bar, select **Constrain** and **Multiple**.
6. As the start point of the copy, select the alignment line at the middle of one of the sinks.
7. Copy the elements to the same alignment line on the next sink, as shown in Figure 9–68.

You can select other points as the start point, just ensure that they are ones that you can place directly on the sinks in the linked architectural model.

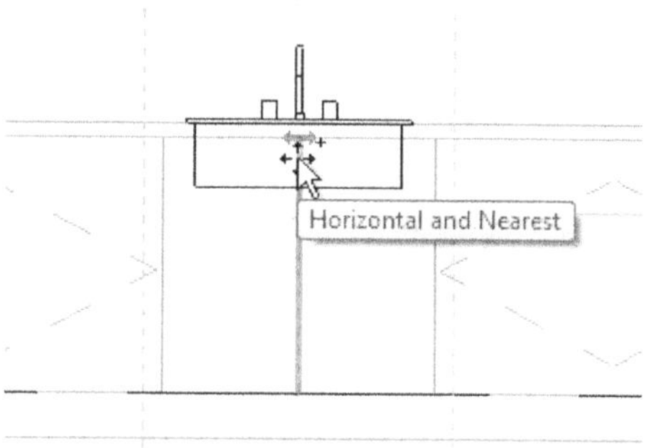

Figure 9–68

8. Continue copying the elements down the hall until all of the new sinks and piping are in place, as shown in Figure 9–69.

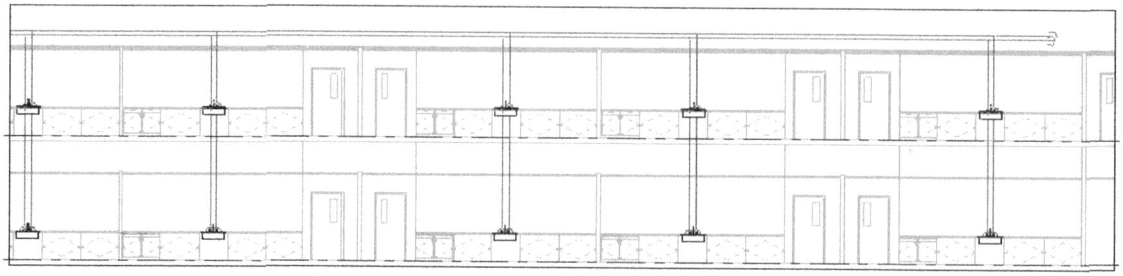

Figure 9–69

9. Click **Modify**.
10. Save the project.

Task 5 - Modify fittings.

1. Continue working in the **Classroom Section** view.
2. Hover the cursor over one of the vertical pipes coming from the original sink and press <Tab>. The full length of the connected pipe should highlight, as shown in Figure 9–70.

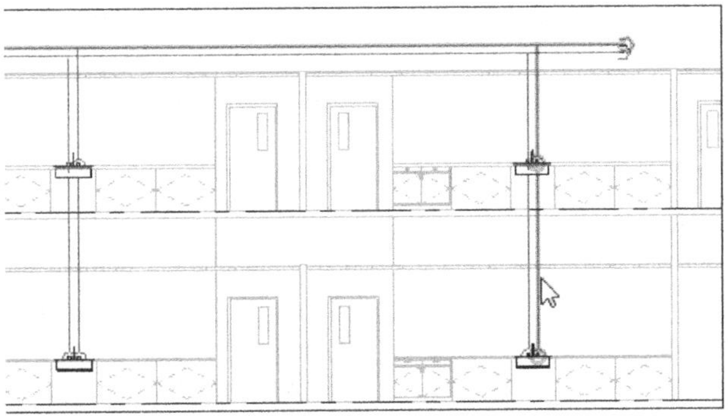

Figure 9–70

3. Hover the cursor over one of the vertical pipes from another sink and press <Tab> until the pipes highlight.
   - If the pipes connect to all of the other pipes, go to Step 8.
   - If the pipes do not connect into the other pipes, go to Step 4.
4. If you continue pressing tab you will see that the two sinks are connected in a Piping System, as shown in Figure 9–71.

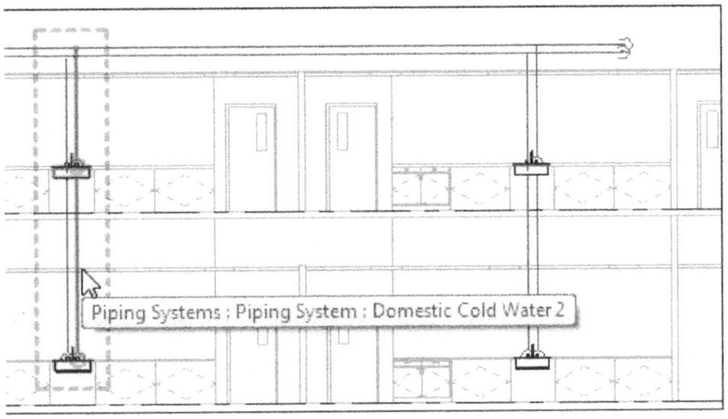

Figure 9–71

5. Zoom in on the fittings.

6. Select the Tee and Transition fittings (as shown in Figure 9–72) and delete them.

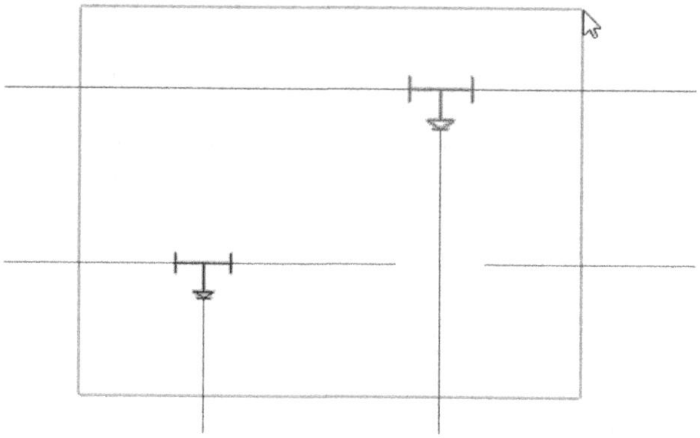

Figure 9–72

7. Select the open end of the vertical pipe and drag it up to the horizontal pipe. The pipes are connected and new fittings are applied. Continue to do this all the way down the hall, including the last set of connections.
   - Alternatively, you can use the **Trim/Extend Multiple Elements** tool. Select the cold water main as the reference and select each of the vertical cold water pipes to extend them to the main. Repeat with the hot water pipes.

8. Delete the extra pipe beyond the last tee fittings. Then, select each tee fitting and click the **Elbow** control, as shown in Figure 9–73.

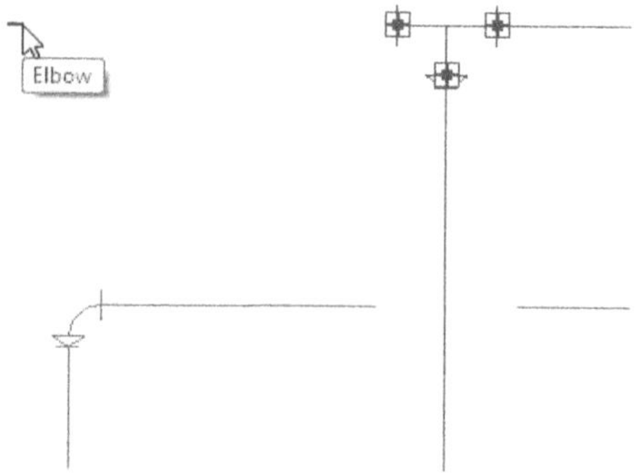

Figure 9–73

9. Zoom out and test the piping for continuity.

10. Save the project.

Task 6 - Optional: Add piping to the rest of the sinks in the south wing.

1. Open the **1 - Plumbing** plan.
2. Select the Classroom Section marker and copy it to the other side.
3. Select the new section and flip it so it faces the sinks, as shown in Figure 9–74.

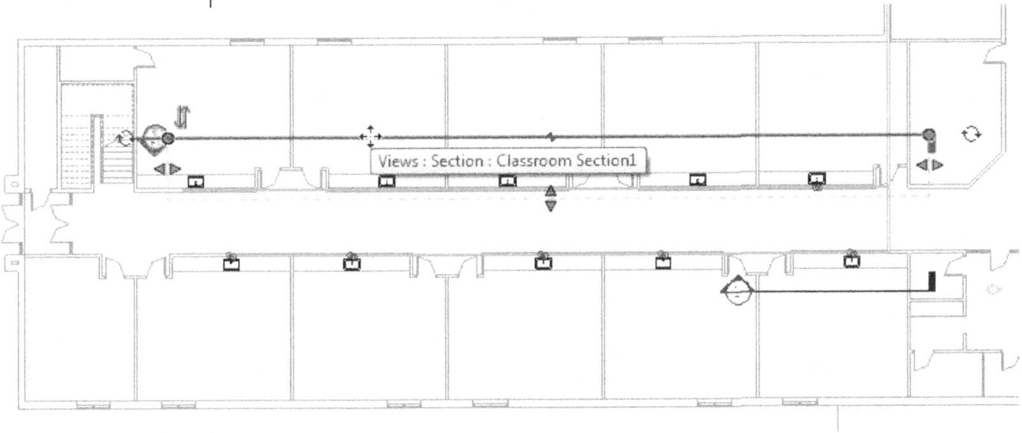

Figure 9–74

4. Repeat the process of connecting the sink to the mains and then copying them along the hall.

9.4 Adding Fire Protection Networks

Fire Protection networks work in much the same way as plumbing and hydronic piping networks. You place sprinkler heads where they are required and add piping to connect them, as shown in Figure 9–75. The systems are created automatically based on the sprinkler type.

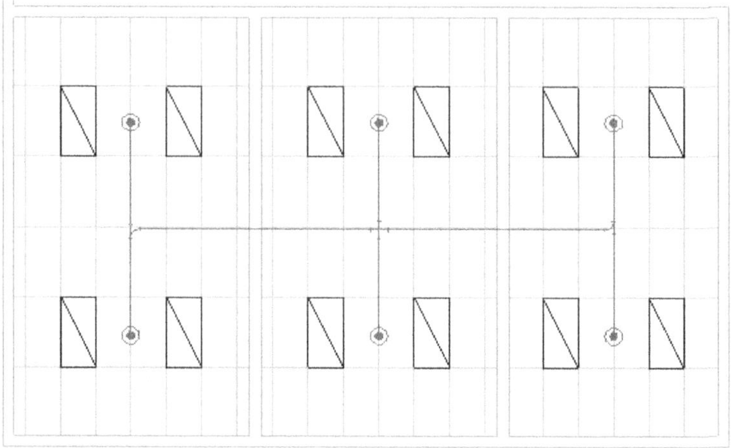

Figure 9–75

- Sprinkler types include wet and dry. All sprinklers in a system must be of the same type.
- To insert sprinklers, in the *Systems* tab>Plumbing & Piping panel, click  (Sprinkler) or type **SK**.
- You can load sprinklers from the *Fire Protection/Sprinklers* folder of the Library.
- Hosted sprinklers need to be placed on ceilings. Therefore, it is best to use a reflected ceiling plan when adding them.

Practice 9d Add Fire Protection Networks

Estimated time for completion: 20 minutes

Practice Objectives

- Add two different types of sprinklers.
- Add piping.

In this practice you will add both wet and dry sprinklers. You will also add piping that connects the sprinklers, as shown in Figure 9–76.

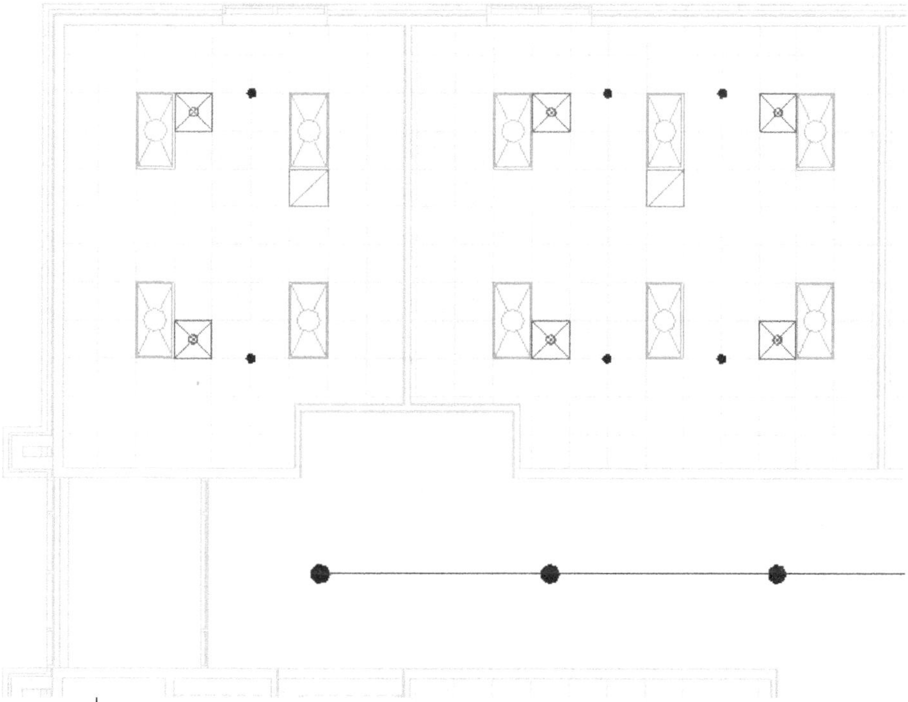

Figure 9–76

Task 1 - Add sprinklers.

1. In the practice files *Plumbing* folder, open **MEP-Elementary-School-Fire-M.rvt**.
2. Open the Plumbing>Fire>Ceiling Plans: **1- Fire RCP** view.
3. Zoom in on the north wing.

4. In the *Systems* tab>Plumbing & Piping panel, click (Sprinkler) or type **SK**.
5. A warning displays noting that no sprinklers are loaded in the project yet. Click **Yes** to load them.

These families are also available in the Plumbing practice files folder.

6. Navigate to the *Fire Protection>Sprinklers* folder and select both **M_Sprinkler - Dry - Pendent - Hosted rfa** and **Sprinkler - Pendent.rfa**. Click **Open**.
7. In the Type Selector, select **M_Sprinkler - Dry - Pendent - Hosted: 15mm Dry Pendent**.
8. In the *Modify | Place Sprinkler* tab>Placement panel, click (Place on Face).
9. Move the cursor over the hallway. A symbol displays because there is no ceiling in this area.
10. Move the cursor into one of the classrooms where there is a ceiling. Note that you can now place the hosted sprinkler type in the ceiling at the intersections of the grids.
11. Add sprinklers in two classrooms similar to that shown in Figure 9–77.

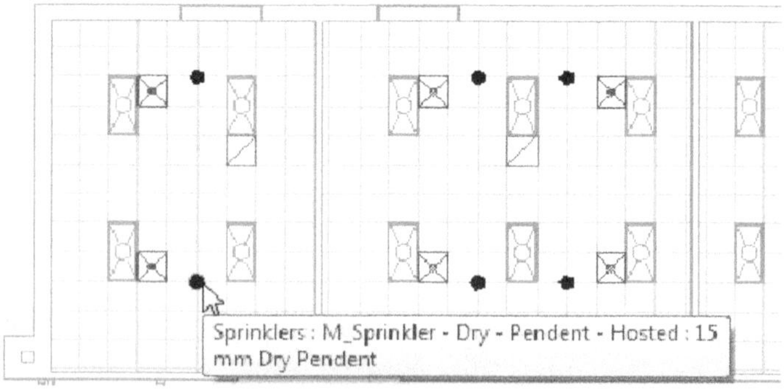

Figure 9–77

12. In the Type Selector, select **M_Sprinkler - Pendent: 15mm Pendent**. This is a non-hosted sprinkler so you can place it in the hall where there is no ceiling.

13. In Properties, set the *Offset* to **2750mm**.

You can use dimensions or reference planes to help you place the first sprinkler.

14. Place sprinklers down the hall at a spacing of **1800mm**off the vestibule door and then **3650mm** on center, as shown in Figure 9–78. You can place the first one and then array or copy the rest.

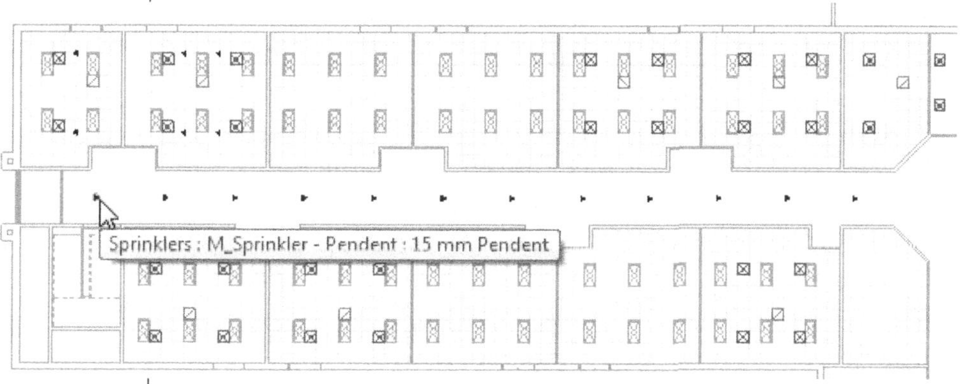

Figure 9–78

- If you array the sprinklers, turn off **Group and Associate** or ungroup the sprinklers after you finish.

15. Save the project.

Task 2 - Add Piping for Fire Protection Systems.

1. Select the left most sprinkler in the hallway. Right-click on the connector and select **Draw Pipe**.
2. In the *Modify | Place Pipe* tab>Sloped Piping panel, select  (Slope: Off) to make sure this piping is not sloped.
3. In the Type Selector, select **Pipe Types: Copper.**
4. In the Options Bar, the *Diameter* and *Offset* match the location of the connector. Change the *Offset* to **3000mm** and press <Enter>. This moves the first segment of the pipe directly up from the sprinkler.

5. Draw the pipe down the hallway and past the last sprinkler as shown in Figure 9–79.

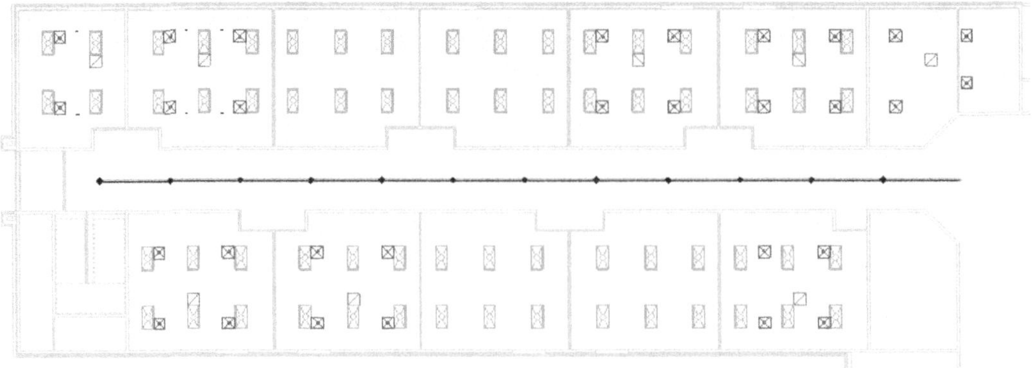

Figure 9–79

6. Open the Plumbing>Fire>Sections (Wall Section)>**Hallway Section** view.
7. Zoom in so that one of the sprinklers is displayed, as shown in Figure 9–80

Toggle on (Thin Lines), if required to see the pipes and fittings clearly.

8. Select the sprinkler. In the *Modify | Sprinklers* tab>Layout panel, click (Connect Into).
9. Select the horizontal pipe to connect into. The new connection is created with appropriate fittings, as shown in Figure 9–81.

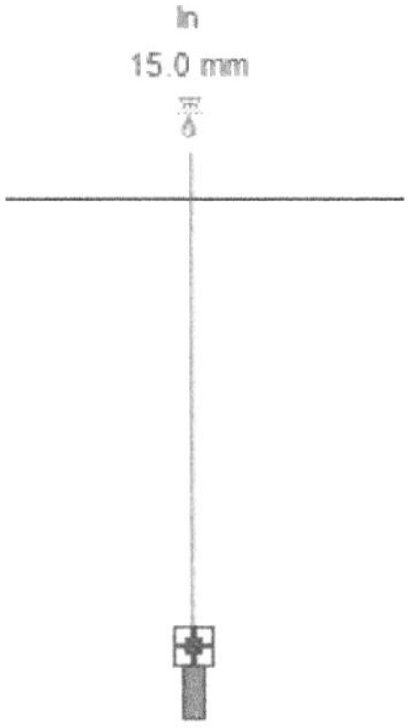

Figure 9–80

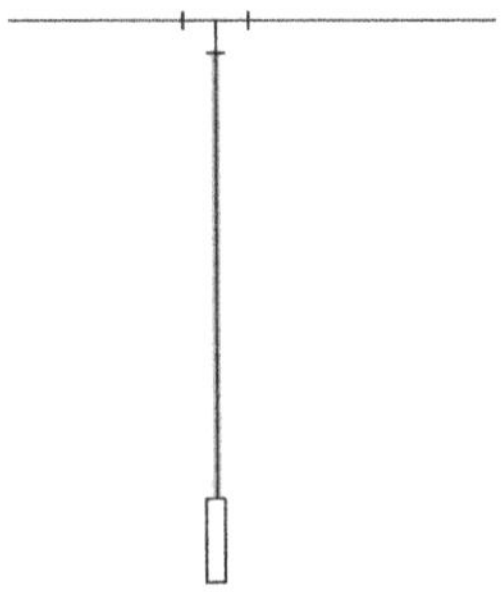

Figure 9–81

10. Continue adding pies from the sprinkler to the horizontal pipe.
11. Save the project.

Chapter Review Questions

1. After tying in piping to a sloped sanitary pipe, the automatically placed fittings are facing the wrong direction, as shown in Figure 9–82. To fix this, select the fitting and...

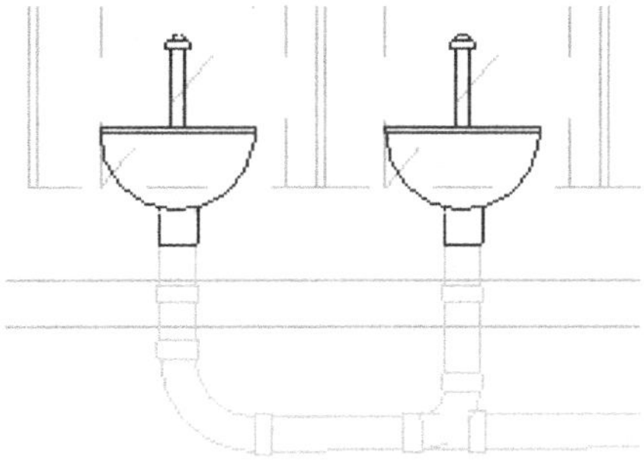

Figure 9–82

   a. Click the **Flip** arrow.
   b. Place its opposite type.
   c. Use **Rotate**.
   d. Click **AutoSlope** in the ribbon.

2. Which placement option can be used for placing a face based plumbing fixture on the wall, as shown in Figure 9–83?

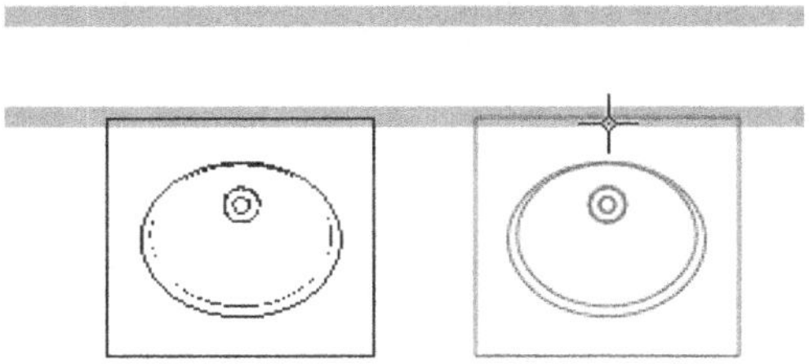

Figure 9–83

   a. **Place on Vertical Face**
   b. **Place on Face**
   c. **Place on Work Plane**

3. How do you specify the direction in which a pipe slopes as you are creating it, as shown in Figure 9–84?

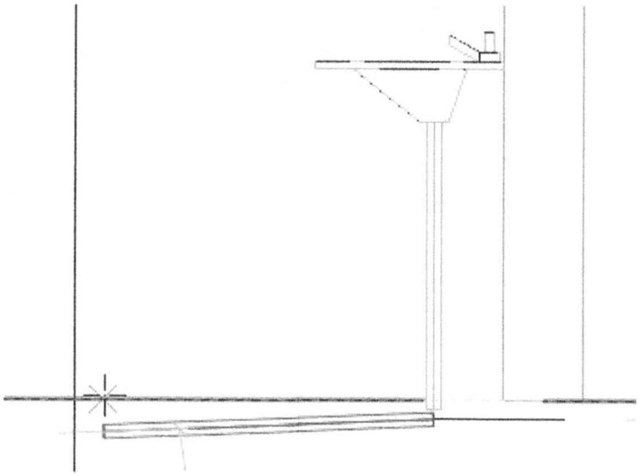

Figure 9–84

a. Set the slope in the Options Bar.

b. Set the slope in the ribbon.

c. Create it flat and slope it later.

d. Draw the pipe in a section view to ensure that it slopes correctly.

4. Piping can be added in a variety of systems. Match the name of the piping system on the left with its corresponding icon on the right.

a. Fire Protection Dry	1. 
b. Hydronic	2. 
c. Plumbing	3. 
d. Fire Protection Wet	4. 

Command Summary

Button	Command	Location
Plumbing & Piping Tools		
	**Flex Pipe**	• **Ribbon:** *Systems* tab>Plumbing & Piping panel • **Shortcut:** FP
	**Mechanical Equipment**	• **Ribbon:** *Systems* tab>Mechanical panel • **Shortcut:** ME
	Mechanical Settings	• **Ribbon:** *Systems* tab>Mechanical panel title • **Shortcut:** MS
	**Parallel Pipes**	• **Ribbon:** *Systems* tab>Plumbing & Piping panel
	**Pipe**	• **Ribbon:** *Systems* tab>Plumbing & Piping panel • **Shortcut:** PI
	**Pipe Accessory**	• **Ribbon:** *Systems* tab>Plumbing & Piping panel • **Shortcut:** PA
	**Pipe Fitting**	• **Ribbon:** *Systems* tab>Plumbing & Piping panel • **Shortcut:** PF
	**Pipe Placeholder**	• **Ribbon:** *Systems* tab>Plumbing & Piping panel
	**Plumbing Fixture**	• **Ribbon:** *Systems* tab>Plumbing & Piping panel • **Shortcut:** PX
	**Sprinkler**	• **Ribbon:** *Systems* tab>Plumbing & Piping panel
Pipe Modification		
	**Add Insulation**	*With one or more Pipes selected*: • **Ribbon:** *Modify* | *Pipe* tab>Edit panel *With Pipes and Pipe Fittings selected*: • **Ribbon:** *Modify* | *Multi-Select* tab>Edit panel
	**Automatically Connect**	• **Ribbon:** *Modify* | *Place Pipe* tab> Placement Tools panel
	**Cap Open Ends**	• **Ribbon:** *(with one or more pipes selected) Modify* | *contextual* tab>Edit panel

	**Change Type**	*With one or more Pipes selected*: • **Ribbon:** *Modify* | *Pipe* tab>Edit panel *With Pipes and Pipe Fittings selected*: • **Ribbon:** *Modify* | *Multi-Select* tab>Edit panel
	**Convert Placeholder**	• **Ribbon:** *Modify* | *Pipe Placeholders* tab>Edit panel
	**Edit Insulation**	*With one or more Pipes selected*: • **Ribbon:** *Modify* | *Pipe* tab>Edit panel *With Pipes and Pipe Fittings selected*: • **Ribbon:** *Modify* | *Multi-Select* tab>Edit panel
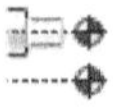	**Inherit Elevation**	• **Ribbon:** *Modify* | *Place Pipe* tab> Placement Tools panel
	**Inherit Size**	• **Ribbon:** *Modify* | *Place Pipe* tab> Placement Tools panel
	**Justification (Settings)**	• **Ribbon:** *Modify* | *Place Pipe* tab> Placement Tools panel
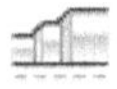	**Justify**	• **Ribbon:** (*with one or more Pipes selected*) *Modify* | *Pipe* tab>Edit panel or (*with Pipes and Pipe Fittings selected*) *Modify* | *Multi-Select* tab>Edit panel
	**Reapply Type**	*With one or more Pipes selected*: • **Ribbon:** *Modify* | *Pipe* tab>Edit panel *With Pipes and Pipe Fittings selected*: • **Ribbon:** *Modify* | *Multi-Select* tab>Edit panel
	**Remove Insulation**	*With one or more Pipes selected*: • **Ribbon:** *Modify* | *Pipe* tab>Edit panel *With Pipes and Pipe Fittings selected*: • **Ribbon:** *Modify* | *Multi-Select* tab>Edit panel
	**Slope**	• **Ribbon**: (*when piping in a system is selected*) *Modify* | *Multi-Select* tab> Edit panel

Advanced Systems for HVAC and Plumbing

HVAC and plumbing networks are automatically placed in systems as you connect the elements. However, there are times when you want to create a system first, and then use automatic layouts to connect everything together with ducts or pipes. It is also important to test the systems to ensure that they are completely connected and the have the correct flow and sizes.

Learning Objectives in this Chapter

- Create duct and piping systems without first connecting the components.
- Modify duct and piping systems by adding or removing elements, renaming them, and dividing them.
- Create automatic duct and piping layouts that connect elements in systems.
- Test systems by showing disconnects, checking systems, using the System Inspector, and viewing schedules.

10.1 Creating and Modifying Systems

When you place components and connect them using ducts or pipes, systems are automatically created, as shown for several duct systems in Figure 10–1. You can also create systems before you connect components, which is especially helpful if you want to use the automatic layout tools that connect components for you.

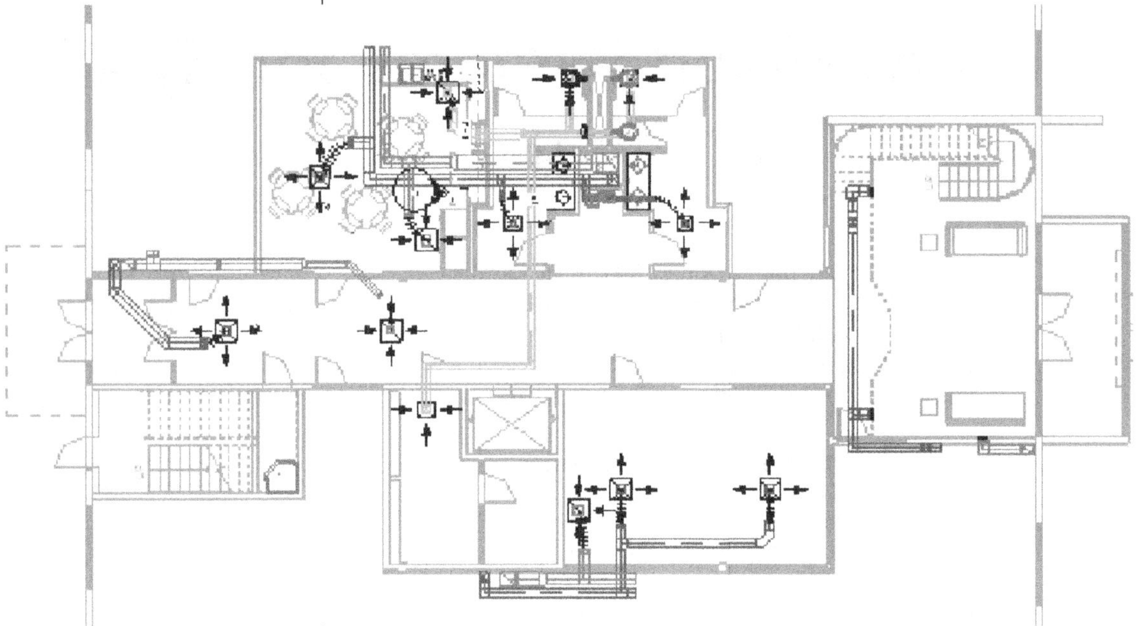

Figure 10–1

How To: Create a Duct or Piping System

1. Select at least one of the components that is to be part of the system, such as air terminals or plumbing fixtures.
    - The elements must all be the same system type.
    - Do not select the source equipment at this time.
2. In the *Modify | contextual* tab>Create Systems panel, click the related systems button, such as (Duct) or (Piping).
    - You can also right-click on an air terminal or plumbing fixture connector and select **Create Duct/Piping System**.

3. Proceed as follows:

If you started the command...	Then...
By right-clicking on a connector	In the Create System dialog box, the *System type* is preset.
Using a button	There are multiple options. Select the type of system you want to create from the drop-down list, as shown in Figure 10–2.

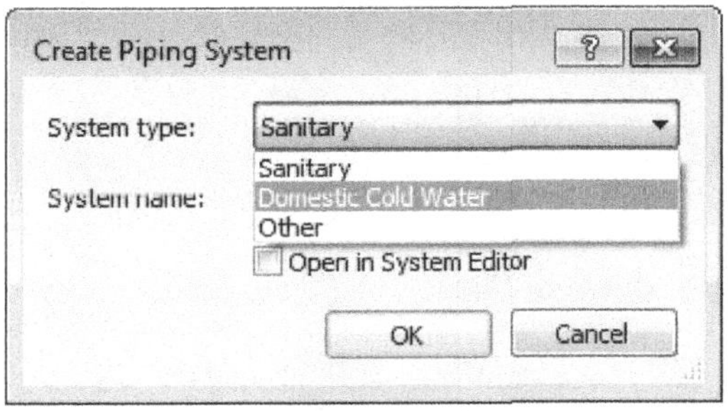

Figure 10–2

- If you want to continue working in the system, select **Open in the System Editor**.

4. In the *System name* field, enter a name and then click **OK**.
5. If you did not open the System Editor in the previous step, in the *Modify | Duct* or *Modify |Piping Systems* tab>System Tools panel, click (Edit System).
6. In the *Edit Duct or Piping System* tab (shown in Figure 10–3), you can:
   - Add and remove elements from the system
   - Select the equipment connected to the system.

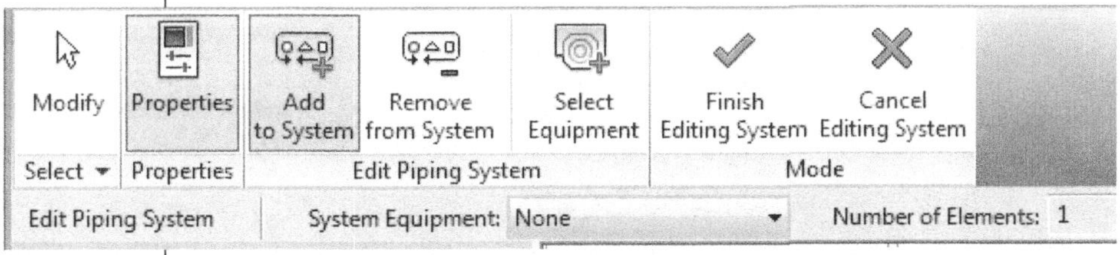

Figure 10–3

   - You can also select the system equipment from the Options Bar *System Equipment* drop-down list.

7. Click (Finish Editing System)

If multiple systems are applied to an element, the color returns to the neutral black.

- The elements take on the color of the system (if specified), as shown for a sanitary system in Figure 10–4.

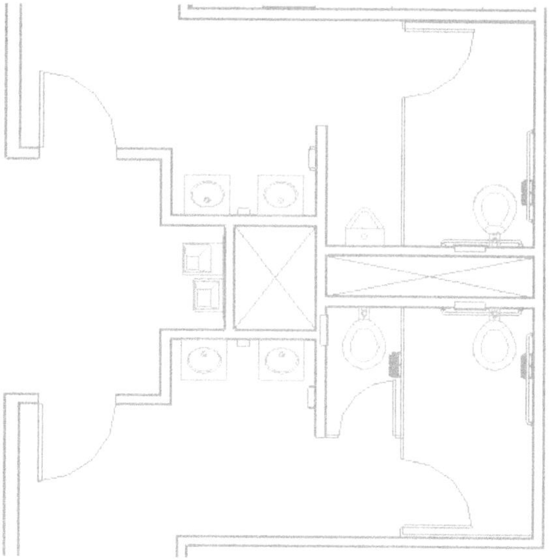

Figure 10–4

Hint: Using the System Browser while Creating Systems

It is helpful to have the System Browser open when you are creating systems because it can help you to identify which elements have been assigned to a system and which still need assignment, as shown in Figure 10–5.

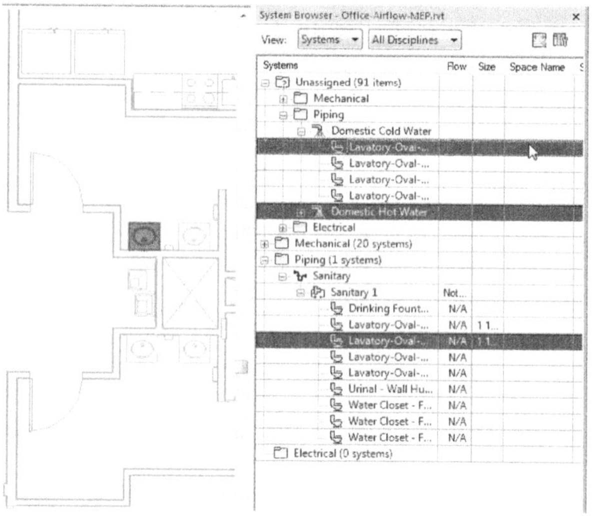

Figure 10–5

Modifying Systems

You can modify a system at any time. Hover the cursor over one of the elements and press <Tab> until you see the system border highlighted (as shown in Figure 10–6), and then select it. The tools you use to modify systems display in the related *Modify | Duct* or *Modify | Piping Systems* tab.

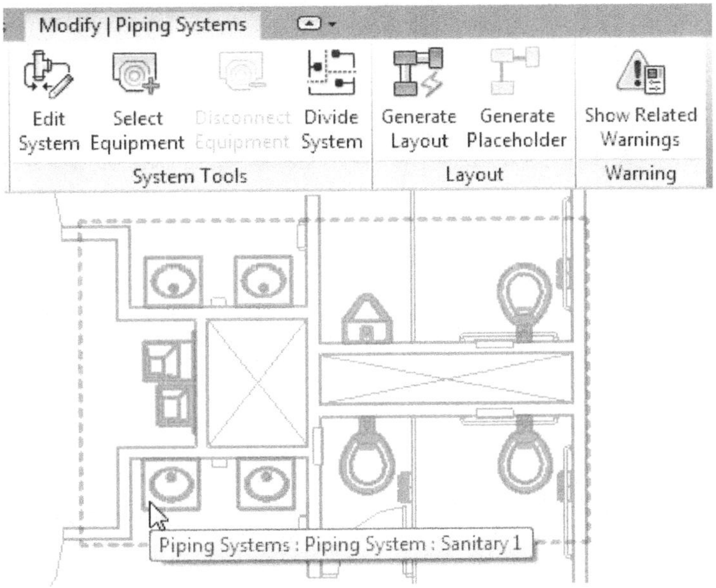

Figure 10–6

- You can change the *System Name* in Properties.
-  (Edit System) takes you to the *Edit Duct or Piping Systems* tab which enables you to add and remove elements from the system and select equipment.
-  (Select Equipment) prompts you to select a mechanical equipment component in the project.

Dividing Systems

Systems can be divided if they have more than one network of ducts or pipes. In the example shown in Figure 10–7, there are three networks of ducts, each of which are connected to a different air handling unit.

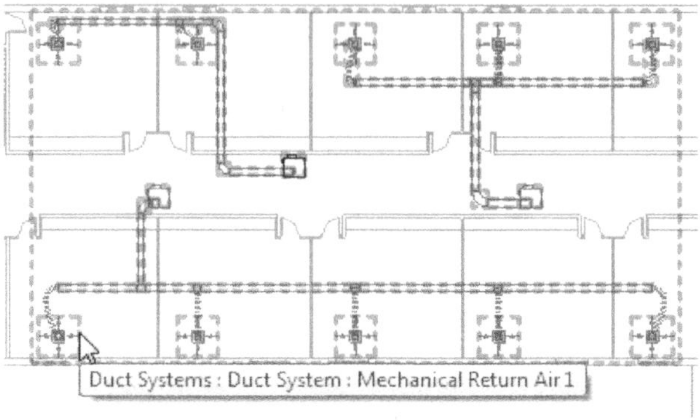

Figure 10–7

- If you need to divide a system even further, add another piece of equipment and connect some of the existing components to it.

How To: Divide Systems

1. Select the system you want to divide.
2. In the *Modify | Duct or Piping Systems* tab>System Tools panel, click (Divide System).
3. An alert box displays indicating the number of networks that are to be converted into individual systems.
4. Click **OK**. The systems are separated as shown in Figure 10–8.

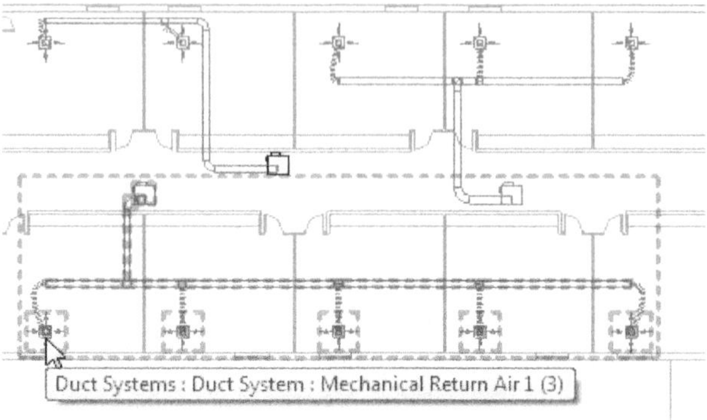

Figure 10–8

Practice 10a Create and Modify HVAC Systems

Practice Objectives

- Review elements in the System Browser.
- Create Duct Systems.

Estimated time for completion: 10 minutes

In this practice you will view unassigned elements in the System Browser and then add them to a new a supply air duct system, as shown in Figure 10–9. You will repeat the process with the return air duct system.

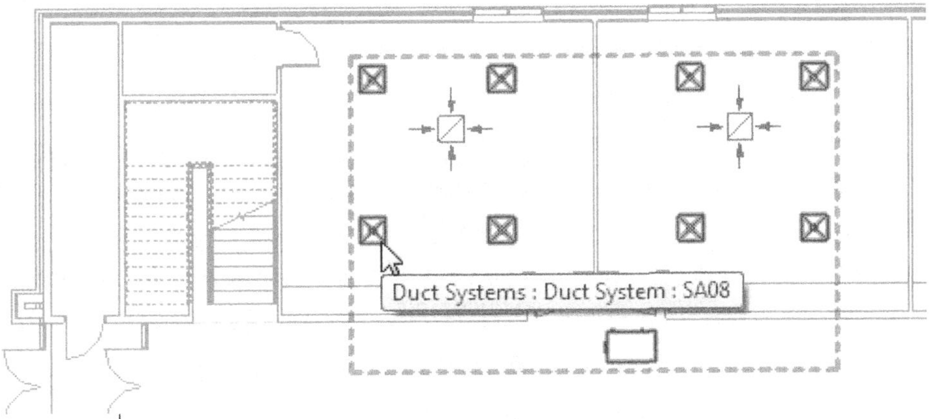

Figure 10–9

Task 1 - Create supply and return air duct systems.

1. In the practice files *Systems* folder, open **MEP-Elementary-School-HVAC-Systems-M.rvt**.
2. Open the System Browser. by pressing <F9>.
3. In the System Browser, set the *View* to **Systems** and the discipline to **Mechanical**, as shown in Figure 10–10.

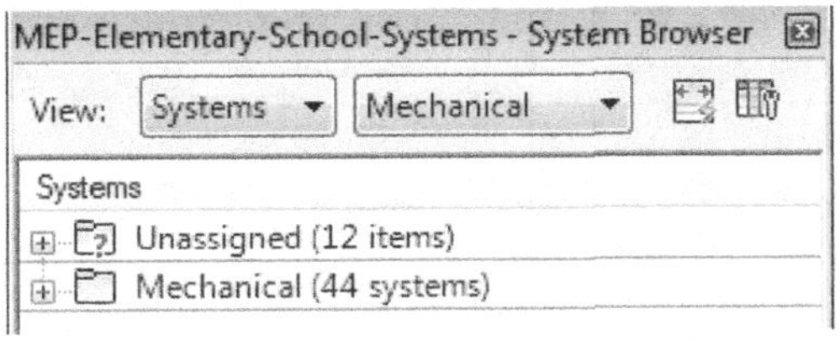

Figure 10–10

4. In the System Browser, expand **Unassigned>Mechanical> Supply Air**. Note that there are several air terminals and an AHU listed, as shown in Figure 10–11.

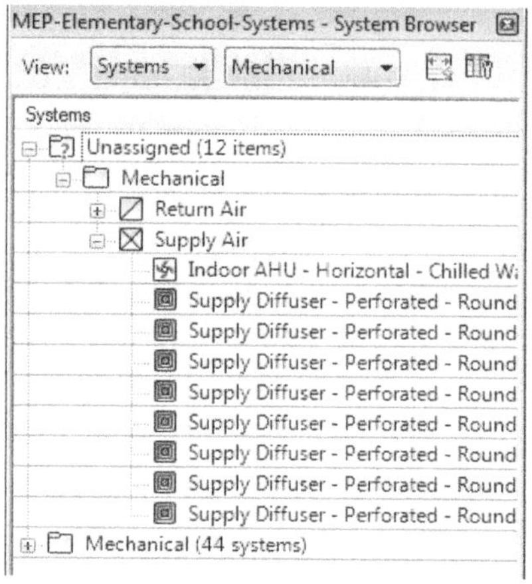

Figure 10–11

5. Select one of the unassigned Supply Diffusers. Right-click and select **Show** to automatically zoom in on the selected diffuser. Click **Close**.

6. Zoom out enough so that you can see the classroom the diffuser is in.

7. In the *Modify | Air Terminals* tab>Create Systems panel, click  (Duct).

8. In the Create Duct System dialog box, type **01 - SA08**. Select **Open in System Editor** and then click **OK**.

9. In the *Edit Duct System* tab>Edit Duct System panel, click  (Select Equipment) and select the nearby AHU unit.

10. Click  (Add to System) and select the air terminals in the other two classrooms, as shown in Figure 10–12.

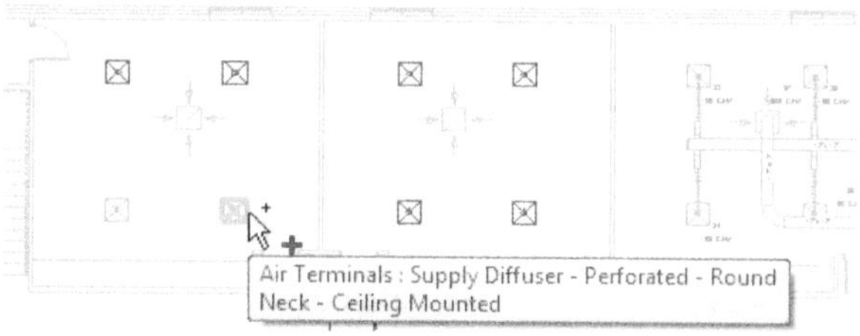

Figure 10–12

11. Click (Finish Editing System).

12. Select one of the air terminals in the new system and in the System Browser, expand the highlighted levels until the new system displays, as shown in Figure 10–13.

This would have been very hard to identify without the selection because the system listing is under the AHU unit.

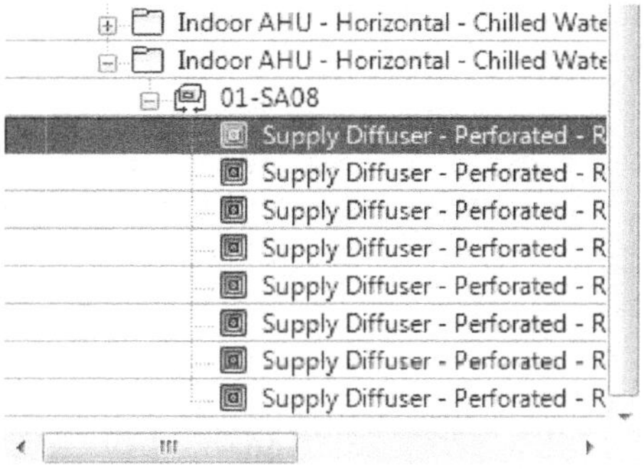

Figure 10–13

13. In the same classrooms, select the two return air terminals.

14. In the *Modify | Air Terminals* tab>Create Systems panel, click (Duct).

15. In the Create Duct System dialog box, type the *System Name* **01 - RA08**. Do not select **Open in System Editor**. Click **OK**.

16. In the *Modify| Duct Systems* tab>System Tools panel, click (Select Equipment) and select the same AHU unit.

17. Hover over one of the return diffusers and press <Tab> until the new system displays, as shown in Figure 10–14.

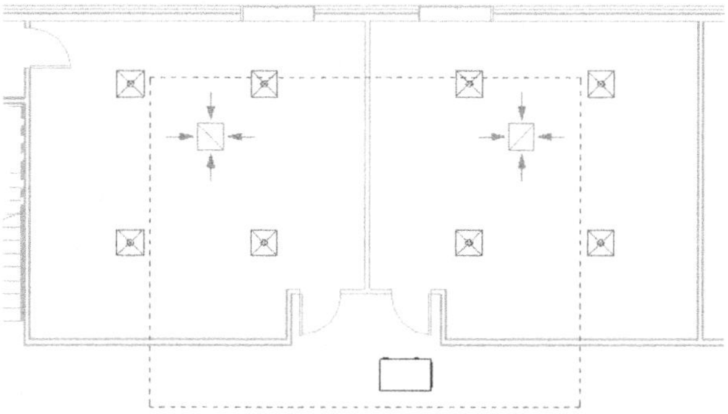

Figure 10–14

18. Save and close the project.

Practice 10b Create and Modify Plumbing Systems

Practice Objective

- Create plumbing and fire protection systems.

Estimated time for completion: 10 minutes

In this practice you will create sanitary and domestic cold water systems for a series of water closets. You will then investigate an existing Fire Protection system and create an additional one, as shown in Figure 10–15.

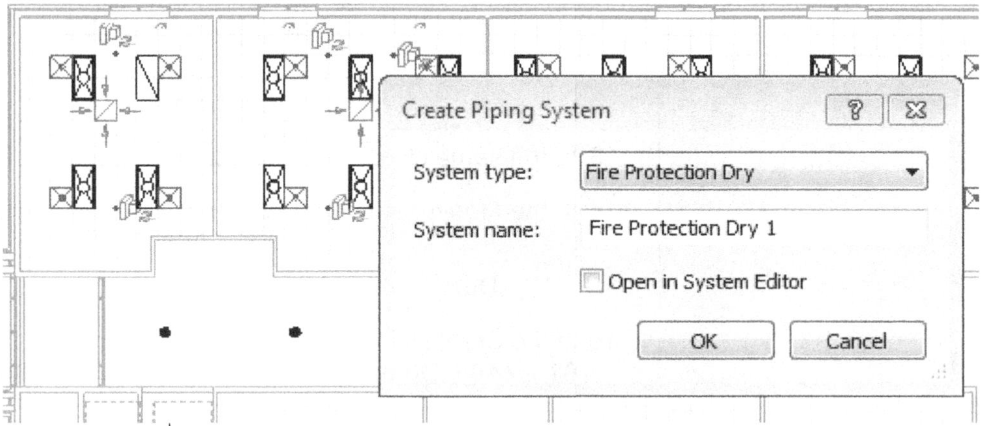

Figure 10–15

Task 1 - Create systems for the water closets.

1. In the practice files *Systems* folder, open the project **MEP-Elementary-School-Plumbing-Systems-M.rvt**.
2. Open the Plumbing>Plumbing>Floor Plans>**1 - Plumbing Plan** view.
3. Zoom in on the Women's restroom closest to the main entrance and select one of the water closets.
4. In the *Modify | Plumbing Fixtures* tab>Create Systems panel, click (Piping).
5. In the Create Piping System dialog box, ensure that the *System Type* is set to **Sanitary**. Accept the default name and select **Open in System Editor**, as shown in Figure 10–16. Click **OK**.

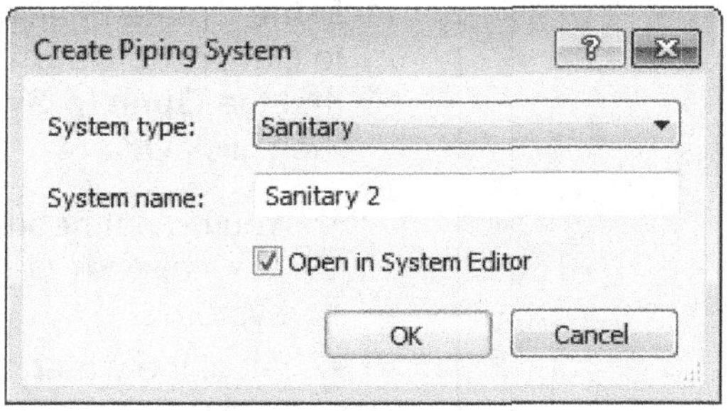

Figure 10–16

6. The *Edit Piping System* tab displays with (Add to System) selected.

7. Select the other water closets in the room.

8. Click (Finish Editing Systems). The new system is created, and all of the water closets display in green to indicate that they are part of the sanitary system, as shown in Figure 10–17.

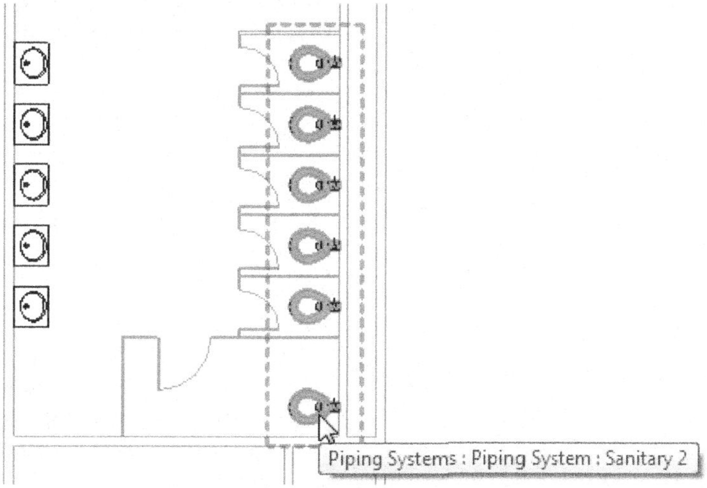

Figure 10–17

9. Select all of the water closets in the room.

10. In the *Modify | Plumbing Fixtures* tab>Create Systems panel, click (Piping). This option is available because there is another system that the water closets can be assigned to.

11. In the Create Piping System dialog box, set the *System Type* to **Domestic Cold Water**. Accept the default name, ensure that the **Open in System Editor** option is not selected, and then click **OK**.
    - You do not need to open the System Editor because you have already selected all of the elements you want in the system.
    - All of the water closets are now part of the Domestic Cold Water and Sanitary systems and display black because they are connected to more than one system.
12. Save the project.

Task 2 - Create a fire protection system.

1. Open the Plumbing>Fire>Ceiling Plans>**1 - Fire RCP** view.
2. Select one of the sprinklers in the hall. Note that the option to create a system is not available because the system was automatically created when the piping was added.
3. Select the *Piping Systems* tab. The System Tools panel displays, as shown in Figure 10–18.

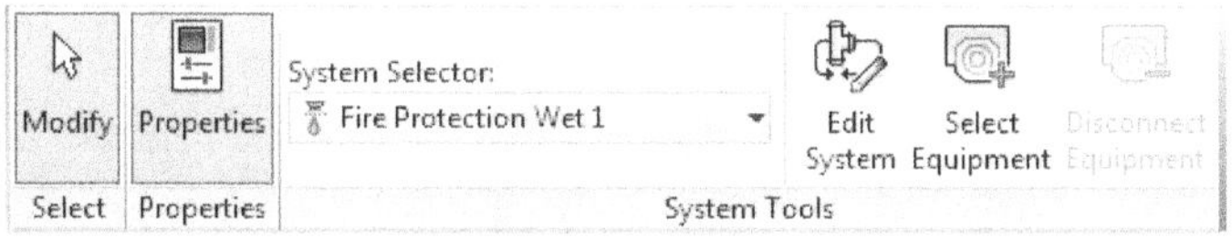

Figure 10–18

4. Click  (Edit System).
5. With  (Add to System) selected, select one of the classroom sprinklers. A warning displays (as shown in Figure 10–19) noting that you cannot add this sprinkler to the Wet System because it belongs in a Dry System. Close the warning box.

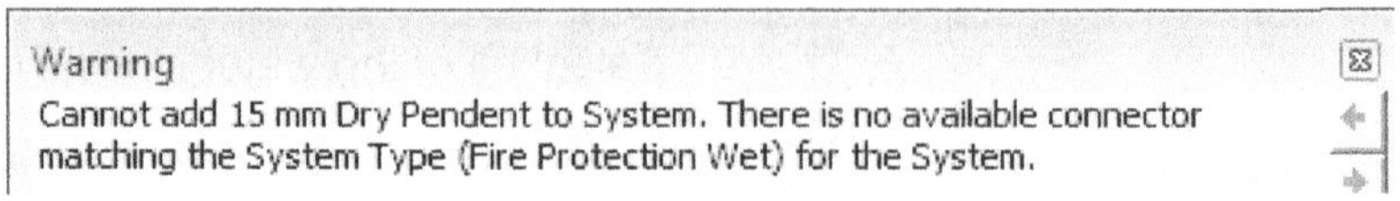

Figure 10–19

6. Click  (Cancel Editing System).

7. Select all of the classroom sprinklers in the two rooms at the end of the hall.

8. In the *Modify | Sprinklers* tab>Create Systems panel, click  (Piping).

9. In the Create Piping System dialog box, ensure that **Open in System Editor** is not selected, and then click **OK**. The software knows that this sprinkler needs to be part of a dry system, as shown in Figure 10–20.

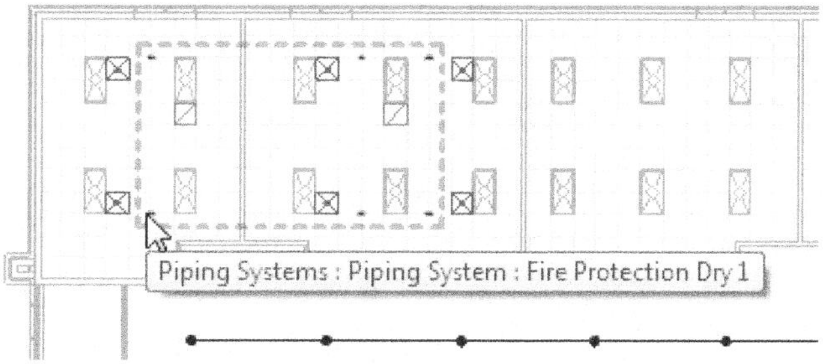

Figure 10–20

10. Save the project.

10.2 Creating Automatic Layouts

Once you have created a duct or piping system, you can automatically create a layout of ducts or pipes. These tools create various routes for the layout as shown for ducts in Figure 10–21.

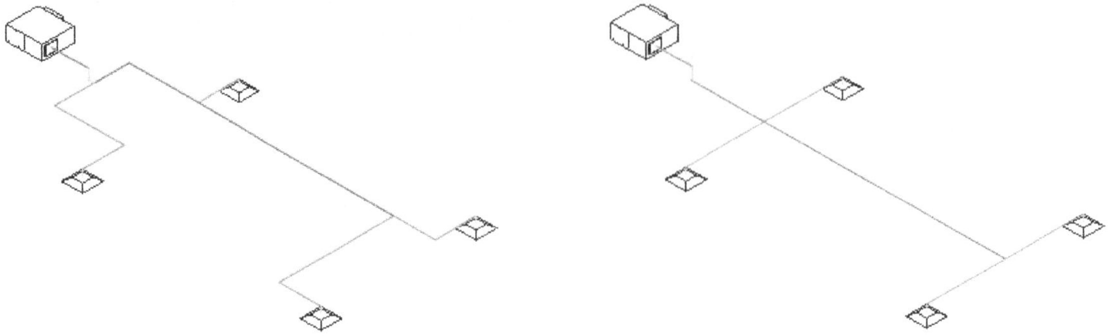

Figure 10–21

How To: Generate an automatic layout

You can view the solutions in the plan or a 3D view.

1. Hover the cursor over one of the elements and press <Tab> until you see the outline of the system, as shown with a duct system in Figure 10–22. Click to select the system.

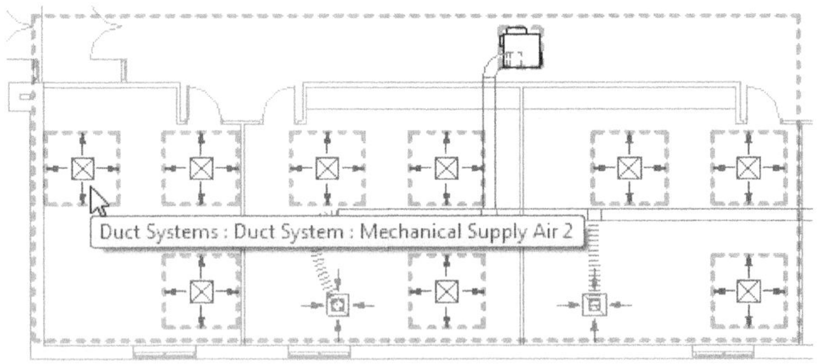

Figure 10–22

2. In the *Modify* | *Duct* or *Pipe Systems* tab>Layout panel, click  (Generate Layout).

3. In the *Generate Layout* tab>Modify Layout panel, click (Place Base). This is used if a system is not connected to equipment (such as the sanitary system shown in Figure 10–23) or in the early stages of setting up the layouts.

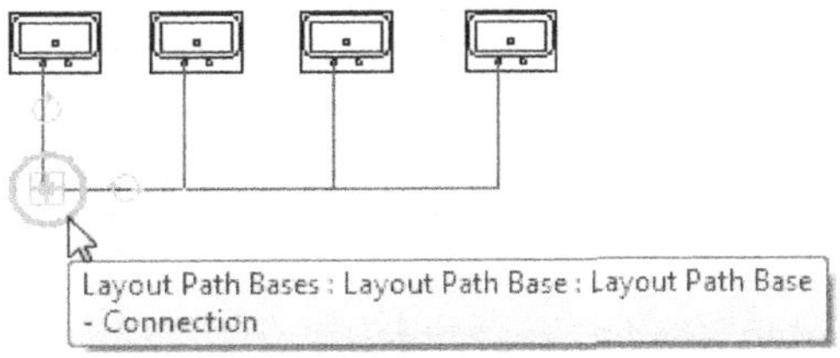

Figure 10–23

- When you place the base, (Modify Base) automatically starts. Make changes to the base including the offset from the level and size.
- Use the rotate controls on the base to ensure that it is pointing in the correct direction
- If you no longer want the base, click (Remove Base).

4. If you need the pipe to slope, before selecting a layout, use the Slope panel to specify the slope for piping systems.
5. In the Options Bar, click **Settings** and set the types and offsets that apply to this layout.
6. In the Options Bar, select a *Solution Type,* as shown in Figure 10–24, and click (Next Solution) or (Previous Solution) to cycle through the possible options.

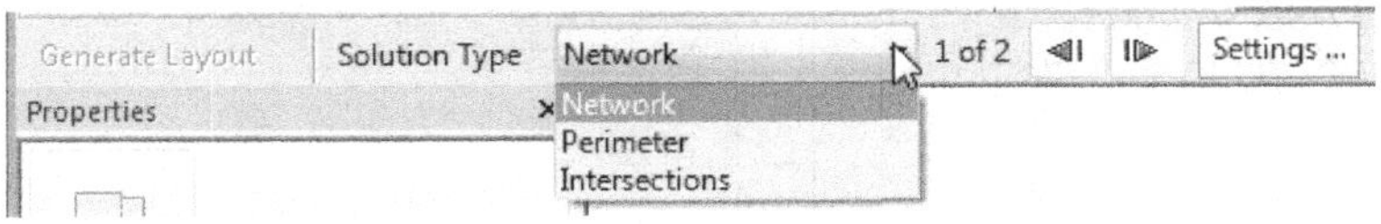

Figure 10–24

Network	Creates a layout with the main segment through the center of a bounding box around the entire system and the branches at 90 degrees from the main branch.
Perimeter	Creates a layout with segments being placed on three of the four sides, and one with segments being placed on all four sides. (The **Inset** value is the offset between the bounding box and components.)
Intersections	Creates a layout with segments extending from each connector of the components. Where they intersect perpendicularly, proposed intersection junctions are created.

- Blue-colored lines identify the main trunk, while green-colored lines identify branches off of the trunk.
- Gold-colored lines indicate a potential open connection that might cause problems when the ducts or pipes are added (as shown in Figure 10–25), or other issues related to adequate space to place the required fittings.

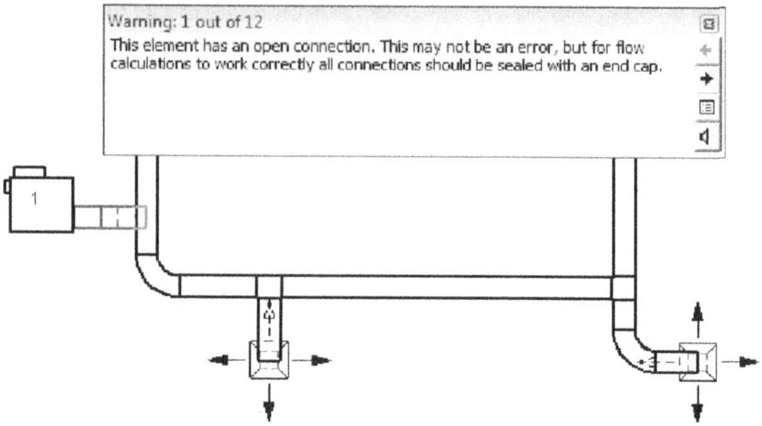

Figure 10–25

7. In the *Generate Layout* tab>Generate Layout panel, click (Finish Layout) when you have a solution that looks best.

- The Conversion Settings dialog box (shown for ducts in Figure 10–26), enables you to set the type of duct or pipe and the offset from the level where you are working.

These settings are specific to this system only. Global settings are defined in Mechanical Settings.

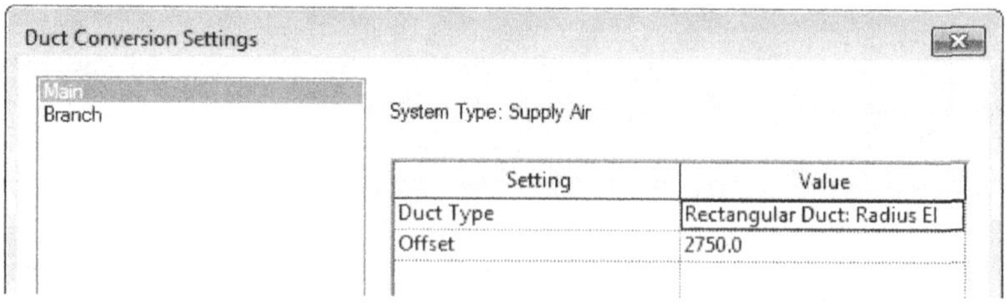

Figure 10–26

- For duct branches, you can also specify a *Flex Duct Type* and *Maximum Flex Duct Length* if you want air terminals automatically connected that way.

How To: Customize the Layout

1. Using (Solutions), select a layout design similar to what you want to use.
2. In the *Generate Layout* tab>Modify Layout panel, click (Edit Layout).
3. Select one of the layout lines. You can use the move control to change the location of the line as shown in Figure 10–27. You can also change the height of the offset by clicking on the number control.

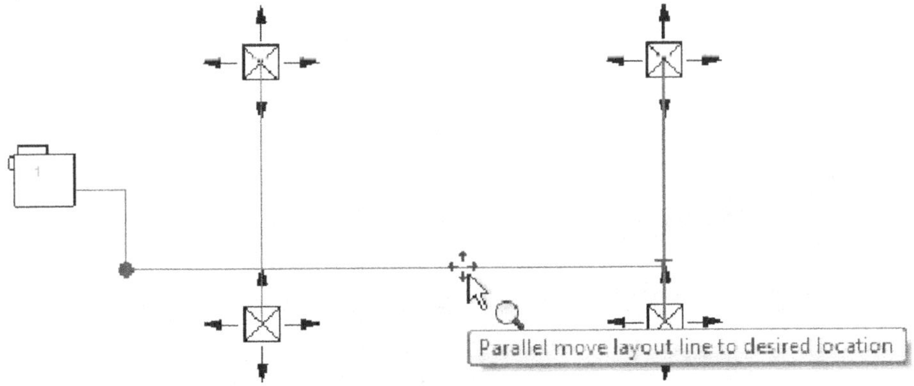

Figure 10–27

4. Click (Solutions) to finish customizing the layout. The Solution Type list now has **Custom** as an additional option to the standard three solution types.
   - The software only permits one custom option at a time.
5. In the *Generate Layout* tab>Generate Layout panel, click (Finish Layout).

- When the automatic/custom layout is completed, it is important to check the entire system to ensure that the layout is correct. Ensure that you check slopes and fitting directions.

Practice 10c Create Automatic HVAC Layouts

Practice Objectives

- Create ducts using the Generate Layout tool with both standard and custom layouts.
- Modify ductwork after it has been placed.

Estimated time for completion: 15 minutes

In this practice you will create supply ducts using the **Generate Layout** tool and modify the ductwork in the layout after it has been placed. You will also create a custom layout for the return ducts and modify the ductwork. The final systems are shown in Figure 10–28.

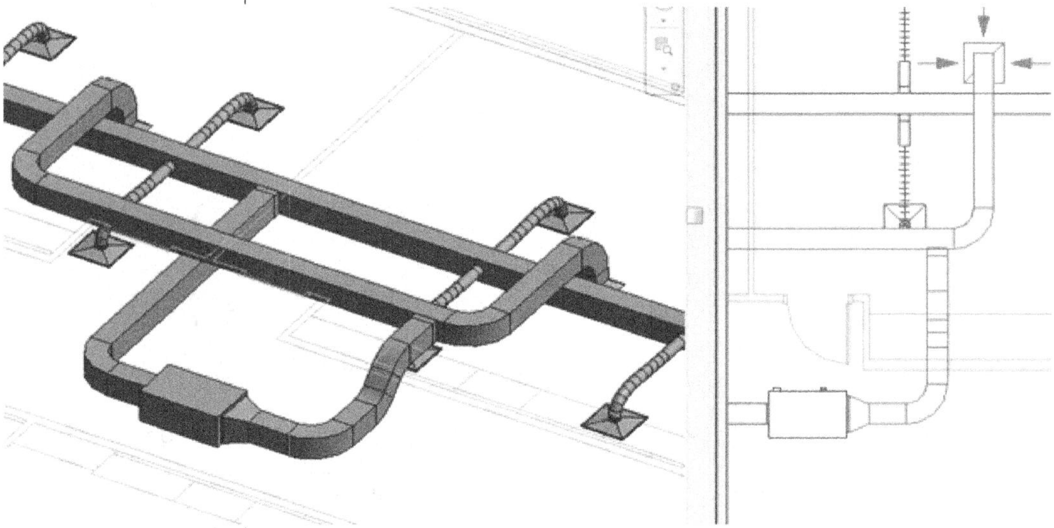

Figure 10–28

Task 1 - Create an automatic ductwork layout.

1. In the practice files *System* folder, open the project **MEP-Elementary-School-HVAC-Layouts-M.rvt.**
2. Verify that you are in the **01 Mechanical Plan** and that no other views are open.
3. Open the Mechanical>HVAC>3D Views>**01 Mechanical - Area B 3D** view.
4. Resize the views so you can see both the 2D plan and 3D views of the new systems area. Type **WT** (Window Tile) if there are no other open views in the Autodesk Revit session.

5. In the plan, roll the cursor over one of the supply air terminals and press <Tab> until the system displays. Click to select it as shown in Figure 10–29.

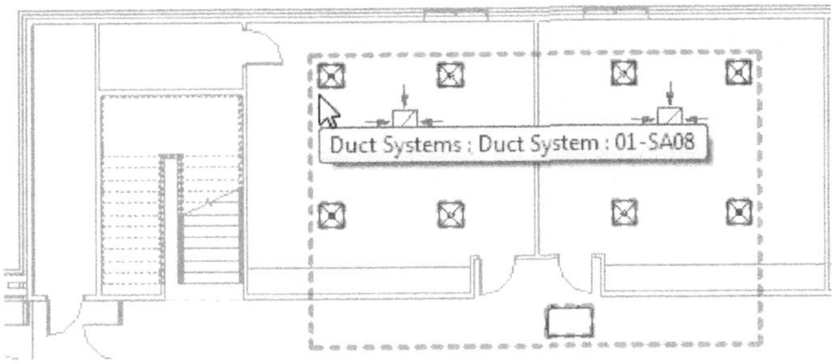

Figure 10–29

6. In the *Modify | Duct Systems* tab>Layout panel, click  (Generate Layout).
7. In the *Generate Layout* tab>Modify Layout panel, click  (Solutions).
8. In the Options Bar, click **Settings...**.
9. In the Duct Conversion Settings dialog box, select **Main** and set the following parameters:
   - *Duct Type:* **Rectangular Duct: Radius Elbows/Taps**
   - *Offset*: **3080mm**
10. Select **Branch** and set the following parameters, as shown in Figure 10–30:
    - *Duct Type*: **Round Duct: Taps / Short Radius**
    - *Offset*: **3080mm**
    - *Flex Duct*: **Flex Duct Round: Flex - Round**
    - *Maximum Flex Duct Length*: **1000mm**

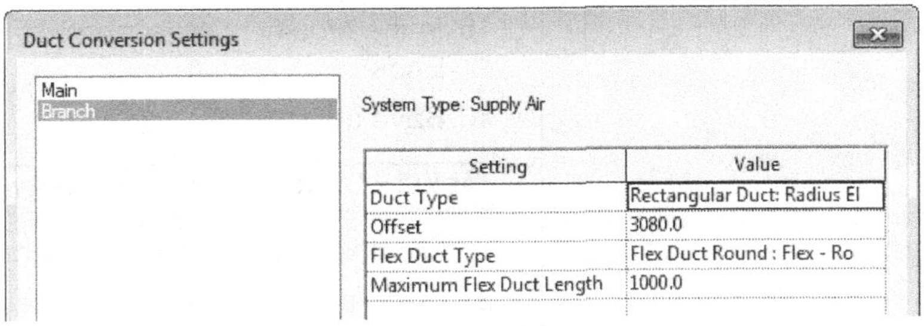

Figure 10–30

11. Click **OK**.

12. In the Options Bar, use the arrow buttons and Solution Types to try out several different solutions. End with the solution Network 1 of 6, shown in Figure 10–31 and click (Finish Layout).

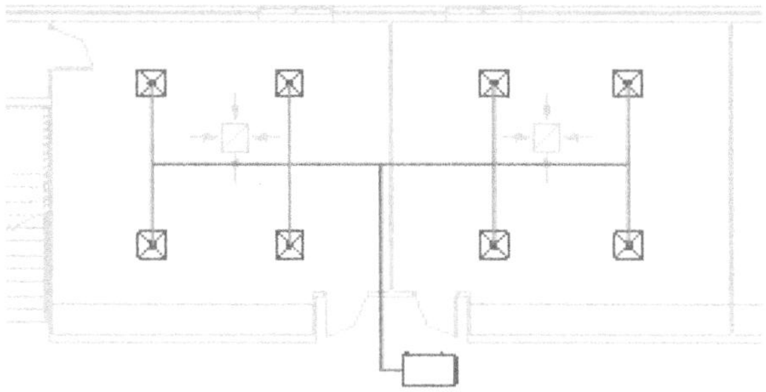

Figure 10–31

13. A Warning displays prompting you that there is an open connection and the horizontal duct is highlighted as shown in Figure 10–32. You can see in the 3D view that it is missing an endcap.

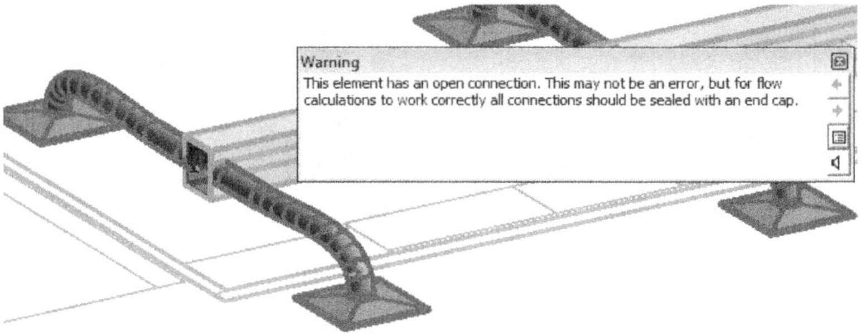

Figure 10–32

14. Click in the 3D view to activate it and select the duct again, if required.
15. In the *Modify | Ducts* tab>Edit panel, click (Cap Open Ends).
16. Save the project.

Task 2 - Create a Custom Ductwork Layout.

1. Continue working with the same two views open.
2. In the plan view, select the Return Air System.
3. In the *Duct Systems* tab>Layout panel, click (Generate Layout).

4. In the *Generate Layout* tab>Modify Layout panel, click (Solutions).
5. View the various solutions. Most of them have some problem with the layout. When the gold lines display it is a warning that the layout could fail in those areas.
6. In the Options Bar, click **Settings...**.
7. In the Duct Conversion Settings dialog box, select **Main** and change the options as follows:
   - *Duct Type*: **Rectangular Duct: Radius Elbow and Taps**
   - *Offset*: **3500mm**
8. Select **Branch** and change the options as follows:
   - *Duct Type*: **Rectangular Duct: Radius Elbow and Taps**
   - *Offset*: **3500mm**
   - *Flex Duct Type*: **None**
9. Click **OK**. This still didn't correct all of the problems but it solved some by changing the heights of the ducts.
10. Cycle through the solutions to review the options.
11. End with Network 3 of 5. In the *Generate Layout* tab>Modify Layout panel, click (Edit Layout).
12. Click (Finish Layout). There are still some problems that need to be corrected as shown in Figure 10–33.

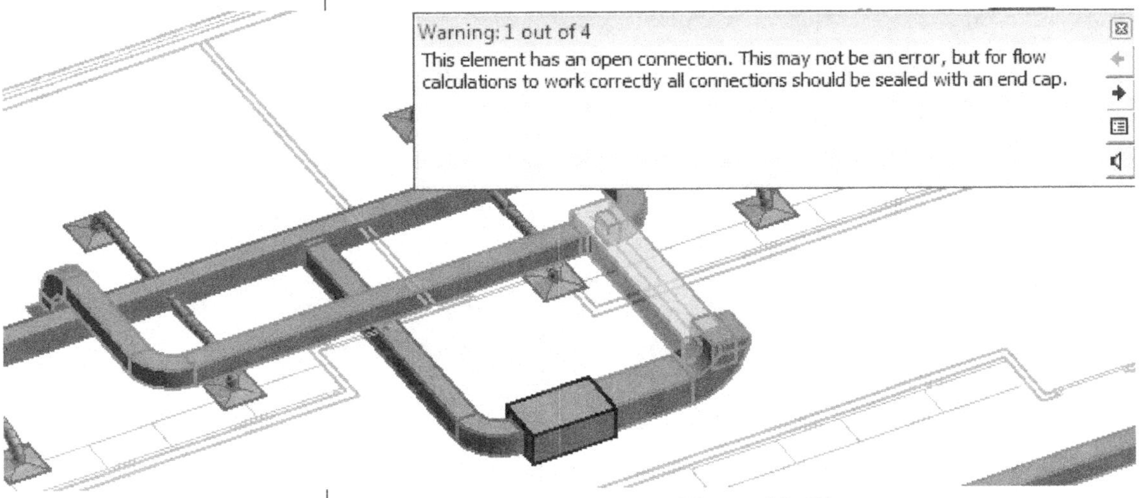

Figure 10–33

13. In the Warning dialog box, click through the various warnings to see the other issues. The corresponding duct is also highlighted. You can see that they are all related to the ducts coming from the air handling unit.
    - If you selected a different layout there will be different issues but the principles of fixing them are still the same.
14. Close the Warning dialog box.
15. Save the project.

Task 3 - Correct issues with the layout.

1. Select the ducts and related duct fittings coming out of the air handling unit and delete them up to the horizontal duct, as shown in Figure 10–34.

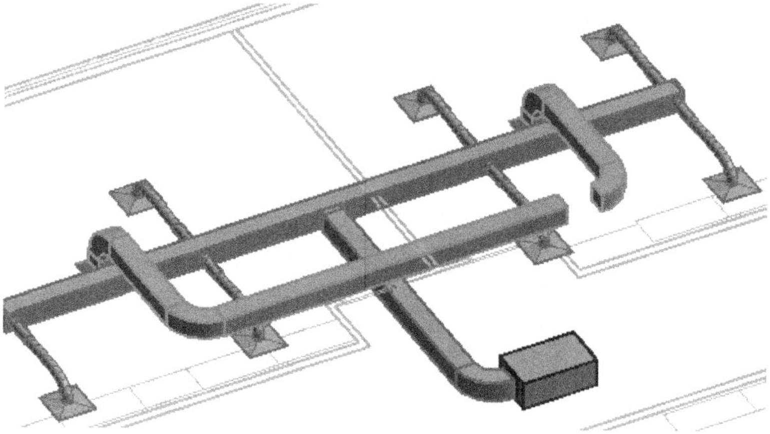

Figure 10–34

2. Drag the horizontal duct over to the duct going to the upper air terminal so that it connects as shown in Figure 10–35.

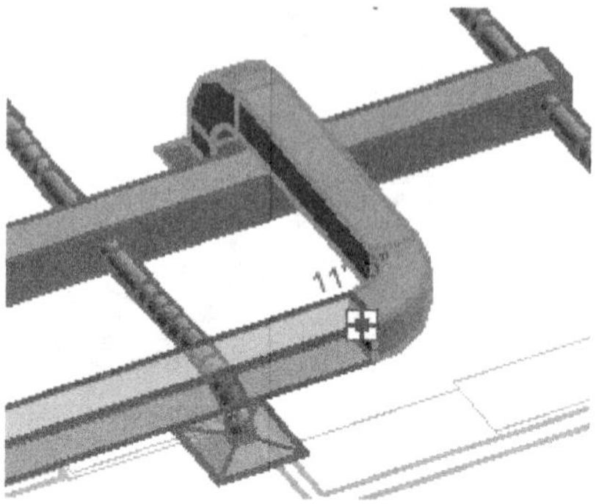

Figure 10–35

3. Select the Mechanical Equipment unit, right-click on the Return Air control and select **Draw Duct**.

4. In the Type Selector, verify that the type is set to **Rectangular Duct: Radius Elbows/Taps**.

5. In the Options Bar, set the *Width* and *Height* to **300mm** and the *Offset* to **3080mm** as shown in Figure 10–36.

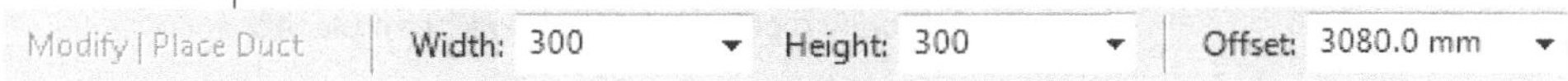

Figure 10–36

6. Draw the duct out **900mm**.

7. In the Options Bar, set *Offset* to **3500mm** and continue drawing the duct until it connects with the horizontal duct. The appropriate fittings are added to resize the duct coming from the AHU and changing the height going to the other duct, as shown in Figure 10–37.

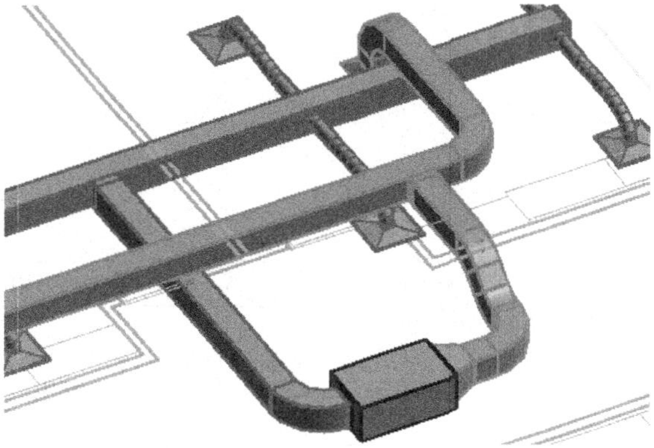

Figure 10–37

8. Save the project.

Practice 10d Create Automatic Plumbing Layouts

Practice Objectives

- Create pipes using the Generate Layout tool with both standard and custom layouts.
- Modify pipes after they have been placed.

Estimated time for completion: 10 minutes

In this practice you will create a piping layout for a sprinkler system. You will then create a sanitary system and use the layout tools, including **Place Base**, to add sloped piping, as shown in Figure 10–38.

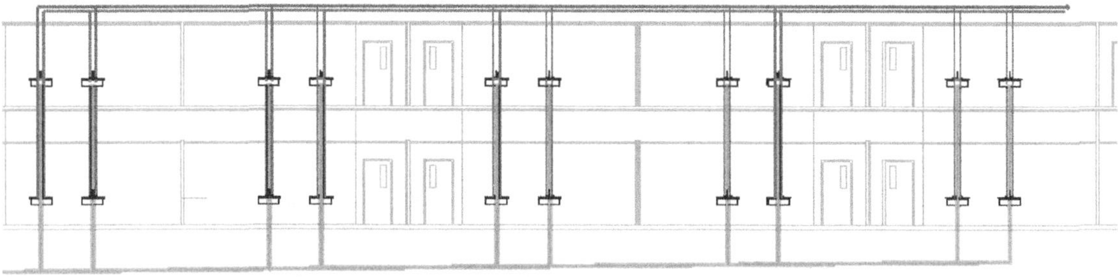

Figure 10–38

Task 1 - Create a piping layout for a sprinkler system.

1. In the practice files *Systems* folder, open the project **MEP-Elementary-School- Plumbing-Layouts-M.rvt**
2. Open the Plumbing>Fire>Ceiling Plans>**1 - Fire RCP** view and that no other views are open.
3. Open the Plumbing>Fire>3D Views>**1- Fire 3D** view.
4. Tile the two windows so that both the 3D view and the north wing of the RCP display.

5. Hover the cursor over one of the sprinklers in the classroom and press <Tab> until the piping systems displays, as shown in Figure 10–39. Click to select the system.

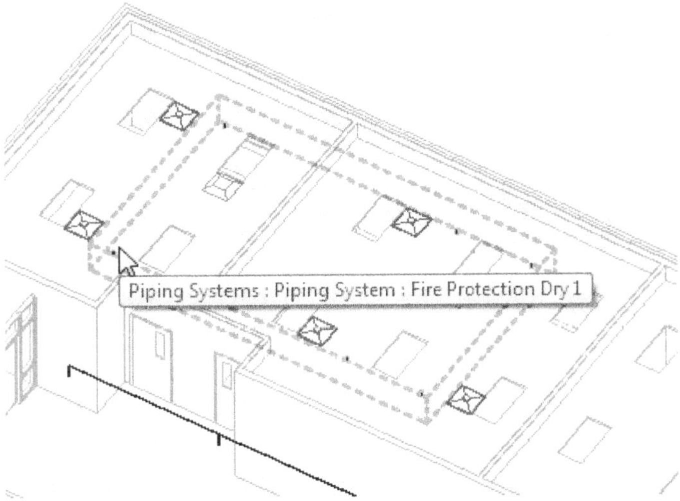

Figure 10–39

6. In the *Modify | Piping Systems* tab>Layout panel, click  (Generate Layout).

7. In the *Generate Layout* tab>Modify Layout panel, click  (Solutions).

8. In the Slope panel, set the *Slope Value* to **0%**.

9. In the Options Bar, click **Settings...**.

10. In the Pipe Conversion Settings dialog box, set the following parameters and then click **OK**.

    Main:

    - *Pipe Type:* **Pipe Types: Copper**
    - *Offset:* **2800mm**

    Branch:

    - *Pipe Type:* **Pipe Types: Copper**
    - *Offset*: **2750mm**

11. In the Options Bar, work through the *Solution Types* and try out several different solutions. Many of them have issues, as shown by the gold lines in Figure 10–40.

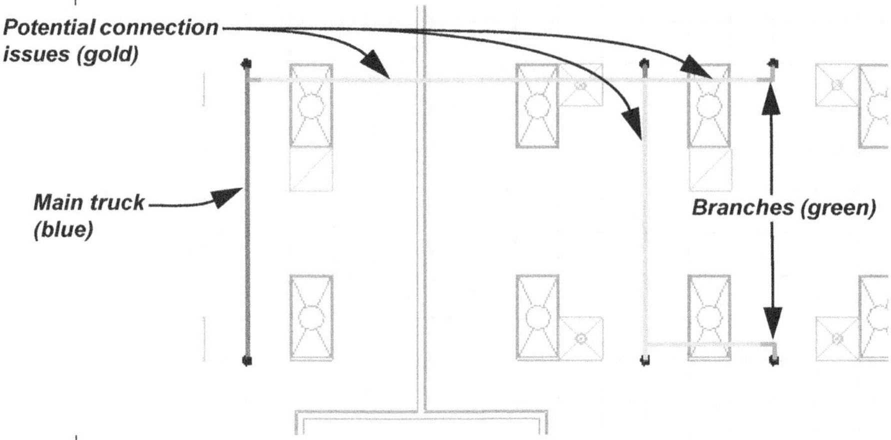

Figure 10–40

12. In this case, the *Offset* specified in the settings does not work. In the Options Bar, click **Settings...**.

13. Change the Branch so that it is *Offset* to **2800mm** and click **OK**.

14. This time the options work. Select one that you like and click (Finish Layout).

15. Save the project.

Task 2 - Create a piping layout for a sanitary system.

1. Open the Plumbing>Plumbing>3D views>**3D Plumbing** view and maximize it.

2. Hover the cursor over one of the sinks in the classroom wing and press <Tab> to highlight the various elements. Note that there are piping networks and domestic hot and cold water systems, but there is no sanitary system.

3. Create a Sanitary System linking all of the sinks, as shown in Figure 10–41. (**Hint:** Select one, right-click, and select **Select All Instances>Visibile in View**.)

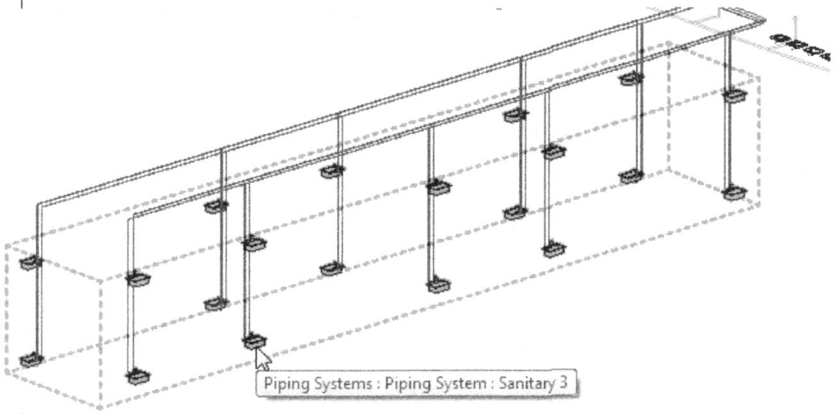

Figure 10–41

4. In the Quick Access Toolbar, click  (Close Hidden Windows).

5. Open the Plumbing>Plumbing>Sections (Building Section)>**Classroom Section Sanitary** view.

6. Type **WT** to tile the two views and arrange them so that the sinks display in each view.

7. Select the sanitary system.

8. In the *Modify | Piping Systems* tab>Layout panel, click  (Generate Layout).

9. In the *Generate Layout* tab>Modify Layout panel, click  (Solutions).

10. In the Options Bar, click **Settings...**.

11. In the Pipe Conversion Settings dialog box, set the following parameters and click **OK**.

    Main:

    - *Pipe Type:* **Pipe Types: PVC - DWV**
    - *Offset:* (negative) **-41200mm**

    Branch:

    - *Pipe Type:* **Pipe Types: PVC - DWV**
    - *Offset*: (negative) **-1200mm**

12. In the Generate Layout tab, set the *Slope Value* to **1%**.

13. In the Modify Layout panel, click (Place Base).

14. Select a point outside and to the left of the building, as shown in Figure 10–42.

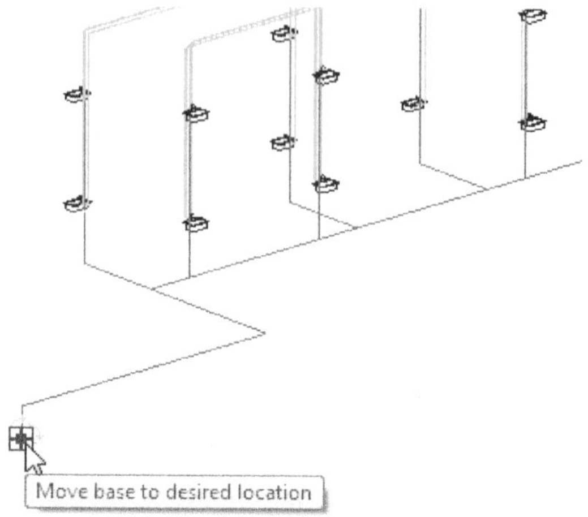

Figure 10–42

15. The **Modify Base** command is automatically selected. In the Options Bar, change the *Offset* to (negative) **-2400mm** and the *Diameter* to **32mm**.

    - If the Base pipe is too large it causes problems with the connections to the sinks. You can change the main trunk pipe sizes after the layout is finished.

16. In the Modify Layout panel, click (Solutions).

17. In the Options Bar, work through the *Solution Types* and try out several different solutions. Select the one you want.

18. Click (Finish Layout).

19. If warnings display, read them and zoom in to see what is wrong. Then, undo until you are back in the layout and try the process again.

20. Save the project.

10.3 Testing Systems

As you start working with connectors and systems, it is important to check how the system is working. For a quick way to test the continuity of a system, hover the cursor over one of the linear connections and press <Tab> until the system highlights. For the example shown in Figure 10–43, one of the ducts is not attached to the fitting and therefore is not highlighted.

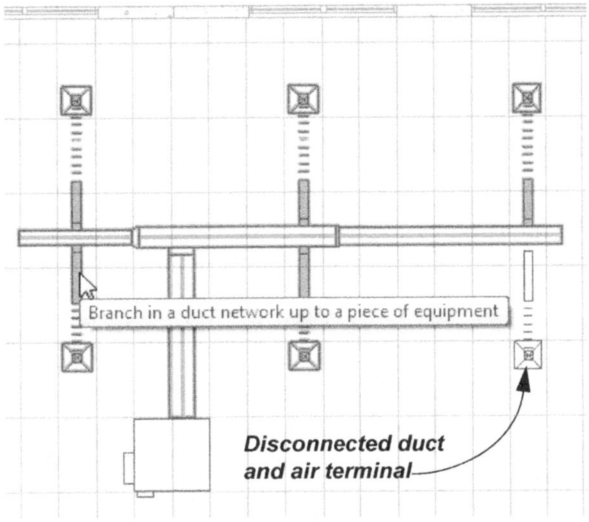

Figure 10–43

If there are issues with a selected system, the Warning panel displays in the related *Modify* toolbar, as shown in Figure 10–44.

Click (Show Related Warnings) to open the dialog box and review the issues.

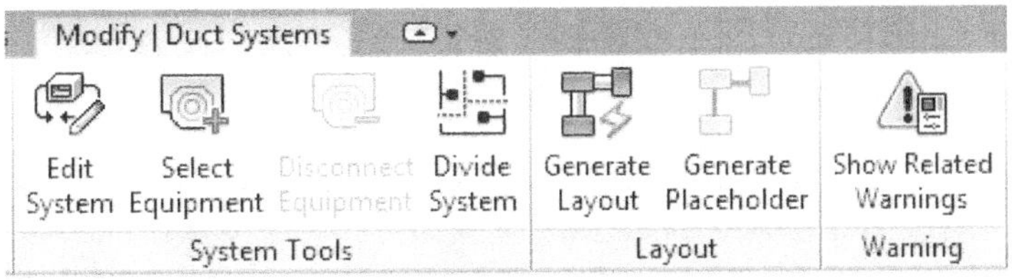

Figure 10–44

Often, these warnings are corrected as you continue working in a system and complete the full connection. However, some errors need to be corrected before the system works as required.

Hint: Displaying Only the MEP Analysis Panels

If you are using a copy of Autodesk Revit that has not been optimized for MEP, it is helpful to turn off the Structural Analysis tools so that you can see the full MEP analysis panels. In the *File* tab, click **Options**. In the Options dialog box, in the User Interface panel, clear the **Structure analysis and tools** checkmark, as shown in Figure 10–45.

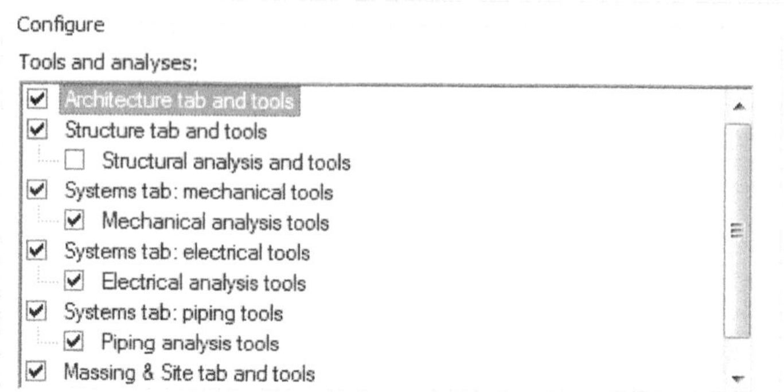

Figure 10–45

Showing Disconnects

Duct and Piping Systems can be analyzed and reviewed for issues. This includes searching for disconnects and checking the various systems. For the example shown in Figure 10–46, there are open connectors at three different places. Once the tee fitting is changed to an elbow fitting, and the flex duct connects the end of the existing duct to the air terminal, the warnings are removed.

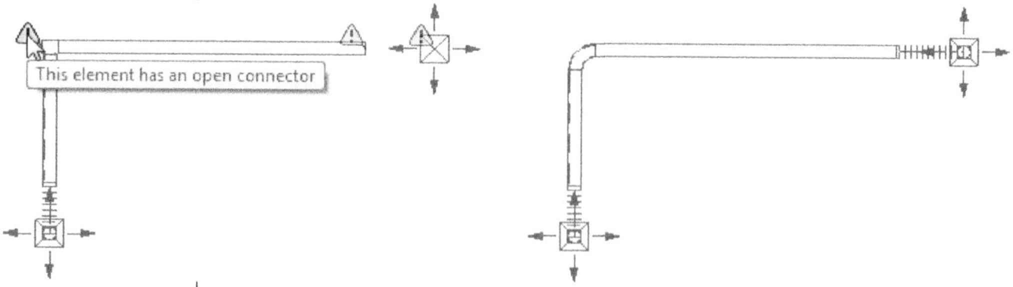

Figure 10–46

How To: Show Disconnects

1. In the *Analyze* tab>Check Systems panel, click (Show Disconnects).
2. In the Show Disconnects Options dialog box, select the types of systems you want to display (as shown in Figure 10–47) and then click **OK**.

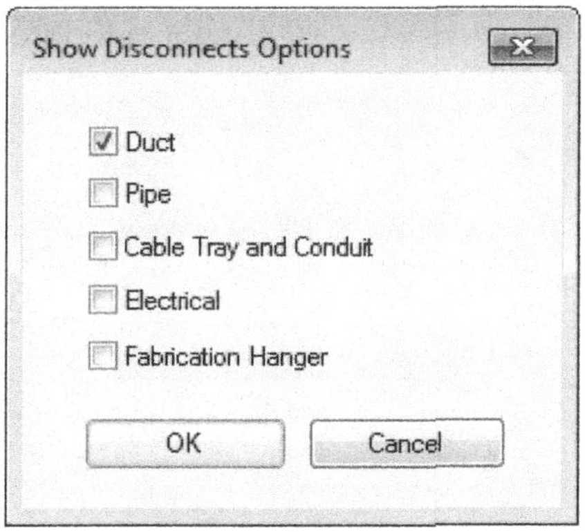

Figure 10–47

3. The disconnects displays (Warning).
   - The disconnects continue to display until you either correct the situation or run **Show Disconnects** again and clear all of the selections.
4. Roll the cursor over the warning icon to display a tooltip with the warning, or click on the icon to open the Warning dialog box, as shown in Figure 10–48.

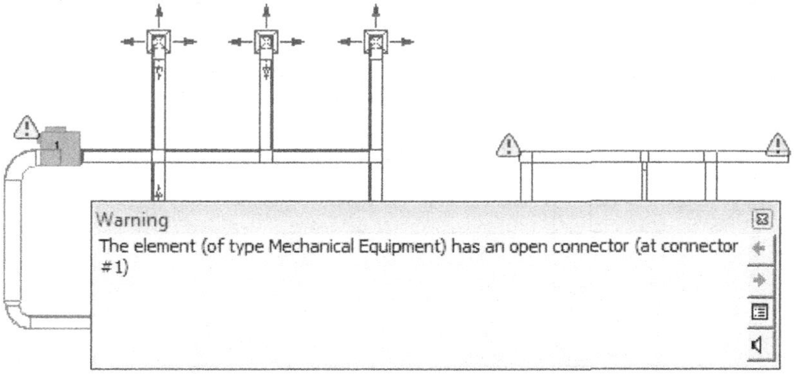

Figure 10–48

How To: Use the Check Systems Tools

1. In the *Analyze* tab>Check Systems panel, click (Check Duct Systems) or (Check Pipe Systems) to toggle them on.
2. The (Warning) icon displays where there are problems. Click one of the icons to open the Warning alert box, as shown in Figure 10–49.

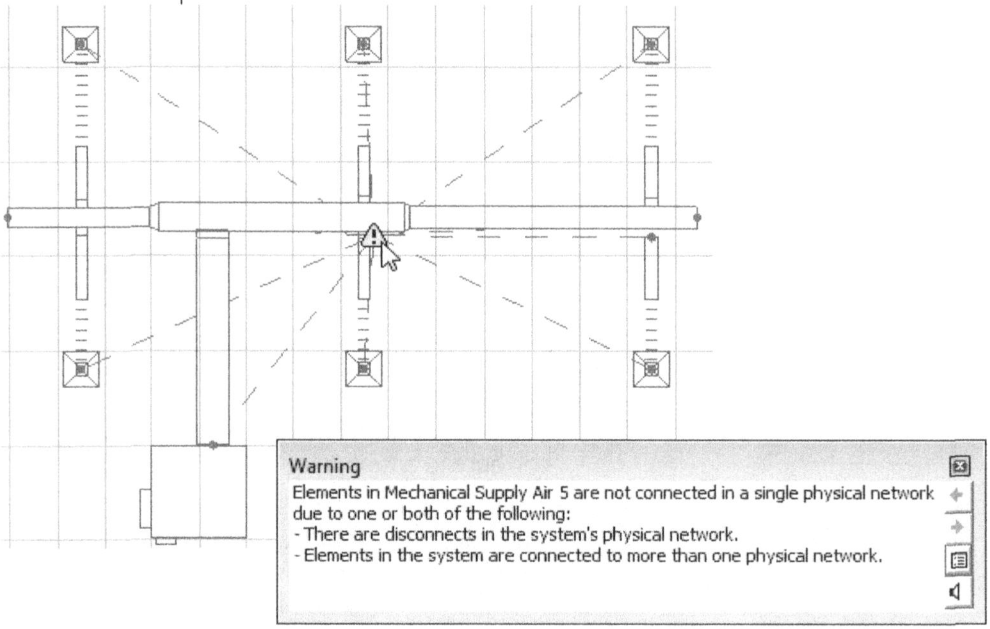

Figure 10–49

- For icons that have more than one warning, in the Warning alert box, click (Next Warning) and (Previous Warning) to search through the list.

3. Click (Expand Warning Dialog) to open the dialog box, as shown in Figure 10–50. You can expand each node in the box and select elements to display or delete.

*If there are a lot of warnings to review, click **Export...** and save the HTML report to review separately.*

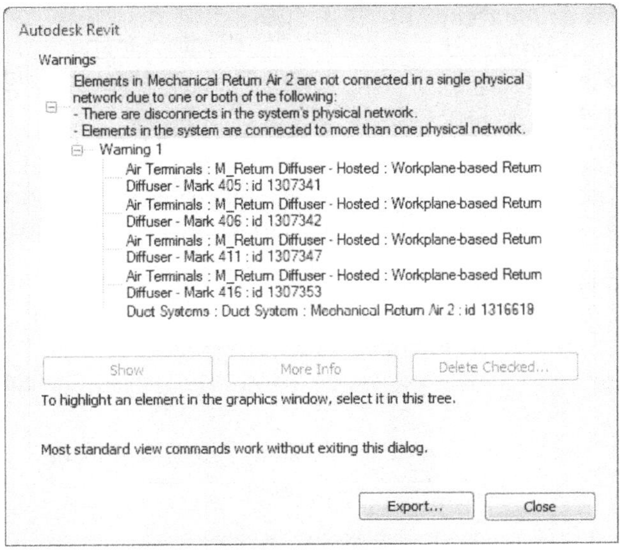

Figure 10–50

System Inspector

The System Inspector provides information such as flow rate, static pressure, and pressure loss at every point in a system, as shown in Figure 10–51 for a domestic cold water system. The System Inspector also enables you to make changes to components of a system as you complete an inspection.

The System Inspector works with all Duct and Piping Systems except Fire Suppression Systems.

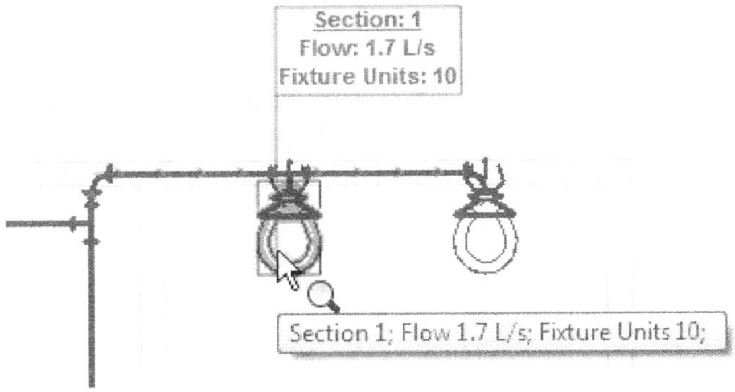

Figure 10–51

- The System Inspector does not display in the ribbon if an open system is selected.
- The pressure loss method settings for duct and pipe fittings and accessories can be setup in Properties.

How To: Use the System Inspector

*In the System Browser, right-click on the top level of a system and select **System Inspector**.*

1. Select any part of a system (e.g., air terminals, ductwork, piping, mechanical equipment, or plumbing fixtures, etc.).
2. In the contextual *Modify* tab>Analysis panel, click (System Inspector), the floating System Inspector panel displays as shown in Figure 10–52.
3. Click (Inspect). The air flow displays in the system, as shown in Figure 10–52. Move the cursor over a section of system to display information, such as the Flow, Static Pressure, and Pressure Loss for duct systems.

The red path displays the greatest static pressure.

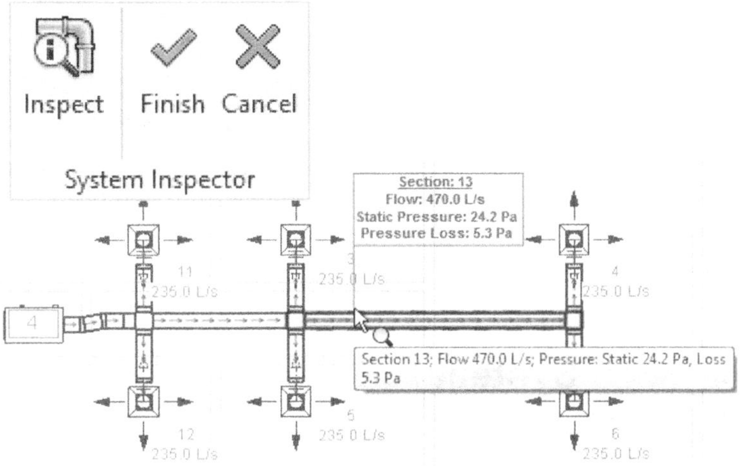

Figure 10–52

4. If you need to change a component of the system, remain in the System Inspector:
    1. In the Select panel, click (Modify).
    2. Select the component.
    3. Make changes to the component on the screen using the controls or in the Properties.
5. Click (Inspect) to return to the flow pattern.
6. When you are finished reviewing the system, click (Finish).

- If you select a piece of mechanical equipment that is attached to more than one duct-based or pipe-based system, the Select a System dialog box displays, as shown in Figure 10–53. Select the system you want to inspect and click **OK**.

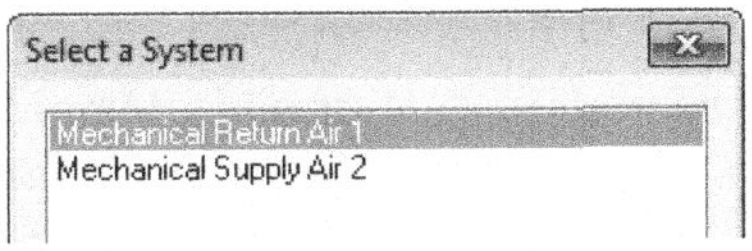

Figure 10–53

- The System Inspector displays in a floating panel by default. You can move it or make it a part of the Ribbon by clicking **Return Panels to Ribbon**, as shown in Figure 10–54.

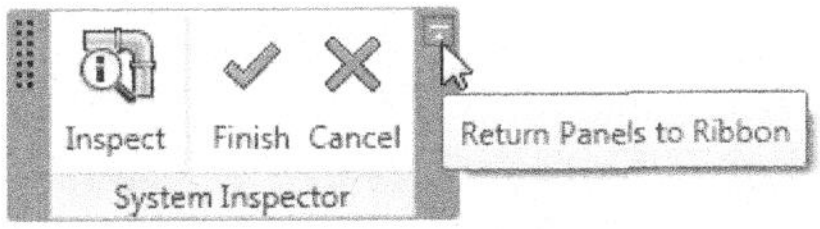

Figure 10–54

Duct and Pipe Color Fill Legends

An additional way to view information about ducts and pipes is to create a Color Fill Legend, as shown in Figure 10–55, for Friction in ducts.

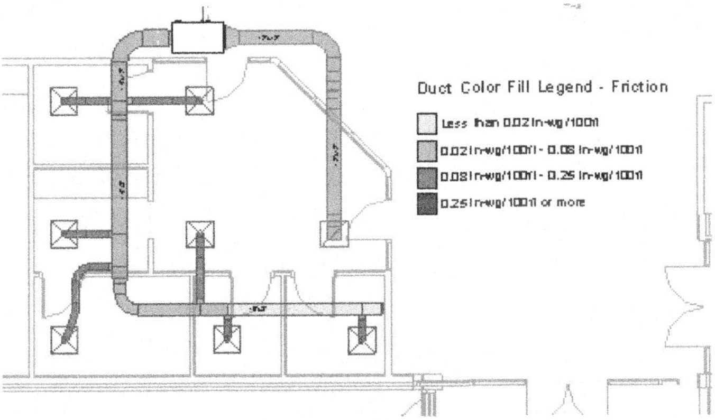

Figure 10–55

- These color fill schemes and legends are similar to those created for spaces and zones.

How To: To Create a Color Fill Legend

1. In the *Annotate* tab>Color Fill Panel, click (Duct Legend) or (Pipe Legend) and place the legend.
2. If a color scheme is not assigned to the view, the Choose Color Scheme dialog box displays. Choose a scheme from the list. When you click **OK**, the view is filled to match the legend, as shown in Figure 10–56.

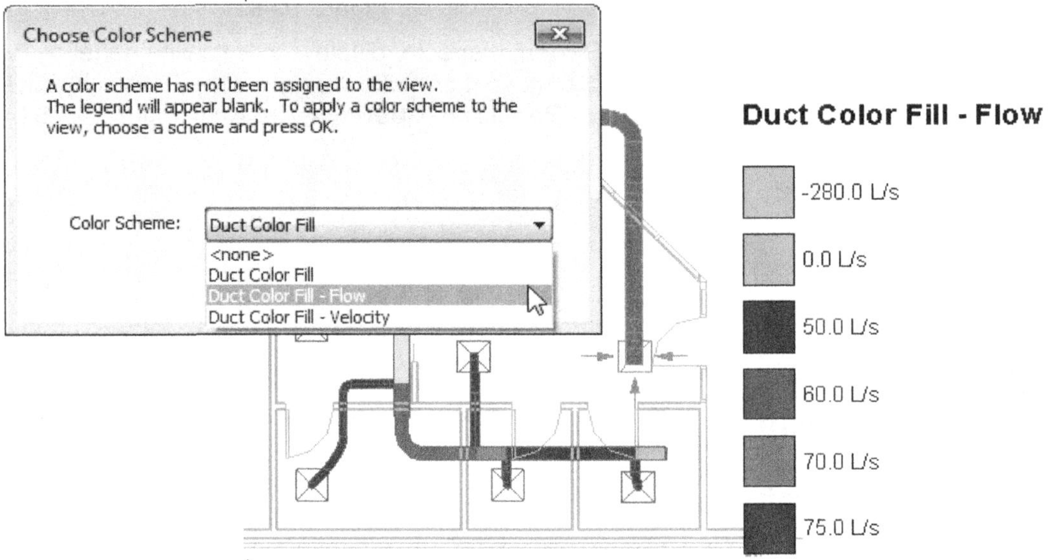

Figure 10–56

3. To make changes to the color fill scheme, select the legend and in the *Modify | Duct/Pipe Color Fill Legends* tab>Scheme panel, click (Edit Scheme).
4. The Edit Color Scheme dialog box opens where you select the color scheme you want to use, as shown in Figure 10–57.

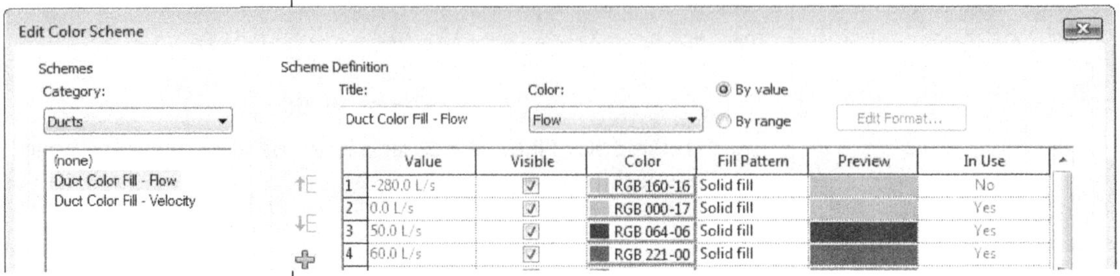

Figure 10–57

5. Click **OK** to apply the changes.

- You can also reach the Edit Color Scheme dialog box through the view. In Properties beside *System Color Schemes*, click **Edit...**. In the Color Schemes dialog box, click the color scheme button for either **Pipes** or **Ducts**. The Edit Color Scheme dialog box displays.

- To create new color schemes or modify existing ones, see the *Defining Color Schemes* topic in Appendix B.

Analyzing Systems with Schedule

No schedules are included with the default MEP templates (**Electrical-Default_Metric.rte, Mechanical-Default_Metric.rte, Plumbing-Default_Metric.rte,** and **Systems-Default_Metric.rte**) provided by the Autodesk® Revit® software, but many firms create typical ones that can be used in most projects. These schedules are helpful for analyzing the systems (such as displaying the flow rate, keeping track of the systems, etc.), as shown in Figure 10–58.

- The **Construction-DefaultMetric.rte** template file includes some useful MEP quantities schedules.

<Plumbing System Schedule>

A	B	C	D
System Classification	System Name	Comments	Flow
Domestic Cold Water	Domestic Cold Water 1		2.7 L/s
Domestic Cold Water	Domestic Cold Water 2		2.2 L/s
Domestic Cold Water	Domestic Cold Water 3		4.8 L/s
Domestic Cold Water	Domestic Cold Water 4		4.8 L/s
Domestic Cold Water	Domestic Cold Water 5		0.9 L/s
Domestic Hot Water	Domestic Hot Water 1		1.2 L/s
Domestic Hot Water	Domestic Hot Water 2		1.2 L/s
Domestic Hot Water	Domestic Hot Water 3		1.1 L/s
Domestic Hot Water	Domestic Hot Water 4		1.1 L/s
Domestic Hot Water	Domestic Hot Water 5		0.4 L/s
Sanitary	Sanitary 1		Not Computed
Sanitary	Sanitary 2		Not Computed
Sanitary	Sanitary 3		Not Computed
Sanitary	Sanitary 4		Not Computed
Sanitary	Sanitary 5		Not Computed
Sanitary	Sanitary 6		Not Computed

Figure 10–58

- Some schedules have highlighting to indicate where something needs to be changed.

Practice 10e Test HVAC Systems

Practice Objectives

- Investigate warnings and use Check Duct Systems.
- Review disconnects.
- Add a duct color fill legend.
- Review a schedule setup to show the airflow in spaces.
- Correct issues discovered by the testing tools

Estimated time for completion: 10 minutes

In this practice, you will review warnings, run **Check Duct Systems**, and **Show Disconnects**. You will then correct any problems and run the **System Inspector**. You will add a color fill legend to test the velocity and make corrections as shown in Figure 10–59. You will also review a schedule that displays the airflow of rooms and add air terminals to spaces where the airflow is negative.

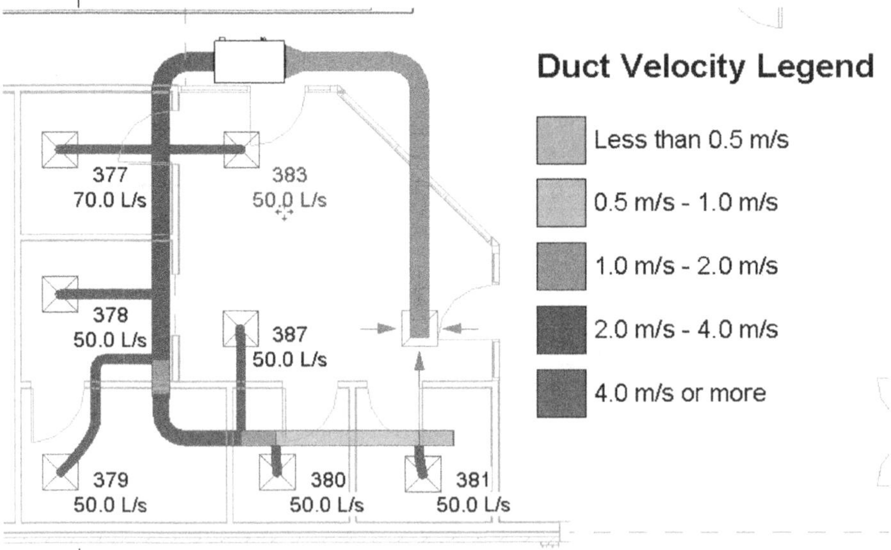

Figure 10–59

Task 1 - Review warnings and check duct systems

1. In the practice files *Systems* folder, open **MEP-Elementary-School-HVAC-Analyze-M.rvt**.
2. Open the Mechanical>HVAC>Floor Plans>**01 Mechanical Plan** view.

3. Zoom in on the office area near the front entrance of the building.
4. Hover over a supply duct and press <Tab> until you see the duct system highlight, as shown in Figure 10–60. Click to select it.

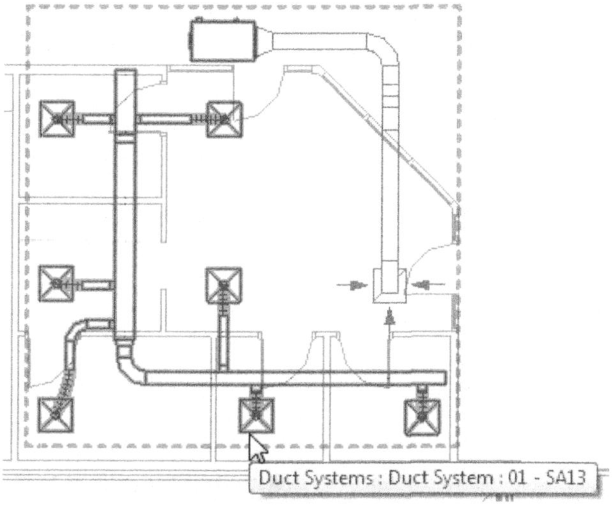

Figure 10–60

5. In the *Modify | Duct Systems* tab>Warning panel, click (Show Related Warnings).
6. Review the contents of the dialog box, as shown in Figure 10–61.

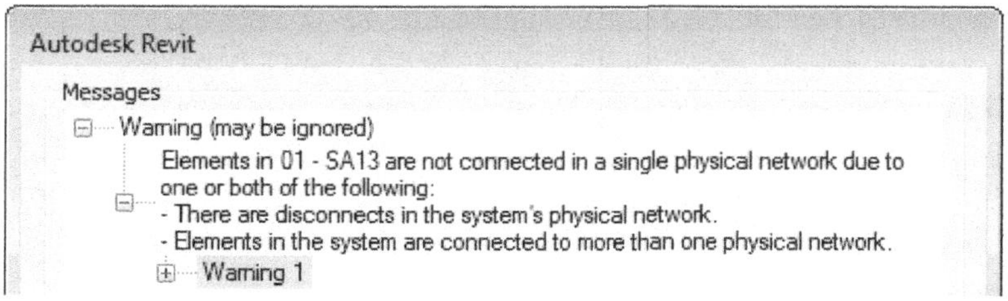

Figure 10–61

7. Close the dialog box.

8. In the *Analyze* tab>Check Systems panel, click (Check Duct Systems). The duct system is not working, as shown in Figure 10–62.

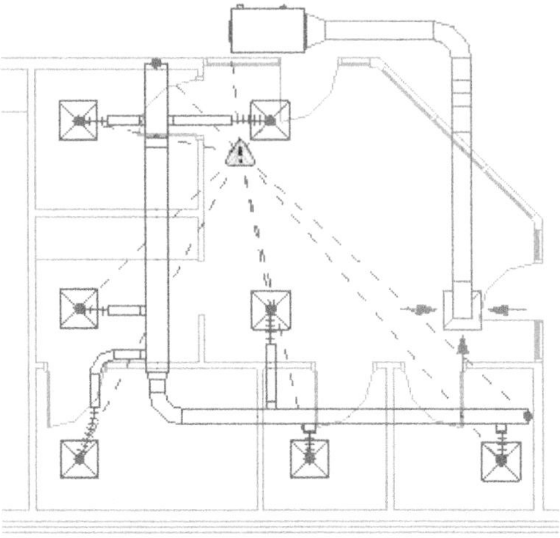

Figure 10–62

9. Note that there is a duct missing, which should be coming out of the air handling unit. Use the **Draw Duct** tool and set the type to **Rectangular Duct: Radius Elbows / Taps**. Then, draw a horizontal duct coming from the AHU (as shown in Figure 10–63).

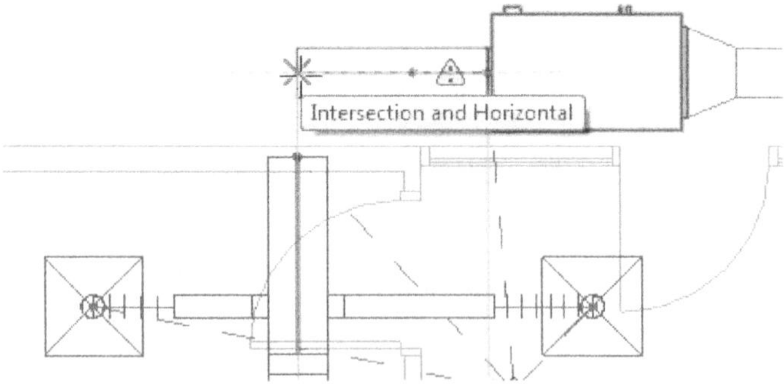

Figure 10–63

10. Use (Trim/Extend to Corner) to clean up the intersection and automatically apply the required elbow fitting.

11. Now that the duct system is working as expected, toggle off **Check Duct Systems**.

12. Save the project.

Task 2 - Check and correct duct disconnects.

1. In the *Analyze* tab>Check Systems panel, click (Show Disconnects).
2. In the Show Disconnects Options dialog box, select **Duct** (as shown in Figure 10–64) and click **OK**.

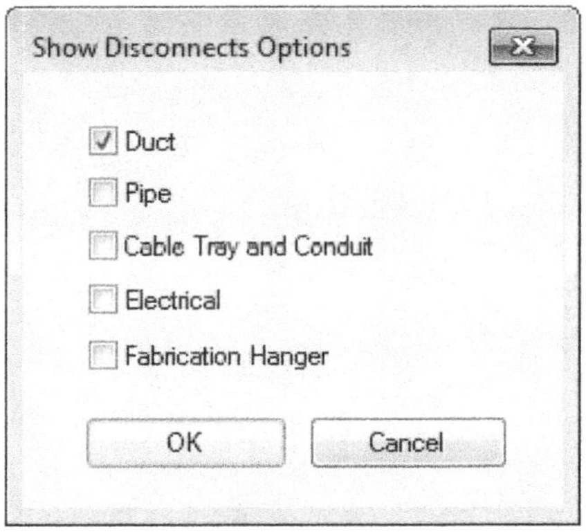

Figure 10–64

3. While the system is now connected correctly, there is still a disconnect at the end of the system, as shown in Figure 10–65.

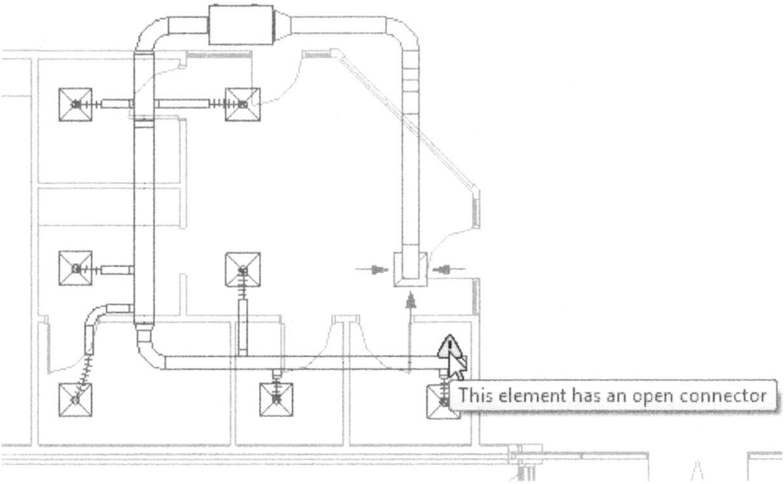

Figure 10–65

4. Select the duct, right-click on the open connector, and select **Cap Open End**, as shown in Figure 10–66. This solves the problem on this end of the system.

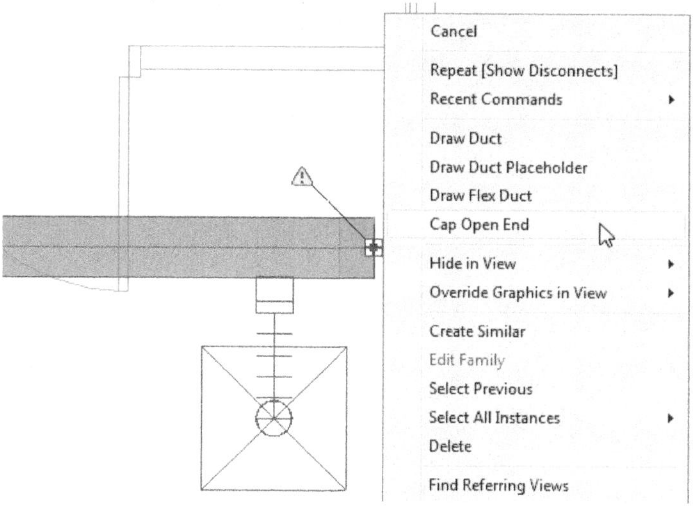

Figure 10–66

5. Hover over a duct and press <Tab> until you see the duct system highlight and then click to select it.
6. The *Modify | Duct Systems* tab>Analysis panel, click (System Inspector).
7. In the System Inspector panel, click (Inspect).
8. Roll the cursor over parts of the system to view the information, as shown in Figure 10–67.

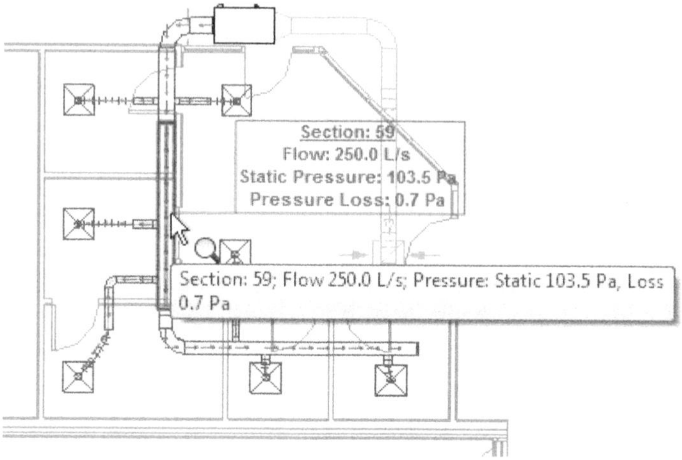

Figure 10–67

9. When you are finished inspecting the system, click (Finish).

10. Toggle off the **Show Disconnects** options for ducts.

11. Save the project.

Task 3 - Add a Duct Color Fill Scheme and Legend.

1. In the *Analyze* tab>Color Fill panel, click (Duct Legend).
2. Place the legend near the office area.
3. In the Choose Color Scheme dialog box, select **Duct Color Fill - Velocity** and click **OK**. The legend and color scheme displays as shown in Figure 10–68.

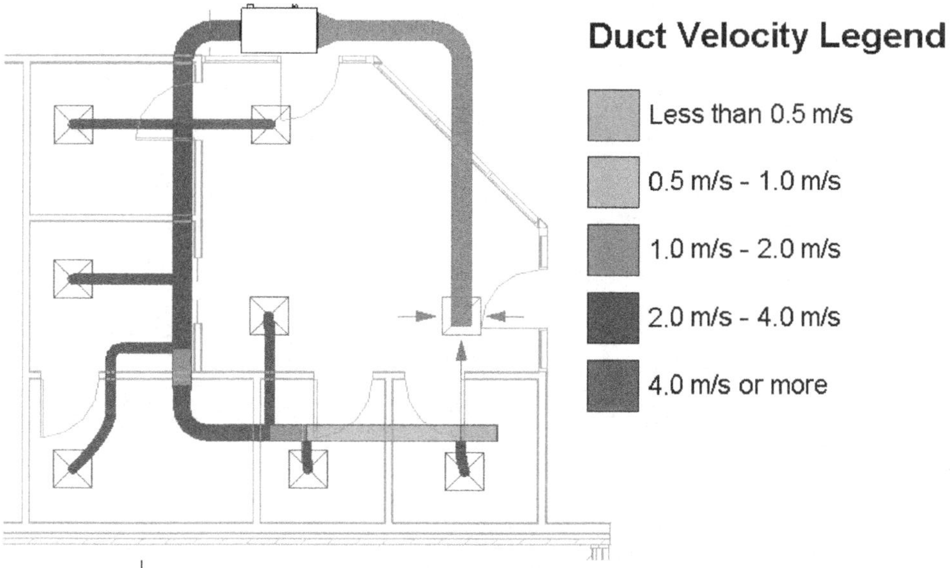

Figure 10–68

4. You can see from the colors that some of the velocity is set too high.

5. Open the Visibility Graphics dialog box and in the *Annotation Categories* tab, toggle on **Air Terminal Tags**. Click **OK**.

6. The tags display the Flow associated with the diffusers. Select the tag of the diffuser with too large of a flow, as shown in Figure 10–69, and change it to **50 L/s**.

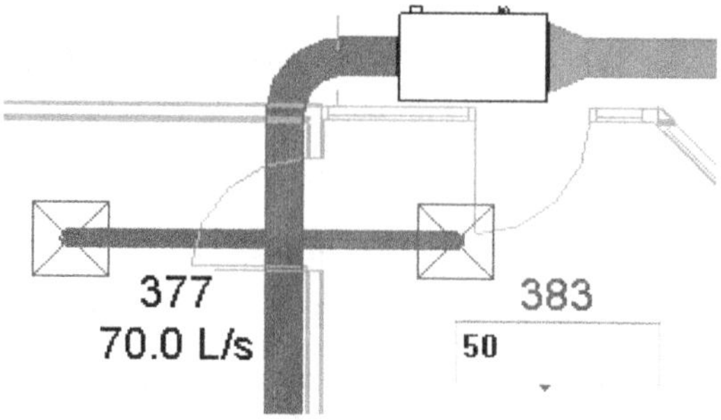

Figure 10–69

7. The colors change to the expected amounts, as shown in Figure 10–70.

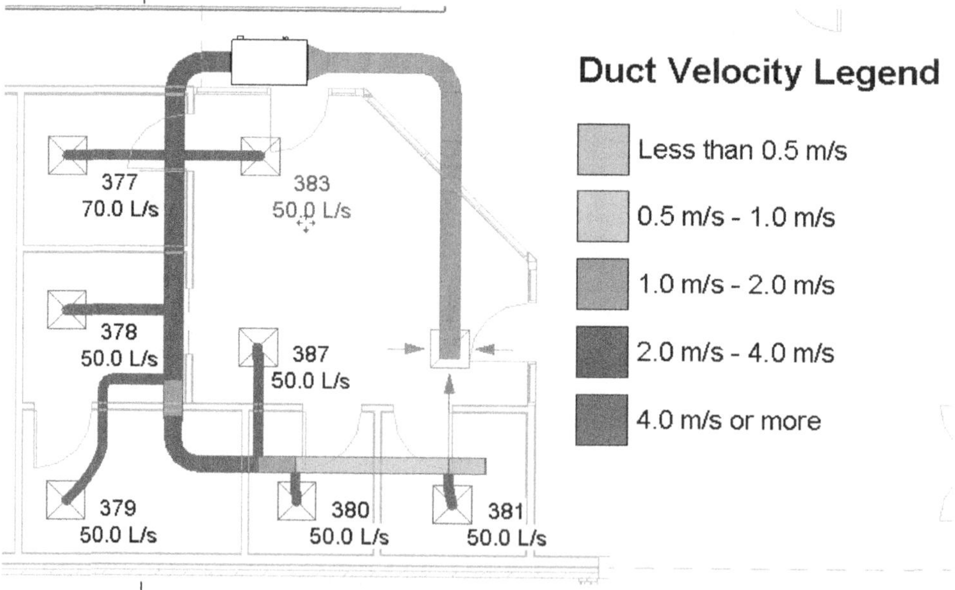

Figure 10–70

8. Zoom out to see the entire building.

9. Save the project

Task 4 - Work with schedules.

1. In the Project Browser, scroll down to the *Schedules* area and open **Space Airflow Check**.

2. Scroll down to *Space Number* **2008** and **2010**. Neither of these spaces have any air terminals and therefore have a negative *Airflow Check* number, as shown in Figure 10–71.

2007	CLASSROOM	Heated and coole	280.0 L/s	240.3 L/s	39.7 L/s
361	Supply Diffuser - Perforated	70.0 L/s			
362	Supply Diffuser - Perforated	70.0 L/s			
363	Supply Diffuser - Perforated	70.0 L/s			
364	Supply Diffuser - Perforated	70.0 L/s			
2008	CLASSROOM	Heated and coole	0.0 L/s	246.7 L/s	-246.7 L/s
2009	CLASSROOM	Heated and coole	280.0 L/s	240.2 L/s	39.8 L/s
357	Supply Diffuser - Perforated	70.0 L/s			
358	Supply Diffuser - Perforated	70.0 L/s			
359	Supply Diffuser - Perforated	70.0 L/s			
360	Supply Diffuser - Perforated	70.0 L/s			
2010	CLASSROOM	Heated and coole	0.0 L/s	192.8 L/s	-192.8 L/s
2011	CORRIDOR	Heated and coole	0.0 L/s	536.1 L/s	-536.1 L/s

Figure 10–71

3. Arrange the view windows to display the **Space Airflow Check** schedule and the **01 Mechanical** view.

4. In the **01 Mechanical** view, open the Visibility/Graphics dialog box. Toggle on **Spaces** and click **OK**.

5. Pan and zoom so that Spaces 2008 and 2010 display in each window. (The spaces are in the lower left of the south wing of the school with space tags.)

6. Select one of the existing supply air terminals. Right-click and select **Create Similar**. This starts the **Air Terminal** command and sets the type and Properties to match the original.

7. In the *Modify | Place Component* tab>Placement panel, click  (Place on Face).

8. Add an air terminal in Classroom 2010. The schedule automatically updates and includes the flow rate of the air terminal in the *Airflow Check*, as shown in Figure 10–72.

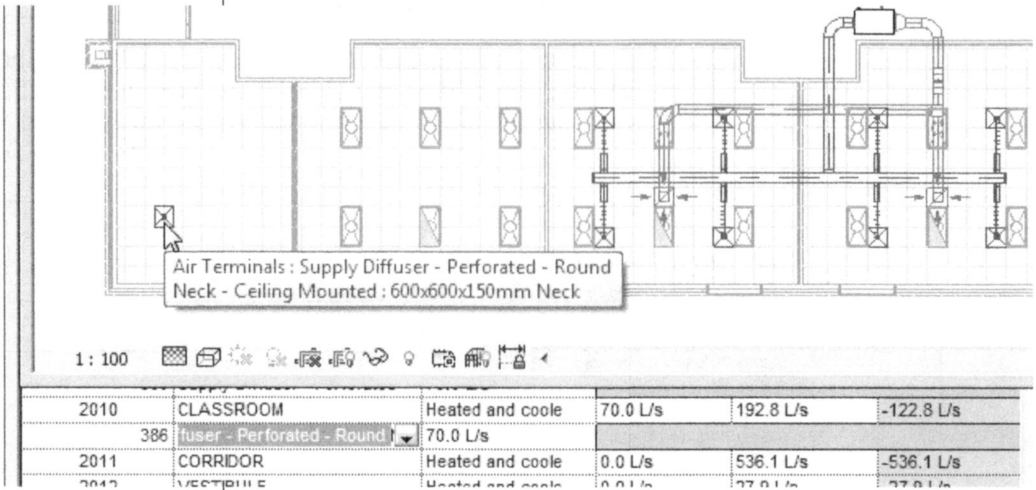

Figure 10–72

9. Add as many air terminals as required to have a positive airflow.

10. Save the project.

Practice 10f Test Plumbing Systems

Practice Objectives

- Investigate warnings and use Check Pipe Systems.
- Review disconnects.
- Correct issues discovered by the testing tools
- Add a Piping Color Fill Legend.

Estimated time for completion: 10 minutes

In this practice, you will review warnings, run **Check Pipe Systems**, and **Show Disconnects**. You will then correct some of the problems in the south wing, as shown in Figure 10–73. You will also add a piping color fill legend that shows the sizes of pipes in the view.

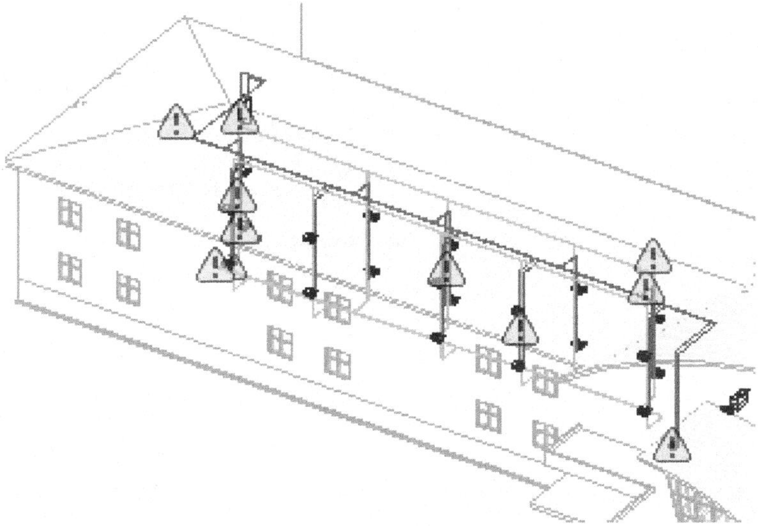

Figure 10–73

Task 1 - Review warnings and check pipe systems

1. In the practice files *Systems* folder, open **MEP-Elementary-School-Plumbing-Analyze-M.rvt**.

2. Hover over a one of the domestic hot or cold water system pipes in the south wing of the building and press <Tab> until you see the system highlight, as shown in Figure 10–74. Click to select it.

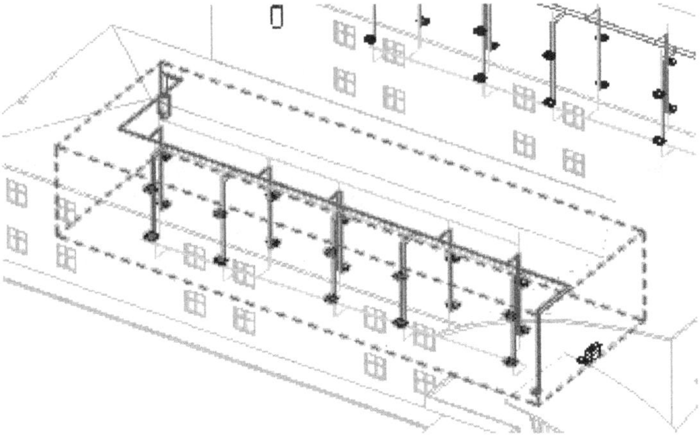

Figure 10–74

3. In the *Modify | Pipe Systems* tab>Warning panel, click (Show Related Warnings).

4. Review the contents of the dialog box, as shown in Figure 10–75.

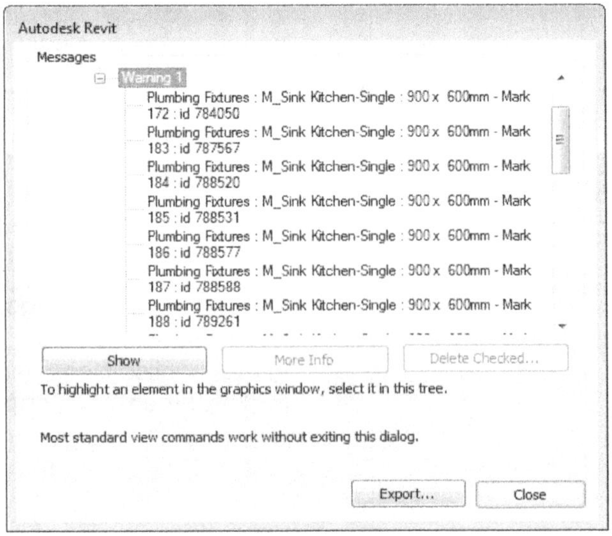

Figure 10–75

5. Close the dialog box.

6. In the *Analyze* tab>Check Systems panel, click (Check Pipe Systems). The pipe system is not working, as shown in Figure 10–76.

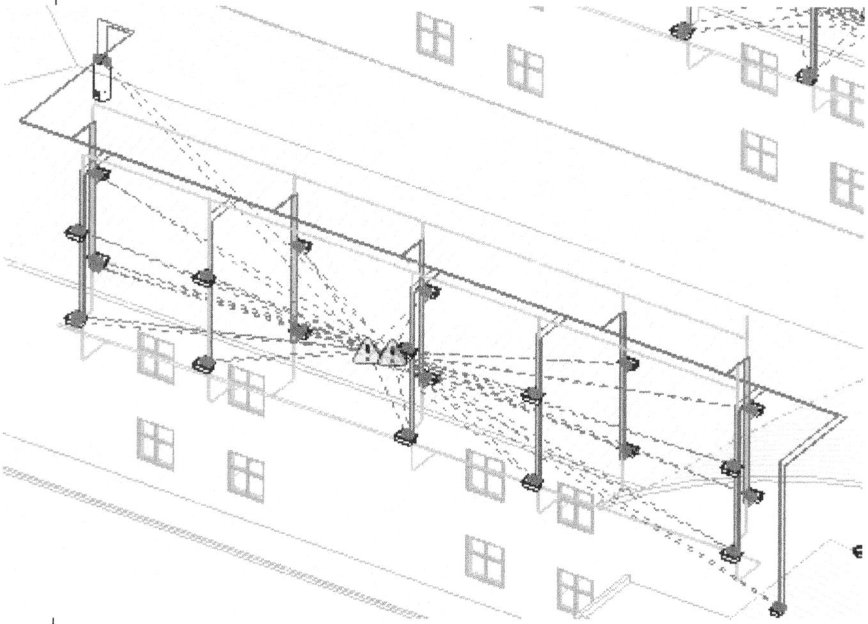

Figure 10–76

7. Toggle off **Check Pipe Systems**.

8. Save the project.

Task 2 - Check and correct pipe disconnects.

1. Continue working in the 3D view.

2. In the *Analyze* tab>Check Systems panel, click (Show Disconnects).

3. In the Show Disconnects Options dialog box, select **Pipe** as shown in Figure 10–77. Click **OK**.

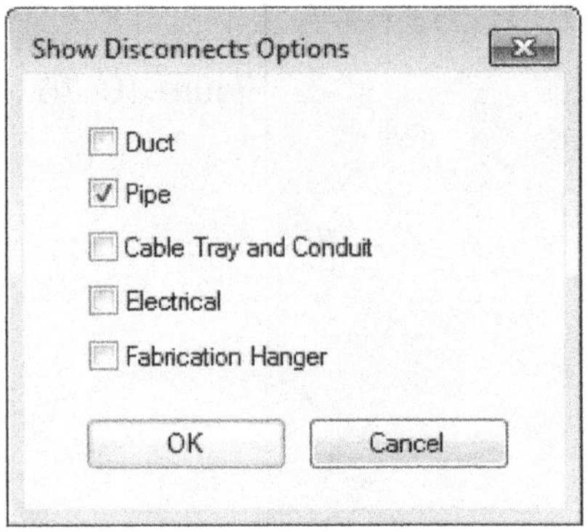

Figure 10–77

4. To see only sanitary systems, in the Visibility Graphics dialog box on the *Filters* tab, toggle off **Domestic Cold Water** and **Domestic Hot Water**.

5. Zoom in on parts of the south wing and discover the issues. Correct the places where there are extra fittings or the pipes are not connected correctly.

6. Open the Mechanical>Plumbing>Floor Plans>**01 Plumbing Plan** view.

7. A number of plumbing systems have open connectors, as shown in Figure 10–78.

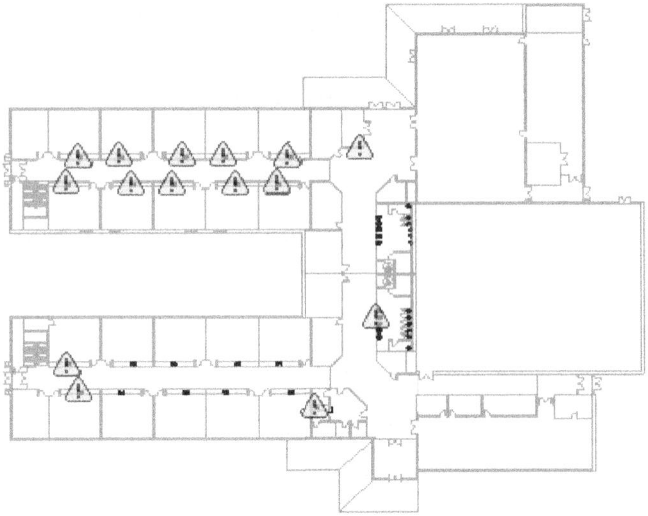

Figure 10–78

8. Zoom in on the office and select the sink in the copy room. Note that the open connector is for sanitary piping.

9. Open the side facing section where you can see the disconnect more clearly, as shown in Figure 10–79.

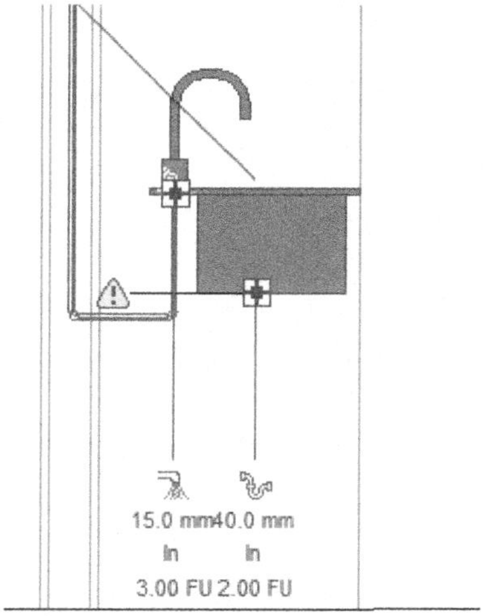

Figure 10–79

10. (Optional) Draw sanitary piping, connect into the existing system, and fix any other disconnects.

11. In the *Analyze* tab>Check Systems panel, click (Show Disconnects). Clear the check from **Pipe** and click **OK**.

12. Save the project.

Task 3 - Add a Pipe Color Fill Scheme and Legend.

1. Open the Plumbing>Plumbing>Floor Plans: **02 Sanitary Plan** view.

2. Change the *Detail Level* to **Coarse**.

3. In the *Analyze* tab>Color Fill panel, click (Pipe Legend).

4. Place the legend in the gym area close to one of the restrooms.

5. In the Choose Color Scheme dialog box, select **Pipe Color Fill Size** and click **OK**. The legend and color scheme displays, as shown in Figure 10–80.

Figure 10–80

- Note that the scale of this figure was changed for clarity.

6. Review the rest of the plan to see the sanitary pipe sizes.
7. Select some of the 32mm diameter pipes and change their size to **25mm** diameter. Note that the color fill of the pipes change.
8. Zoom out to see the entire building.
9. Save the project

Chapter Review Questions

1. How many elements must be selected before you can create a duct or piping system?
    a. One
    b. Two
    c. Three
    d. None need to be selected first.
2. How do you specify which type of system you want to create when the element has multiple options, such as the lavatory shown in Figure 10–81?

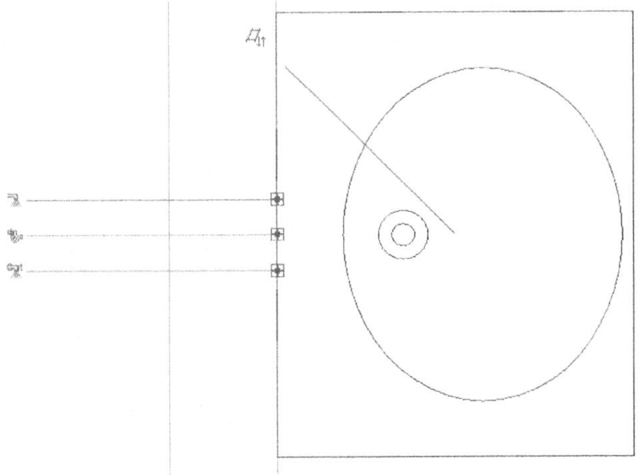

Figure 10–81

    a. Select the appropriate connector to start the system.
    b. In the contextual tab, select the appropriate system button.
    c. In the Options Bar, select the system type from the drop-down list.
    d. Select the system type from the drop-down list in the dialog box that opens when you start a system.
3. The purpose of a Base is to serve as a placeholder equipment connection point when generating an automatic layout.
    a. True
    b. False

4. Match the color of a line when generating a layout with what the color indicates.

Color	**Indicates**
a. Gold	_____ Branch
b. Blue	_____ Modeling Error
c. Green	_____ Main

5. Flex duct can be placed automatically on which of the following components of a layout?
   a. Main lines
   b. Branch lines
   c. Both
6. What is a common problem when generating layouts?
   a. Unable to edit standard solutions into custom layouts.
   b. The direction of the connector does not match how the automatic layout wants to connect to it.
   c. Cannot specify which family/type for the main and branch lines to use separately.
7. What is required before you can create an automatic ductwork layout?
   a. Duct System
   b. Air Terminals only
   c. Duct placeholders
   d. All air terminals and equipment placed for the entire project.

Command Summary

Button	Command	Location
System Tools		
	**Add to System**	• **Ribbon:** *Edit Duct or Piping System* tab>Edit Duct or Piping System panel
	**Disconnect Equipment**	• **Ribbon:** *Edit Duct or Piping Systems* tab> System Tools panel
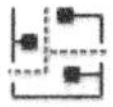	**Divide Systems**	• **Ribbon:** *Modify | Duct or Piping Systems* tab>Systems Tools panel
	**Duct (System)**	• **Ribbon:** *Modify | contextual* tab>Create Systems panel • Right-click: Create Duct System
	**Edit System**	• **Ribbon:** *Duct or Piping System* tab>System Tools panel
	**Remove from System**	• **Ribbon:** *Edit Duct or Piping System* tab>Edit Duct *or Piping* System panel and *Generate Layout* tab>Modify Layout panel
	**Select Equipment**	• **Ribbon:** *Duct or Piping System* tab>System Tools and *Edit Duct or Piping Systems* tab>Edit Duct *or Piping* System panel
	**System Browser**	• **Ribbon:** *View* tab>Windows panel, expand User Interface • **Shortcut:** <F9>
Automatic Duct or Piping Layout		
	**Edit Layout**	• **Ribbon:** *Generate Layout* tab>Modify Layout panel
	**Generate Layout**	• **Ribbon:** *Duct or Piping System* tab>Layout panel
	**Modify Base**	• **Ribbon:** *Generate Layout* tab>Modify Layout panel
	**Place Base**	• **Ribbon:** *Generate Layout* tab>Modify Layout panel
	**Remove Base**	• **Ribbon:** *Generate Layout* tab>Modify Layout panel
	**Solutions**	• **Ribbon:** *Generate Layout* tab>Modify Layout panel

Testing Systems		
	**Check Duct Systems**	• **Ribbon**: *Analyze* tab>Check Systems panel
	**Check Pipe Systems**	• **Ribbon**: *Analyze* tab>Check Systems panel
	**Show Disconnects**	• **Ribbon:** *Analyze* tab>Check Systems panel
	**Show Related Warnings**	• **Ribbon:** Modify contextual tab>Warning panel
	**System Inspector**	• **Ribbon:** (When an element in a system is selected) *Modify* contextual tab>Analysis panel

Chapter 11

Electrical Systems

Electrical systems consist of components such as lighting fixtures, electrical fixtures, fire alarms, security systems, telephone devices, and power equipment. Frequently, the various elements are connected via a power circuit or related systems. Cable trays or conduits can be added to a project, but these do not create system connections between elements.

Learning Objectives in this Chapter

- Establish electrical settings.
- Place electrical equipment, devices, and lighting fixtures.
- Create power circuits, switch systems, and other circuit systems.
- Create and modify electrical panel schedules.
- Add cable trays and conduits, including parallel conduit runs and fittings.

11.1 About Electrical Systems

Electrical systems in the Autodesk® Revit® software are circuits consisting of devices, lighting fixtures, and other electrical equipment. They are elements in a project and are added to the model using the tools in the Ribbon. There can be different types of electrical plan views based on the type of information required. A typical electrical view plan might display power, systems, or lighting layouts as shown in Figure 11–1.

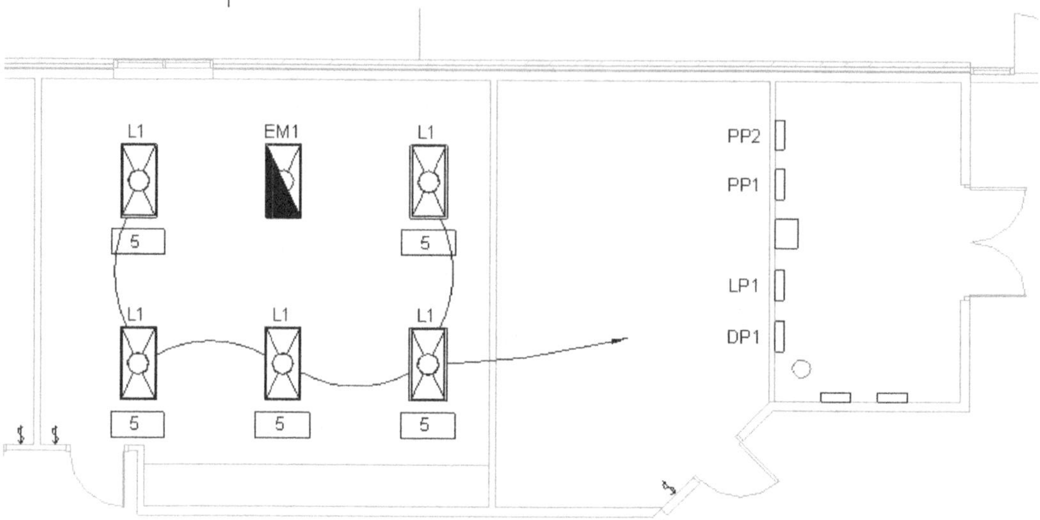

Figure 11–1

There are several steps in the process of creating an Electrical system:

1. Place electrical equipment such as distribution panels.
2. Define the Distribution System in the Properties of the electrical equipment.
3. Place electrical devices, such as receptacles and lighting fixtures. Each device represents an electrical load in the system.
4. Select an electrical device or lighting fixture, and create a power circuit for it and similar devices in the same room or area of the building.
5. Assign circuits to electrical equipment (e.g. Panel).

To make room for the Electrical tools, in the File tab, click ***Options****. In the Options dialog box, on the User Interface pane, clear the checks from* ***Systems tab: mechanical tools*** *and* ***Systems tab: piping tools****.*

The tools for creating and placing Electrical components and circuits are located in the *Systems* tab>Electrical panel, as shown in Figure 11–2.

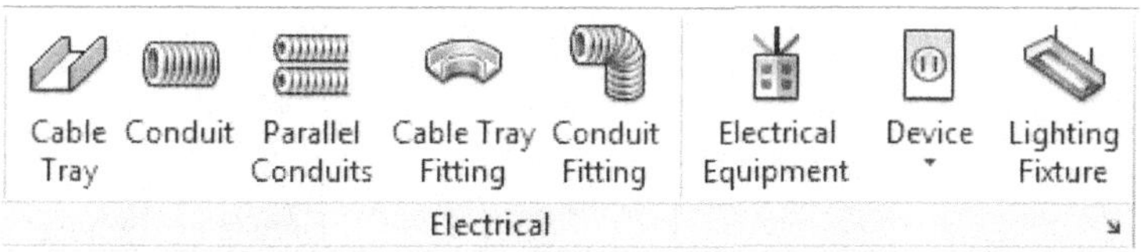

Figure 11–2

Electrical Settings

Electrical settings contain many parameters used for various electrical component placement and system/circuit creation. They include wiring parameters, voltage definitions, distribution systems, cable tray and conduit settings, load calculation settings, and circuit naming settings.

In *Manage* tab>Settings panel, expand (MEP Settings) and click (Electrical Settings), or in the *Systems* tab>Electrical panel, click (Electrical Settings), to open the Electrical Settings dialog box, as shown in Figure 11–3.

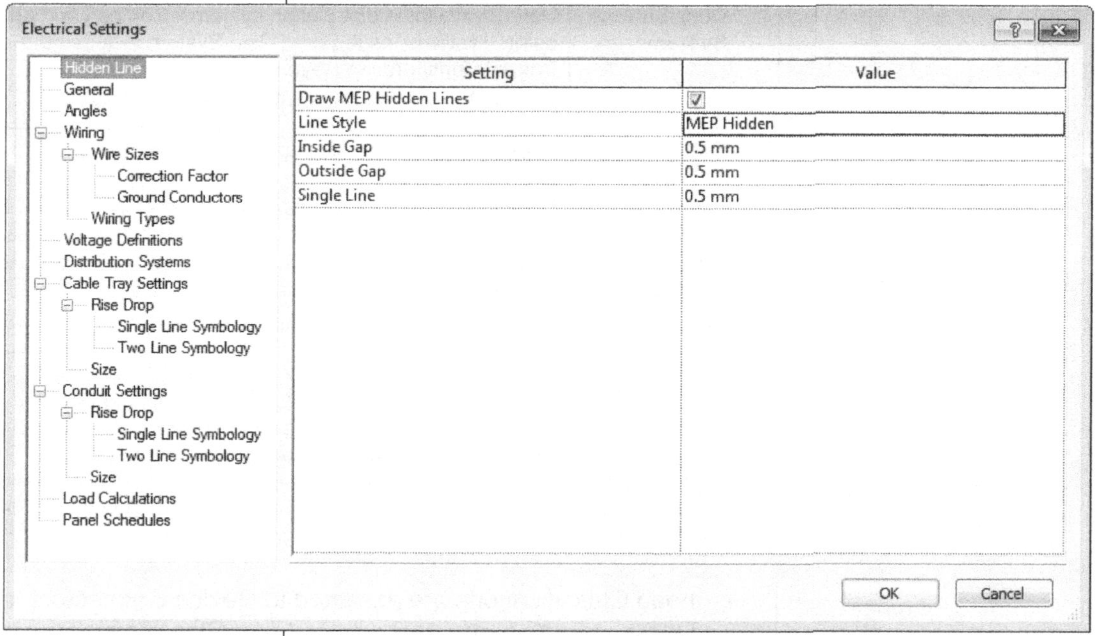

Figure 11–3

The different categories in the left pane have their own specific settings that are available when the category is selected.

Hidden Line	Settings for cable tray and conduit hidden line styles and gaps.
General	Parameters and formats for symbols and styles for various electrical component values, including phase naming. Enables you to specify the sequence in which power circuits are generated (i.e., **Numerical**, **Group by Phase**, or **Odd then Even**). You can also set the default Circuit Rating to match the country for which you are designing. Some engineers like to set this to **0** so they know which circuits they have not yet reviewed.
Angles	Enables to set angle increments or specify the use of specific angles for drawing cable trays and conduit. This is typically used to match industry standards.
Wiring	Determines how wires and wire sizes are displayed and calculated. Includes type of wires available based on material, temperature, and insulation ratings. Specifies which wire types can be used in a project.
Voltage Definitions	Lists the ranges of voltages that can be assigned to the Distribution Systems.
Distributions Systems	Defines available distribution systems. You can add and delete systems, as required. The System includes the Phase, Configuration (Wye or Delta), number of wires, and the **L-L Voltage** and **L-G Voltage** options.
Cable Tray Settings	Specifies annotative scaling for cable tray fittings and rise/drop symbology. Specifies cable tray sizes available in a project.
Conduit Settings	Specifies annotative scaling for conduit fittings, size prefix and suffix, and rise/drop symbology. Specifies conduit sizes available in a project.
Load Calculations	Specifies whether to enable load calculations for loads in spaces, and defines Load Classifications and Demand Factors. Available methods include Sum true load and reactive load, as well as Sum apparent load.
Panel Schedules	Specifies settings for spares and spaces, and for merging multi-poled circuits

- Load Classifications are assigned to Device Connectors, and Demand Factors are assigned to Load Classifications.

11.2 Placing Electrical Components

There are many different types of electrical components that can be added to a model, as shown in Figure 11–4. Components consist of panels, transformers, switches, receptacles, various communication and safety devices, and lighting fixtures. There are different commands for different types of electrical components and devices.

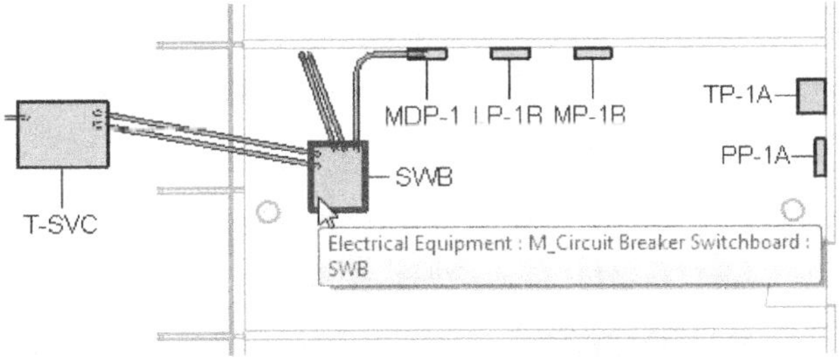

Figure 11–4

- Electrical components can be placed in any view, including plan, elevation, and 3D.
- There are three primary types of electrical components: Electrical Equipment, Electrical Devices, and Lighting Fixtures. The process of adding the components to the project is essentially the same.

Electrical Equipment

Electrical equipment includes panels and transformers, which can be placed either as hosted or unhosted components. Panels are typically hosted onto a wall, surface or flush mount, as shown in Figure 11–5, and a transformer could be placed anywhere including ceiling hung. Other electrical equipment includes motor control centers, switchboards, and generators.

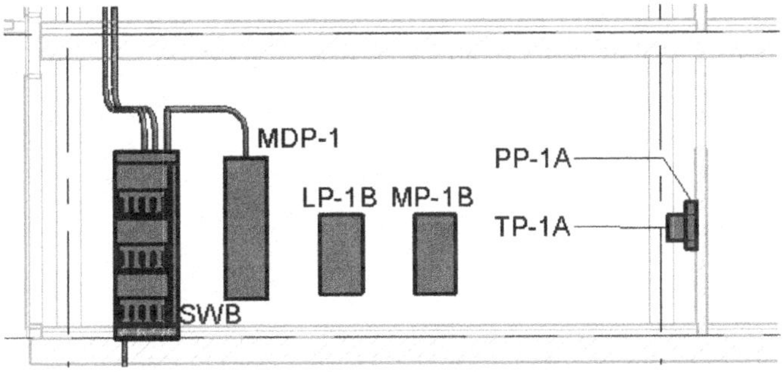

Figure 11–5

Electrical Devices

Electrical devices include a variety of devices, including receptacles, switches, telephone/communication/data terminal devices, junction boxes, nurse call devices, wall speakers, starters, smoke detectors, and fire alarm manual pull stations, shown in Figure 11–6. These devices are typically face-based components, and are often placed on a wall.

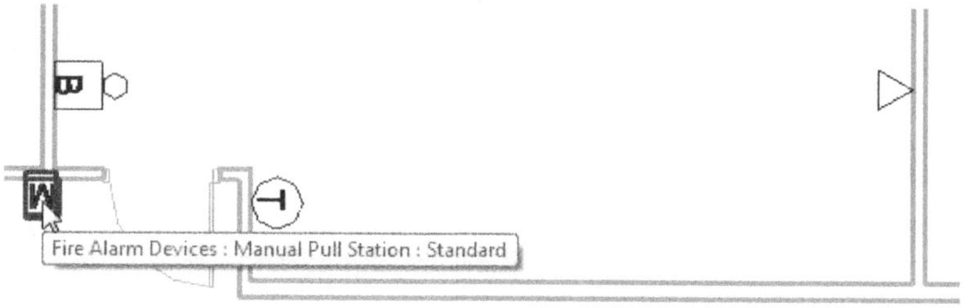

Figure 11–6

Lighting Fixtures

Most lighting fixtures are face-based components, and are therefore placed on a ceiling or on a wall. Examples of lighting fixtures are shown in Figure 11–7.

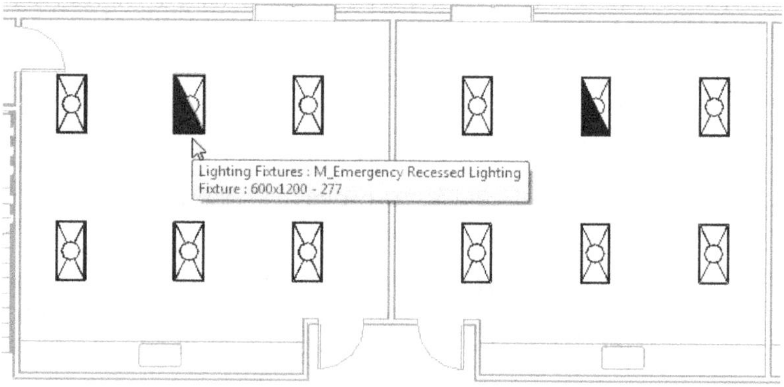

Figure 11–7

- Lighting fixtures can also be copied and monitored from a linked architectural file.

How To: Place Electrical Components

1. In the *Systems* tab>Electrical panel, click on one of the following, or type the associated shortcut:

(Electrical Equipment (EE))	Device> (Fire Alarm)
(Lighting Fixture (LF))	Device> (Nurse Call)
Device> (Electrical Fixture)	Device> (Security)
Device> (Communication)	Device> (Telephone)
Device> (Lighting (Switch))	Device> (Data)

2. In Type Selector, select the type you want to use.
3. In Properties, set any applicable parameters.

Automatically placing the tags is typically recommended for electrical equipment.

4. In the *Modify | contextual* tab>Tag panel, click (Tag on Placement) to select or clear, as required. If you have selected **Tag on Placement**, set the parameters for the tags in the Options Bar.
5. In the Placement panel, click (Place on Vertical Face), (Place on Face), or (Place on Work Plane).
    - The placement panel does not display for some components. These are placed on the current level with an offset as required.
6. Place the component. Use alignment lines, temporary dimensions, and snaps to aid placement.
7. Continue to place additional components, or click (Modify) to exit the command.

- After placing components, you can move them to a different location by clicking and dragging it to the new location, as required.

Hint: Placing Devices Directly Beside or Above Each Other

Electrical device families are model families with an embedded annotation family. This is so that the actual device box displays in sections and 3D views and a symbol displays in plan view, as shown in Figure 11–8.

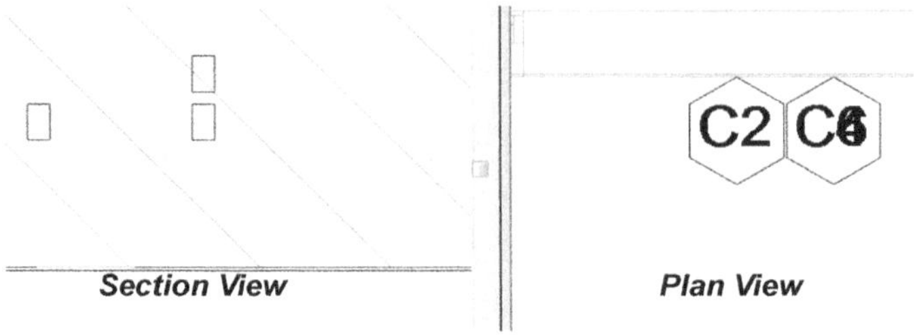

Figure 11–8

Some families do not work well if two devices need to be placed directly next to or above each other. For example, in Figure 11–9, devices that are placed correctly in a section view result in overlapping, illegible symbols in plan. Moving the symbol in the plan view also moves the device in the model.

Figure 11–9

Many offices create custom device families, which include offset parameters so that the annotation family can move separately from the model family as shown in Figure 11–10.

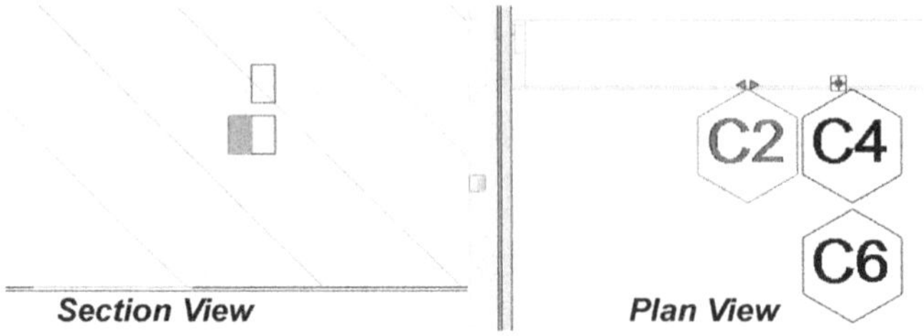

Figure 11–10

Working with Lighting Fixtures

- Hosted fixtures have an **Elevation** parameter. For example, if the fixture is being placed on a vertical face (e.g., a sconce on a wall), this value can be set to control the height above the level.

- If the fixture is being placed on a face, such as a ceiling, the **Elevation** parameter is automatically determined by the height of the light fixture, which in this case is the same as the ceiling height.

- Some fixtures have an additional **Offset** parameter. This enables you to specify that the fixture be offset from the host, such as a fluorescent fixture, which hangs below the ceiling. In this case, adjust the elevation value to reflect the new elevation of the fixture, as shown in Figure 11–11.

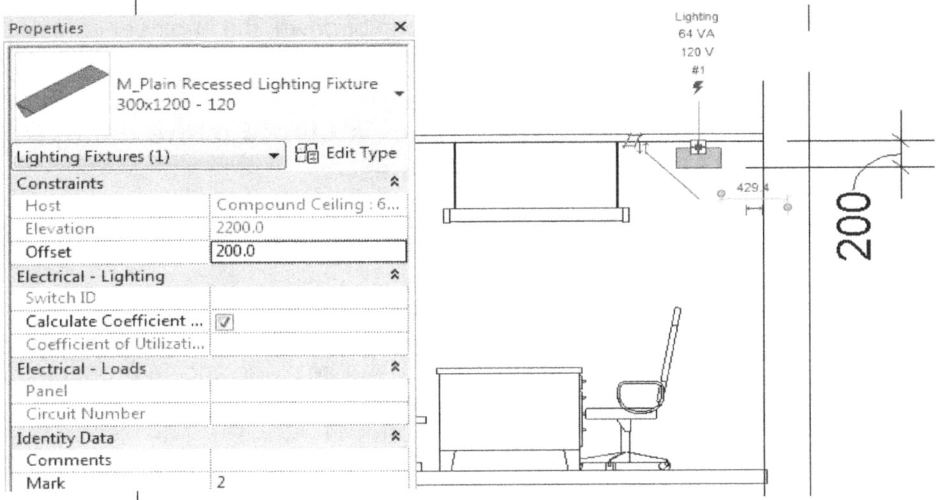

Figure 11–11

- Light fixtures that are hosted by a ceiling in a linked model move automatically with any changes that the architects make to the ceiling height. This can be an advantage of using face-based fixtures.

- If the architect deletes the ceiling and puts a new one in the linked model, the hosted lighting fixtures are orphaned and do not move with changes in the ceiling height. A warning box opens when you reload the linked model or reopen the MEP project, as shown in Figure 11–12. Use the **Coordination Monitoring** tools to address the issue.

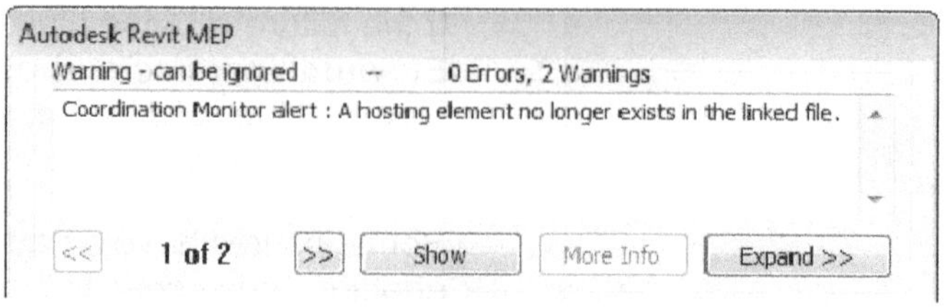

Figure 11–12

- Some firms add reference planes and place the hosted families on them instead of in the ceiling. This gives them control over the height of the families. If the architect moves the ceilings up or down, the engineer adjusts the height of the reference plane to match.

How To: Place a Light Fixture using Reference Planes

1. Cut a section through the area where you are placing the light fixtures.
2. In the *Systems* tab>Work Plane panel, click (Ref Plane).
3. Draw a reference plane at the ceiling height.
4. Select the reference plane and, in Properties, type in a name. When you select the reference plane the name displays as shown in Figure 11–13.

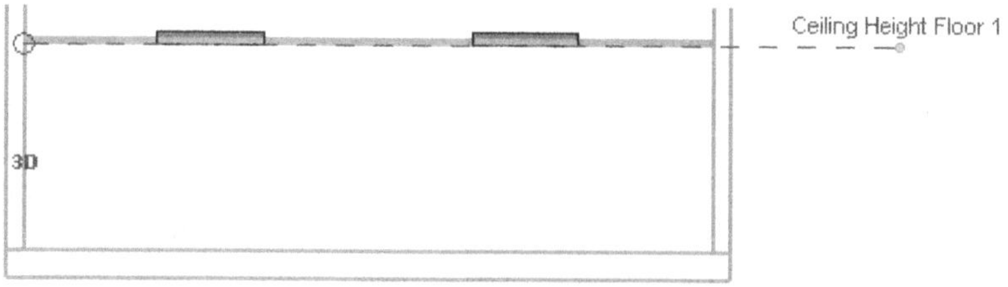

Figure 11–13

5. Switch to a ceiling plan view.
6. Start the **Lighting Fixture** command.
7. In the Type Selector, select a lighting fixture.
8. In the *Modify | Place Fixture* tab>Placement panel, click (Place on Workplane).

9. In the Work Plane dialog box, select the named reference plane you just created, as shown in Figure 11–14, and click **OK**.

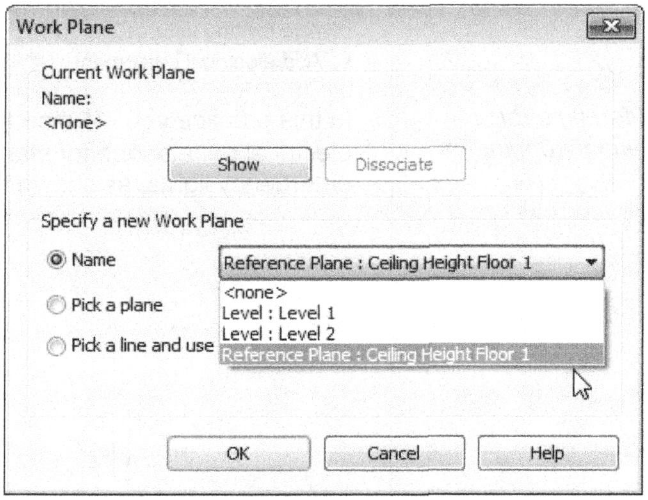

Figure 11–14

10. Add the lighting fixtures. They align to ceiling grids even though they are not hosted by the ceiling.

- Architectural light fixtures cut holes in the architectural ceiling. If the electrical engineer needs to put fixtures in a different place, they usually turn off the visibility of the linked architectural light fixtures first. This results in holes in the ceiling, as shown in Figure 11–15. To correct this issue, the engineer needs to request that the architect move the architectural lighting fixtures to the final, agreed on location.

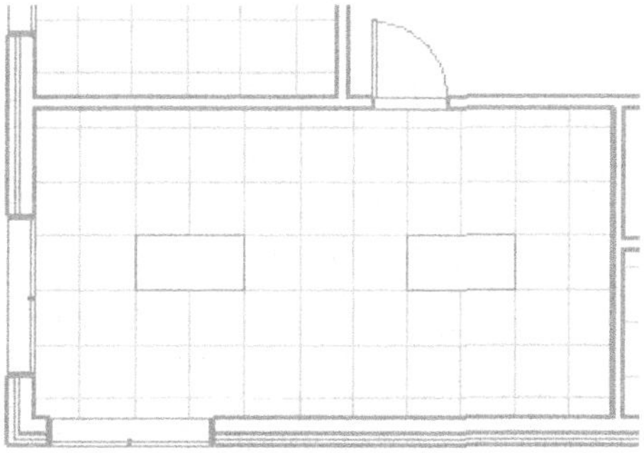

Figure 11–15

Practice 11a Place Electrical Components

Estimated time for completion: 10 minutes

Practice Objectives

- Add lighting fixtures.
- Add electrical equipment.

In this practice you will insert lighting fixtures and add two electrical panels, one for standard lights and the other for emergency lights, as shown in Figure 11–16.

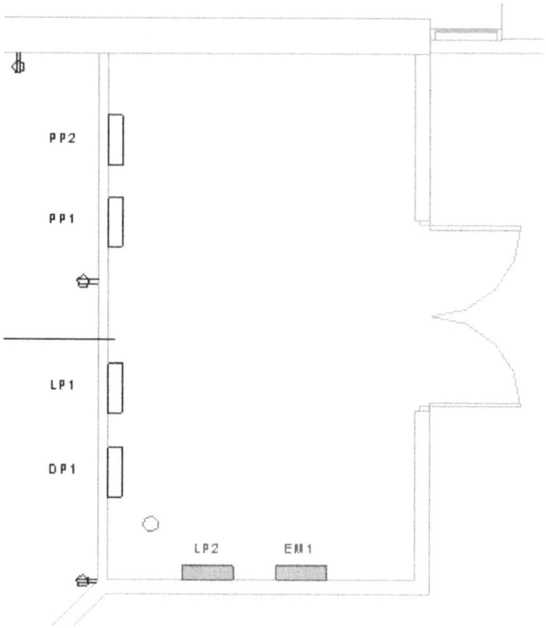

Figure 11–16

Task 1 - Add lighting fixtures.

1. In the practice files *Electrical* folder, open **MEP-Elementary-School-Electrical-M.rvt**.
2. In the *Systems* tab>Electrical panel title bar, click (Electrical Settings).
3. In the Electrical Settings dialog box, click **Distribution Systems**. Review the list of systems available (as shown in Figure 11–17) and then click **OK**.

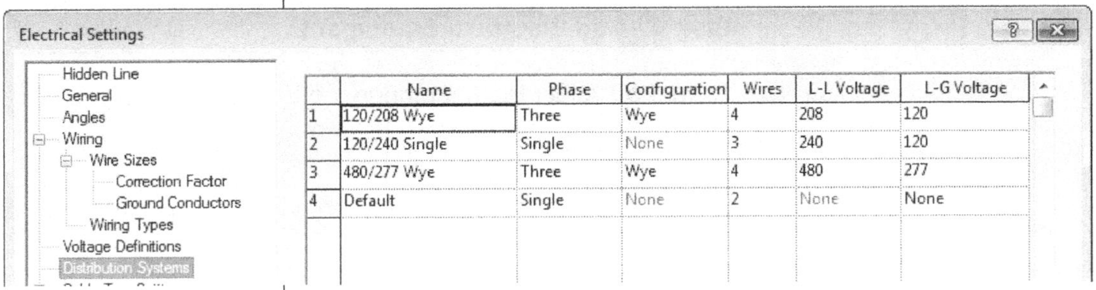

Figure 11–17

4. Open the Coordination>MEP>Ceiling Plans>**01 Electrical RCP** view and zoom to the upper left room.

5. In *Systems* tab>Electrical panel, click (Lighting Fixture).

6. In Type Selector, select **M_Troffer Light - Parabolic Rectangular: 0600x1200mm(2 Lamp) - 277V**.

7. In the *Modify | Place Fixture* tab>Placement panel, click (Place on Face).

8. Place three lighting fixtures in the upper left room. (Hint: Press <Spacebar> to rotate the fixtures before placing them.)

9. In the Type Selector, change the type to **M_Emergency Recessed Lighting Fixture: 600x1200 - 277** and place one of these lighting fixtures, as shown in Figure 11–18.

Figure 11–18

10. Click (Modify) to exit the command.

Task 2 - Add Electrical Equipment.

1. In the Project Browser, open the Electrical>Power>Floor Plans>**01 Electrical Room** view.

2. In *Systems* tab>Electrical panel, click (Electrical Equipment).

3. In the *Modify | Place Equipment*>Tag panel, click (Tag on Placement).

4. In Type Selector, select **M_Lighting and Appliance Panelboard - 480V MLO - Surface: 125 A**.

5. Place one panelboard on the bottom wall of the room, as shown in Figure 11–19. Note that the tag displays with a question mark because the name has not been added.

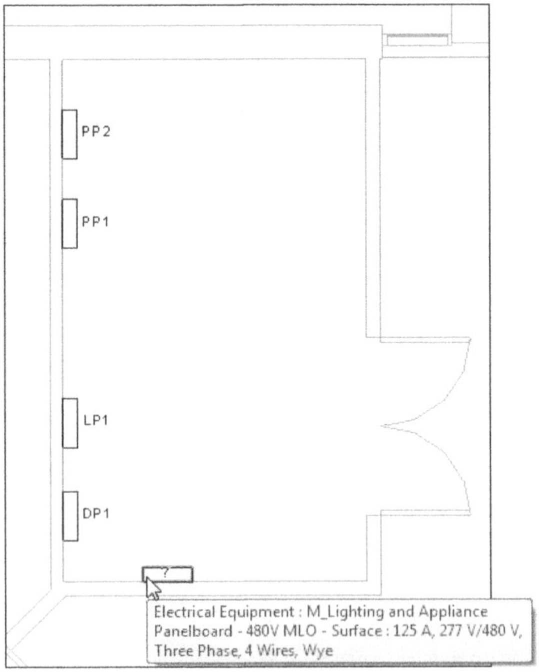

Figure 11–19

6. Click **Modify** and select the newly added panel in the active view.

7. In Properties, scroll down to the *General* area, set *Panel Name* to **LP2**, as shown in Figure 11–20.

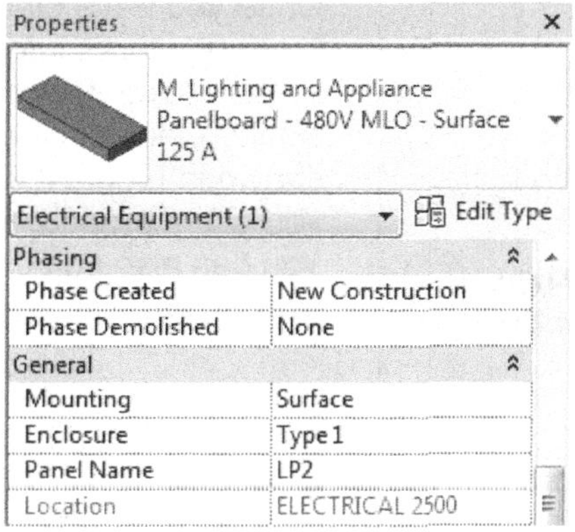

Figure 11–20

8. While still in Properties, scroll further down to the *Electrical - Circuiting* area and expand the *Distribution System* list. The only choice is **480/277 Wye** as this is the only distribution system that fits this panel.

9. Click **Modify**.

10. Start the **Electrical Equipment** command again. In the Type Selector, select **M_Lighting and Appliance Panelboard - 480V MLO- Surface: 400 A**. Place the panel beside the other one you just added.

11. Click **Modify** and double-click on the tag. Change the name of the tag to **EM1**. (Do not double-click on the tag too quickly or it will open the tag in the family editor, instead of allowing you to change the name.)

12. Select the tags for the LP2 and EM1 panels and move them above the panels, as shown in Figure 11–21.

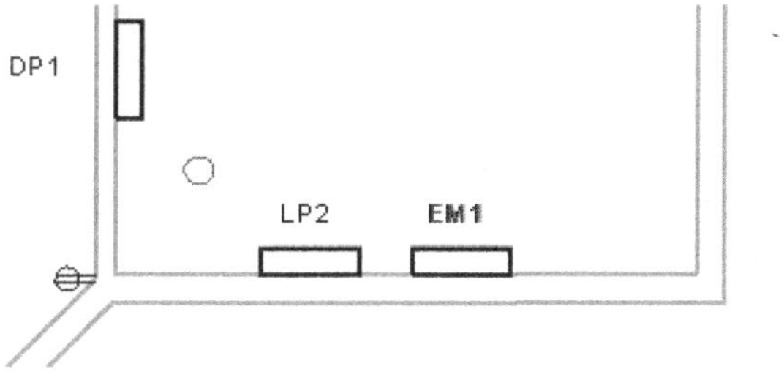

Figure 11–21

13. Save the project.

11.3 Creating Electrical Circuits

New in 2018

Once you have placed the electrical equipment, devices, and lighting fixtures into the model, you need to create the electrical system (circuit) from these components. Circuits connect the similar electrical components to form the electrical system, as shown in Figure 11–22. Once the electrical system is created, you can then add, remove, or modify any of the components. You can also edit the circuit path to establish the accurate length used in voltage drop calculations and wire sizing.

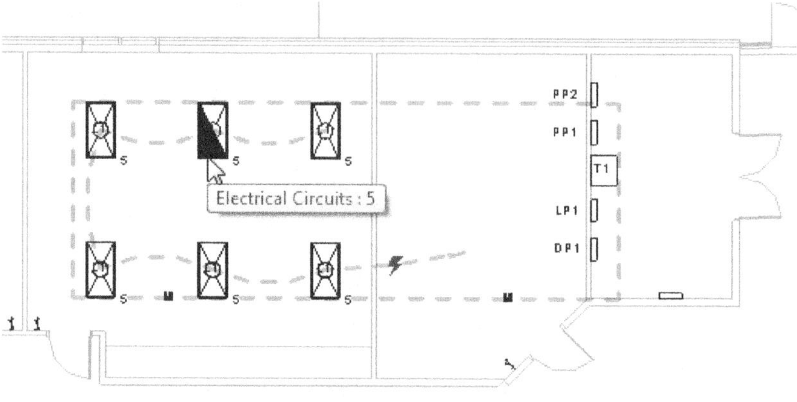

Figure 11–22

Components that are to be connected in a circuit must be of compatible voltage and distribution system.

- Circuits can be created for power, lighting, switches, data, telephones, fire alarms, nurse call or security systems, and controls. The process is similar no matter which type of circuit you are creating.
- Power systems connect compatible electrical devices and lighting fixtures in a circuit to an electrical equipment panel, as shown in Figure 11–23.

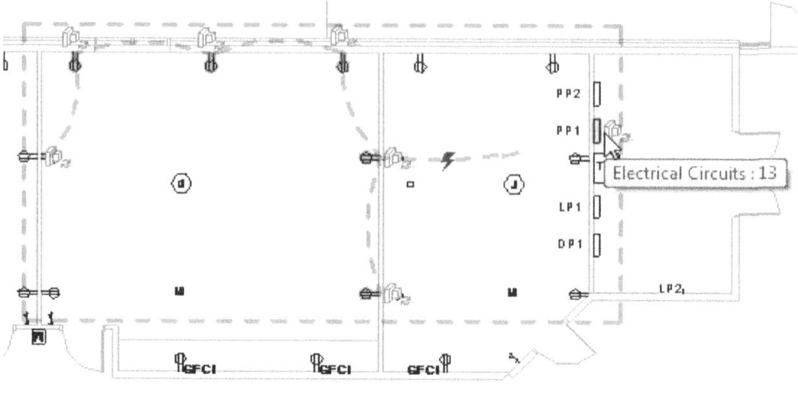

Figure 11–23

- Switch systems enable you to indicate which lights and switches are linked, as shown in Figure 11–24. This is especially useful for those cases where there are multiple lights on the same circuit that are controlled by different switches.

Linking lines are for reference only and do not plot.

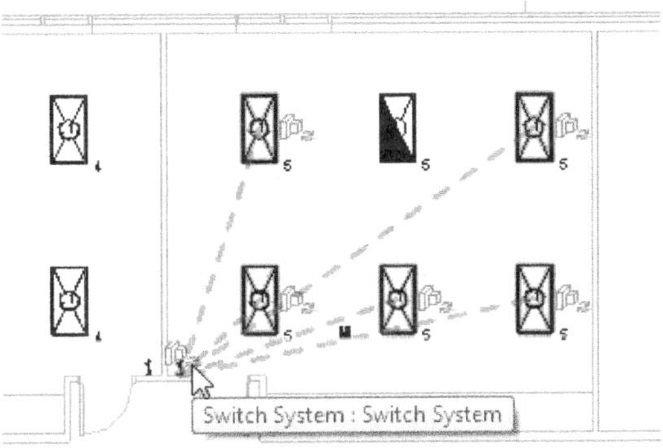

Figure 11–24

How To: Create a Circuit

1. Select at least one of the components that is to be part of the circuit.
2. In the *Modify | contextual* tab>Create Systems panel, click the related system button (i.e., (Power), (Switch), or (Data)).
3. In the *Electrical Circuits* tab>System Tools panel, either:
   - Accept the existing panel,
   - Either select a panel from the drop-down list (as shown in Figure 11–25, or select a panel in the project and click (Select Panel).

When you create a circuit, the program automatically connects to the most recently used panel in the current session of the Autodesk Revit software.

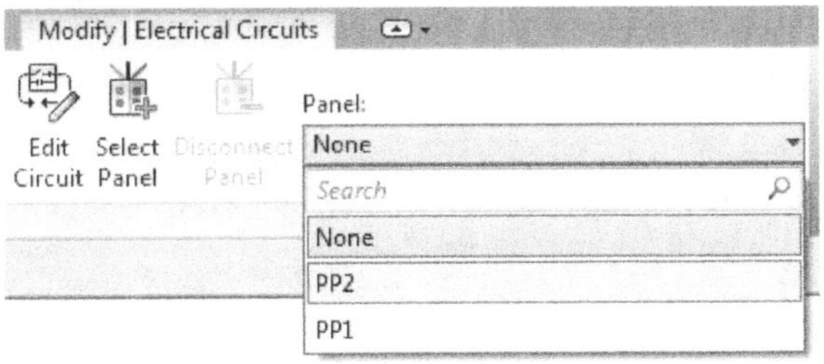

Figure 11–25

   - Switch systems are not connected to a panel.
4. In the *Electrical Circuits* tab>System Tools panel, click (Edit Circuit).

5. In the *Edit Circuit* tab>Edit Circuit panel, click (Add to Circuit) and select the other components for that circuit.

    - To remove components from a circuit, click (Remove from Circuit) and select the component.

6. Click (Finish Editing Circuit).

- If a component has more than one electrical connector, a Select Connector dialog box opens, as shown in Figure 11–26. Select the connector for which you want to make a circuit and click **OK**.

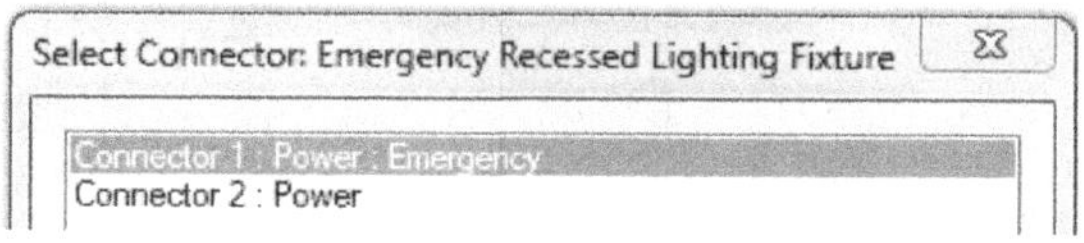

Figure 11–26

Editing Circuit Paths

You can edit circuit paths in plan or 3D views.

When you add a circuit, an automatic route is processed and the length information (used to calculate the voltage drop and wire sizing) is automatically available. Note that the results might not be what you are expecting (as shown in Figure 11–27) and you can edit the path of the circuit to ensure that it runs in the direction and height you expect, as shown in Figure 11–28. Then the length automatically updates to provide you with the correct information.

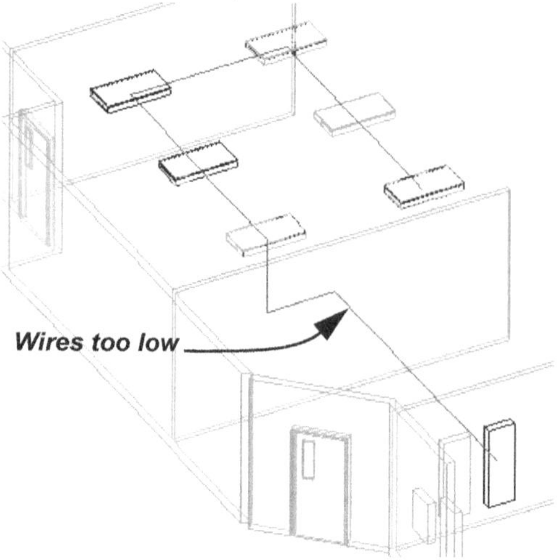

Figure 11–27

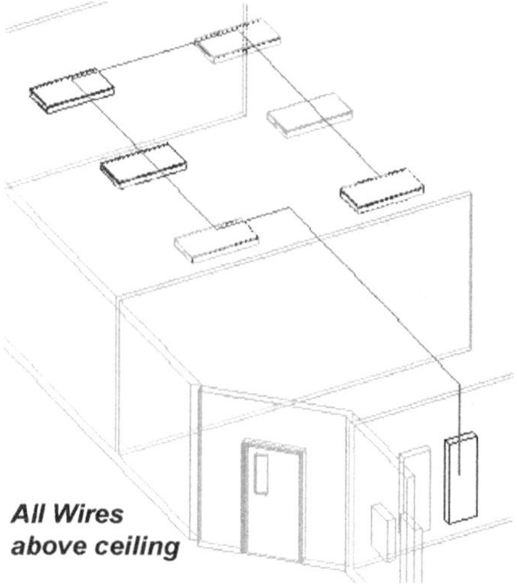

Figure 11–28

New in 2018

How To: Edit the Path of a Circuit

1. Hover the cursor over a circuit component and press <Tab> until you can select the circuit.
2. Select the *Electrical Circuits* tab in the ribbon.
3. In the System Tools panel, click (Edit Path). The Edit Path tab displays, as shown in Figure 11–29
   - The *Length* automatically updates as you make changes.
   - The *Number of Elements* in the circuit displays in the Options Bar.

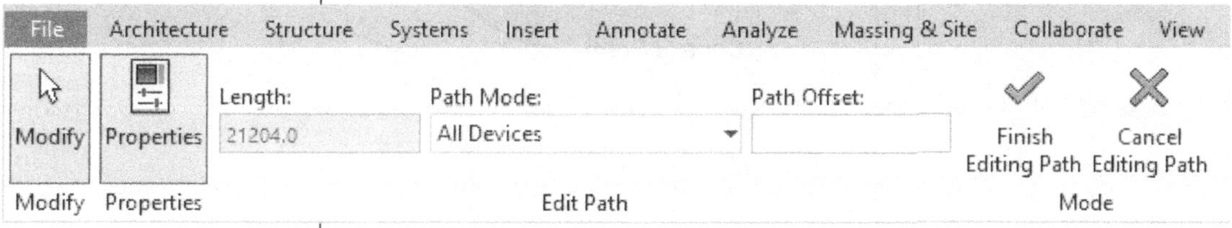

Figure 11–29

4. In the Edit Path panel, set the *Path Mode* to **All Devices**, **Farthest Device** (as shown in Figure 11–30) or **Custom** (if you have already edited the path).

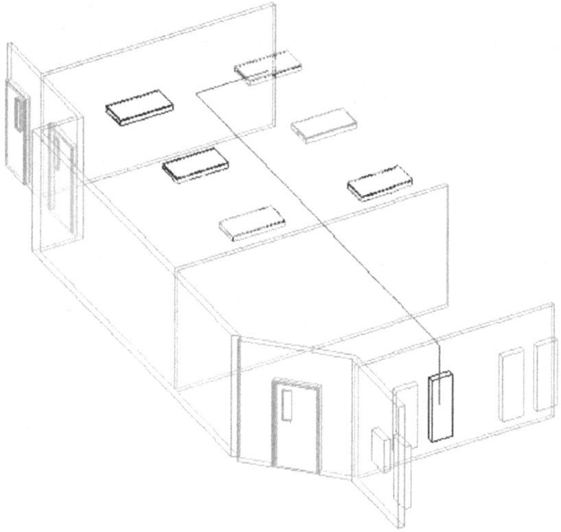

Figure 11–30

5. Change the *Path Offset* in the ribbon to modify the entire circuit path. This is especially useful to get the entire path above the ceiling.

6. Select individual circuit paths to modify the route. You can drag the path line or control points or change the path offset, as shown in Figure 11–31.

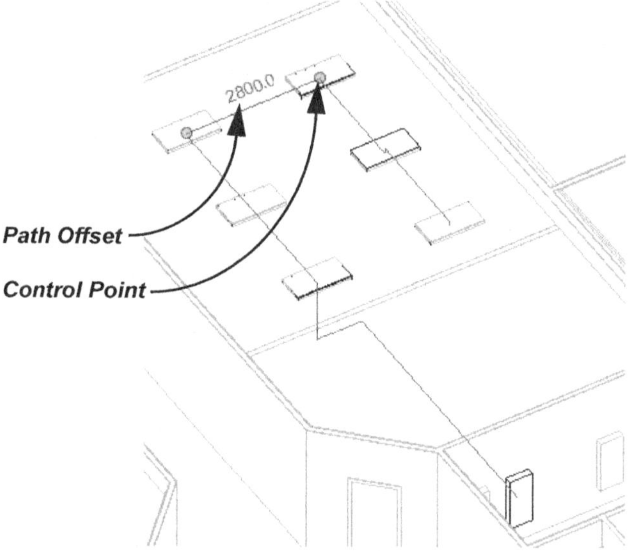

Figure 11–31

7. To add or remove control points, right-click on a control point and select **Delete Control Point** or right-click on a path line and select **Insert Control Point.**
8. When you have finished adjusting the path, in the *Edit Path* tab>Mode panel, click (Finish Editing Path)

Adding Wires

Wiring is typically schematic, frequently used in wiring plans such as that shown in Figure 11–32. You can create wires once you have added circuits.

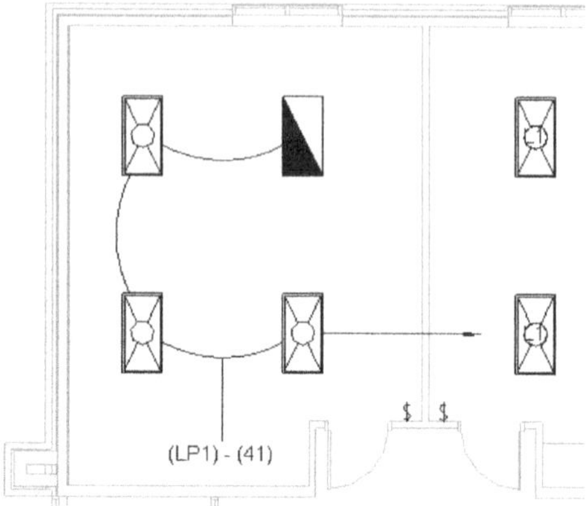

Figure 11–32

- Wires stay connected if you move a fixture, adjusting to the new location.
- Wires are view specific.
- Add conduits or cable trays to show the exact location where the wires will run.

How To: Add Wires to a View

1. Create the circuits that connect the fixtures and panel.
2. Create a duplicated view in which you want to display the wires.
3. Hover the cursor over one of the elements in the circuit. Press < Tab> to highlight the circuit and then click to select it.
4. In the *Modify | Electrical Circuits* tab>Convert to Wire panel, click (Arc Wire) or (Chamfered Wire). Alternatively, you can click on the **Generate arc** (or **chamfered**) **type wiring** control in the drawing area, as shown in Figure 11–33.

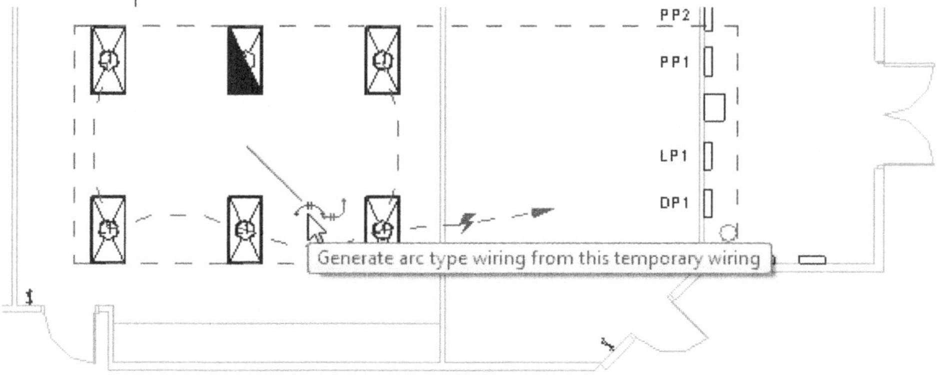

Figure 11–33

5. Click **Modify** and select the wiring. Use the controls to add, remove, and move vertices as required, as shown in Figure 11–34.

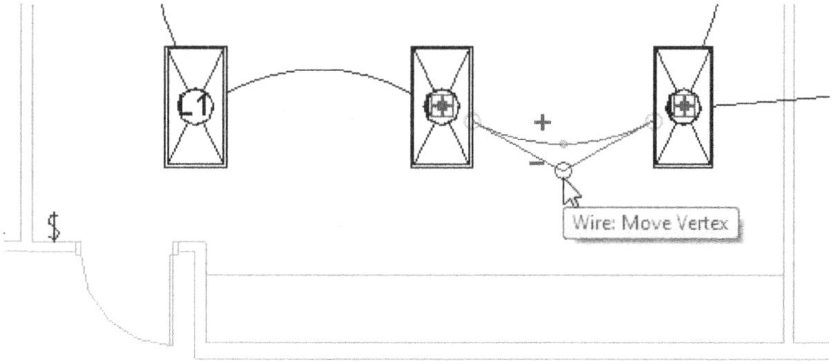

Figure 11–34

Practice 11b Create Electrical Circuits

Practice Objectives

- Create electrical circuits for standard and emergency lighting.
- Edit the Circuit Path.
- Display wire connections for a wiring plan.

Estimated time for completion: 10 minutes

In this practice you will connect light fixtures together in a power circuit. You will also create an emergency power circuit and add light fixtures to the circuit, as shown in Figure 11–35. You will edit the path of the circuit and view the changes to the length. You will also add a transformer and connect panels to it. Finally, you will display wire connections to create a wiring plan.

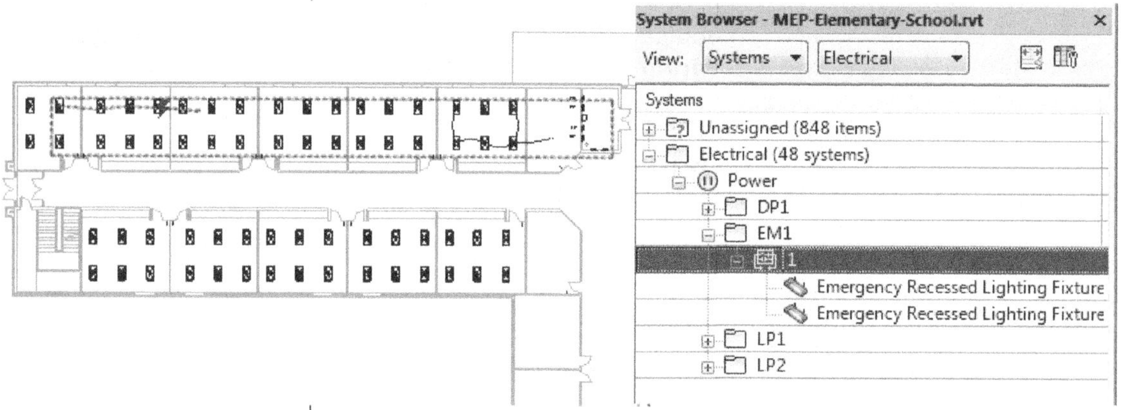

Figure 11–35

Task 1 - Create an electrical circuit system.

1. In the practice files *Electrical* folder, open **MEP-Elementary-School-Circuits-M.rvt**.
2. Open the Electrical>Lighting>Floor Plans>**01 Lighting Plan** view and zoom to the upper left room.
3. Select the upper left light and in the *Modify | Lighting Fixtures* tab>Create Systems panel, click (Power).
4. In the *Modify | Electrical Circuits* tab>System Tools panel, expand the *Panel* list, and select **LP2**.
5. In the System Tools panel, click (Edit Circuit).

6. In the *Edit Circuit* tab>Edit Circuit panel, ensure that (Add to Circuit) is selected. Select the other two standard lights in the room but not the emergency light, as shown in Figure 11–36.

Do not select the emergency light fixture until the next step.

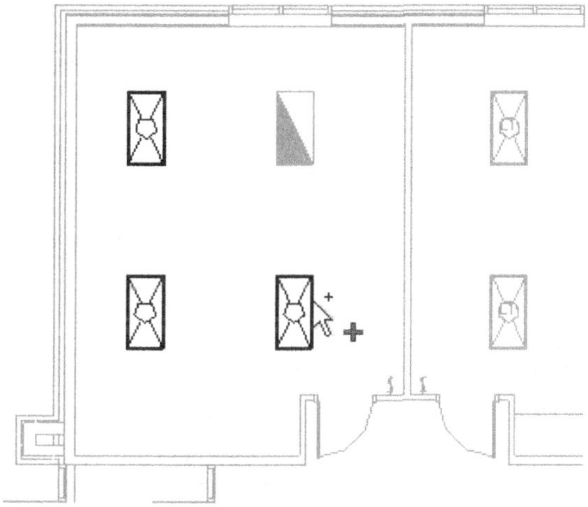

Figure 11–36

7. While still in the same circuit, select the emergency light. In the Select Connector dialog box, select **Connector 2: Power** and click **OK**.

8. Click (Finish Editing Circuit).

9. Open the System Browser.(**Hint:** Press <F9>.)

10. In the System Browser, in the *View* area, filter the list by **Systems** and **Electrical**, as shown in Figure 11–37.

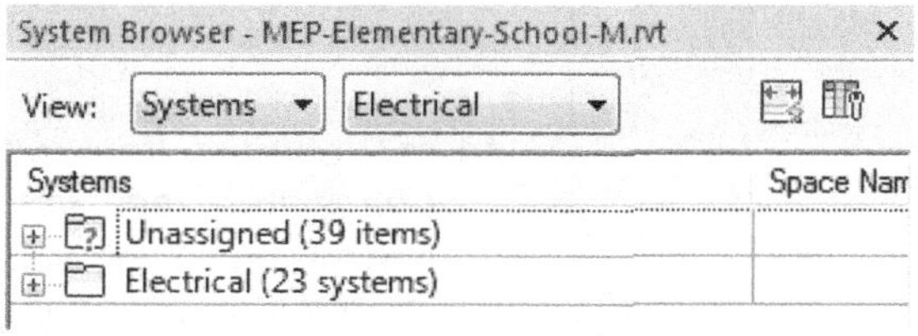

Figure 11–37

11. In the view, select one of the Troffer light fixtures which you just circuited.

12. In the Systems Browser, expand the highlighted nodes to display the selected light fixtures, as shown in Figure 11–38. Only one light is highlighted in the project.

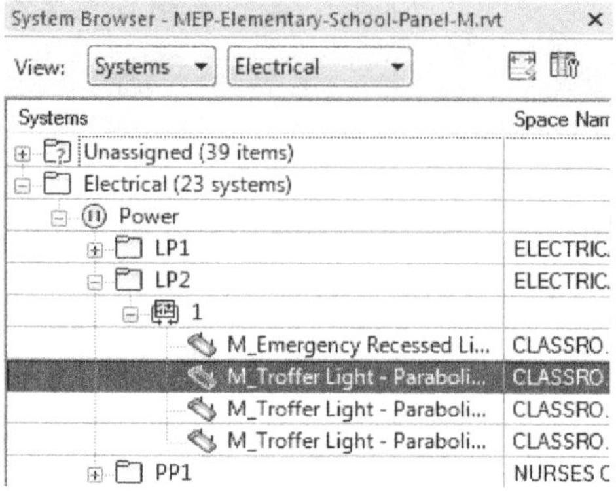

Figure 11–38

13. In the Systems Browser, select the related circuit **1**. The selection in the view changes to display the circuit outline, as shown in Figure 11–39.

The extents box surrounds the system and the panel with connecting arcs to each fixture in this circuit.

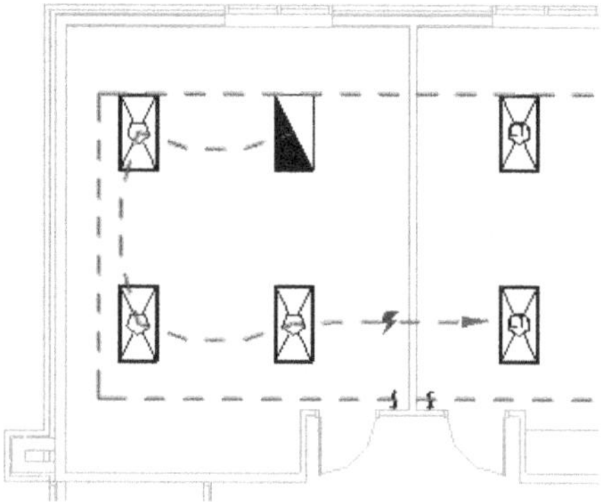

Figure 11–39

14. In Properties, review the circuit properties. In the *Electrical - Loads* area, the *Circuit Number* should be set to **1** as it is the first circuit added to this panel. This field is editable in the related panel schedule.

15. Scroll down to note the *Length* of the circuit. This is read only, but updates when you edit the circuit path.

16. Clear the selection.

17. Select the **M_Emergency Recessed Lighting Fixture**. In the Systems Browser, note that the Unassigned node highlights as well. This is because the fixture has two connectors, and you have only circuited one of them. This will be resolved in the next task.

18. Save the project

Task 2 - Add and move emergency lighting fixtures to an emergency circuit and panel.

1. Continue working in the **01 Lighting Plan** view.

Because there is now only one uncircuited connector on this fixture, the Select Connector dialog box does not open.

2. Select the emergency lighting fixture added earlier.

3. In the *Modify | Lighting Fixtures* tab>Create Systems panel, click (Power).

4. In the *Modify | Electrical Circuits* tab>Systems Tools panel, expand the Panel drop-down list and select **EM1**.

5. With the same light selected, in the Systems Tool panel, click (Edit Circuit).

6. In the *Edit Circuit* tab>Edit Circuit panel, verify that (Add to Circuit) is selected.

7. Select the emergency fixture in the room directly to the right of the room that you are working in.

8. In the Select Connector dialog box, select **Connection 1: Power : Emergency**.

   - Many emergency lighting fixtures have a battery backup. This is the method used when the fixtures are connected to an emergency circuit.

9. Click (Finish Editing Circuit).

10. Save the project.

Task 3 - Edit the Circuit Path

1. Hover the cursor over one of the standard light fixtures in the same room and press <Tab> to select the circuit.
2. In the *Modify | Electrical Circuits* tab>System Tools panel click (Edit Path).
3. In the Edit Path panel, note the *Length*, *Path Mode*, and *Path Offset* as shown in Figure 11–40.

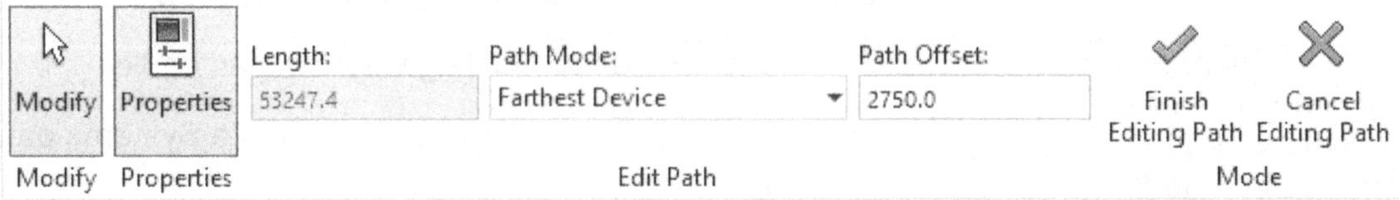

Figure 11–40

4. Change the *Path Mode* to **All Devices** and the *Path Offset* to **3000mm**. The *Length* also changes, as shown in Figure 11–41.

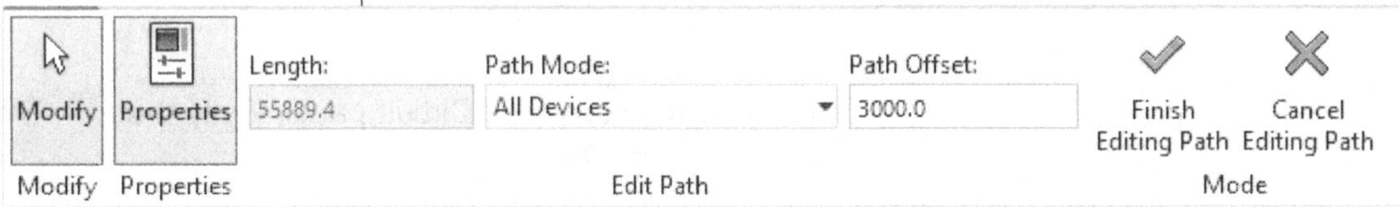

Figure 11–41

5. Modify the individual circuit path lines as desired.
6. Click (Finish Editing Path).
7. Save the project.

Task 4 - Add a step down transformer.

1. Open the **01 Electrical Room** view.
2. In the *Systems* tab>Electrical panel, click (Electrical Equipment).
3. In the Type Selector, select **M_Dry Type Transformer - 480-208Y120 - NEMA Type 3R: 15 kVA**.

4. Place the transformer between PP1 and LP1, as shown in Figure 11–42.

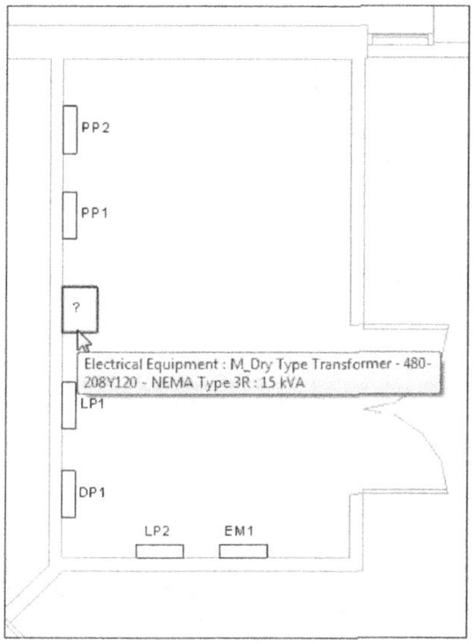

Figure 11–42

5. Click **Modify** and select the new transformer.

6. In Properties, in the *General* area, set the *Panel Name* to **TR1-1**.

7. In the *Electrical - Loads* area, set the *Secondary Distribution System* to **120/208 Wye**.

The transformer has a primary and secondary distribution system; both are set as properties of the transformer.

8. In the *Electrical - Circuiting* area, verify that the *Distribution System* is set to **480/277 Wye**.

9. Click **Modify** and select the panel **PP1**.

10. In the *Modify | Electrical Equipment* tab>Create Systems panel, click (Power).

11. In the *Modify | Electrical Circuits* tab>System Tools panel, click (Select Panel).

12. Select the new TR1-1 panel. The load from panel PP-1 is now assigned to the transformer TR1-1

13. Clear the selection and select **TR1-1**.

14. Right-click on the **Power** connector and select **Create Power Circuit.**

15. In the System Tools panel, in the *Panel* list, select **DP1**. The system displays as shown in Figure 11–43.

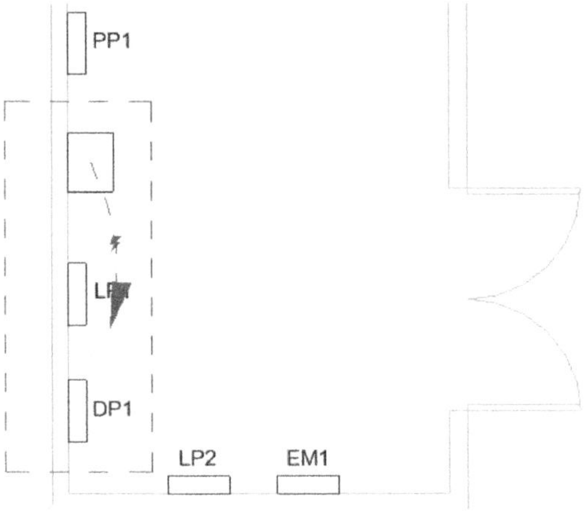

Figure 11–43

16. Release the selection.

17. Save the project.

Task 5 - Create a Wiring Plan

1. Duplicate (with Detailing) the Electrical>Lighting>Floor Plans>**01 Lighting Plan** view and name it **01 Wiring Plan**.

2. Zoom into the area near the electrical room but the nearby classroom should also be displayed.

3. Hover the cursor over one of the lights in the classroom and press <Tab> to highlight the circuit. Click to select it, as shown in Figure 11–44.

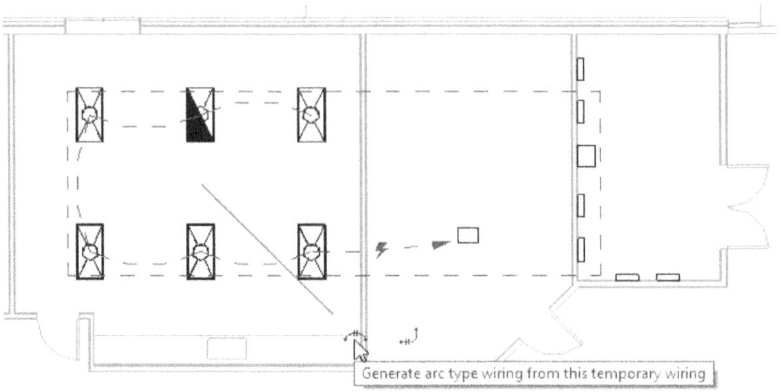

Figure 11–44

4. In the *Modify | Electrical Circuits* tab>Convert to Wire panel, click  (Arc Wire). Alternatively, click on the Generate arc type wiring control in the drawing, as shown in Figure 11–44.
5. Wire displaying schematic routing of the circuit is automatically drawn. Adjust the wire arcs manually by pulling the add, remove, and move vertex controls, as shown in Figure 11–45.

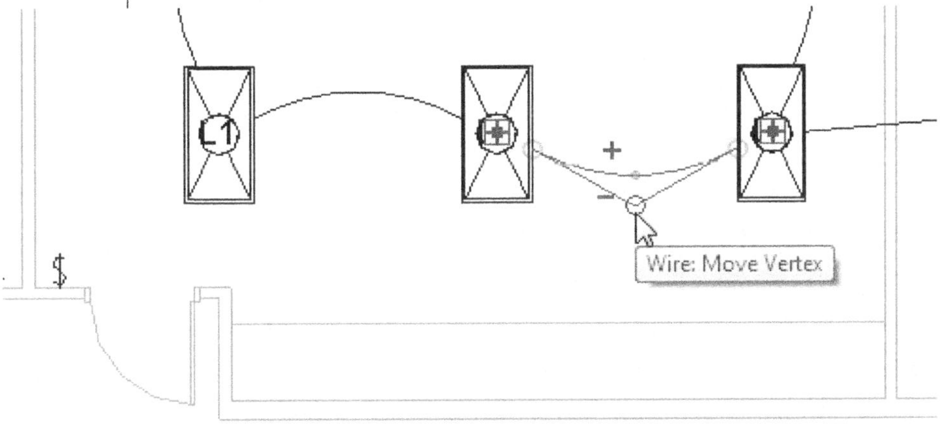

Figure 11–45

The fixture that remains in place is in the linked file.

6. Move a fixture and observe that the wire stays connected adjusting to the new fixture location. Wires are view specific.
7. Undo the move.
8. Continue adding the schematic wiring throughout the north wing of the building. Add additional circuits, if required.
9. If you have time you can also create Switch Systems for the same wing.
10. Save the project.

11.4 Setting up Panel Schedules

Panel schedules are used to concisely present information about panels and the components connected to them through their corresponding circuits. They also list the load values of these circuits, as shown in Figure 11–46. The Autodesk Revit software creates panel schedules and automatically update them as the panel's circuits change.

Branch Panel: LP1

Location: ELECTRICAL 2500A
Supply From:
Mounting: Surface
Enclosure: Type 3R

Volts: 480/277 Wye
Phases: 3
Wires: 4

A.I.C. Rating:
Mains Type:
Mains Rating: 100 A
MCB Rating: 400 A

Notes:

CKT	Circuit Description	Trip	Poles	A		B		C		Poles	Trip	Circuit Description	CKT
1	Lighting - Dwelling Unit CLASSROOM 1509	20 A	1	496 VA	496 VA					1	20 A	Lighting - Dwelling Unit CLASSROOM 1507	2
3	Lighting - Dwelling Unit CLASSROOM 1505	20 A	1			496 VA	496 VA			1	20 A	Lighting - Dwelling Unit CLASSROOM 1503	4
5	Lighting - Dwelling Unit CLASSROOM 1501	20 A	1					496 VA	496 VA	1	20 A	Lighting - Dwelling Unit CLASSROOM 1508	6
7	Lighting - Dwelling Unit CLASSROOM 1506	20 A	1	496 VA	496 VA					1	20 A	Lighting - Dwelling Unit CLASSROOM 1504	8
9	Lighting - Dwelling Unit CLASSROOM 1502	20 A	1			496 VA	496 VA			1	20 A	Lighting - Dwelling Unit CLASSROOM 1500	10
11	Lighting - Dwelling Unit CLASSROOM 2009	20 A	1					496 VA	496 VA	1	20 A	Lighting - Dwelling Unit CLASSROOM 2007	12
13	Lighting - Dwelling Unit CLASSROOM 2005	20 A	1	496 VA	496 VA					1	20 A	Lighting - Dwelling Unit CLASSROOM 2003	14
15	Lighting - Dwelling Unit CLASSROOM 2001	20 A	1			496 VA	496 VA			1	20 A	Lighting - Dwelling Unit CLASSROOM 2008	16
17	Lighting - Dwelling Unit CLASSROOM 2006	20 A	1					496 VA	496 VA	1	20 A	Lighting - Dwelling Unit CLASSROOM 2004	18
19	Lighting - Dwelling Unit CLASSROOM 2002	20 A	1	496 VA	496 VA					1	20 A	Lighting - Dwelling Unit CLASSROOM 2000	20
21	Lighting - Dwelling Unit CLASSROOM 5009	20 A	1			496 VA	496 VA			1	20 A	Lighting - Dwelling Unit CLASSROOM 5008	22
23	Lighting - Dwelling Unit CLASSROOM 5004	20 A	1					496 VA	496 VA	1	20 A	Lighting - Dwelling Unit CLASSROOM 5003	24
25	Lighting - Dwelling Unit CLASSROOM 5000	20 A	1	496 VA	496 VA					1	20 A	Lighting - Dwelling Unit CLASSROOM 5010	26
27	Lighting - Dwelling Unit CLASSROOM 5007	20 A	1			496 VA	496 VA			1	20 A	Lighting - Dwelling Unit CLASSROOM 5006	28
29	Lighting - Dwelling Unit CLASSROOM 5002	20 A	1					496 VA	496 VA	1	20 A	Lighting - Dwelling Unit CLASSROOM 5001	30
31	Lighting - Dwelling Unit CLASSROOM 4509	20 A	1	496 VA	496 VA					1	20 A	Lighting - Dwelling Unit CLASSROOM 4508	32
33	Lighting - Dwelling Unit CLASSROOM 4504	20 A	1			496 VA	496 VA			1	20 A	Lighting - Dwelling Unit CLASSROOM 4503	34
35	Lighting - Dwelling Unit CLASSROOM 4500	20 A	1					496 VA	496 VA	1	20 A	Lighting - Dwelling Unit CLASSROOM 4510	36
37	Lighting - Dwelling Unit CLASSROOM 4507	20 A	1	496 VA	496 VA					1	20 A	Lighting - Dwelling Unit CLASSROOM 4506	38
39	Lighting - Dwelling Unit CLASSROOM 4502	20 A	1			496 VA	496 VA			1	20 A	Lighting - Dwelling Unit CLASSROOM 4501	40
41	Spare	0 A	1					0 VA					42
			Total Load:	6944 VA		6944 VA		5952 VA					
			Total Amps:	25 A		25 A		21 A					

Legend:

Load Classification	Connected Load	Demand Factor	Estimated Demand	Panel Totals	
Lighting	3840 VA	100.00%	3840 VA		
Lighting - Dwelling Unit	16000 VA	47.19%	7550 VA	Total Conn. Load:	19840 VA
				Total Est. Demand:	11390 VA
				Total Conn.:	24 A
				Total Est. Demand:	14 A

Figure 11–46

Creating Panel Schedules

Panel schedules can be created for each panel in the model, and it can be created anytime before or after circuits are created for the panel. Once created, panel schedules are listed in the Project Browser, in the **Panel Schedule** node, as shown in Figure 11–47.

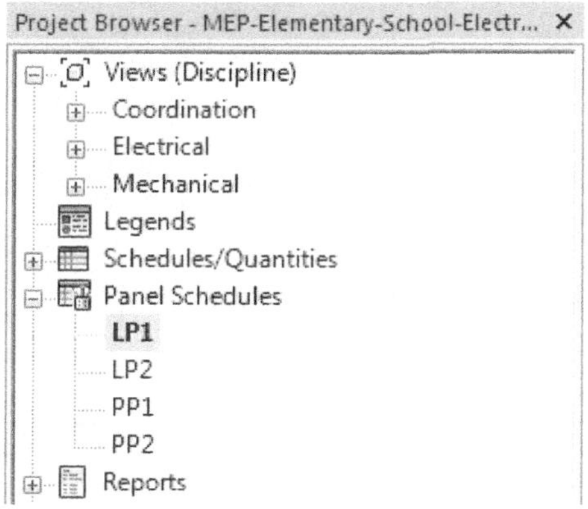

Figure 11–47

How To: Create a panel schedule

If a panel schedule has already been created for the selected equipment, the command is grayed out.

1. Select the panel for which you want to create the panel schedule.
2. In the *Modify | Electrical Equipment* tab>Electrical panel, expand (Create Panel Schedule) and click either (Use Default Template or (Choose a Template).

   A new panel schedule is created. Its view opens, and is listed in the Project Browser.

- Panel schedules can be placed on sheets for construction documentation.
- Panel Schedule Templates specify the formating and information displayed in the schedule. They can be created and edited. In the *Manage* tab>Settings panel, expand (Panel Schedules Templates) and click (Manage Templates) or (Edit at Template).

Modifying Panel Schedules

Circuits in a panel schedule can be rearranged, locked, grouped, or renamed. You can also balance loads across phases and add spares to the panel.

How To: Modify a Panel Schedule

1. In the panel schedule view, select the particular circuit(s) or empty slot(s) that you want to modify.
2. In the *Modify Panel Schedule* tab, click the particular command that you want to conduct:

Icon	Command	Function
	**Change Template**	Opens a dialog box where you can choose from a list of available templates.
	**Rebalance Loads**	Rearranges the panels circuits to redistribute the loads evenly across each phase.
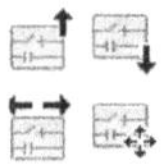	**Move Up, Down, Across, To**	Moves the selected circuit up, down, across, or to a new slot on the circuit panel without disturbing the other circuit locations.
	**Assign/Remove Spare/Space**	Assigns a slot as either a spare or a space (and are automatically locked), or removes a spare or space from a slot.
	**Lock/Unlock**	Locks or unlocks circuits, spares, or spaces in a specific slot location.
	**Group/Ungroup**	Groups single-pole circuits/spares together to act as a multi-pole circuit (or ungroups them).
	**Update Names**	Updates the names of the circuits on panel schedules.
	**Edit Font**	Opens the Edit Font dialog box where you can select a font and modify the font size, style, and color.
	**Horizontally Align and Vertically Align**	Select the alignment of the text in the selected cells

Practice 11c Set Up Panel Schedules

Practice Objective

- View and create panel schedules.

Estimated time for completion: 10 minutes

In this practice you will view an existing electrical panel schedule, shown in Figure 11–48. You will also create a new panel schedule and add a power system that connects to that panel.

Branch Panel: LP1

Location: ELECTRICAL 2500A
Supply From:
Mounting: Surface
Enclosure: Type 3R

Volts: 480/277 Wye
Phases: 3
Wires: 4

Notes:

CKT	Circuit Description	Trip	Poles	A		B		C		Pole
1	Lighting - Dwelling Unit CLASSROOM 1509	20 A	1	400 VA	400 VA					1
3	Lighting - Dwelling Unit CLASSROOM 1505	20 A	1			400 VA	400 VA			1
5	Lighting - Dwelling Unit CLASSROOM 1501	20 A	1					400 VA	400 VA	1
7	Lighting - Dwelling Unit CLASSROOM 1506	20 A	1	400 VA	400 VA					1
9	Lighting - Dwelling Unit CLASSROOM 1502	20 A	1			400 VA	400 VA			1
11	Lighting - Dwelling Unit CLASSROOM 2009	20 A	1					400 VA	496 VA	1
13	Lighting - Dwelling Unit CLASSROOM 2005	20 A	1	496 VA	496 VA					1
15	Lighting - Dwelling Unit CLASSROOM 2001	20 A	1			496 VA	496 VA			1
17	Lighting - Dwelling Unit CLASSROOM 2006	20 A	1					496 VA	496 VA	1

Figure 11–48

Task 1 - Viewing and creating panel schedules.

1. In the practice files *Electrical* folder, open **MEP-Elementary-School-Panel-M.rvt**.
2. In the Project Browser, expand the **Panel Schedules** node and double-click on the **LP1** panel schedule to open it.
3. Select circuit **39**, and note its description **Lighting - Dwelling Unit CLASSROOM 4502**.
4. In the *Modify Panel Schedule* tab>Circuits panel, click  (Move Across). It switches place with circuit **40** on the right (**Lighting - Dwelling Unit CLASSROOM 4501**).

5. Continue to move it up, down, or across, and then **Lock** it and try to move others near it. The locked one will not move.

6. Select an empty circuit in the panel schedule.

7. Click (Assign Spare) and a Spare is inserted into that circuit. Note that it is automatically **Locked**, but you can unlock it and move it if required.

8. Close Panel Schedule **LP1**.

Task 2 - Create a panel schedule.

1. Open the Electrical>Power>**01 Electrical Room** view.

2. Select electrical panel **LP2**.

3. In the *Modify | Electrical Equipment* tab>Electrical panel, expand (Create Panel Schedules) and click (Use Default Template).

4. The Panel Schedule **LP2** is created and automatically opened, as shown in Figure 11–49. It is also listed in the Panel Schedules node in the Project Browser. There are no values assigned to the schedule.

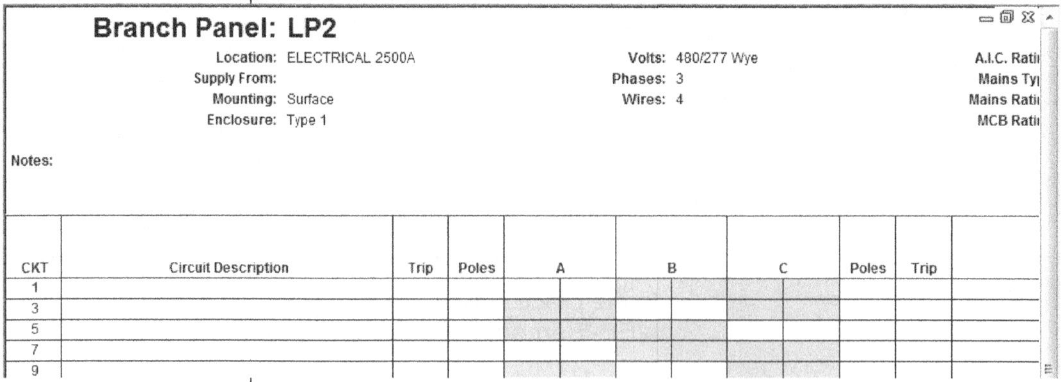

Figure 11–49

5. Open the Electrical>Power>**01 Power Plan** view.

6. Select one of the Ceiling Occupancy Sensors, as shown in Figure 11–50.

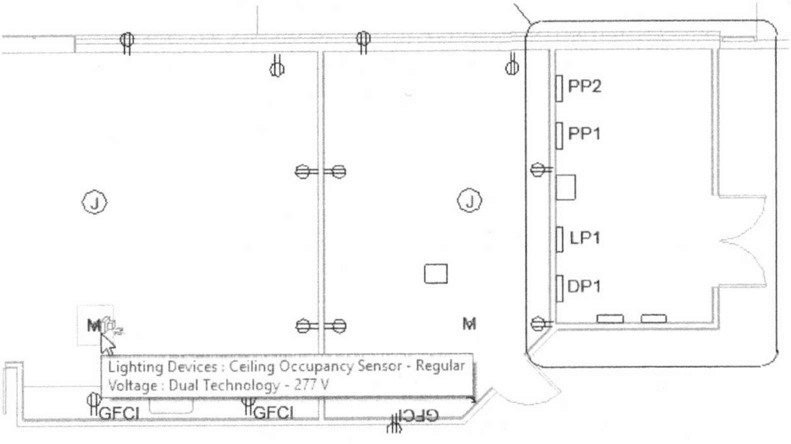

Figure 11–50

7. Right-click and select **Select All Instances>Visible in View**.

8. In the *Modify | Lighting Devices* tab>Create Systems panel, click (Power).

9. In the *Modify | Electrical Circuits* tab>System Tools panel, expand the Panel drop-down list and select **LP2**.

10. Open the Panel Schedule LP2. Note that the items are added to the *Circuit Description*, as shown in Figure 11–51.

CKT	Circuit Description	Trip	Poles	A	
1	Other Room 1509, 1507, 1505, 1503, 1501, 2501, ...	20 A	1	0 VA	
3					
5					
7					
9					
11					

Figure 11–51

11. Save the project.

11.5 Adding Cable Trays and Conduit

Cable tray and conduit, as shown in Figure 11–52, hold electrical wiring either for power or data. The wiring that connects electrical equipment, devices, and lighting fixtures is schematic. Cable tray and conduit are not directly connected to the components in the same way that ducts and pipes are.

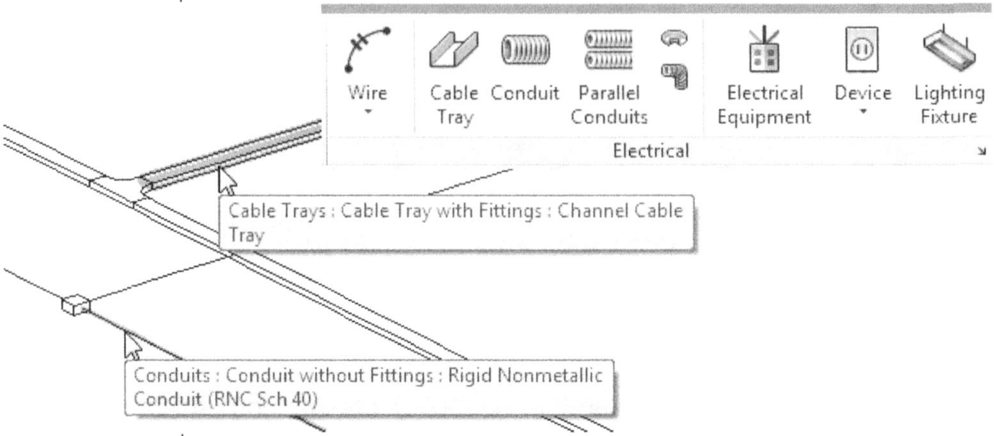

Figure 11–52

- The commands to create and place cable trays, conduits, and their appropriate fittings, are located in the *Systems* tab>Electrical panel, as shown in Figure 11–52.
- Cable trays, conduits, and fittings can be placed in any view, including plan, elevation, and 3D.

How To: Add Cable Tray or Conduit

1. In the *Systems* tab>Electrical panel, click (Cable Tray) or (Conduit).
2. In Type Selector, select a type to insert. You can select a type that includes fittings, or a type that does not include fittings.
3. In the Options Bar, for Cable Tray, set the *Width*, *Height*, *Offset* (as shown in Figure 11–53), tagging options, and *Bend Radius*.

Figure 11–53

For Conduit, set the *Diameter*, *Offset* (as shown in Figure 11–54), and tagging options.

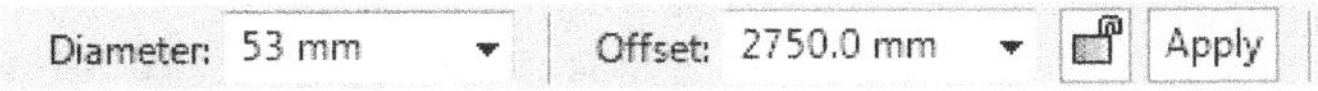

Figure 11–54

- Using (Lock/unlock Specified Elevation) enables the locked segment elevations to maintain their current elevation. However, they cannot connect to segments on different elevations.
- To draw a vertical segment, specify a new *Offset* value in the Options Bar and click **Apply**.

4. In the *Modify | Place Cable Tray (Conduit)* tab>Tag panel, toggle (Tag on Placement) off or on as required.
5. Set the appropriate Placement Tools.
6. In the drawing, click at the required location to begin the cable tray or conduit run.
7. Move to a second location and click to place the other end point of the cable tray or conduit. Continue to click at other points to create additional cable tray segments starting from the last end point. Fittings are automatically added where required.
8. Click (Modify) to end and exit the command.

- In the *Modify | Place Cable Tray (Conduit)* tab>Placement Tools panel, click (Automatically Connect) if you want a cable tray or conduit to connect to a lower segment and put in all of the right fittings as shown in the background in Figure 11–55. Turn it off if you want to draw a tray that remains at the original elevation as shown in the foreground in Figure 11–55.

*When you snap to a connector, if **Automatically Connect** is not on, any changes in height and size are applied with the appropriate fittings.*

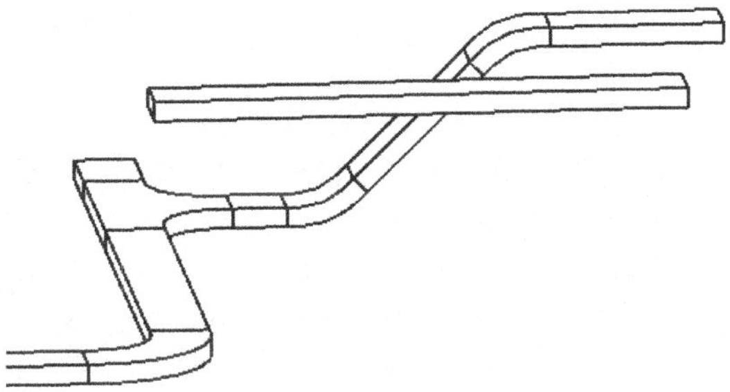

Figure 11–55

- To connect a conduit to a cable tray, start the conduit segment on a cable tray, regardless of elevation.

- For conduit, the **Placement Tools** option, (Ignore Slope to Connect) draws conduit directly from a higher point to a lower point without any fittings, as shown on the right in Figure 11–56. If the option is off, then the conduit does not slope but bends down at the point of connection, as shown on the left in Figure 11–56.

Ignore Slope ***Allow Slope***

Figure 11–56

Cable Tray and Conduit With and Without Fittings

The process of placing cable tray and conduit is the same whether you select a type with fittings (separate elbows and tees) or a type without fittings (in the field the elements are bent to create curves and bends). In both cases, the software adds fitting components, but the one with fittings includes options to create tees and crosses, as shown on the left in Figure 11–57. The type without fittings does not, as shown on the right in Figure 11–57.

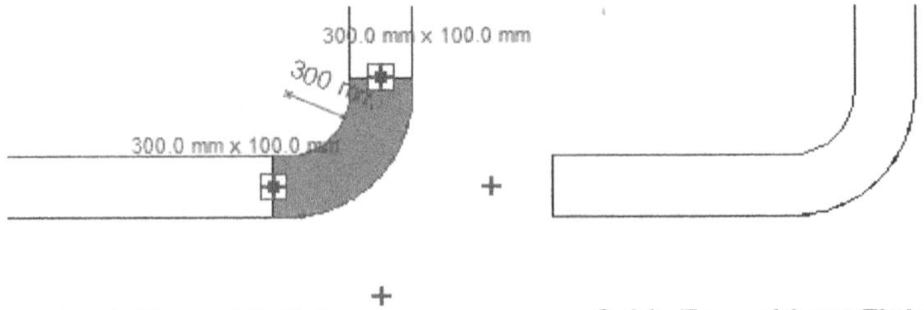

Cable Tray with Fittings ***Cable Tray without Fittings***

Figure 11–57

- The without fittings type also displays as a continuous element without lines between the straight segments and the fittings. It can use the special Conduit Runs or Cable Tray Runs schedules to schedule each run for a real-life length of conduit that is going to be used at the site.

Cable Tray and Conduit Placement Options

	**Justification Settings**	Opens the Justification Setting dialog box where you can specify the default settings for the **Horizontal Justification**, **Horizontal Offset**, and **Vertical Justification**.
	**Inherit Elevation**	An on/off toggle. If the tool is toggled on and you start drawing a cable tray/conduit by snapping to an existing element, the new cable tray/conduit takes on the elevation of the existing one regardless of what is specified, as shown in Figure 11–58.
	**Inherit Size**	An on/off toggle. If the tool is toggled on and you start drawing a cable tray/conduit by snapping to an existing element, the new cable tray/conduit takes on the size of the existing one regardless of what is specified, as shown in Figure 11–58.

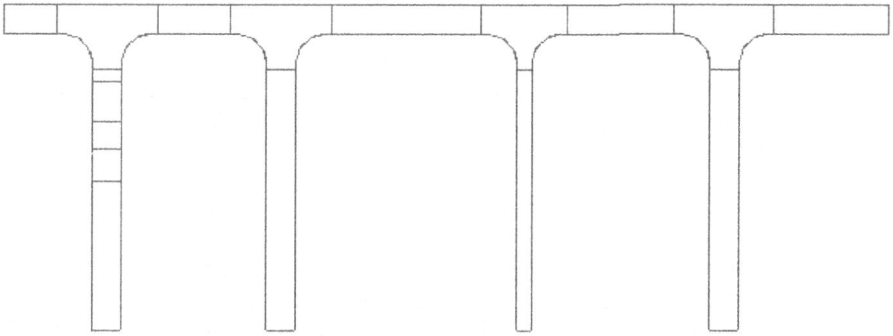

Figure 11–58

Creating Parallel Conduit Runs

The **Parallel Conduits** tool facilitates the creation of conduit runs parallel to an existing run, as shown in Figure 11–59. This saves time because only one run needs to be laid out, and the tool generates the parallel runs for you.

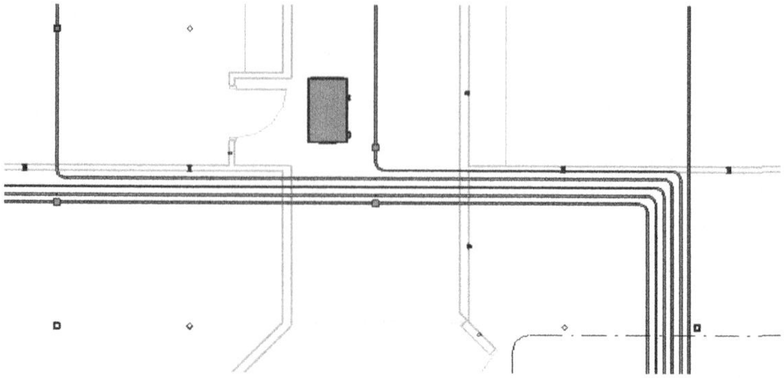

Figure 11–59

- Parallel conduit can be created in plan, section, elevation, and 3D views.

How To: Create Parallel Conduit Runs

1. Create the initial single run of conduit as required.
2. In the *Systems* tab>Electrical panel, click (Parallel Conduits).
3. In the *Modify | Place Parallel Conduits* tab>Parallel Conduits panel, set the options as required (see below).
4. Hover the cursor over the existing conduit and press <Tab> to select the existing run.
   - If you do not press <Tab>, the parallel conduit is only created for the single piece of existing conduit.
5. When the preview displays as required, click to create the parallel runs.
   - The preview and resulting parallel conduit varies depending on which side of the existing run you hover the cursor.

Parallel Conduit Creation Options

	**Bend Radius**	Parallel runs use the same bend radius as the original.
	**Concentric Bend Radius**	The bend radius of the parallel runs varies in order to remain concentric to the original run. This option results in concentric bend radii only when used with parallel conduit types without fittings. For conduit types with fittings, it gives the same result as the Same Bend Radius option.
n/a	**Horizontal Number**	The total number of parallel conduit runs in the horizontal direction.
n/a	**Horizontal Offset**	The distance between parallel conduit runs in the horizontal direction.
n/a	**Vertical Number**	The total number of parallel conduit runs in the vertical direction.
n/a	**Vertical Offset**	The distance between parallel conduit runs in the vertical direction.

- In section and elevation views, horizontal refers to parallel to the view (visually up, down, left or right from the original conduit). Vertical creates parallel conduit runs perpendicular to the view, in the direction of the user.

Modifying Cable Tray and Conduit

Cable tray and conduit can be modified using a variety of standard modifying tools. You can also change type, modify the justification, and (in the case of conduits) ignore slope to connect.

You can modify cable tray and conduit using universal methods by making changes in Properties, in the Options bar, and by using temporary dimensions, controls, and connectors. Modify tools, such as **Move**, **Rotate**, **Trim/Extend**, and **Align** enable you to place the elements in the correct locations.

Often a change using these tools automatically applies the correct fittings. For example, in Figure 11–60, the *Edit End Offset* control is changed from **2800mm** on the left to **2500mm** on the right and the appropriate cable tray fittings are automatically placed to facilitate the change in elevation.

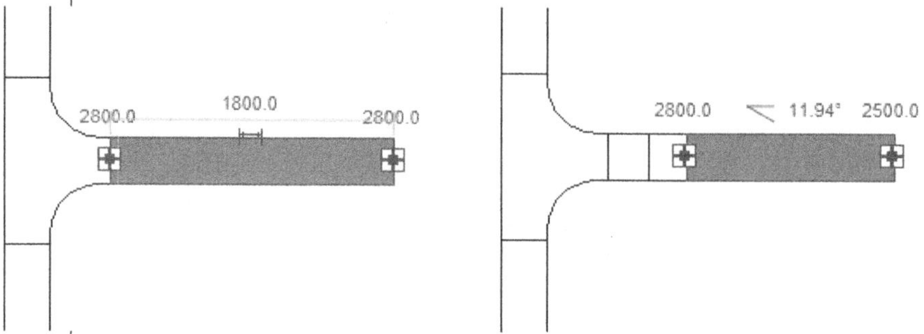

Figure 11–60

How To: Change the Type of Cable Tray and Conduit Runs

1. Select the cable tray or conduit run. Ensure that you filter out everything except related elements and fittings.
2. In the *Modify | Multi-Select* tab>Edit panel, click (Change Type).
3. In the Type Selector, select a new type of conduit or cable tray. This changes the cable tray or conduit and also any related fittings. For example, as shown in Figure 11–61, a solid bottom cable tray is changed to a ladder cable tray.

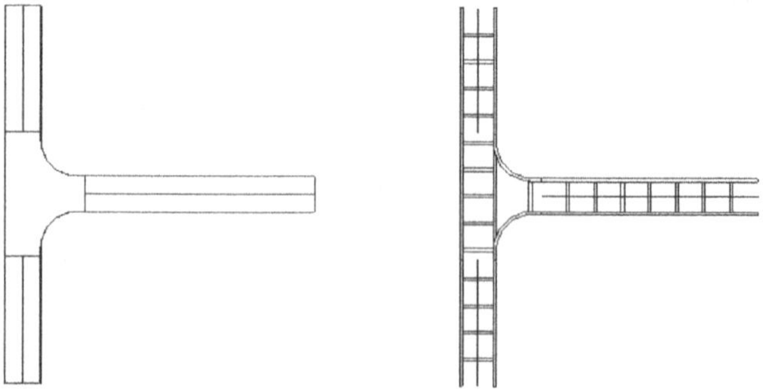

Figure 11–61

Modifying the Justification

If a cable tray or conduit run has different sizes along its run, you can modify the justification of the cable tray or conduit, as shown in Figure 11–62.

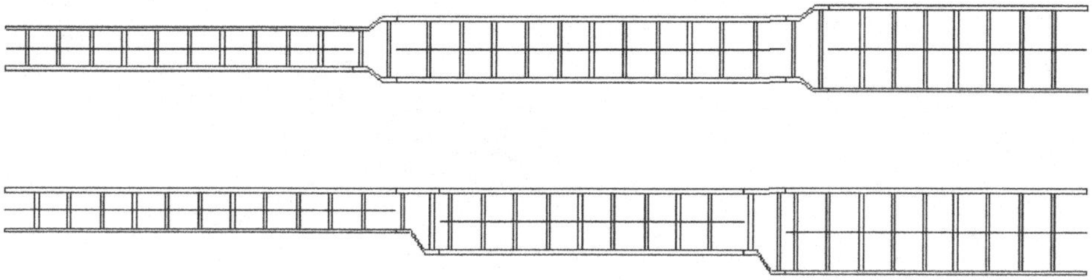

Figure 11–62

- While you can justify conduit, it is not typically required.

How To: Modify Cable Tray Justifications

1. Select the cable tray run.
2. In the *Modify | Multi-Select* tab>Edit Panel, click (Justify).
3. To specify the point on the cable tray you want to justify around, in the *Justification Editor* tab>Justify panel, click (Control Point) to cycle between the end point references. The alignment location displays as an arrow, as shown in Figure 11–63.

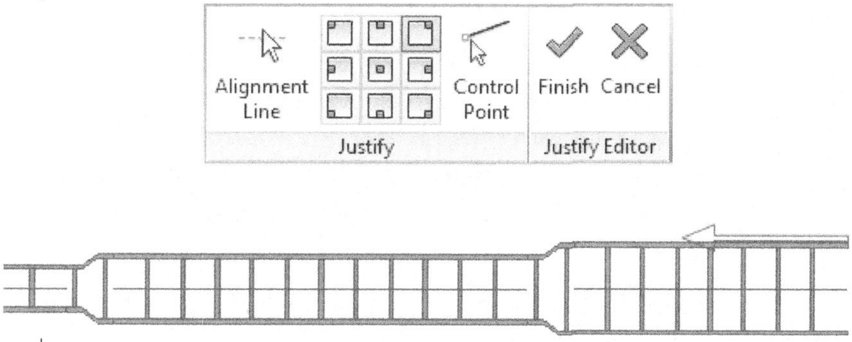

Figure 11–63

4. To indicate the required alignment, either click one of the nine alignment buttons in the Justify panel, or in a 3D view, use (Alignment Line) to select the required dashed line, as shown in Figure 11–64.

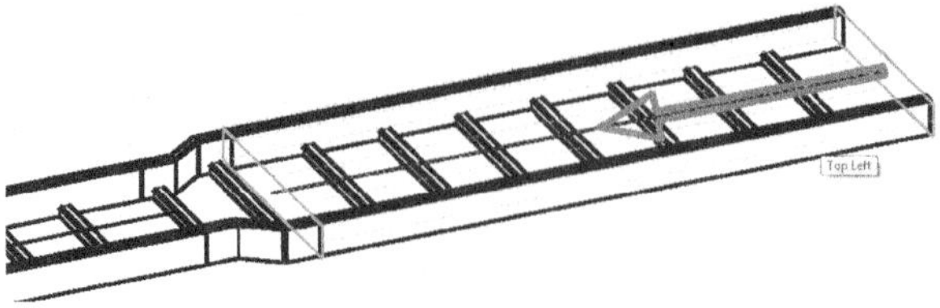

Figure 11–64

5. In the Justification Editor, click (Finish).

Adding Fittings

Revit MEP software automatically adds fittings to cable tray and conduit segments during their creation. It is also possible to manually add cable tray and conduit fittings to any existing segment or segment run. You can also use the controls on the fittings to modify the type, as shown in Figure 11–65.

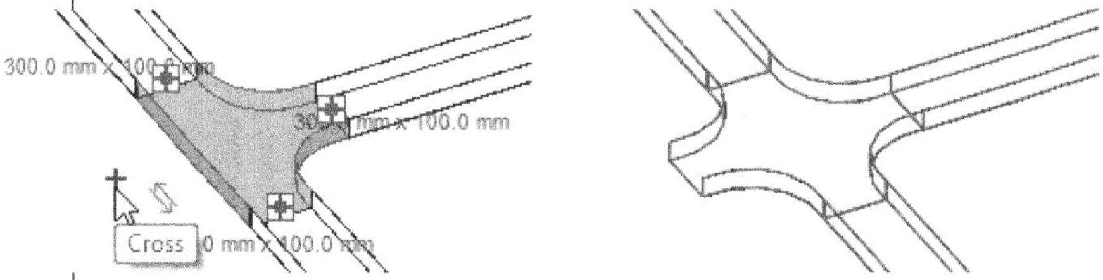

Figure 11–65

- Only Cable Tray and Conduit types with fittings display **+** to turn elbows into tees and tees into crosses.

How To: Manually add a Cable Tray or Conduit Fitting to a plan view

1. Open the view in which you are going to place the fitting.
2. In the *Systems* tab>Electrical panel, click either (Cable Tray Fitting) or (Conduit Fitting).
3. In the Type Selector, select the appropriate type you want to place.
4. In Properties, verify that the *Level* and *Offset* values are set as required.
5. Click in the view where you want to place the fitting.
6. Click (Modify) to end and exit the command.

11.6 Testing Electrical Layouts

These tools along with schedules based on spaces and lighting fixture properties can be used to help you perform lighting analysis.

As you are working with electrical circuits, cable trays, and conduits, the **Show Disconnects** (shown in Figure 11–66) and **Check Circuits** tools can help you find areas that might need to be corrected.

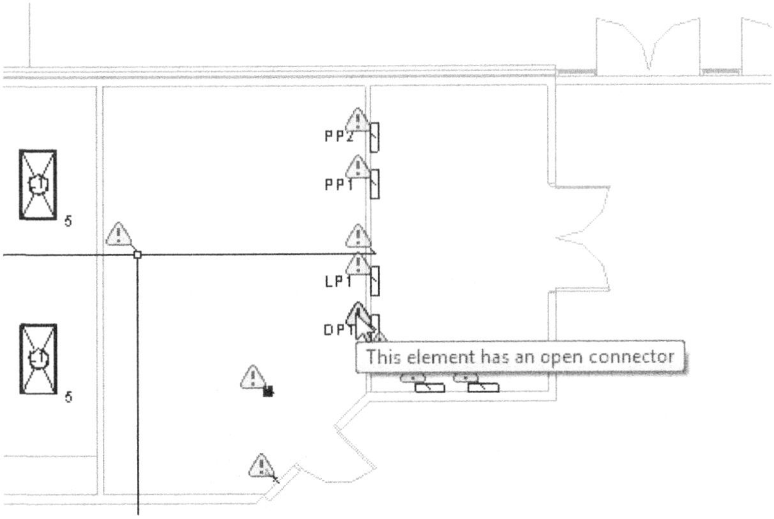

Figure 11–66

Often, these warnings are corrected as you continue working in a circuit and complete the full connection. However, some need to be corrected before the circuit works as required.

Hint: Displaying Only the MEP Analysis Panels

If you are using a copy of Autodesk Revit that has not been optimized for MEP, it is helpful to turn off the Structural Analysis tools so that you can see the full MEP analysis panels. Expand the *File* tab and click **Options**. In the Options dialog box, in the User Interface panel, in *Tools and analysis*, clear **Structure analysis and tools**, as shown in Figure 11–67.

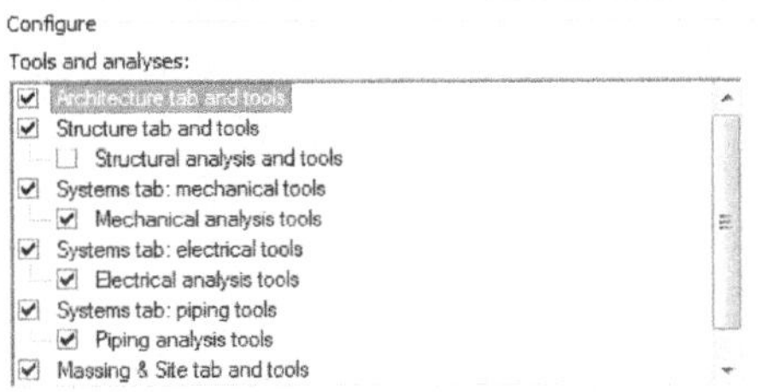

Figure 11–67

How To: Use the Show Disconnects Tool

1. In the *Analyze* tab>Check Systems panel, click (Show Disconnects).
2. In the Show Disconnects Options dialog box, select the types of systems you want to display, as shown in Figure 11–68. Click **OK**.

Figure 11–68

3. The disconnects display (Warning).
   - The disconnects continue to display until you either correct the situation or run **Show Disconnects** again and clear all of the selections.
4. Hover the cursor over the warning icon to display a tooltip with the warning. You can also click on the icon to open the Warning dialog box, shown in Figure 11–69.

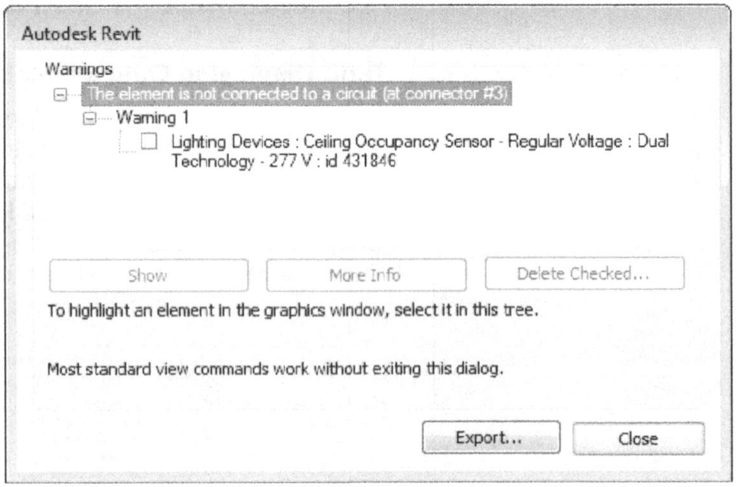

Figure 11–69

How To: Use the Check Circuits Tool

1. In the *Analyze* tab>Check Systems panel, click (Check Circuits) to toggle it on.
2. The (Warning) icon displays wherever there is an issue. Click on one of the icons to open the Warning alert box, shown in Figure 11–70.

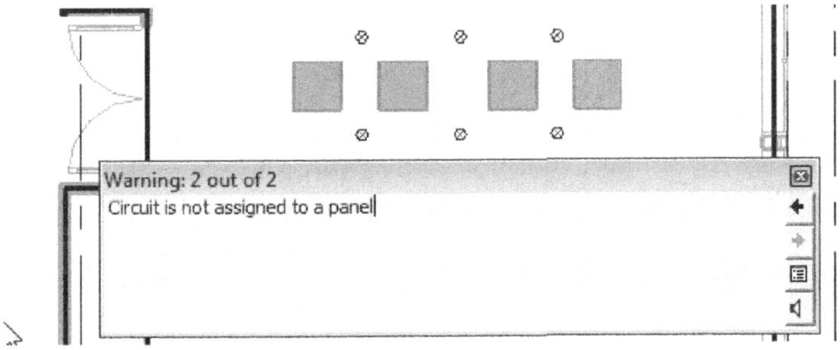

Figure 11–70

- For icons that have more than one warning, in the Warning alert box, click (Next Warning) and (Previous Warning) to search through the list.
- Click (Expand Warning Dialog) to open the dialog box, shown in Figure 11–71. You can expand each node in the box and select elements to display or delete.

*If there are a lot of warnings to review, you can click **Export...** and save an HTML report*

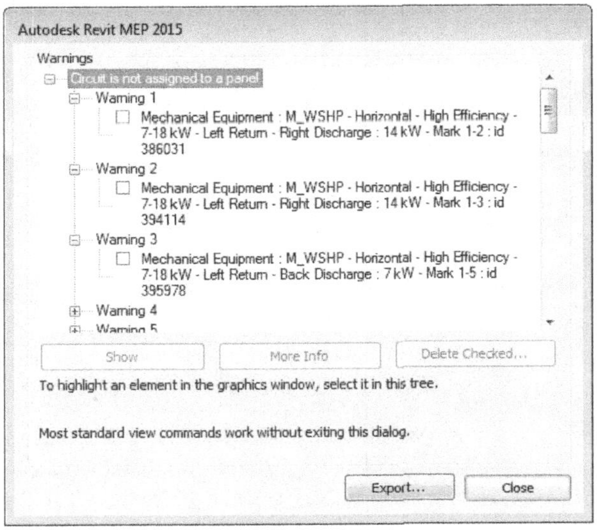

Figure 11–71

Hint: Color Fill Legends for Analysis

An additional way to analyze information about lighting and power is to create a Color Fill Legend. Electrical color fills are typically created from spaces and can be set for parameters such as the Average Estimated Illumination or Specified Lighting load for the spaces.

How To: Place a Color Fill Legend

1. Set the appropriate *Color Scheme* in the Properties of the view.
2. In the *Annotate* tab>Color Fill panel, click (Color Fill Legend) to place the appropriate legend.

Practice 11d

Add Conduit

Practice Objective

- Add conduit to a lighting plan.

Estimated time for completion: 15 minutes

In this practice you will add conduit and fittings to a project, as shown in Figure 11–72.

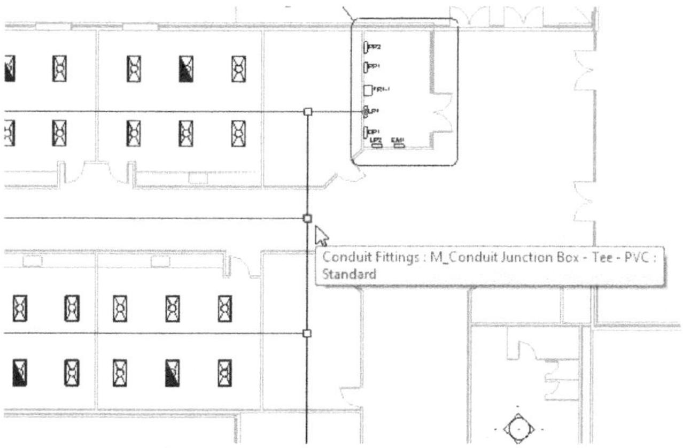

Figure 11–72

Task 1 - Modify electrical settings.

1. In the practice files *Electrical* folder, open **MEP-Elementary-School-Conduit-M.rvt**.
2. In the *Systems* tab>Electrical panel title bar, click ↘ (Electrical Settings).
3. In the Electrical Settings dialog box, select **Angles**.

4. In the **Angles** pane, select **Use specific angles** and clear the **22.50** and **11.25** checkmarks, as shown in Figure 11–73. This limits the angles that you can draw.

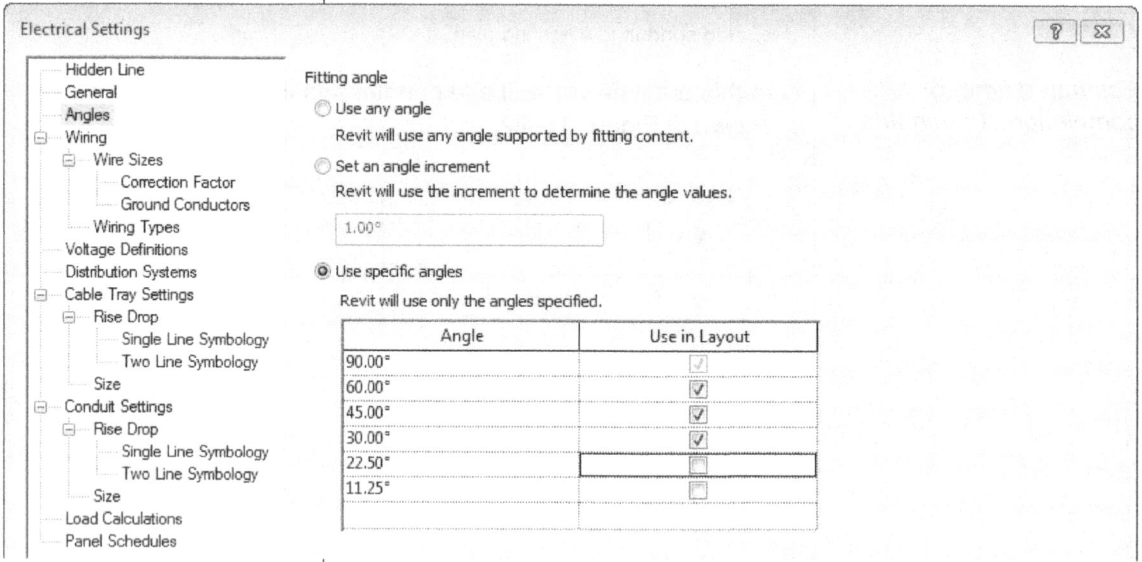

Figure 11–73

5. Click **OK** to close the dialog box.

6. Open the Electrical>Lighting>Floor Plans>**01 Lighting Plan** view, if it is not already open.

7. Zoom into the electrical room area so that some portion of the classroom wing is also displayed.

8. In the *Systems* tab>Electrical panel, click (Conduit).

9. In the Type Selector, select **Conduit with Fittings - Rigid Nonmetallic Conduit (RNC Sch 40)**.

10. In the Options Bar, verify that the *Diameter* is set to **53mm** and the *Offset* is set to **2900mm**.

11. In the Electrical Room, select the panel **LP1**. The program zooms in on the connector and the *Surface Connection* tab displays in the Ribbon, as shown in Figure 11–74.

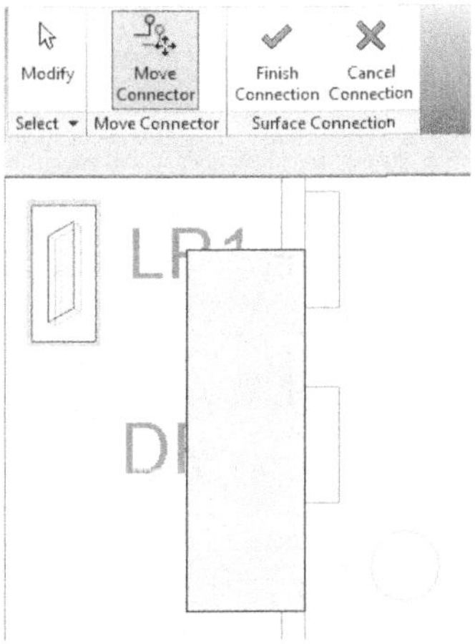

Figure 11–74

12. Click  (Finish Connection).

13. Draw the conduit down the length of the wing.

14. Press <Esc> once to release the end of the conduit, but remain in the **Conduit** command. Draw another line of conduit vertically and then horizontally across the bottom of the other classroom wing, as shown in Figure 11–75.

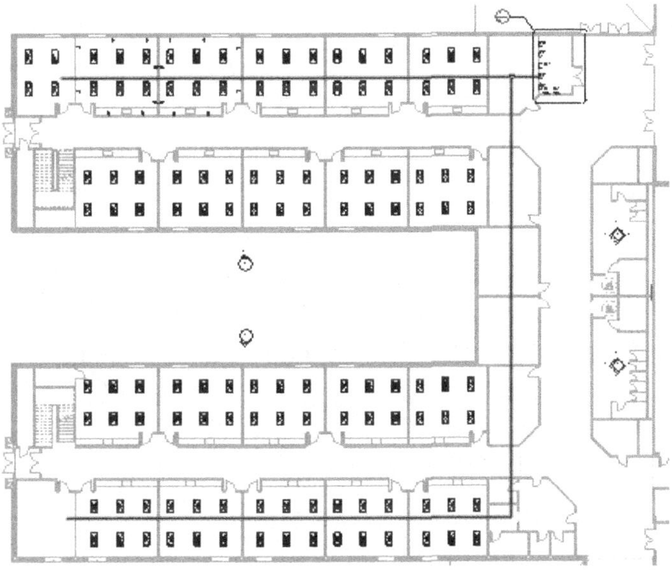

Figure 11–75

15. Draw additional lines of conduit from the vertical line down each of the hallways and the other classrooms. Click **Modify** to end the command.

16. Zoom in so that you can see where the junction boxes are automatically placed, as shown in Figure 11–76.

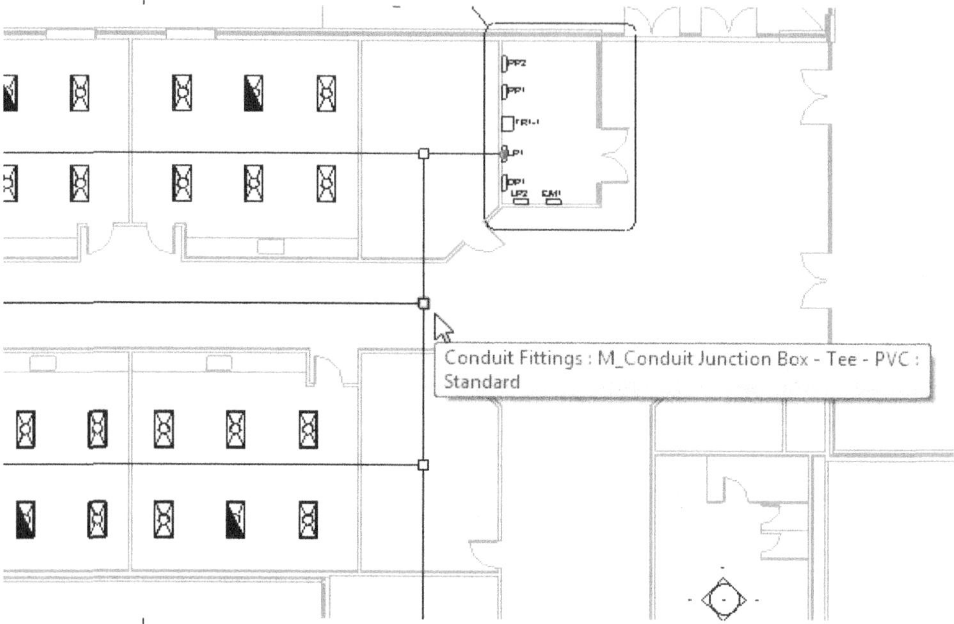

Figure 11–76

17. Pan over to the end of one of the runs.

18. In the *Systems* tab>Electrical panel, click  (Conduit Fitting).

19. In the Type Selector, select **Conduit Junction Box - Cross - Aluminum - Standard**.

20. Place the junction box at the end of the conduit segment you just created. Select the endpoint of the conduit so that the junction box takes on the height and size of the conduit.

21. Add other junction boxes as required along the lines of conduit. Snap to the conduit (Nearest) to place it correctly.

22. Save the project.

Chapter Review Questions

1. Which of the following is NOT a type of system that can be created in the Autodesk Revit MEP software?
   a. Power
   b. Communications
   c. Low Voltage
   d. Lighting

2. Which of the following are electrical devices that can be added to a project? (Select all that apply.)
   a. Lighting switches
   b. Communication
   c. Electrical Panels
   d. Data

3. What happens to hosted, face-based lighting fixtures in an Autodesk Revit MEP project if the ceiling (as shown in Figure 11–77) is deleted and then a new one is added at a different height in the architectural linked model?

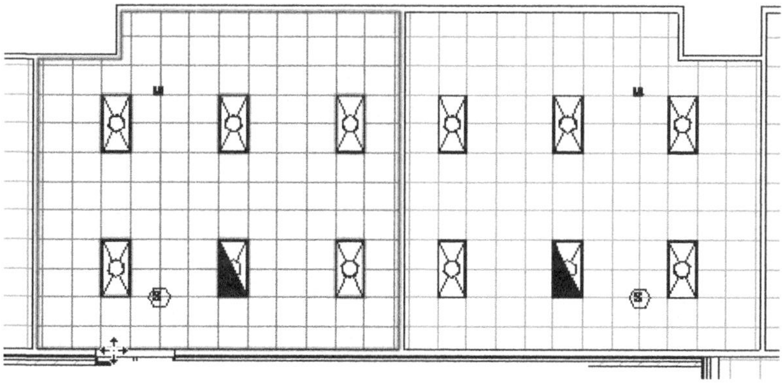

Figure 11–77

   a. The hosted lighting fixtures are deleted.
   b. A warning displays that you need a coordination review.
   c. A warning displays that the hosting element no longer exists in the linked model.
   d. Nothing happens, but in the 3D view, the light fixtures are not connected to the ceiling.

4. To change the type of a cable tray or conduit run, as shown in Figure 11–78, you must...

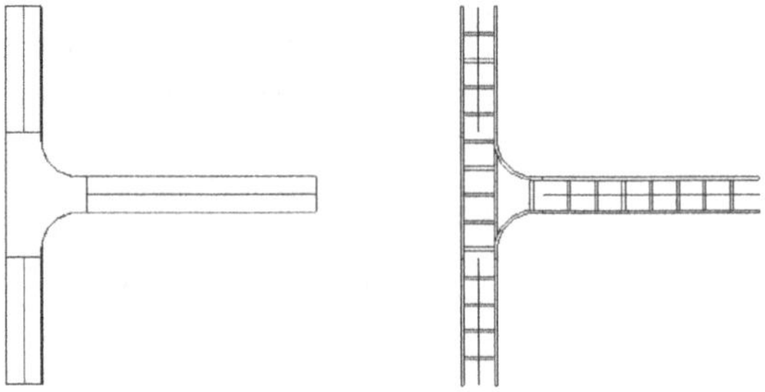

Figure 11–78

   a. Redraw the run using the correct type.
   b. Select one element in the run and change it in the Type Selector.
   c. Select all of the elements in the run and change it in the Type Selector.
   d. Select all the elements in the run and use **Change Type**.

5. Can a panel schedule, such as that shown in Figure 11–79, be modified once a circuit has been added to it?

Branch Panel: LP1

Location: ELECTRICAL 2500A
Supply From:
Mounting: Surface
Enclosure: Type 3R

Notes:

CKT	Circuit Description	Trip	Poles
1	Lighting - Dwelling Unit CLASSROOM 1509	20 A	1
3	Lighting - Dwelling Unit CLASSROOM 1505	20 A	1
5	Lighting - Dwelling Unit CLASSROOM 1501	20 A	1

Figure 11–79

   a. Yes
   b. No

6. How do you move a spare circuit in a panel schedule?
   a. Select it and use the **Move** tool in the *Modify* tab.
   b. Select it and use **Move Up**, **Move Down**, or **Move Across**.
   c. Unlock it and use the **Move** tools in the Circuits panel.
   d. Move the circuit in the plan view. The panel schedule updates accordingly.

Command Summary

Button	Command	Location
Electrical Devices and Components		
	**Communication**	• **Ribbon:** *Systems* tab>Electrical panel>expand Device
	**Data**	• **Ribbon:** *Systems* tab>Electrical panel>expand Device
	**Electrical Equipment**	• **Ribbon:** *Systems* tab>Electrical panel
	**Electrical Fixture**	• **Ribbon:** *Systems* tab>Electrical panel>expand Device
	**Fire Alarm**	• **Ribbon:** *Systems* tab>Electrical panel>expand Device
	**Lighting (switch)**	• **Ribbon:** *Systems* tab>Electrical panel>expand Device
	**Lighting Fixture**	• **Ribbon:** *Systems* tab>Electrical panel
	**Nurse Call**	• **Ribbon:** *Systems* tab>Electrical panel>expand Device
	**Security**	• **Ribbon:** *Systems* tab>Electrical panel>expand Device
	**Telephone**	• **Ribbon:** *Systems* tab>Electrical panel>expand Device
Electrical Circuits		
	**Add to Circuit**	• **Ribbon:** *Edit Circuit* tab>Edit Circuit panel
	**Create Panel Schedule**	• **Ribbon:** *Modify | Electrical Equipment* tab>Electrical panel
	**Edit Circuit**	• **Ribbon:** *Modify | Electrical Circuits* tab>System Tools panel
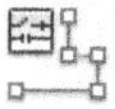	**Edit Path (Circuits)**	• **Ribbon:** *Modify | Electrical Circuits* tab>System Tools panel
	**Edit a Template**	• **Ribbon:** *Manage* tab>Settings panel expand **Panel Schedule Templates**
	**Manage Templates**	• **Ribbon:** *Manage* tab>Settings panel expand **Panel Schedule Templates**

	**Power**	• **Ribbon:** *Modify* | *Lighting Fixtures* tab or *Modify Electrical Equipment* tab> Create Systems panel
	**Remove from Circuit**	• **Ribbon:** *Edit Circuit* tab>Edit Circuit panel
	**Select Panel**	• **Ribbon:** *Modify* | *Electrical Circuits* tab>System Tools panel
Cable Tray and Conduit		
	**Automatically Connect**	• **Ribbon:** *Modify* | *Place Cable Tray* or *Place Conduit* tab>Placement Tools panel
	**Cable Tray**	• **Ribbon:** *Systems* tab>Electrical panel
	**Cable Tray Fitting**	• **Ribbon:** *Systems* tab>Electrical panel
	**Conduit**	• **Ribbon:** *Systems* tab>Electrical panel
	**Conduit Fitting**	• **Ribbon:** *Systems* tab>Electrical panel
	**Ignore Slope to Connect (Conduit only)**	• **Ribbon:** *Modify* | *Place Conduit* tab> Placement Tools panel
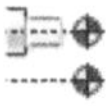	**Inherit Elevation**	• **Ribbon:** *Modify* | *Place Cable Tray* or *Place Conduit* tab>Placement Tools panel
	**Inherit Size**	• **Ribbon:** *Modify* | *Place Cable Tray* or *Place Conduit* tab>Placement Tools panel
	**Justification**	• **Ribbon:** *Modify* | *Place Cable Tray* or *Place Conduit* tab>Placement Tools panel
	**Parallel Conduits**	• **Ribbon:** *Systems* tab>Electrical panel

Chapter 12

Creating Construction Documents

The accurate creation of construction documents in the Autodesk® Revit® software ensures that the design is correctly communicated to downstream users. Construction documents are created primarily in special views call sheets. Knowing how to select titleblocks, assign titleblock information, place views, and print the sheets are essential steps in the construction documentation process.

Learning Objectives in this Chapter

- Add Sheets with titleblocks and views of a project.
- Enter the titleblock information for individual sheets and for an entire project.
- Place and organize views on sheets.
- Print sheets using the default Print dialog box.

12.1 Setting Up Sheets

While you are modeling a project, the foundations of the working drawings are already in progress. Any view (such as a floor plan, section, callout, or schedule) can be placed on a sheet, as shown in Figure 12–1.

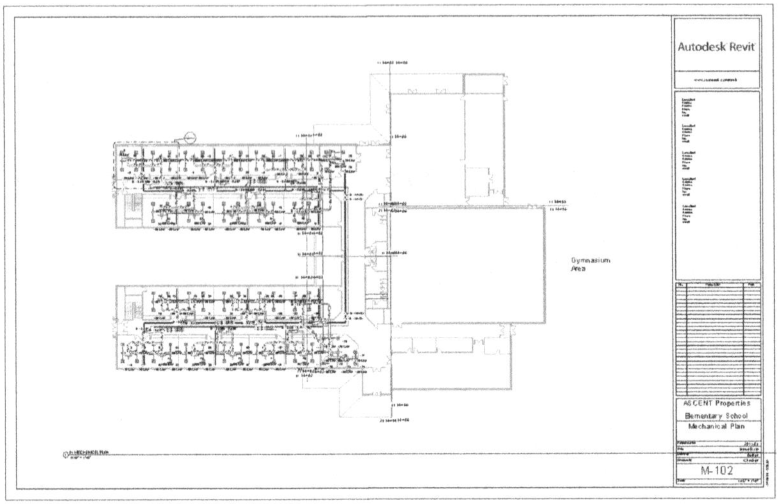

Figure 12–1

- Company templates can be created with standard sheets using the company (or project) titleblock and related views already placed on the sheet.
- The sheet size is based on the selected title block family.
- Sheets are listed in the *Sheets* area in the Project Browser.
- Most information on sheets is included in the views. You can add general notes and other non-model elements directly to the sheet, though it is better to add them using drafting views or legends, as these can be placed on multiple sheets.

How To: Set Up Sheets

1. In the Project Browser, right-click on the *Sheets* area header and select **New Sheet...** or in the *View* tab>Sheet Composition panel, click (Sheet).

2. In the New Sheet dialog box, select a titleblock from the list as shown in Figure 12–2. Alternatively, if there is a list of placeholder sheets, select one or more from the list.

*Click **Load...** to load a sheet from the Library.*

Hold <Ctrl> to select multiple placeholder sheets.

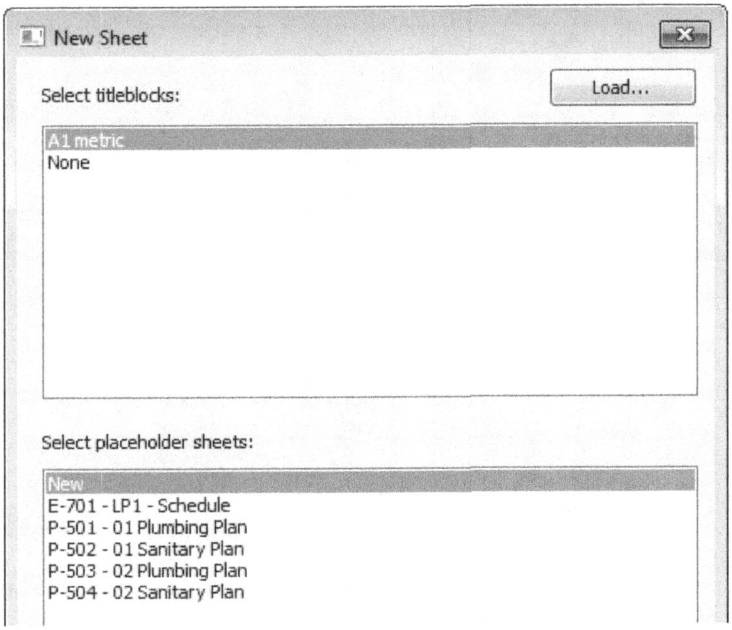

Figure 12–2

3. Click **OK**. A new sheet is created using the preferred title block.
4. Fill out the information in the title block as required.
5. Add views to the sheet.

- When you create sheets, the next sheet is incremented numerically.
- When you change the *Sheet Name* and/or *Number* in the title block, it automatically changes the name and number of the sheet in the Project Browser.
- The plot stamp on the side of the sheet automatically updates according to the current date and time. The format of the display uses the regional settings of your computer.
- The Scale is automatically entered when a view is inserted onto a sheet. If a sheet has multiple views with different scales, the scale displays **As Indicated.**

Sheet (Title Block) Properties

Each new sheet includes a title block. You can change the title block information in Properties, as shown in Figure 12–3 or by selecting any blue label you want to edit (Sheet Name, Sheet Number, Drawn by, etc.), as shown in Figure 12–4.

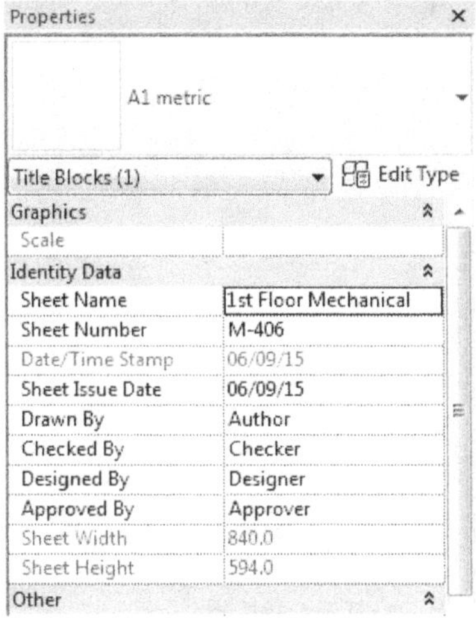

Figure 12–3

Figure 12–4

Properties that apply to all sheets can be entered in the Project Properties dialog box (as shown in Figure 12–5). In the *Manage* tab>Settings panel, click (Project Information).

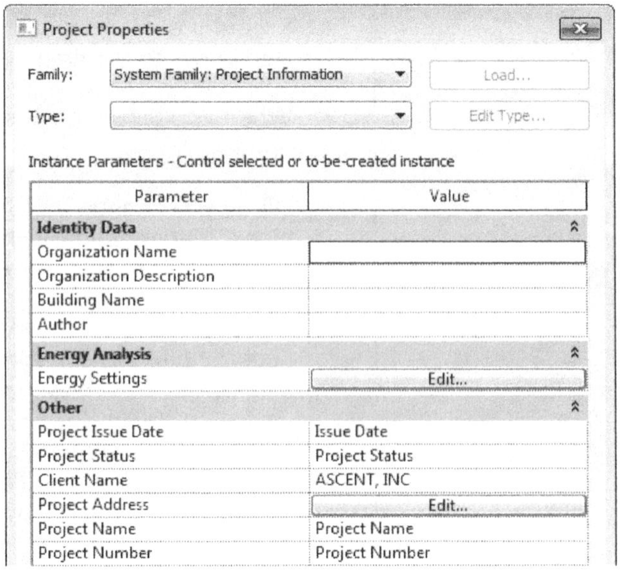

Figure 12–5

12.2 Placing and Modifying Views on Sheets

The process of adding views to a sheet is simple. Drag and drop a view from the Project Browser onto the sheet. The new view on the sheet is displayed at the scale specified in the original view. The view title displays the name, number, and scale of the view, as shown in Figure 12–6.

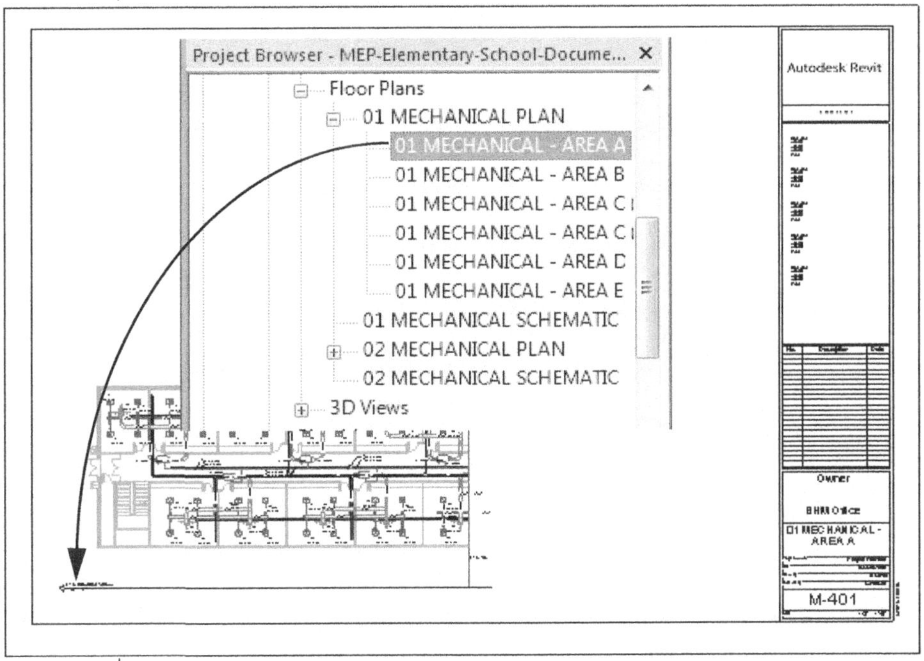

Figure 12–6

How To: Place Views on Sheets

Alignment lines from existing views display to help you place additional views.

1. Set up the view as you want it to display on the sheet, including the scale and visibility of elements.
2. Create or open the sheet where you want to place the view.
3. Select the view in the Project Browser, and drag and drop it onto the sheet.
4. The center of the view is attached to the cursor. Click to place it on the sheet.

Placing Views on Sheets

- Views can only be placed on a sheet once. However, you can duplicate the view and place that copy on a sheet.
- Views on a sheet are associative. They automatically update to reflect changes to the project.
- Each view on a sheet is listed under the sheet name in the Project Browser, as shown in Figure 12–7.

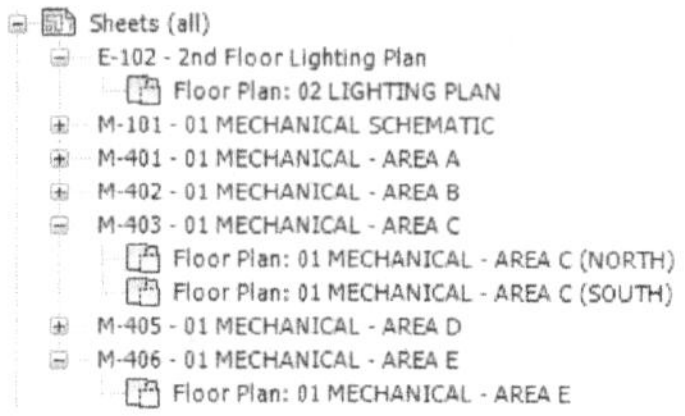

Figure 12–7

- You can also use two other methods to place views on sheets:
  - In the Project Browser, right-click on the sheet name and select **Add View...**
  - In the *View* tab>Sheet Composition panel click (Place View).

  Then, in the Views dialog box (shown in Figure 12–8), select the view you want to use and click **Add View to Sheet.**

This method lists only those views which have not yet been placed on a sheet.

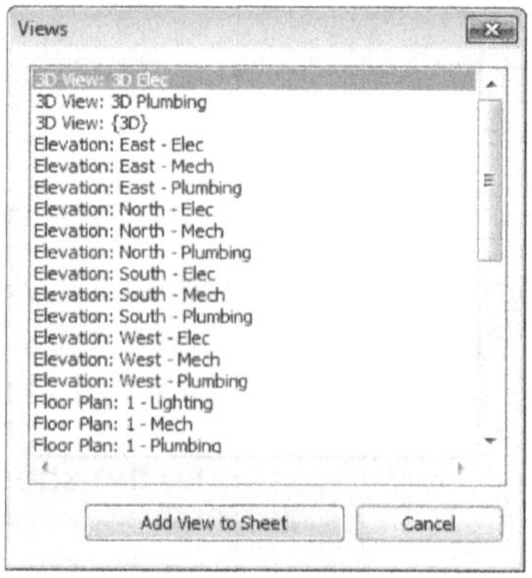

Figure 12–8

- To remove a view from a sheet, select it and press <Delete>. Alternatively, in the Project Browser, expand the individual sheet information to show the views, right-click on the view name and select **Remove From Sheet**.

> **Hint: Setting up the Project Browser**
>
> To view and change the Project Browser's types, select the top level node of the Project Browser (which is set to *Discipline* by default) and select the type you want to use from the Type Selector. For example, you can set the Browser to only display views that are not on sheets, as shown in Figure 12–9.
>
> 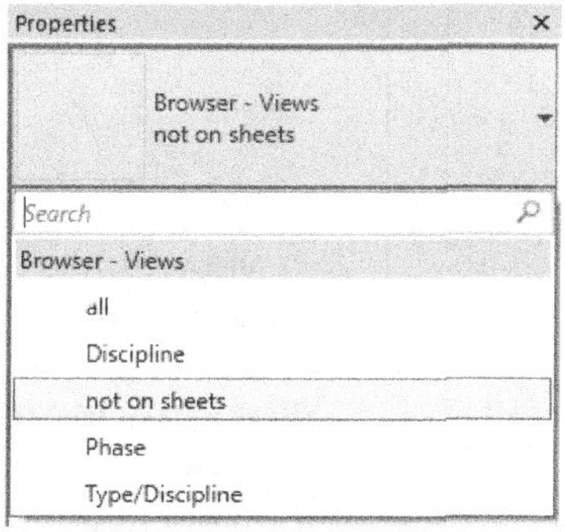
>
>
> **Figure 12–9**

Moving Views and View Titles

*You can also use the **Move** command or the arrow keys to move a view.*

- To move a view on a sheet, select the edge of the view and drag it to a new location. The view title moves with the view.
- To move only the view title, select the title and drag it to the new location.
- To modify the length of the line under the title name, select the edge of the view and drag the controls, as shown in Figure 12–10.

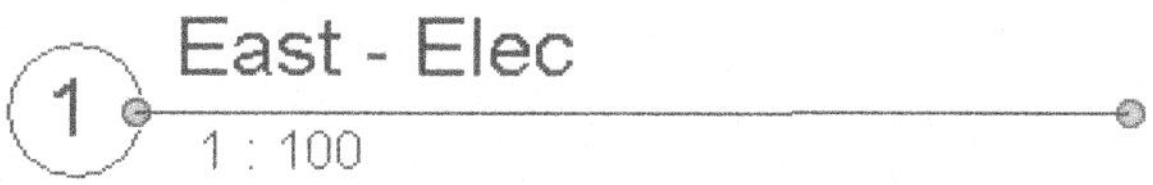

Figure 12–10

- To change the title of a view on a sheet without changing its name in the Project Browser, in Properties, in the *Identity Data* area, type a new title for the *Title on Sheet* parameter, as shown in Figure 12–11.

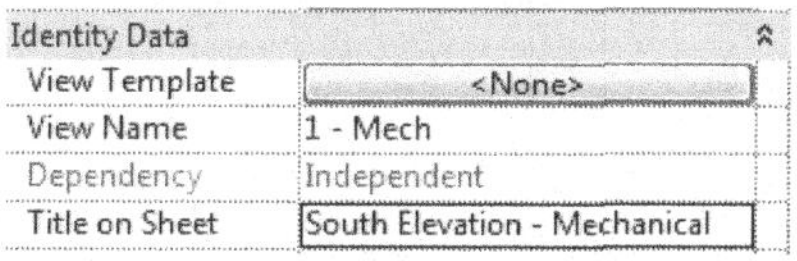

Figure 12–11

Rotating Views

- When creating a vertical sheet, you can rotate the view on the sheet by 90 degrees. Select the view and set the direction of rotation in the Rotation on Sheet drop-down list in the Options Bar, as shown in Figure 12–12.

Figure 12–12

- To rotate a view to an angle other than 90 degrees, open the view, toggle on and select the crop region and use the **Rotate** command to change the angle.

Working Inside Views

To make small changes to a view while working on a sheet:

- Double-click *inside* the view to activate it.
- Double-click *outside* the view to deactivate it.

Only elements in the viewport are available for modification. The rest of the sheet is grayed out, as shown in Figure 12–13.

Only use this method for small changes. Significant changes should be made directly in the view.

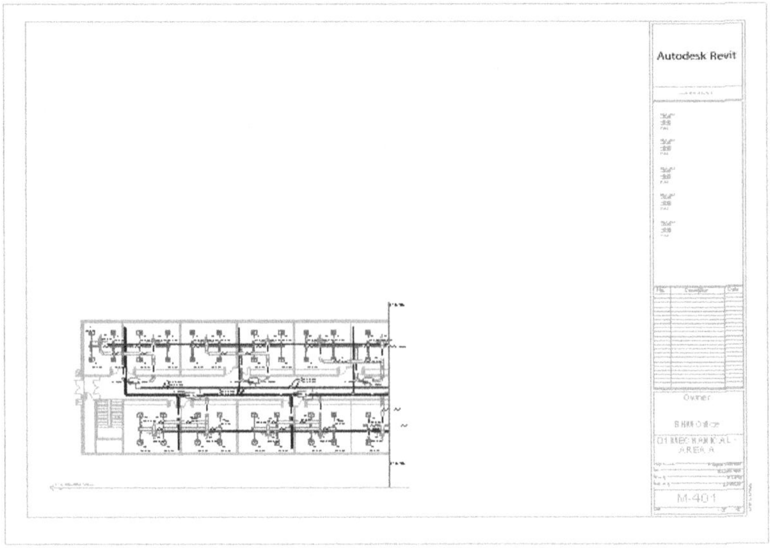

Figure 12–13

- You can activate and deactivate views by right-clicking on the edge of the view or by using the tools found on the *Modify | Viewports* and *Views* tab>Sheet Composition panel.
- Changes you make to elements when a view is activated also display in the original view.
- If you are unsure which sheet a view is on, right-click on the view in the Project Browser and select **Open Sheet**. This item is grayed out if the view has not been placed on a sheet and is not available for schedules and legends which can be placed on more than one sheet.

Resizing Views on Sheets

Each view displays the extents of the model or the elements contained in the crop region. If the view does not fit on a sheet (as shown in Figure 12–14), you might need to crop the view or move the elevation markers closer to the building.

If the extents of the view change dramatically based on a scale change or a crop region, it is easier to delete the view on the sheet and drag it over again.

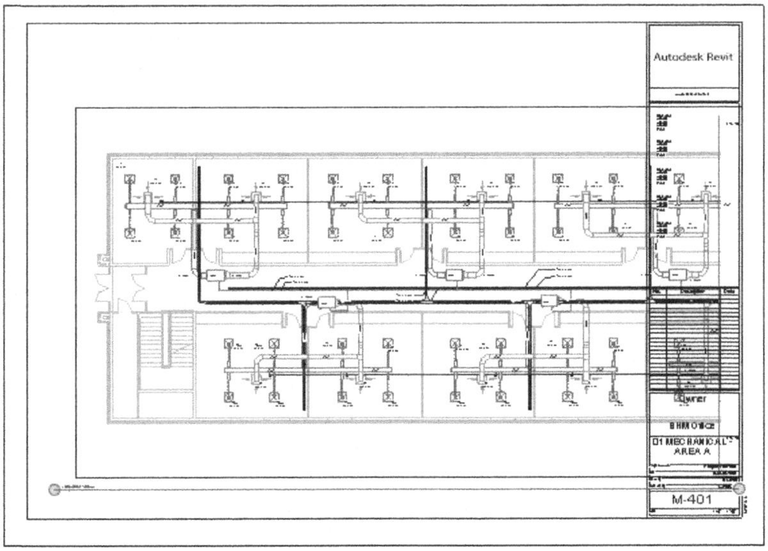

Figure 12–14

Hint: Add an Image to a Sheet

Company logos and renderings saved to image files (such as .JPG and .PNG) can be added directly on a sheet or in a view.

1. In the *Insert* tab>Import panel, click (Image).
2. In the Import Image dialog box, select and open the image file. The extents of the image display as shown in Figure 12–15.

Figure 12–15

3. Place the image where you want it.
4. The image is displayed. Pick one of the grips and extend it to modify the size of the image.

- In Properties, you can adjust the height and width and also set the *Draw Layer* to either **Background** or **Foreground**, as shown in Figure 12–16.

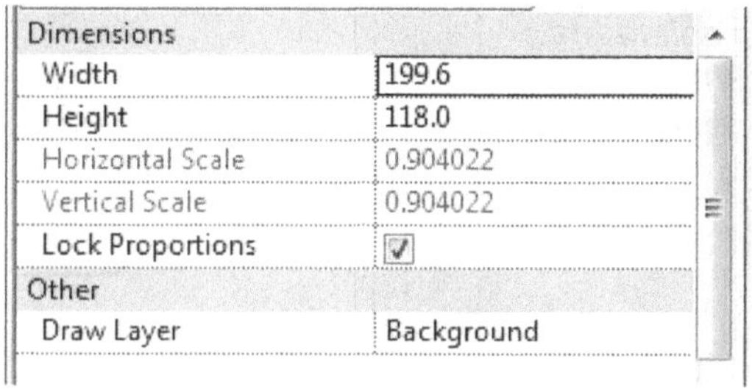

Figure 12–16

- You can select more than one image at a time and move them as a group to the background or foreground.

Practice 12a Create Construction Documents

Practice Objectives

- Set up project properties.
- Create sheets individually.
- Modify views to prepare them to be placed on sheets.
- Place views on sheets.

Estimated time for completion: 20 minutes

In this practice you will complete the project information, add new sheets and use existing sheets. You will fill in title block information and then add views to sheets, such as the Lighting Plan sheet shown in Figure 12–17. Complete as many sheets as you have time for.

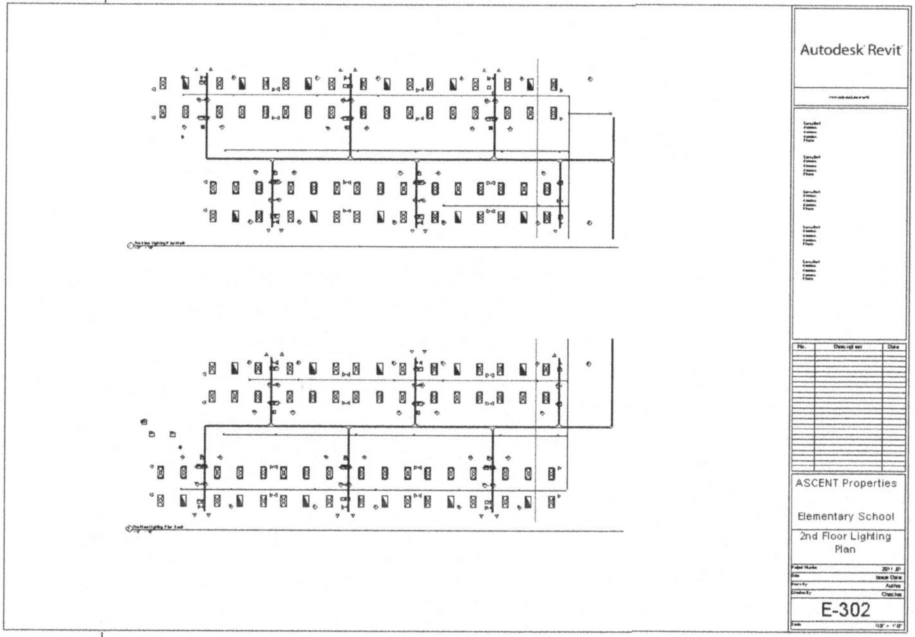

Figure 12–17

Task 1 - Complete the project information.

1. In the practice files *Documents* folder, open **MEP-Elementary-School-Documents-M.rvt**.

2. In the *Manage* tab>Settings panel, click (Project Information).

3. In the Project Properties dialog box, add the following values, as shown in Figure 12–18.
   - *Client Name:* **School District ABC**
   - *Project Name:* **Elementary School**
   - *Project Number:* **1234.56**

These values are added automatically to any sheet you create.

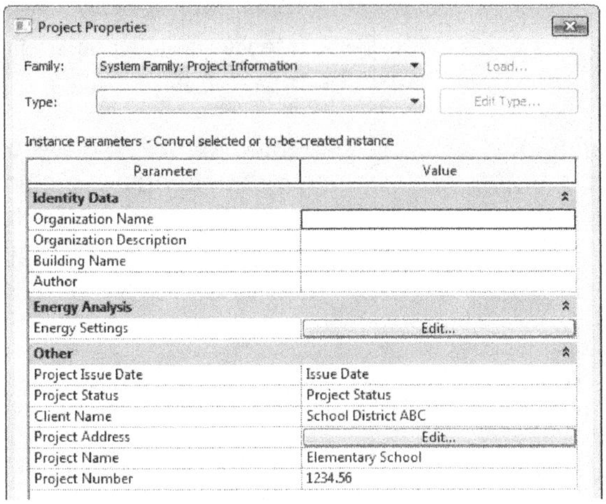

Figure 12–18

4. Click **OK**.

5. In the Project Browser, expand the *Sheets (all)* area and open **M-101 - 01 Mechanical Schematic**. There is already a view placed on the sheet.

6. Zoom in on the title block and review the contents. The Project Parameters that you added are automatically applied to the sheet, as shown in Figure 12–19.

*The Scale is automatically entered when a view is inserted onto a sheet. If a sheet has multiple scales, the scale reads **As Indicated**.*

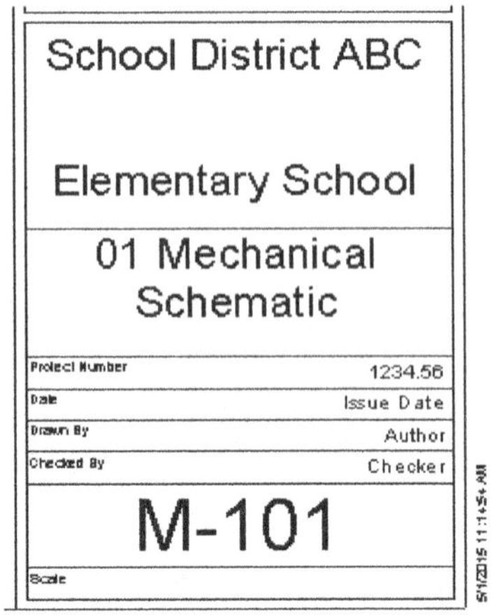

Figure 12–19

7. Set *Drawn by* to your initials. Leave the *Checked by* and *Issue Date* parameters as is.

8. Open another sheet. The project parameter values are repeated but note that the *Drawn By* value is not added because it is a by sheet parameter.

9. Review the other existing Mechanical sheets and save the project.

Task 2 - Add Sheets.

1. In the *View* tab>Sheet Composition panel, click (Sheet).

2. In the New Sheet dialog box, select the titleblock **A0 Metric** and click **OK**.

3. In the Project Browser, select the new sheet, right-click, and select **Rename**.

4. In the Sheet Title dialog box, set *Number* as **C-101**, *Name* as **Cover Sheet**, and click **OK**. The titleblock updates as shown in Figure 12–20.

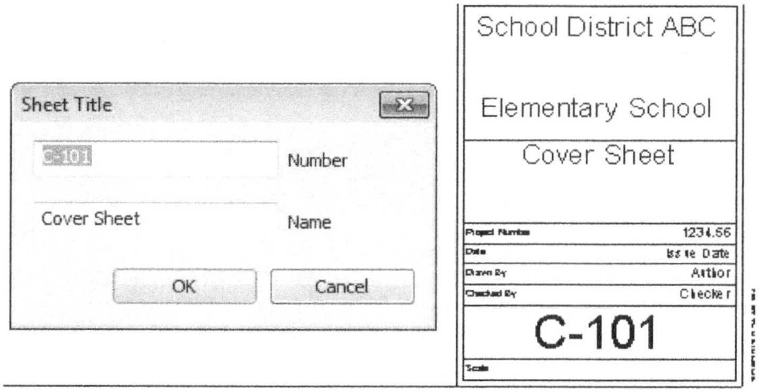

Figure 12–20

5. In the Project Browser, right-click on Sheets (all) and select **New Sheet....**

You can change the sheet number and name in the titleblock or by renaming it in the Project Browser.

6. Using the same title block, create the following sheets:
   - E-301 - 1st Floor Lighting Plan
   - E-302 - 2nd Floor Lighting Plan
   - E-303 - Power Panel Plan Detail
   - P-509 - Plumbing 3D

7. In the Project Browser, in the *Sheets (all)* area, note that these new sheets, the other sheets that you created, and the M-# sheets that were already created for you are displayed.

8. Save the project.

Task 3 - Set up and add views to sheets.

1. In the Project Browser, in the Electrical>Lighting>Floor Plans, right click on the **02 Lighting Plan** view and using **Duplicate as Dependent** create two copies. Name them as **02 Lighting Plan - North** and **02 Lighting Plan - South**.

2. Open the **02 Lighting Plan - North** view, display the crop region, and resize it to fit the north classroom wing, as shown in Figure 12–21.

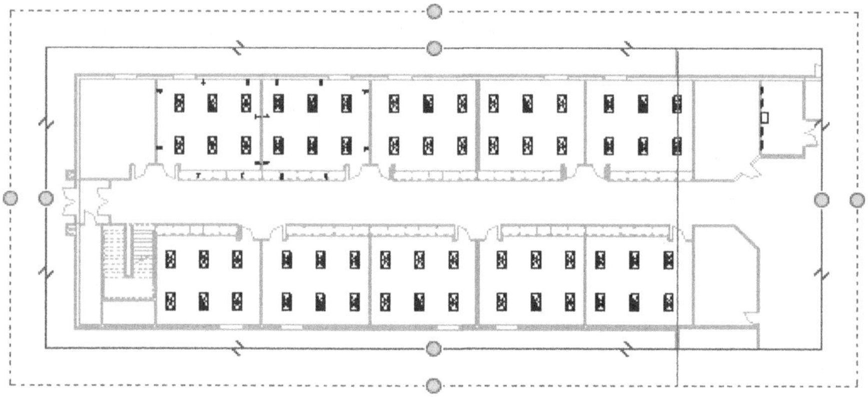

Figure 12–21

3. Toggle the crop region off.

4. Repeat the steps with the **02 Lighting Plan - South** view.

5. Open the sheet **E-302 - 2nd Floor Lighting Plan** and drag and drop the **2nd Floor Lighting Plan North** and **South** views you just created onto it.

6. Open the **E-303 - Power Panel Plan Detail** sheet and drag and drop the **Power Panel Callout** view onto it.

7. Switch to the **01Power Plan** view. Zoom in on the callout marker by the power panels. Notice that it has now been automatically assigned a detail and sheet number, as shown in Figure 12–22.

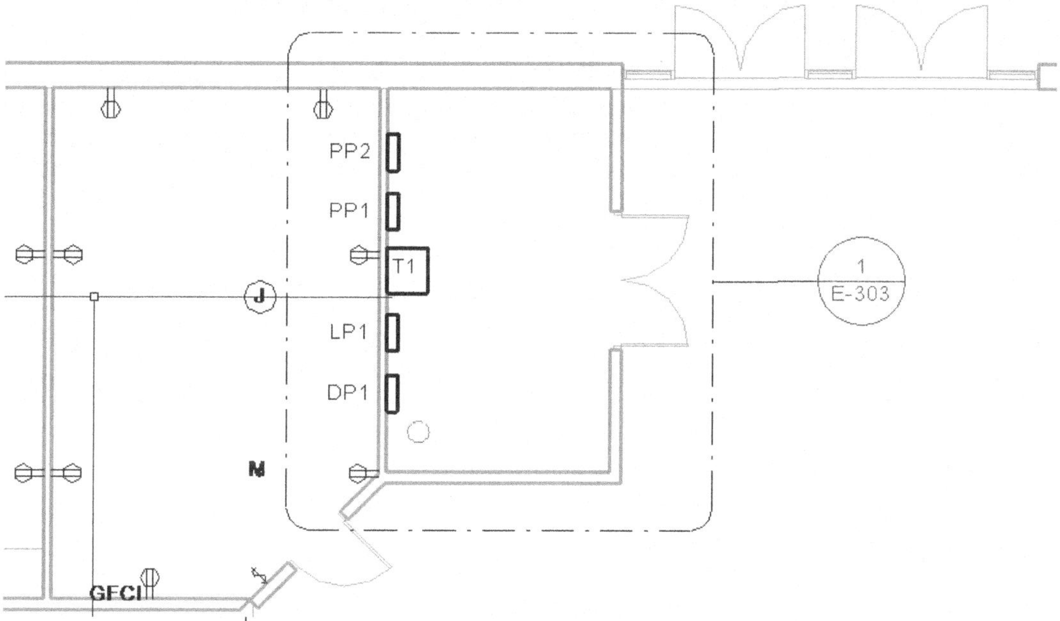

Figure 12–22

8. Repeat the process of adding views and schedules to sheets using the views and schedules you have available.
   - Modify crop regions and hide unnecessary elements in the views. Toggle off crop regions after you have modified them.
   - Verify the scale of a view in Properties before placing it on a sheet.
   - Use alignment lines to help place multiple views on one sheet.
   - Change the view title if required, to more accurately describe what is on the sheet.
   - To make minor changes to a view once it is on a sheet, right-click on the view and select **Activate View.** To return to the sheet, right-click on the view and select **Deactivate View**.
   - To make larger changes to a view on a sheet, return to the original view.
   - If you modify the size of a view that is already placed on a sheet, delete the view from the sheet and replace it with the updated view.
9. Save the project.

12.3 Printing Sheets

With the **Print** command, you can print individual sheets or a list of selected sheets. You can also print an individual view or a portion of a view for check prints or presentations. To open the Print dialog box (shown in Figure 12–23), in the *File* tab, click (Print).

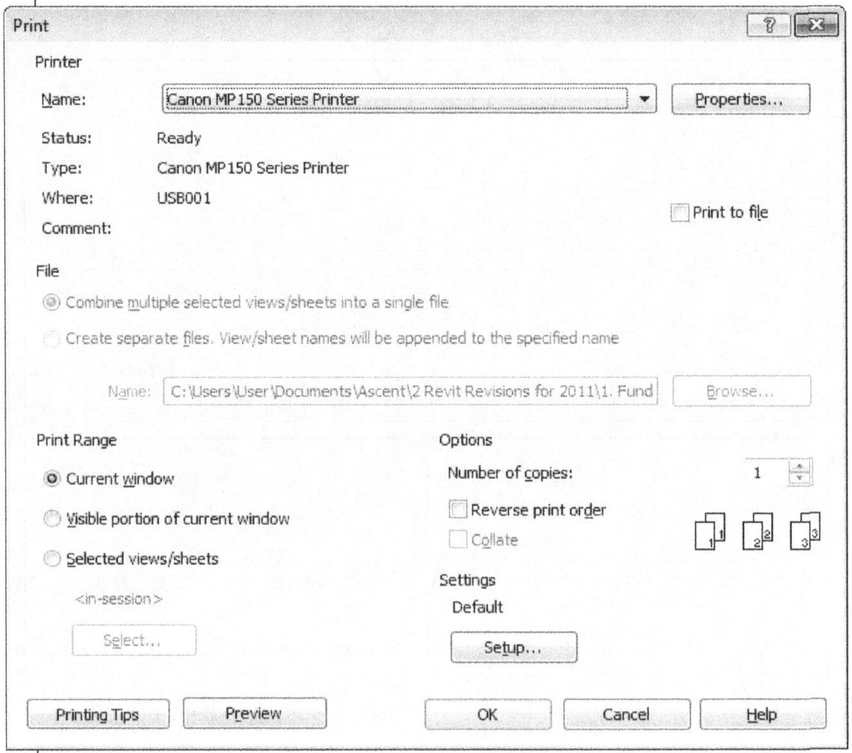

Figure 12–23

Printing Options

The Print dialog box is divided into the following areas: *Printer*, *File*, *Print Range, Options*, and *Settings*. Modify them as required to produce the plot you want.

- **Printing Tips**: Opens Autodesk WikiHelp online, in which you can find help with troubleshooting printing issues.
- **Preview**: Opens a preview of the print output so that you can see what is going to be printed.

You must have a .PDF print driver installed on your system to print to PDF.

Printer

Select from the list of available printers, as shown in Figure 12–24. Click **Properties...** to adjust the properties of the selected printer. The options vary according to the printer. Select the **Print to file** option to print to a file rather than directly to a printer. You can create .PLT or .PRN files.

Figure 12–24

File

The *File* area is only available if the **Print to file** option has been selected in the *Printer* area or if you are printing to an electronic-only type of printer. You can create one file or multiple files depending on the type of printer you are using, as shown in Figure 12–25. Click **Browse...** to select the file location and name.

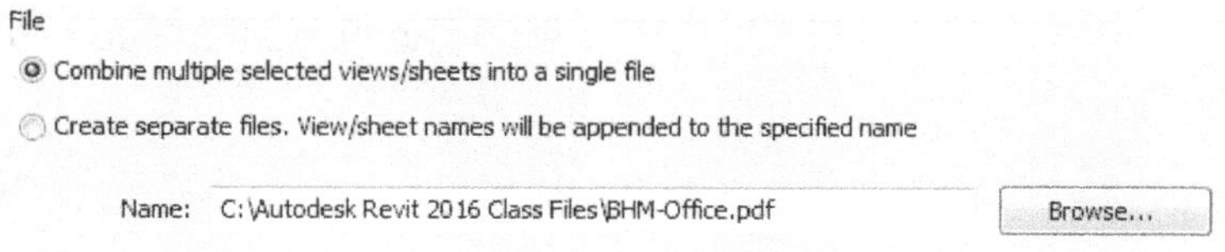

Figure 12–25

Print Range

The *Print Range* area enables you to print individual views/sheets or sets of views/sheets, as shown in Figure 12–26.

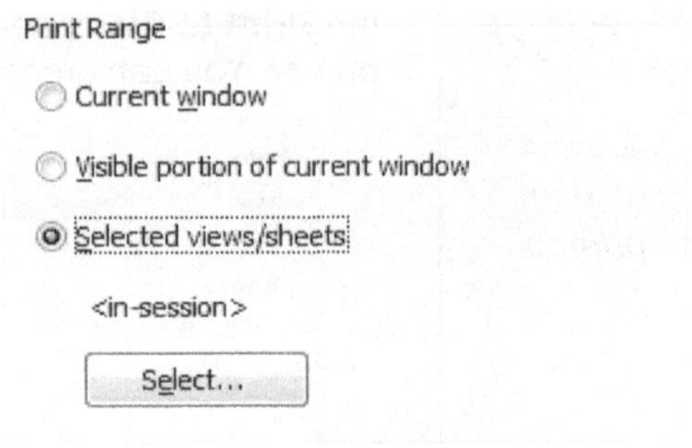

Figure 12–26

- **Current window**: Prints the entire current sheet or view you have open.
- **Visible portion of current window**: Prints only what is displayed in the current sheet or view.
- **Selected views/sheets**: Prints multiple views or sheets. Click **Select...** to open the View/Sheet Set dialog box to choose what to include in the print set. You can save these sets by name so that you can more easily print the same group again.

Options

If your printer supports multiple copies, you can specify the number in the *Options* area, as shown in Figure 12–27. You can also reverse the print order or collate your prints. These options are also available in the printer properties.

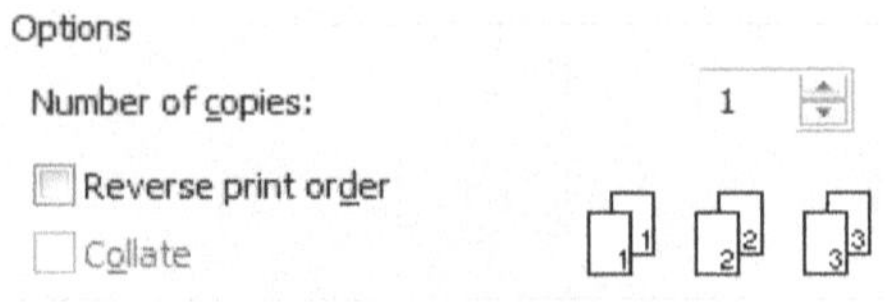

Figure 12–27

Settings

Click **Setup**... to open the Print Setup dialog box, as shown in Figure 12–28. Here, you can specify the *Orientation* and *Zoom* settings, among others. You can also save these settings by name.

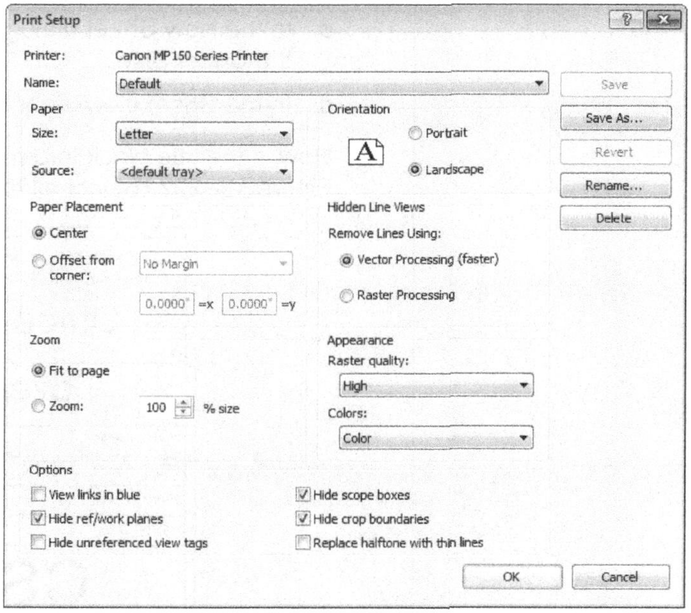

Figure 12–28

- In the *Options* area specify the types of elements you want to print or not print. Unless specified, all of the elements in a view or sheet print.

Chapter Review Questions

1. How do you specify the size of a sheet?
   a. In the Sheet Properties, specify the **Sheet Size**.
   b. In the Options Bar, specify the **Sheet Size**.
   c. In the New Sheet dialog box, select a title block to control the Sheet Size.
   d. In the Sheet view, right-click and select **Sheet Size**.
2. How is the title block information filled in as shown in Figure 12–29? (Select all that apply.)

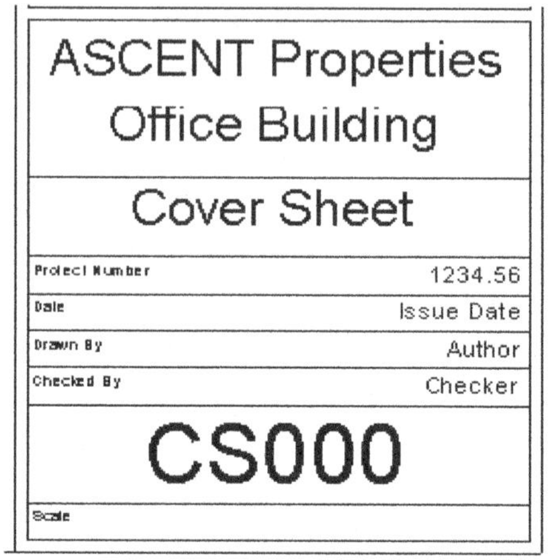

Figure 12–29

   a. Select the title block and select the label that you want to change.
   b. Select the title block and modify it in Properties.
   c. Right-click on the Sheet in the Project Browser and select **Information**.
   d. Some of the information is filled in automatically.
3. On how many sheets can a floor plan view be placed?
   a. 1
   b. 2-5
   c. 6+
   d. As many as you want.

4. Which of the following is the best method to use if the size of a view is too large for a sheet, as shown in Figure 12–30?

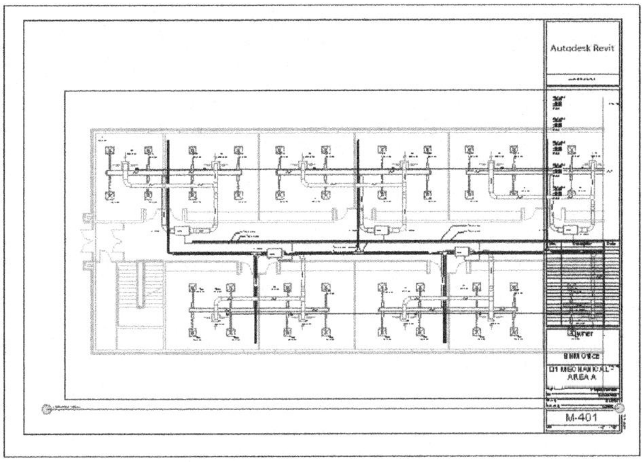

Figure 12–30

   a. Delete the view, change the scale and place the view back on the sheet.

   b. Activate the view and change the View Scale.

5. How do you set up a view on a sheet that only displays part of a floor plan, as shown in Figure 12–31?

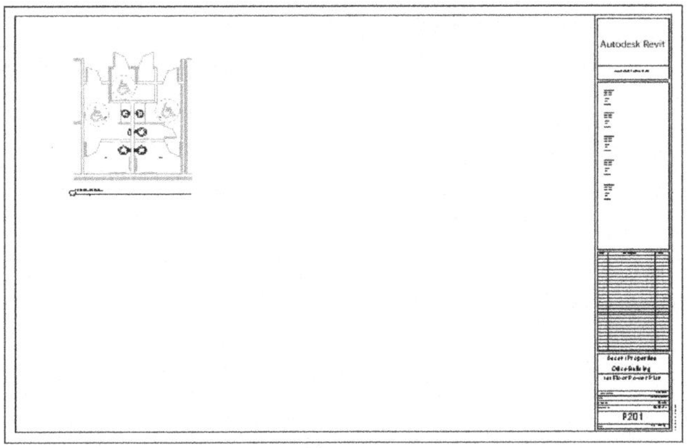

Figure 12–31

   a. Drag and drop the view to the sheet and use the crop region to modify it.

   b. Activate the view and rescale it.

   c. Create a callout view displaying the part that you want to use and place the callout view on the sheet.

   d. Open the view in the Project Browser and change the View Scale.

Command Summary

Button	Command	Location
	**Activate View**	• **Ribbon:** (*select the view*) *Modify | Viewports* tab>Viewport panel • **Double-click:** *(in viewport)* • **Right-click:** (*on view*) Activate View
	**Deactivate View**	• **Ribbon:** *View* tab>Sheet Composition panel>expand Viewports • **Double-click:** *(on sheet)* • **Right-click:** (*on view*) Deactivate View
	**Place View**	• **Ribbon:** *View* tab>Sheet Composition panel
	**Print**	• **Ribbon:** File tab
	**Sheet**	• **Ribbon:** *View* tab>Sheet Composition panel

Annotating Construction Documents

When you create construction documents, annotations are required to show the design intent. Annotations such as dimensions and text can be added to views at any time during the creation of a project. Detail lines and symbols can also be added to views as you create the working drawing sheets, while Legends can be created to provide a place to document any symbols that are used in a project

Learning Objectives in this Chapter

- Add dimensions to the model as a part of the working drawings.
- Add text to a view and use leaders to create notes pointing to a specific part of the model.
- Create Text Types using different fonts and sizes to suit your company standards.
- Draw detail lines to further enhance the documentation view.
- Add view-specific annotation symbols for added clarity.
- Create legend views and populate them with symbols of elements in the project.

13.1 Working with Dimensions

You can create permanent dimensions using aligned, linear, angular, radial, diameter, and arc length dimensions. These can be individual or a string of dimensions, as shown in Figure 13–1. With aligned dimensions, you can also dimension entire walls with openings, grid lines, and/or intersecting walls.

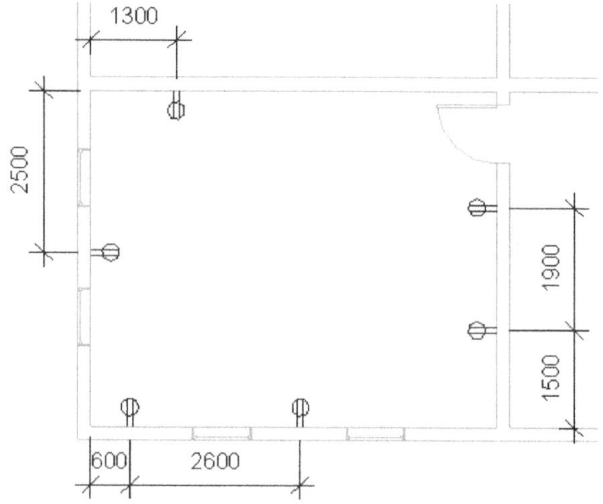

Figure 13–1

- Dimensions referencing model elements must be added to the model in a view. You can dimension on sheets, but only to items added directly on the sheets.

- Dimensions are available in the *Annotate* tab>Dimension panel and the *Modify* tab>Measure panel, as shown in Figure 13–2.

 *(Aligned) is also located in the Quick Access Toolbar.*

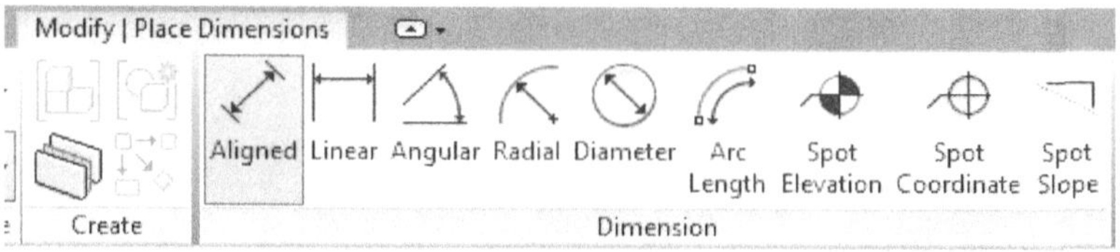

Figure 13–2

How To: Add Aligned Dimensions with Options

1. Start the  (Aligned) command or type **DI**.
2. In the Type Selector, select a dimension style.

3. In the Options Bar, select the location line of the wall to dimension from, as shown in Figure 13–3.
   - This option can be changed as you add dimensions.

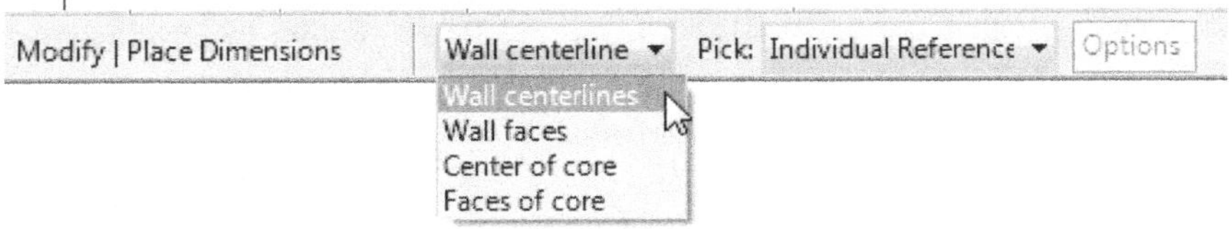

Figure 13–3

   - Most MEP fixtures have alignment lines along their centerline. You can also dimension to individual parts of components, as shown in Figure 13–4.

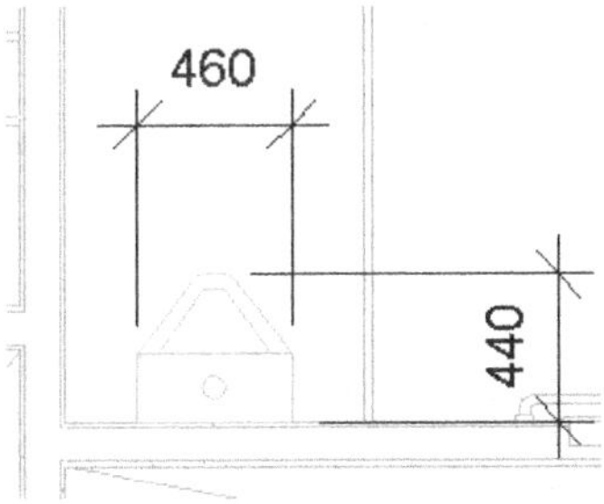

Figure 13–4

4. In the Options Bar, select your preference from the Pick drop-down list:
   - **Individual References**: Select the elements in order (as shown in Figure 13–5) and then click in empty space to position the dimension string.

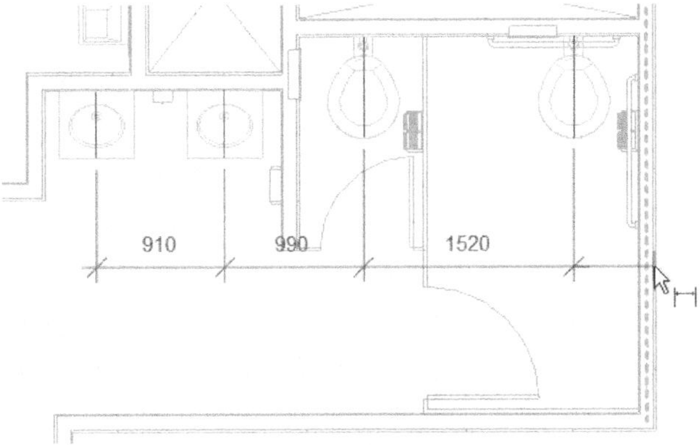

Figure 13–5

   - **Entire Walls**: (Walls only) Select the wall you want to dimension.

- When dimensioning entire walls you can specify how you want *Openings*, *Intersecting Walls*, and *Intersecting Grids* to be treated by the dimension string. In the Options Bar, click **Options**. In the Auto Dimension Options dialog box (shown in Figure 13–6), select the references you want to have automatically dimensioned.

*If the **Entire Wall** option is selected without additional options, it places an overall wall dimension.*

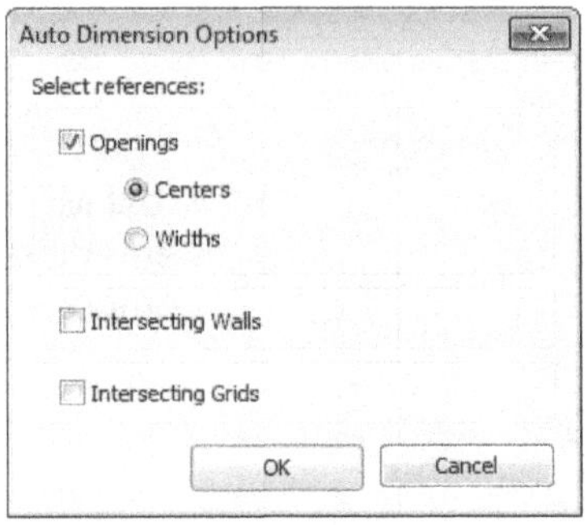

Figure 13–6

How To: Add Other Types of Dimensions

*When the **Dimension** command is active, the dimension methods are also accessible in the Modify | Place Dimensions tab> Dimension panel.*

1. In the *Annotate* tab>Dimension panel, select a dimension method.

	Aligned	Most commonly used dimension type. Select individual elements or entire walls to dimension.
	Linear	Used when you need to specify certain points on elements.
	Angular	Used to dimension the angle between two elements.
	Radial	Used to dimension the radius of circular elements.
	Diameter	Used to dimension the diameter of circular elements.
	Arc Length	Used to dimension the length of the arc of circular elements.

2. In the Type Selector, select the dimension type.
3. Follow the prompts for the selected method.

Modifying Dimensions

When you move elements that are dimensioned, the dimensions automatically update. You can also modify dimensions by selecting a dimension or dimension string and making changes, as shown in Figure 13–7.

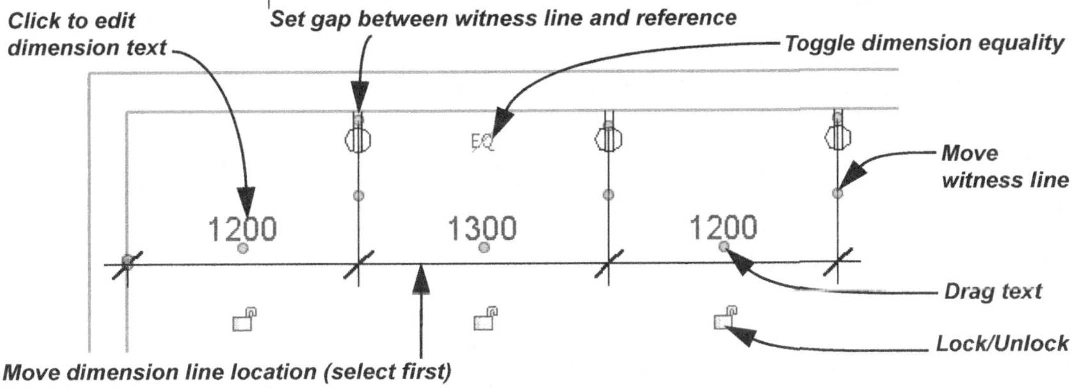

Figure 13–7

- To move the dimension text, select the **Drag text** control under the text and drag it to a new location. It automatically creates a leader from the dimension line if you drag it away. The style of the leader (arc or line) depends on the dimension style.
- To move the dimension line (the line parallel to the element being dimensioned) simply drag the line to a new location or select the dimension and drag the ✥ (Move) control.
- To change the gap between the witness line and the element being dimensioned, drag the control at the end of the witness line.
- To move the witness line (the line perpendicular to the element being dimensioned) to a different element or face of a wall, use the **Move Witness Line** control in the middle of the witness line. Click repeatedly to cycle through the various options. You can also drag this control to move the witness line to a different element, or right-click on the control and select **Move Witness Line**.

Adding and Deleting Dimensions in a String

- To add a witness line to a string of dimensions, select the dimension and, in the *Modify | Dimensions* tab>Witness Lines panel, click (Edit Witness Lines). Select the element(s) you want to add to the dimension, as shown in Figure 13–8. Click in space to finish.

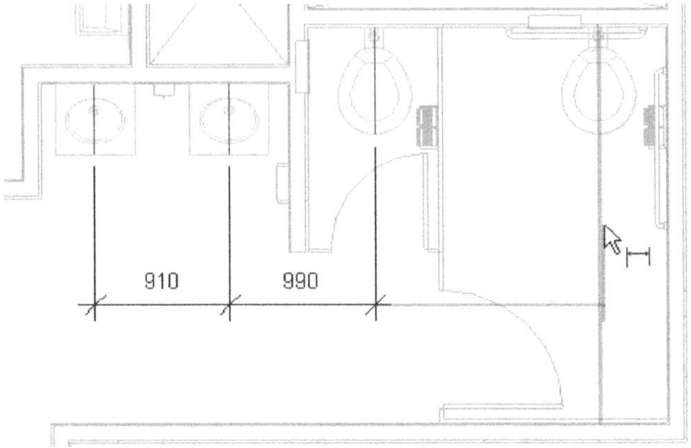

Figure 13–8

- To delete a witness line, drag the **Move Witness Line** control to a nearby element. Alternatively, you can hover the cursor over the control, right-click, and select **Delete Witness Line**.

- To delete one dimension in a string and break the string into two separate dimensions, select the string, hover over the dimension that you want to delete, and press <Tab>. When it highlights (as shown in Figure 13–9), pick it and press <Delete>. The selected dimension is deleted and the dimension string is separated into two elements as shown in Figure 13–10.

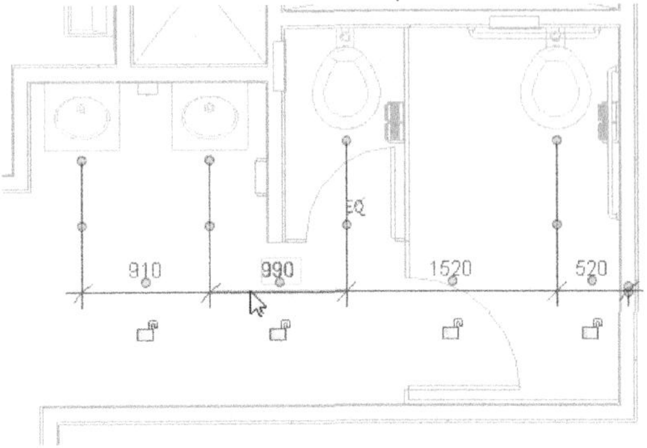

Figure 13–9

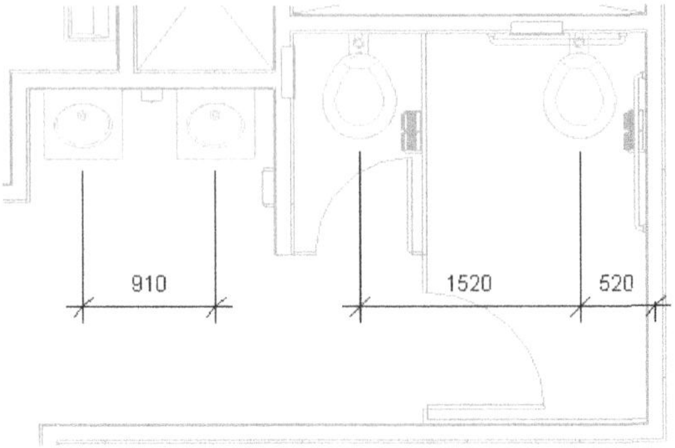

Figure 13–10

Modifying the Dimension Text

Because the Autodesk® Revit® software is parametric, changing the dimension text without changing the elements dimensioned would cause problems throughout the project. These issues could cause problems beyond the model if you use the project model to estimate materials or work with other disciplines.

You can append the text with prefixes and suffixes (as shown in Figure 13–11), which can help you in renovation projects.

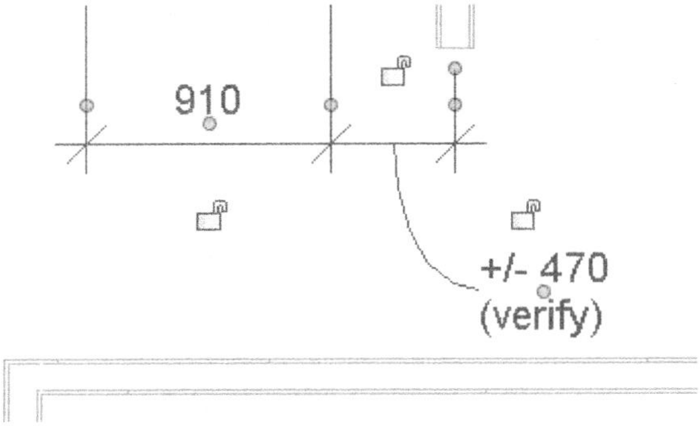

Figure 13–11

Double-click on the dimension text to open the Dimension Text dialog box, as shown in Figure 13–12, and make modifications as required.

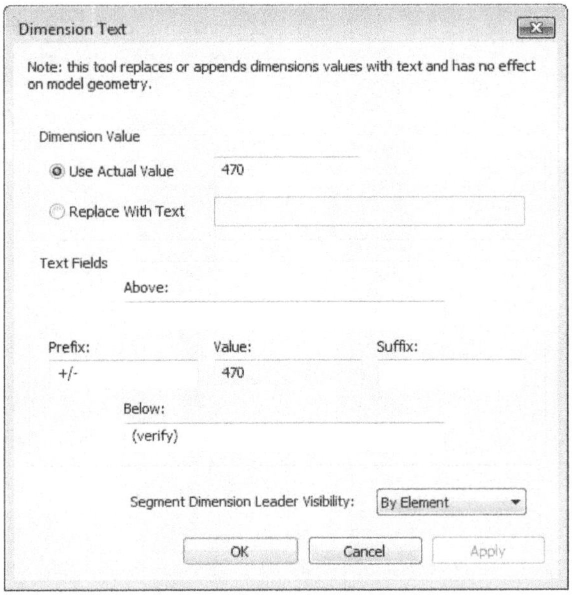

Figure 13–12

Setting Constraints

The three types of constraints that work with dimensions are locks and equal settings (as shown in Figure 13–13), as well as labels.

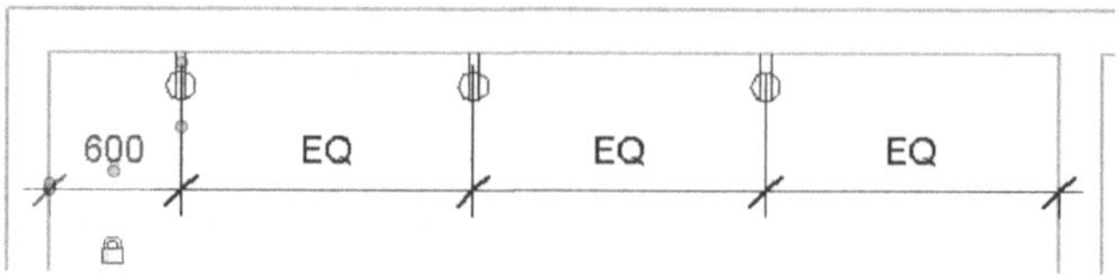

Figure 13–13

Locking Dimensions

When you lock a dimension, the value is set and you cannot make a change between it and the referenced elements. If it is unlocked, you can move it and change its value.

- Note that when you use this and move an element, any elements that are locked to the dimension also move.

Setting Dimensions Equal

For a string of dimensions, select the **EQ** symbol to constrain the elements to be at an equal distance apart. This actually moves the elements that are dimensioned.

- The equality text display can be changed in Properties, as shown in Figure 13–14. The style for each of the display types is set in the dimension type.

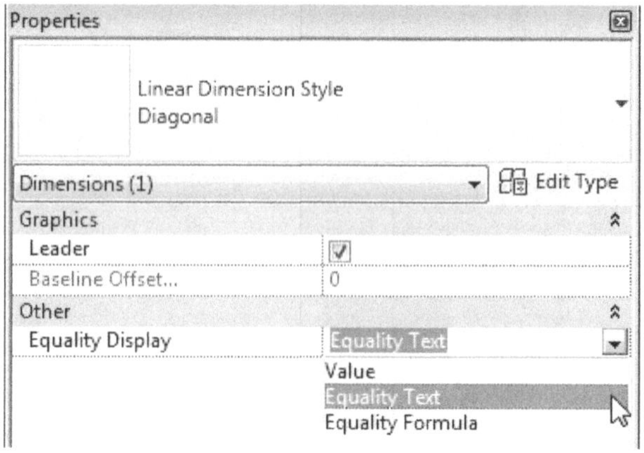

Figure 13–14

Labeling Dimensions

If you have a distance that needs to be repeated multiple times, such as the *Wall to AT* label shown in Figure 13–15, or one where you want to use a formula based on another dimension, you can create and apply a global parameter, also called a label, to the dimension.

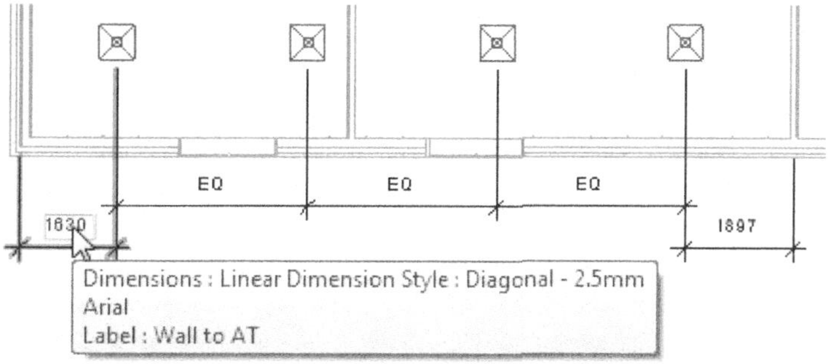

Figure 13–15

- To apply an existing label to a dimension, select the dimension and in the *Modify | Dimension* tab>Label Dimension panel, select the label in the drop-down list, as shown in Figure 13–16.

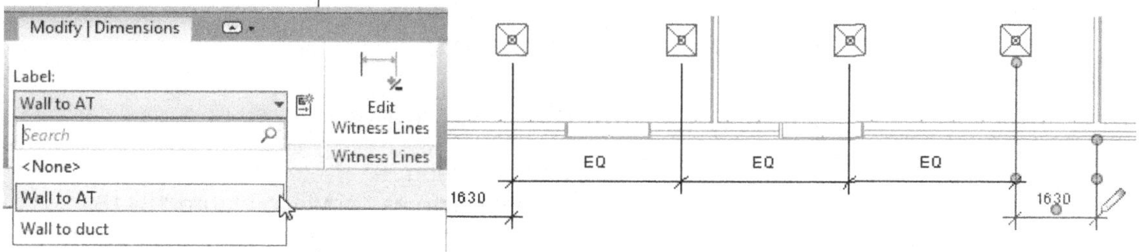

Figure 13–16

How To: Create a Label

1. Select a dimension.
2. In the *Modify | Dimension* tab>Label Dimension panel click (Create Parameter)
3. In the Global Parameter Properties dialog box type in a *Name* as shown in Figure 13–17 and click **OK**.

Figure 13–17

4. The label is applied to the dimension.

How To: Edit the Label Information

1. Select a labeled dimension.
2. Click **Global Parameters**, as shown in Figure 13–18.
3. In the Global Parameters dialog box, in the *Value* column, enter the new distance, as shown in Figure 13–19.

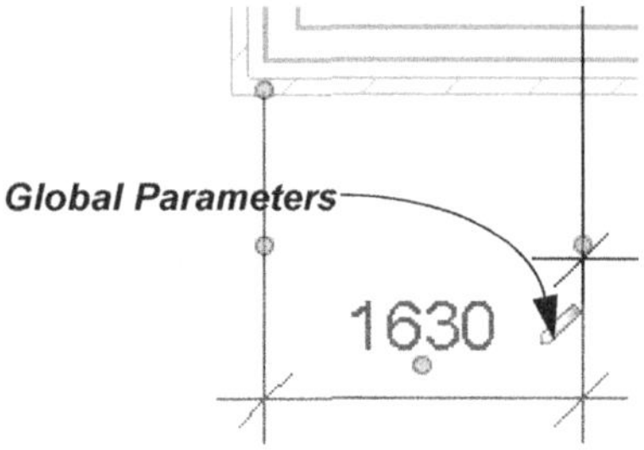

Figure 13–18

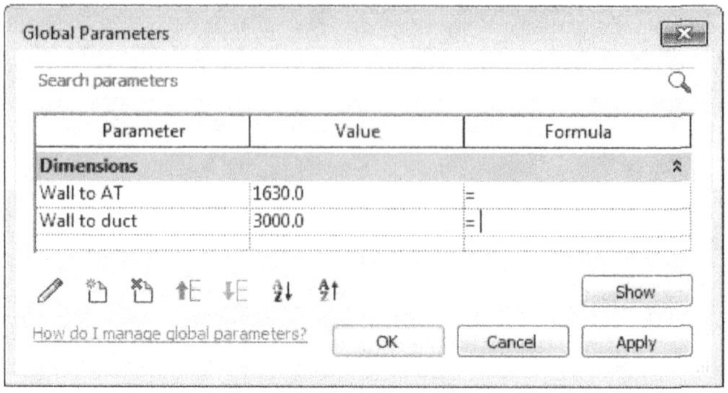

Figure 13–19

4. Click **OK**. The selected dimension and any other dimensions using the same label are updated.

- You can also edit, create, and delete Global Parameters in this dialog box.

Working with Constraints

To find out which elements have constraints applied to them, in the View Control Bar, click (Reveal Constraints). Constraints display as shown in Figure 13–20.

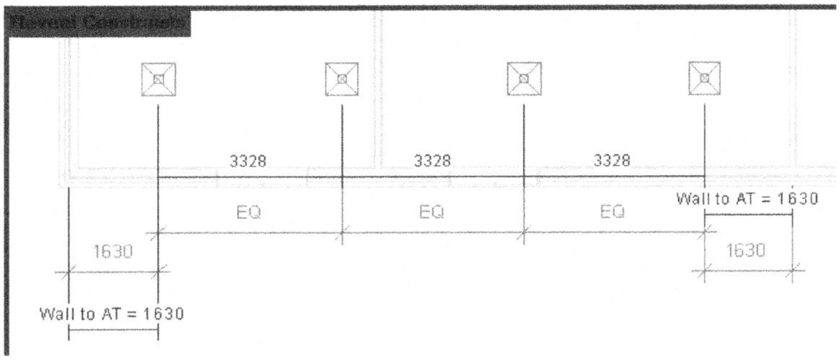

Figure 13–20

- If you try to move the element beyond the appropriate constrains, a warning dialog box displays, as shown in Figure 13–21.

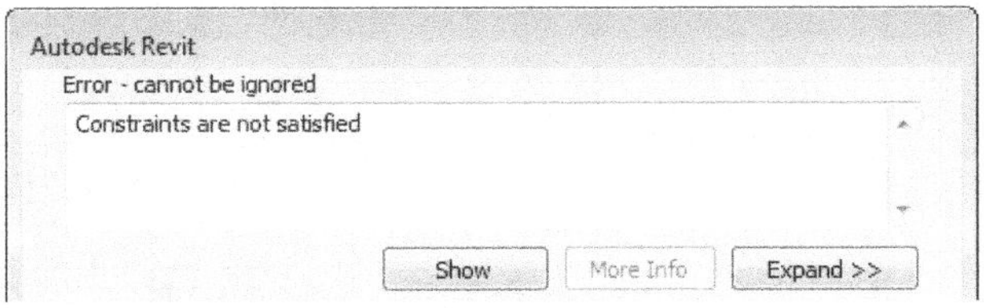

Figure 13–21

- If you delete dimensions that are constrained, a warning dialog box displays, as shown in Figure 13–22. Click **OK** to retain the constraint or **Unconstrain** to remove the constraint.

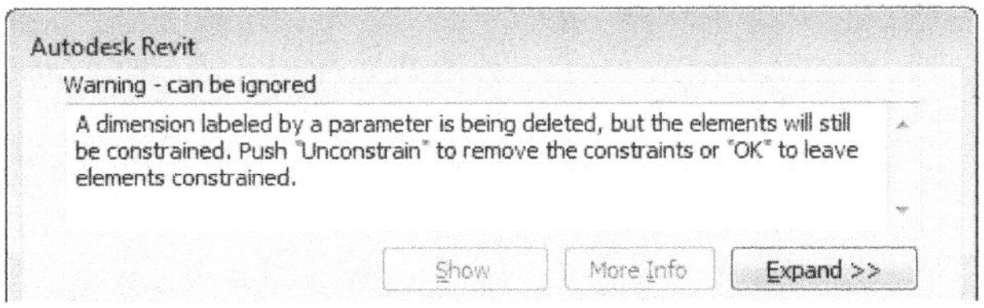

Figure 13–22

Practice 13a Work with Dimensions

Estimated time for completion: 10 minutes

Practice Objective

- Add dimensions to a mechanical plan.

In this practice you will add dimensions to the duct branches, and then modify those dimensions, as shown in Figure 13–23.

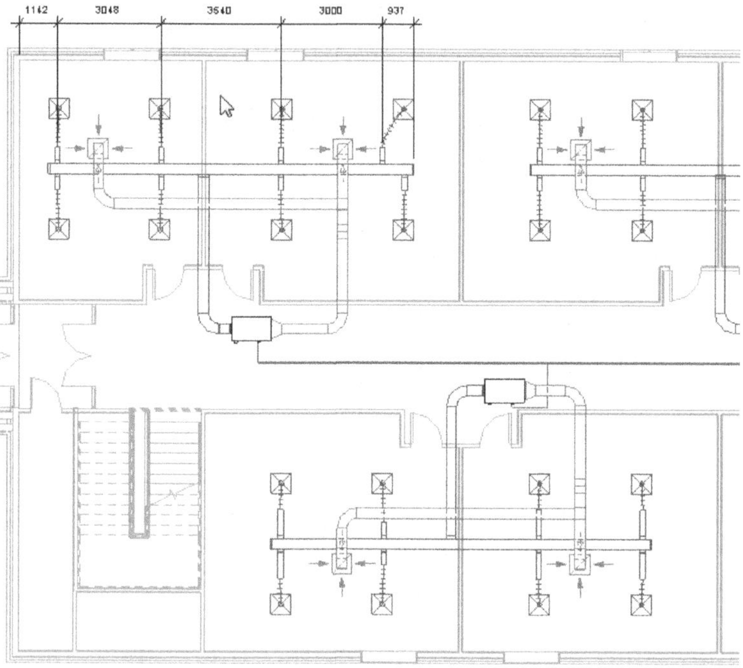

Figure 13–23

Task 1 - Add and Modify duct branch spacing Dimensions.

1. In the practice files *Annotating* folder, open **MEP-Elementary-School-Annotation-M.rvt**.
2. Open the Mechanical>HVAC>Floor Plans> **01 Mechanical Plan** view.
3. In the *Annotate* tab>Dimension panel, click  (Aligned).
4. In the Options Bar, verify that the **Wall centerlines** is selected.

5. Dimension the first four duct branches (not the diffusers) on the top side of the North wing, starting from the left side wall, as shown in Figure 13–24.

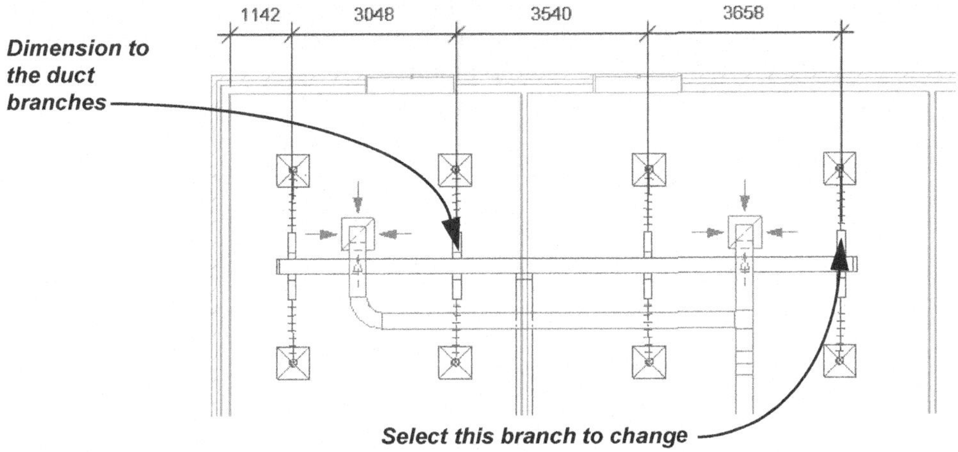

Figure 13–24

6. Click **Modify**.
7. Select the far right duct branch, as shown in Figure 13–24.
8. The corresponding dimension text turns blue. Select the dimension and change its value from *3658mm* to **3000mm**. The duct branch and the flex ductwork move accordingly, but the air terminal maintains its original position, as shown in Figure 13–25.

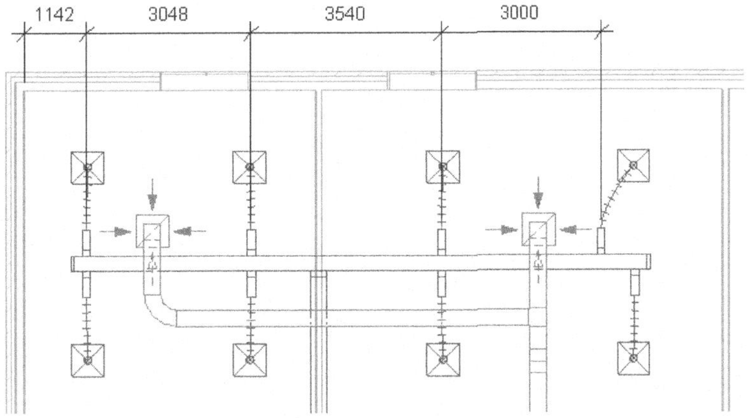

Figure 13–25

9. Click **Modify** and select the dimension line.

10. In the *Modify | Dimensions* tab>Witness Lines panel, click  (Edit Witness Lines).
11. Select the end of the main duct to add a fifth dimension to the string of dimensions, as shown in Figure 13–26. Click anywhere in the empty space away from any objects to finish the command.

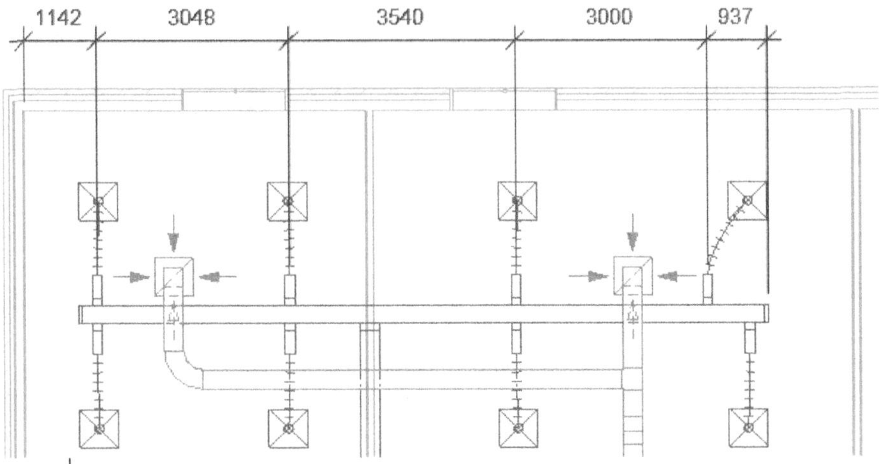

Figure 13–26

12. Click **Modify**.
13. Save the project.

13.2 Working With Text

The **Text** command enables you to add notes to views or sheets, such as the detail shown in Figure 13–27. The same command is used to create text with or without leaders.

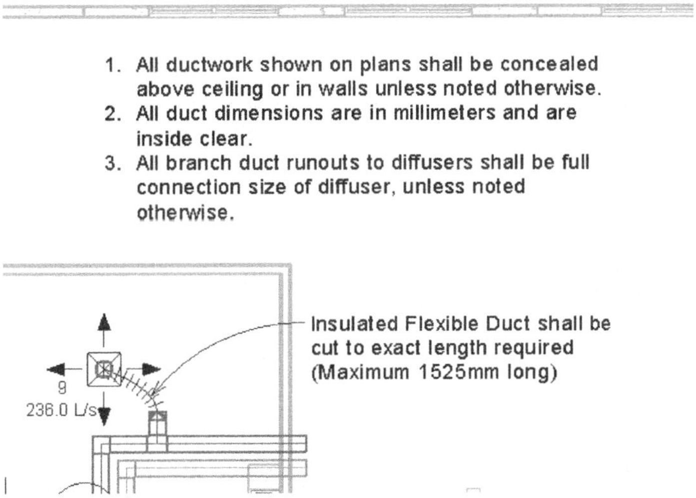

Figure 13–27

The text height is automatically set by the text type in conjunction with the scale of the view (as shown in Figure 13–28, using the same size text type at two different scales). Text types display at the specified height, both in the views and on the sheet.

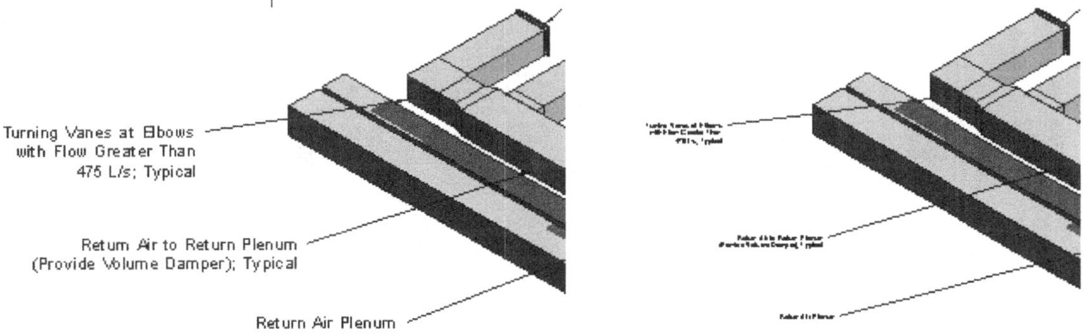

Scale 1:200 ***Scale: 1:100***

Figure 13–28

How To: Add Text

1. In the Quick Access Toolbar or *Annotate* tab>Text panel, click A (Text).

The text type sets the font and height of the text.

2. In the Type Selector, set the text type.
3. In the *Modify | Place Text* tab>Leader panel, select the method you want to use: A (No Leader), A (One Segment), A (Two Segments), or A (Curved).
4. In the Paragraph panel, set the overall justification for the text and leader, as shown in Figure 13–29.

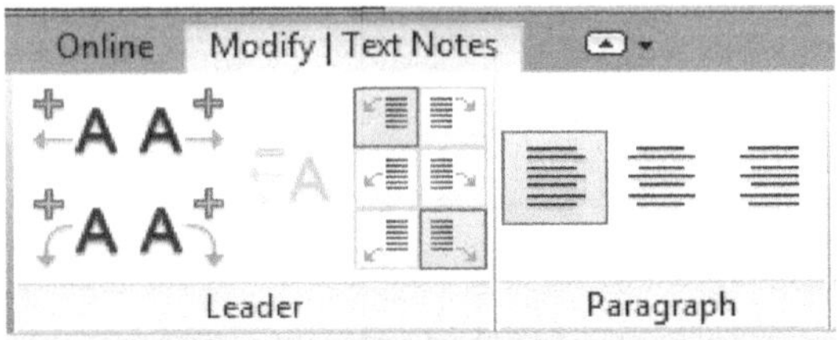

Figure 13–29

Use alignment lines to help you align the text with other text elements.

5. Select the location for the leader and text.
   - If **No leader** is selected, select the start point for the text and begin typing.
   - If using a leader, the first point places the arrow and you then select points for the leader. The text starts at the last leader point.
   - To set a word wrapping distance, click and drag to set the start and end points of the text.
6. Type the required text. In the *Edit Text* tab, specify additional options for the font and paragraph, as shown in Figure 13–30.

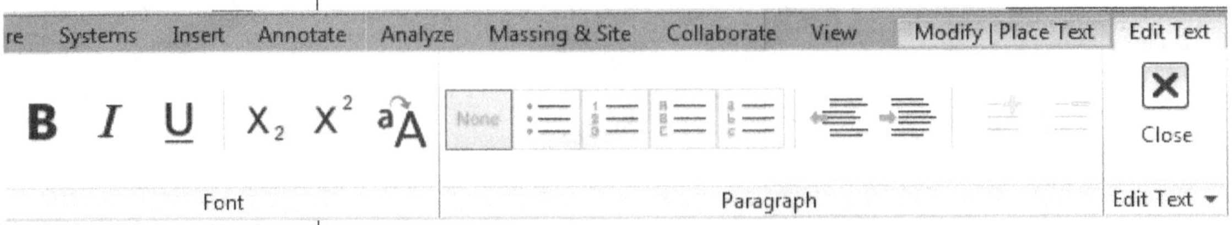

Figure 13–30

7. In the *Edit Text* tab>Edit Text panel, click (Close) or click outside the text box to complete the text element.
   - Pressing <Enter> after a line of text starts a new line of text in the same text window.

How To: Add Text Symbols

New in 2018

1. Start the **Text** command and click to place the text.
2. As you are typing text and need to insert a symbol, right-click and select **Symbols** from the shortcut menu. Select from the list of commonly used symbols, as shown in Figure 13–31.

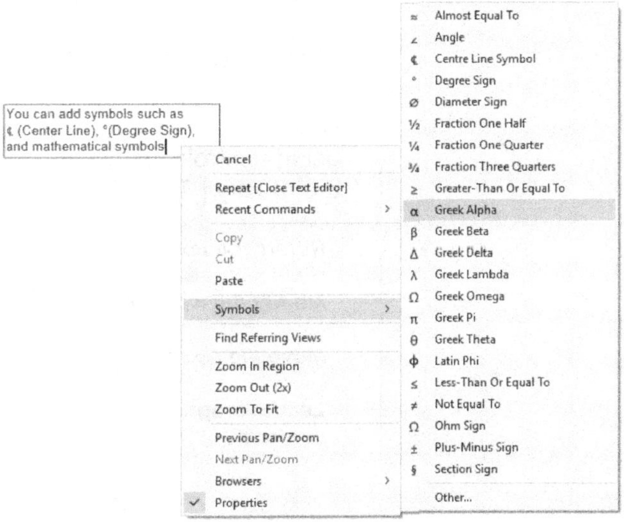

Figure 13–31

3. If the symbol you need is not listed, click **Other**.
4. In the Character Map dialog box, click on a symbol and click **Select**, as shown in Figure 13–32.

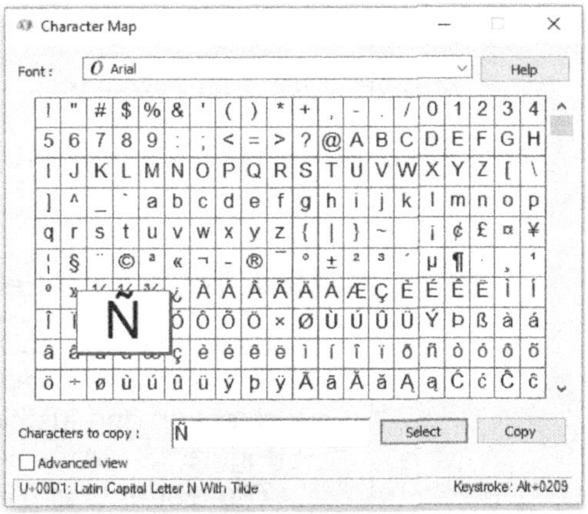

Figure 13–32

5. Click **Copy** to copy the character to the clipboard and paste it into the text box.

- The Font in the Character Map must match the font used by the text type. You cannot use a different font for symbols.

Editing Text

Editing text notes takes place at two levels:

- Modifying the text note, which includes the **Leader** and **Paragraph** styles.
- Editing the text, which includes changes to individual letters, word, and paragraphs in the text note.

Modifying the Text Note

Click once on the text note to modify the text box and leaders using controls, as shown in Figure 13–33, or using the tools in the *Modify | Text Notes* tab.

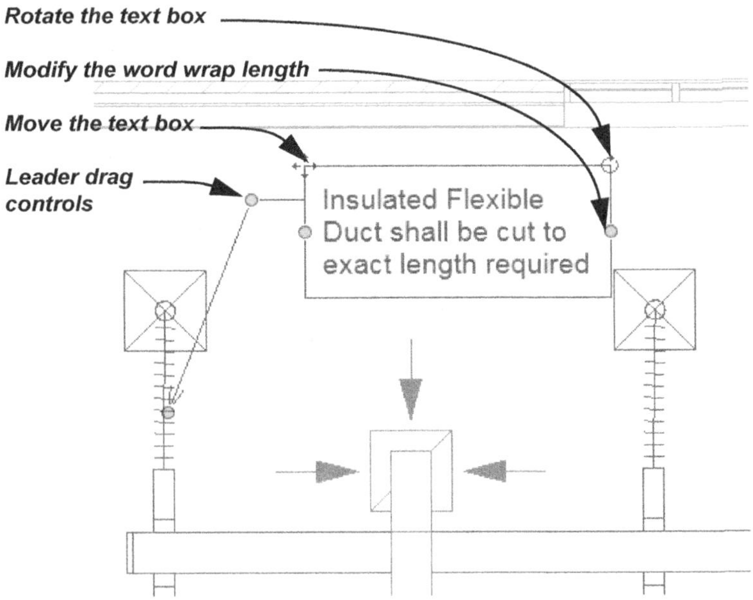

Figure 13–33

How To: Add a Leader to Text Notes

1. Select the text note.
2. In the *Modify | Text Notes* tab>Leader panel, select the direction and justification for the new leader, as shown in Figure 13–34.
3. The leader is applied, as shown in Figure 13–35. Use the drag controls to place the arrow as required.

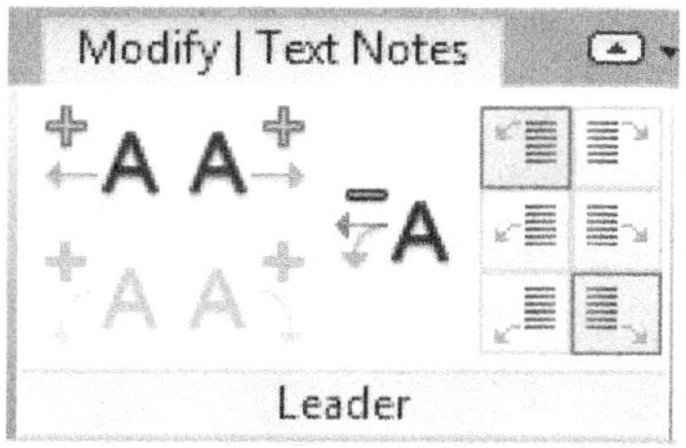

Figure 13–34

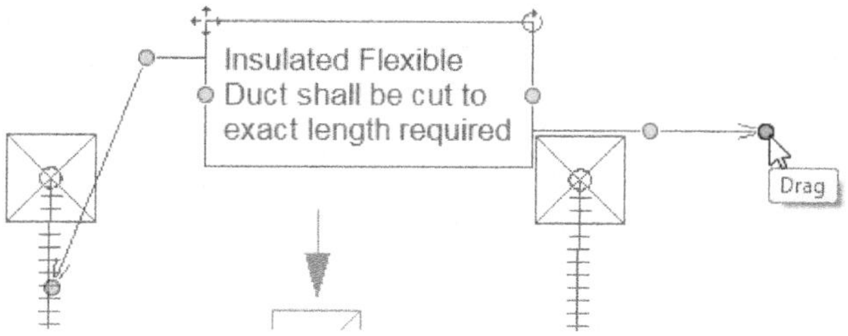

Figure 13–35

- You can remove leaders by clicking (Remove Last Leader).

Editing the Text

The *Edit Text* tab enables you to make various customizations. These include modifying the font of selected words as well as creating bulleted and numbered lists, as shown in Figure 13–36.

General Notes
1. Notify designer of intention to start construction at least 10 days prior to start of site work.
2. Installer shall provide the following:
   - 24-hour notice of start of construction
   - Inspection of bottom of bed or covering required by state inspector
   - All environmental management inspection sheets must be emailed to designer's office within 24 hours of inspection.

Figure 13–36

- You can **Cut**, **Copy**, and **Paste** text using the clipboard. For example, you can copy text from a document and then paste it into the text editor in Revit.

- To help you see the text better as you are modifying it, in the *Edit Text* tab, expand the Edit Text panel, and select one or both of the options, as shown in Figure 13–37.

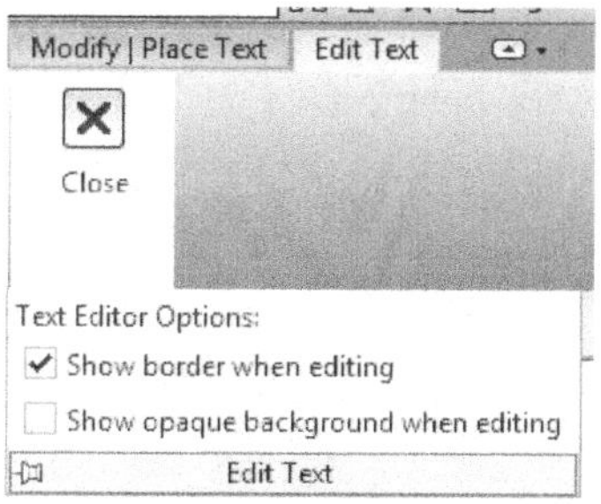

Figure 13–37

How To: Modify the Font

1. Select Individual letters or words.
2. Click on the font modification you want to include:

B (Bold)	X_2 (Subscript)
I (Italic)	X^2 (Superscript)
U (Underline)	aA (All Caps)

- When pasting text from a document outside of Autodesk Revit, font modifications (e.g, Bold, Italic, etc.) are retained.

How To: Create Lists

1. In Edit Text mode, place the cursor in the line where you want to add to a list.
2. In the *Edit Text* tab>Paragraph panel, click the type of list you want to create:

(Bullets)	(Uppercase Letters)
(Numbers)	(Lowercase Letters)

3. As you type, press <Enter> and the next line in the list is incremented.
4. To include sub-lists, at the beginning of the next line, click (Increase Indent). This indents the line and applies the next level of lists, as shown in Figure 13–38.

The indent distance is setup by the Text Type Tab Size.

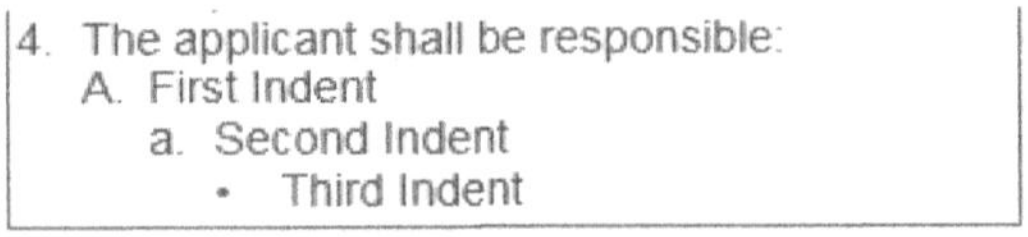

Figure 13–38

   - You can change the type of list after you have applied the first increment. For example, you might want to use a list of bullets instead of letters, as shown in Figure 13–39.

5. Click (Decrease Indent) to return to the previous list style.

- Press <Shift>+<Enter> to create a blank line in a numbered list.

- To create columns or other separate text boxes that build on a numbering system (as shown in Figure 13–39), create the second text box and list. Then, place the cursor on one of the lines and in the Paragraph panel click (Increment List Value) until the list matches the next number in the sequence.

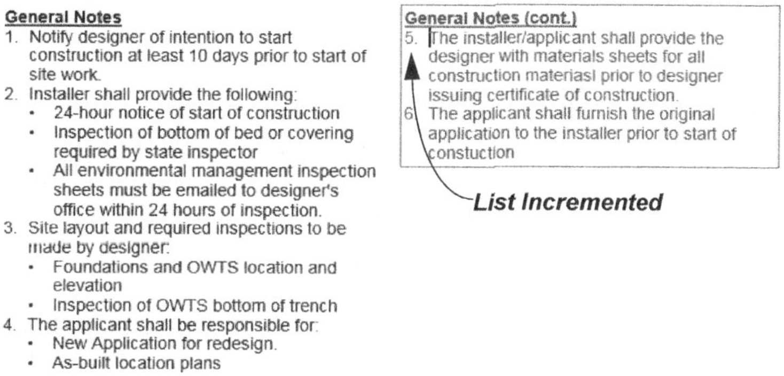

Figure 13–39

6. Click (Decrement List Value) to move back a number.

Spell Checking

The Spelling dialog box displays any misspelled words in context and provides several options for changing them, as shown in Figure 13–40.

You can also check the spelling in selected text. With text selected, in the Modify | Text Notes tab>Tools panel, click (Check Spelling).

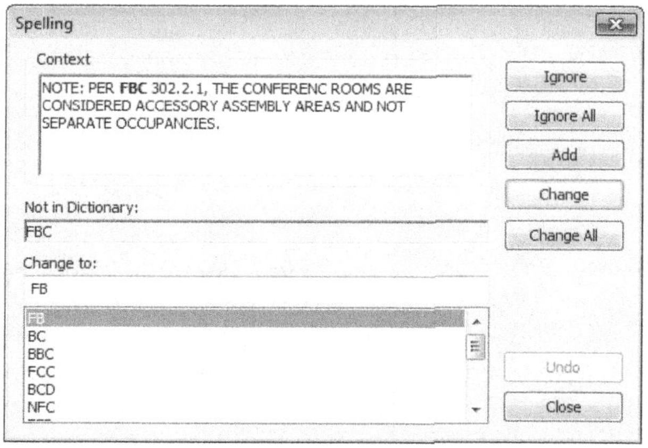

Figure 13–40

- To spell check all text in a view, in the *Annotate* tab>Text panel, click (Spelling) or press <F7>. As with other spell checkers, you can **Ignore**, **Add**, or **Change** the word.

Creating Text Types

If you need new text types with a different text size or font (such as for a title or hand-lettering), you can create new ones, as shown in Figure 13–41. It is recommended that you create these in a project template so they are available in future projects.

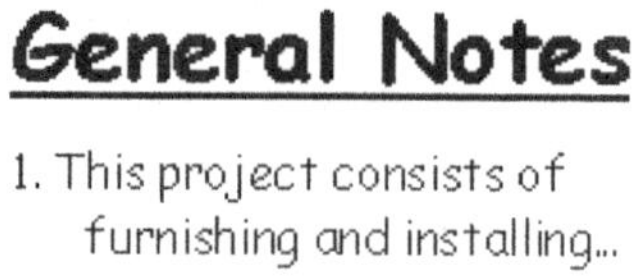

Figure 13–41

- You can copy and paste text types from one project to another or use **Transfer Project Standards**.

How To: Create Text Types

1. In the *Annotate* tab>Text panel, click (Text Types).
2. In the Type Properties dialog box, click **Duplicate**.
3. In the Name dialog box, type a new name and click **OK**.
4. Modify the text parameters, as required. The parameters are shown in Figure 13–42.

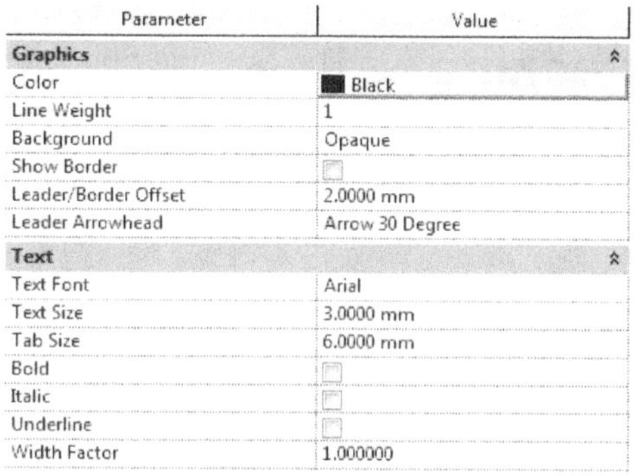

Parameter	Value
Graphics	
Color	Black
Line Weight	1
Background	Opaque
Show Border	☐
Leader/Border Offset	2.0000 mm
Leader Arrowhead	Arrow 30 Degree
Text	
Text Font	Arial
Text Size	3.0000 mm
Tab Size	6.0000 mm
Bold	☐
Italic	☐
Underline	☐
Width Factor	1.000000

Figure 13–42

5. Click **OK** to close the Type Properties dialog box.

- The **Background** parameter can be set to **Opaque** or **Transparent**. An opaque background includes a masking region that hides lines or elements beneath the text.
- In the *Text* area, the **Width Factor** parameter controls the width of the lettering, but does not affect the height. A width factor greater than **1** spreads the text out and a width factor less than **1** compresses it.
- The **Show Border** parameter, when selected, includes a rectangle around the text.

13.3 Adding Detail Lines and Symbols

While annotating views for construction documents, you might need to add detail lines and symbols to clarify the design intent or show information, such as the life safety plan exit information, as shown in Figure 13–43.

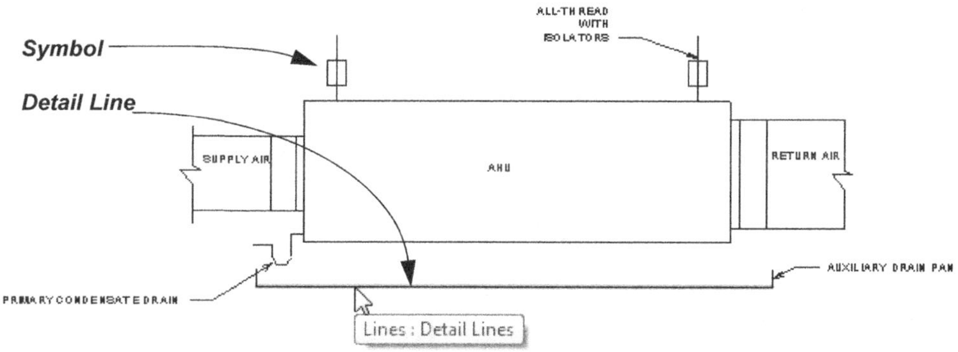

Figure 13–43

- Detail lines and symbols are view-specific, which means that they only display in the view in which they were created.

How To: Draw Detail Lines

1. In the *Annotation* tab>Detail panel, click (Detail Line).
2. In the *Modify | Place Detail Lines* tab>Line Style panel, select the type of line you want to use, as shown in Figure 13–44.

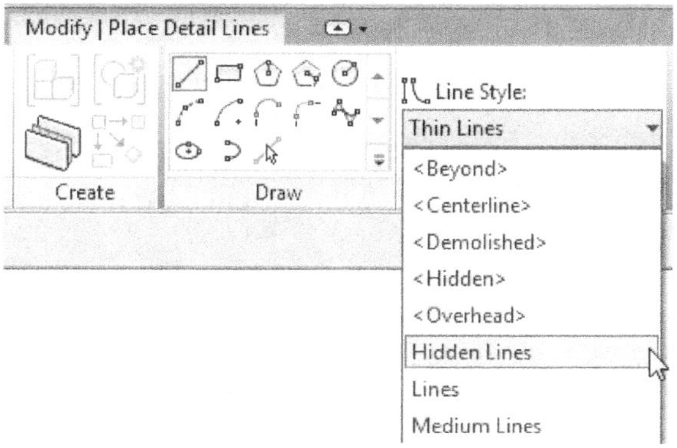

Figure 13–44

3. Use the tools in the Draw panel to create the detail lines.

Draw Options

When you are in Drawing mode, several options display in the Options Bar, as shown in Figure 13–45.

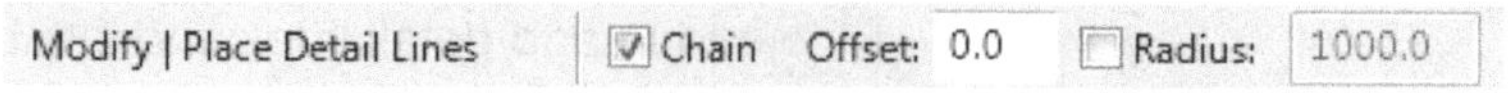

Figure 13–45

- **Chain**: Controls how many segments are created in one process. If this option is not selected, the **Line** and **Arc** tools only create one segment at a time. If it is selected, you can continue adding segments until you select the command again.
- **Offset**: Enables you to enter values so you can create linear elements at a specified distance from the selected points or element.
- **Radius**: Enables you to enter values when using a radial tool.

Draw Tools

	Line	Draws a straight line defined by the first and last points. If Chain is enabled, you can continue selecting end points for multiple segments.
	Rectangle	Draws a rectangle defined by two opposing corner points. You can adjust the dimensions after selecting both points.
	Inscribed Polygon	Draws a polygon inscribed in a hypothetical circle with the number of sides specified in the Options Bar.
	Circumscribed Polygon	Draws a polygon circumscribed around a hypothetical circle with the number of sides specified in the Options Bar.
	Circle	Draws a circle defined by a center point and radius.
	Start-End-Radius Arc	Draws a curve defined by a start, end, and radius of the arc. The outside dimension shown is the included angle of the arc. The inside dimension is the radius.
	Center-ends Arc	Draws a curve defined by a center, radius, and included angle. The selected point of the radius also defines the start point of the arc.
	Spline	Draws a spline curve based on selected points. The curve does not actually touch the points (Model and Detail Lines only).

	Tangent End Arc	Draws a curve tangent to another element. Select an end point for the first point, but do not select the intersection of two or more elements. Then select a second point based on the included angle of the arc.
	Fillet Arc	Draws a curve defined by two other elements and a radius. Because it is difficult to select the correct radius by clicking, this command automatically moves to edit mode. Select the dimension and modify the radius of the fillet.
	Ellipse	Draws an ellipse from a primary and secondary axis (Model and Detail Lines only).
	Partial Ellipse	Draws only one side of the ellipse, like an arc. A partial ellipse also has a primary and secondary axis (Model and Detail Lines only).
	Pick Lines	Use this option to select existing linear elements in the project. This is useful when you start the project from an imported 2D drawing.

Using Symbols

Symbols are 2D elements that only display in one view, while components can be in 3D and display in many views.

Many of the annotations used in working drawings are frequently repeated. Several of them have been saved as symbols in the Autodesk Revit software, such as the North Arrow, Center Line, and Graphic Scale annotations as shown in Figure 13–46.

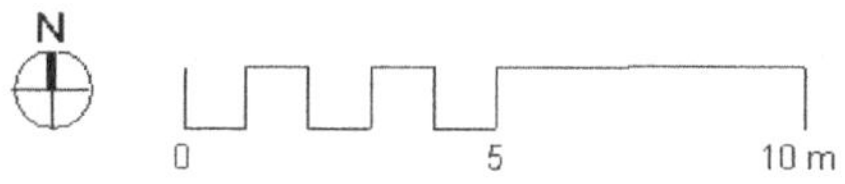

Figure 13–46

- You can also create or load custom annotation symbols.

How To: Place a Symbol

1. In the *Annotate* tab>Symbol panel, click (Symbol).
2. In the Type Selector, select the symbol you want to use.
3. In the *Modify | Place Symbol* tab>Mode panel, click (Load Family) if you want to load other symbols.
4. In the Options Bar, as shown in Figure 13–47, set the *Number of Leaders* and select **Rotate after placement** if you want to rotate the symbol as you insert it.

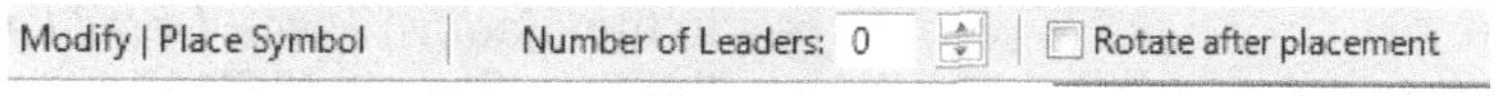

Figure 13–47

5. Place the symbol in the view. Rotate it if you selected the **Rotate after placement** option. If you specified leaders, use the controls to move them into place.

Practice 13b Annotate Construction Documents

Estimated time for completion: 10 minutes

Practice Objectives

- Add detail lines and text in a callout view.
- Paste in text and modify text formatting.

In this practice, you will add detail lines and text to indicate the boundaries of an access area, as shown in Figure 13–48. You will also add a symbol to a sheet and a bulleted list of general notes.

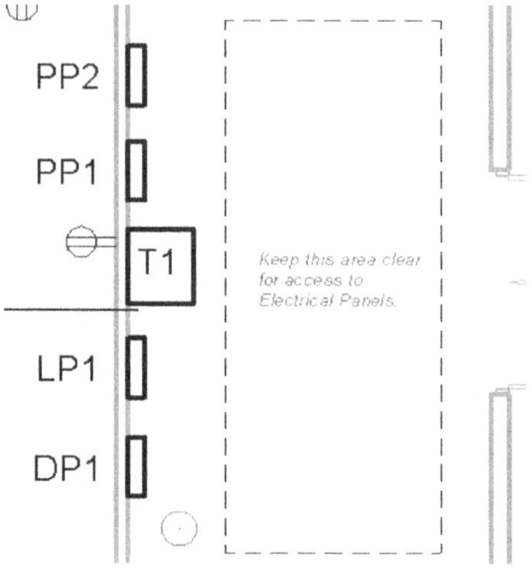

Figure 13–48

Task 1 - Add detail lines and text.

1. In the practice files *Annotating* folder, open **MEP-Elementary-School-Annotation-M.rvt**.
2. Open the Electrical>Power>Floor Plans>**01 Power Plan** view, and zoom in on the Electrical Distribution Room in the upper right corner.
3. In the *Annotate* tab>Detail panel, click (Detail Line).
4. In the *Modify | Place Detail Lines* tab>Line Style panel, set the *Line Style* to **MEP Hidden**.

5. Draw a rectangle from the upper left corner of the room to the lower right corner of the room, approximately **500mm x 1800mm**, as shown in Figure 13–49.

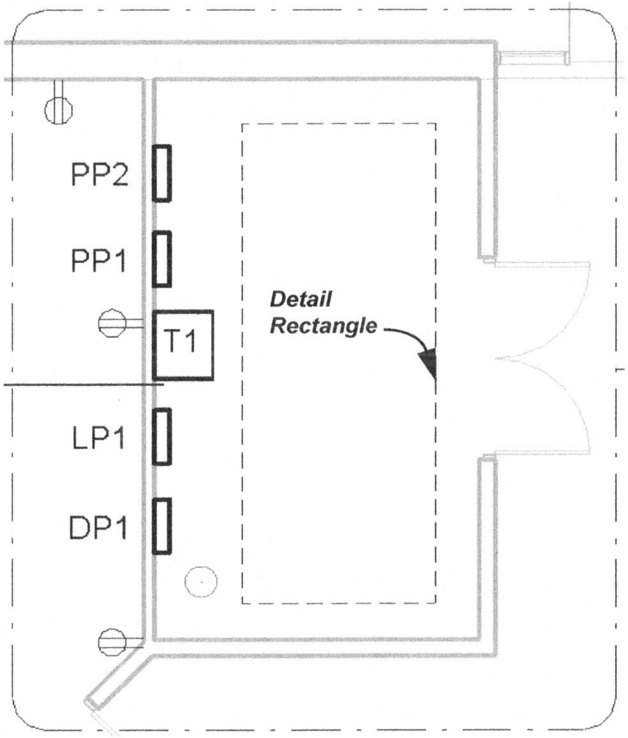

Figure 13–49

6. In the *Annotate* tab>Text panel, click A (Text).
7. In the Type Selector, select **Text: 3.5mm Arial**.
8. In Properties, click **Edit Type**. In the Type Properties dialog box, click **Duplicate**. Type **4mm Arial - Red** for the name and click **OK**.
9. Set the following properties:
   - *Color*: **Red**
   - *Text Font*: **Arial**
   - *Text Size*: **4mm**
   - Select **Italic**.

10. Click **OK** to save and close the Type Properties dialog box.

11. Add text using the **4mm Arial - Red** text type, to the inside of the Detail rectangle you drew, as shown in Figure 13–50.

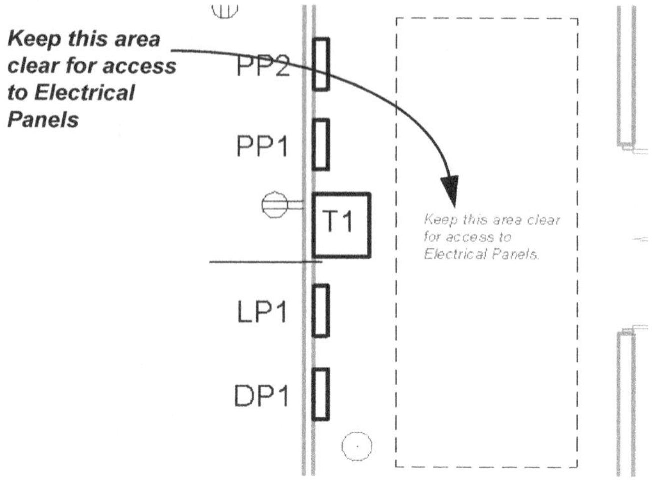

Figure 13–50

12. Save the project.

Task 2 - Add a symbol.

1. Zoom out to fit.
2. In the *Annotate* tab>Symbol panel, click (Symbol).
3. In the *Modify | Place Symbol* tab>Mode panel, click (Load Family).
4. In the Autodesk Revit library>*Annotations* folder, select the **N_North Arrow 1.rfa** symbol and click **Open**.
5. Insert a North Arrow near the bottom left of the model.
6. Save the project.

Task 3 - Create Text with a List.

1. Open the sheet **C-101 - Cover Sheet**.
2. Open a text editor and navigate to the practice files folder. Open either **General Notes.docx** or **General Notes.txt**.
3. Copy the entire contents of the file to the clipboard.
4. In Autodesk Revit, start the **Text** command.
5. Verify that no leader is selected, set the text type to **3.5mm Arial**, and draw a text box similar to the one shown in Figure 13–51.

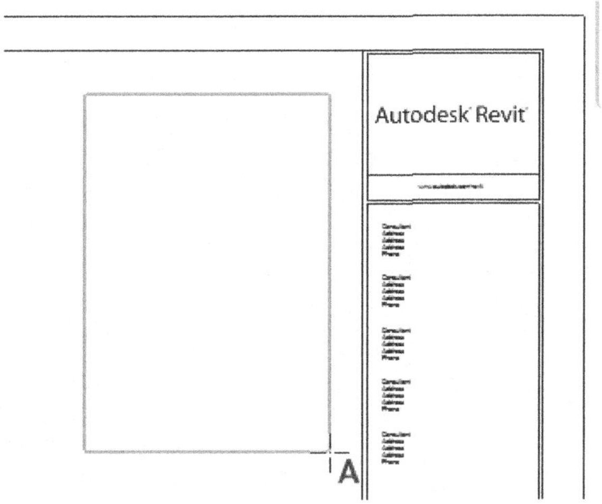

Figure 13–51

6. In the Edit Text dialog box>Clipboard panel, click  (Paste).
7. Remain in Edit Text mode and zoom in on the text box. Note that there are numbered and lettered lists in the text but that they are not quite correct.

8. Select all of the text and in the *Edit Text* tab>Paragraph panel, click (List: Numbers).

   The paragraphs are recognized and numbered but, the existing numbers and letters are still there.

9. Select the lettered paragraphs and in the *Edit Text* tab> Paragraph panel, click (List: Lowercase letters). This changes that list to a lettered list.

10. Zoom in and remove the additional numbers and letters, as shown in Figure 13–52.

If you copied the text from the .TXT file, then you might need to increase the indent and change the list type.

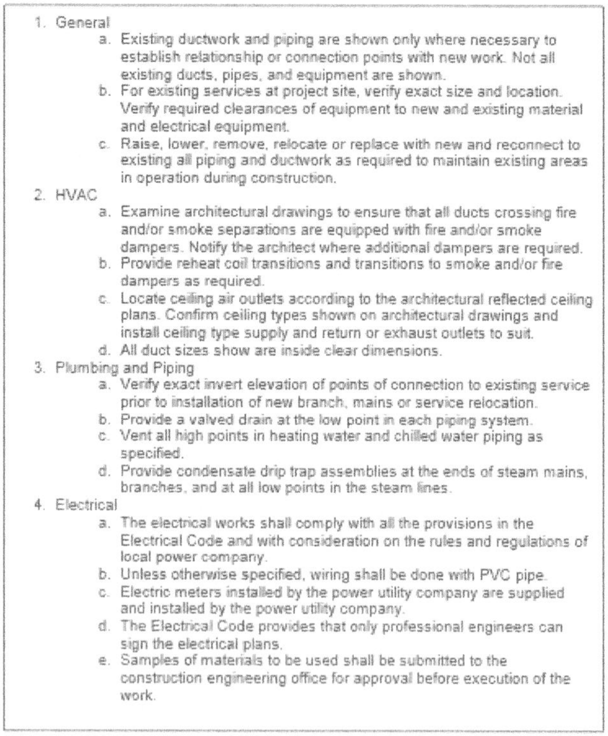
1. General
   a. Existing ductwork and piping are shown only where necessary to establish relationship or connection points with new work. Not all existing ducts, pipes, and equipment are shown.
   b. For existing services at project site, verify exact size and location. Verify required clearances of equipment to new and existing material and electrical equipment.
   c. Raise, lower, remove, relocate or replace with new and reconnect to existing all piping and ductwork as required to maintain existing areas in operation during construction.
2. HVAC
   a. Examine architectural drawings to ensure that all ducts crossing fire and/or smoke separations are equipped with fire and/or smoke dampers. Notify the architect where additional dampers are required.
   b. Provide reheat coil transitions and transitions to smoke and/or fire dampers as required.
   c. Locate ceiling air outlets according to the architectural reflected ceiling plans. Confirm ceiling types shown on architectural drawings and install ceiling type supply and return or exhaust outlets to suit.
   d. All duct sizes show are inside clear dimensions.
3. Plumbing and Piping
   a. Verify exact invert elevation of points of connection to existing service prior to installation of new branch, mains or service relocation.
   b. Provide a valved drain at the low point in each piping system.
   c. Vent all high points in heating water and chilled water piping as specified.
   d. Provide condensate drip trap assemblies at the ends of steam mains, branches, and at all low points in the steam lines.
4. Electrical
   a. The electrical works shall comply with all the provisions in the Electrical Code and with consideration on the rules and regulations of local power company.
   b. Unless otherwise specified, wiring shall be done with PVC pipe.
   c. Electric meters installed by the power utility company are supplied and installed by the power utility company.
   d. The Electrical Code provides that only professional engineers can sign the electrical plans.
   e. Samples of materials to be used shall be submitted to the construction engineering office for approval before execution of the work.

Figure 13–52

11. At the beginning of the list, add the text **General Notes**. Make it bold and underlined, as shown in Figure 13–53.

12. Place the cursor at the end sentence of the **1. General** section. Hold <Shift> and press <Enter>. A new line is created without disrupting the numbering sequence.

13. Repeat this at the end of the discipline sections, as shown in Figure 13–53.

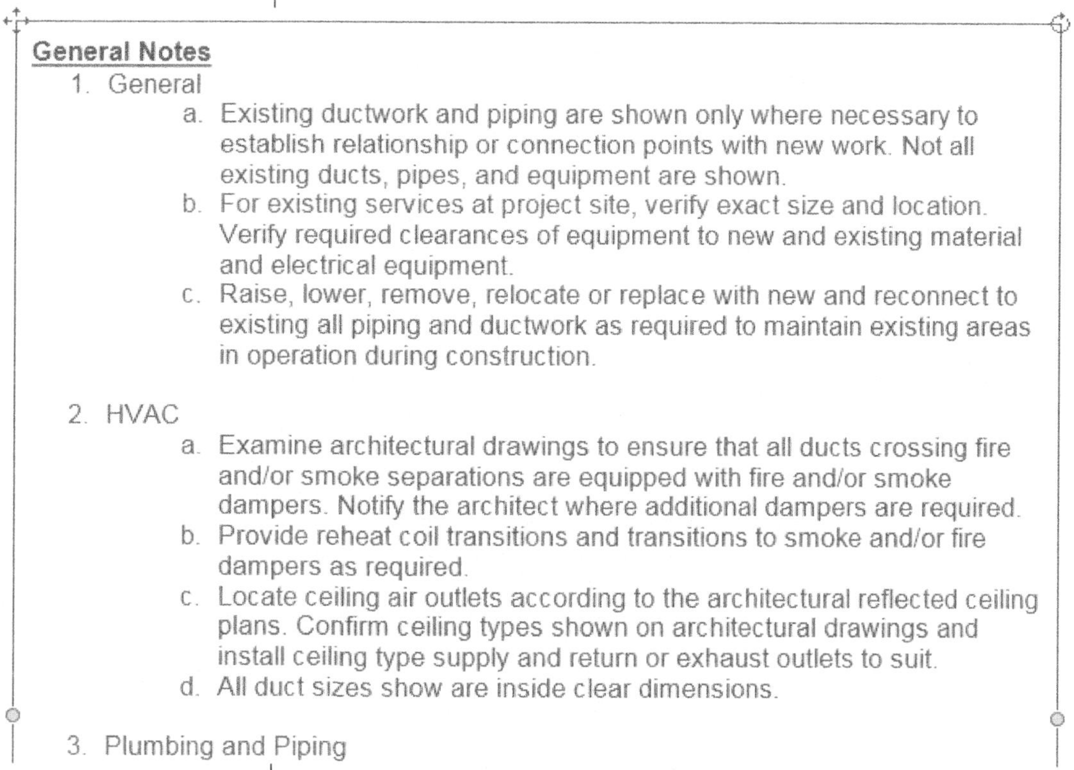

General Notes

1. General
   a. Existing ductwork and piping are shown only where necessary to establish relationship or connection points with new work. Not all existing ducts, pipes, and equipment are shown.
   b. For existing services at project site, verify exact size and location. Verify required clearances of equipment to new and existing material and electrical equipment.
   c. Raise, lower, remove, relocate or replace with new and reconnect to existing all piping and ductwork as required to maintain existing areas in operation during construction.

2. HVAC
   a. Examine architectural drawings to ensure that all ducts crossing fire and/or smoke separations are equipped with fire and/or smoke dampers. Notify the architect where additional dampers are required.
   b. Provide reheat coil transitions and transitions to smoke and/or fire dampers as required.
   c. Locate ceiling air outlets according to the architectural reflected ceiling plans. Confirm ceiling types shown on architectural drawings and install ceiling type supply and return or exhaust outlets to suit.
   d. All duct sizes show are inside clear dimensions.

3. Plumbing and Piping

Figure 13–53

14. Use the controls if required to relocate or resize the text note.

15. Zoom out to see the full sheet.

16. Save the project.

13.4 Creating Legends

A legend is a separate view that can be placed on multiple sheets. Legends can be used to hold installation notes that need to be placed on a sheet with each floor plan, key plans, or any 2D items that need to be repeated. You can also create and list the symbols that are used in your project, and provide explanatory notes next to the, as shown in Figure 13–54. Additionally, legends can provide a list of materials, or elevations of window types used in the project.

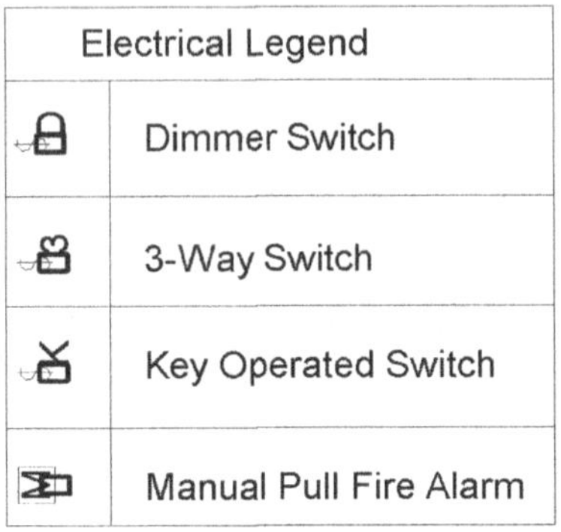

Figure 13–54

- You use (Detail Lines) and (Text) to create the table and explanatory notes. Once you have a legend view, you can use commands, such as (Legend Component), (Detail Component), and (Symbol), to place elements in the view.
- Unlike other views, legend views can be attached to more than one sheet.
- You can set a legend's scale in the View Status Bar.
- Elements in legends can be dimensioned.

How To: Create a Legend

1. In the *View* tab>Create panel, expand (Legends) and click (Legend) or in the Project Browser, right-click on the *Legends* area title and select **New Legend**.

2. In the New Legend View dialog box, enter a name and select a scale for the legend, as shown in Figure 13–55, and click **OK**.

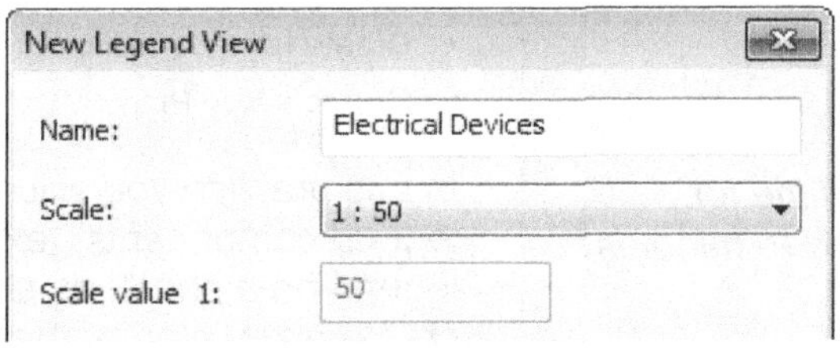

Figure 13–55

3. Place the components in the view first, and then sketch the outline of the table when you know the sizes. Use **Ref Planes** to line up the components.

How To: Use Legend Components

1. In the *Annotate* tab>Detail panel, expand (Component) and click (Legend Component).
2. In the Options Bar, select the *Family* type that you want to use, as shown in Figure 13–56.
   - This list contains all of the elements in a project that can be used in a legend.

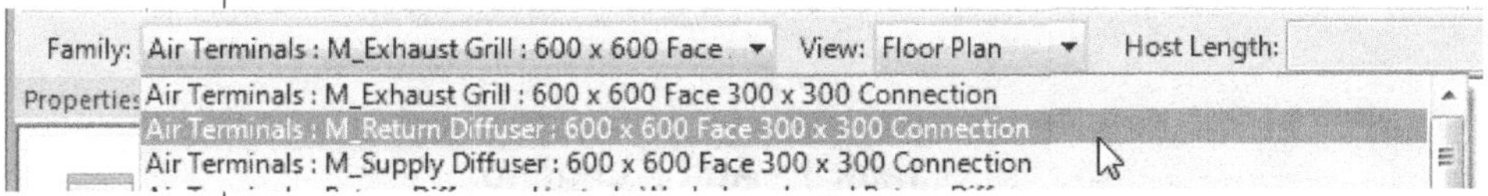

Figure 13–56

3. Select the *View* of the element that you want to use.
4. Place the component anywhere in the view.
   - Note that legend components are not counted in schedules and material takeoffs.
5. Add symbols (such as those shown in Figure 13–57), text, and detail lines to complete the legend.

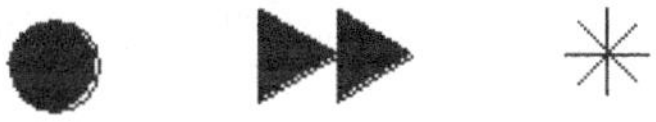

Figure 13–57

- Elements that are full size, such as plumbing fixtures, electrical equipment, or air terminals, come in at their full size.

Practice 13c Create Legends

Practice Objectives

- Create legends using legend components and text.
- Create a Key Plan.

Estimated time for completion: 10 minutes

In this practice you will create a Plumbing Fixture legend using legend components, text and detail lines. You will then put the legend on a sheet, as shown in Figure 13–58. You will also create a key plan of the building using a Legend view and add it to several sheets.

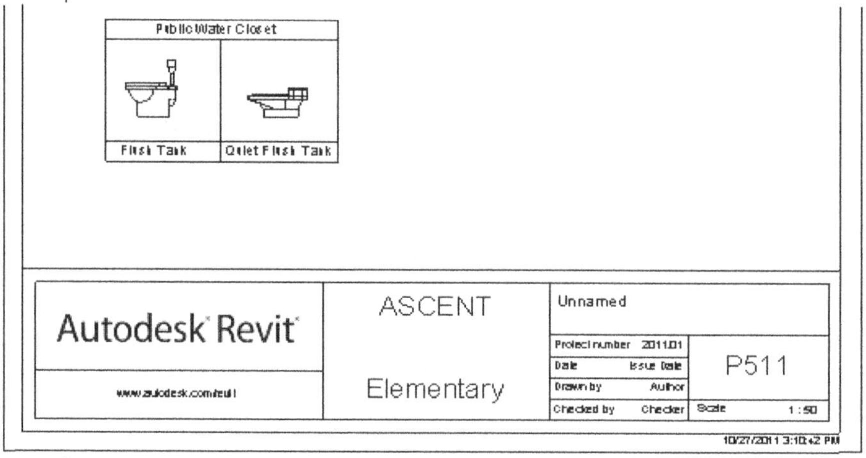

Figure 13–58

Task 1 - Add a Legend.

1. In the practice files *Annotating* folder open **MEP-Elementary-School-Annotation-M.rvt**.
2. In the *View* tab>Create panel, expand (Legends) and click (Legend) to create a new Legend view.
3. Name the legend **Plumbing Fixture - Flush Tank** and set the *Scale* to **1:50**. The new legend is created and placed in the *Legends* node of the Project Browser.
4. In the *Annotate* tab>Detail panel, expand (Component) and click (Legend Component).

5. In the Options Bar, set *Family* to **Plumbing Fixtures: M_Water Closet - Flush Tank: Public - 6.1 Lpf** and set *View* to **Elevation - Front**. Add a single instance to the current Legend view.

6. In the Options Bar, set *Family* to **Plumbing Fixtures: M_Water Closet - Quiet Flush Tank: Public - 6.1 Lpf** and set *View* to **Elevation - Front**. Add a single instance next to the first one, as shown in Figure 13–59. Click (Modify) to finish.

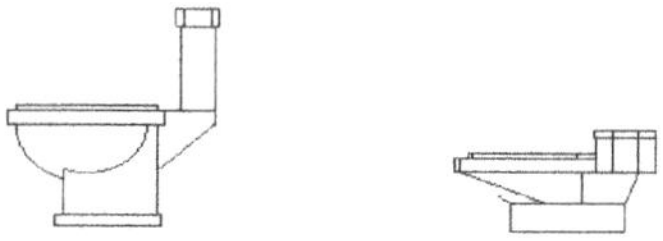

Figure 13–59

7. In the *Annotate* tab>Text panel, click A (Text) and label the elements, as shown in Figure 13–60.

8. Click (Detail Line) in the *Annotate* tab>Detail panel. Use the tools on the *Modify | Place Detail Lines* tab>Draw panel to add the boxes around the elements and text, as shown in Figure 13–60.

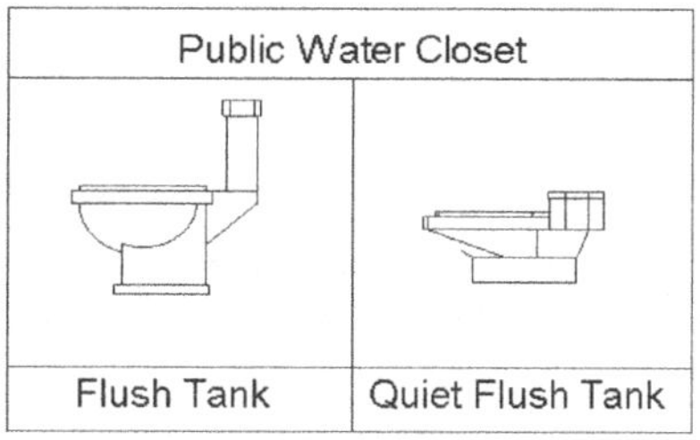

Figure 13–60

9. In the *View* tab>Sheet Composition panel, click (Sheet) to create a new sheet. Use the **A4 metric** titleblock, loading the titleblock if required.

10. Place the **Plumbing Fixture - Flush Tank** legend on the sheet, as shown at the beginning of the practice in Figure 13–58.

11. Save the project.

Task 2 - Create a Key Plan.

1. Create another legend view. Name it **Key Plan** and set the *Scale* to **1: 1000**.
2. Open the Coordination>All>Floor Plans: **Site** view.
3. Hide the views and other annotations so that you just display the roof lines, as shown in Figure 13–61

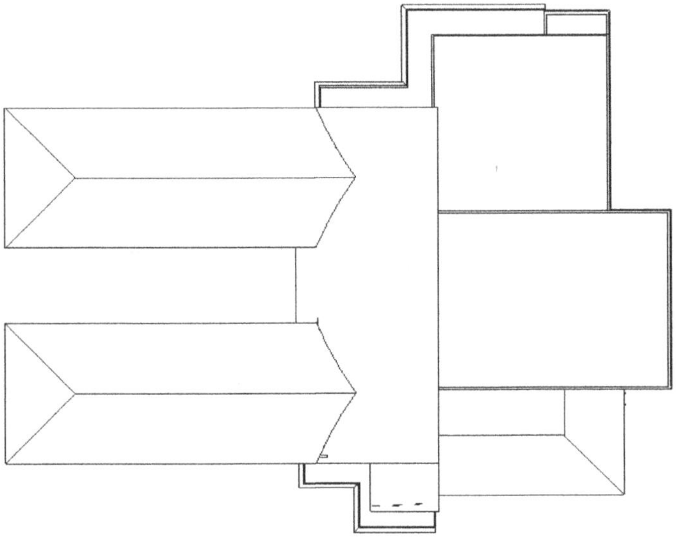

Figure 13–61

4. In the Quick Access Toolbar, click (Thin Lines). Ensure that the line width displays for the next steps.
5. In the *Annotate* tab>Detail panel, click (Detail Line).
6. In the *Modify | Place Detail Line* tab>Line Style panel, select **Outline**.
7. In the Draw panel, click (Line).

8. Trace over the outer edges of the building following the outline shown in Figure 13–62. It does not have to be exactly on the edges of the building.

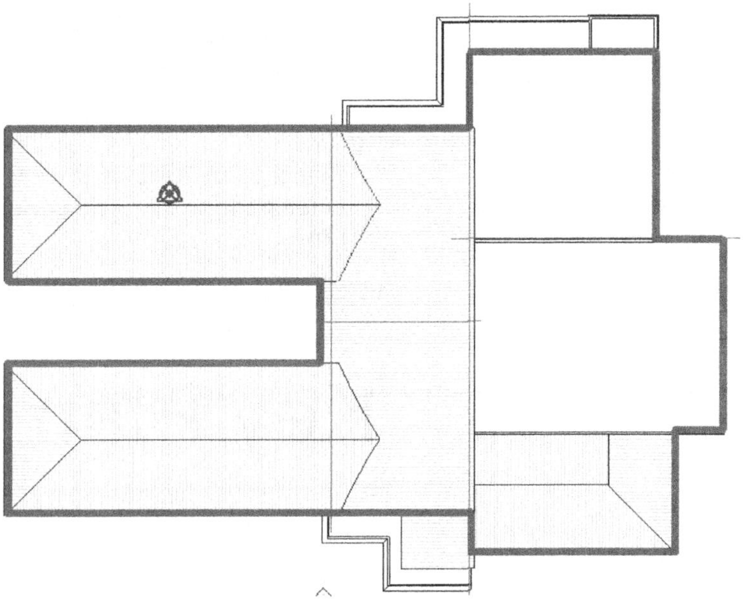

Figure 13–62

9. Click **Modify**.

10. Window around the entire building.

11. In the *Modify | Multi-Select* tab>Selection Window, click (Filter).

12. In the Filter dialog box, click **Check None** and select **Lines (Outline)**, as shown in Figure 13–63.

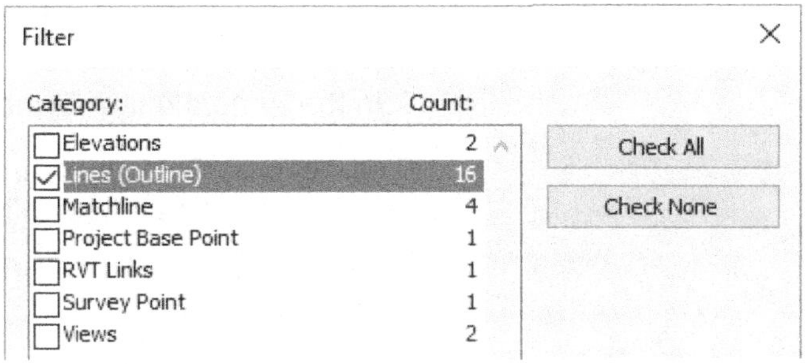

Figure 13–63

13. In the *Modify | Lines* tab>Clipboard panel, click (Cut to Clipboard).

14. Return to the Key Plan view and press <Ctrl>+<V> to paste from the clipboard. Click to place the elements and then in the *Modify | Detail Groups* tab>Edit Pasted panel, click (Finish).

15. Select all of the lines (they will be very thick). In the *Modify | Lines* panel>Line Style panel, change the *Line Style* to **Wide Lines**.

16. Use the modify tools to clean up the edges and add text, as shown in Figure 13–64.

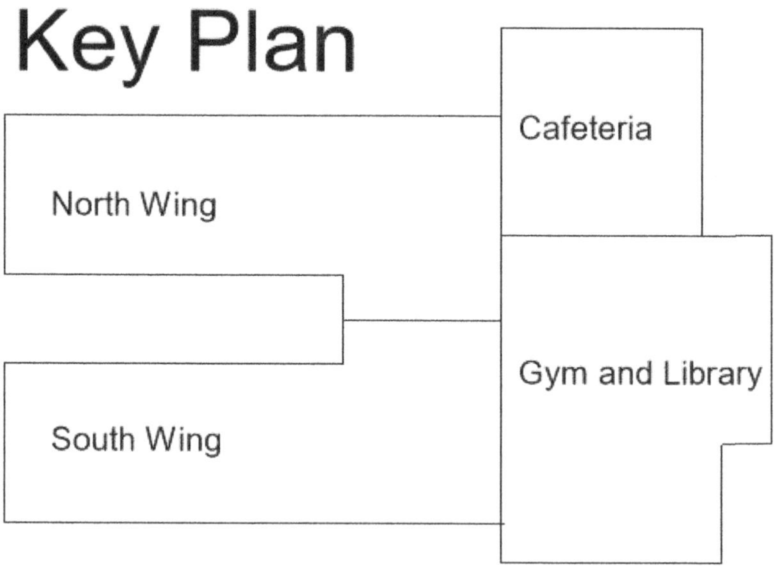

Figure 13–64

17. In the *Annotate* tab>Symbol panel, click (Symbol).

18. In the Type Selector search path start typing **North**. Select North Arrow 2 and place it near the word Key Plan.

19. Save the project.

Task 3 - Add Legends to sheets.

1. Open the sheet **C-101 - Cover Sheet**.
2. Drag and drop the Key Plan legend above the Revision Table in the title block
3. With the Legend still selected, in the Type, select **Viewport: No Title** so there is no title below the key plan, as shown in Figure 13–65.

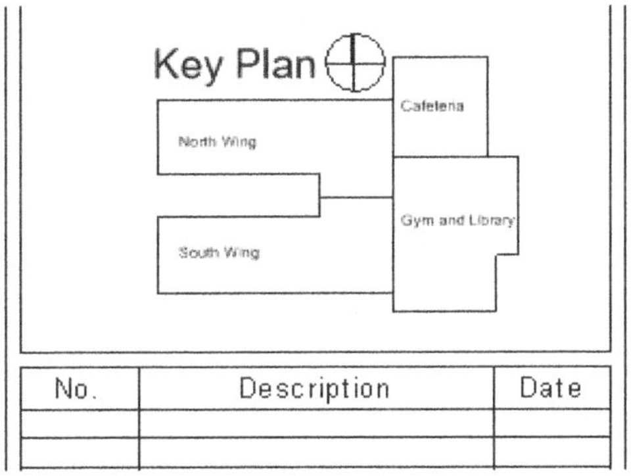

Figure 13–65

4. Open another sheet and place a key plan on that sheet and adjust the viewport to **No Title**.
5. Zoom out to display the full sheet.
6. If time permits, add the Key Plan to other sheets.
7. Save the project.

Chapter Review Questions

1. When a fixture is moved (as shown in Figure 13–66), how do you update the dimension?

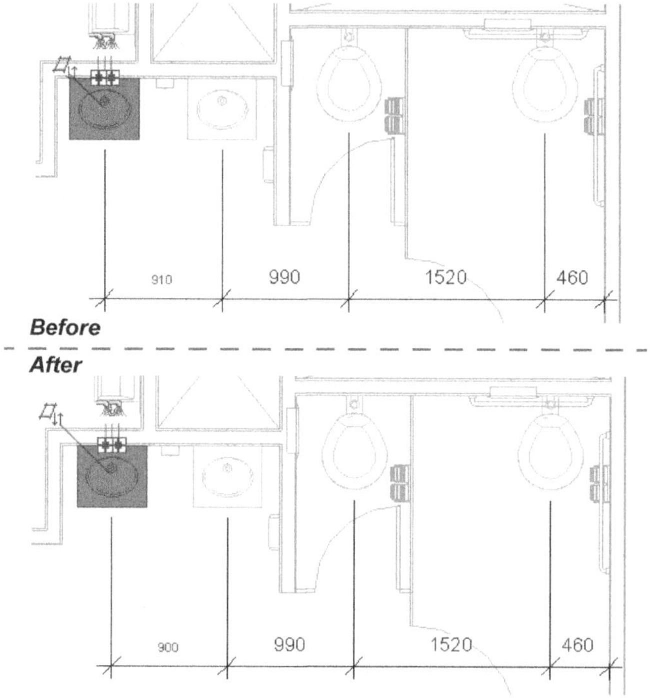

Figure 13–66

   a. Edit the dimension and move it over.
   b. Select the dimension and then click **Update** in the Options Bar.
   c. The dimension automatically updates.
   d. Delete the existing dimension and add a new one.

2. How do you create new text styles?
   a. Using the **Text Styles** command.
   b. Duplicate an existing type.
   c. They must be included in a template.
   d. Using the **Format Styles** command.

3. When you edit text, how many leaders can be added using the leader tools shown in Figure 13–67?

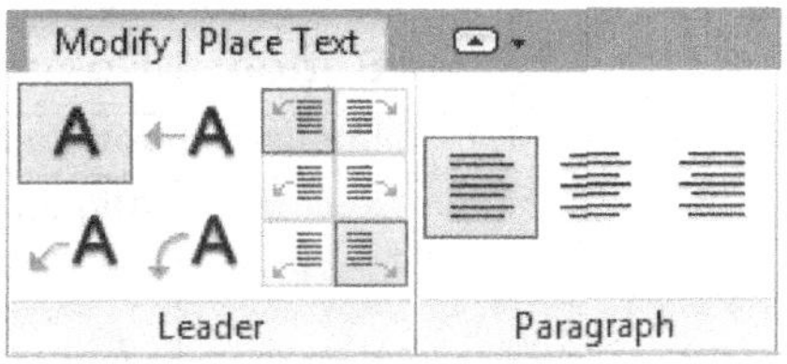

Figure 13–67

   a. One
   b. One on each end of the text.
   c. As many as you want at each end of the text.

4. Detail Lines created in one view also display in the related view.
   a. True
   b. False

5. Which of the following describes the difference between a symbol and a component?
   a. Symbols are 3D and only display in one view. Components are 2D and display in many views.
   b. Symbols are 2D and only display in one view. Components are 3D and display in many views.
   c. Symbols are 2D and display in many views. Components are 3D and only display in one view.
   d. Symbols are 3D and display in many views. Components are 2D and only display in one view.

6. When creating a Legend, which of the following elements cannot be added?
   a. Legend Components
   b. Tags
   c. Rooms
   d. Symbols

Command Summary

Button	Command	Location
Dimensions and Text		
	**Aligned (Dimension)**	• **Ribbon:** *Annotate* tab>Dimension panel or *Modify* tab>Measure panel, expanded drop-down list • **Quick Access Toolbar** • **Shortcut:** DI
	**Angular (Dimension)**	• **Ribbon:** *Annotate* tab>Dimension panel or *Modify* tab>Measure panel, expanded drop-down list
	**Arc Length (Dimension)**	• **Ribbon:** *Annotate* tab>Dimension panel or *Modify* tab>Measure panel, expanded drop-down list
	**Diameter (Dimension)**	• **Ribbon:** *Annotate* tab>Dimension panel or *Modify* tab>Measure panel, expanded drop-down list
	**Linear (Dimension)**	• **Ribbon:** *Annotate* tab>Dimension panel or *Modify* tab>Measure panel, expanded drop-down list
	**Radial (Dimension)**	• **Ribbon:** *Annotate* tab>Dimension panel or *Modify* tab>Measure panel, expanded drop-down list
	**Text**	• **Ribbon:** *Annotate* tab>Text panel • **Shortcut:** TX
Detail Lines and Symbols		
	**Detail Line**	• **Ribbon:** *Annotate* tab>Detail panel • **Shortcut:** DL
	**Stair Path**	• **Ribbon:** *Annotate* tab>Symbol panel
	**Symbol**	• **Ribbon:** *Annotate* tab>Symbol panel
Legends		
	**Legend (View)**	• **Ribbon:** *View* tab>Create panel> expand Legends
	**Legend Component**	• **Ribbon:** *Annotate* tab>Detail panel> expand Component

Adding Tags and Schedules

Adding tags to your views helps you to identify elements such as air terminals, plumbing fixtures, and electrical equipment in the model. Tags are typically added when you insert an element, but can also be added at any point of the design process. The information captured in the elements in a project is used to populate schedules, which can be added to sheets to complete the construction documents.

Learning Objectives in this Chapter

- Add tags to elements in 2D and 3D views to prepare the views to be placed on sheets.
- Load tags that are required for projects.
- Modify schedule content including the instance and type properties of related elements.
- Add schedules to sheets as part of the construction documents.

14.1 Adding Tags

Tags identify elements that are listed in schedules. Some tags are inserted automatically if you use the **Tag on Placement** option when inserting the elements. You can also add them later to specific views as required. Many other types of tags are available in the Autodesk® Revit® software, such as air terminal, duct, mechanical equipment and piping tags, as shown in Figure 14–1.

Additional tags are stored in the Library in the Annotations folder.

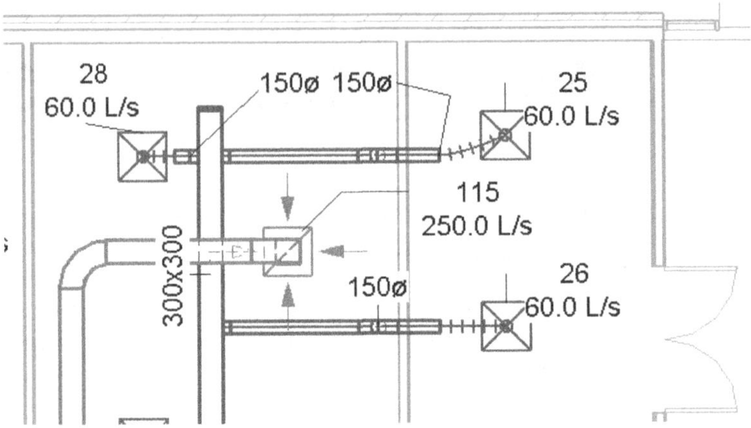

Figure 14–1

- The **Tag by Category** command works for most elements, except for a few that have separate commands.
- Tags can be letters, numbers, or a combination of the two.

You can place three types of tags, as follows:

-  (Tag by Category): Tags according to the category of the element. It places door tags on doors and wall tags on walls.
-  (Multi-Category): Tags elements belonging to multiple categories. The tags display information from parameters that they have in common.
-  (Material): Tags that display the type of material. They are typically used in detailing.

How To: Add Tags

1. In the *Annotate* tab>Tag panel, click (Tag by Category), (Multi-Category), or (Material Tag) depending on the type of tag you want to place.
2. In the Options Bar, set the options as required, as shown in Figure 14–2.

Figure 14–2

3. Select the element you want to tag. If a tag for the selected element is not loaded, you are prompted to load it from the Library.

Tag Options

- You can set tag options for leaders and tag rotation, as shown in Figure 14–3. You can also press <Spacebar> to toggle the orientation while placing or modifying the tag.

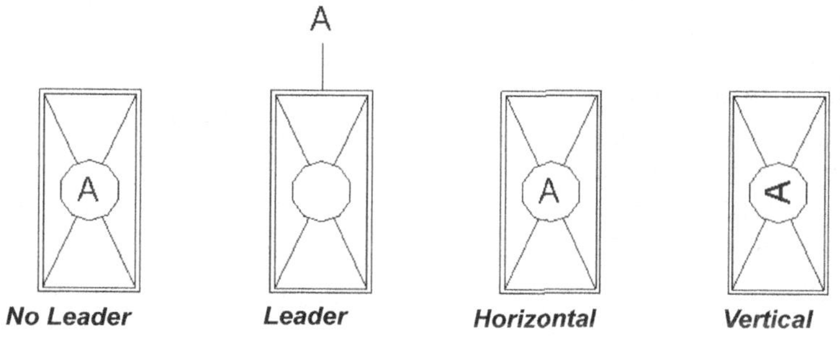

Figure 14–3

- Leaders can have an **Attached End** or a **Free End**, as shown in Figure 14–4. The attached end must be connected to the element being tagged.

A free end has an additional drag control where the leader touches the element.

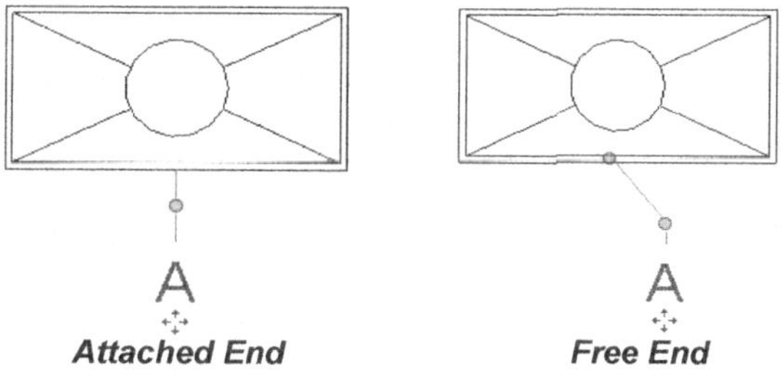

Figure 14–4

- If you change between **Attached End** and **Free End**, the tag does not move and the leader does not change location.
- The **Length** option specifies the length of the leader in plotting units. It is grayed out if **Leader** is not selected or if a **Free End** leader is defined.
- If a tag is not loaded a warning box opens. Click **Yes** to open the Load Family dialog box in which you can select the appropriate tag.
- Tags can be pinned to they stay in place if you move the element that is tagged. This is primarily used when tags have leaders.

How To: Add Multiple Tags

Enhanced in 2018

1. In the *Annotate* tab>Tag panel, click (Tag All).
2. In the Tag All Not Tagged dialog box (shown in Figure 14–5), select the checkbox beside one or more categories to tag. Selecting the checkbox beside the Category title selects all of the tags.

*To tag only some elements, select them before starting this command. In the Tag All Not Tagged dialog box, select **Only selected objects in current view**.*

Figure 14–5

3. Set the *Leader* and *Tag Orientation* as required.
4. Click **Apply** to apply the tags and stay in the dialog box. Click **OK** to apply the tags and close the dialog box.

- When you select a tag, the properties of that tag display. To display the properties of the tagged element, in the *Modify | <contextual>* tab>Host panel click (Select Host).

How To: Load Tags

1. In the *Annotate* tab, expand the Tag panel and click (Loaded Tags And Symbols) or, when a Tag command is active, in the Options Bar click **Tags...**
2. In the Loaded Tags And Symbols dialog box (shown in Figure 14–6), click **Load Family...**

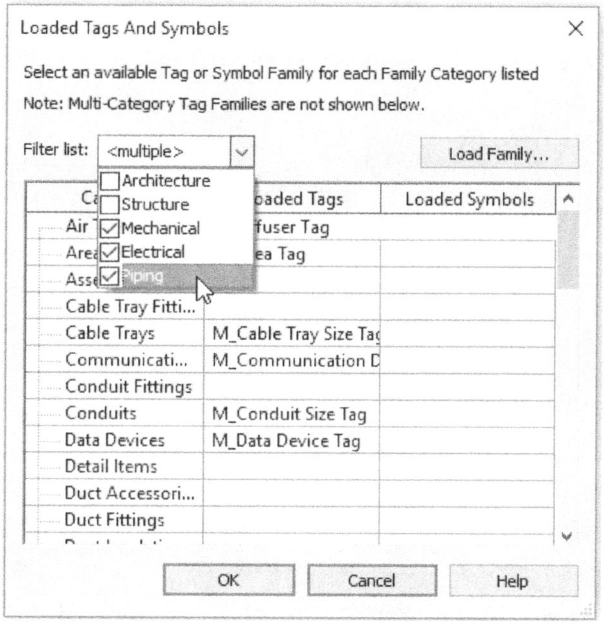

Figure 14–6

3. In the Load Family dialog box, navigate to the appropriate *Annotations* folder, select the tag(s) required and click **Open**.
4. The tag is added to the category in the dialog box. Click **OK**.

Instance vs.Type Based Tags

Many elements are tagged in a numbered sequence, with each instance of the element having a separate tag number. Other elements are tagged by type. Changing the information in one tag changes all instances of that element.

- Both Instance and Type tags can be modified by double-clicking on the tag number, as shown Figure 14–7.

Instance Tag ***Type Tag***

Figure 14–7

Alternatively, you can change the tag information by selecting the element (not the tag) and changing the values in Properties (for Instance tags, as shown in Figure 14–8) or Type Properties (for type tags, as shown in Figure 14–9).

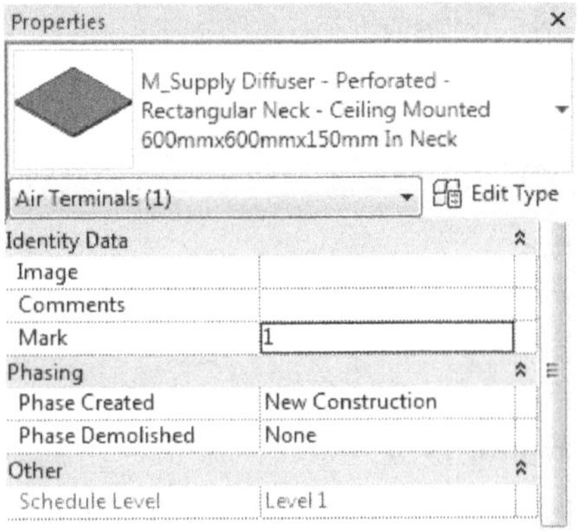

Figure 14–8

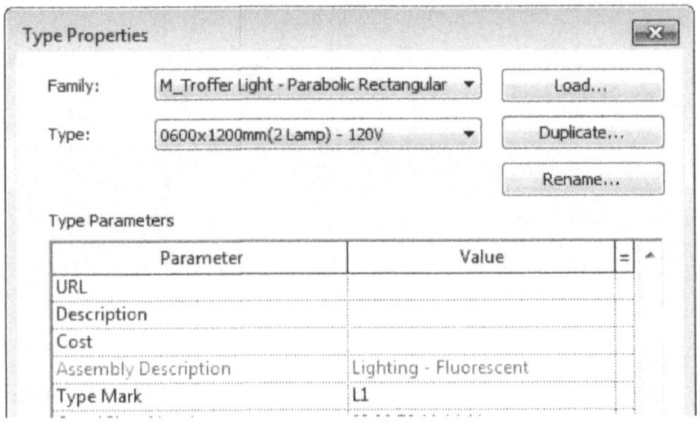

Figure 14–9

- If a type tag displays with a question mark, it means that no Type Mark has been assigned yet.
- When you change a type tag, an alert box opens to warn you that changing a type parameter may affect other elements.

- When you select a tag, the properties of that tag display. To display the properties of the tagged element, in the *Modify* | *<contextual>* tab>Host panel, click (Select Host).

Tagging in 3D Views

You can add tags (and some dimensions) to 3D views, as shown in Figure 14–10, as long as the views are locked first. You can only add tags in isometric views.

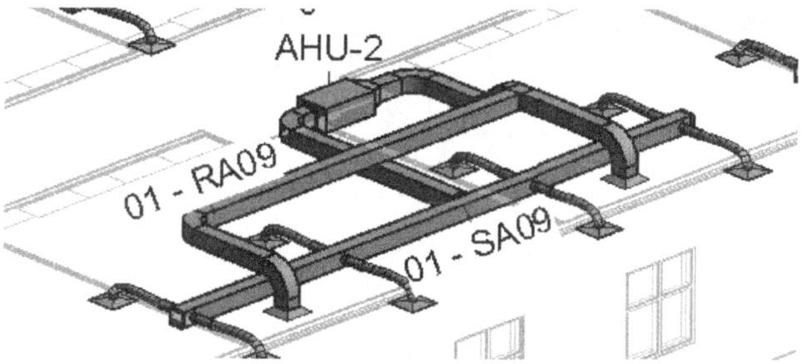

Figure 14–10

- Locked views can be used with perspective views. This enables you to create the view as you want it and then save it from being modified.

How To: Lock a 3D View

1. Open a 3D view and set it up as you want it to display.
2. In the View Control Bar, expand (Unlocked 3D View) and click (Save Orientation and Lock View).

- If you are using the default 3D view and it has not been saved, you are prompted to name and save the view first.
- You can modify the orientation of the view, expand (Locked 3D View) and click (Unlock View). This also removes any tags you have applied.
- To return to the previous locked view, expand (Unlocked 3D View) and click (Restore Orientation and Lock View).

Practice 14a Add Tags - Mechanical and Electrical

Practice Objectives

- Add tags to lighting fixtures and conduits in a floor plan.
- Add duct, pipe, and air terminal tags in a separate floor plan.

Estimated time for completion: 15 minutes

In this practice, you will add lighting fixture tags and conduit tags to electrical floor plans. You will then add duct, pipe, and air terminal tags to a mechanical floor plan, as shown in Figure 14–11.

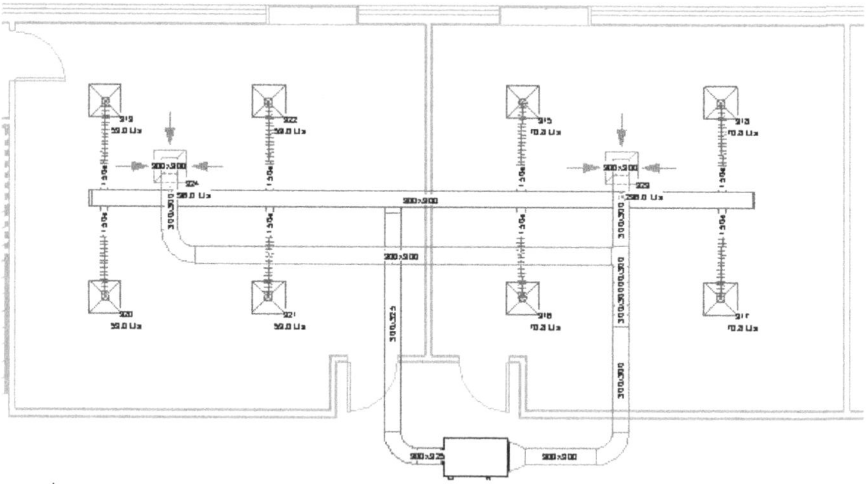

Figure 14–11

Task 1 - Add tags to a floor plan.

1. In the practice files *Schedules* folder, open **MEP-Elementary-School-Tags-M.rvt**.
2. Open the Electrical>Lighting>Floor Plans>**01 Lighting Plan** view.
3. Zoom into the classroom at the far upper left corner of the building.
4. In the *Annotate* tab>Tag panel, click (Tag by Category).

*The default **M_Lighting Fixture Tag: Standard** is used.*

5. In the Options Bar, select **Leader** and set the leader length to **2mm**. Tag the light fixtures as shown in Figure 14–12.

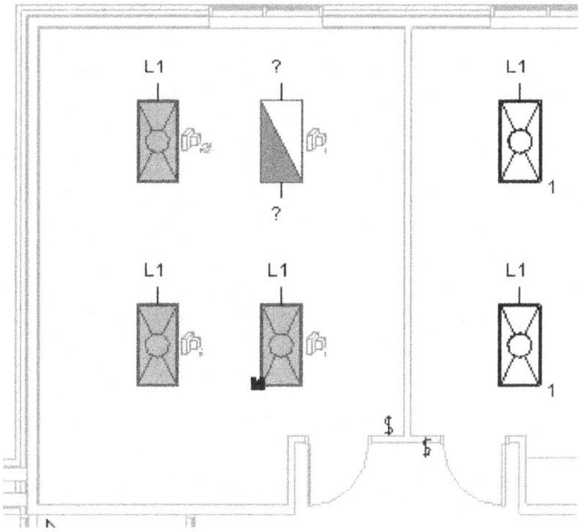

Figure 14–12

6. Tag the light fixtures again by placing the tag below each of the lights.

7. Click **Modify** and select the tags below the lights.

Because the lights are not connected to a circuit, they display a question mark.

8. In the Type Selector, select **M_Lighting Fixture Circuit Tag: m_Standard**. The tag information changes from displaying the lighting fixture number to the circuit number.

9. With the tags still selected, toggle off the leader and move them to the lower right of the fixture, as shown in Figure 14–13, so that they match the tags in the room next door.

Alignment lines display when the cursor lines up with other tags.

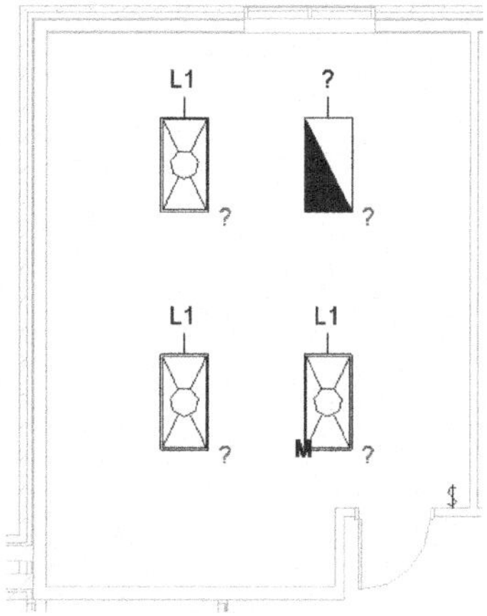

Figure 14–13

Task 2 - Update Tag information.

1. Click **Modify** and select the emergency recessed lighting fixture. In Properties, click  (Edit Type).
2. In the Type Properties dialog box, in the *Identity Data* area, set the *Type Mark* to **E1** and click **OK**. All of the emergency lighting fixture tags update to display this information, as shown in Figure 14–14.
3. In the next room, hover the cursor over one of the light fixtures and press <tab> until the circuit displays. Click to select the circuit.
4. In the *Modify | Electrical Circuits* tab>System Tools panel, click  (Edit Circuit).
5. The  (Add to Circuit) command is active. Select the three standard light fixtures (not the emergency fixture).
6. Select the emergency fixture. When the Select Connector dialog box displays select **Connector 1: Power: Emergency** and click **OK**.
7. Click  (Finish Editing Circuit). The Circuit tags now display with the circuit number, as shown in Figure 14–14.

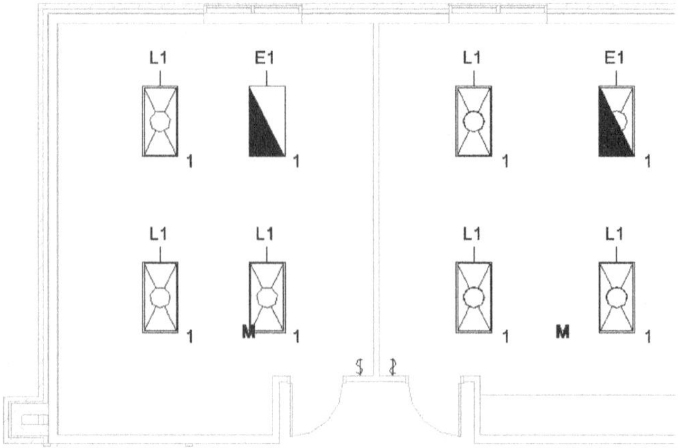

Figure 14–14

8. Save the project.

Task 3 - Load and use a Tag.

1. Open the Electrical>Power>Floor Plans>**01 Power Plan** view.

2. Zoom in on the same rooms you worked in with the lighting fixtures.

3. Using (Tag by Category), click on the conduit that runs horizontally along the classrooms.

4. An alert box displays, warning you that no tag is loaded for Conduits. Click **Yes** to load one now.

5. In the Load Family dialog box, navigate to the *Annotations>Electrical>Conduit* folder and select **M_Conduit Size Tag.rfa**. Click **Open**.

6. The **Tag by Category** tool is still running.

7. In the Options Bar, select **Leader** and in the drop-down list select **Free End**.

8. Add two tags to the conduit in the classroom, as shown in Figure 14–15.

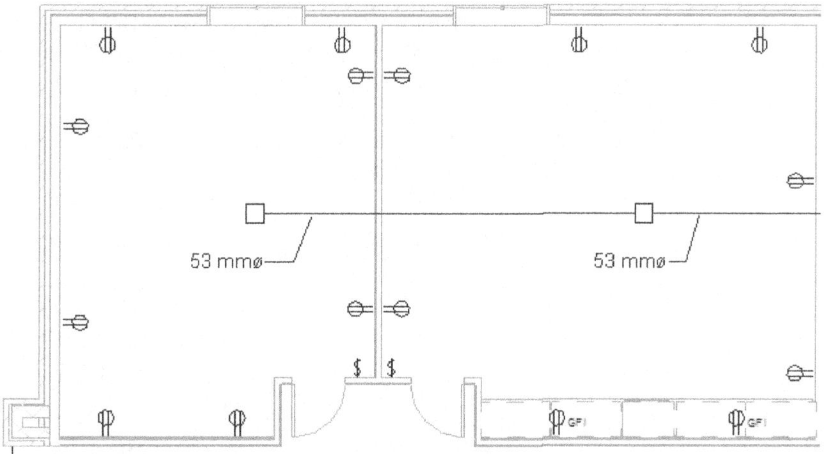

Figure 14–15

9. Click **Modify** and select the conduit in the smaller classroom.

10. In the Options Bar, change the *Diameter* to **35mm**. The tag updates automatically as shown in Figure 14–16.

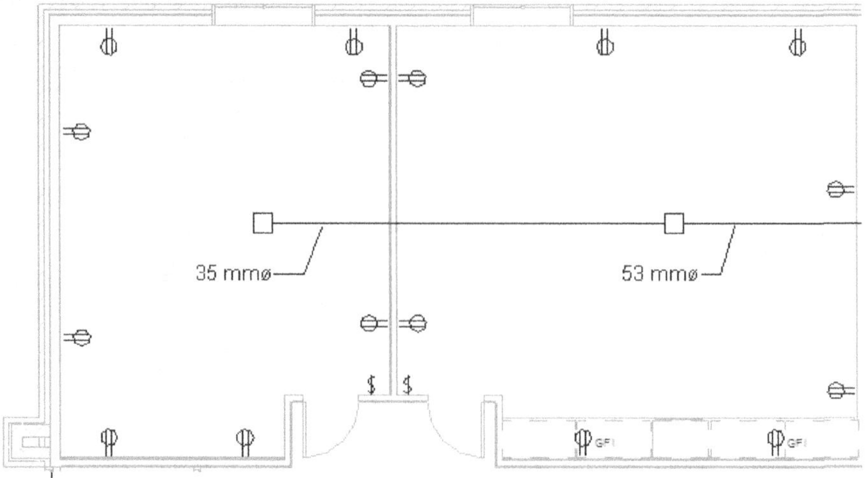

Figure 14–16

11. Type **ZF** to zoom out to fit the view.

12. Save the project.

Task 4 - Tag All not Tagged.

1. Open the Mechanical>HVAC>Floor Plans>01 Mechanical Plan>**01 Mechanical - AREA A** view. There are tags on the ducting and the air terminals.

2. Open **01 Mechanical - AREA B** view. This view is missing its tags.

3. In the *Annotate* tab>Tag panel, click (Tag All).

4. In the Tag All Not Tagged dialog box, select the following (hold <Ctrl> to select more than one):
   - *Air Terminal Tags:* **M_Diffuser Tag**
   - *Duct Tags:* **M_Duct Size Tag**
   - *Pipe Tags:* **M_Pipe Size Tag**

5. Verify that the **Leader** is cleared and click **OK**.

6. If a warning box displays about Elements Have Hidden Tags, click **OK**.

7. All of the air terminals, pipes and ducts are now tagged in this view, as shown in part in Figure 14–17. Move the tags around as required, to clarify the view.

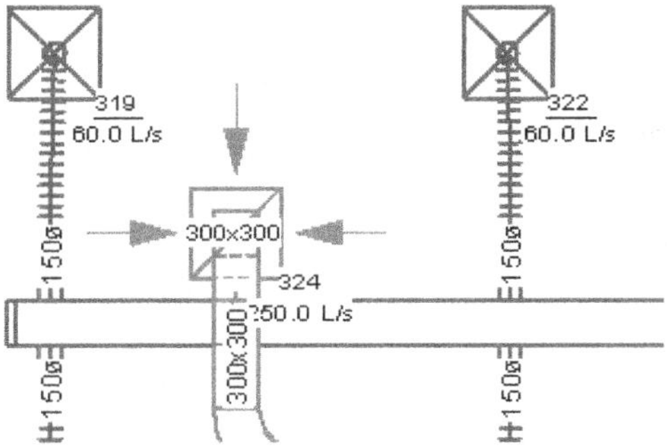

Figure 14–17

8. Select the crop region and then modify the Annotation Crop Region on the right so that the extra tags do not display.

9. Hide the crop region.

10. Save the project.

14.2 Working with Schedules

Schedules extract information from a project and display it in table form. Each schedule is stored as a separate view and can be placed on sheets, as shown in Figure 14–18. Any changes you make to the project elements that affect the schedules are automatically updated in both views and sheets.

Schedules are typically included in project templates. Ask your BIM Manager for more information about your company's schedules.

Creating basic building component schedules is covered in the appendix. For more information about creating schedules, refer to the ASCENT student guide Autodesk Revit: BIM Management: Template and Family Creation.

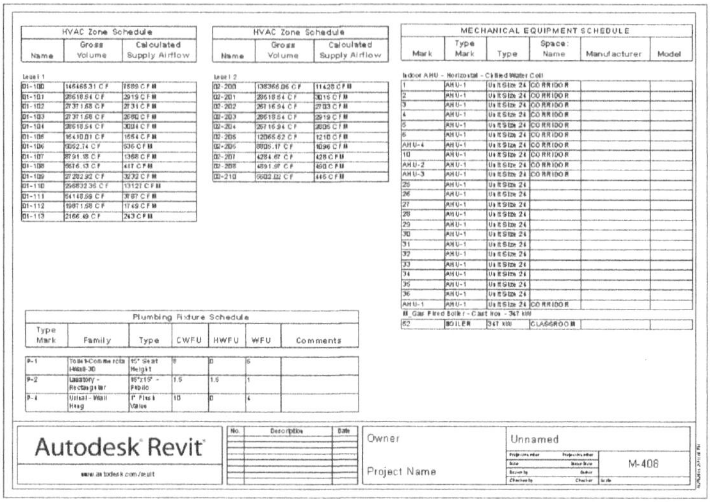

Figure 14–18

- The default MEP templates do not include any schedules. The **Construction-DefaultMetric.rte** template file does include schedules, but they are more geared toward quantity takeoffs.

How To: Work with Schedules

1. In the Project Browser, expand the *Schedules/Quantities* area, as shown in Figure 14–19, and double-click on the schedule you want to open.

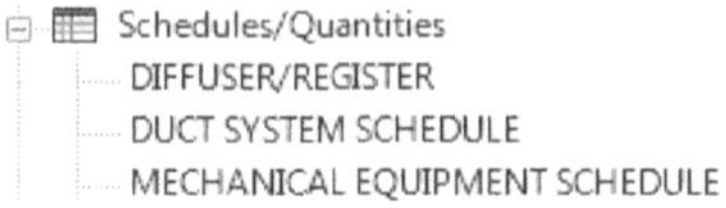

Figure 14–19

2. Schedules are automatically filled out with the information stored in the instance and type parameters of related elements that are added to the model.
3. Fill out additional information in either the schedule or Properties.
4. Drag and drop the schedule onto a sheet.

Modifying Schedules

Information in schedules is bi-directional:

- If you make changes to elements, the schedule automatically updates.

- If you change information in the cells of the schedule, it automatically updates the elements in the project.

How To: Modify Schedule Cells

1. Open the schedule view.
2. Select the cell you want to change. Some cells have drop-down lists, as shown in Figure 14–20. Others have edit fields.
    - If you change a Type Property in the schedule, it applies to all elements of that type. If you change an Instance Property, it only applies to that one element.

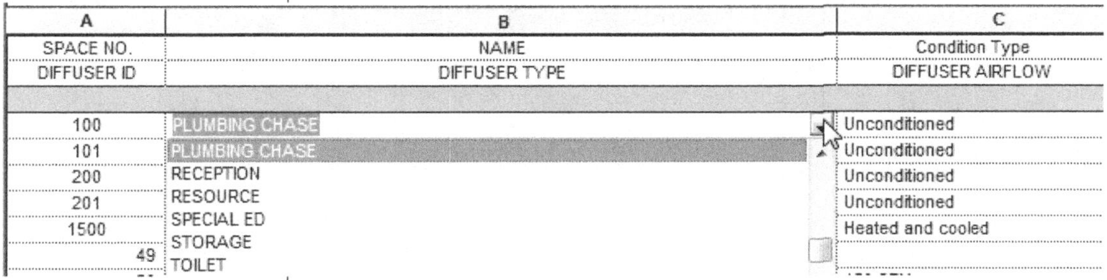

Figure 14–20

3. Add the new information. The change is reflected in the schedule, on the sheet, and in the elements of the project.

- If you change a Type Property, an alert box opens, as shown in Figure 14–21.

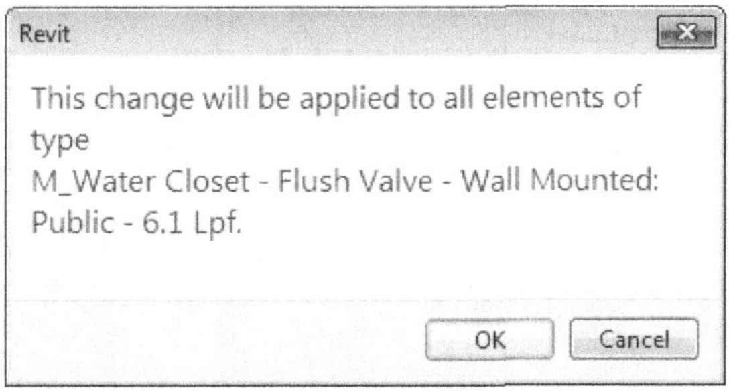

Figure 14–21

- When you select an element in a schedule, in the *Modify Schedule/Quantities* tab>Element panel, you can click  (Highlight in Model). This opens a close-up view of the element with the Show Element(s) in View dialog box, as shown in Figure 14–22. Click **Show** to display more views of the element. Click **Close** to finish the command.

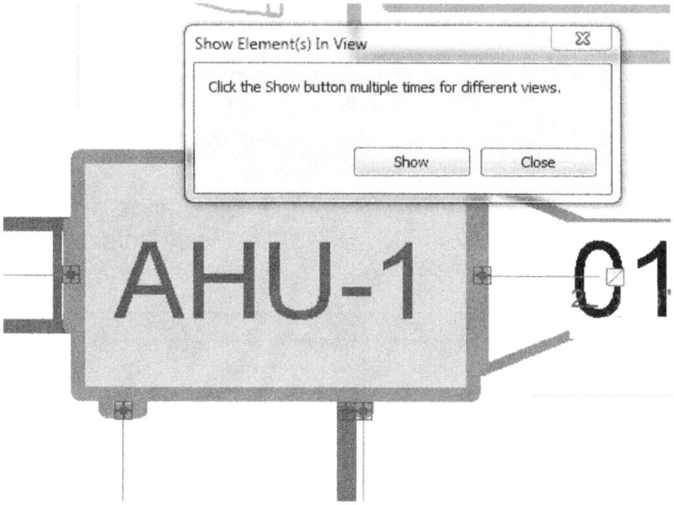

Figure 14–22

Modifying a Schedule on a Sheet

Once you have placed a schedule on a sheet, you can manipulate it to fit the information into the available space. Select the schedule to display the controls that enable you to modify it, as shown in Figure 14–23.

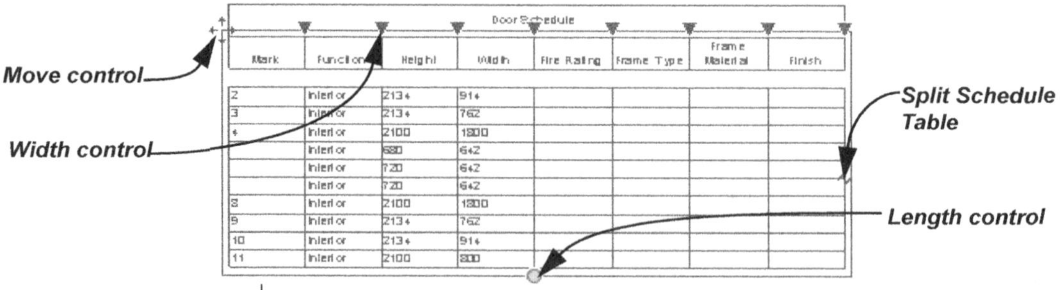

Figure 14–23

- The blue triangles modify the width of each column.
- The break mark splits the schedule into two parts.

- In a split schedule you can use the arrows in the upper left corner to move that portion of the schedule table. The control at the bottom of the first table changes the length of the table and impacts any connected splits, as shown in Figure 14–24.

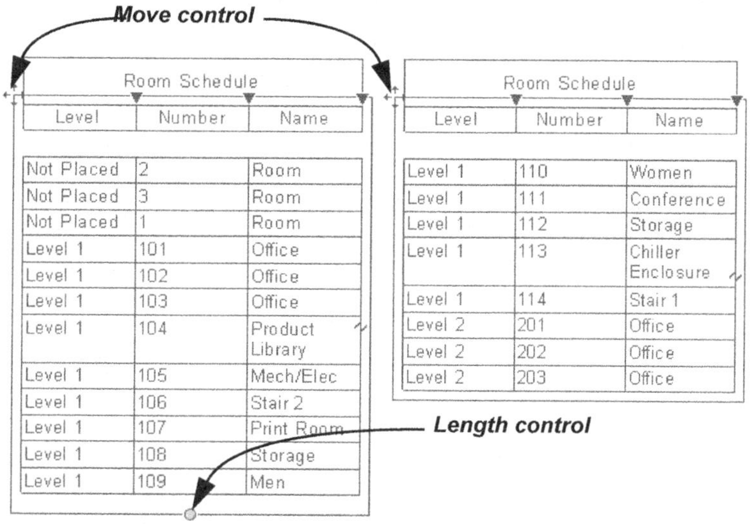

Figure 14–24

- To unsplit a schedule, drag the Move control from the side of the schedule that you want to unsplit back to the original column.

Practice 14b Work with Schedules - Mechanical

Estimated time for completion: 10 minutes

Practice Objectives

- Update schedule information.
- Add a schedule to a sheet.

In this practice you will update a schedule and place it on a sheet., as shown in Figure 14–25.

Mechanical Equipment Schedule					
Type Mark	Mark	Space: Name	Manufacturer	Model	Comments
AHU-1	1	CORRIDOR	ME Unlimited		
AHU-1	2	CORRIDOR	ME Unlimited		
AHU-1	3	CORRIDOR	ME Unlimited		
AHU-1	4	CORRIDOR	ME Unlimited		
AHU-3	5	CORRIDOR	ME Unlimited		
AHU-1	6	CORRIDOR	ME Unlimited		
AHU-1	7	CORRIDOR	ME Unlimited		
AHU-1	8	CORRIDOR	ME Unlimited		
AHU-1	9	CORRIDOR	ME Unlimited		
AHU-1	10	CORRIDOR	ME Unlimited		
AHU-2	11	CORRIDOR	ME Unlimited		
AHU-1	12	CORRIDOR	ME Unlimited		
HW-1	13	STORAGE			
HW-1	14	JANITOR			
HW-1	15	JANITOR			
HW-1	16	STORAGE			

Figure 14–25

Task 1 - Fill in schedules.

1. In the practice files *Schedules* folder, open **MEP-Elementary-School-Schedules-M.rvt**.
2. In the Project Browser, expand *Schedules/Quantities* and open **MECHANICAL EQUIPMENT SCHEDULE**. The schedule is already populated with some information, as shown in Figure 14–26.

<MECHANICAL EQUIPMENT SCHEDULE>					
A	B	C	D	E	F
Type Mark	Mark	Space: Name	Manufacturer	Model	Comments
AHU-1	1	CORRIDOR			
AHU-1	2	CORRIDOR			
AHU-1	3	CORRIDOR			
AHU-1	4	CORRIDOR			
AHU-1	5	CORRIDOR			
AHU-1	6	CORRIDOR			
AHU-1	7	CORRIDOR			

Figure 14–26

3. Several Type Marks are empty. Click in one of the empty *Type Mark* cells. In the *Modify Schedules/Quantities* tab> Element panel, click (Highlight in Model).
4. If an alert box displays about no open views, click **OK** to search and open a view.
5. In the view that comes up, click **Close** in the Show Element(s) in View dialog box.
6. Zoom out so that you can see the elements (i.e., a hot water heater) in context.
7. In Properties, click (Edit Type).
8. In the Type Properties dialog box, in the *Identity Data* area, set the *Type Mark* to **HW-1**.
9. Click **OK** to finish.
10. Return to the Mechanical Equipment Schedule (press <Ctrl>+<Tab> to switch between open windows).
11. All of the hot water heaters in the project now have a *Type Mark* set, as shown in Figure 14–27.

<MECHANICAL EQUIPMENT SCHEDULE>

A	B	C	D	E	F
Type Mark	Mark	Space: Name	Manufacturer	Model	Comments
AHU-1	1	CORRIDOR			
AHU-1	2	CORRIDOR			
AHU-1	3	CORRIDOR			
AHU-1	4	CORRIDOR			
AHU-1	5	CORRIDOR			
AHU-1	6	CORRIDOR			
AHU-1	7	CORRIDOR			
AHU-1	8	CORRIDOR			
AHU-1	9	CORRIDOR			
AHU-1	10	CORRIDOR			
AHU-1	11	CORRIDOR			
AHU-1	12	CORRIDOR			
HW-1	49	STORAGE			
HW-1	50	STORAGE			
HW-1	51	JNTR.			
HW-1	52	JNTR.			
AHU-1	53	CORRIDOR			

Figure 14–27

12. In the *Mark* column you can see that the numbers are out of sequence. The numbering of hot water heaters and one air handling unit (AHU-1) is incorrect, starting at 49.
13. Change the *Mark* of the incorrectly numbered AHU-1 to **13**.

14. Modify the *Mark* of the hot water heaters to match the sequence.

15. In the schedule view, change the name of the Manufacturer of one of the AHUs. An alert displays warning that changing this changes all of the elements of this type, as shown in Figure 14–28. Click **OK**.

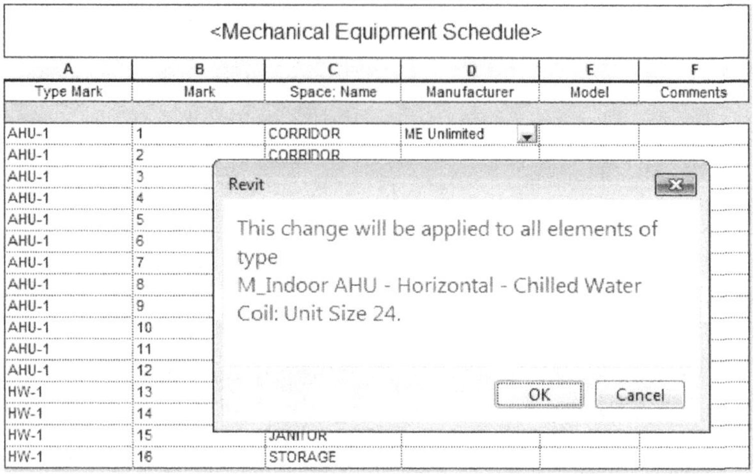

Figure 14–28

16. Open the Mechanical>HVAC>Floor Plans>**01 Mechanical** view and zoom in on the office area.

17. Select the AHU that is connected to the Office duct system. In the Type Selector, change it to **M_Indoor AHU - Horizontal - Chilled Water Coil: Unit Size 12**.

18. While it is still selected, edit the type and set the *Type Mark* to **AHU-2**.

19. Switch back to the schedule view to see the change.

20. In the *Manufacturer* column, use the drop-down list to select the same *Manufacturer* for the modified AHU, as shown in Figure 14–29.

<MECHANICAL EQUIPMENT SCHEDULE>					
A	B	C	D	E	F
Type Mark	Mark	Space: Name	Manufacturer	Model	Comments
AHU-1	1	CORRIDOR	ME Unlimited		
AHU-1	2	CORRIDOR	ME Unlimited		
AHU-1	3	CORRIDOR	ME Unlimited		
AHU-1	4	CORRIDOR	ME Unlimited		
AHU-1	5	CORRIDOR	ME Unlimited		
AHU-1	6	CORRIDOR	ME Unlimited		
AHU-1	7	CORRIDOR	ME Unlimited		
AHU-1	8	CORRIDOR	ME Unlimited		
AHU-1	9	CORRIDOR	ME Unlimited		
AHU-1	10	CORRIDOR	ME Unlimited		
AHU-1	11	CORRIDOR	ME Unlimited		
AHU-1	12	CORRIDOR	ME Unlimited		
AHU-2	13	CORRIDOR			
HW-1	14	STORAGE	ME Unlimited		
HW-1	15	STORAGE			
HW-1	16	JNTR.			
HW-1	17	JNTR.			

Figure 14–29

21. Fill in the other information.

22. Save the project.

Task 2 - Add schedules to a sheet.

1. In the Project Browser, right-click on Sheets (all) and select **New Sheet**. Select the **A0 metric** title block and click **OK**.

2. In the Project Browser, right-click on the new sheet (which is bold) and select Rename. In the Sheet Title dialog box, set the *Number* to **M-801** and the *Name* to **Schedules** and click **OK**.

3. Drag and drop the **MECHANICALEQUIPMENT SCHEDULE** view onto the sheet, as shown in Figure 14–30.

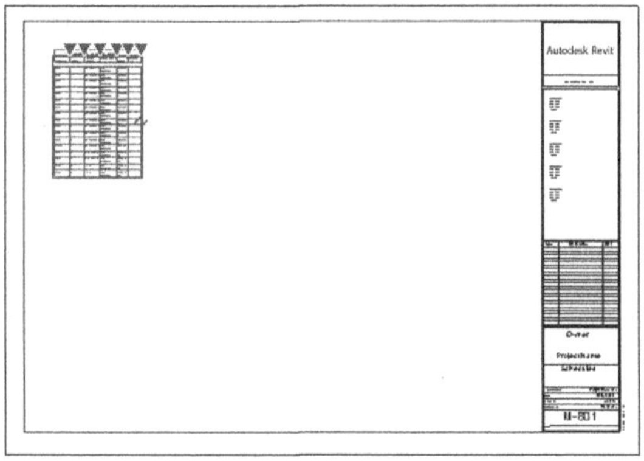

Figure 14–30

4. Zoom in and use the arrows at the top to modify the width of the columns so that the titles display correctly.

5. Click in empty space on the sheet to finish placing the schedule.

6. Switch back to the Mechanical>HVAC>Floor Plans> **01 Mechanical** view and select one of the Classroom AHUs.

7. In the Type Selector, change the size to **Unit Size 36**. In Type Properties add the *Model*, *Manufacturer*, and *Type Mark.*

8. Return to the Schedule sheet. The information is automatically populated.

9. Save the project.

Practice 14c Work with Schedules - Electrical

Practice Objectives

- Update schedule information.
- Add a schedule to a sheet.

Estimated time for completion: 10 minutes

In this practice, you will update a schedule and place it on a sheet, as shown in Figure 14–31.

LIGHTING FIXTURE SCHEDULE								
Type Mark	Description	Count	Manufacturer	Model	Lamp			Electrical Data
					Lamp	Wattage	Illuminance	
EM-1	M_Emergency Recessed Lighting Fixture: 600x1200 - 277	22				96 W	73 lx	277 V/1-96 VA- 277 V/1-32 VA
L1	M_Troffer Light - Parabolic Rectangular: 0600x1200mm(2 Lamp) - 277V	106	XYZ lighting		T-12	80 W	54 lx	277 V/1-80 VA
L2	M_Troffer Light - Parabolic Square: 0600x0600mm(2 Lamp) - 120V	8	XYZ lighting		T-12	40 W	22 lx	120 V/1-40 VA
L3	M_Sconce Light - Uplight: 60W - 120V	5			A-19	60 W	7 lx	120 V/1-60 VA
Grand total: 141								

Figure 14–31

Task 1 - Fill in schedules.

1. In the practice files *Schedules* folder, open **MEP-Elementary-School-Schedules-M.rvt**.
2. In the Project Browser, expand **Schedules/Quantities**. Several schedules have been added to this project.
3. Double-click on **LIGHTING FIXTURE SCHEDULE** to open it. The schedule is already populated with some of the basic information, as shown in part in Figure 14–32.

<LIGHTING FIXTURE SCHEDULE>							
A	B	C	D	E	F	G	H
					Lamp		
Type Mark	Description	Count	Manufacturer	Model	Lamp	Wattage	Illuminance
		30					
L1	M_Troffer Light - Parabolic Rectangular: 0600x1200	106			T-12	80 W	54 lx
Grand total: 136							

Figure 14–32

4. Click in the empty *Type Mark* cell. In the *Modify Schedules/ Quantities* tab>Element panel, click (Highlight in Model).
5. If an alert box displays about no open views, click **OK** to search and open a useful view.

6. In the view that comes up, click **Close** in the Show Element(s) in View dialog box.

7. In Properties, you can see that Multiple Families are selected, as shown in Figure 14–33. More than one lighting fixture type is selected and you cannot edit the types.

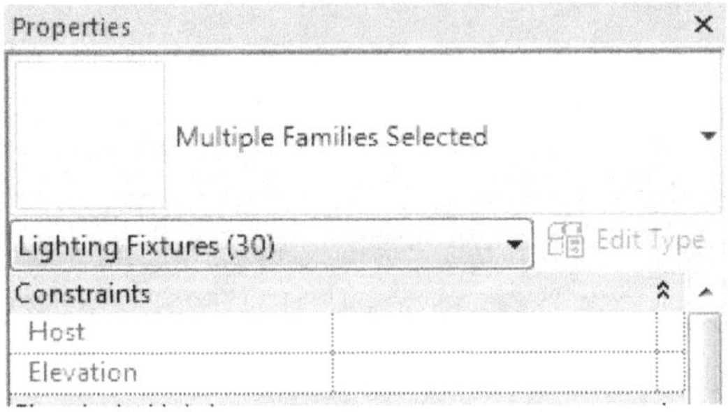

Figure 14–33

Isolating the category would show all lighting fixtures.

8. In the View Control Bar, expand (Temporary Hide/Isolate) and select **Isolate Elements**.

   The selected fixtures display and you can easily see that there are at least two different types of lights, as shown for the south wing of the building in Figure 14–34.

Figure 14–34

9. Click **Modify** and select one of the rectangular fixtures.
10. In Properties, you can see that it is an emergency light fixture. Click (Edit Type).
11. In the Type Properties dialog box, in the *Identity Data* area, set the *Type Mark* to **EM-1**.
12. Click **OK** to finish.
13. Return to the Lighting Fixture Schedule (press <Ctrl>+<Tab> to switch between open windows).

    All of the emergency lighting fixtures in the project now have a *Type Mark* set, as shown in Figure 14–35.

<LIGHTING FIXTURE SCHEDULE>							
A	B	C	D	E	F	G	H
					Lamp		
Type Mark	Description	Count	Manufacturer	Model	Lamp	Wattage	Illuminance
	M_Troffer Light - Parabolic Square: 0600x0600mm(2	8			T-12	40 W	22 lx
EM-1	M_Emergency Recessed Lighting Fixture: 600x1200	22				96 W	73 lx
L1	M_Troffer Light - Parabolic Rectangular: 0600x1200	106			T-12	80 W	54 lx
Grand total: 136							

Figure 14–35

14. There is still a lighting fixture type without a type mark. Type **L2** in the *Type Mark* column. An alert displays warning that this action changes all of the elements of this type, as shown in Figure 14–36. Click **OK**.

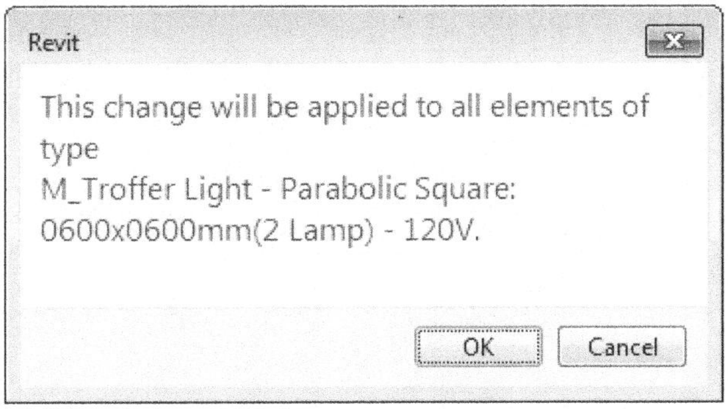

Figure 14–36

15. Select one of the square lighting fixtures and in the Type Properties, assign a name in the *Manufacturer* column and click **OK**.

16. While still zoomed into the office, add several new wall sconce fixtures. (You will need to load them from the library.)

17. Return to the Lighting Fixture Schedule. The new sconce lights and the manufacture name of the L2 lights are added as shown in Figure 14–37.

<LIGHTING FIXTURE SCHEDULE>							
A	B	C	D	E	F	G	H
					Lamp		
Type Mark	Description	Count	Manufacturer	Model	Lamp	Wattage	Illuminance
	M_Sconce Light - Uplight: 60W - 120V	5			A-19	60 W	7 lx
EM-1	M_Emergency Recessed Lighting Fixture: 600x1200	22				96 W	73 lx
L1	M_Troffer Light - Parabolic Rectangular: 0600x1200	106			T-12	80 W	54 lx
L2	M_Troffer Light - Parabolic Square: 0600x0600mm(2	8	XYZ lighting		T-12	40 W	22 lx
Grand total: 141							

Figure 14–37

18. In the *Manufacturer* column, use the drop-down list to select the same *Manufacturer* for the other Troffer light.

19. Fill in some of the other information.

20. Save the project.

Task 2 - Add a schedule to a sheet.

1. In the Project Browser, right-click on **Sheets** (all) and select **New Sheet**. Select the **A0 metric** title block and click **OK**.

2. In the Project Browser, right-click on the new sheet (which is bold) and select **Rename**. In the Sheet Title dialog box, set the *Number* to **E-801** and the *Name* to **Schedules**. Click **OK**.

3. Drag and drop the **LIGHTING FIXTURESCHEDULE** view onto the sheet, as shown in Figure 14–38.

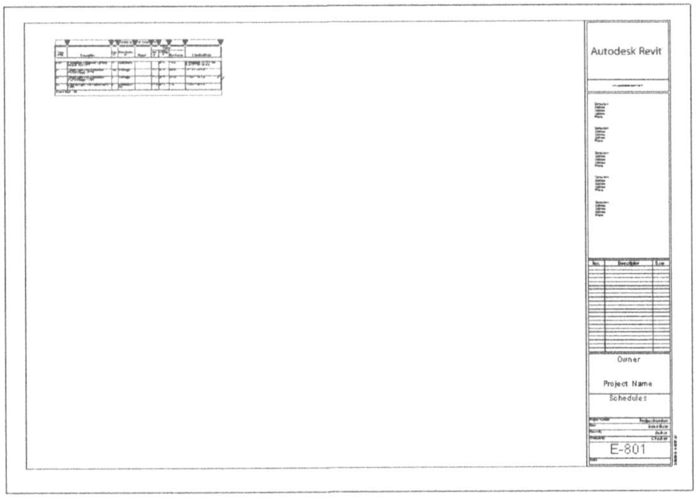

Figure 14–38

4. Zoom in and use the arrows at the top to modify the width of the columns so that the titles display correctly.

5. Click in empty space on the sheet to finish placing the schedule.

6. Save the project.

Chapter Review Questions

1. Which of the following elements cannot be tagged using **Tag by Category**?
    a. Spaces
    b. Ducts
    c. Plumbing Fixtures
    d. Communication Devices
2. What happens when you delete an air terminal in an Autodesk Revit model, as shown in Figure 14–39?

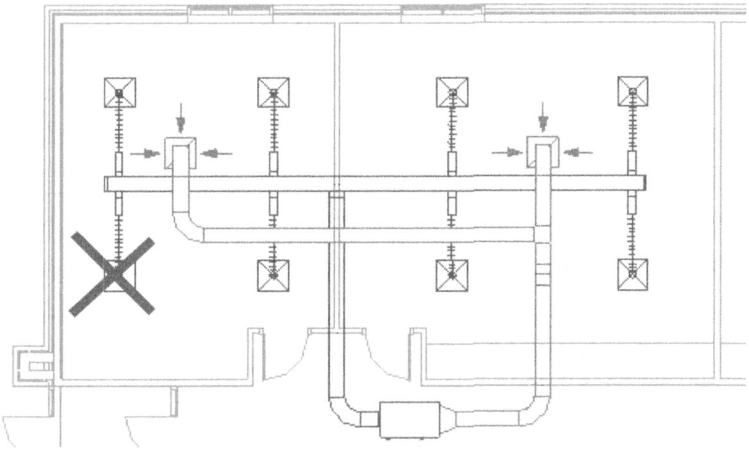

Figure 14–39

    a. You must delete the air terminal on the sheet.
    b. You must delete the air terminal from the schedule.
    c. The air terminal is removed from the model, but not from the schedule.
    d. The air terminal is removed from the model and the schedule.
3. In a schedule, if you change type information (such as a Type Mark) all instances of that type update with the new information.
    a. True
    b. False

Command Summary

Button	Command	Location
	**Material Tag**	**Ribbon:** *Annotate* tab>Tag panel
	**Multi-Category**	**Ribbon:** *Annotate* tab>Tag panel
	**Tag All Not Tagged**	**Ribbon:** *Annotate* tab>Tag panel
	**Tag by Category**	**Ribbon:** *Annotate* tab>Tag panel **Shortcut:** TG

Chapter 15

Creating Details

Creating details is a critical part of the design process, as it is the step where you specify the exact information that is required to build a construction project. The elements that you can add to a model include detail components, detail lines, text, keynotes, tags, symbols, and filled regions for patterning. Details can be created from views in the model, but you can also add 2D details in separate views.

Learning Objectives in this Chapter

- Create drafting views where you can add 2D details.
- Add detail components that show the typical elements in a detail.
- Annotate details using detail lines, text, tags, symbols, and patterns that define materials.

15.1 Setting Up Detail Views

Most of the work you do in the Autodesk® Revit® software is exclusively with *smart* elements that interconnect and work together in the model. However, the software does not automatically display how elements should be built to fit together. For this, you need to create detail drawings, as shown in Figure 15–1.

Details are created either in 2D drafting views, or in callouts from plan, elevation, or section views.

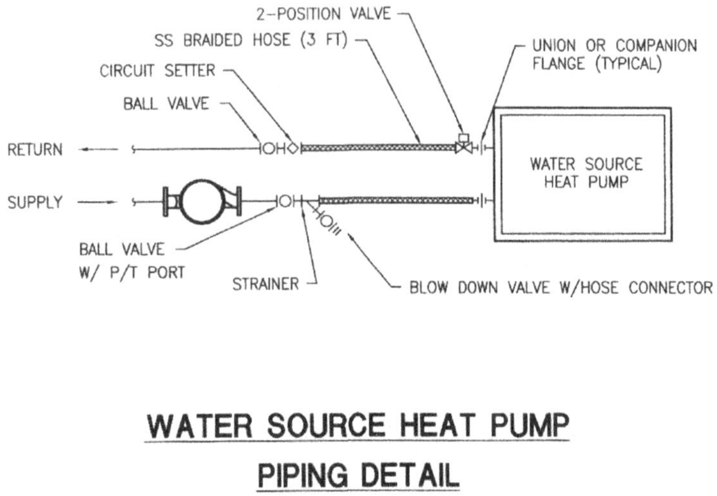

Figure 15–1

How To: Create a Drafting View

1. In the *View* tab>Create panel, click (Drafting View).
2. In the New Drafting View dialog box, enter a *Name* and set a *Scale*, as shown in Figure 15–2.

Drafting views are listed in their own section in the Project Browser.

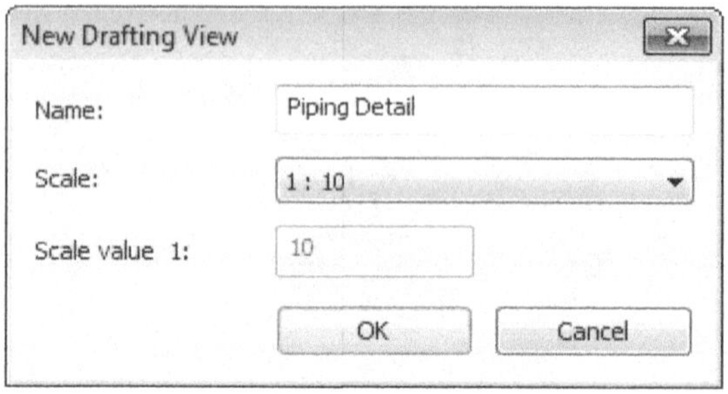

Figure 15–2

3. Click **OK**. A blank view is created with space in which you can sketch the detail.

Callouts also have a Detail View Type that can be used in the same way.

How To: Create a Detail View from Model Elements

1. Start the **Section** or **Callout** command.
2. In the Type Selector, select the **Detail View: Detail** type.
   - The marker indicates that it is a detail, as shown for a section in Figure 15–3.

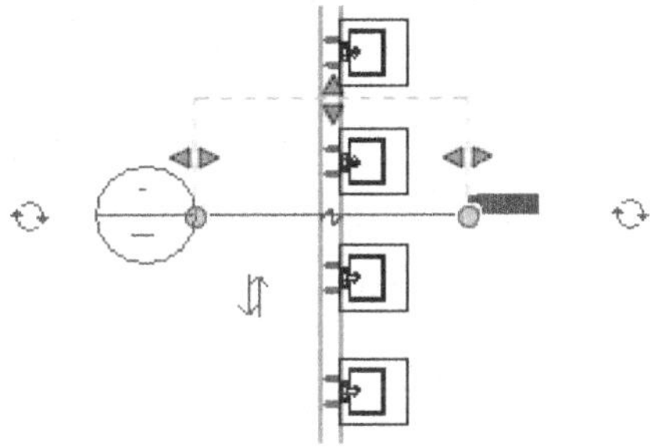

Figure 15–3

3. Place the section or a callout of the area you want to use for the detail.
4. Open the new detail. Use the tools to sketch on top of or add to the building elements.

- In this type of detail view when the building elements change, the detail changes as well, as shown in Figure 15–4.

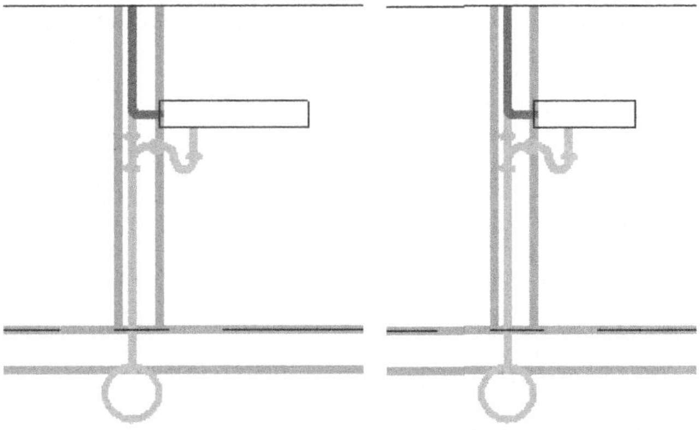

Figure 15–4

- You can create detail elements on top of the model and then toggle the model off so that it does not show in the detail view. In Properties, in the *Graphics* area, change *Display Model* to **Do not display**. You can also set the model to **Halftone**, as shown in Figure 15–5.

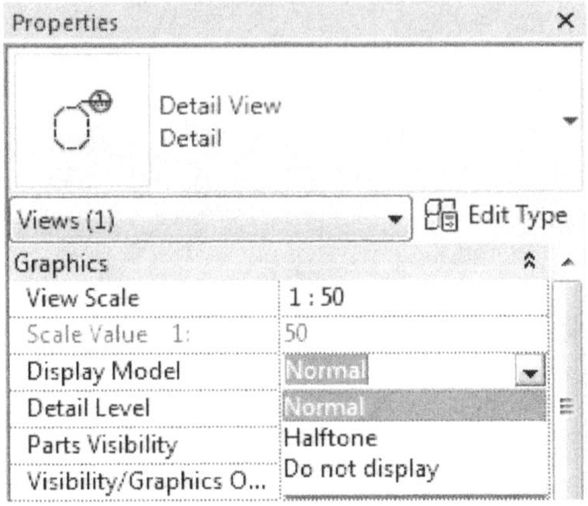

Figure 15–5

Referencing a Drafting View

Once you have created a drafting view, you can reference it in another view (such as a callout, elevation, or section view), as shown in Figure 15–6. For example, in a section view, you might want to reference an existing roof detail. You can reference drafting views, sections, elevations, and callouts.

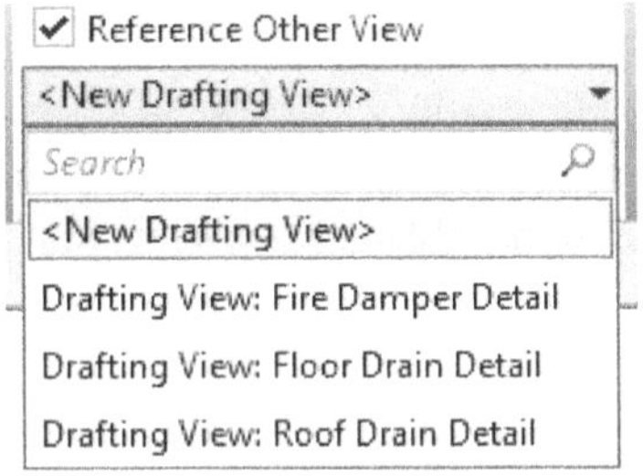

Figure 15–6

- You can use the search feature to limit the information displayed.

How To: Reference a Drafting View

1. Open the view in which you want to place the reference.
2. Start the **Section, Callout,** or **Elevation** command.
3. In the *Modify* | *<contextual>* tab>Reference panel select **Reference Other View**.

4. In the drop-down list, select **<New Drafting View>** or an existing drafting view.
5. Place the view marker.
6. When you place the associated drafting view on a sheet, the marker in this view updates with the appropriate information.

- If you select **<New Drafting View>** from the drop-down list, a new view is created in the *Drafting Views (Detail)* area in the Project Browser. You can rename it as required. The new view does not include any model elements.
- When you create a detail based on a section, elevation, or callout, you do not need to link it to a drafting view.
- You can change a referenced view to a different referenced view. Select the view marker and in the ribbon, select the new view from the list.

Saving Drafting Views

To create a library of standard details, save the non-model specific drafting views to your server. They can then be imported into a project and modified to suit. They are saved as .RVT files.

Drafting views can be saved in two ways:

- Save an individual drafting view to a new file.
- Save all of the drafting views as a group in one new file.

How To: Save One Drafting View to a File

1. In the Project Browser, right-click on the drafting view you want to save and select **Save to New File...**, as shown in Figure 15–7.

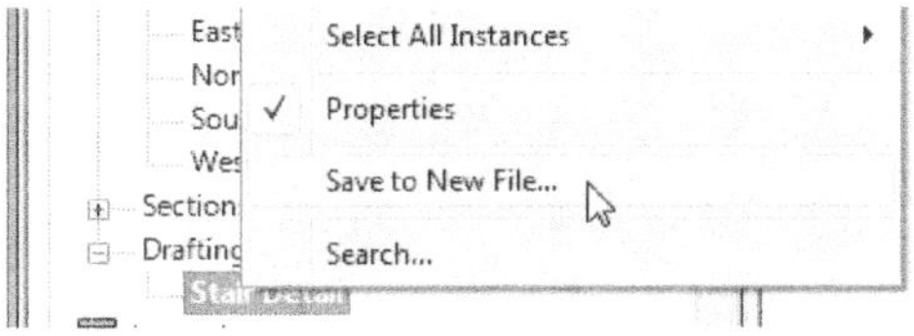

Figure 15–7

2. In the Save As dialog box, specify a name and location for the file and click **Save**.

How To: Save a Group of Drafting Views to a File

You can save sheets, drafting views, model views (floor plans), schedules, and reports.

1. In the *File* tab, expand (Save As), expand (Library) and then click (View).
2. In the Save Views dialog box, in the *Views:* pane, expand the list and select **Show drafting views only**.
3. Select the drafting views that you want to save as shown in Figure 15–8.

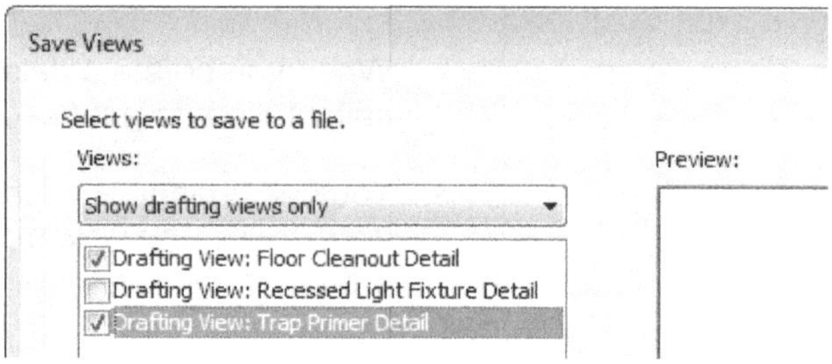

Figure 15–8

4. Click **OK**.
5. In the Save As dialog box, specify a name and location for the file and click **Save**.

How To: Use a Saved Drafting View in another Project

1. Open the project to which you want to add the drafting view.
2. In the *Insert* tab>Import panel, expand (Insert from File) and click (Insert Views from File).
3. In the Open dialog box, select the project in which you saved the detail and click **Open**.
4. In the Insert Views dialog box, limit the types of views to **Show drafting views only**, as shown in Figure 15–9.

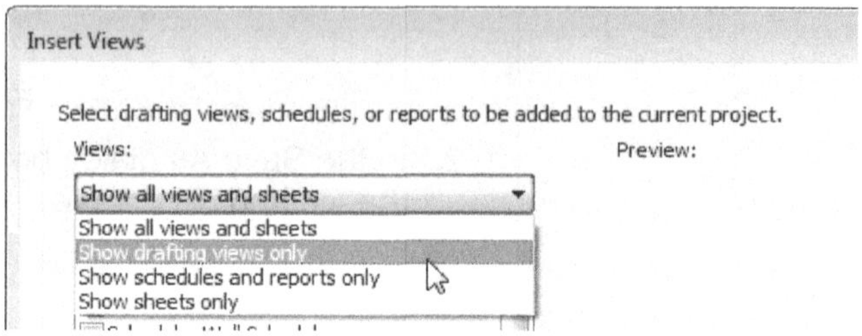

Figure 15–9

5. Select the view(s) that you want to insert and click **OK**.

Hint: Importing Details from Other CAD Software

You might already have a set of standard details created in a different CAD program, such as the AutoCAD® software. You can reuse the details in the Autodesk Revit software by importing them into a temporary project. Once you have imported the detail, it helps to clean it up and save it as a view before bringing it into your active project.

1. In a new project, create a drafting view and make it active.
2. In the *Insert* tab>Import panel, click (Import CAD).
3. In the Import CAD dialog box, select the file to import. Most of the default values are what you need. You might want to change the *Layer/Level colors* to **Black and White**.
4. Click **Open**.

- If you want to modify the detail, select the imported data. In the *Modify | [filename]* tab>Import Instance panel, expand (Explode) and click (Partial Explode) or (Full Explode). Click (Delete Layers) before you explode the detail. A full explode greatly increases the file size.
- Modify the detail using tools in the Modify panel. Change all the text and line styles to Autodesk Revit specific elements.

15.2 Adding Detail Components

Autodesk Revit elements typically require additional information to ensure that they are constructed correctly. To create details (such as the one shown in Figure 15–10), you add detail components, detail lines, and various annotation elements.

- Detail elements are not directly connected to the model, even if model elements display in the view.

Figure 15–10

Detail Components

Detail components are families made of 2D and annotation elements. Over 500 detail components organized by CSI format are found in the *Detail Items* folder of the library, as shown in Figure 15–11.

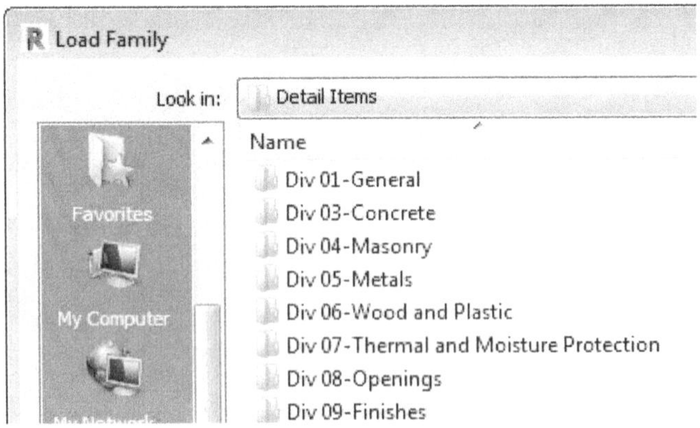

Figure 15–11

How To: Add a Detail Component

1. In the *Annotate* tab>Detail panel, expand  (Component) and click  (Detail Component).
2. In the Type Selector, select the detail component type. You can load additional types from the Library.
3. Many detail components can be rotated as you insert them by pressing <Spacebar>. Alternatively, select **Rotate after placement** in the Options Bar, as shown in Figure 15–12.

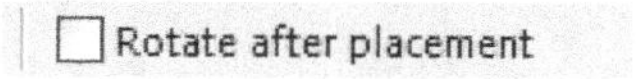

Figure 15–12

4. Place the component in the view.

Adding Break Lines

The Break Line is a detail component found in the *Detail Items\ Div 01-General* folder. It consists of a rectangular area (shown highlighted in Figure 15–13) which is used to block out elements behind it. You can modify the size of the area that is covered and change the size of the cut line using the controls.

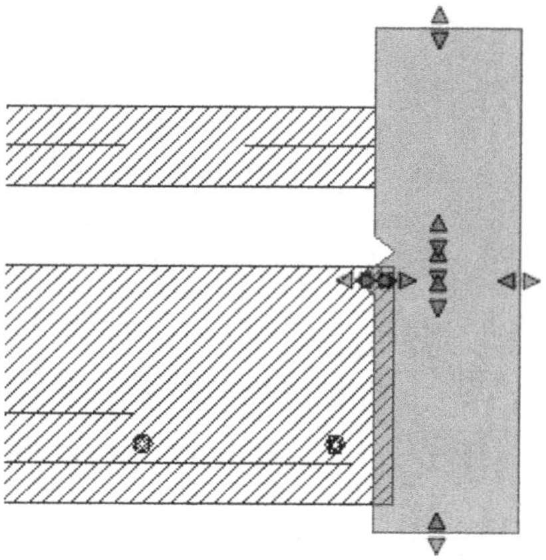

Figure 15–13

Hint: Working with the Draw Order of Details

When you select detail elements in a view, you can change the draw order of the elements in the *Modify | Detail Items* tab> Arrange panel. You can bring elements in front of other elements or place them behind elements, as shown in Figure 15–14.

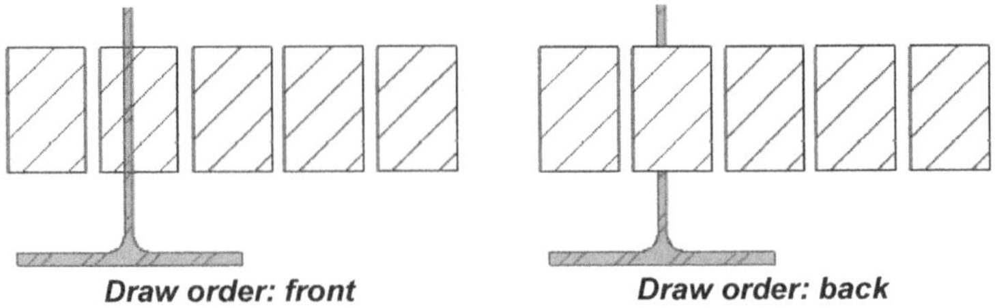

Figure 15–14

-  **(Bring to Front):** Places element in front of all other elements.
-  **(Send to Back):** Places element behind all other elements.
-  **(Bring Forward):** Moves element one step to the front.
-  **(Send Backward):** Moves element one step to the back.
- You can select multiple detail elements and change the draw order of all of them in one step. They keep the relative order of the original selection.

Repeating Details

Instead of having to insert a component multiple times (such as with a brick or concrete block), you can use (Repeating Detail Component) and create a string of components, as shown in Figure 15–15.

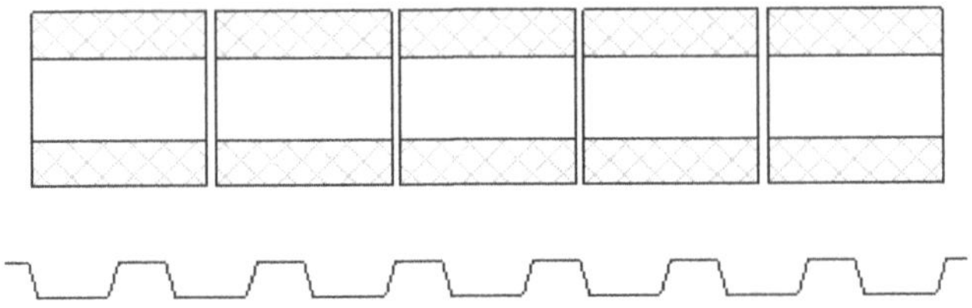

Figure 15–15

How To: Insert a Repeating Detail Component

1. In the *Annotate* tab>Detail panel, expand (Component) and click (Repeating Detail Component).
2. In the Type Selector, select the detail you want to use.
3. In the Draw panel, click (Line) or (Pick Lines).
4. In the Options Bar, type a value for the *Offset*, if required.
5. The components repeat as required to fit the length of the sketched or selected line, as shown in Figure 15–16. You can lock the components to the line.

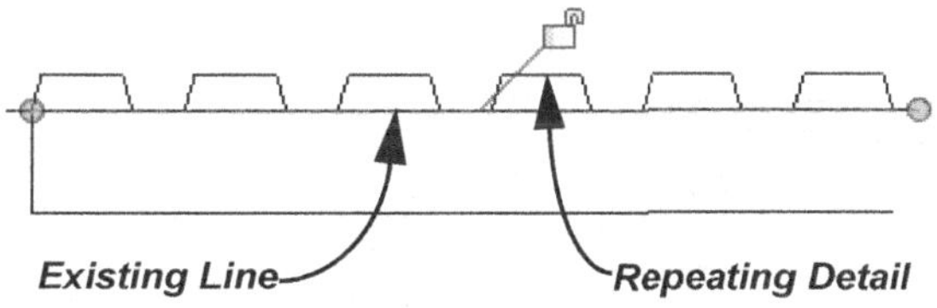

Figure 15–16

Hint: (Insulation)

Adding batt insulation is similar to adding a repeating detail component, but instead of a series of bricks or other elements, it creates the linear batting pattern, shown in Figure 15–17.

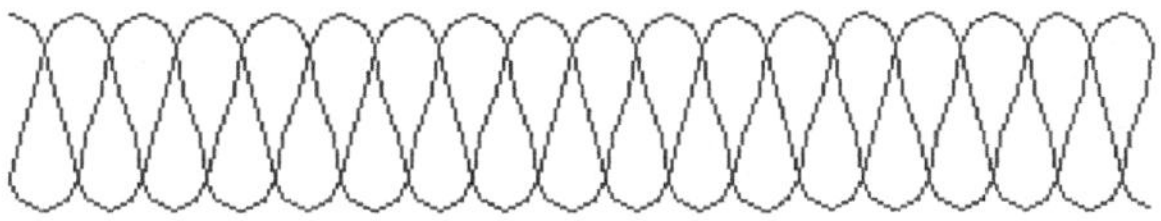

Figure 15–17

Before you place the insulation in the view, specify the *Width* and other options in the Options Bar, as shown in Figure 15–18.

Figure 15–18

15.3 Annotating Details

After you have added components and sketched detail lines, you need to add annotations to the detail view. You can place text notes and dimensions as shown in Figure 15–19, as well as symbols and tags. Filled regions are used to add hatching or poche.

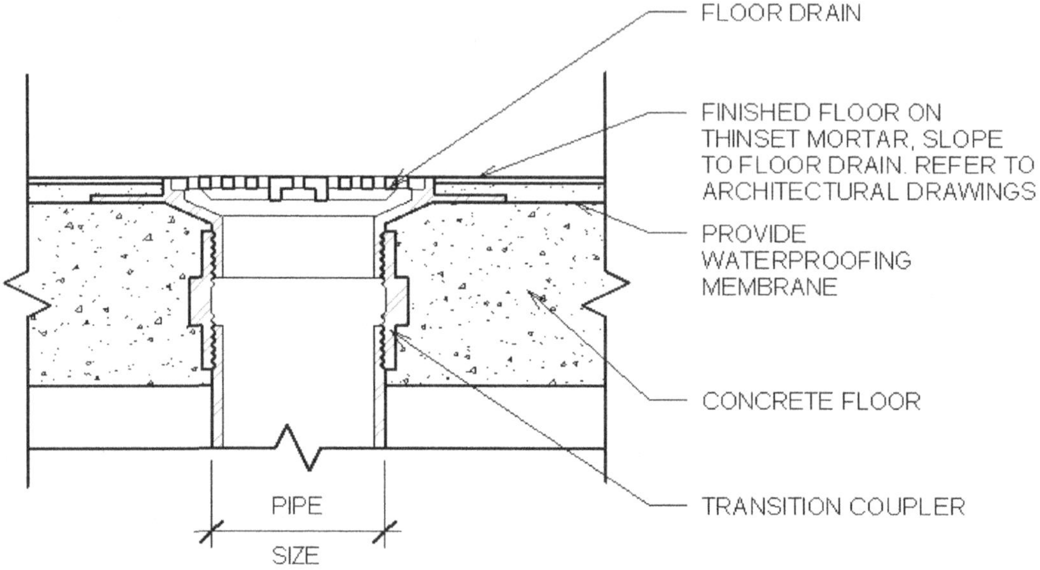

Figure 15–19

Creating Filled Regions

Many elements include material information that displays in plan and section views, while other elements need such details to be added. For example, the concrete wall shown in Figure 15–20 includes material information, while the earth to the left of the wall needs to be added using the **Filled Region** command.

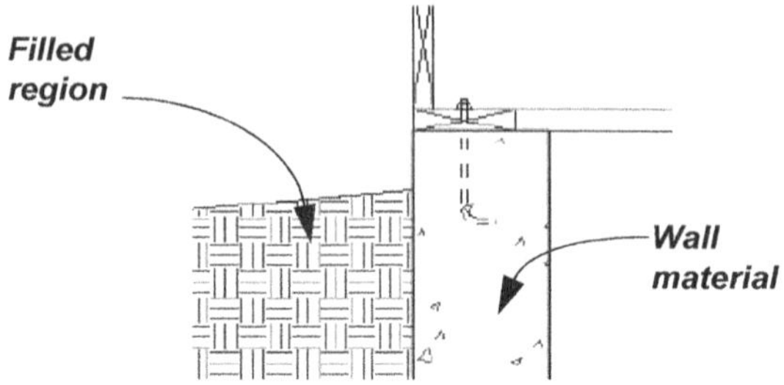

Figure 15–20

The patterns used in details are *drafting patterns*. They are scaled to the view scale and update if you modify it. You can also add full-size *model patterns*, such as a Flemish Bond brick pattern, to the surface of some elements.

How To: Add a Filled Region

1. In the *Annotate* tab>Detail panel, expand (Region) and click (Filled Region).
2. Create a closed boundary using the Draw tools.
3. In the Line Style panel, select the line style for the outside edge of the boundary. If you do not want the boundary to display, select the <Invisible lines> style.
4. In the Type Selector, select the fill type, as shown in Figure 15–21.

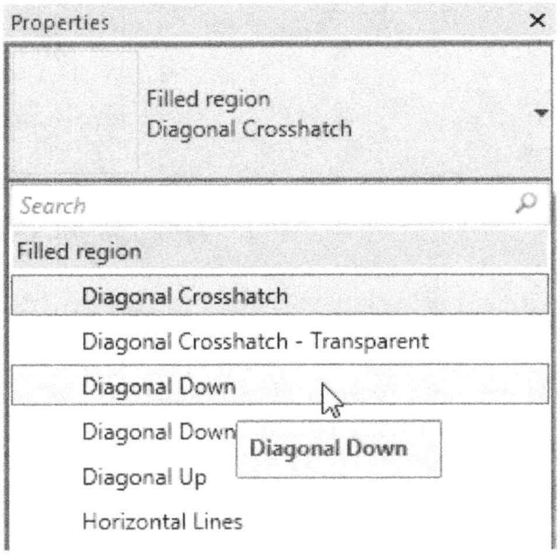

Figure 15–21

5. Click (Finish Edit Mode).

- You can modify a region by changing the fill type in the Type Selector or by editing the sketch.
- Double-click on the edge of the filled region to edit the sketch.

  If you have the Selection option set to (Select elements by face) you can select the pattern.

Adding Detail Tags

Besides adding text to a detail, you can tag detail components using (Tag By Category). The tag name is set in the Type Parameters for that component, as shown in Figure 15–22. This means that if you have more than one copy of the component in your project, you do not have to rename it each time you place its tag.

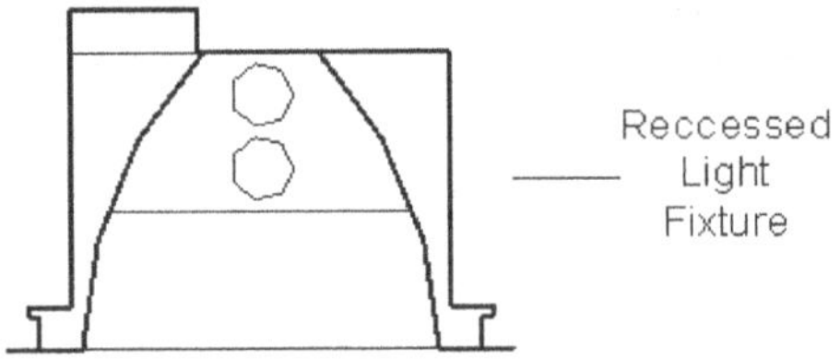

Type Parameters

Parameter	Value
Identity Data	
Keynote	26 51 00.A1
Type Image	
Model	
Manufacturer	
Type Comments	
URL	
Description	
Assembly Code	
Cost	
Assembly Description	
Type Mark	Reccessed Light Fixture
OmniClass Number	
OmniClass Title	

Figure 15–22

- The M_**Detail Item Tag.rfa** tag is located in the *Annotations* folder in the Library.

Hint: Multiple Dimension Options

If you are creating details that show one element with multiple dimension values, as shown in Figure 15–23, you can easily modify the dimension text.

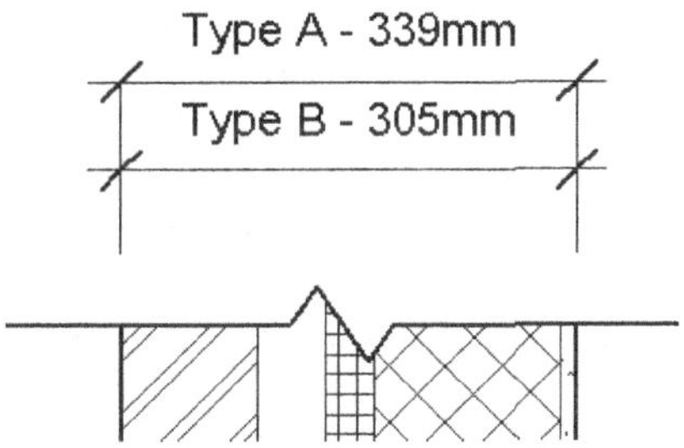

Figure 15–23

Select the dimension and then the dimension text. The Dimension Text dialog box opens. You can replace the text, as shown in Figure 15–24, or add text fields above or below, as well as a prefix or suffix.

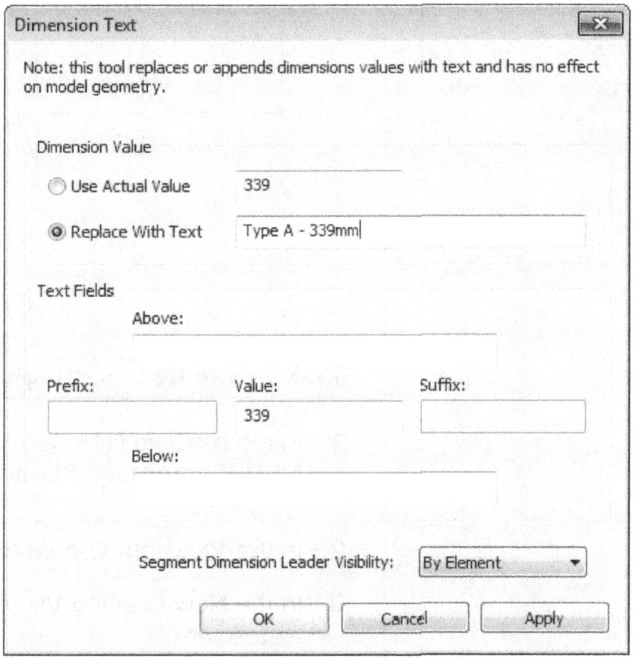

Figure 15–24

- This also works with Equality Text Labels.

Practice 15a Create a Fire Damper Detail

Estimated time for completion: 10 minutes

Practice Objectives

- Create a drafting view.
- Add detail lines, components, filled regions, and text.

In this practice you will create a drafting view. In the new view you will add detail lines of different weights, insulation, and filled regions. You will also add detail components, including Break Lines and text notes. Finally, you will place the detail view on a sheet (as shown in Figure 15–25) and place a reference section.

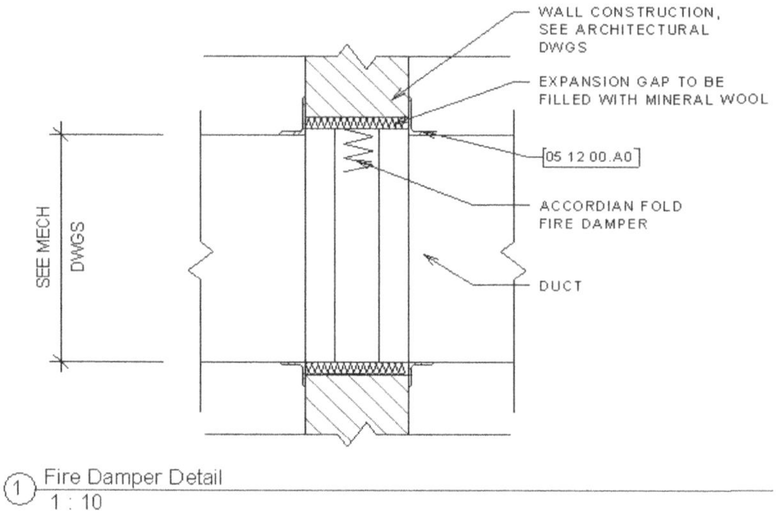

Figure 15–25

Task 1 - Create a drafting view.

1. In the practice files *Detailing* folder, open **MEP-Elementary-School-Detailing-M.rvt**.
2. In the *View* tab>Create panel, click (Drafting View).
3. In the New Drafting View dialog box, set the name and scale as follows:
   - *Name*: **Fire Damper Detail**
   - *Scale*: **1:10**

4. In the Project Browser, expand the **Coordination** node until you can see the new detail view. Select the view, as shown in Figure 15–26.

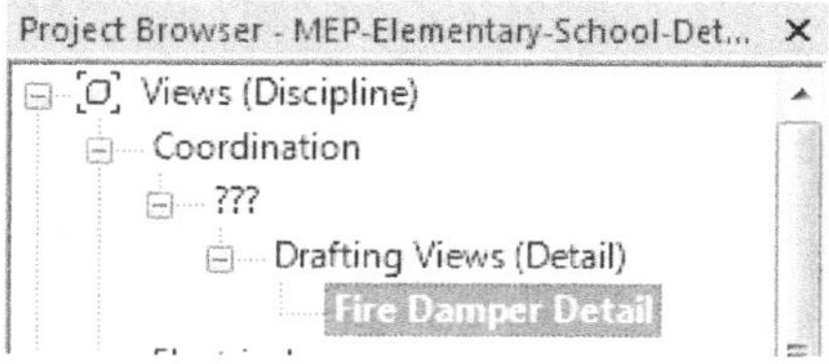

Figure 15–26

5. In Properties, change *Discipline* to **Mechanical** and *Sub-Discipline* to **HVAC**. The new view moves to that node in the Project Browser.

Task 2 - Draw detail lines.

1. In the *Annotate* tab>Detail panel, click (Detail Line).
2. In the *Modify | Place Detail Lines tab*, ensure that the *Line Style* is set to **Thin Lines**. Draw the two vertical lines shown in Figure 15–27.
3. Change the *Line Style* to **Wide Lines** and draw the two horizontal lines shown in Figure 15–27. These become the primary duct and wall lines.
   - If the difference in the line weights does not display clearly, zoom in and, in the Quick Access Toolbar, toggle off (Thin Lines).

The dimensions are for information only.

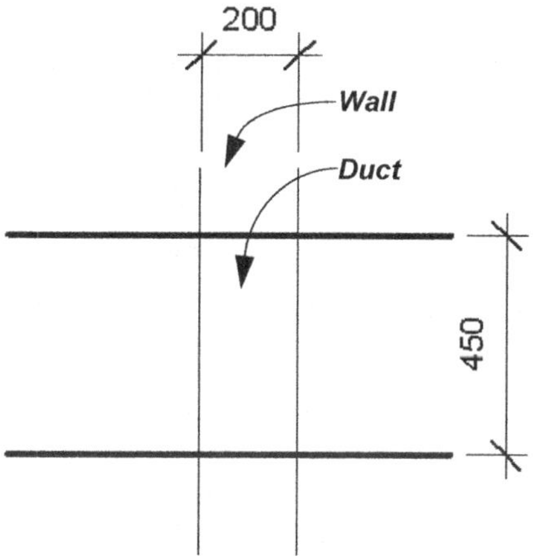

Figure 15–27

4. Continue adding and modifying detail lines to create the elements shown in Figure 15–28. Use modify commands (such as **Split** and **Offset**) and the draw tools.

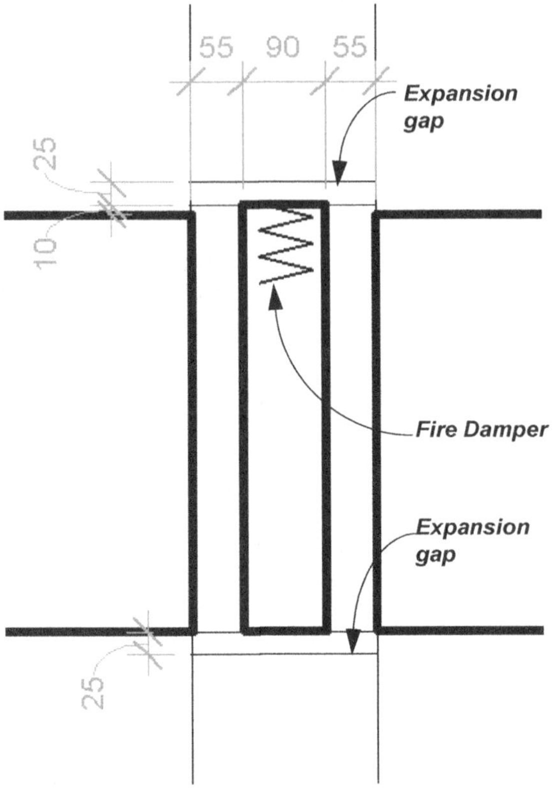

Figure 15–28

5. Save the project.

Task 3 - Add detail components.

1. In the *Annotate* tab>Detail panel, expand (Component) and select (Detail Component).
2. In the Type Selector, select **M_Angle Shapes - Section L75x50x6**.

3. Place the angle on the top left. as shown in Figure 15–29.
   - Press <Spacebar> to rotate the angle before placing it.
4. Change the type **to M_Angle Shapes - Section L50x50x6** and place the angle on the bottom of the duct, as shown in Figure 15–29.

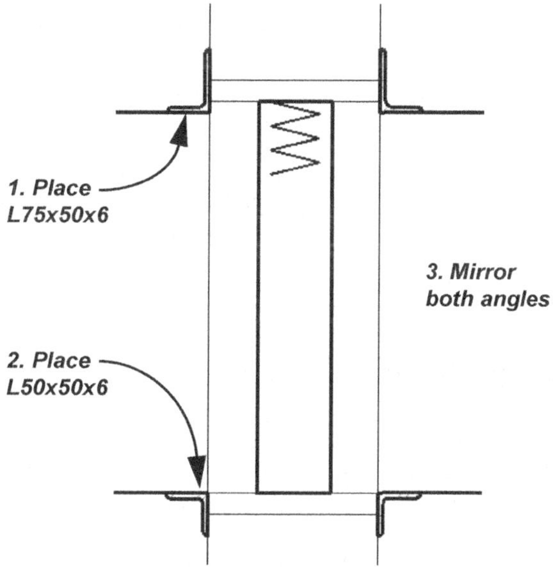

Figure 15–29

5. Select the two angle components and mirror them to the other side, as shown in Figure 15–29.
6. Add four Break Line components. Rotate and use the controls to modify the size until all of your excess lines are covered, as shown in Figure 15–30

The exact location and size of your break lines might vary.

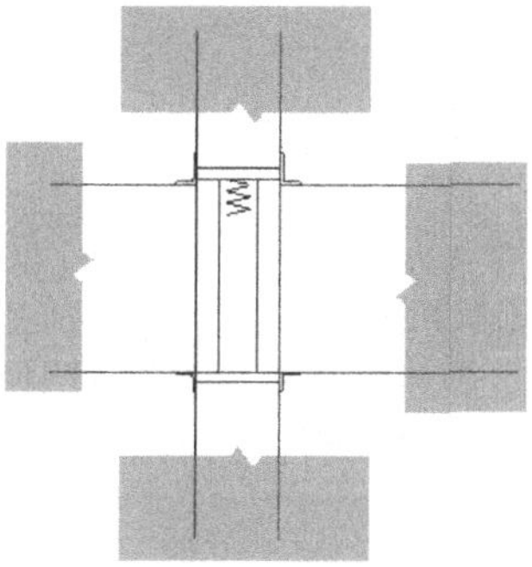

Figure 15–30

7. Save the project.

Task 4 - Add insulation and filled regions.

1. In the *Annotate* tab>Detail panel, click (Insulation).
2. In the Options Bar, set the *Width* to **25mm**.
3. Draw the insulation lines in the two expansion gaps, as shown in Figure 15–31.
4. In the *Annotate* tab>Detail panel, click (Filled Region)
5. In the Type Selector, select F**illed region: Diagonal Down**.
6. Draw rectangles around the wall areas as shown in Figure 15–31.
7. Click (Finish). The filled regions display.

The filled region pattern does not display until you finish the process.

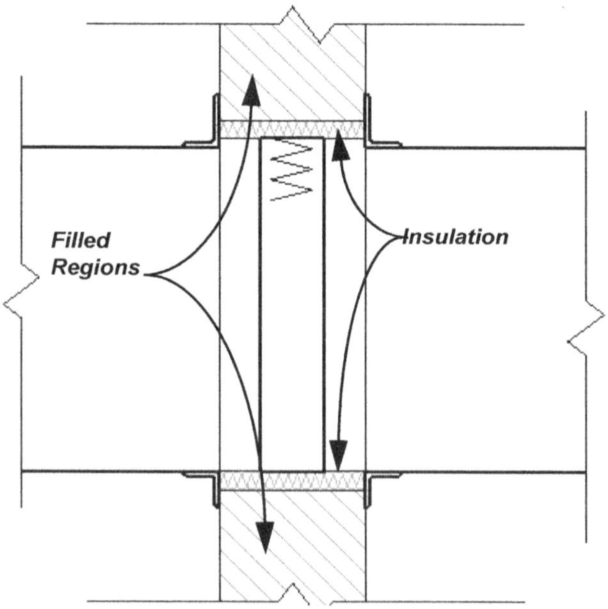

Figure 15–31

8. Save the project.

Task 5 - Add text notes.

1. In the *Annotate* tab>Text panel, click A (Text).
2. In the *Modify | Place Text* tab>Leader panel, select (Two Segments) as the leader style.
3. In the Type Selector, select **Text: 2.5mm Arial**.
4. Add text notes, as shown in Figure 15–32.

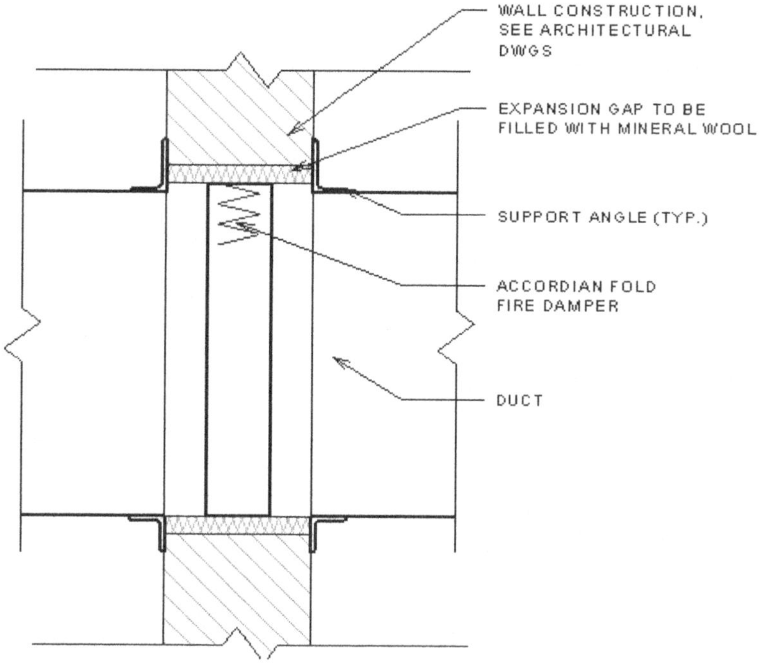

Figure 15–32

5. Save the project.

Task 6 - Place the detail on a sheet and reference it in the project.

1. In the Project Browser, open the sheet **M601 - HVAC Details**.
2. In the Project Browser, drag the **Fire Damper Detail** view to the sheet.
3. Open the Mechanical>HVAC>**1 - Mech** view.

4. Zoom in on one of the duct systems.
5. In the *View* tab>Create panel, click (Callout).
6. In the *Modify | Callout* tab>Reference panel, select **Reference Other View**.
7. Expand the drop-down list and select the new **Fire Damper Detail**, as shown in Figure 15–33.
8. Place the callout at the intersection of a duct and the wall, as shown in Figure 15–33. The information is filled out based on the location of the detail view on the sheet.

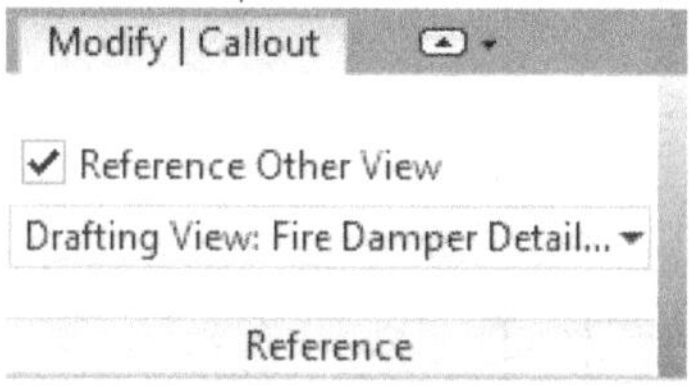

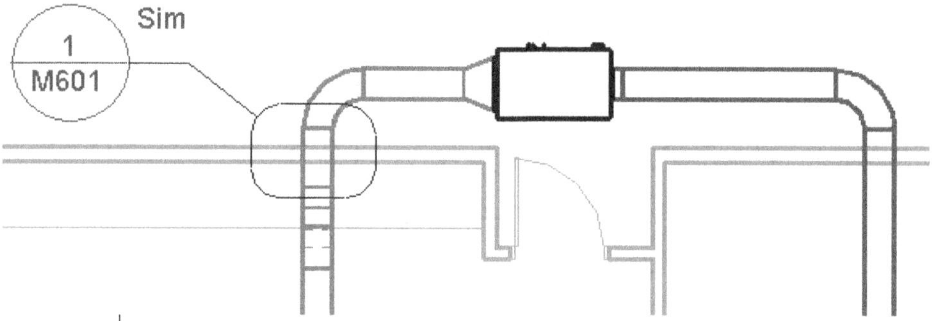

Figure 15–33

9. Save the project.

Practice 15b Create a Floor Drain Detail

Estimated time of completion: 10 minutes

Practice Objective

- Create and annotate details.

In this practice you will create a floor drain detail using detail components. You will then annotate the floor drain detail with text and a dimension, as shown in Figure 15–34. This practice is designed without individual steps.

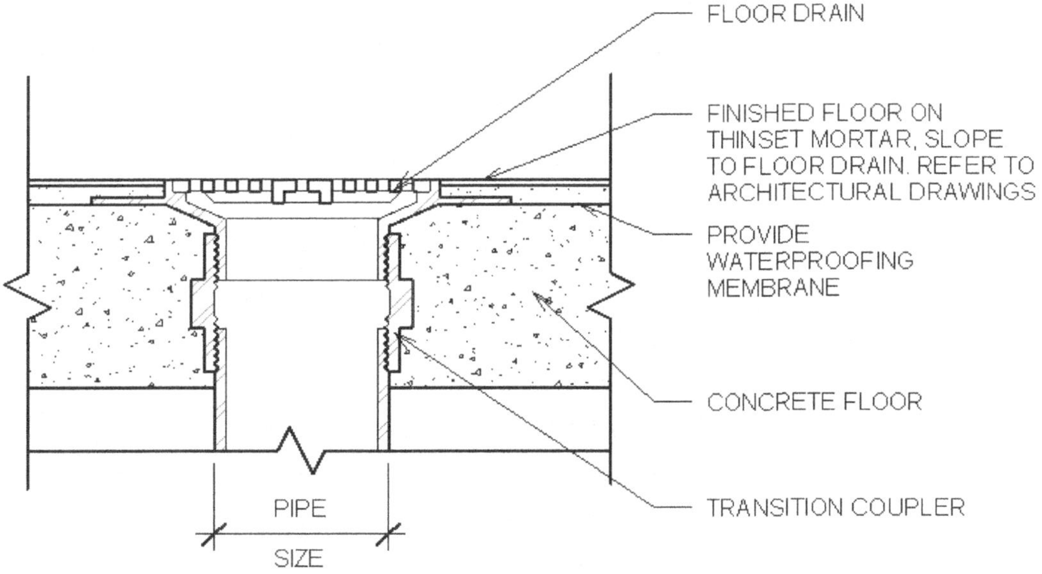

Figure 15–34

Use the **MEP-Elementary-School-Detailing-M.rvt** project as the base file for these tasks.

The following components and pattern are included in the practice file:

- Floor Drain - Section
- Resilient Flooring - Section
- Slab with Optional Haunch-Section
- Filled Region: Grout

Chapter Review Questions

1. Which of the following are ways in which you can create a detail? (Select all that apply.)
   a. Make a callout of a section and sketch over it.
   b. Draw all of the elements from scratch.
   c. Import a CAD detail and modify or sketch over it.
   d. Insert an existing drafting view from another file.
2. In which type of view (access shown in Figure 15–35) can you NOT add detail lines?

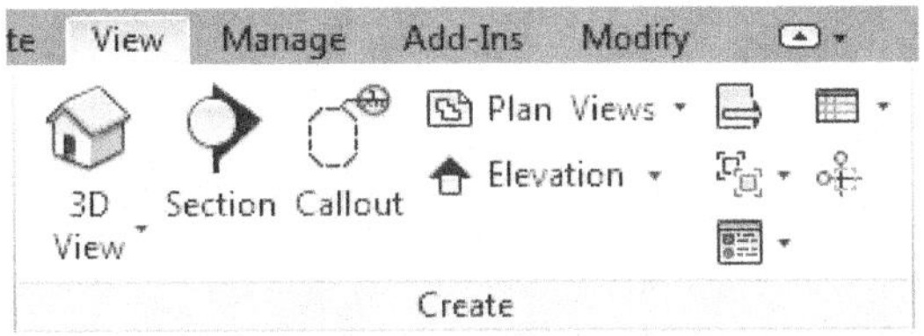

Figure 15–35

   a. Plans
   b. Elevations
   c. 3D views
   d. Legends
3. How are detail components different from building components?
   a. There is no difference.
   b. Detail components are made of 2D lines and annotation only.
   c. Detail components are made of building elements, but only display in detail views.
   d. Detail components are made of 2D and 3D elements.
4. When you sketch detail lines they are...
   a. Always the same width.
   b. Vary in width according to the view.
   c. Display in all views associated with the detail.
   d. Display only in the view in which they were created.

5. Which command do you use to add a pattern (such as concrete or earth as shown in Figure 15–36) to part of a detail?

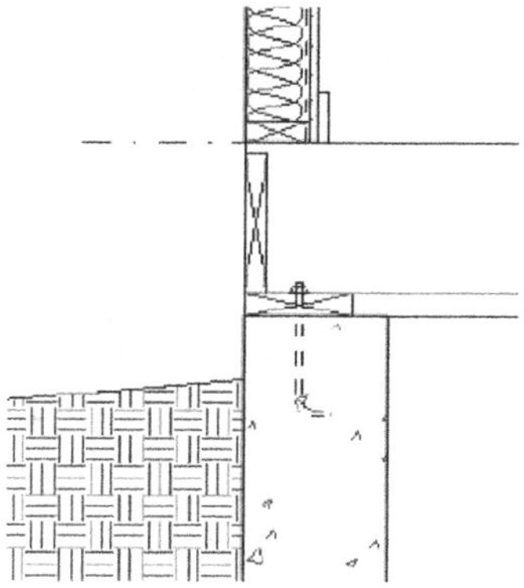

Figure 15–36

   a. Region
   b. Filled Region
   c. Masking Region
   d. Pattern Region

Command Summary

Button	Command	Location
CAD Import Tools		
	**Delete Layers**	• **Ribbon:** *Modify* | *<imported filename>* tab>Import Instance panel
	**Full Explode**	• **Ribbon:** *Modify* | *<imported filename>* tab>Import Instance panel> expand Explode
	**Import CAD**	• **Ribbon:** *Insert* tab>Import panel
	**Partial Explode**	• **Ribbon:** *Modify* | *<imported filename>* tab>Import Instance panel> expand Explode
Detail Tools		
	**Detail Component**	• **Ribbon:** *Annotate* tab>Detail panel> expand Component
	**Detail Line**	• **Ribbon:** *Annotate* tab>Detail panel
	**Insulation**	• **Ribbon:** *Annotate* tab>Detail panel
	**Filled Region**	• **Ribbon:** *Annotate* tab>Detail panel
	**Repeating Detail Component**	• **Ribbon:** *Annotate* tab>Detail panel> expand Component
View Tools		
	**Bring Forward**	• **Ribbon:** *Modify* | *Detail Items* tab> Arrange panel
	**Bring to Front**	• **Ribbon:** *Modify* | *Detail Items* tab> Arrange panel
	**Drafting View**	• **Ribbon:** *View* tab>Create panel
	**Insert from File: Insert Views from File**	• **Ribbon:** *Insert* tab>Import panel> expand Insert from File
	**Send Backward**	• **Ribbon:** *Modify* | *Detail Items* tab> Arrange panel
	**Send to Back**	• **Ribbon:** *Modify* | *Detail Items* tab> Arrange panel

Introduction to Worksets

Worksharing is a workflow used in the Autodesk® Revit® software when multiple people are working on a single project model. The model is broken up into worksets. Individuals open and work on in local files that are synchronized to a central file upon saving.

Learning Objectives in this Appendix

- Review worksharing principles.
- Open a local file to make changes to your part of a project.
- Synchronize your local file with the central file, which contains changes from all the local files.

A.1 Introduction to Worksets

Establishing and using Worksets is covered in the Autodesk Revit Collaboration Tools student guide.

When a project becomes too big for one person, it needs to be subdivided so that a team of people can work on it. Since Autodesk Revit projects include the entire building model in one file, the file needs to be separated into logical components, as shown in Figure A–1, without losing the connection to the whole. This process is called *worksharing* and the main components are worksets.

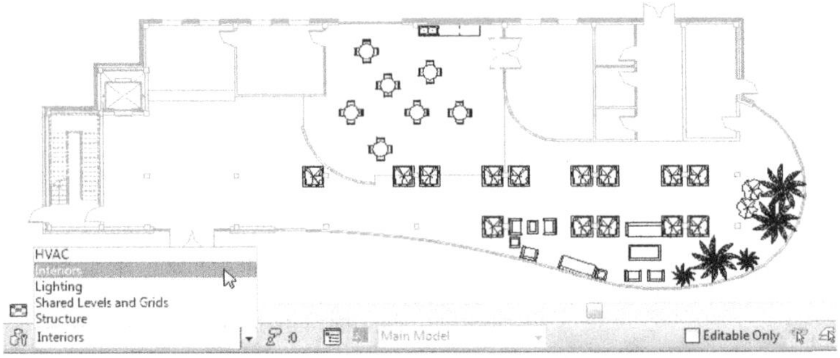

Figure A–1

When worksets are established in a project, there is one **central file** and as many **local files** as required for each person on the team to have a file, as shown in Figure A–2.

*The **central file** is created by the BIM Manager, Project Manager, or Project Lead, and is stored on a server, enabling multiple users to access it. A **local file** is a copy of the central file that is stored on your computer.*

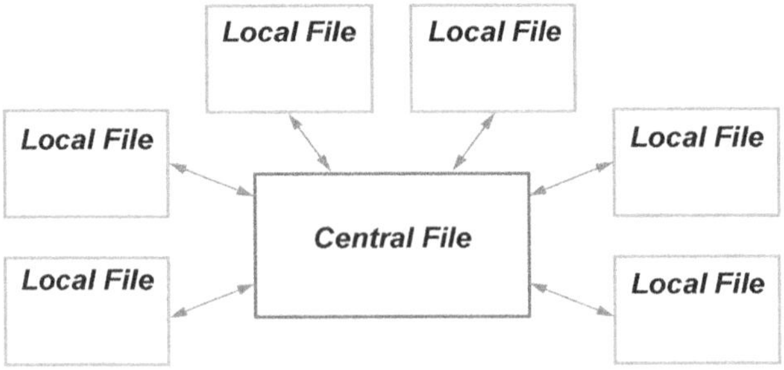

Figure A–2

- All local files are saved back to the central file, and updates to the central file are sent out to the local files. This way, all changes remain in one file, while the project, model, views, and sheets are automatically updated.

How To: Create a Local File

1. In the *File* tab or Quick Access Toolbar click (Open). You must use this method to be able to create a local file from the central file.
2. In the Open dialog box, navigate to the central file server location, and select the central file. Do not work in this file. Select **Create New Local**, as shown in Figure A–3.
3. Verify that this option is selected and click **Open**.

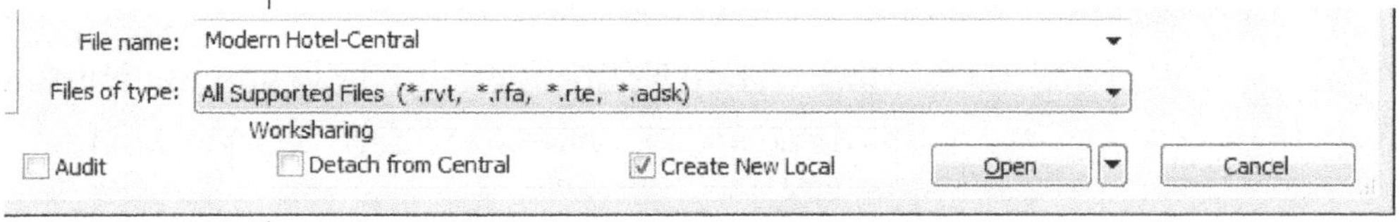

Figure A–3

User Names can be assigned in Options.

4. A copy of the project is created. It is named the same as the central file, but with your *User Name* added to the end.

- You can save the file using the default name, or use (Save As) and name the file according to your office's standard. It should include *Local* in the name to indicate that it is saved on your local computer, or that you are the only one working with that version of the file.
- Delete any old local files to ensure that you are working on the latest version.

How To: Work in a Workset-Related File

1. Open your local file.
2. In the Status Bar, expand the Active Workset drop-down list and select a workset, as shown in Figure A–4. By setting the active workset, other people can work in the project but cannot edit elements that you add to the workset.

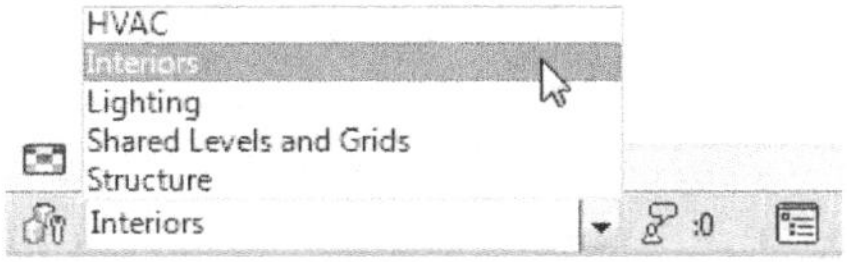

Figure A–4

3. Work on the project as required.

Saving Workset-Related Files

When you are using a workset-related file, you need to save the file locally and centrally.

- Save the local file frequently (every 15-30 minutes). In the Quick Access Toolbar, click (Save) to save the local file just as you would any other project.
- Synchronize the local file with the central file periodically (every hour or two) or after you have made major changes to the project.

Hint: Set up Notifications to Save and Synchronize

You can set up reminders to save and synchronize files to the central file in the Options dialog box, on the *General* pane, as shown in Figure A–5.

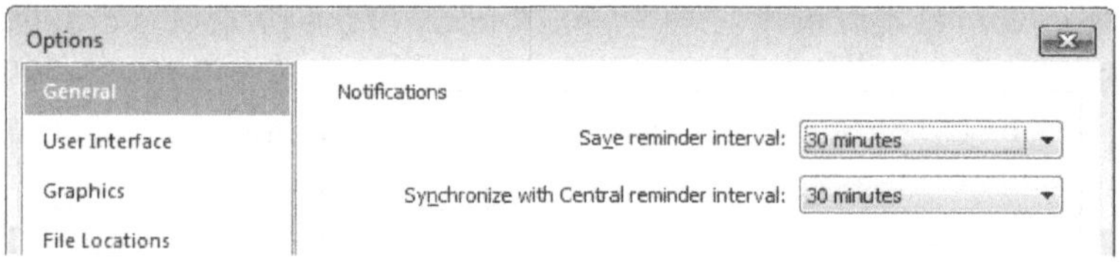

Figure A–5

Synchronizing to the Central File

There are two methods for synchronizing to the central file. They are located in the Quick Access Toolbar or the *Collaborate* tab> Synchronize panel.

Click (Synchronize Now) to update the central file and then the local file with any changes to the central file since the last synchronization. This does not prompt you for any thing. It automatically relinquishes elements borrowed from a workset used by another person, but retains worksets used by the current person.

Click (Synchronize and Modify Settings) to open the Synchronize with Central dialog box, as shown in Figure A–6, where you can set the location of the central file, add comments, save the file locally before and after synchronization, and set the options for relinquishing worksets and elements.

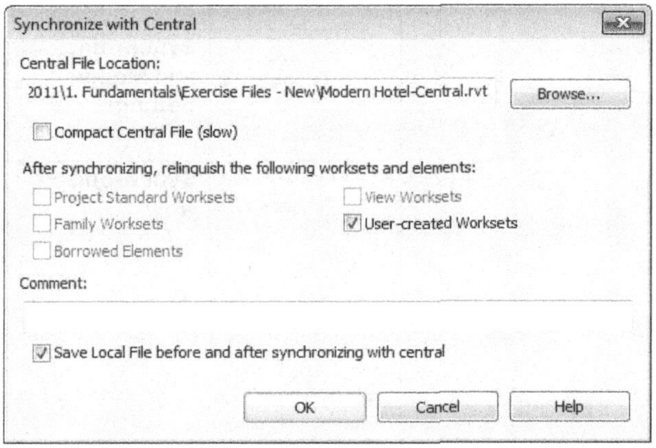

Figure A–6

- Ensure that **Save Local file before and after synchronizing with central** is checked before clicking **OK**. Changes from the central file might have been copied into your file.
- When you close a local file without saving to the central file, you are prompted with options, as shown in Figure A–7.

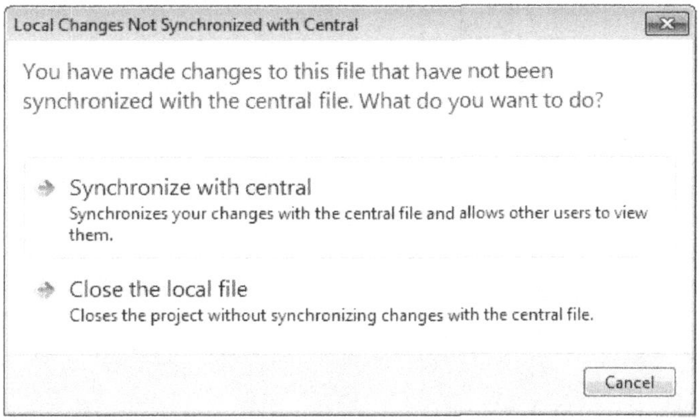

Figure A–7

Command Summary

Button	Command	Location
	**Save**	• **Quick Access Toolbar** • **Ribbon:** *File* tab • **Shortcut:** <Ctrl>+<S>
	**Synchronize and Modify Settings**	• **Quick Access Toolbar** • **Ribbon:** *Collaborate* tab>Synchronize panel>expand Synchronize with Central
	**Synchronize Now**	• **Quick Access Toolbar** • **Ribbon:** *Collaborate* tab>Synchronize panel>expand Synchronize with Central

Appendix B

Additional Tools

There are many other tools available in the Autodesk® Revit® software that you can use when creating and using models. This appendix provides details about several tools and commands that are related to those covered in this student guide.

Learning Objectives in this Appendix

- Linking and Importing CAD files.
- Customize Building Type Settings for Heating and Cooling Loads.
- Define Color Schemes
- Creating custom ducts and piping types.
- Modify system graphics using filters and overrides.
- Produce Pressure Loss Reports
- Use guide grids to help place views on sheets.
- Add revision clouds, tags, and information.
- Annotate dependent views with matchlines and view references.
- Import and export schedules.
- Create basic building component schedules.

B.1 Linking and Importing CAD Files

While the Autodesk® Revit® software has become a major player in the AEC community, many firms have legacy drawings from other CAD programs and could be working with consultants that use other programs. You can import, link, and export data from a variety of programs. These can include 2D details (as shown in Figure B–1) and 3D models.

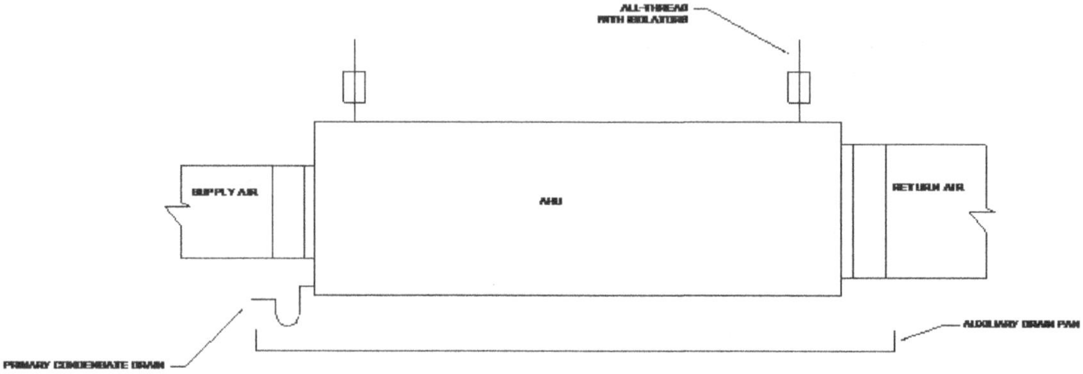

Figure B–1

- CAD files that can be linked or imported include AutoCAD .DWG and .DXF, Microstation .DGN, ACIS .SAT, and Sketchup .SKP files.

Linking vs. Importing

- **Linked files:** Become part of the project, but are still connected to the original file. Use them if you expect the original drawing to change. The link is automatically updated when you open the project.

- **Imported files:** Become part of the project and are not connected to the original file. Use them if you know that the original drawing is not going to change.

How To: Link or Import a CAD File

1. Open the view into which you want to link or import the file.
   - For a 2D file, this should be a 2D view. For a 3D file, open a 3D view.
2. In the *Insert* tab>Link panel, click  (Link CAD), or in the *Insert* tab>Import panel, click  (Import CAD).
3. In the Link CAD Formats or Import CAD Formats dialog box (shown in Figure B–2), select the file that you want to import.

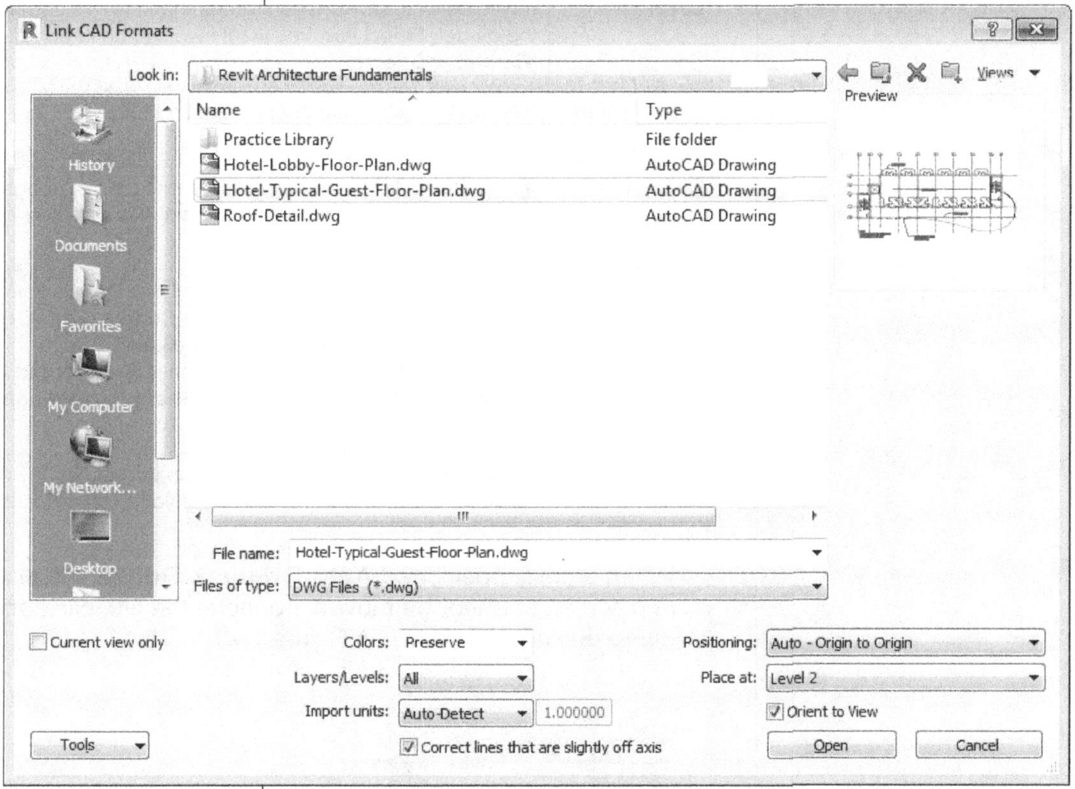

Figure B–2

- The dialog boxes for Link CAD Formats and Import CAD Formats are the same.
- Select a file format in the **Files of Type** drop-down list to limit the files that are displayed.

4. Set the other options as outlined below.
5. Click **Open**.

Link and Import Options

Current view only	Determine whether the CAD file is placed in every view, or only in the current view. This is especially useful if you are working with a 2D floor plan that you only need to have in one view.
Colors	Specify the color settings. Typical Autodesk Revit projects are mainly black and white. However, other software frequently uses color. You can **Invert** the original colors, **Preserve** them, or change everything to **Black and White**.
Layers	Indicates which CAD layers are going to be brought into the model. Select how you want layers to be imported: **All**, **Visible**, or **Specify...**.
Import units	Select the units of the original file, as required. **Auto-Detect** works in most cases.
Correct Lines...	If lines in a CAD file are off axis by less than 0.1 degree selecting this option straightens them. It is selected by default.
Positioning	Specify how you want the imported file to be positioned in the current project: **Auto-Center to Center**, **Auto-Origin to Origin**, **Manual-Origin**, **Manual-Base Point**, or **Manual-Center**. The default position is **Auto-Origin to Origin.** If linking the file, **Auto-By Shared Coordinates** is also available.
Place at	Select a level in which to place the imported file. If you selected **Current view only**, this option is grayed out.

- When a file is positioned **Auto-Origin to Origin**, it is pinned in place and cannot be moved. To move the file, click on the pin to unpin it, as shown in Figure B–3.

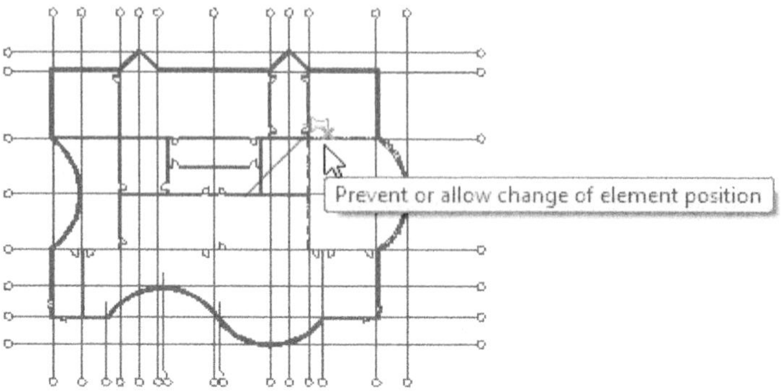

Figure B–3

Hint: Opening Building Component Files

Building Component files, such as the blower created in Inventor shown in Figure B–4, can be imported as a family into an Autodesk Revit project. They display the real size of the equipment and can also include connectors to related MEP elements. They must first be saved in the original program as an Autodesk® Exchange (ADSK) file.

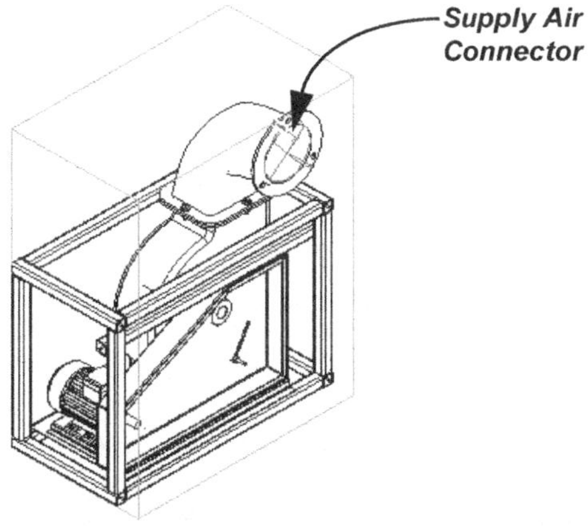

Figure B–4

To use the ADSK file, click (Component) and then click (Load Family). In the Load Family dialog box, select any file with the extension .ADSK, as shown in Figure B–5.

Figure B–5

- ADSK files can be saved as an RFA family file. In the *File* tab, expand (Open), expand (Building Component) and select the ADSK file to open. Then, in the *File* tab, expand (Save As) and click (Family).

B.2 Building Type Settings

For even more control over Heating and Cooling Load analysis, you can customize the Building Types using the Building/Space and Type Settings dialog box, as shown in Figure B–6.

Enhanced in **2018**

- To open the dialog box, in the *Manage* tab>Settings panel, expand (MEP Settings) and click (Building/Space and Type Settings), or in the *Analyze* tab, click in the Reports & Schedules panel title.

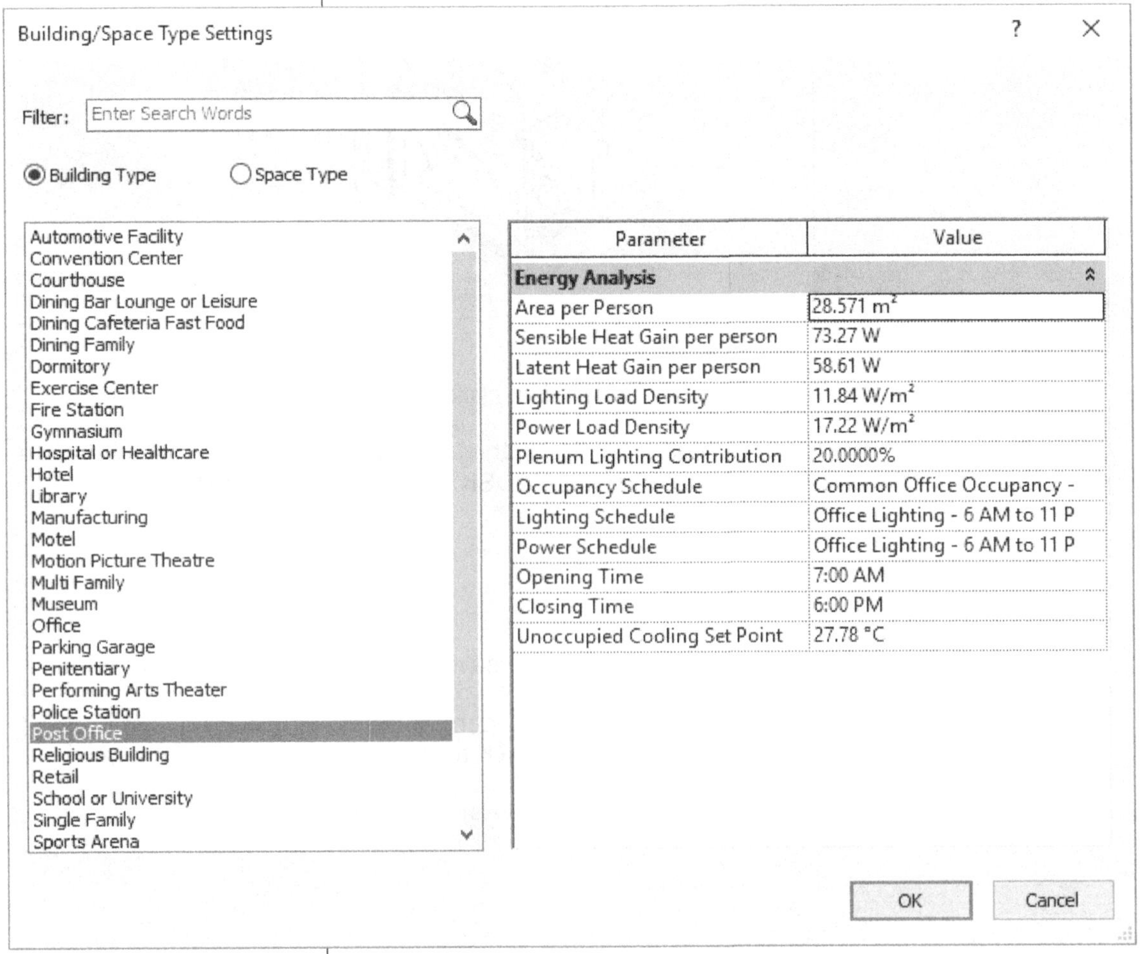

Figure B–6

New in **2018**

- You can add, duplicate, rename and delete Building and Space Types.

- For each type of building or space you can specify energy analysis information, such as the number of people and expected heat gain per person, as well as the schedules of typical times that the building is occupied, as shown for a Warehouse in Figure B–7.

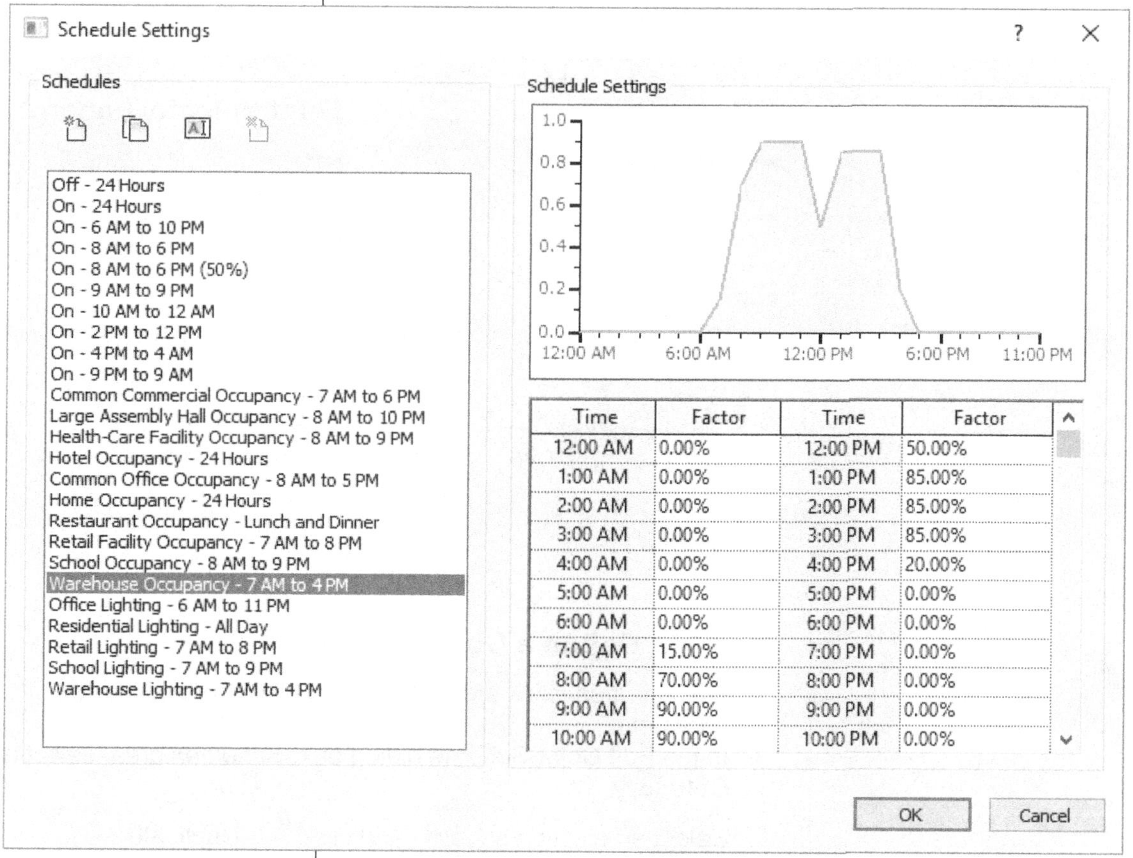

Figure B–7

New
in 2018

- Building/Space type names are exported when you export a project to gbXML for further processing in other energy analysis programs.

B.3 Defining Color Schemes

Color Schemes are uses with Space, Zones, ducts and pipes. You can define colors using many of the properties connected to the elements such as the Duct Friction Color Fill, as shown in Figure B–8.

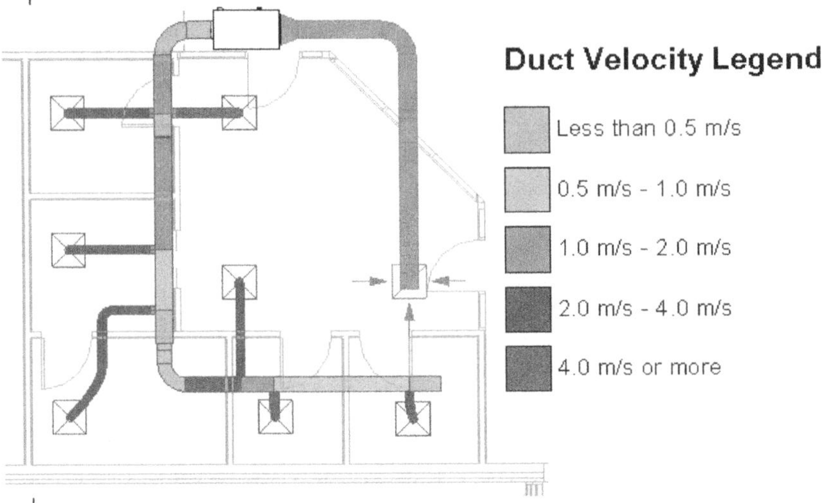

Figure B–8

How To: Define a Color Scheme

1. In Properties, click the button next to the **Color Scheme** parameter.
2. In the Edit Color Scheme dialog box, *Schemes* area, select a **Category**.
3. Select an existing scheme and click (Duplicate).
4. In the New color scheme dialog box, enter a new name and click **OK**. If the Colors Not Preserved warning displays, click **OK** again.
5. In the Edit Color Scheme dialog box, in the *Scheme Definition* area, type a name for the *Title* of the color scheme. This displays when the legend is placed in the view.

6. In the Color drop-down list, select an option, as shown in Figure B–9. The available parameters depend on the type of scheme you are creating.

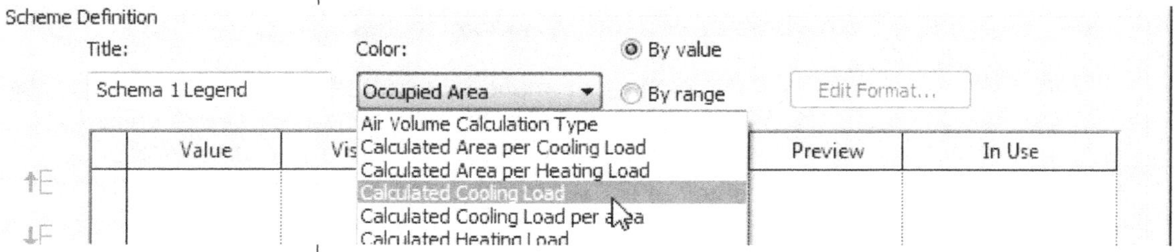

Figure B–9

7. Select the **By value** or **By range** options to set how the color scheme displays. Depending on the selection made in the Color drop-down list, **By range** might not be available.

8. If required, click (Add Value) to add more rows to the scheme, as shown in Figure B–10. Modify the visibility (*Visible* column), *Color*, and *Fill Pattern* as required.

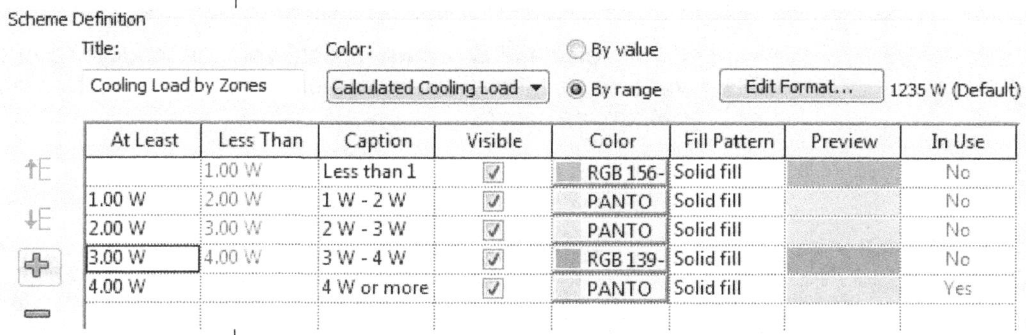

Figure B–10

9. In the *Options* area, select **Include elements from linked files** if you are using linked models.
10. Click **OK** to end the command.

Color Schemes By Value

If you select the **By value** option, you can modify the visibility, color, and fill pattern of the scheme. The value is assigned by the parameter data in the room or area object.

- Values are automatically updated when you add data to the parameters used in the color scheme. For example, if you create a color by space name and then add another space name in the project, it is also added to the color scheme.
- Click (Move Rows Up) and (Move Rows Down) to change the order of rows in the list.
- To remove a row, select it and click (Remove Value). This is only available if the parameter data is not being used in the room or area elements in the project.

Color Schemes By Range

If you select the **By range** option, you can modify the *At Least* variable and the *Caption*, as well as the visibility, color, and fill pattern, as shown in Figure B–11.

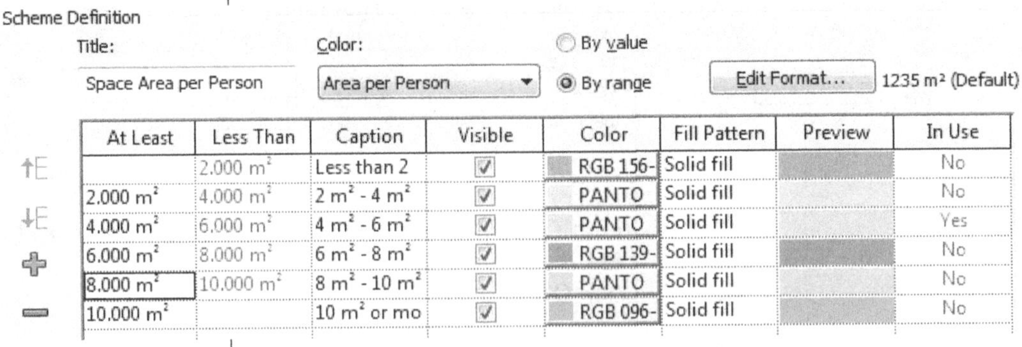

Figure B–11

- Click **Edit Format...** to modify the units display format.
- To add rows, select the row above the new row and click (Add Value). The new row increments according to the previous distances set or by double the value of the first row.

B.4 Custom Duct and Piping Types

Duct/Pipe Types and Settings

You can create additional duct/pipe types. Ducts and pipes are system families, therefore you need to duplicate an existing family in the Type Properties, as shown in Figure B–12.

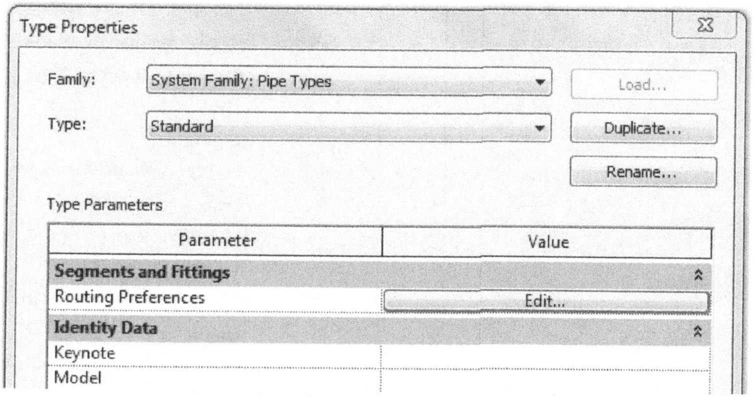

Figure B–12

Routing Preferences

The Routing Preferences dialog box enables you to specify the kind of pipe and pipe fittings to use. You can have a simple pipe type with one kind of pipe segment used for all sizes and one family for each kind of pipe fitting. Alternatively, you can set up the pipe type so that as the pipe size increases, different pipe and different fittings are used. Use (Add Row) and (Remove Row) to create or remove rows, and the arrows to re-order items.

- Duct routing preferences are similar.

The Routing Preferences dialog box is shown in Figure B–13.

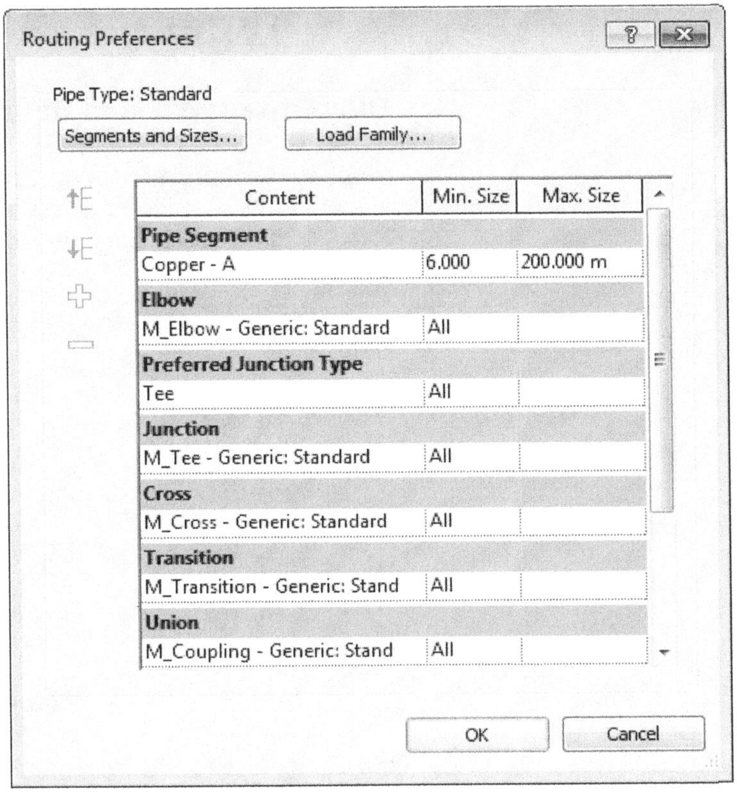

Figure B–13

- **Segments and Sizes...** enables you to create named segments with corresponding standard pipe sizes.
- **Load Family...** enables you to load additional pipe fittings as required.

B.5 Work with System Graphics

Default system colors are setup by graphic overrides at the system family level. These can be modified to suit your company standards. Another useful graphic override is to create filters that display only the systems you want to see in a view. For example, use graphic override filters to display the sanitary piping only and not the hot and cold water piping, as shown in Figure B–14.

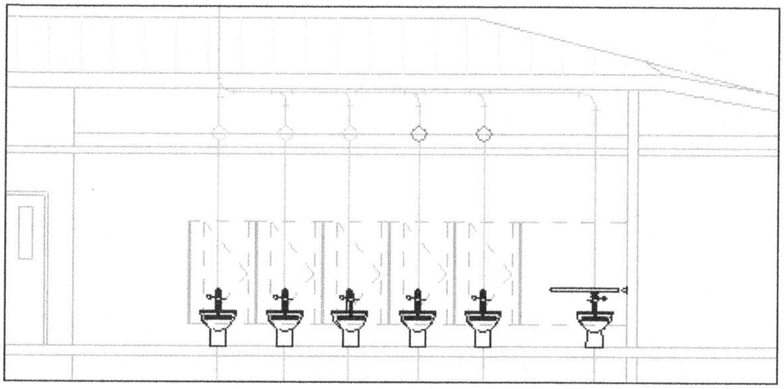

Figure B–14

System Graphic Overrides

By default, in the Autodesk Revit templates, the Return Air Systems are magenta and Supply Air Systems are blue. In Figure B–15, Hydronic Supply and Return Systems also have the colors specified. System colors display in all views including 3D views.

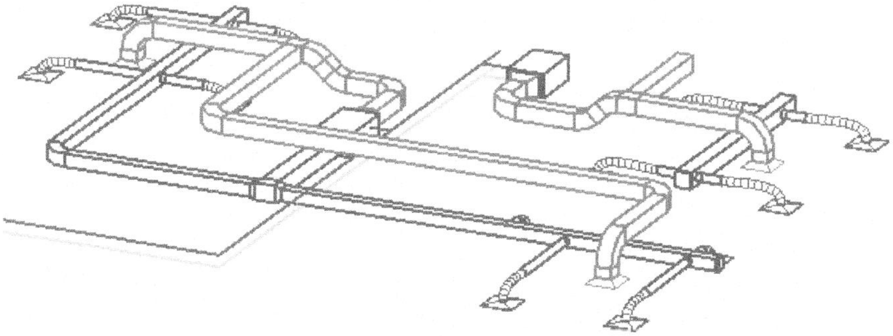

Figure B–15

- System graphic overrides are consistent across a project. They are not view dependent.

How To: Setup System Graphic Overrides

To create a new system family, in the Project Browser, right-click on an existing type and duplicate it.

1. In the Project Browser, expand **Families>Piping (or Duct) Systems> Piping (or Duct) System**, as shown in Figure B–16.
2. Double-click on the one that you want to modify or right-click and select **Type Properties**.

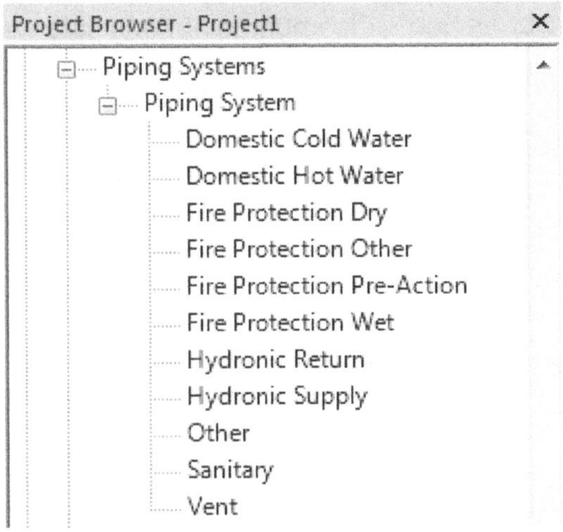

Figure B–16

3. In Type Properties, next to *Graphic Overrides*, click **Edit...**.
4. In the Line Graphics dialog box (shown in Figure B–17), make changes to the *Weight*, *Color*, and/or *Pattern*.

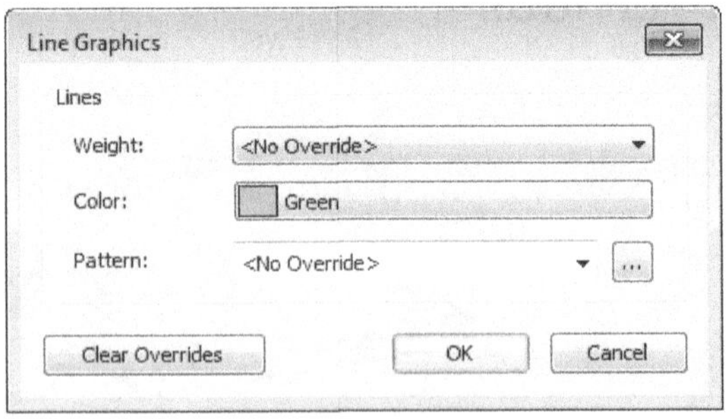

Figure B–17

5. Click **OK** twice to apply the changes.

Using Graphic Override Filters

Any view can be set to display specific systems by using filters. In the example in Figure B–18, the view on the left displays all of the systems along with extra elements such as data components. The view on the right has graphic overrides that toggle off extraneous elements and filter out all systems except duct and hydronic piping.

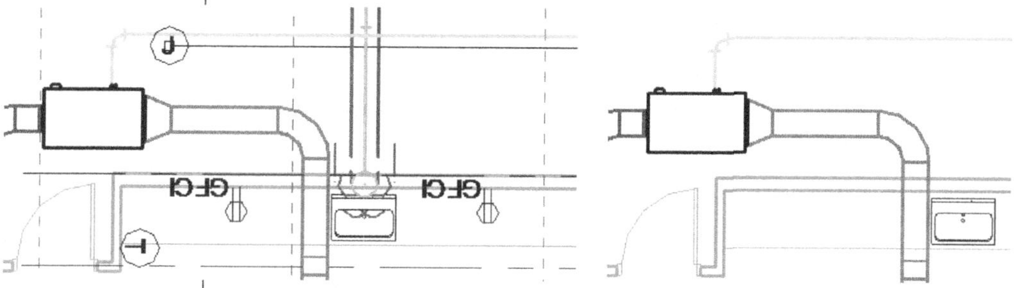

Figure B–18

How To: Apply a View Filter to Override a View

1. Open the Visibility/Graphic Overrides dialog box.
2. In the dialog box, select the *Filters* tab.
3. In the *Visibility* column, select the overrides you want to display. In Figure B–19, the Domestic Cold and Hot Water have been toggled off while the Sanitary and Vent systems display.

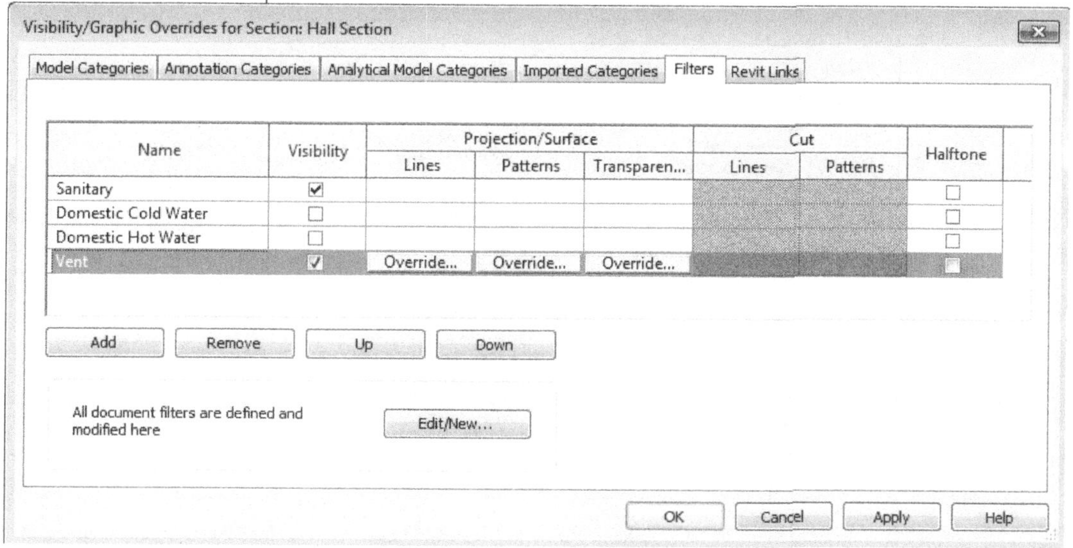

Figure B–19

4. To add a new filter to this view, click **Add**.
5. In the Add Filters dialog box (shown in Figure B–20), select the type of systems you want to modify and click **OK**.

The list might vary depending on the filters set up in the project.

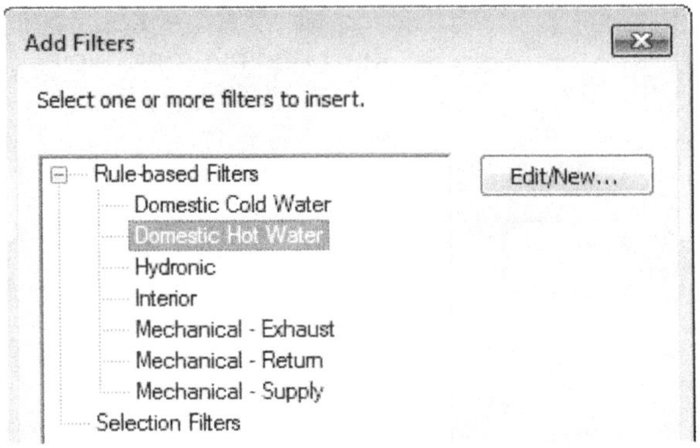

Figure B–20

- View Filters override system graphics so any colors you set in this dialog box supersede those specified in the System Type.

- If you need to change information about the filter itself, click **Edit/New...** in the Add Filters or Filters dialog box. Then, modify the *Categories* or *Filter Rules*. For example, the **Mechanical - Exhaust Filter** does not include *Air Terminals* by default so you need to select it, as shown in Figure B–21.

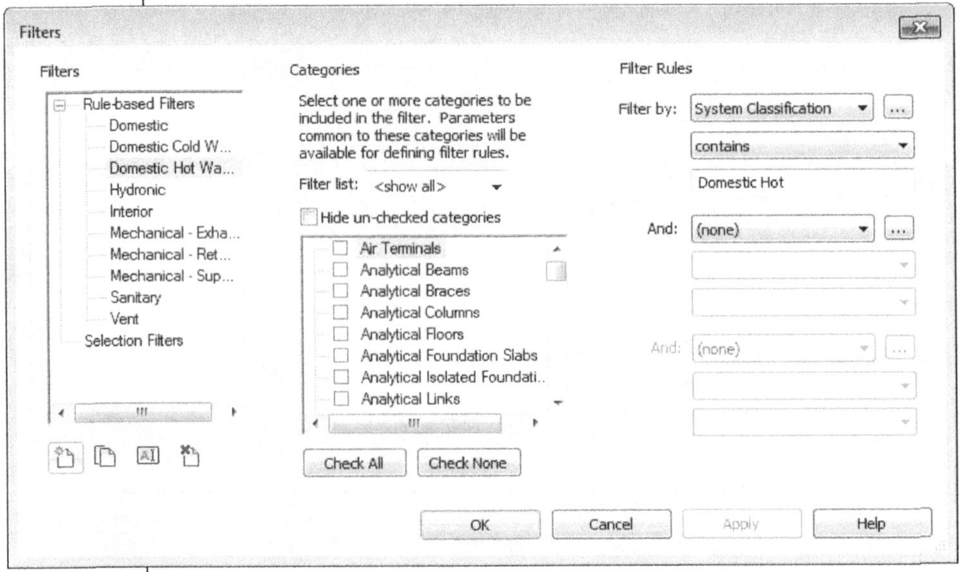

Figure B–21

B.6 Pressure Loss Reports

Pressure Loss Reports are HTML files (as shown in Figure B–22), that include all of the data that can be viewed dynamically in the System Inspector. The reports can be set up to export exactly the information you need. They can be created for Duct or Pipe systems. The analysis for each system includes total pressure loss for the system and detailed information for various sections of duct or pipe.

01 - RA01

System Information	
System Classification	Return Air
System Type	Return Air
System Name	01 - RA01
Abbreviation	

Total Pressure Loss Calculations by Sections							
Section	Element	Flow	Size	Velocity	Velocity Pressure	Length	Lc
1	Fittings	236.0 L/s	-	2.6 m/s	4.1 Pa	-	0.
	Air Terminal	236.0 L/s	-	-	-	-	-
2	Duct	236.0 L/s	305x305	2.5 m/s	-	193	-
	Fittings	236.0 L/s	-	2.5 m/s	3.9 Pa	-	0.
3	Duct	236.0 L/s	300x300	2.6 m/s	-	999	-
	Fittings	236.0 L/s	-	2.6 m/s	4.1 Pa	-	0.
4	Duct	471.9 L/s	300x300	5.2 m/s	-	3803	-
	Fittings	471.9 L/s	-	5.2 m/s	16.5 Pa	-	0.
5	Fittings	471.9 L/s	-	2.1 m/s	2.6 Pa	-	0
	Equipment	471.9 L/s	-	-	-	-	-
6	Fittings	236.0 L/s	-	2.6 m/s	4.1 Pa	-	0.
	Air Terminal	236.0 L/s	-	-	-	-	-
7	Duct	236.0 L/s	305x305	2.5 m/s	-	193	-
	Fittings	236.0 L/s	-	2.5 m/s	3.9 Pa	-	0.
8	Duct	236.0 L/s	300x300	2.6 m/s	-	7291	-
	Fittings	236.0 L/s	-	2.6 m/s	4.1 Pa	-	0.
Critical Path : 6-7-8-4-5 ; Total Pressure Loss : 35.5 Pa							

Detail Information of Straight Segment by Sections					
Section	Element ID	Flow	Size	Velocity	Velocity Pressure
2	711207	236.0 L/s	305x305	2.5 m/s	3.9 Pa
3	711206	236.0 L/s	300x300	2.6 m/s	4.1 Pa
	711215	471.9 L/s	300x300	5.2 m/s	16.5 Pa

Figure B–22

How To: Create a Duct/Pipe Pressure Loss Report

1. When a system is selected, in the contextual *Modify Duct (Pipe) System* tab>Duct (Pipe) System Report panel, click (Duct Pressure Loss Report) or (Pipe Pressure Loss Report). These tools are also found in the *Analyze* tab> Reports & Schedules panel.

2. In the Duct (Pipe) Pressure Loss Report - System Selector dialog box (shown in Figure B–23), select the systems that you want to include in the report.

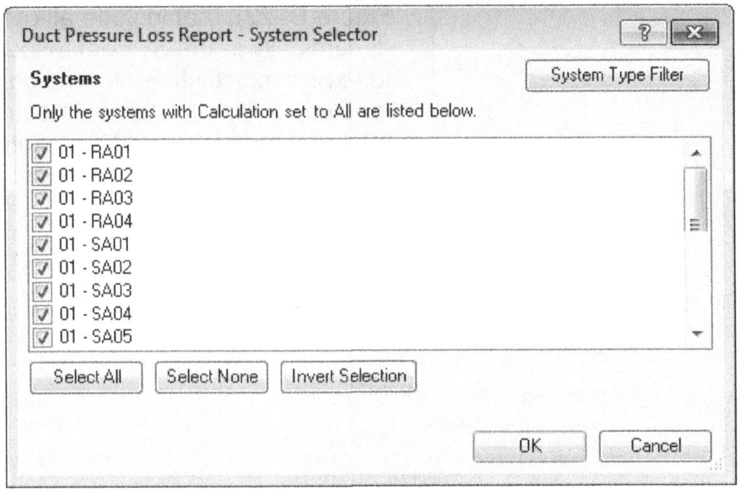

Figure B–23

- To limit the systems displayed in the System Selector, click **System Type Filter** to open the dialog box shown in Figure B–24. Select the types of systems you want to include in the report and click **OK** to return to the main dialog box.

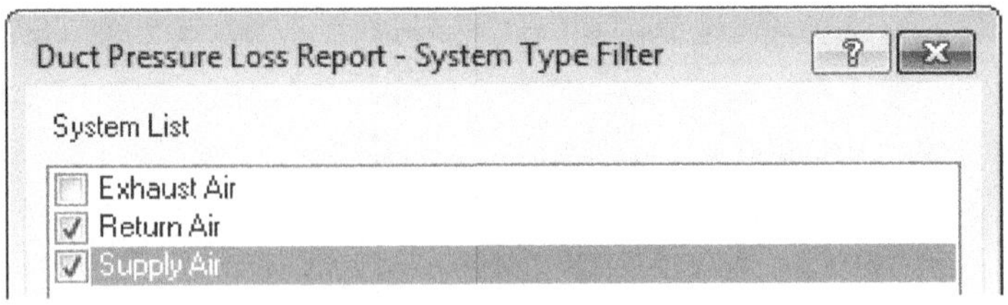

Figure B–24

- Use **Select All**, **Select None**, and **Invert Selection** to help with the selection as required.

3. When you have finished selecting the systems to include, click **OK**.

4. In the Duct/Pipe Pressure Loss Reports Settings dialog box, specify the type of Report Format and the Reports Fields, and other information as shown in Figure B–25.

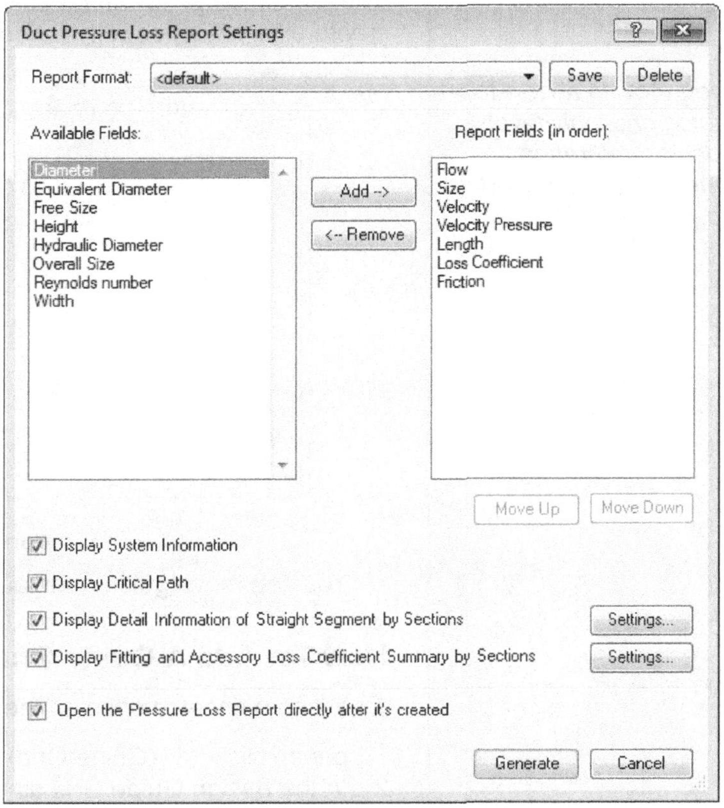

Figure B–25

5. Click **Generate**.

B.7 Guide Grids and Sheets

Guide grids, as shown in Figure B–26, help you place views on sheets,. Guide grids can be set up per sheet. You can also create different types with various grid spacings.

When moving a view to a guide grid, only levels, grids and reference planes snap to the guide grid.

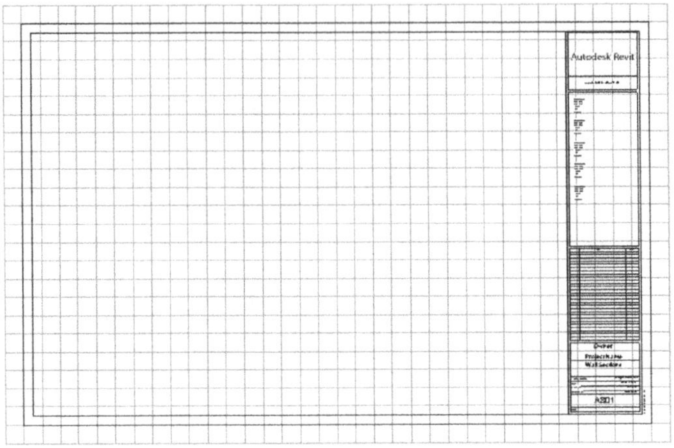

Figure B–26

- You can move guide grids and resize them using controls.

How To: Add A Guide Grid

1. When a sheet is open, in the *View* tab>Sheet Composition panel, click (Guide Grid).
2. In the Assign Guide Grid dialog box, select from existing guide grids (as shown in Figure B–27), or create a new one.
3. The guide grid displays. You can change the size and name in Properties, as shown in Figure B–28.

Figure B–27

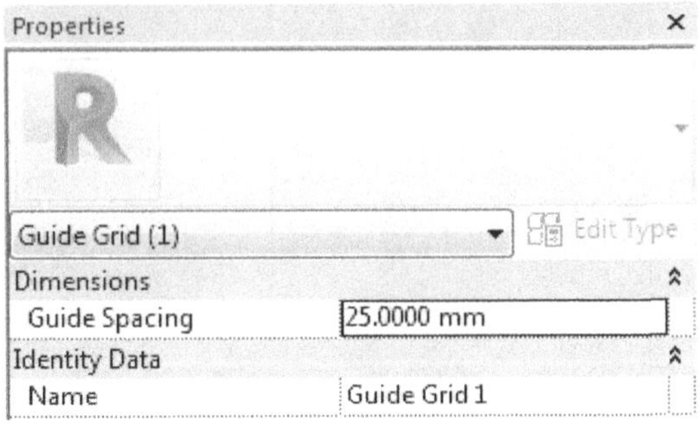

Figure B–28

B.8 Revision Tracking

When a set of working drawings has been put into production, you need to show where changes are made. Typically, these are shown on sheets using revision clouds and tags along with a revision schedule in the title block, as shown in Figure B–29. The revision information is setup in the Sheet Issues/Revisions dialog box.

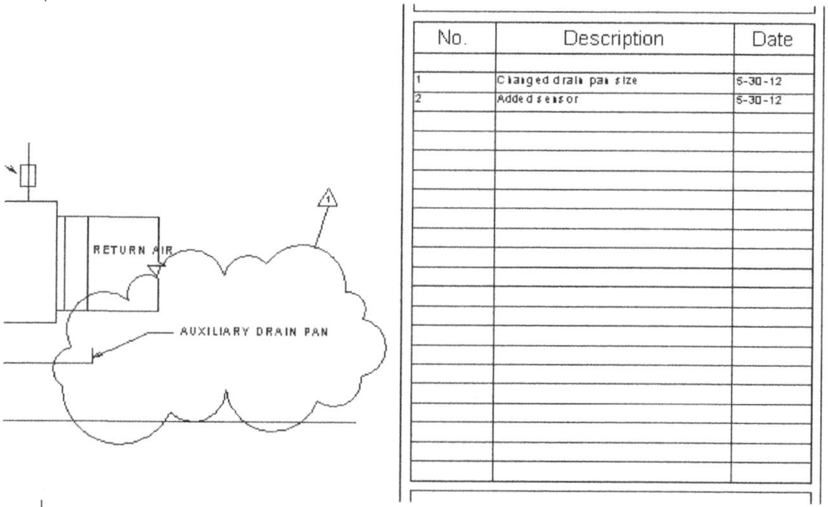

Figure B–29

- More than one revision cloud can be associated with a revision number.
- The title blocks that come with the Autodesk Revit software already have a revision schedule inserted into the title area. It is recommended that you also add a revision schedule to your company title block.

How To: Add Revision Information to the Project

1. In the *View* tab>Sheet Composition panel, click (Sheet Issues/Revisions).
2. In the Sheet Issues/Revisions dialog box, set the type of *Numbering* you want to use.
3. Click **Add** to add a new revision.

4. Specify the *Date* and *Description* for the revision, as shown in Figure B–30.

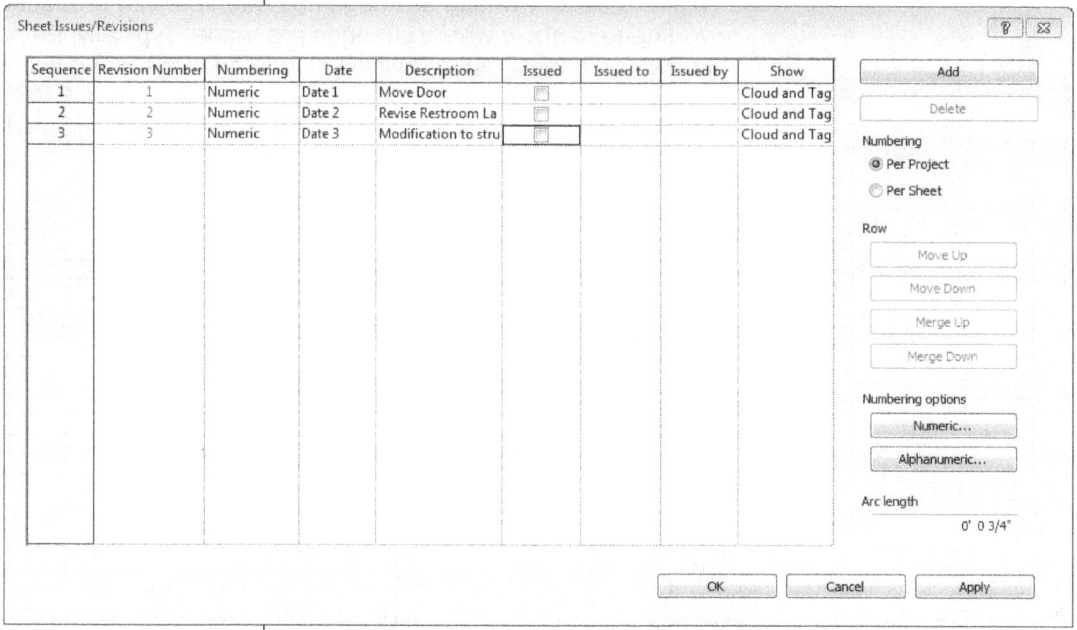

Figure B–30

- Do not modify the *Issued*, *Issued by*, or *Issued to* columns. You should wait to issue revisions until you are ready to print the sheets.

5. Click **OK** when you have finished adding revisions.
   - To remove a revision, select its *Sequence* number and click **Delete**.

Revision Options

- *Numbering:* specify **Per Project** (the numbering sequence is used throughout the project) or **Per Sheet** (the number sequence is per sheet).
- *Row*: To reorganize the revisions, select a row and click **Move Up** and **Move Down**, or use **Merge Up** and **Merge Down** to combine the revisions into one.

- *Numbering Options:* Click **Numeric...** or **Alphanumeric...** to bring up the Customize Numbering Options dialog box where you can specify the numbers or letters used in the sequence as well as any prefix or suffix, as shown for the *Alphanumeric* tab in Figure B–31.

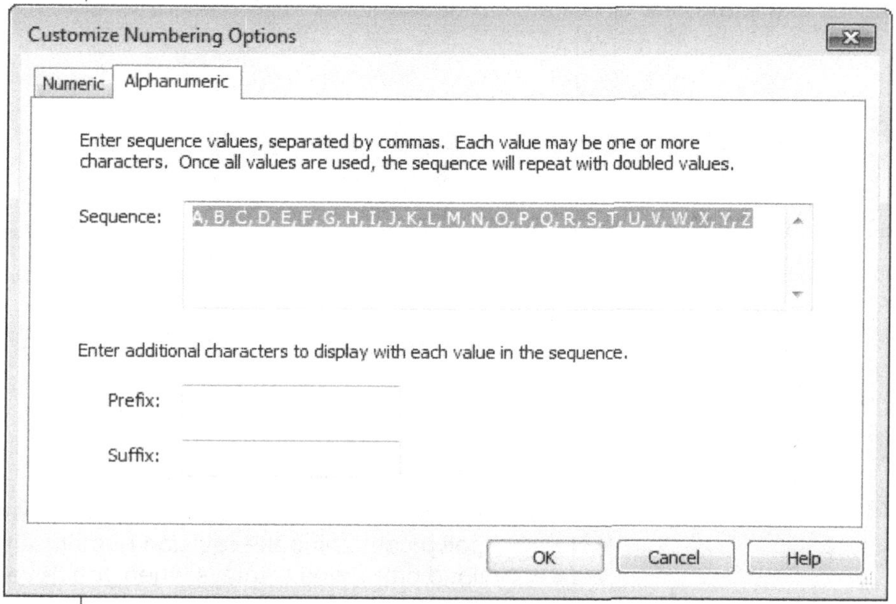

Figure B–31

- *Arc length:* Specify the length of the arcs that form the revision cloud. It is an annotation element and is scaled according to the view scale.

How To: Add Revision Clouds and Tag

1. In the *Annotate* tab>Detail panel, click (Revision Cloud).
2. In the *Modify | Create Revision Cloud Sketch* tab>Draw panel, use the draw tools to create the cloud.
3. Click (Finish Edit Mode).

4. In the Options Bar or Properties, expand the Revision drop-down list and select from the Revision list, as shown in Figure B–32.

If the revision table has not be set up, you can do this at a later date.

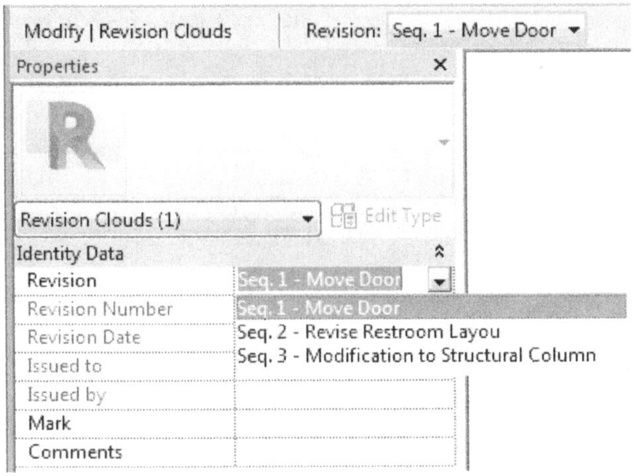

Figure B–32

5. In the *Annotate* tab>Tag panel, click (Tag By Category).
6. Select the revision cloud to tag, as shown in Figure B–33. A tooltip containing the revision number and revision from the cloud properties displays when you hover the cursor over the revision cloud.

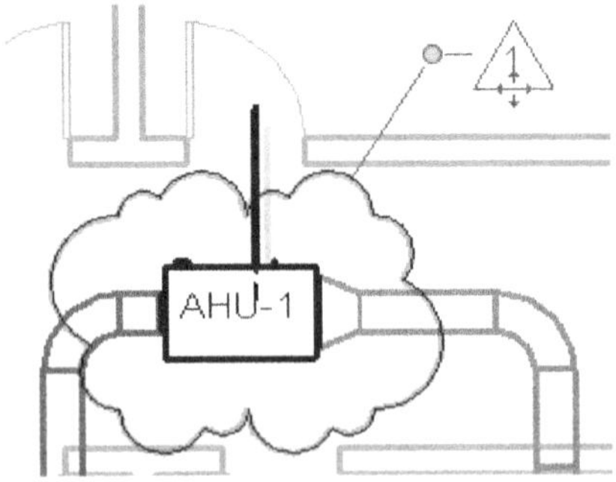

Figure B–33

- If the revision cloud tag is not loaded, load **M_Revision Tag.rfa** from the *Annotations* folder in the Library.
- The *Revision Number* and *Date* are automatically assigned according to the specifications in the revision table.
- Double-click on the edge of revision cloud to switch to the Edit Sketch mode and modify the size or location of the revision cloud arcs.

Issuing Revisions

When you have completed the revisions and are ready to submit new documents to the field, you should first lock the revision for the record. This is called issuing the revision. An issued revision is noted in the tooltip of a revision cloud, as shown in Figure B–34.

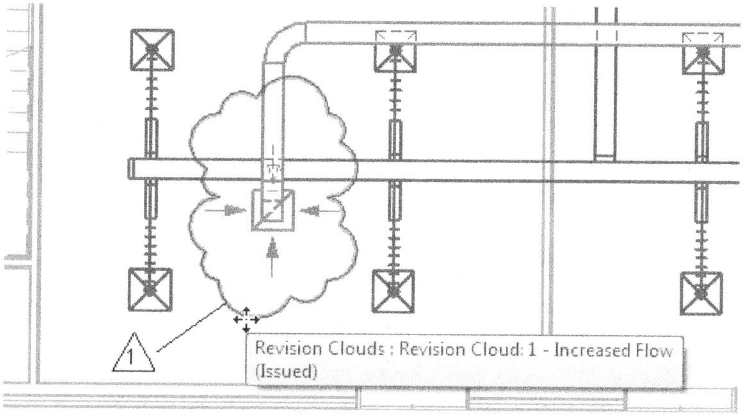

Figure B–34

How To: Issue Revisions

1. In the Sheet Issues/Revisions dialog box, in the row for the revision that you are issuing, type a name in the *Issued to* and *Issued by* fields, as required.
2. In the same row, select **Issued**.
3. Continue issuing any other revisions, as required.
4. Click **OK** to finish.

- Once **Issued** is selected, you cannot modify that revision in the Revisions dialog box or by moving the revision cloud(s). The tooltip on the cloud(s) note that it is **Issued**.

- You can unlock the revision by clearing the **Issued** option. Unlocking enables you to modify the revision after it has been locked.

B.9 Annotating Dependent Views

The **Duplicate as a Dependent** command creates a copy of the view and links it to the selected view. Changes made to the original view are also made in the dependent view and vice-versa. Use dependent views when the building model is so large you need to split the building up on separate sheets, as shown in Figure B–35.

Figure B–35

- Using one overall view with several dependent views makes it easier to see changes, such as *to the scale* or *detail level.*
- Dependent views display in the Project Browser under the top-level view, as shown in Figure B–36.

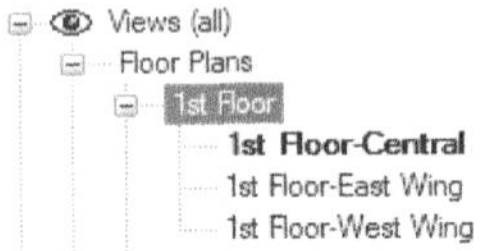

Figure B–36

How To: Duplicate Dependent Views

1. Select the view you want to use as the top-level view.
2. Right-click and select **Duplicate View>Duplicate as a Dependent**.
3. Rename the dependent views as required.
4. Modify the crop region of the dependent view to show the specified portion of the model.

- If you want to separate a dependent view from the original view, right-click on the dependent view and select **Convert to independent view**.

Annotating Views

To clarify and annotate dependent views, use **Matchlines** and **View References**, as shown in Figure B–37.

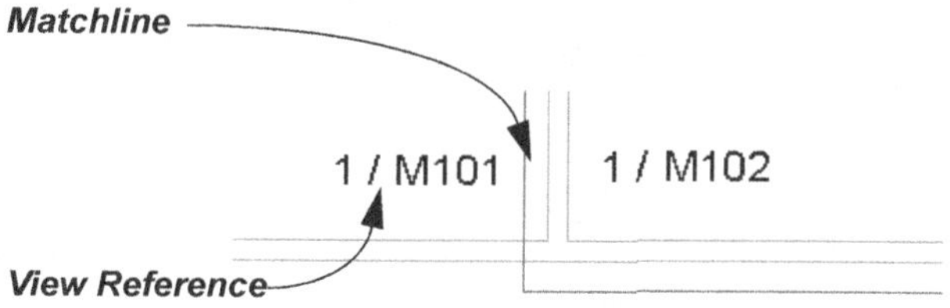

Figure B–37

- Sketch Matchlines in the primary view to specify where dependent views separate. They display in all related views and extend through all levels of the project by default.
- View References are special tags that display the sheet location of the dependent views.

How To: Add Matchlines

1. In the *View* tab>Sheet Composition panel, click (Matchline).
2. In the Draw panel, click (Line) and sketch the location of the matchline.
3. In the Matchline panel, click (Finish Edit Mode) when you are finished.

- To modify an existing matchline, select it and click (Edit Sketch) in the *Modify | Matchline* tab>Mode panel.

- To modify the color and linetype of Matchlines, in the *Manage* tab>Settings panel, click (Object Styles). In the Object Styles dialog box that opens, in the *Annotation Objects* tab, you can make changes to Matchline properties.

How To: Add View References

1. In the *View* tab>Sheet Composition panel or *Annotate* tab> Tag panel, click (View Reference).
2. In the *Modify | View Reference* tab>View Reference panel specify the *View Type* and *Target View*, as shown in Figure B–38.

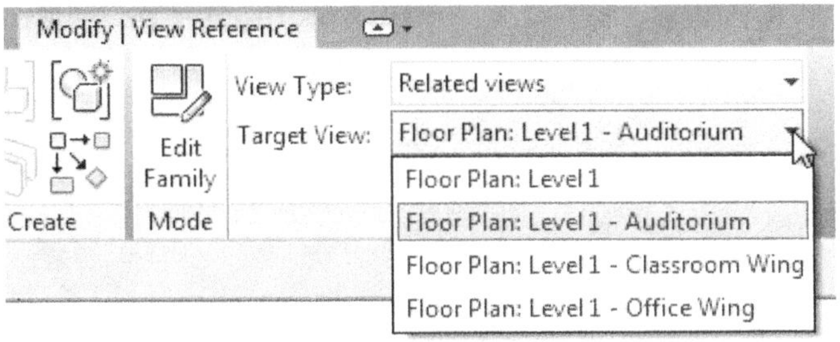

Figure B–38

3. Place the tag on the side of the matchline that corresponds to the target view.
4. Select another target view from the list and place the tag on the other side of the matchline.
5. The tags display as empty dashes until the views are placed onto sheets. They then update to include the detail and sheet number, as shown in Figure B–39.

1 / M102

- / ---

Figure B–39

- Double-click on the view reference to open the associated view.

B.10 Importing and Exporting Schedules

Schedules are views that can be copied into your project from other projects. Only the formatting information is copied; the information about individually scheduled items is not included. That information is automatically added by the project the schedule is copied into. You can also export the schedule information to be used in spreadsheets.

How To: Import Schedules

1. In the *Insert* tab>Import panel, expand (Insert from File) and click (Insert Views from File).
2. In the Open dialog box, locate the project file containing the schedule you want to use.
3. Select the schedules you want to import, as shown in Figure B–40.

If the referenced project contains many types of views, change Views: to ***Show schedules and reports only****.*

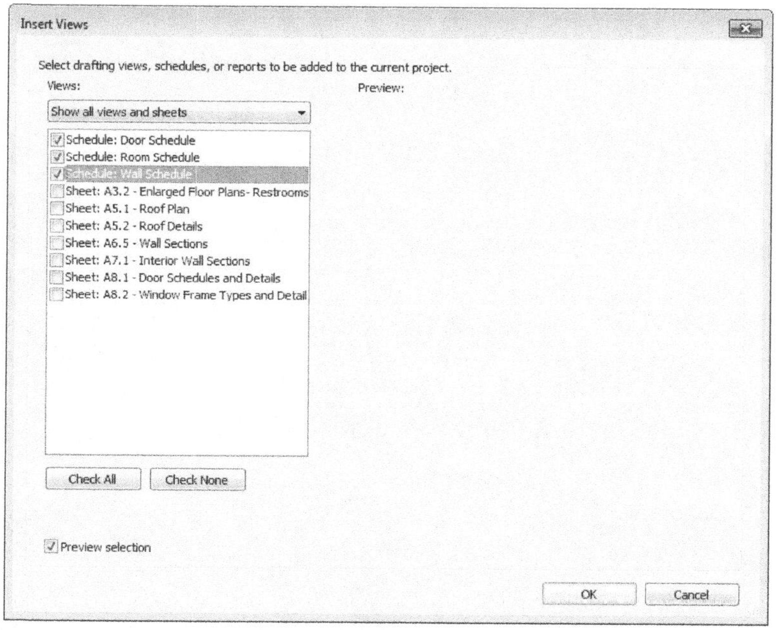

Figure B–40

4. Click **OK**.

How To: Export Schedule Information

1. Switch to the schedule view that you want to export.
2. In the *File* tab, click (Export)> (Reports)> (Schedule).
3. Select a location and name for the text file in the Export Schedule dialog box and click **Save**.
4. In the Export Schedule dialog box, set the options in the *Schedule appearance* and *Output options* areas that best suit your spreadsheet software, as shown in Figure B–41.

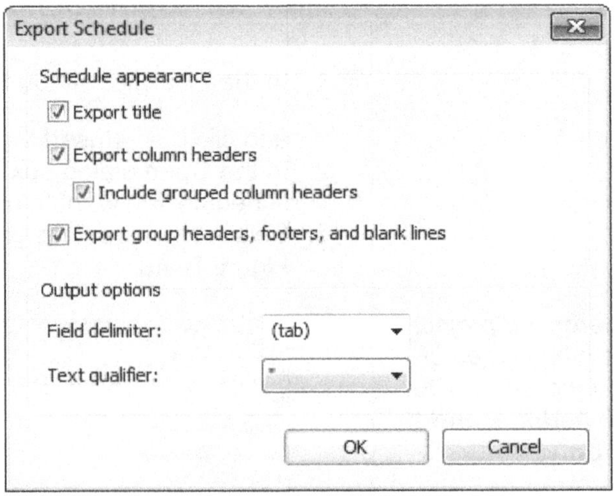

Figure B–41

5. Click **OK**. A new text file is created that you can open in a spreadsheet, as shown in Figure B–42.

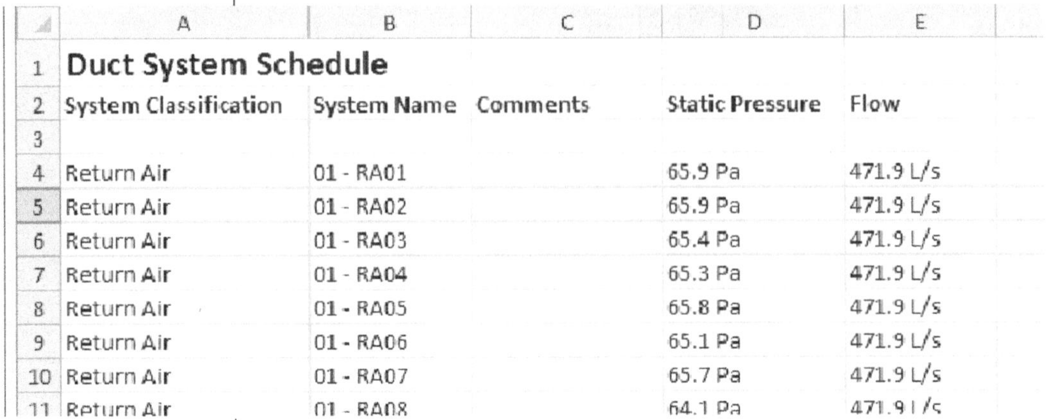

	A	B	C	D	E
1	Duct System Schedule				
2	System Classification	System Name	Comments	Static Pressure	Flow
3					
4	Return Air	01 - RA01		65.9 Pa	471.9 L/s
5	Return Air	01 - RA02		65.9 Pa	471.9 L/s
6	Return Air	01 - RA03		65.4 Pa	471.9 L/s
7	Return Air	01 - RA04		65.3 Pa	471.9 L/s
8	Return Air	01 - RA05		65.8 Pa	471.9 L/s
9	Return Air	01 - RA06		65.1 Pa	471.9 L/s
10	Return Air	01 - RA07		65.7 Pa	471.9 L/s
11	Return Air	01 - RA08		64.1 Pa	471.9 L/s

Figure B–42

B.11 Creating Building Component Schedules

A Building Component schedule, as shown in Figure B–43, is a table view of the type and instance parameters of a specific element. You can specify the parameters (fields) you want to include in the schedule. All of the parameters found in the type of element you are scheduling are available to use.

<Air Terminal Schedule>

A	B	C	D	E	F
Mark	Family	Type	Flow	Manufacturer	Model
RD-1	Return Diffuser - Hosted	Workplane-based Return Diffuser	250.0 L/s	XYZ Air Supply	1456R
SD-1	Supply Diffuser - Sidewall	600 x 300mm	240.0 L/s	XYZ Air Supply	1246S
SD-2	Supply Diffuser - Perforated - Round Neck - C	600x600x150mm Neck		XYZ Air Supply	1234S
Grand total					

Figure B–43

How To: Create a Building Component Schedule

1. In the *View* tab>Create panel, expand (Schedules) and click (Schedule/Quantities), or in the Project Browser, right-click on the **Schedule/Quantities** node and select **New Schedule/Quantities**.
2. In the New Schedule dialog box, select a category from the list, as shown in Figure B–44.

In the Filter list drop-down list, you can specify the discipline(s) to show only the categories that you want to display.

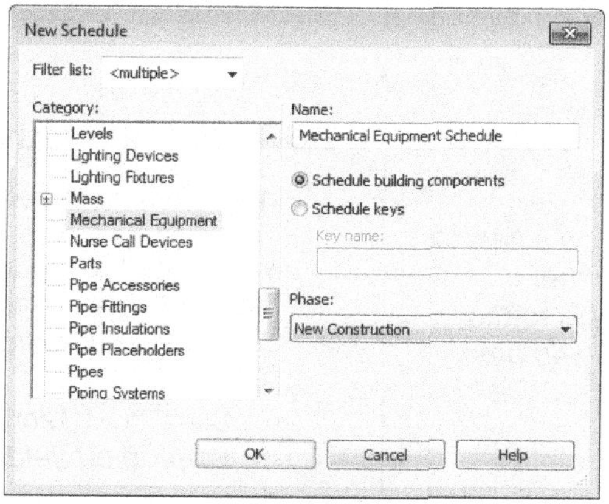

Figure B–44

3. Type a new *Name*, if the default does not suit.
4. Select **Schedule building components**.
5. Specify the *Phase*, as required.

6. Click **OK**.
7. Fill out the information in the Schedule Properties dialog box, in the *Fields*, *Filter*, *Sorting/Grouping*, *Formatting*, and *Appearance* tabs.
8. Click **OK**. A schedule report is created in its own view.

Fields Tab

In the *Fields* tab, select from a list of available fields and organize them in the order you want them to display in the schedule, as shown in Figure B–45.

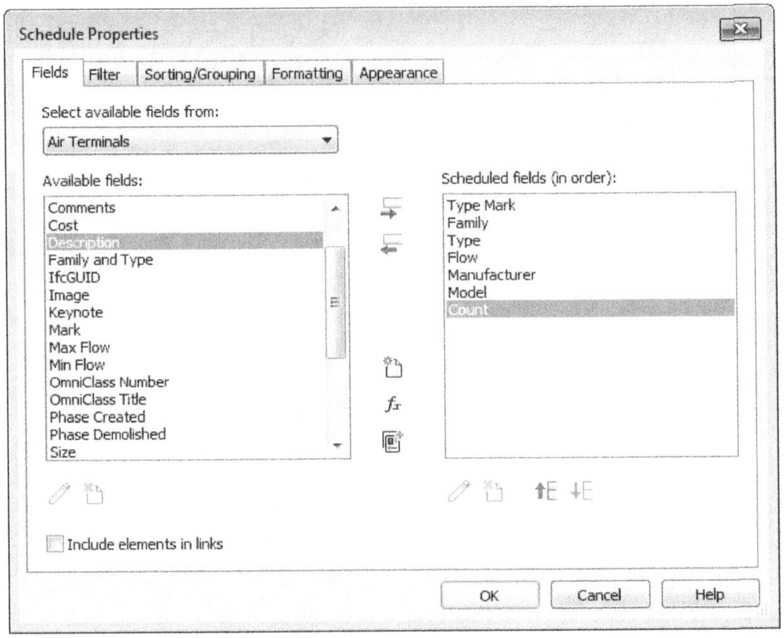

Figure B–45

How To: Fill out the Fields Tab

You can also double-click on a field to move it from the Available fields to the Scheduled fields area.

1. In the *Available fields* area, select one or more fields you want to add to the schedule and click (Add parameter(s)). The field(s) are placed in the *Scheduled fields (in order)* area.
2. Continue adding fields, as required.
   - Click (Remove parameter(s)) to move a field from the *Scheduled fields* area back to the *Available fields* area.
   - Use (Move parameter up) and (Move parameter down) to change the order of the scheduled fields.

Fields Tab Options

Select available fields from	Select additional category fields for the schedule. The available list of fields depends on the original category of the schedule.
Include elements in links	Enables you to include elements from a linked file in the schedule.
(New parameter)	Adds a new field according to your specification. New fields can be placed by instance or by type.
fx **(Add Calculated parameter)**	Creates a formula based field made up of other fields.
(Combine parameters)	Combines two or more parameters in one column.You can put any fields together even if they are used in another column.
(Edit parameter)	Enables you to edit custom fields. This is grayed out if you select a standard field.
(Delete parameter)	Deletes selected custom fields. This is grayed out if you select a standard field.

Filter Tab

You can create filters for up to eight values. All values must be satisfied for the elements to display.

In the *Filter* tab, set up filters so that only elements meeting specific criteria are included in the schedule. For example, you might only want to show information for one level, as shown in Figure B–46.

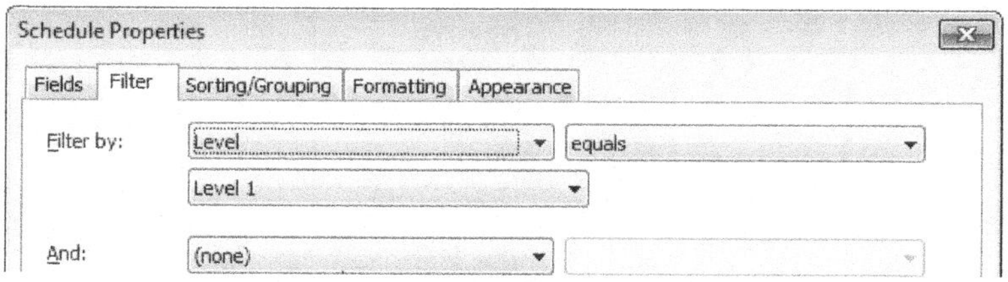

Figure B–46

- The parameter you want to use as a filter must be included in the schedule. You can hide the parameter once you have completed the schedule, if required.

Filter by	Select the field to filter. Not all fields can be filtered.
Condition	Select the condition that must be met. This includes **equal**, **not equal**, **greater than**, and **less than**.
Value	Select the value of the element to be filtered from a drop-down list of appropriate values. For example, if you set *Filter By* to **Level**, it displays the list of levels in the project.

Sorting/ Grouping Tab

In the *Sorting/Grouping* tab, you can set how you want the information to be sorted, as shown in Figure B–47. For example, you can sort by **Mark** (number) and then by **Type**.

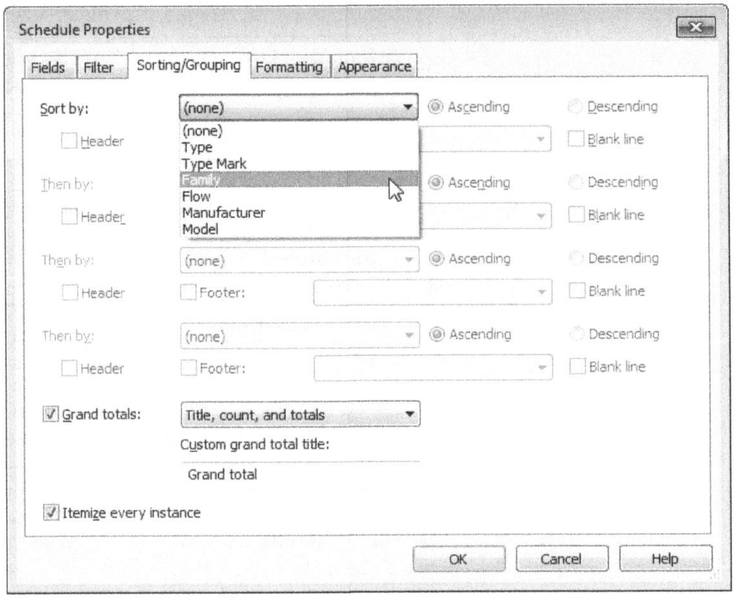

Figure B–47

Sort by	Select the field(s) you want to sort by, up to four levels.
Ascending/ Descending	Sorts fields in **Ascending** or **Descending** order.
Header/ Footer	Group similar information and separate it by a **Header** with a title and/or a **Footer** with quantity information.
Blank line	Adds a blank line between groups.
Grand totals	Select from a list of totals to display and specify a name to display in the schedule for the grand total.
Itemize every instance	If selected, displays each instance of the element in the schedule. If not selected, displays only one instance of each type.

Formatting Tab

In the *Formatting* tab, you can control how the headers of each field display, as shown in Figure B–48.

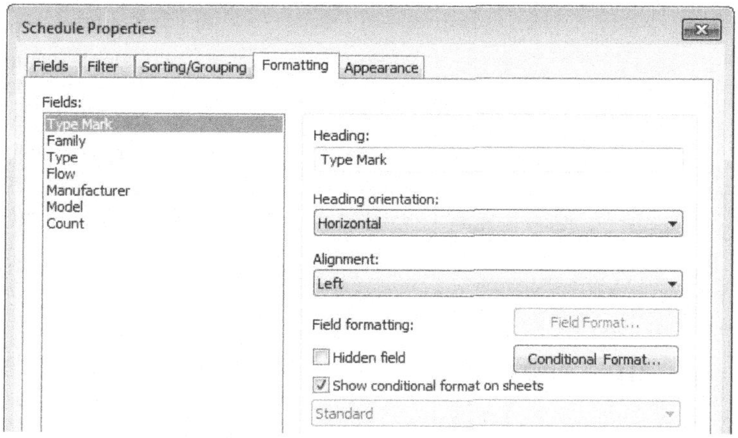

Figure B–48

Fields	Enables you to select the field for which you want to modify the formatting.
Heading	Enables you to change the heading of the field if you want it to be different from the field name. For example, replace **Mark** (a generic name) with the more specific **Door Number** in a door schedule.
Heading orientation	Enables you to set the heading on sheets to **Horizontal** or **Vertical**.
Alignment	Aligns the text in rows under the heading to be **Left**, **Right**, or **Center**.
Field Format...	Sets the units format for the length, area, volume, angle, or number field. By default, this is set to use the project settings.
Conditional Format...	Sets up the schedule to display visual feedback based on the conditions listed.
Hidden field	Enables you to hide a field. For example, you might want to use a field for sorting purposes, but not have it display in the schedule.
Show conditional format on sheets	Select if you want the color code set up in the Conditional Format dialog box to display on sheets.

Calculation options	Select the type of calculation you want to use. All values in a field are: • **Standard** - Calculated separately. • **Calculate totals** - Added together. • **Calculate minimum** - Reviewed and only the smallest amount is displayed. • **Calculate maximum** - Reviewed and only the largest amount is displayed. • **Calculate minimum and maximum** - Reviewed and both the smallest and largest amounts are displayed. • This is often used with rebar sets.

Appearance Tab

In the *Appearance* tab, you can set the text style and grid options for a schedule, as shown in Figure B–49.

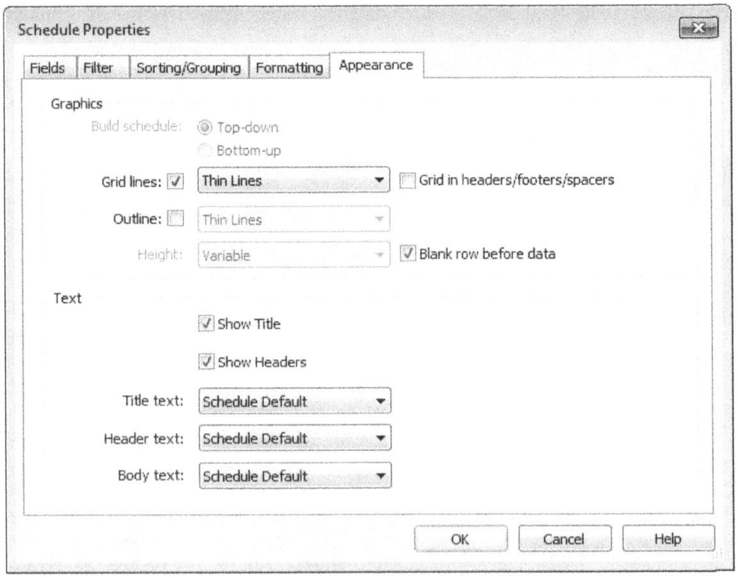

Figure B–49

Grid lines	Displays lines between each instance listed and around the outside of the schedule. Select the style of lines from the drop-down list; this controls all lines for the schedule, unless modified.
Grid in headers/ footers/spacers	Extends the vertical grid lines between the columns.
Outline	Specify a different line type for the outline of the schedule.

Blank row before data	Select this option if you want a blank row to be displayed before the data begins in the schedule.
Show Title/Show Headers	Select these options to include the text in the schedule.
Title text/Header text/Body Text	Select the text style for the title, header, and body text.

Schedule Properties

Schedule views have properties including the *View Name*, *Phases* and methods of returning to the Schedule Properties dialog box as shown in Figure B–50. In the *Other* area, select the button next to the tab that you want to open in the Schedule Properties dialog box. In the dialog box, you can switch from tab to tab and make any required changes to the overall schedule.

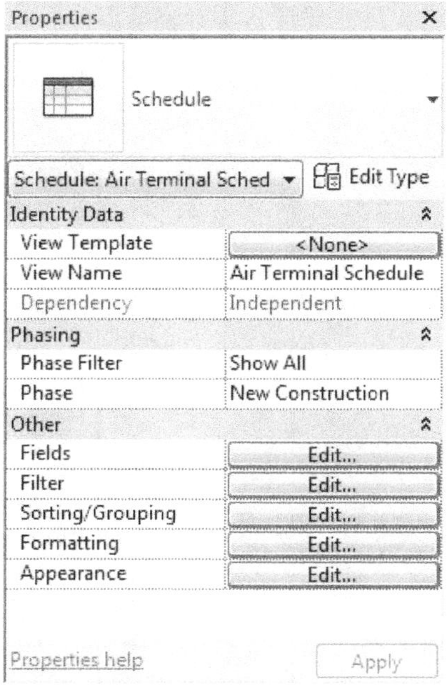

Figure B–50

Command Summary

Button	Command	Location
Annotations		
	Matchline	• **Ribbon:** *View* tab>Sheet Composition panel
	View Reference	• **Ribbon:** *View* tab>Sheet Composition panel or *Annotate* tab>Tag panel
CAD Files		
	Import CAD	• **Ribbon:** *Insert* tab> Import panel
	Link CAD	• **Ribbon:** *Insert* tab> Link panel
Pressure Loss Reports		
	Duct Pressure Loss Report	• **Ribbon:** *Analyze* tab> Reports & Schedules panel
	Pipe Pressure Loss Report	• **Ribbon:** *Analyze* tab> Reports & Schedules panel
Revisions		
	Revision Cloud	• **Ribbon:** *Annotate* tab>Detail panel
	Sheet Issues/ Revisions	• **Ribbon:** *Manage* tab>Settings panel> expand Additional Settings
Schedules		
	Insert Views from File	• **Ribbon**: *Insert* tab>expand **Insert from File**
n/a	**Schedule (Export)**	• **Ribbon:** *File* tab>expand Export> Reports>Schedule
	Schedule/ Quantities	• **Ribbon:** *View* tab>Create panel> expand Schedules • **Project Browser:** right-click on Schedule/Quantities node> New Schedule/Quantities...

Appendix C

Autodesk Revit MEP Mechanical Certification Exam Objectives

The following table will help you to locate the exam objectives in the chapters of the Autodesk® Revit® student guides to help you prepare for the Autodesk Revit MEP Mechanical Certified Professional exam.

Exam Topic	Exam Objective	Student Guide	Chapter & Section(s)
Collaboration	Import AutoCAD files into Revit	• Revit Collaboration Tools	• 3.1
	Link Revit models	• Revit MEP Fundamentals	• 4.1
	Copy levels and setup monitoring	• Revit MEP Fundamentals	• 4.2 & 4.3
	Create floor plans	• Revit MEP Fundamentals	• 4.2
	Use Worksets	• Revit Collaboration Tools	• 4.1 to 4.3
	Resolve Coordination Review Errors	• Revit MEP Fundamentals	• 4.5
Documentation	Mechanical: Tag ducts and piping	• Revit MEP Fundamentals	• 14.1
	Create sheets	• Revit MEP Fundamentals	• 12.1
	Add and modify text	• Revit MEP Fundamentals	• 13.2
	Add and modify dimensions	• Revit MEP Fundamentals	• 13.1
	Mechanical: Create duct/pipe legends	• Revit MEP Fundamentals	• B.3

Exam Topic	Exam Objective	Student Guide	Chapter & Section(s)
Elements	Differentiate system and component families	• Revit BIM Management	• 3.1 • 4.1
	Edit Family Connectors	• Revit BIM Management	• 5.1
	Create a new family type	• Revit BIM Management	• 4.4
Modeling	Mechanical: Add and use mechanical equipment	• Revit MEP Fundamentals	• 8.1
	Mechanical: Add and modify air terminals	• Revit MEP Fundamentals	• 8.1
	Mechanical: Add and modify ducts	• Revit MEP Fundamentals	• 8.2 & 8.3
	Mechanical: Add and modify return ducts	• Revit MEP Fundamentals	• 8.2 & 8.3
	Mechanical: Add and modify duct accessories and fittings	• Revit MEP Fundamentals	• 8.3
	Mechanical: Work with heating and cooling zones	• Revit MEP Fundamentals	• 7.1
	Plumbing: Add and modify fixtures	• Revit MEP Fundamentals	• 9.1
	Plumbing: Add and modify piping	• Revit MEP Fundamentals	• 9.2
	Plumbing: Add and use plumbing equipment	• Revit MEP Fundamentals	• 9.1
	Plumbing: Create a plumbing system	• Revit MEP Fundamentals	• 10.1
	Plumbing: Add and modify pipe accessories	• Revit MEP Fundamentals	• 9.3
	Mechanical: Add and modify placeholder duct	• Revit MEP Fundamentals	• 8.2
	Mechanical: Define a duct system	• Revit MEP Fundamentals	• 10.1
	Mechanical: Add and modify placeholder duct	• Revit MEP Fundamentals	• 8.2 & 8.3
	Mechanical: Define a duct system	• Revit MEP Fundamentals	• 10.1
	Mechanical: Work with spaces	• Revit MEP Fundamentals	• 6.1 to 6.3
	Plumbing: Add and modify placeholder pipe	• Revit MEP Fundamentals	• 9.2
	Size duct and pipe systems	• Revit MEP Fundamentals	• 8.3
	Perform interference check	• Revit Collaboration Tools	• 2.4
	Check duct and pipe systems and disconnects	• Revit MEP Fundamentals	• 10.3

Exam Topic	Exam Objective	Student Guide	Chapter & Section(s)
Views	View models	• Revit MEP Fundamentals	• 1.4
	Apply view templates	• Revit MEP Fundamentals	• 6.1
	Create detail views	• Revit MEP Fundamentals	• 15.1
	Mechanical: Create and label HVAC plans	• Revit MEP Fundamentals	• 5.2 • 13.1 to 13.3 • 14.1
	Plumbing: Create a plumbing view	• Revit MEP Fundamentals	• 5.1
	Plumbing: Create and label plumbing plans	• Revit MEP Fundamentals	• 5.2 • 13.1 to 13.3 • 14.1

Appendix D

Autodesk Revit MEP Electrical Certification Exam Objectives

The following table will help you to locate the exam objectives in the chapters of the Autodesk® Revit® student guides to help you prepare for the Autodesk Revit MEP Electrical Certified Professional exam.

Exam Topic	Exam Objective	Student Guide	Chapter & Section(s)
Collaboration	Import AutoCAD files into Revit	• Revit Collaboration Tools	• 3.1
	Link Revit models	• Revit MEP Fundamentals	• 4.1
	Copy levels and setup monitoring	• Revit MEP Fundamentals	• 4.2 & 4.3
	Create floor plans	• Revit MEP Fundamentals	• 4.2
	Use Worksets	• Revit Collaboration Tools	• 4.1 to 4.3
	Resolve Coordination Review Errors	• Revit MEP Fundamentals	• 4.5
Documentation	Electrical: Tag components	• Revit MEP Fundamentals	• 14.1
	Create sheets	• Revit MEP Fundamentals	• 12.1
	Electrical: Create panel schedules	• Revit MEP Fundamentals	• 11.4
	Add and modify text	• Revit MEP Fundamentals	• 13.2
	Add and modify dimensions	• Revit MEP Fundamentals	• 13.1
Elements	Differentiate system and component families	• Revit BIM Management	• 3.1 • 4.1
	Edit Family Connectors	• Revit BIM Management	• 5.1
	Create a new family type	• Revit BIM Management	• 4.4

Exam Topic	Exam Objective	Student Guide	Chapter & Section(s)
Modeling	Electrical: Add and modify receptacles	• Revit MEP Fundamentals	• 11.2
	Electrical: Add and modify panels	• Revit MEP Fundamentals	• 11.2
	Electrical: Create and modify circuits	• Revit MEP Fundamentals	• 11.3
	Electrical: Add and modify lighting fixtures	• Revit MEP Fundamentals	• 11.2
	Electrical: Add and modify switches	• Revit MEP Fundamentals	• 11.2
	Electrical: Create and modify lighting circuits	• Revit MEP Fundamentals	• 11.3
	Electrical: Create and modify switching circuits	• Revit MEP Fundamentals	• 11.3
	Electrical: Add and modify conduit	• Revit MEP Fundamentals	• 11.5
	Electrical: Use cable trays	• Revit MEP Fundamentals	• 11.5
	Electrical: Add and modify switch systems	• Revit MEP Fundamentals	• 11.3
	Electrical: Create Distribution System	• Revit MEP Fundamentals	• 11.1
	Electrical: Add and modify security devices	• Revit MEP Fundamentals	• 11.2
	Electrical: Add and modify wiring	• Revit MEP Fundamentals	• 11.3
	Electrical: Generate automatic wire layouts	• Revit MEP Fundamentals	• 11.3
	Electrical: Check circuits and disconnects	• Revit MEP Fundamentals	• 11.6
	Perform interference check	• Revit Collaboration Tools	• 2.4
	Electrical: Work with Spaces	• Revit MEP Fundamentals	• 6.1 to 6.3
	Electrical: Perform a Lighting Analysis	• Revit MEP Fundamentals	• 11.6
	Electrical: Work with Fire Alarm Devices	• Revit MEP Fundamentals	• 11.2
	Electrical: Work with Site Lighting	• Revit MEP Fundamentals	• 11.2
Views	View models	• Revit MEP Fundamentals	• 1.4
	Apply view templates	• Revit MEP Fundamentals	• 6.1
	Create detail views	• Revit MEP Fundamentals	• 15.1
	Electrical: Create and label wiring plans	• Revit MEP Fundamentals	• 5.2 • 11.3 • 13.1 to 13.3 • 14.1

Index

Made in United States
North Haven, CT
04 November 2026

21727467R00383